THE

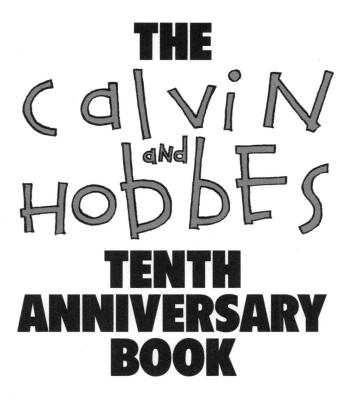

TENTH
ANNIVERSARY
BOOK

OTHER BOOKS BY BILL WATTERSON

Calvin and Hobbes
Something Under the Bed Is Drooling
Yukon Ho!
Weirdos From Another Planet!
The Revenge of the Baby-Sat
Scientific Progress Goes "Boink"
Attack of the Deranged Mutant Killer Monster Snow Goons
The Days Are Just *Packed*
Homicidal Psycho Jungle Cat

TREASURY COLLECTIONS

The Essential Calvin and Hobbes
The Calvin and Hobbes Lazy Sunday Book
The Authoritative Calvin and Hobbes
The Indispensable Calvin and Hobbes

THE Calvin and Hobbes

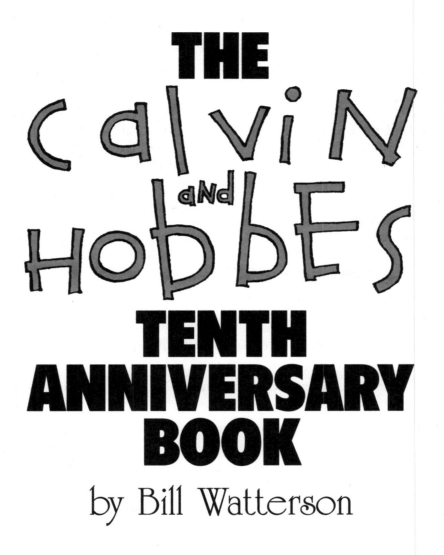

TENTH ANNIVERSARY BOOK

by Bill Watterson

Andrews and McMeel
A Universal Press Syndicate Company
Kansas City

Calvin and Hobbes is distributed internationally by Universal Press Syndicate.

For information, write Andrews and McMeel, a Universal Press Syndicate Company, 4900 Main Street, Kansas City, Missouri 64112.

ISBN: 0-8362-0438-7 (paperback)
0-8362-0440-9 (hardback)

Library of Congress Catalog Card Number: 95-77563

ACKNOWLEDGMENTS

BLONDIE © 1990 King Features Syndicate. Reprinted with special permission of King Features Syndicate.

FOXTROT © 1990 Bill Amend. Reprinted with permission of Universal Press Syndicate. All rights reserved.

HEATHCLIFF © 1990 Tribune Media Services, Inc. Reprinted with permission of Tribune Media Services, Inc.

THE LOCKHORNS © 1990 King Features Syndicate. Reprinted with special permission of King Features Syndicate.

THE WIZARD OF ID © 1990 Johnny Hart. Reprinted with special permission of Johnny Hart and Creators Syndicate.

The front page of the comics section of the *Chicago Sunday Tribune* of May 31, 1931, is reprinted with the special permission of the *Chicago Tribune*.

The page from the comics section of *The Philadelphia Inquirer* of September 30, 1990, is reprinted with the special permission of *The Philadelphia Inquirer*.

TO MELISSA

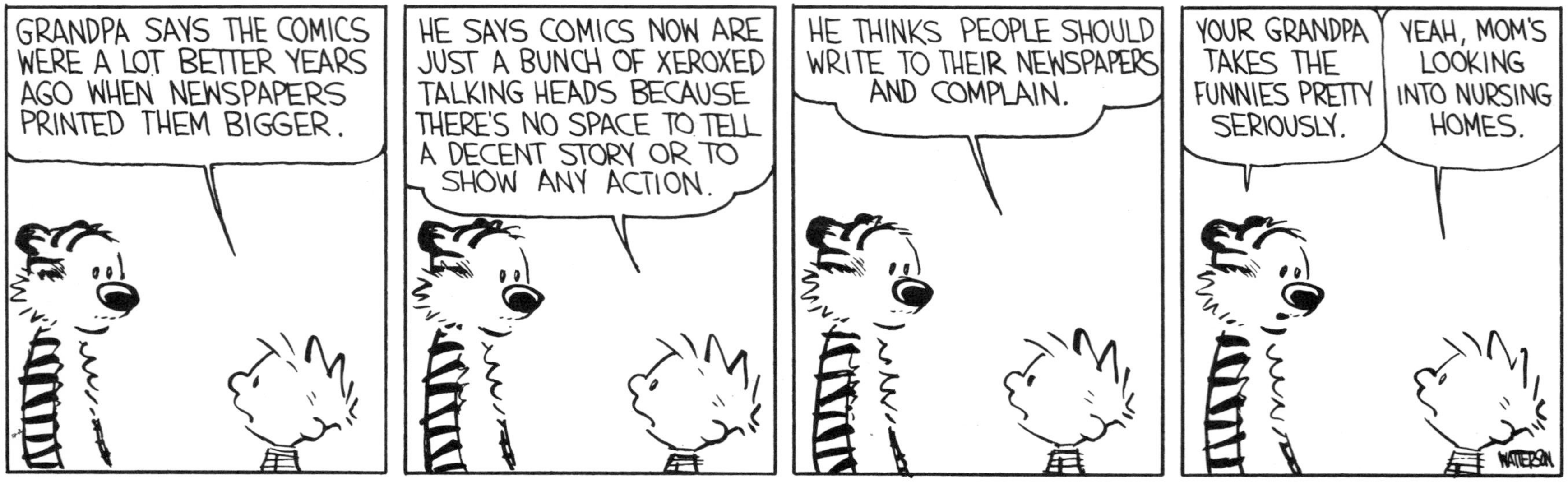
GRANDPA SAYS THE COMICS WERE A LOT BETTER YEARS AGO WHEN NEWSPAPERS PRINTED THEM BIGGER.
HE SAYS COMICS NOW ARE JUST A BUNCH OF XEROXED TALKING HEADS BECAUSE THERE'S NO SPACE TO TELL A DECENT STORY OR TO SHOW ANY ACTION.
HE THINKS PEOPLE SHOULD WRITE TO THEIR NEWSPAPERS AND COMPLAIN.
YOUR GRANDPA TAKES THE FUNNIES PRETTY SERIOUSLY.
YEAH, MOM'S LOOKING INTO NURSING HOMES.
WATTERSON

THE COMICS IN TRANSITION

Comics are a wonderfully versatile medium. With the potent combination of words and pictures, the comic strip can depict anything a cartoonist has the imagination to envision.

Of course, the newspaper business puts severe constraints on comic strips. Comics are produced on an inflexible daily deadline and are given very little space for writing or drawing. Moreover, because comics are frequently assumed to be children's entertainment, and because comics must attract a huge and diverse readership to be profitable, there are editorial constraints as well: controversial subjects and opinions are rarely tolerated. The commercial, mass-market needs of newspapers are not often sympathetic to the concerns of artistic expression.

It is difficult for a new strip to get into newspapers, and few strips survive long even then. Newspapers already have their comics pages filled with popular strips, and the only way for a paper to bring in a new strip is to dump an old strip. The new strip must quickly establish itself in the hearts of readers, or it's the first one to go when another new strip comes along. The competition far exceeds the available spaces, and the results are Darwinian.

The top strips, however, can go on decade after decade. *Blondie* has been in the papers for sixty-five years, and *Beetle Bailey*, *Dennis the Menace*, and *Peanuts* are all in their forties. Even *Doonesbury* has been around for twenty-five years—that is to say, a quarter of the comics' entire existence. There is very little turnover at the top of this business. The most popular strips become institutions and can hold their spaces in the paper for generations.

I think the permanence of familiar strips and the lack of change *within* the strips account for much of their popularity. In a newspaper full of surprising horrors, it's a comforting little ritual to see our favorite characters each morning for a few seconds over coffee. They become friends of sorts. We care about them when they're in trouble, and we count on them to look at life with a slightly amusing twist that may even help us do the same. They are there for us seven days a week, year after year.

Adding to that consistency, comic characters typically stay the same age and maintain the same appearance (often right down to the same outfit every day), no matter how things change in the real world. In most strips, certain predictable events and situations recur frequently with only minor variations. In most strips, every story can be expected to end with the characters right back where they began. In most strips, the regular cast is unvarying. The world of a comic strip is simple and enduring, a tiny oasis of stability in a mixed-up, ever-changing world.

Or, at least they used to be. Lately, more strips have been addressing controversial subjects, and there have been sabbaticals, early retirements, size and format demands, and fights over issues of creative control. Some commentators (including a few cartoonists) explain these recent events as the self-indulgent tantrums of the profession's nine-hundred-pound gorillas, but I believe these critics are missing the bigger picture. On the hundredth anniversary of the American newspaper comic strip, the comics are in a period of major transition.

The first transition is a simple one: the comics are beginning one of their rare generation shifts. When a popular strip can easily last forty or fifty years, the top cartoonists define the profession that long. Cartoonists who started in the 1950s and 1960s changed the direction of the comic strip and have set the standards ever since. Recently, new talents have worked their ways to the top ranks, bringing along some different ideas about what cartooning should be.

The second transition is one of artistic interpretation. Over the course of the last century, the line between commercial art and fine art has been greatly blurred. Whereas original comic strip drawings were once given away to fans or were destroyed to save storage space, today original cartoons are sold in galleries for hundreds or thousands of dollars. Whereas cartoonists were once considered replaceable workers, now—in certain cases—syndicates are recognizing that only the original creator is capable of producing the strip's unique vision. Academics now write about the comics as social history and commentary. There are several cartoon collections and museums. Comics have been awarded Pulitzer prizes. Whether or not most comics are Great Art can be debated, but there is no denying that cartoonists and the public take the comics more seriously than they used to. Increasingly, cartoonists are regarding their creations as a form of personal expression. Issues of creative control are becoming relevant to cartoonists, and old assumptions about the way business is conducted are being questioned.

Third, the newspaper business itself is changing. The comics were invented in the late 1800s, when large cities had as many as a half-dozen newspapers, each trying to outdo the other to attract the readership of huge new immigrant populations. The comics were visual, easy to understand, funny, boisterous, and lowbrow by design and hence immediately popular. Cartoonists had few pretensions about the artistic or cultural significance of their work. From the beginning, the comics were regarded as a commercial product that existed for the purpose of increasing newspaper readership. Cartoonists considered themselves newspapermen, not artists. Their job, pure and simple, was to help sell newspapers.

Since that time:

• *Syndicates have turned the comics into big business.* At first, cartoonists were hired by individual newspapers to produce comics exclusively for that paper. Today, cartoonists work for syndicates that sell their strips to newspapers worldwide. That means a strip today needs very broad appeal. Whereas the early cartoonists experimented, starting and stopping strips as their interests changed and discovering what appealed to the local audience along the way, syndication has encouraged the calculated production of strips to mirror trends and capitalize on the specific interests of desirable demographic groups. Marketing strips on a large scale encourages comics to be conservative, easily categorized, and imitative of previous successes. The comics have gained immense readerships and have become very profitable this way, but at some cost to the comics' early exuberance.

• *There is now much less newspaper competition.* Each big city used to have several papers battling each other for readers, and a well-liked comic strip could dramatically help a paper's circulation. Popular strips would go to the highest bidding newspaper, and the other papers would scramble to buy other strips that might help them compete. Today, most cities have just one newspaper, and the surviving paper can have any strip it wants. It will obviously buy the most popular strips, and without other papers to grab other strips, the big strips get huge, and the small strips play musical chairs and vanish. There is little room any more for a peculiar "cult" strip with a small but devoted following. There are fewer openings for new strips, fewer opportunities for marginal strips to survive, and there is less time for a strip to find its audience.

• *Television has replaced newspapers as the source of most people's information.* Newspaper production costs have gone up, circulations have not, and some of the big advertising accounts have abandoned newspapers. A comic strip might once have lured readers from one newspaper to another, but comics don't lure people away from televisions. The comics are less helpful to newspapers than they used to be, so papers look at the comics page as one more place to cut costs. They cram more strips into less space, forcing cartoonists to write and draw more simply to stay legible. With fewer words and cruder drawings, the comics become less imaginative and less entertaining. The irony of this is that newspapers are desperate to attract readers reared on the visual impact of television. Papers have spent a lot of money to improve layouts and add colorful maps, charts, and photographs, while the comics—the one graphic feature unique to newspapers—typically languish on a single page of tiny black-and-white boxes arranged in a boring grid. By unimaginatively imposing standardized, reduced formats on all comics, papers give the comics cost-efficient space, not graphically effective space.

Because of all these developments, the traditional relationship between cartoonist, syndicate, and newspaper has been strained. As circumstances change, each party tries to protect its own interests. Newspapers are trimming costs by cutting space and features. Syndicates respond by diversifying into licensing and publishing. The top cartoonists are demanding greater control over their work, and some are leaving the business altogether. With fewer common goals and needs, there is less trust and cooperation.

As a cartoonist who's done his share of aggravating the situation, it seems to me that good comics are in the interest of readers, newspapers, syndicates, and cartoonists. Yet the best strips of the past would have a tough time in newspapers today. The esoteric but brilliant *Krazy Kat,* barely marketable in its own day, would be hard pressed to find a publisher willing to champion its unique vision today. Adventure strips like *Terry and the Pirates* would be unlikely to sweep readers into their exotic stories now that beautiful illustration is stifled by the little boxes available to strips. *Popeye* relied on up to twenty panels on Sunday to create its raucous energy, a sheer impossibility in today's quarter-page Sunday slots. Continuous "soap opera" strips are all but gone now, unable to keep their plots gripping with the reduction of dialogue necessary in small panels. The comics are losing their variety.

Sixty years ago, the best strips weren't just amusingly drawn, they were beautiful to look at. I can't think of a single strip today that comes close to that standard of craftsmanship. Now we have plenty of simply drawn gag strips, but not much else. We've lost an essential part of what makes comics fun to read. As animated cartoons and comic books are becoming more sophisticated, more lavishly produced, and more popular than ever, newspaper comic strips are enervated.

I've heard it argued that today's readers do not have the patience for involved storylines and rich artwork in comics anymore. Popularity polls are cited to show that comics are doing just fine the way they are. I disagree and I think it's a mistake to underestimate readers' appetite for quality. The comics can be much more than they presently are. Better strips could attract larger audiences, and this would help newspapers. The comics' potential—as a seller of newspapers, and as an art form—is great if cartoonists will challenge themselves to create extraordinary work and if the business will work to create a sustaining environment for it.

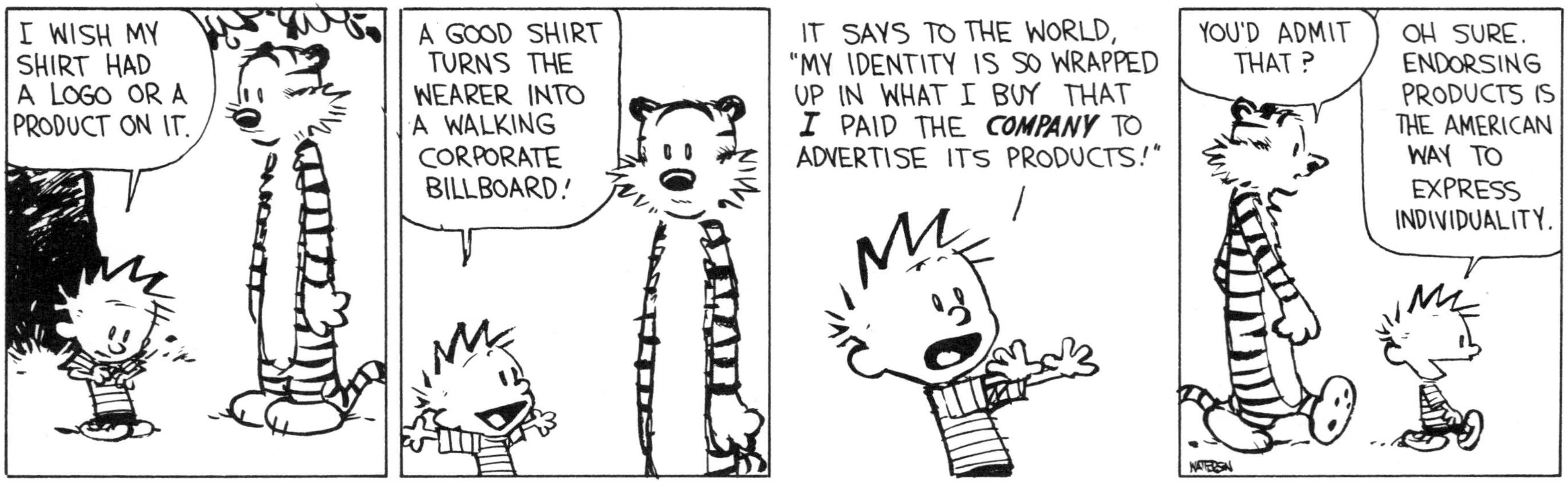
I WISH MY SHIRT HAD A LOGO OR A PRODUCT ON IT.
A GOOD SHIRT TURNS THE WEARER INTO A WALKING CORPORATE BILLBOARD!
IT SAYS TO THE WORLD, "MY IDENTITY IS SO WRAPPED UP IN WHAT I BUY THAT I PAID THE COMPANY TO ADVERTISE ITS PRODUCTS!"
YOU'D ADMIT THAT?
OH SURE. ENDORSING PRODUCTS IS THE AMERICAN WAY TO EXPRESS INDIVIDUALITY.

LICENSING

Comic strips have been licensed from the beginning, but today the merchandising of popular cartoon characters is more profitable than ever. Derivative products—dolls, T-shirts, TV specials, and so on—can turn the right strip into a gold mine. Everyone is looking for the next Snoopy or Garfield, and Calvin and Hobbes were imagined to be the perfect candidates. The more I thought about licensing, however, the less I liked it. I spent nearly five years fighting my syndicate's pressure to merchandise my creation.

In an age of shameless commercialism, my objections to licensing are not widely shared. Many cartoonists view the comic strip as a commercial product itself, so they regard licensing as a natural extension of their work. As most people ask, what's wrong with comic strip characters appearing on calendars and coffee mugs? If people want to buy the stuff, why not give it to them?

I have several problems with licensing. First of all, I believe licensing usually cheapens the original creation. When cartoon characters appear on countless products, the public inevitably grows bored and irritated with them, and the appeal and value of the original work are diminished. Nothing dulls the edge of a new and clever cartoon like saturating the market with it.

Second, commercial products rarely respect how a comic strip works. A wordy, multiple-panel strip with extended conversation and developed personalities does not condense to a coffee mug illustration without great violation to the strip's spirit. The subtleties of a multi-dimensional strip are sacrificed for the one-dimensional needs of the product. The world of a comic strip ought to be a special place with its own logic and life. I don't want some animation studio giving Hobbes an actor's voice, and I don't want some greeting card company using Calvin to wish people a happy anniversary, and I don't want the issue of Hobbes's reality settled by a doll manufacturer. When everything fun and magical is turned into something for sale, the strip's world is diminished. *Calvin and Hobbes* was designed to be a comic strip and that's all I want it to be. It's the one place where everything works the way I intend it to.

Third, as a practical matter, licensing requires a staff of assistants to do the work. The cartoonist must become a factory foreman, delegating responsibilities and overseeing the production of things he does not create. Some cartoonists don't mind this, but I went into cartooning to draw cartoons, not to run a corporate empire. I take great pride in the fact that I write every word, draw every line, color every Sunday strip, and paint every book illustration myself. My strip is a low-tech, one-man operation, and I like it that way. I believe it's the only way to preserve the craft and to keep the strip personal. Despite what some cartoonists say, approving someone else's work is not the same as doing it yourself.

Beyond all this, however, lies a deeper issue: the corruption of a strip's integrity. All strips are supposed to be entertaining, but some strips have a point of view and a serious purpose behind the jokes. When the cartoonist is trying to talk honestly and seriously about life, then I believe he has a responsibility to think beyond satisfying the market's every whim and desire. Cartoonists who think they can be taken seriously as artists while using the strip's protagonists to sell boxer shorts are deluding themselves.

The world of a comic strip is much more fragile than most people realize or will admit. Believable characters are hard to develop and easy to destroy. When a cartoonist licenses his characters, his voice is co-opted by the business concerns of toy makers, television producers, and advertisers. The cartoonist's job is no longer to be an original thinker; his job is to keep his characters profitable. The characters become "celebrities," endorsing companies and products, avoiding controversy, and saying whatever someone will pay them to say. At that point, the strip has no soul. With its integrity gone, a strip loses its deeper significance.

My strip is about private realities, the magic of imagination, and the specialness of certain friendships. Who would believe in the innocence of a little kid and his tiger if they cashed in on their popularity to sell overpriced knickknacks that nobody needs? Who would trust the honesty of the strip's observations when the characters are hired out as advertising hucksters? If I were to undermine my own characters like this, I would have taken the rare privilege of being paid to express my own ideas and given it up to be an ordinary salesman and a hired illustrator. I would have sold out my own creation. I have no use for that kind of cartooning.

Unfortunately, the more popular *Calvin and Hobbes* became, the less control I had over its fate. I was presented with licensing possibilities before the strip was even a year old, and the pressure to capitalize on its success mounted from then on. Succeeding beyond anyone's wildest expectations had only inspired wilder expectations.

To put the problem simply, trainloads of money were at stake—millions and millions of dollars could be made with a few signatures. Syndicates are businesses, and no business passes up that kind of opportunity without an argument.

Undermining my position, I had signed a contract giving my syndicate all exploitation rights to *Calvin and Hobbes* into the next century. Because it is virtually impossible to get into daily newspapers without a syndicate, it is standard practice for syndicates to use their superior bargaining position to demand rights they neither need nor deserve when contracting with unknown cartoonists. The cartoonist has few alternatives to the syndicate's terms: he can take his work elsewhere on the unlikely chance that a different syndicate would be more inclined to offer concessions, he can self-syndicate and attempt to attract the interest of newspapers without the benefit of reputation or contacts, or he can go back home and find some other job. Universal would not sell my strip to newspapers unless I gave the syndicate the right to merchandise the strip in other media. At the time, I had not thought much about licensing and the issue was not among my top concerns. Two syndicates had already rejected *Calvin and Hobbes*, and I worried more about the contractual consequences if the strip failed than the contractual consequences if the strip succeeded. Eager for the opportunity to publish my work, I signed the contract, and it was not until later, when the pressure to commercialize focused my opinions on the matter, that I understood the trouble I'd gotten myself into.

I had no legal recourse to stop the syndicate from licensing. The syndicate preferred to have my cooperation, but my approval was by no means necessary. Our arguments with each other grew more bitter as the stakes got higher, and we had an ugly relationship for several years.

The debate had its ridiculous aspects. I am probably the only cartoonist who resented the popularity of his own strip. Most cartoonists are more than eager for the exposure, wealth, and prestige that licensing offers. When cartoonists fight their syndicates, it's usually to make more money, not less. And making the whole issue even more absurd, when I didn't license, bootleg *Calvin and Hobbes* merchandise sprung up to feed the demand. Mall stores openly sold T-shirts with drawings illegally lifted from my books, and obscene or drug-related shirts were rife on college campuses. Only thieves and vandals have made money on *Calvin and Hobbes* merchandise.

For years, Universal pressured me to compromise on a "limited" licensing program. The syndicate would agree to rule out the most offensive products if I would agree to go along with the rest. This would be, in essence, my only shot at controlling what happened to my work. The idea of bartering principles was offensive to me and I refused to compromise. For that matter, the syndicate and I had nothing to trade anyway: I didn't care if we made more money, and the syndicate didn't care about my notions of artistic integrity. With neither of us valuing what the other had to offer, compromise was impossible. One of us was going to trample the interests of the other.

By the strip's fifth year, the debate had gone as far as it could possibly go, and I prepared to quit. If I could not control what *Calvin and Hobbes* stood for, the strip was worthless to me. My contract was so one-sided that quitting would have allowed Universal to replace me with hired writers and artists and license my creation anyway, but at this point, the syndicate agreed to renegotiate my contract. The exploitation rights to the strip were returned to me, and I will not license *Calvin and Hobbes*.

SABBATICALS

I never expected, much less demanded, time off from the strip, but exhausted and disgusted after the licensing fight, I readily accepted the syndicate's offer of two nine-month sabbaticals. By taking them within three years of each other, I became the Lazy Cartoonist poster boy, but in fact, I am not a big advocate of long breaks, or for that matter, of reruns.

Garry Trudeau and Gary Larson had previously taken sabbaticals, so I became the third cartoonist to announce a long break from his strip. Some other cartoonists have publicly denounced these vacations as unnecessary and self-indulgent. I find these criticisms incredibly presumptuous. Some cartoonists can meet their own standards of quality and be on the golf course by noon, but that's not the case for everyone. In my opinion, any creative person can be forgiven some occasional time off to recharge the batteries and pursue other interests.

That said, sabbaticals definitely strain the cartoonist's relationship with newspaper editors and readers. Reruns are tedious, and after several months of them, there is always the risk that readers will break their habit of reading the strip and discover that they don't miss it. Editors, of course, don't like paying for the same material twice, and with such limited space for comics and great competition among new strips, an editor can hardly be blamed for dropping the reruns and substituting a fresher strip. To justify their place in the newspaper, the reruns have to be more popular than the other strips available as a replacement. This is one reason why there will never be many sabbaticals.

A better solution, obviously, is periodic short vacations. To its credit, this last year Universal Press Syndicate offered *all* its cartoonists four weeks off each year. Each cartoonist can decide for himself the need for time off and the risk of stopping the strip. With more frequent breaks, cartoonists may be able to preserve their sanity without long sabbaticals, and readers and editors will undoubtedly find shorter periods of reruns less irritating. I think this is more reasonable all around.

THE SUNDAY STRIP

The format for Sunday strips is a rigid one, and as *Calvin and Hobbes* became more visually complex, I found that I could not design the strip to the story's best advantage. I would often need to eliminate dialogue or simplify the drawings so they'd fit in the arbitrary space the format allotted. At times, this threatened to ruin the idea, and it frequently made for an ugly, graceless strip. It aggravated me to think that I could draw a better strip than my readers were seeing, so I took advantage of my first sabbatical to propose a newly designed Sunday strip.

The prevailing Sunday format was invented to standardize comic strip layouts so as to give newspapers the utmost flexibility in printing them. The strip is drawn in three rows. Printed full size, this will fill half a newspaper page. Most papers are reluctant to run a strip that big, so they remove the top row of panels, which makes the strip take up only a third of a page. Because the cartoonist cannot count on readers seeing the top panels, he must waste them on "throw-away" gags that have little to do with the rest of the strip. To make the strip smaller still, editors can reduce the panels and line them up in two rows, so the strip takes only a quarter of a page. Some papers cut and reduce even more, at which point the strip is virtually illegible. To neatly accommodate all these variations, the panel divisions are specific and unyielding. The strip will fit the different space needs of different newspapers this way, but the cartoonist loses the ability to design his strip effectively.

Before all this, up until the 1940s, a Sunday strip often filled an *entire* newspaper page. I don't think it's coincidental that this was the "golden age" of comics. With all that space to fill, cartoonists produced works of extraordinary beauty and power. There has been nothing remotely like them since. It seemed to me that if readers in the 1990s were given a glimpse

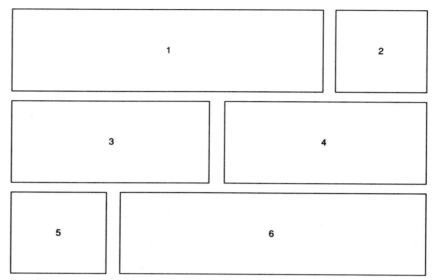

Sunday format as ½ page.

of what they'd been missing, they might read the comics with more interest, and this would benefit newspapers. I believed I could offer newspapers a better cartoon for their money.

Universal agreed to sell my strip exclusively as a half-page feature with no panel restrictions. I was thrilled, but the syndicate warned me that many newspapers would balk at being told they couldn't reduce and rearrange my work anymore. We talked in terms of losing half my Sunday client list, but I figured it would be worth the loss in income if I could work at the limits of my abilities for a change.

The syndicate was right: a number of editors were enraged. They threw syndicate sales people out of their offices and inundated Universal with cancellation threats.

Editors informed me that cartoonists had no business making space decisions on their behalf. They reminded me that newspaper space was expensive and the industry was

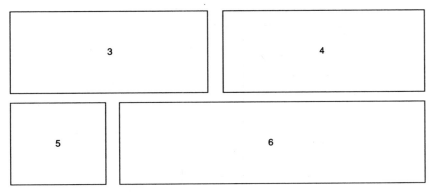

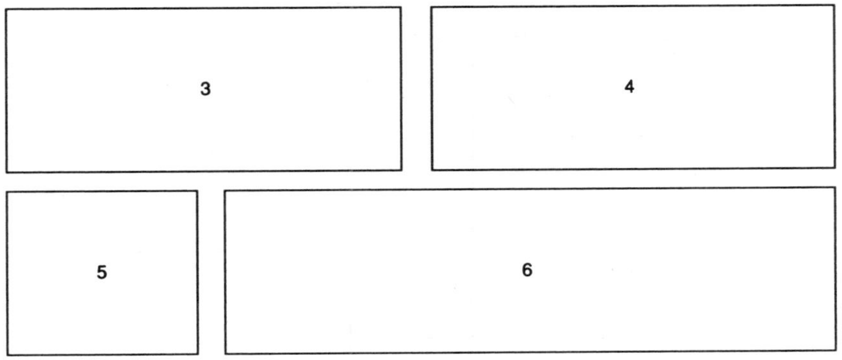

Sunday format as 1/3 page.

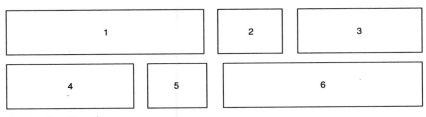

Sunday format as 1/4 page.

was a curious oversight that no one bothered to ask what newspaper readers thought of a larger Sunday *Calvin and Hobbes*.

I still believe that the editors' response was poorly reasoned and absurdly hot-tempered. I was in no way telling editors what to do. I was simply establishing the conditions upon which I would sell my work, just as one sets a price. If an editor found my conditions unacceptable, he was perfectly free to cancel my strip and run something else. Any pressure he felt to take my strip came from his paper's readers, not from me, and I do not apologize for offering papers a popular strip.

I also believe that with a little imagination, most Sunday comic sections could be redesigned to run one half-page strip without dumping others. Moreover, I expected my strip would be canceled in many papers, and that would have opened those spaces to other cartoonists.

And as for my sinister motives and my insensitivity to the newspaper industry's struggles, I can only argue that I was willing to do more work for less income, and I could easily have gotten more freedom *and* more money by abandoning newspapers altogether and publishing elsewhere.

With a firestorm of ill will directed at the syndicate, Universal compromised on the size issue and offered the strip two ways: as the half-page and as a much reduced version of the same thing. I was disappointed, but this still freed me from the panel constraints of the old format. I do not have to waste any panels on throw-away gags and I can design the space more effectively, even if the whole strip is ultimately reduced. Very few papers canceled, but many took the smaller strip. In some cases, this means *Calvin and Hobbes* actually lost space.

Despite that setback, with this new format I've drawn many strips I never could have drawn before. In some of my new Sunday strips, I've been able to draw large panels or as many as twenty small panels, and that has opened up new ways of storytelling. I do many wordless Sunday strips now,

struggling already. They worried what ridiculous demands would come next if this became a precedent. They pointed out that they had just paid for nine months of reruns. They argued that, so long as they paid for the strip, it should serve their needs, not mine. They questioned my familiarity with the real world and wondered if my ego had any boundaries at all. They threatened to cancel other Universal features in wholesale retaliation. They insisted that other popular strips would have to be canceled to make room for mine and that this was an unconscionable grab for more of the newspaper. On this last point, several cartoonists joined in.

I was sorry to see that none of these objections addressed the issue of the graphic needs of comic strips. I also thought it

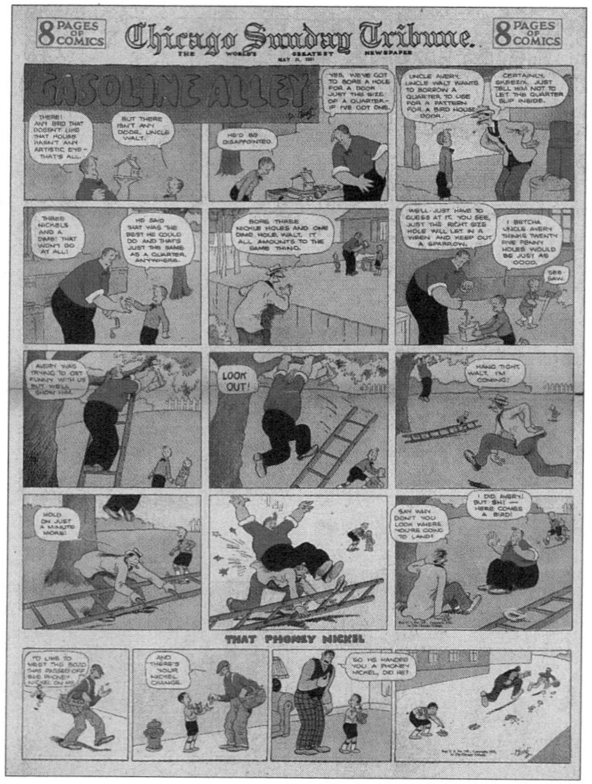
8 PAGES OF COMICS
Chicago Sunday Tribune.
8 PAGES OF COMICS
GASOLINE ALLEY
LOOK OUT!
THAT PHONEY NICKEL
Sample Sunday Page, *Chicago Tribune*, May 31, 1931.

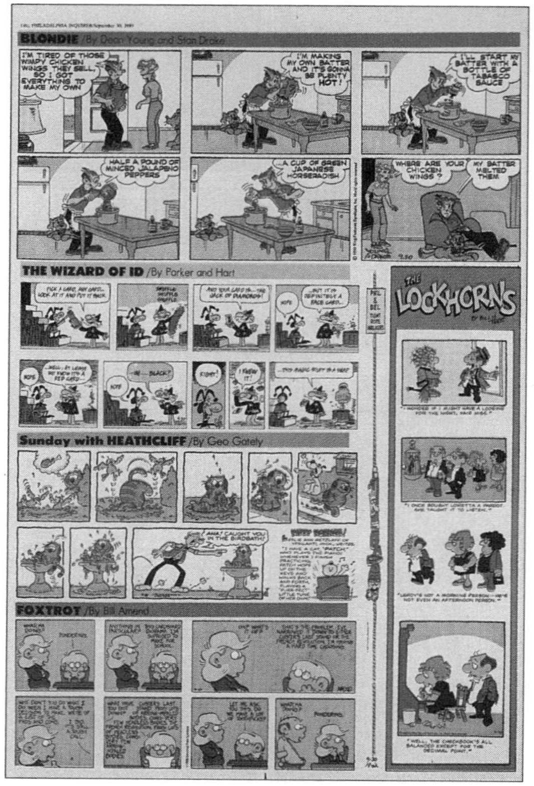
BLONDIE /By Dean Young and Stan Drake
THE WIZARD OF ID /By Parker and Hart
THE LOCKHORNS
Sunday with HEATHCLIFF /By Geo Gately
FOXTROT /By Bill Amend
Sample Sunday Page, *The Philadelphia Inquirer*, September 30, 1990.

because the drawings can finally hold their own. I think I've been able to make Calvin's world more vivid, and I think I've made the space more exciting to look at. These are not esoteric concerns; these are what make a comic strip fun to read.

Over the last several decades, comic strips have been reduced and reduced and reduced. Cartoonists have acquiesced, believing that cutting everyone's size is better than cutting the number of strips a paper will print. Up to a point, that's true, but I think the reductions have now gone so far as to take a serious toll on the art. The possibilities for expression are diminishing, and as a consequence, we don't have well-drawn comics any more. It's hard for me to argue that maintaining the quantity of comics is a reasonable substitute for maintaining their quality.

INFLUENCES

Three comic strips have been tremendously inspirational to me: *Peanuts* by Charles Schulz, *Pogo* by Walt Kelly, and *Krazy Kat* by George Herriman. These strips have very different sensibilities, but they've helped me discover what a comic strip can do.

Peanuts books were among the first things I ever read, and once I saw them, I knew I wanted to be a cartoonist. I instantly related to the flat, spare drawings, the honesty of the children's insecurities, and to Snoopy's bizarre and separate world. At the time, I didn't appreciate how innovative all that was—I just knew it had a kind of humor and truth that other strips lacked. Now when I reread the old books, I'm amazed at what a melancholy comic strip it was in the '60s. Surely no other strip has presented a world so relentlessly cruel and heartless. Charlie Brown's self-torture in the face of constant failure is funny in a bitter, hopelessly sad way. I think the most important thing I learned from *Peanuts* is that a comic strip can have an emotional edge to it and that it can talk about the big issues of life in a sensitive and perceptive way.

Pogo, in some ways, is the opposite of *Peanuts*. Whereas *Peanuts* is a visually spare strip about private insecurities, *Pogo* was a lushly drawn strip, full of bombast and physical commotion. The strip's dialogue was a stew of dialect, pun, and nonsense, and word balloons were often filled with gothic type or circus poster letters to suggest the character's personality and voice. With the possible exception of Porkypine, there was not a soul-searching character in a cast of dozens. The drawings were beautifully animated and the stories wandered down back roads, got lost, and forgot their destinations. Kelly's animals satirized the day's politics, back when comics were expected to avoid controversy altogether. Beneath the chaos and bluster though, the strip had a basic faith in human decency and an optimism for bumbling through. *Pogo* had a pace and an atmosphere that will probably never be seen again. The strip is a wonderful lesson in what a lively, rich world the comics can present.

It is *Krazy Kat*, however, that fills me with the most awe today. *Krazy Kat* is more poetic than funny, with a charm that's impossible to describe. Everything about the strip is idiosyncratic and peculiar—the wonderful, scratchy drawings, the bold design and color of the Sunday strips, the kooky, austere Arizona landscapes, and the bizarre conglomeration of Spanish, slang, literary allusion, dialect, and mispronunciation that makes up the dialogue. The circular plot, such as it is, can be interpreted (and over-interpreted) as an allegory about good and evil, love and hate, society and individual . . . or it can simply be enjoyed for its lunatic machinery. For me, the magic of the strip is not so much in what it says, but how it says it. In its singular, uncompromised vision, its subtle whimsy and its odd beauty, *Krazy Kat* stands alone.

Other cartoonists and artists have inspired me as well, but these three strips shaped my idea of what a comic strip could be. All the strips work on several levels, entertaining while they deal with bigger issues of life. Most important, these strips reflect uniquely personal views of the world. They argue that comics can be vehicles for beautiful artwork and serious, intelligent expression. They set the example I wanted to follow.

The challenge of any cartoonist is not just to duplicate the achievements of the past, but to build on them as well. Comic strips have a short history, but their traditions are important. Cartoonists learn about cartooning by reading cartoons. Unfortunately, the history of comics is not very accessible. Popular strips were not regularly collected in books until very recently. *Peanuts* and *Pogo* collections are often difficult to find and are increasingly expensive. *Krazy Kat* still has not been adequately published in book form. It has only been in the last few years that I've seen any extended runs of the true classics of the medium. Early strips are amazing—some are far more inventive than today's—but they can't educate future cartoonists if they're not collected and republished. Sometimes I wonder what strips would be like if every generation didn't have to reinvent the wheel.

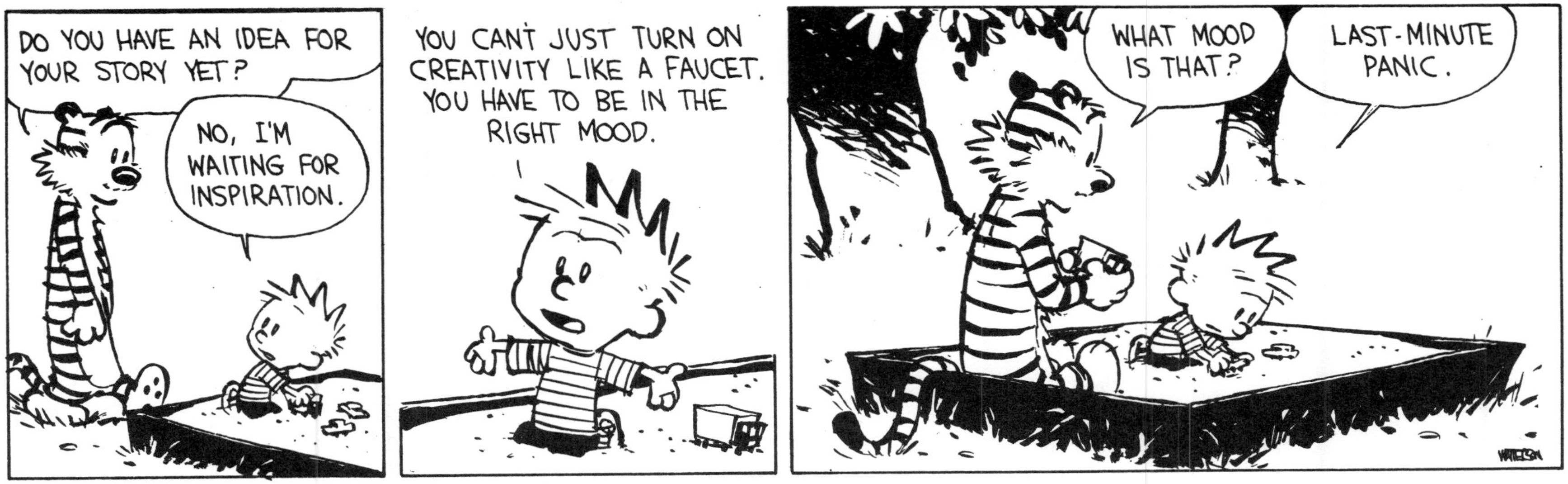
DO YOU HAVE AN IDEA FOR YOUR STORY YET?
NO, I'M WAITING FOR INSPIRATION.
YOU CAN'T JUST TURN ON CREATIVITY LIKE A FAUCET. YOU HAVE TO BE IN THE RIGHT MOOD.
WHAT MOOD IS THAT?
LAST-MINUTE PANIC.

THE PROCESS

I think I learned to be a writer so I could draw for a living. Actually, I enjoy writing as much as drawing, but working on a deadline, the drawing is easier and faster.

People always ask how cartoonists come up with ideas, and the answer is so boring that we're usually tempted to make up something sarcastic. The truth is, we hold a blank sheet of paper, stare into space, and let our minds wander. (To the layman, this looks remarkably like goofing off.) When something interests us, we play around with it. Sometimes this yields a funny observation; sometimes it doesn't, but that's about all there is to it. Once in a while the cartoonist will find himself in a beam of light and angels will appear with a great idea, but not often.

Occasionally I'll have a subject or issue in mind that I want to talk about, but if I don't have a ready topic, I try to think of what I'd like to draw. My goal is to feel enthusiastic about some aspect of the work. I think one can always tell when an artist is engaged and having a good time: the energy and life comes through in the work. I like to sit outside when I write, partly because it seems less like a job that way, and partly because there are bugs and birds and rocks around that may suggest an idea. I never know what will trigger a workable idea, so my writing schedule varies a great deal. Sometimes I can write several strips in an afternoon; sometimes I can't write anything at all. I never know if another hour sitting there will be wasted time or the most productive hour of the day.

When I come up with a topic, I look at it through Calvin's

eyes. Calvin's personality dictates a range of possible reactions to any subject, so I just tag along and see what he does. The truth of the matter is that my characters write their own material. I put them in situations and listen to them. A line for Hobbes never works for Calvin or Susie, because Hobbes reacts differently and he expresses himself in a different voice. Virtually all the strip's humor comes from the characters' personalities: I would never think of Calvin's retort if Calvin weren't the one saying it.

I write my ideas in an ordinary school notebook. I spend a lot of time fussing with the wording, juggling the various concerns of timing, clarity, brevity, and so on. I write in pencil, and go through erasers at an alarming rate. Once I bang an idea into form, I make a small doodle of the characters to give the strip a rough outline. My purpose at this point is mostly to show who's speaking each line, but I try to suggest gestures and rough compositions, so I will think about the idea in visual terms when it comes time to ink it up. I reevaluate the roughs over several days, when I'm fresher and more objective. Often the writing needs more work, and sometimes I just cross the whole thing out. On occasion, I've ripped up entire stories—weeks of material—that I didn't think were good. Obviously, if I'm right on deadline, that kind of editing becomes a luxury, so I try to write well ahead of due dates. It's very embarrassing to send out a strip I think is bad, so I like a long lead time and, given the need to fill newspaper space every day, I weed out as much mediocre work as possible.

After I have about thirty daily strips, I show them to my wife. She can usually intuit what I'm trying to say, even when I don't get it right, so she's a good editor, and a pretty accurate Laugh-o-meter. After reworking or scrapping weak strips, I ink up the ones I like.

I typically ink six daily strips, or one Sunday strip, in a long day. I'd enjoy the inking more if I could take more time,

but I need to draw efficiently in order to gain back the time lost writing bad ideas. I lightly pencil in the dialogue first, as that determines the space left for drawing. Next, I sketch in the characters very loosely, establishing the composition of each panel. I frequently make revisions, so I use a light pencil and I erase as needed. If the picture is unusually complex, I'll render the difficult parts completely, but generally, I try to do as little pencil work as possible. That way, the inking stays spontaneous and fun, because I'm not simply tracing pencil lines. Inking mistakes and accidents are whited out.

I draw the strip with a small sable brush and waterproof India ink on Strathmore bristol board. I letter the dialogue with a Rapidograph fountain pen, and I use a crowquill pen for odds and ends. It's about as low-tech as you can get.

The Sunday strips also need to be colored. This is a time-consuming and rather tedious task, but the color is an integral part of my Sunday strips, so I think it's important to choose all the colors myself. (Foreign collections of my work are sometimes recolored, and the results rarely please me.) When I first started *Calvin and Hobbes*, there were 64 colors available for Sunday strips; now we have 125 colors, as well as the ability to fade colors into each other. The colors are incremental percentage combinations of red, yellow, and blue, and we have a pretty good range, although I wish there were more pale colors. Each color has a number, so I color my strip on an overlay, and mark the corresponding numbers. The syndicate sends this to American Color, a company that processes all the Sunday comics into color negatives for newspaper printing.

After a batch of strips is inked and colored, I send them to the syndicate, where my editor corrects my spelling and grammar, and looks for anything offensive. A copyright sticker is affixed and the strip is printed up and sent to subscribing newspapers. Then I start writing again.

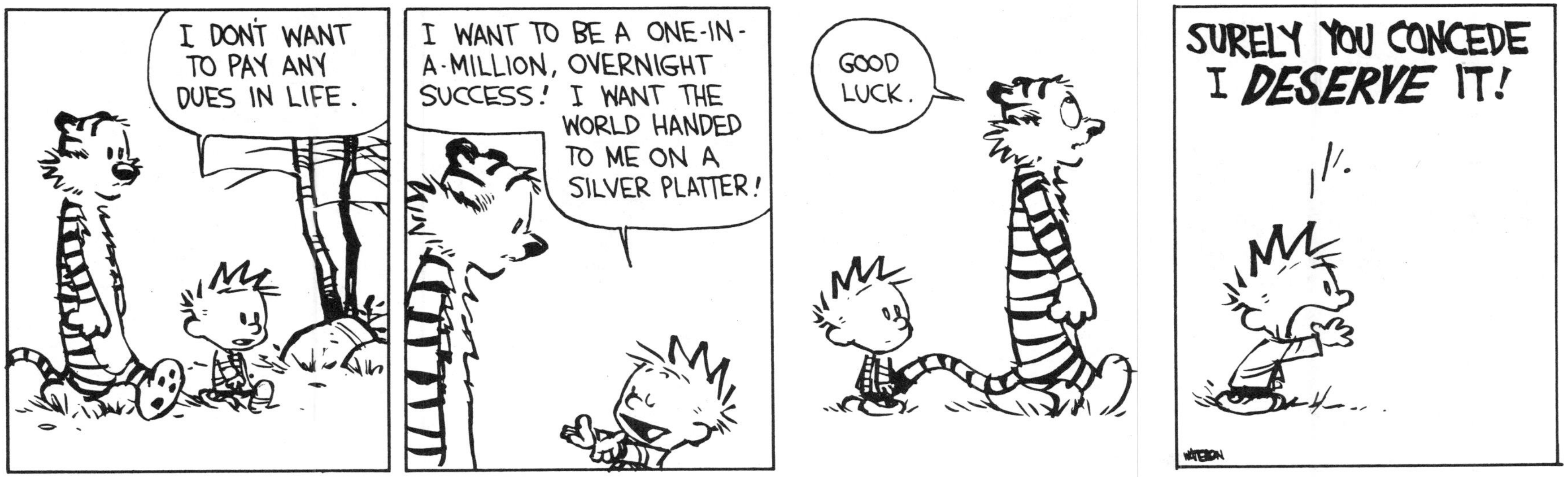
I DON'T WANT TO PAY ANY DUES IN LIFE.
I WANT TO BE A ONE-IN-A-MILLION, OVERNIGHT SUCCESS! I WANT THE WORLD HANDED TO ME ON A SILVER PLATTER!
GOOD LUCK.
SURELY YOU CONCEDE I DESERVE IT!

THE CAST

Calvin: Calvin is named for a sixteenth-century theologian who believed in predestination. Most people assume that Calvin is based on a son of mine, or based on detailed memories of my own childhood. In fact, I don't have children, and I was a fairly quiet, obedient kid—almost Calvin's opposite. One of the reasons that Calvin's character is fun to write is that I often don't agree with him.

Calvin is autobiographical in the sense that he thinks about the same issues that I do, but in this, Calvin reflects my adulthood more than my childhood. Many of Calvin's struggles are metaphors for my own. I suspect that most of us get old without growing up, and that inside every adult (sometimes not very far inside) is a bratty kid who wants everything his own way. I use Calvin as an outlet for my immaturity, as a way to keep myself curious about the natural world, as a way to ridicule my own obsessions, and as a way to comment on human nature. I wouldn't want Calvin in my house, but on paper, he helps me sort through my life and understand it.

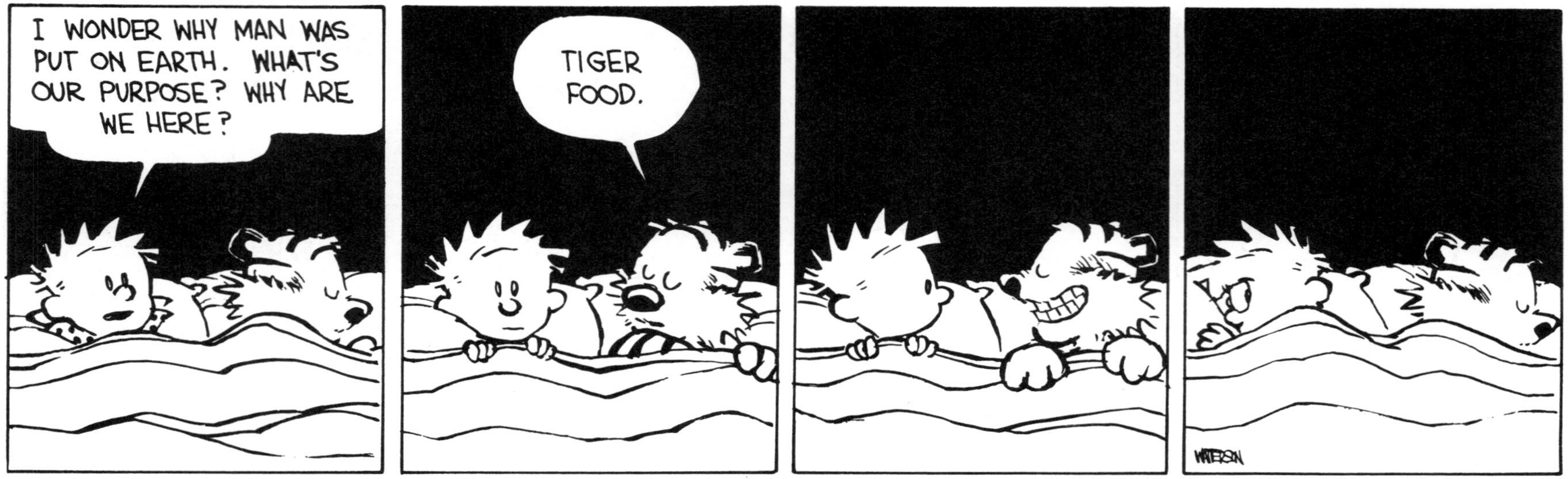
I WONDER WHY MAN WAS PUT ON EARTH. WHAT'S OUR PURPOSE? WHY ARE WE HERE?
TIGER FOOD.
WATERSON

Hobbes: Named after a seventeenth-century philosopher with a dim view of human nature, Hobbes has the patient dignity and common sense of most animals I've met. Hobbes was very much inspired by one of our cats, a gray tabby named Sprite. Sprite not only provided the long body and facial characteristics for Hobbes, she also was the model for his personality. She was good-natured, intelligent, friendly, and enthusiastic in a sneaking-up-and-pouncing sort of way. Sprite suggested the idea of Hobbes greeting Calvin at the door in midair at high velocity.

With most cartoon animals, the humor comes from their humanlike behavior. Hobbes stands upright and talks of course, but I try to preserve his feline side, both in his physical demeanor and his attitude. His reserve and tact seem very catlike to me, along with his barely contained pride in not being human. Like Calvin, I often prefer the company of animals to people, and Hobbes is my idea of an ideal friend.

The so-called "gimmick" of my strip—the two versions of Hobbes—is sometimes misunderstood. I don't think of Hobbes as a doll that miraculously comes to life when Calvin's around. Neither do I think of Hobbes as the product of Calvin's imagination. The nature of Hobbes's reality doesn't interest me, and each story goes out of its way to avoid resolving the issue. Calvin sees Hobbes one way, and everyone else sees Hobbes another way. I show two versions of reality, and each makes complete sense to the participant who sees it. I think that's how life works. None of us sees the world in exactly the same way, and I just draw that literally in the strip. Hobbes is more about the subjective nature of reality than about dolls coming to life.

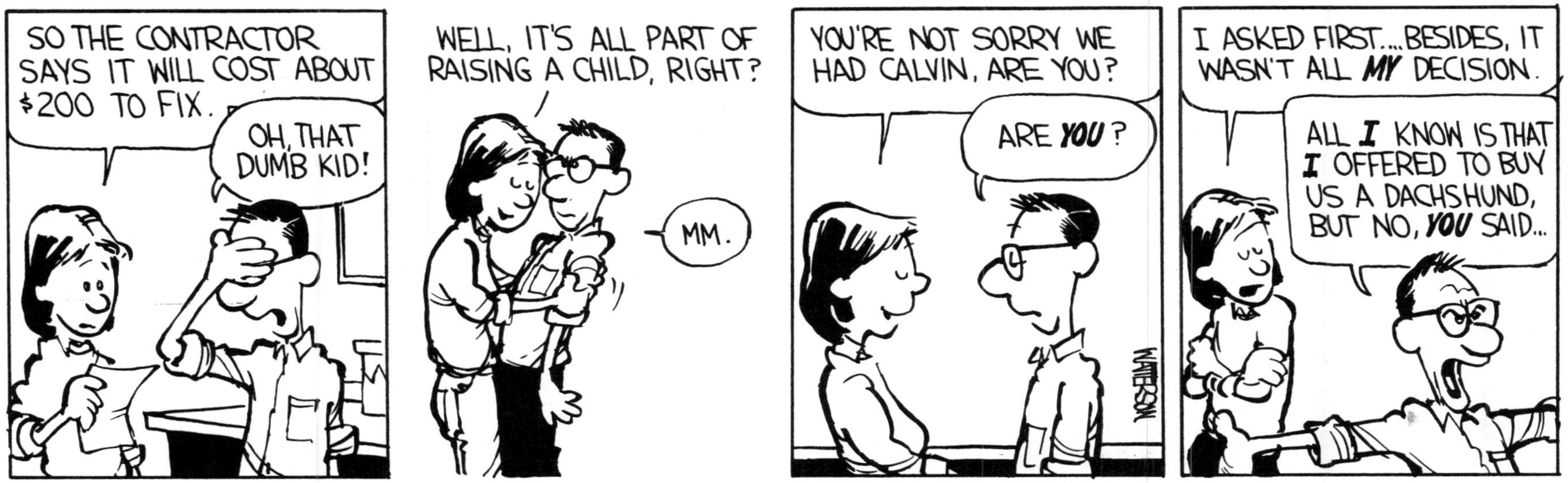
SO THE CONTRACTOR SAYS IT WILL COST ABOUT $200 TO FIX.
OH, THAT DUMB KID!
WELL, IT'S ALL PART OF RAISING A CHILD, RIGHT?
MM.
YOU'RE NOT SORRY WE HAD CALVIN, ARE YOU?
ARE YOU?
WATTERSON
I ASKED FIRST.... BESIDES, IT WASN'T ALL MY DECISION.
ALL I KNOW IS THAT I OFFERED TO BUY US A DACHSHUND, BUT NO, YOU SAID...

Calvin's parents: I've never given Calvin's parents names, because as far as the strip is concerned, they are important only as Calvin's mom and dad. Calvin's dad has been rumored to be a self-portrait. All my characters are half me, so it's true in some ways, but Calvin's dad is also partly a satire of my own father. Any strip about how suffering "builds character" is usually a verbatim transcript of my dad's explanations for why we were all freezing, exhausted, hungry, and lost on camping trips. These things are a lot funnier after twenty-five years have passed.

Calvin's mom is the daily disciplinarian, a job that taxes her sanity, so I don't think we get to see her at her best. I regret that the strip mostly shows her impatient side, but I try to hint at other aspects of her personality and her interests by what she's doing when Calvin barges in.

Early on, Calvin's parents were criticized by readers for being unloving and needlessly sarcastic. (Calvin's dad has remarked that what he really wanted was a dog.) At the time, I think it was unusual for a comic strip to concentrate on the exasperating aspects of kids without a lot of hugs and sentimentality to leaven it. We usually only see Calvin's parents when they're reacting to Calvin, so as secondary characters, I've tried to keep them realistic, with a reasonable sense of humor about having a kid like Calvin. I think they do a better job than I would.

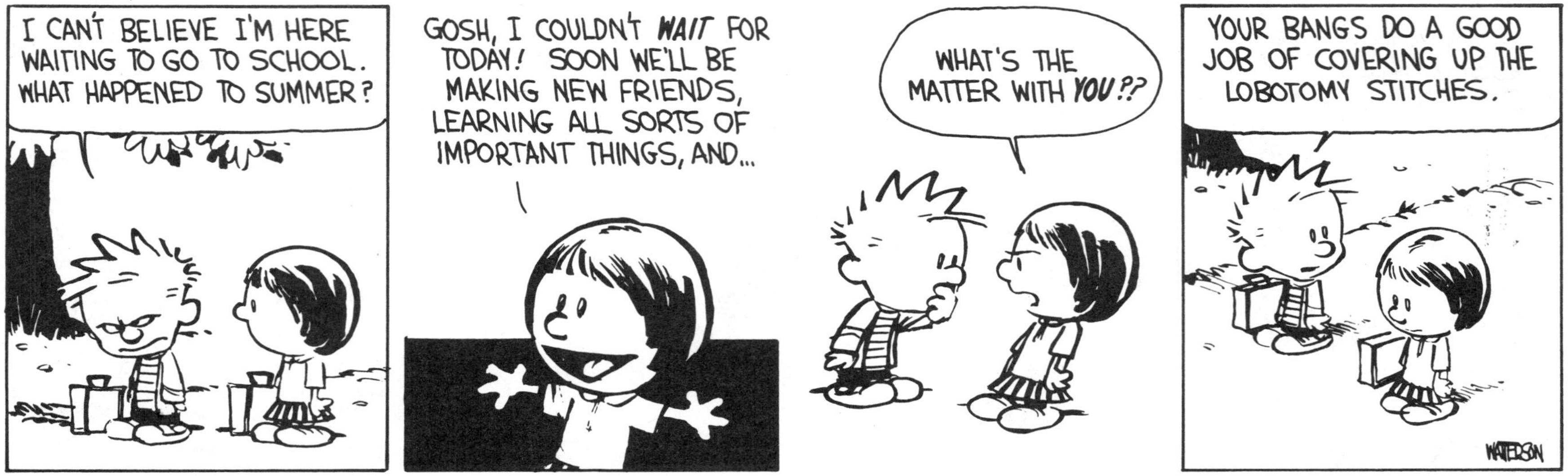
I CAN'T BELIEVE I'M HERE WAITING TO GO TO SCHOOL. WHAT HAPPENED TO SUMMER?
GOSH, I COULDN'T WAIT FOR TODAY! SOON WE'LL BE MAKING NEW FRIENDS, LEARNING ALL SORTS OF IMPORTANT THINGS, AND...
WHAT'S THE MATTER WITH YOU?!?
YOUR BANGS DO A GOOD JOB OF COVERING UP THE LOBOTOMY STITCHES.
WATTERSON

Susie Derkins: Susie is earnest, serious, and smart—the kind of girl I was attracted to in school and eventually married. "Derkins" was the nickname of my wife's family's beagle. The early strips with Susie were heavy-handed with the love-hate conflict, and it's taken me a while to get a bead on Susie's relationship with Calvin. I suspect Calvin has a mild crush on her that he expresses by trying to annoy her, but Susie is a bit unnerved and put off by Calvin's weirdness. This encourages Calvin to be even weirder, so it's a good dynamic. Neither of them quite understands what's going on, which is probably true of most relationships. I sometimes imagine a strip from Susie's point of view would be interesting, and after so many strips about boys, I think a strip about a little girl, drawn by a woman, could be great.

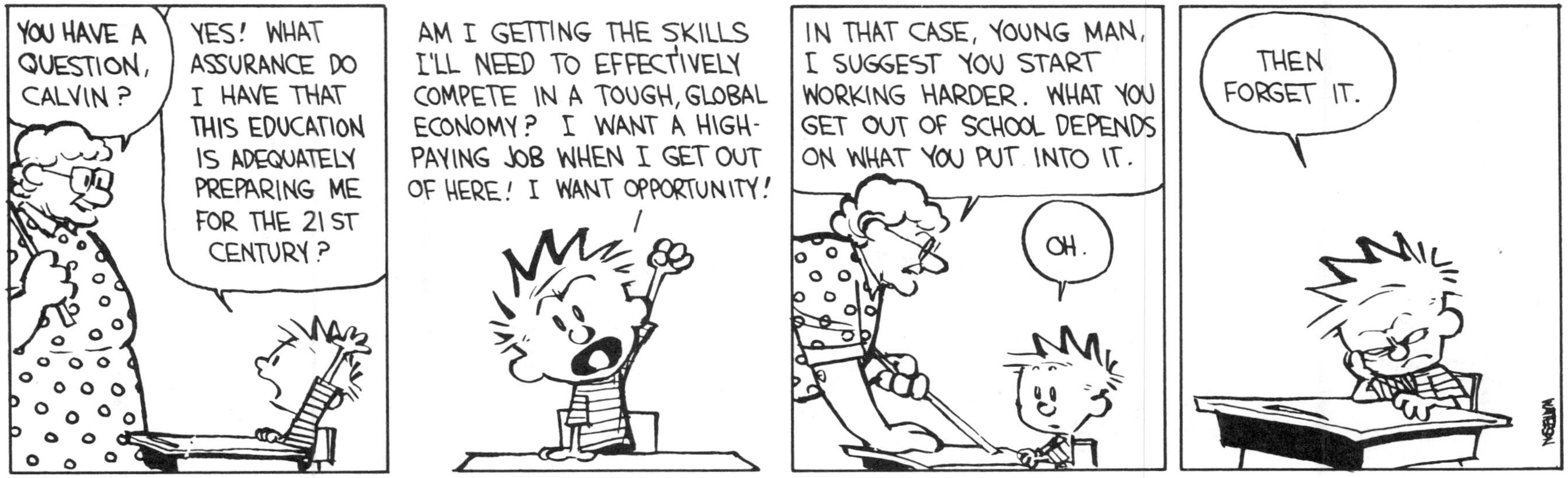
YOU HAVE A QUESTION, CALVIN?
YES! WHAT ASSURANCE DO I HAVE THAT THIS EDUCATION IS ADEQUATELY PREPARING ME FOR THE 21ST CENTURY?
AM I GETTING THE SKILLS I'LL NEED TO EFFECTIVELY COMPETE IN A TOUGH, GLOBAL ECONOMY? I WANT A HIGH-PAYING JOB WHEN I GET OUT OF HERE! I WANT OPPORTUNITY!
IN THAT CASE, YOUNG MAN, I SUGGEST YOU START WORKING HARDER. WHAT YOU GET OUT OF SCHOOL DEPENDS ON WHAT YOU PUT INTO IT.
OH.
THEN FORGET IT.
WATTERSON

Miss Wormwood: As a few readers guessed, Miss Wormwood is named after the apprentice devil in C. S. Lewis's *The Screwtape Letters*. I have a lot of sympathy for Miss Wormwood. We see hints that she's waiting to retire, that she smokes too much, and that she takes a lot of medication. I think she seriously believes in the value of education, so needless to say, she's an unhappy person.

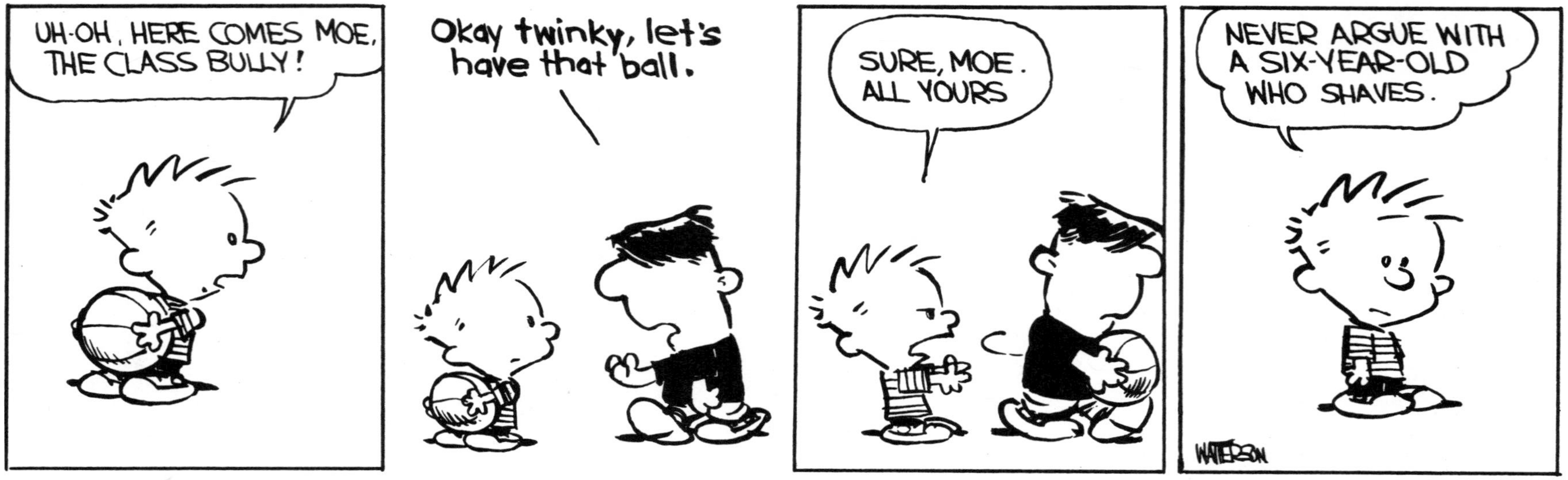
UH-OH, HERE COMES MOE, THE CLASS BULLY!
Okay twinky, let's have that ball.
SURE, MOE. ALL YOURS
NEVER ARGUE WITH A SIX-YEAR-OLD WHO SHAVES.
WATTERSON

Moe: Moe is every jerk I've ever known. He's big, dumb, ugly, and cruel. I remember school being full of idiots like Moe. I think they spawn on damp locker room floors.

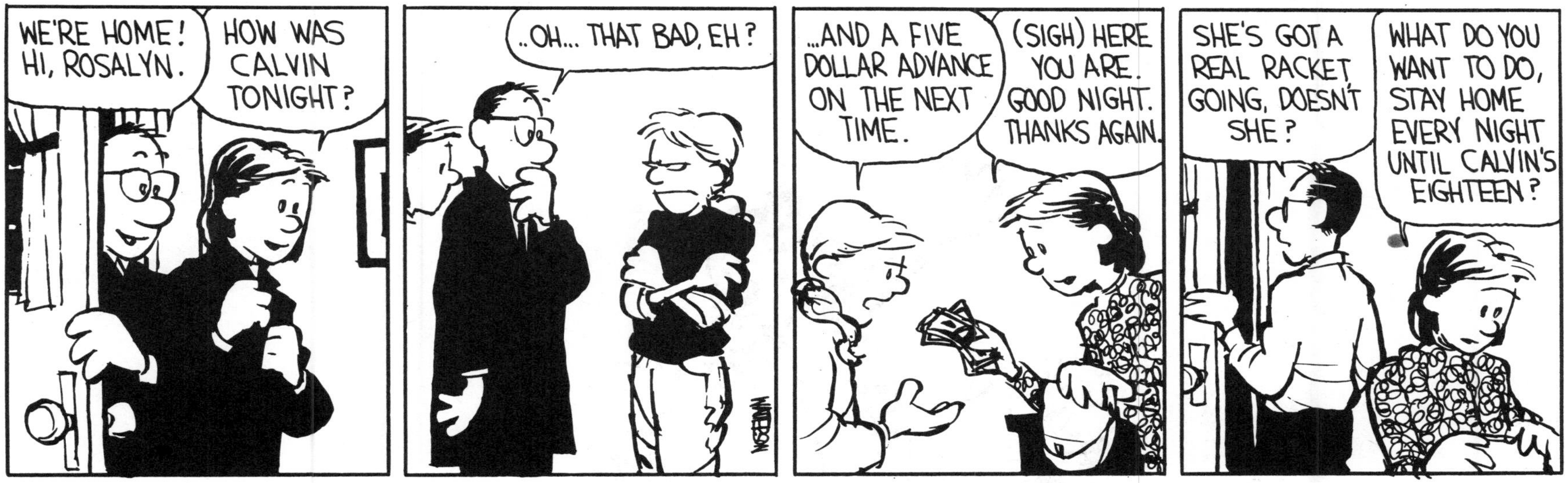

WE'RE HOME! HI, ROSALYN.
HOW WAS CALVIN TONIGHT?
..OH... THAT BAD, EH?
...AND A FIVE DOLLAR ADVANCE ON THE NEXT TIME.
(SIGH) HERE YOU ARE. GOOD NIGHT. THANKS AGAIN.
SHE'S GOT A REAL RACKET GOING, DOESN'T SHE?
WHAT DO YOU WANT TO DO, STAY HOME EVERY NIGHT UNTIL CALVIN'S EIGHTEEN?

Rosalyn: Probably the only person Calvin fears is his baby-sitter. I put her in a Sunday strip early on, never thinking of her as a regular character, but her intimidation of Calvin surprised me, so she's made a few appearances since. Rosalyn even seems to daunt Calvin's parents, using their desperation to get out of the house to demand advances and raises. Rosalyn's relationship with Calvin is pretty one-dimensional, so baby-sitter stories get harder and harder to write, but for a later addition to the strip, she's worked pretty well.

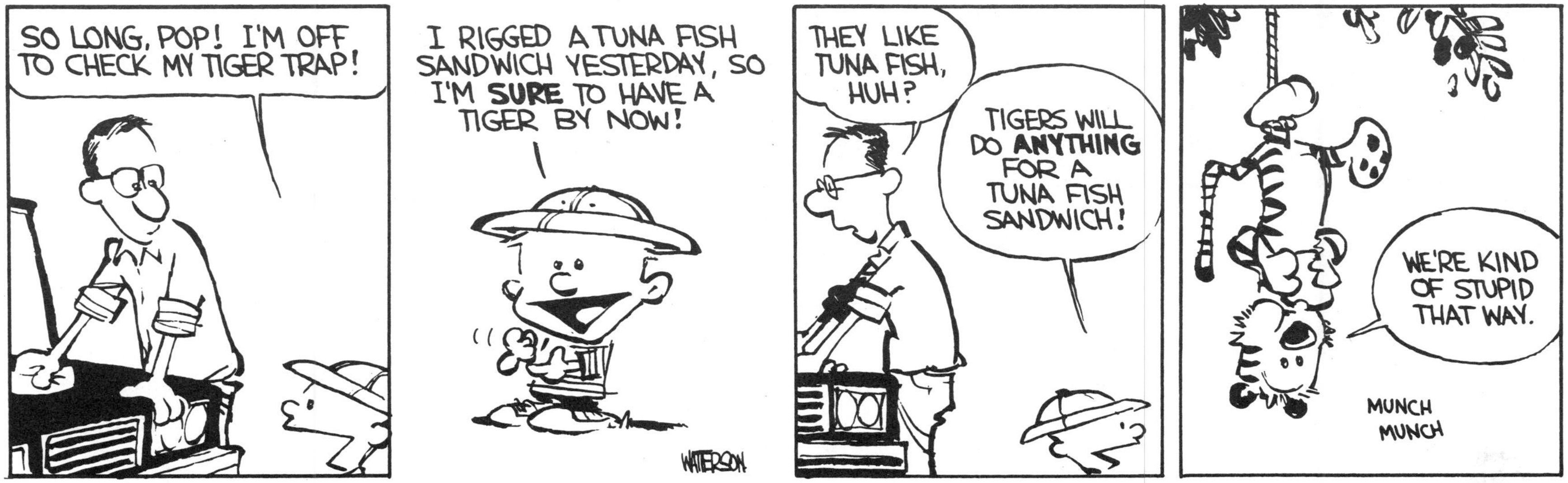
SO LONG, POP! I'M OFF TO CHECK MY TIGER TRAP!
I RIGGED A TUNA FISH SANDWICH YESTERDAY, SO I'M **SURE** TO HAVE A TIGER BY NOW!
WATTERSON
THEY LIKE TUNA FISH, HUH?
TIGERS WILL DO **ANYTHING** FOR A TUNA FISH SANDWICH!
WE'RE KIND OF STUPID THAT WAY.
MUNCH MUNCH

This was the first *Calvin and Hobbes* strip, published November 18, 1985. At the time, I thought it was important to establish how Calvin and Hobbes got together, but now I think this was unnecessary. Of course, when *Calvin and Hobbes* started, it appeared in about thirty-five newspapers, so not many people saw the first strip anyway. My hometown paper didn't pick up the strip for several months, so I didn't see this strip in the newspaper either. This is one reason I've been grateful for the book collections.

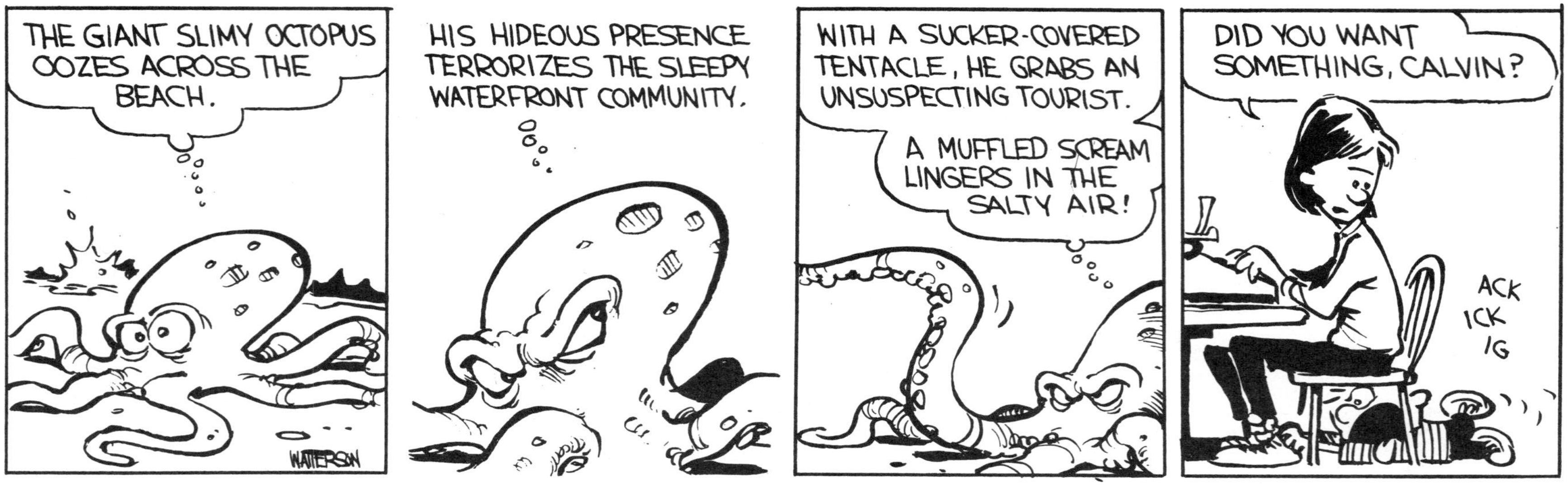
THE GIANT SLIMY OCTOPUS OOZES ACROSS THE BEACH.
HIS HIDEOUS PRESENCE TERRORIZES THE SLEEPY WATERFRONT COMMUNITY.
WITH A SUCKER-COVERED TENTACLE, HE GRABS AN UNSUSPECTING TOURIST.
A MUFFLED SCREAM LINGERS IN THE SALTY AIR!
DID YOU WANT SOMETHING, CALVIN?
ACK
ICK
IG
WATTERSON

The look of the strip has changed over the years as the drawings evolved to meet the changing needs of the strip. At the very beginning, the strip had a more cartoony, flat look. The fantasies were originally drawn that way too. At some point, I realized that the fantasies could be drawn in other styles, and, in fact, it added a funny layer to the strip when the fantasies looked more "realistic" than "reality." As the fantasies became more visually complex, I needed the characters to be more three-dimensional, so I could draw them from different perspectives. This gradually changed their appearance.

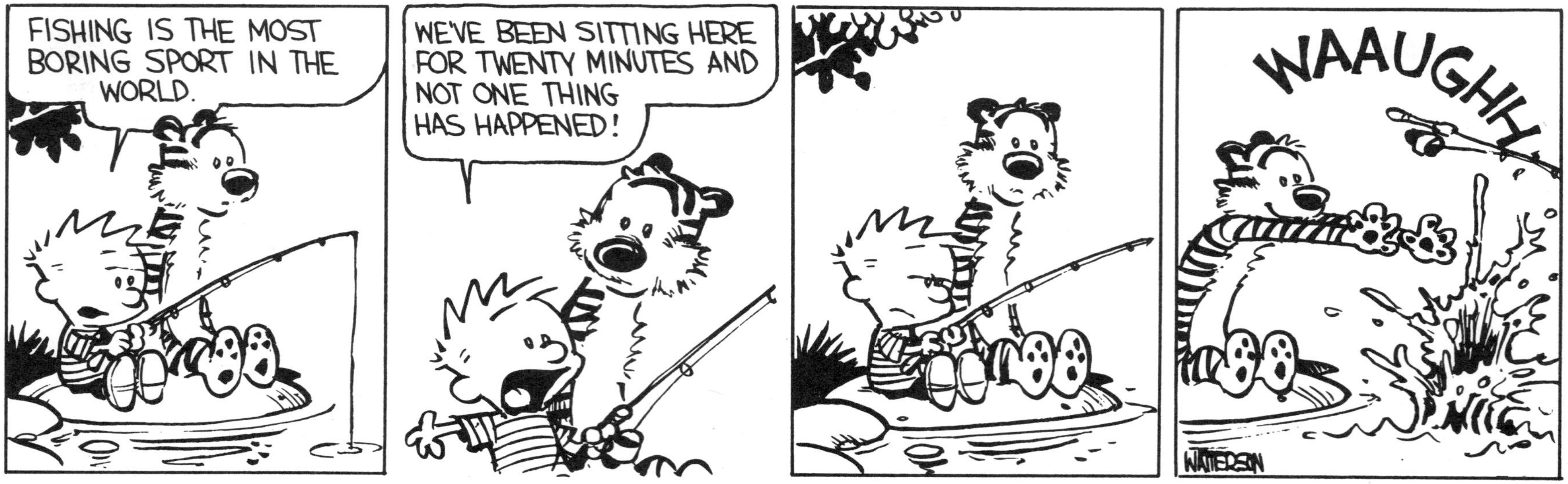
FISHING IS THE MOST BORING SPORT IN THE WORLD.
WE'VE BEEN SITTING HERE FOR TWENTY MINUTES AND NOT ONE THING HAS HAPPENED!
WAAUGHH!
WATTERSON

Over the years, Hobbes got sleeker and more catlike, so he could function either horizontally (sneaking up and pouncing) or vertically (walking). In a few early strips, Hobbes had pads on his hands, similar to the pads on his feet. I liked the pads because they made Hobbes's hands look more like paws, but they were visually distracting. Hobbes's hands read better when they were simple and plain white. The strip adapted to its needs by trial and error, and now, the early strips look very strange to me.

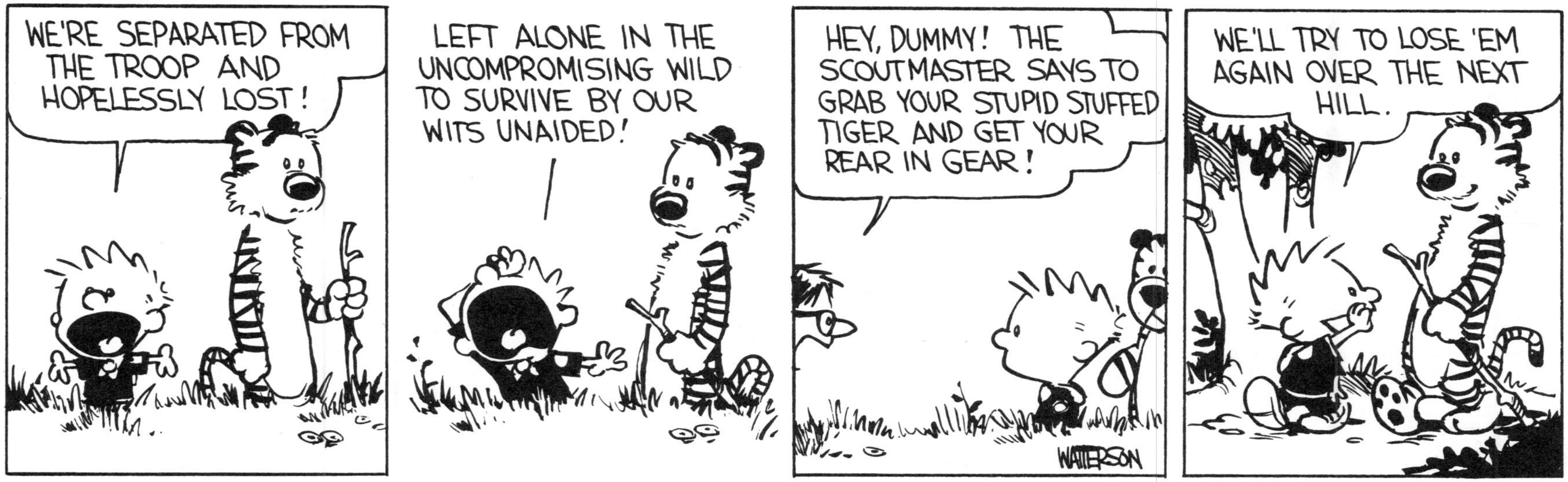
WE'RE SEPARATED FROM THE TROOP AND HOPELESSLY LOST!
LEFT ALONE IN THE UNCOMPROMISING WILD TO SURVIVE BY OUR WITS UNAIDED!
HEY, DUMMY! THE SCOUTMASTER SAYS TO GRAB YOUR STUPID STUFFED TIGER AND GET YOUR REAR IN GEAR!
WATTERSON
WE'LL TRY TO LOSE 'EM AGAIN OVER THE NEXT HILL.

In the beginning of a comic strip, the characters are vaguely defined, and they can develop in almost any direction. That's kind of exciting, but the cartoonist can write himself into corners if he's not careful. The characters are established by their actions, so it's important to make choices that won't limit the strip later on. I made a mistake in the early strips by putting Calvin in the Cub Scouts. I originally thought that hiking and camping trips might offer some humorous stories, but the situation was always awkward. Calvin and Hobbes need to be in their own world, so putting a troop of kids around them didn't provide much material. Eventually, I realized that Calvin is not the kind of kid who would join a group anyway. The strips worked against Calvin's personality, so I abandoned them. Later I sent Calvin camping with his family, and that fits the strip's world much better.

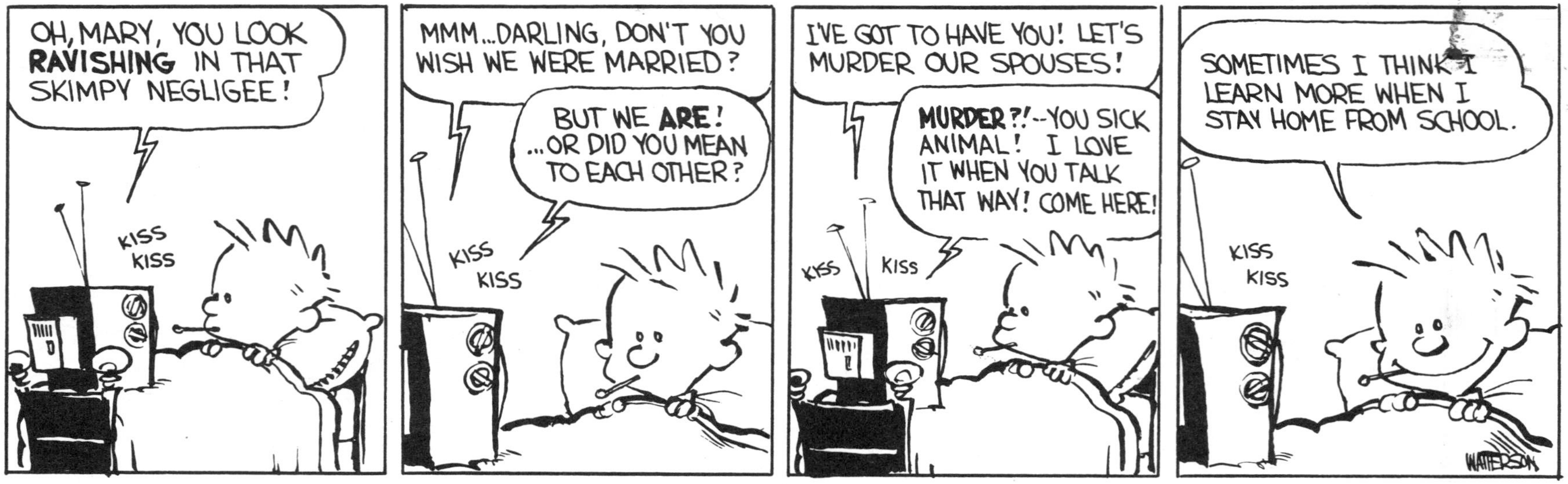
OH, MARY, YOU LOOK **RAVISHING** IN THAT SKIMPY NEGLIGEE!
KISS KISS
MMM...DARLING, DON'T YOU WISH WE WERE MARRIED?
BUT WE **ARE**! ...OR DID YOU MEAN TO EACH OTHER?
KISS KISS
I'VE GOT TO HAVE YOU! LET'S MURDER OUR SPOUSES!
MURDER?!--YOU SICK ANIMAL! I LOVE IT WHEN YOU TALK THAT WAY! COME HERE!
KISS KISS
SOMETIMES I THINK I LEARN MORE WHEN I STAY HOME FROM SCHOOL.
KISS KISS
WATTERSON

The best comics have funny writing and funny drawings, but sometimes the strength of one can make up for the weakness of the other. Great writing will save boring artwork better than great drawings will save boring ideas, but comics are a visual medium, and a funny picture can pull more weight than most people think. Whenever deadlines force me to go with a mediocre idea, I go for broke on the illustration.

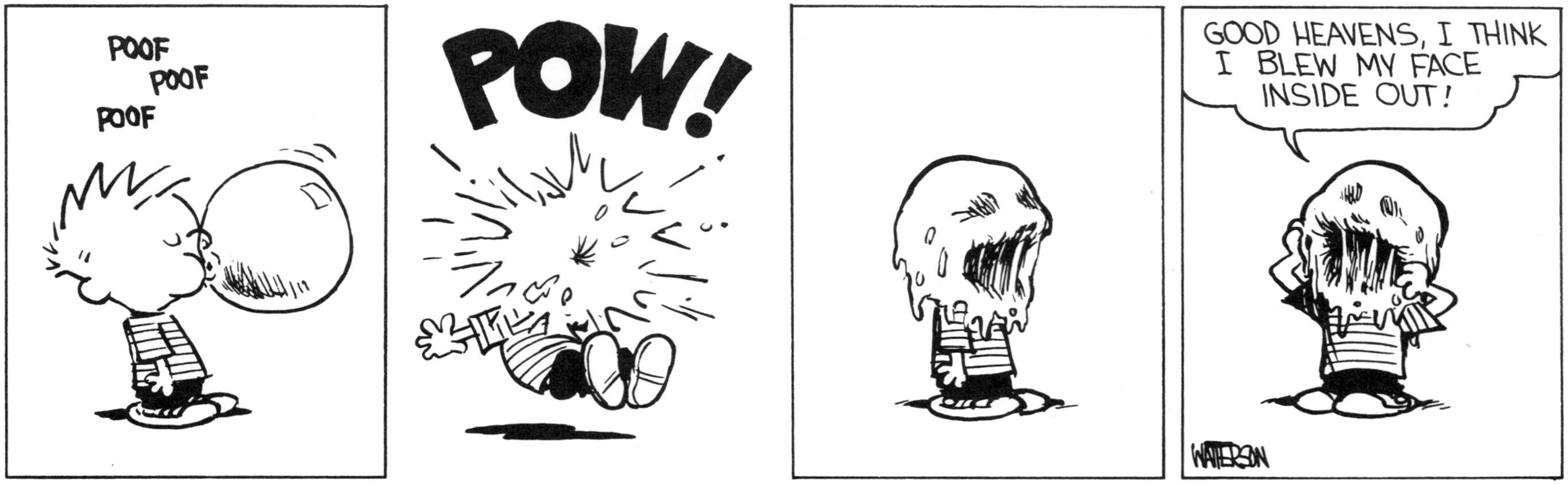
POOF
POOF
POOF
POW!
GOOD HEAVENS, I THINK I BLEW MY FACE INSIDE OUT!
WATTERSON

This early story lasted only a week, but people wrote worried letters about Hobbes before the story was resolved. It was a good sign that readers were connecting with the characters.

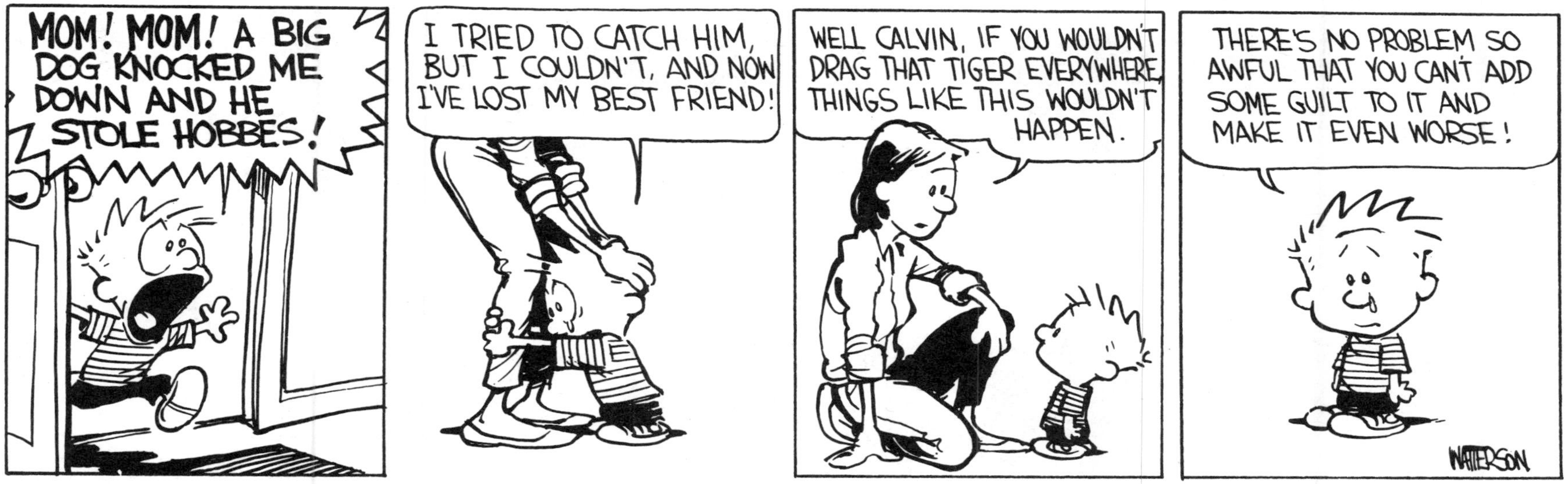
MOM! MOM! A BIG DOG KNOCKED ME DOWN AND HE STOLE HOBBES!
I TRIED TO CATCH HIM, BUT I COULDN'T, AND NOW I'VE LOST MY BEST FRIEND!
WELL CALVIN, IF YOU WOULDN'T DRAG THAT TIGER EVERYWHERE, THINGS LIKE THIS WOULDN'T HAPPEN.
THERE'S NO PROBLEM SO AWFUL THAT YOU CAN'T ADD SOME GUILT TO IT AND MAKE IT EVEN WORSE!
WATTERSON

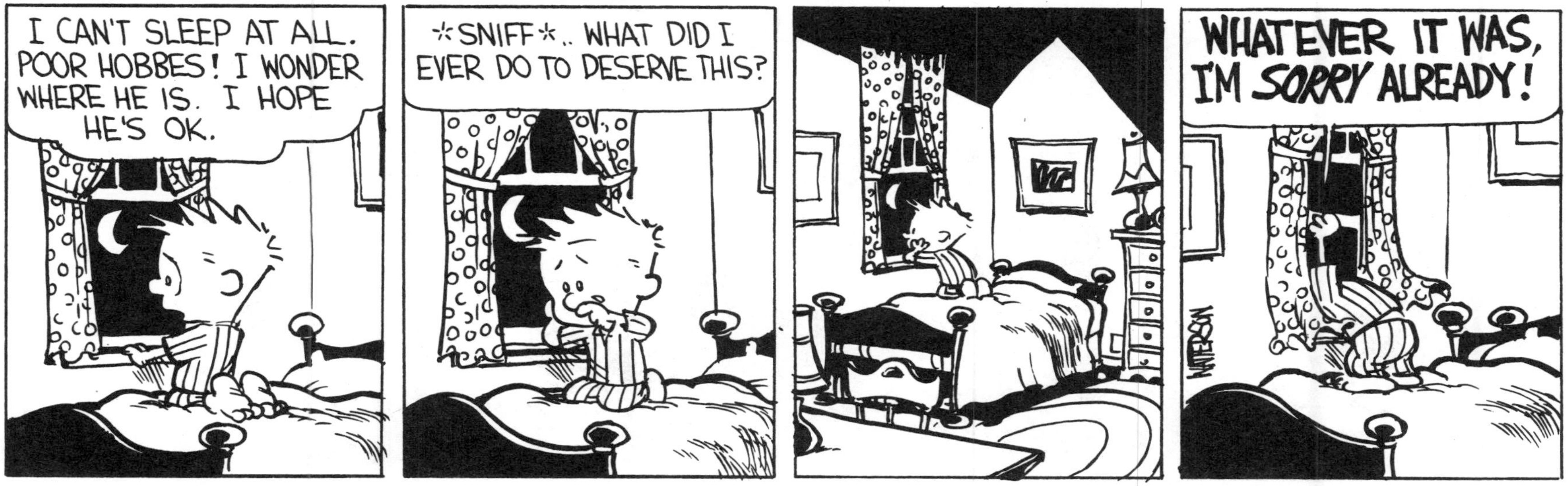
I CAN'T SLEEP AT ALL. POOR HOBBES! I WONDER WHERE HE IS. I HOPE HE'S OK.
SNIFF.. WHAT DID I EVER DO TO DESERVE THIS?
WATTERSON
WHATEVER IT WAS, I'M SORRY ALREADY!

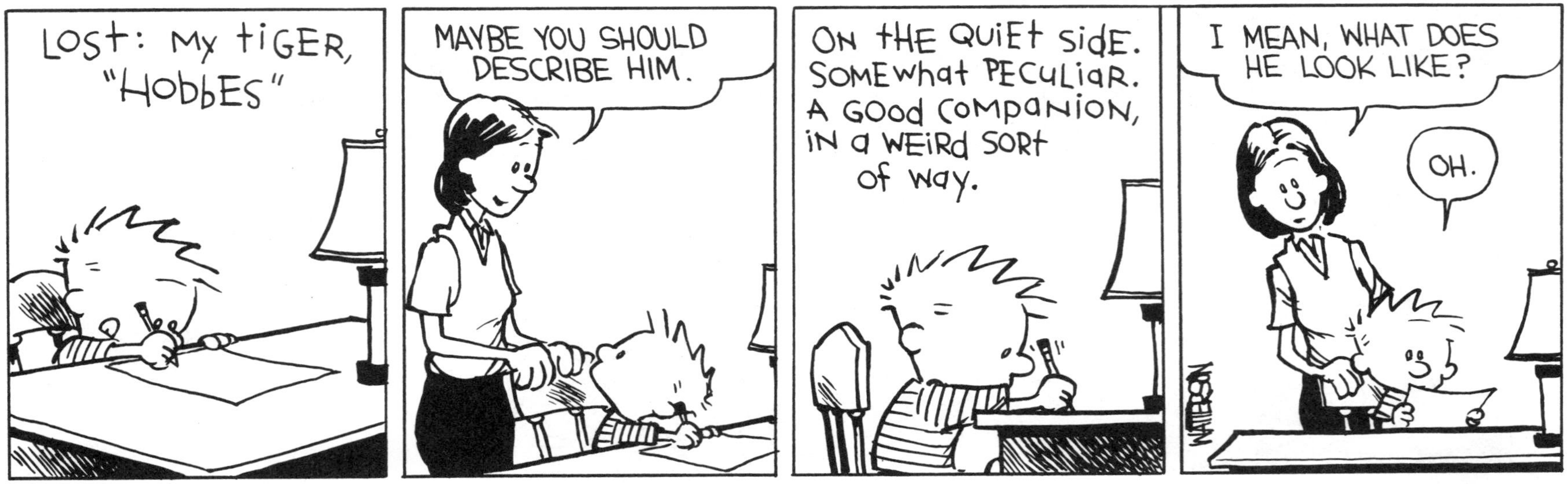
LOST: MY TIGER, "HOBBES"
MAYBE YOU SHOULD DESCRIBE HIM.
ON THE QUIET SIDE. SOMEWHAT PECULIAR. A GOOD COMPANION, IN A WEIRD SORT OF WAY.
I MEAN, WHAT DOES HE LOOK LIKE?
OH.
WATTERSON

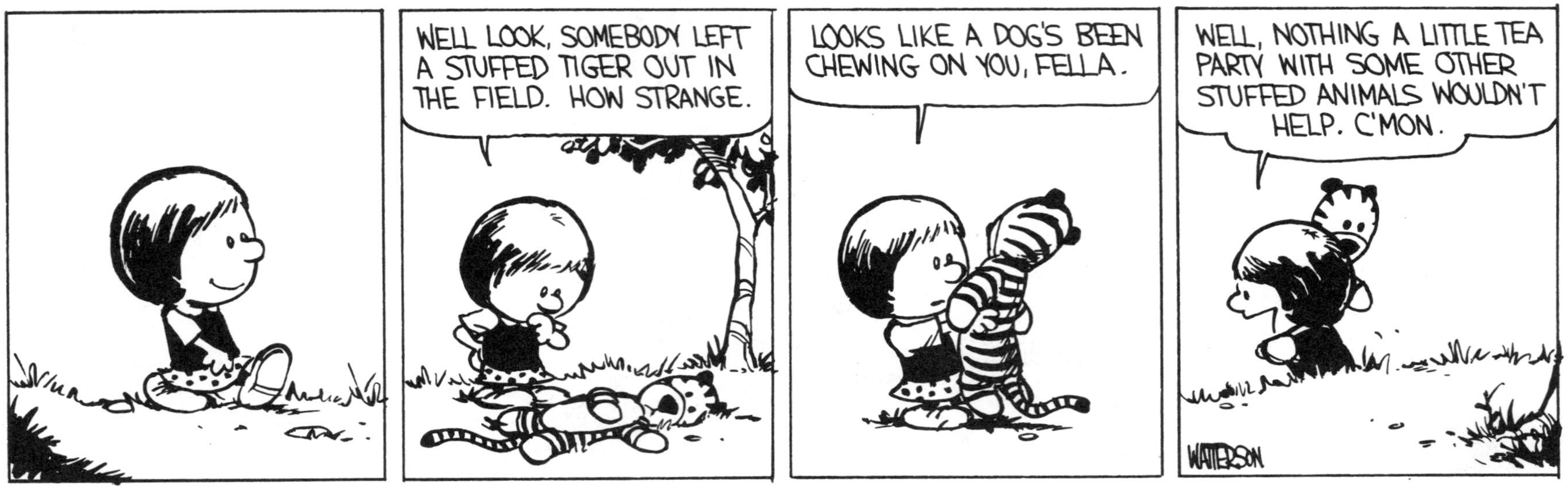
WELL LOOK, SOMEBODY LEFT A STUFFED TIGER OUT IN THE FIELD. HOW STRANGE.
LOOKS LIKE A DOG'S BEEN CHEWING ON YOU, FELLA.
WELL, NOTHING A LITTLE TEA PARTY WITH SOME OTHER STUFFED ANIMALS WOULDN'T HELP. C'MON.
WATTERSON

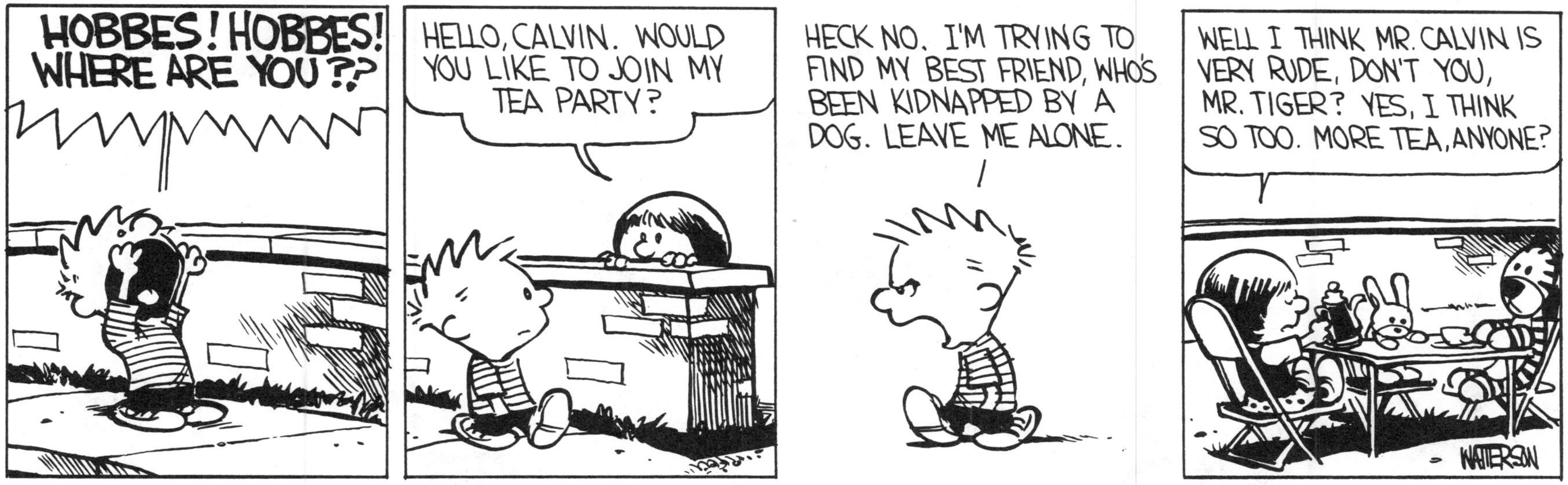
HOBBES! HOBBES! WHERE ARE YOU?!?
HELLO, CALVIN. WOULD YOU LIKE TO JOIN MY TEA PARTY?
HECK NO. I'M TRYING TO FIND MY BEST FRIEND, WHO'S BEEN KIDNAPPED BY A DOG. LEAVE ME ALONE.
WELL I THINK MR. CALVIN IS VERY RUDE, DON'T YOU, MR. TIGER? YES, I THINK SO TOO. MORE TEA, ANYONE?
WATTERSON

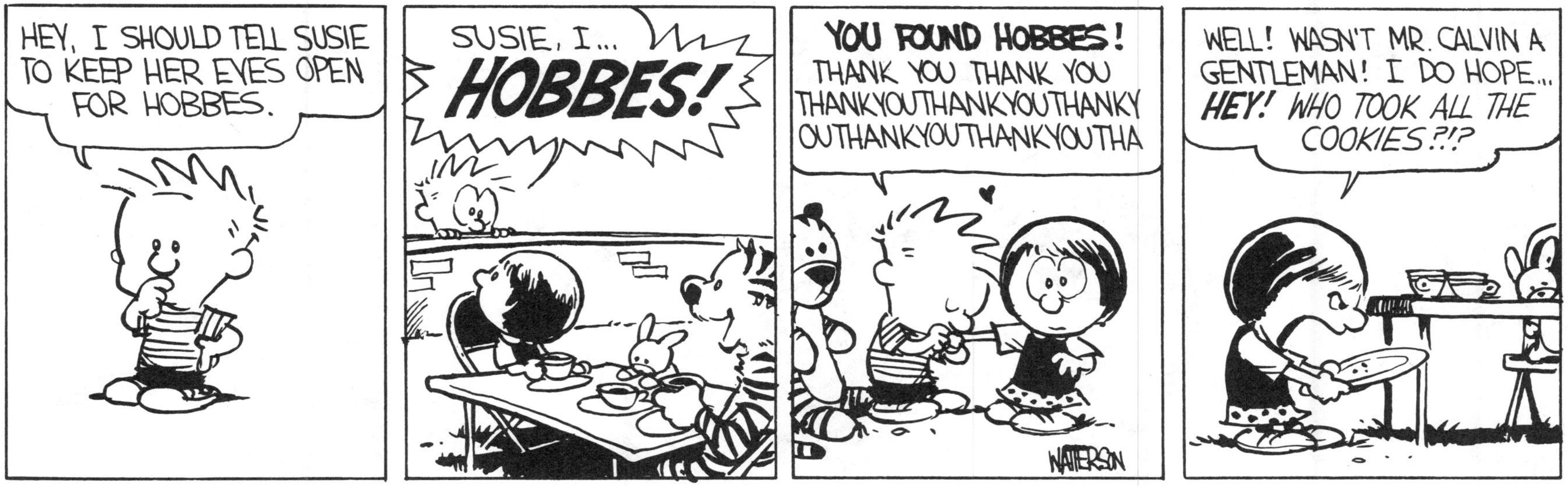
HEY, I SHOULD TELL SUSIE TO KEEP HER EYES OPEN FOR HOBBES.
SUSIE, I...
HOBBES!
YOU FOUND HOBBES! THANK YOU THANK YOU THANKYOUTHANKYOUTHANKY OUTHANKYOUTHANKYOUTHA
WELL! WASN'T MR. CALVIN A GENTLEMAN! I DO HOPE... HEY! WHO TOOK ALL THE COOKIES?!?
WATTERSON

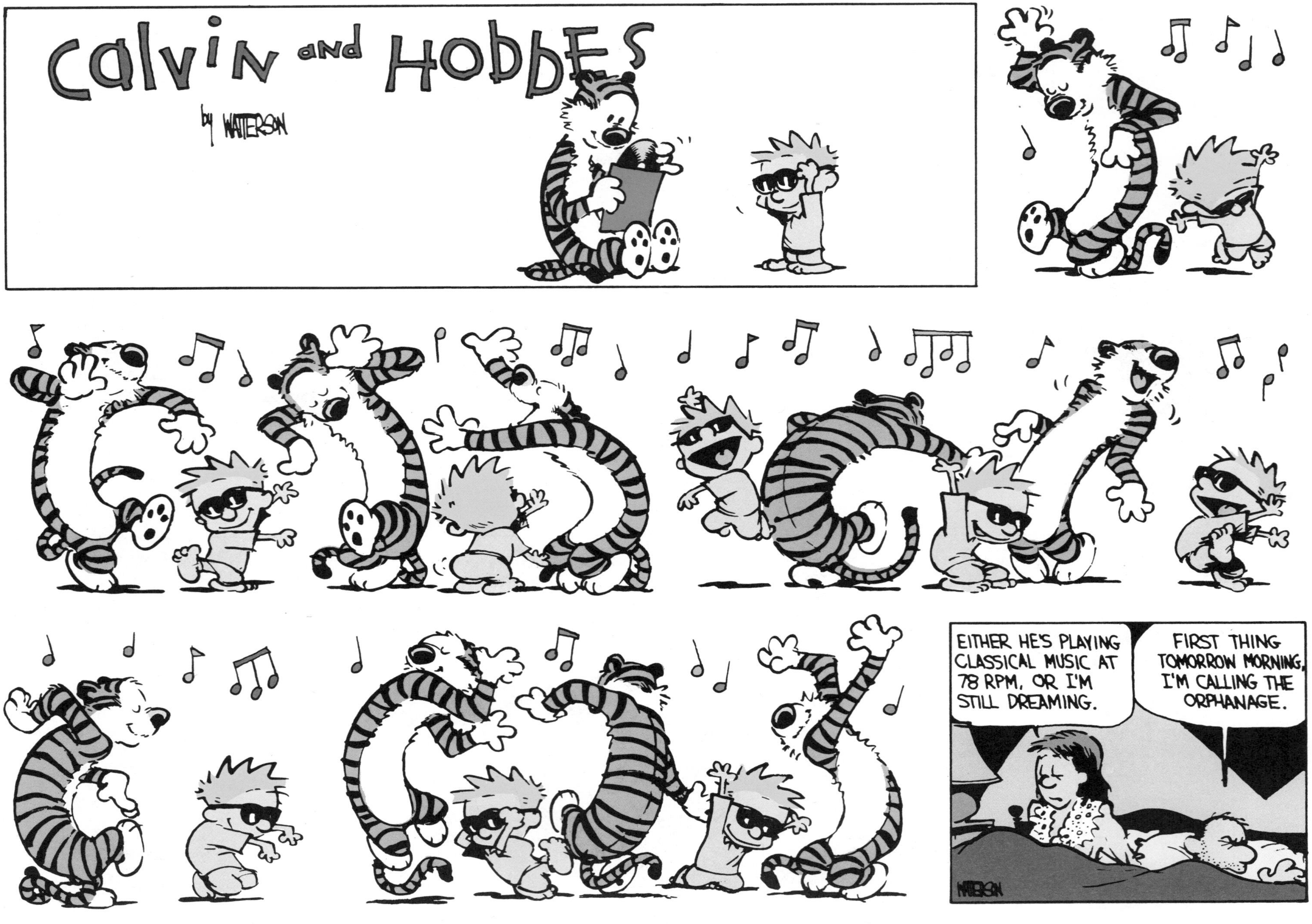
Calvin and HOBBES
by WATTERSON
EITHER HE'S PLAYING CLASSICAL MUSIC AT 78 RPM, OR I'M STILL DREAMING.
FIRST THING TOMORROW MORNING, I'M CALLING THE ORPHANAGE.
WATTERSON

Even at this early date, I was trying to escape the tyranny of panels. Illustrations from this strip were popular for copyright violations.

My wife found a dead kitten outside one morning and this story almost wrote itself. Most of my earlier strips had simple gags, so this was a big departure in tone. Death, of course, is not a common subject for a "kid" strip. This story not only revealed new facets of Calvin's personality but it also suggested to me that the strip was broad enough to handle a wide range of subjects, ideas, and emotions. The strip's world suddenly opened up.

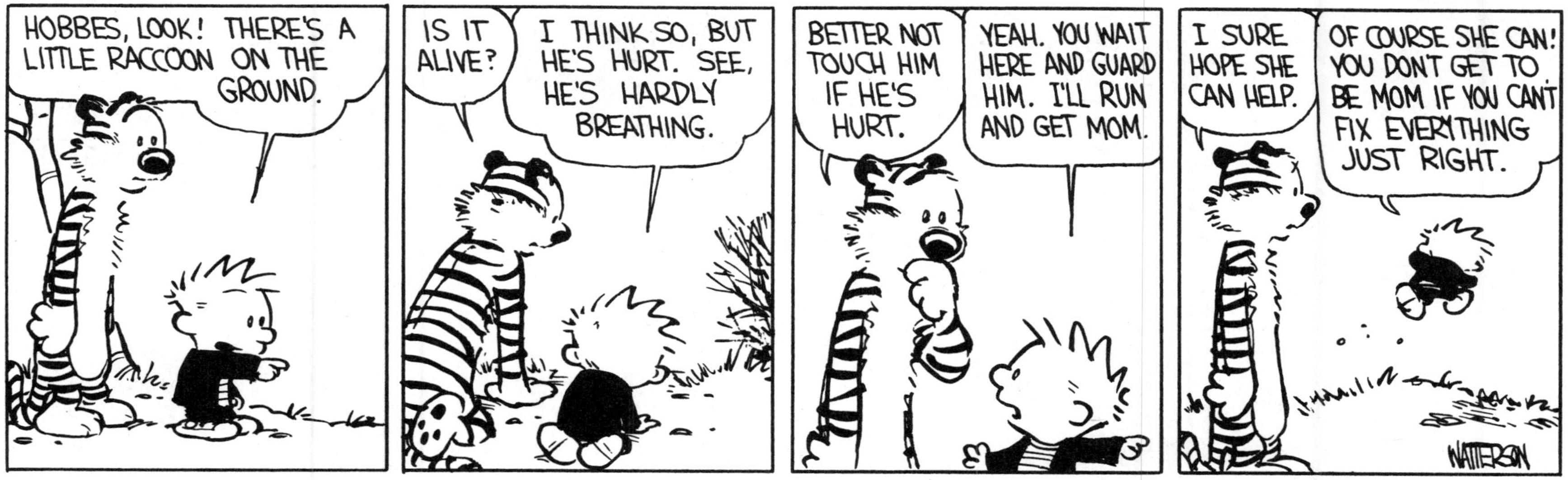

HOBBES, LOOK! THERE'S A LITTLE RACCOON ON THE GROUND.
IS IT ALIVE?
I THINK SO, BUT HE'S HURT. SEE, HE'S HARDLY BREATHING.
BETTER NOT TOUCH HIM IF HE'S HURT.
YEAH. YOU WAIT HERE AND GUARD HIM. I'LL RUN AND GET MOM.
I SURE HOPE SHE CAN HELP.
OF COURSE SHE CAN! YOU DON'T GET TO BE MOM IF YOU CAN'T FIX EVERYTHING JUST RIGHT.
WATTERSON

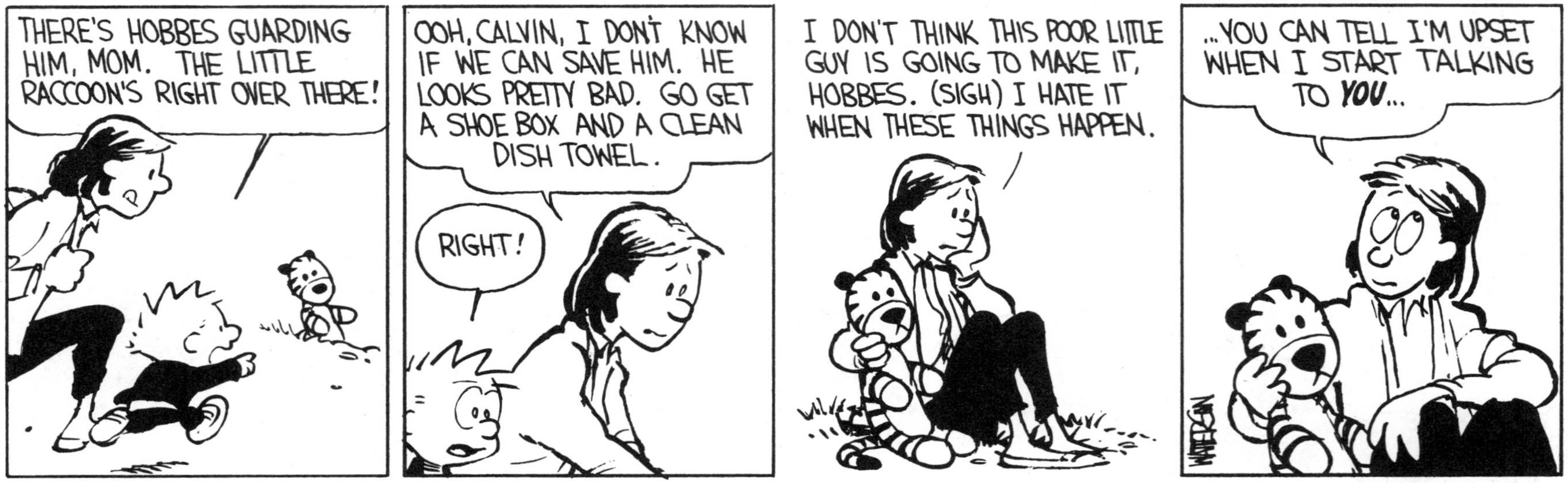
THERE'S HOBBES GUARDING HIM, MOM. THE LITTLE RACCOON'S RIGHT OVER THERE!
OOH, CALVIN, I DON'T KNOW IF WE CAN SAVE HIM. HE LOOKS PRETTY BAD. GO GET A SHOE BOX AND A CLEAN DISH TOWEL.
RIGHT!
I DON'T THINK THIS POOR LITTLE GUY IS GOING TO MAKE IT, HOBBES. (SIGH) I HATE IT WHEN THESE THINGS HAPPEN.
...YOU CAN TELL I'M UPSET WHEN I START TALKING TO **YOU**...
WATTERSON

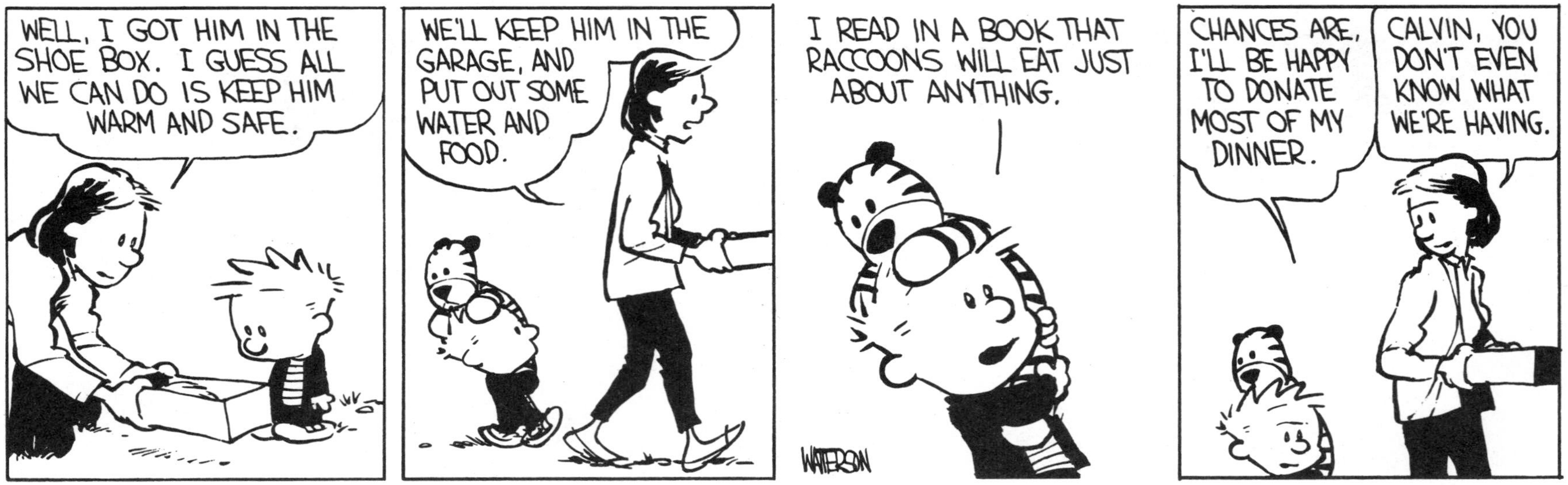
WELL, I GOT HIM IN THE SHOE BOX. I GUESS ALL WE CAN DO IS KEEP HIM WARM AND SAFE.
WE'LL KEEP HIM IN THE GARAGE, AND PUT OUT SOME WATER AND FOOD.
I READ IN A BOOK THAT RACCOONS WILL EAT JUST ABOUT ANYTHING.
WATTERSON
CHANCES ARE, I'LL BE HAPPY TO DONATE MOST OF MY DINNER.
CALVIN, YOU DON'T EVEN KNOW WHAT WE'RE HAVING.

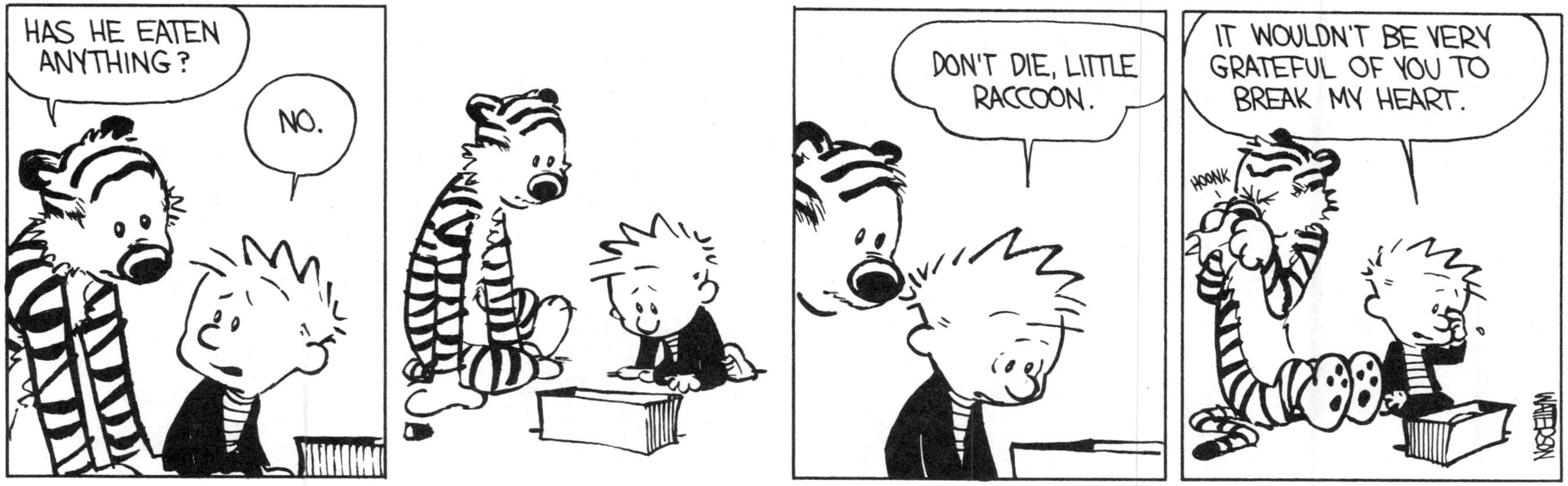
HAS HE EATEN ANYTHING?
NO.
DON'T DIE, LITTLE RACCOON.
IT WOULDN'T BE VERY GRATEFUL OF YOU TO BREAK MY HEART.
HOONK

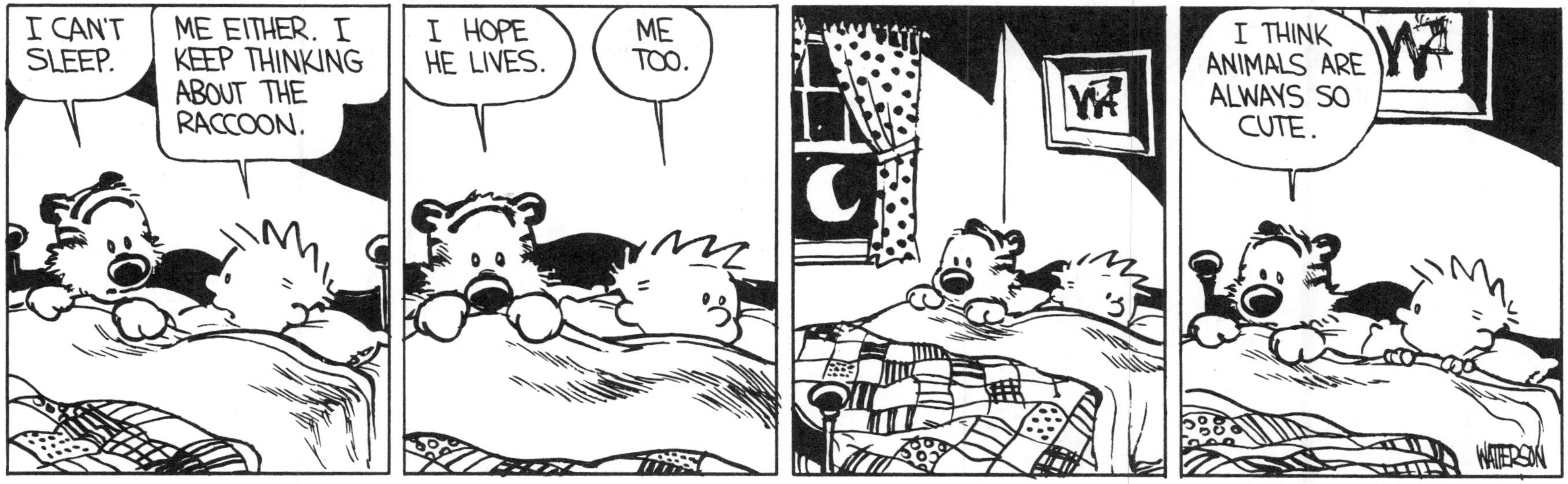
I CAN'T SLEEP.
ME EITHER. I KEEP THINKING ABOUT THE RACCOON.
I HOPE HE LIVES.
ME TOO.
I THINK ANIMALS ARE ALWAYS SO CUTE.

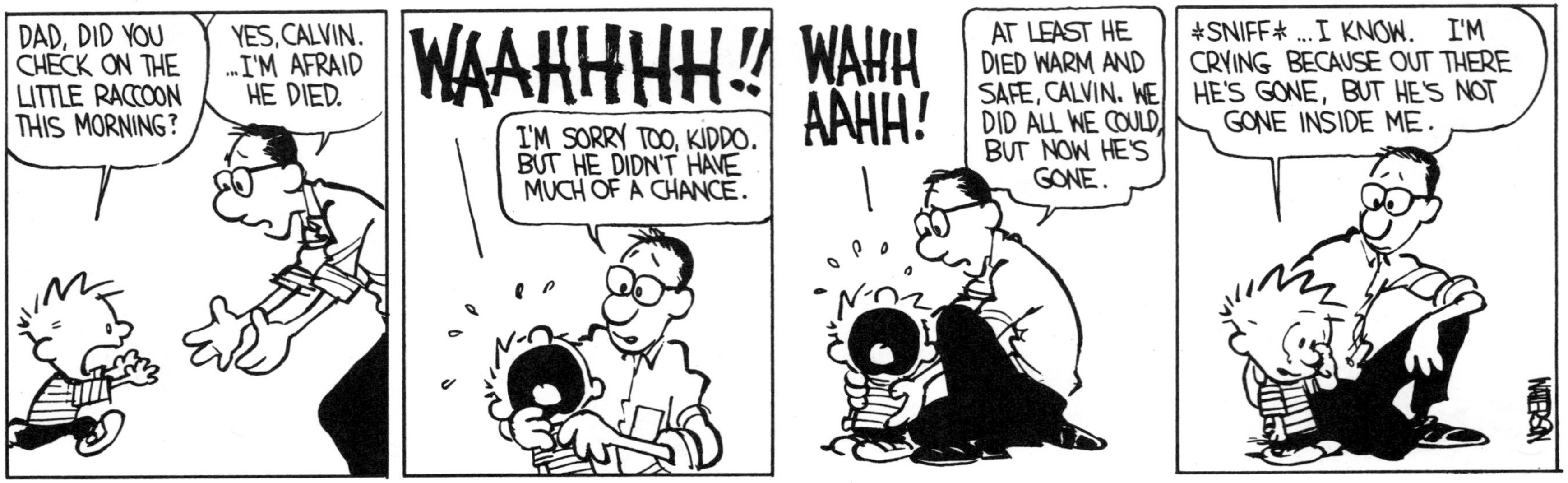
DAD, DID YOU CHECK ON THE LITTLE RACCOON THIS MORNING?
YES, CALVIN. ...I'M AFRAID HE DIED.
WAAHHHH!!
I'M SORRY TOO, KIDDO. BUT HE DIDN'T HAVE MUCH OF A CHANCE.
WAHH AAHH!
AT LEAST HE DIED WARM AND SAFE, CALVIN. WE DID ALL WE COULD, BUT NOW HE'S GONE.
SNIFF ...I KNOW. I'M CRYING BECAUSE OUT THERE HE'S GONE, BUT HE'S NOT GONE INSIDE ME.
WATTERSON

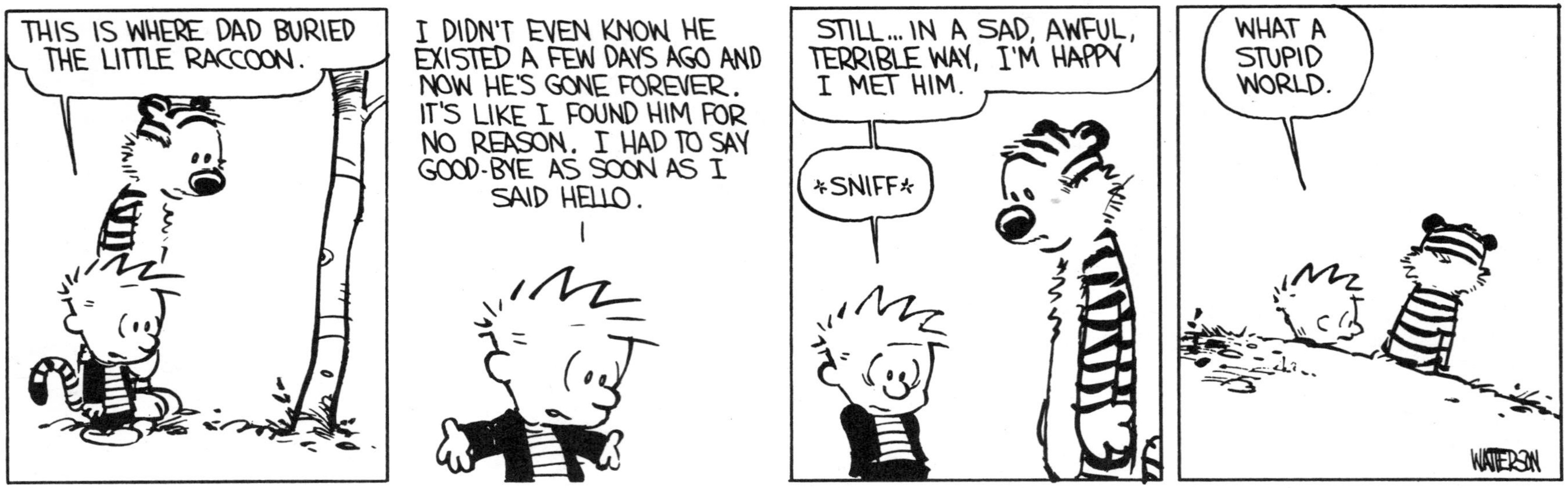
THIS IS WHERE DAD BURIED THE LITTLE RACCOON.
I DIDN'T EVEN KNOW HE EXISTED A FEW DAYS AGO AND NOW HE'S GONE FOREVER. IT'S LIKE I FOUND HIM FOR NO REASON. I HAD TO SAY GOOD-BYE AS SOON AS I SAID HELLO.
STILL... IN A SAD, AWFUL, TERRIBLE WAY, I'M HAPPY I MET HIM.
SNIFF
WHAT A STUPID WORLD.
WATTERSON

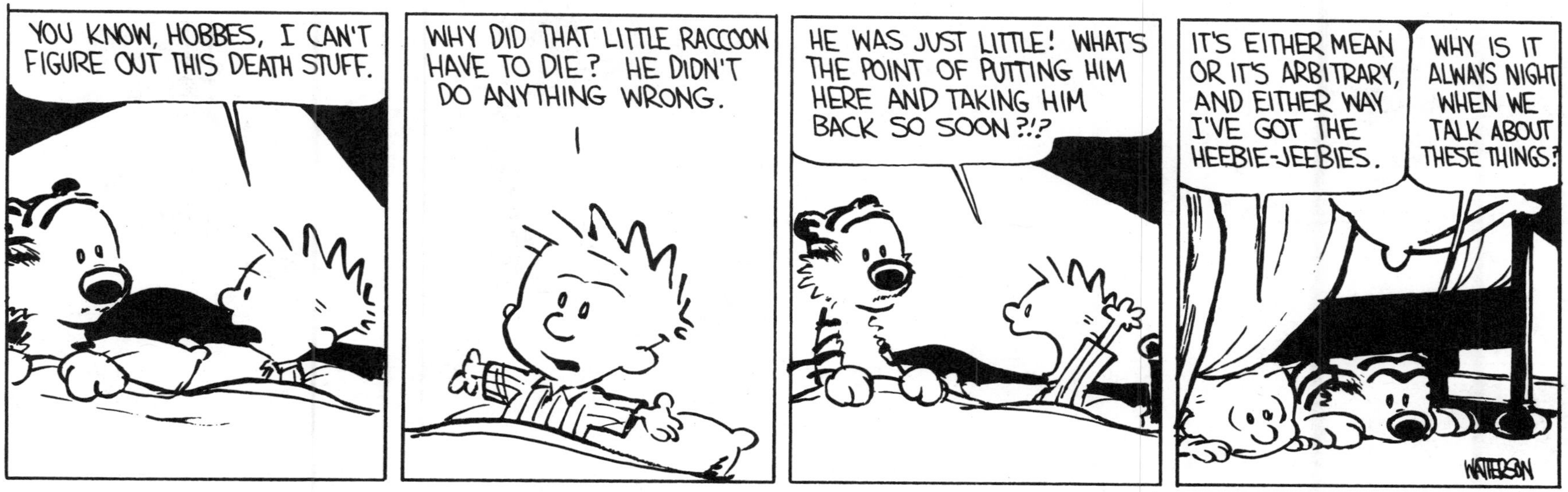
YOU KNOW, HOBBES, I CAN'T FIGURE OUT THIS DEATH STUFF.
WHY DID THAT LITTLE RACCOON HAVE TO DIE? HE DIDN'T DO ANYTHING WRONG.
HE WAS JUST LITTLE! WHAT'S THE POINT OF PUTTING HIM HERE AND TAKING HIM BACK SO SOON?!?
IT'S EITHER MEAN OR IT'S ARBITRARY, AND EITHER WAY I'VE GOT THE HEEBIE-JEEBIES.
WHY IS IT ALWAYS NIGHT WHEN WE TALK ABOUT THESE THINGS?
WATTERSON

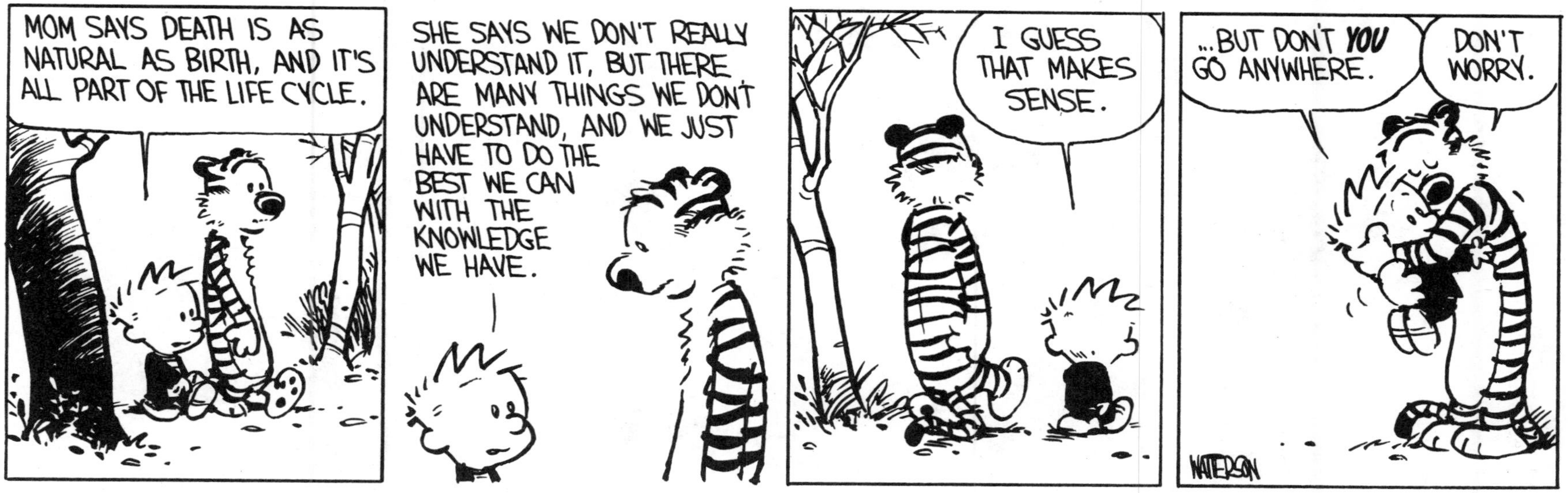
MOM SAYS DEATH IS AS NATURAL AS BIRTH, AND IT'S ALL PART OF THE LIFE CYCLE.
SHE SAYS WE DON'T REALLY UNDERSTAND IT, BUT THERE ARE MANY THINGS WE DON'T UNDERSTAND, AND WE JUST HAVE TO DO THE BEST WE CAN WITH THE KNOWLEDGE WE HAVE.
I GUESS THAT MAKES SENSE.
...BUT DON'T **YOU** GO ANYWHERE.
DON'T WORRY.
WATTERSON

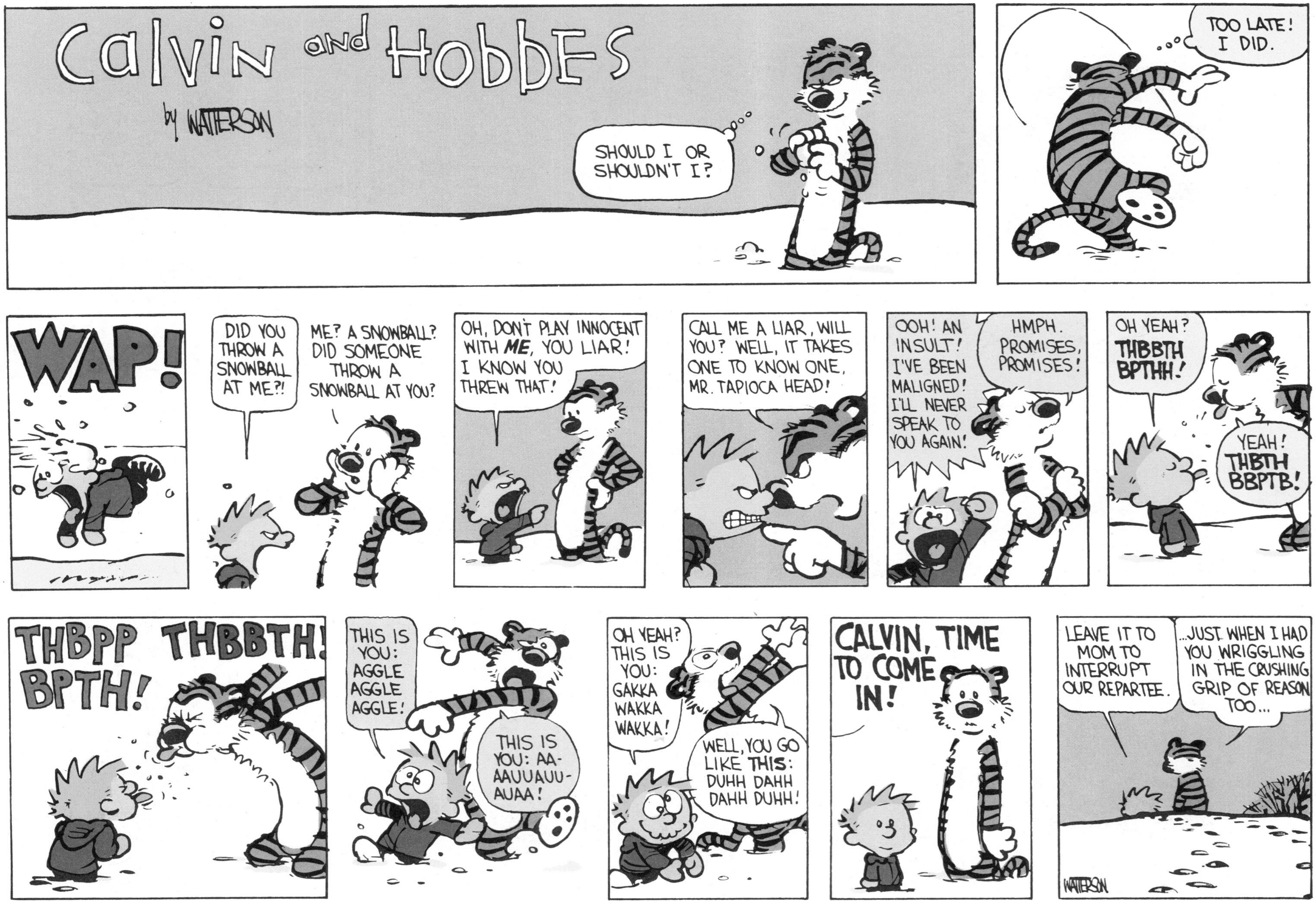
Calvin and Hobbes
by WATTERSON
SHOULD I OR SHOULDN'T I?
TOO LATE! I DID.
WAP!
DID YOU THROW A SNOWBALL AT ME?!
ME? A SNOWBALL? DID SOMEONE THROW A SNOWBALL AT YOU?
OH, DON'T PLAY INNOCENT WITH ME, YOU LIAR! I KNOW YOU THREW THAT!
CALL ME A LIAR, WILL YOU? WELL, IT TAKES ONE TO KNOW ONE, MR. TAPIOCA HEAD!
OOH! AN INSULT! I'VE BEEN MALIGNED! I'LL NEVER SPEAK TO YOU AGAIN!
HMPH. PROMISES, PROMISES!
OH YEAH? THBBTH BPTHH!
YEAH! THBTH BBPTB!
THBPP BPTH! THBBTH!
THIS IS YOU: AGGLE AGGLE AGGLE!
THIS IS YOU: AA-AAUUAUU-AUAA!
OH YEAH? THIS IS YOU: GAKKA WAKKA WAKKA!
WELL, YOU GO LIKE THIS: DUHH DAHH DAHH DUHH!
CALVIN, TIME TO COME IN!
LEAVE IT TO MOM TO INTERRUPT OUR REPARTEE.
...JUST WHEN I HAD YOU WRIGGLING IN THE CRUSHING GRIP OF REASON TOO...
WATTERSON

I always enjoy it when Calvin and Hobbes argue. Few strips play with real back-and-forth dialogue. A funny conversation is more interesting to me than a one-liner.

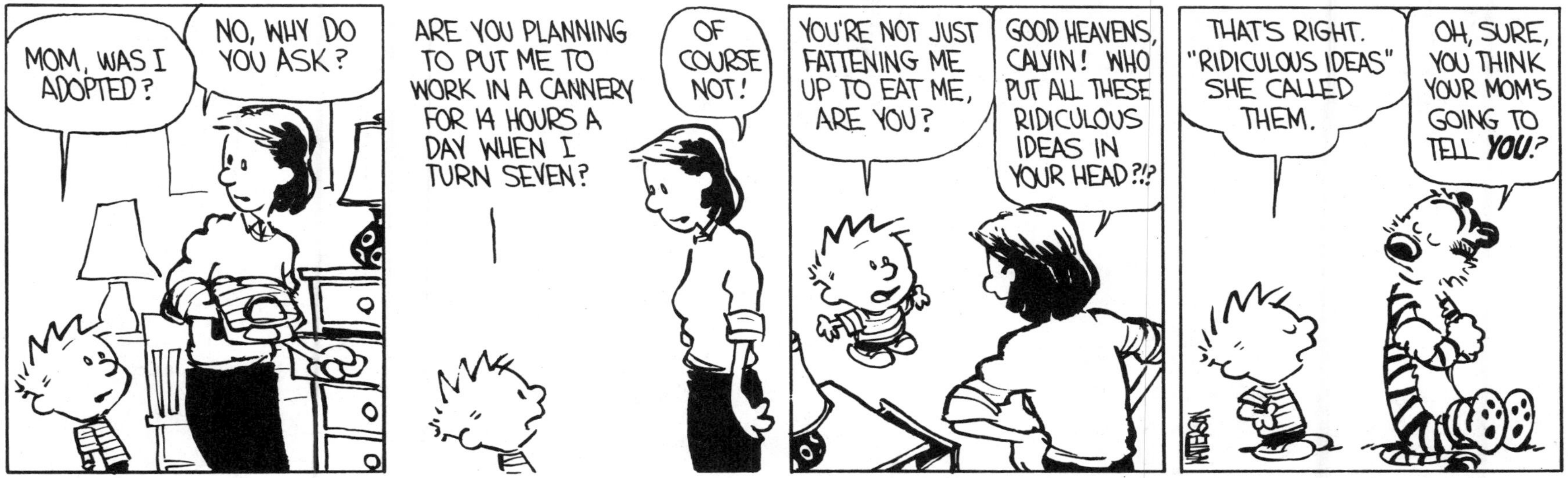
MOM, WAS I ADOPTED?
NO, WHY DO YOU ASK?
ARE YOU PLANNING TO PUT ME TO WORK IN A CANNERY FOR 14 HOURS A DAY WHEN I TURN SEVEN?
OF COURSE NOT!
YOU'RE NOT JUST FATTENING ME UP TO EAT ME, ARE YOU?
GOOD HEAVENS, CALVIN! WHO PUT ALL THESE RIDICULOUS IDEAS IN YOUR HEAD?!?
THAT'S RIGHT. "RIDICULOUS IDEAS" SHE CALLED THEM.
OH, SURE, YOU THINK YOUR MOM'S GOING TO TELL **YOU**?
WATTERSON

Boy, did I get letters about this one. Some readers felt I was maligning adoption by placing it in the same context as child labor and cannibalism. I thought the juxtaposition was ludicrous enough that no one would take it seriously, but as I've learned, some people take *everything* seriously.

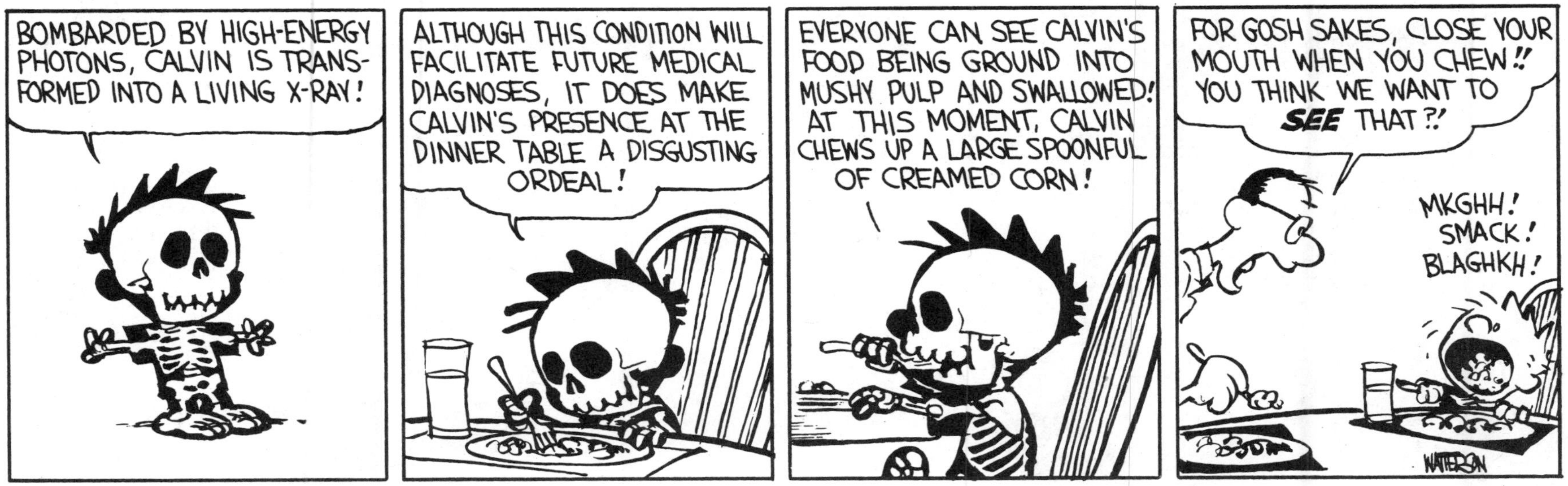
BOMBARDED BY HIGH-ENERGY PHOTONS, CALVIN IS TRANSFORMED INTO A LIVING X-RAY!
ALTHOUGH THIS CONDITION WILL FACILITATE FUTURE MEDICAL DIAGNOSES, IT DOES MAKE CALVIN'S PRESENCE AT THE DINNER TABLE A DISGUSTING ORDEAL!
EVERYONE CAN SEE CALVIN'S FOOD BEING GROUND INTO MUSHY PULP AND SWALLOWED! AT THIS MOMENT, CALVIN CHEWS UP A LARGE SPOONFUL OF CREAMED CORN!
FOR GOSH SAKES, CLOSE YOUR MOUTH WHEN YOU CHEW!! YOU THINK WE WANT TO **SEE** THAT?!
MKGHH! SMACK! BLAGHKH!
WATTERSON

Calvin's proportions make for a bizarre skeleton.

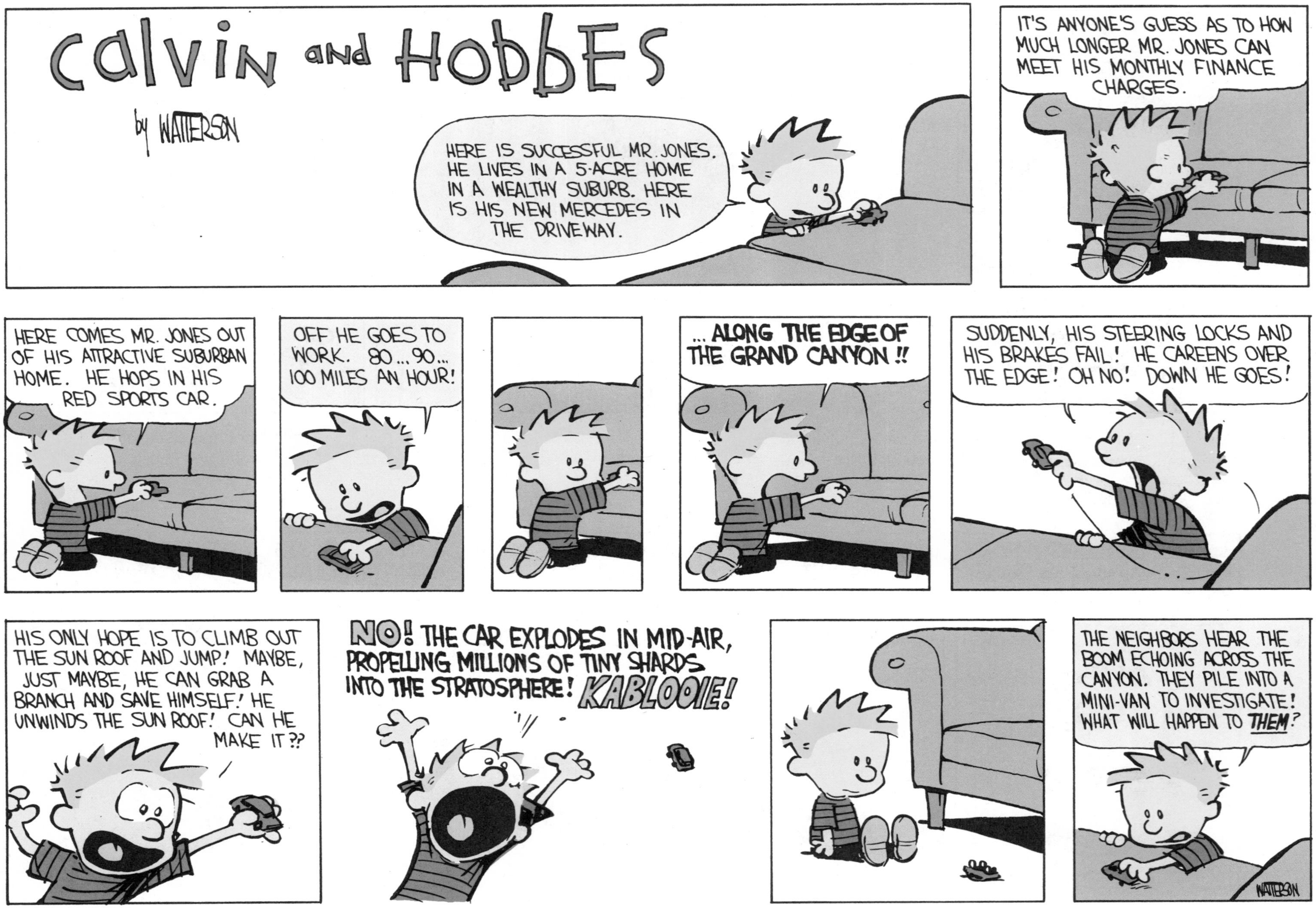
Calvin and HOBBES
by WATTERSON
HERE IS SUCCESSFUL MR. JONES. HE LIVES IN A 5-ACRE HOME IN A WEALTHY SUBURB. HERE IS HIS NEW MERCEDES IN THE DRIVEWAY.
IT'S ANYONE'S GUESS AS TO HOW MUCH LONGER MR. JONES CAN MEET HIS MONTHLY FINANCE CHARGES.
HERE COMES MR. JONES OUT OF HIS ATTRACTIVE SUBURBAN HOME. HE HOPS IN HIS RED SPORTS CAR.
OFF HE GOES TO WORK. 80...90... 100 MILES AN HOUR!
...ALONG THE EDGE OF THE GRAND CANYON!!
SUDDENLY, HIS STEERING LOCKS AND HIS BRAKES FAIL! HE CAREENS OVER THE EDGE! OH NO! DOWN HE GOES!
HIS ONLY HOPE IS TO CLIMB OUT THE SUN ROOF AND JUMP! MAYBE, JUST MAYBE, HE CAN GRAB A BRANCH AND SAVE HIMSELF! HE UNWINDS THE SUN ROOF! CAN HE MAKE IT??
NO! THE CAR EXPLODES IN MID-AIR, PROPELLING MILLIONS OF TINY SHARDS INTO THE STRATOSPHERE! KABLOOIE!
THE NEIGHBORS HEAR THE BOOM ECHOING ACROSS THE CANYON. THEY PILE INTO A MINI-VAN TO INVESTIGATE! WHAT WILL HAPPEN TO THEM?
WATTERSON

I like the timing on this strip.

This is a page from "A Nauseous Nocturne," a poem I did as a special feature for the first treasury collection. The treasuries reprinted all the cartoons that the annual books had already reprinted from the newspaper, so I named the treasuries *The Essential*, *The Authoritative*, and *The Indispensable Calvin and Hobbes*, because the books were obviously none of these things. In an effort to give the treasuries more reason for their existence, I took it upon myself to draw extra stories and poems for them. Books offer considerably more design freedom than newspapers, and I took advantage of the opportunity to paint all the illustrations in watercolor, which permitted various subtleties and effects that I couldn't get in the Sunday strips. Unfortunately, this was an insane amount of extra work on top of the newspaper strip and the other books. Insisting, as I do, that I write and draw everything myself, this extra work kept me in a perpetual deadline panic and it wore me into the ground. This exhausting schedule contributed to the need for a sabbatical several years later.

Oh, blood-red eyes and tentacles!
Throbbing, pulsing ventricles!
Mucus-oozing pores and frightful claws!

Worse, in terms of outright scariness,
Are the suckers multifarious
That grab and force you in its mighty jaws!

I rarely laugh when I'm drawing, but I did when I drew the results of Calvin's haircut. I like the contrast of Calvin's and Hobbes's reactions, and as a bonus, this story introduced Tracer Bullet. Would that I could write like this more often.

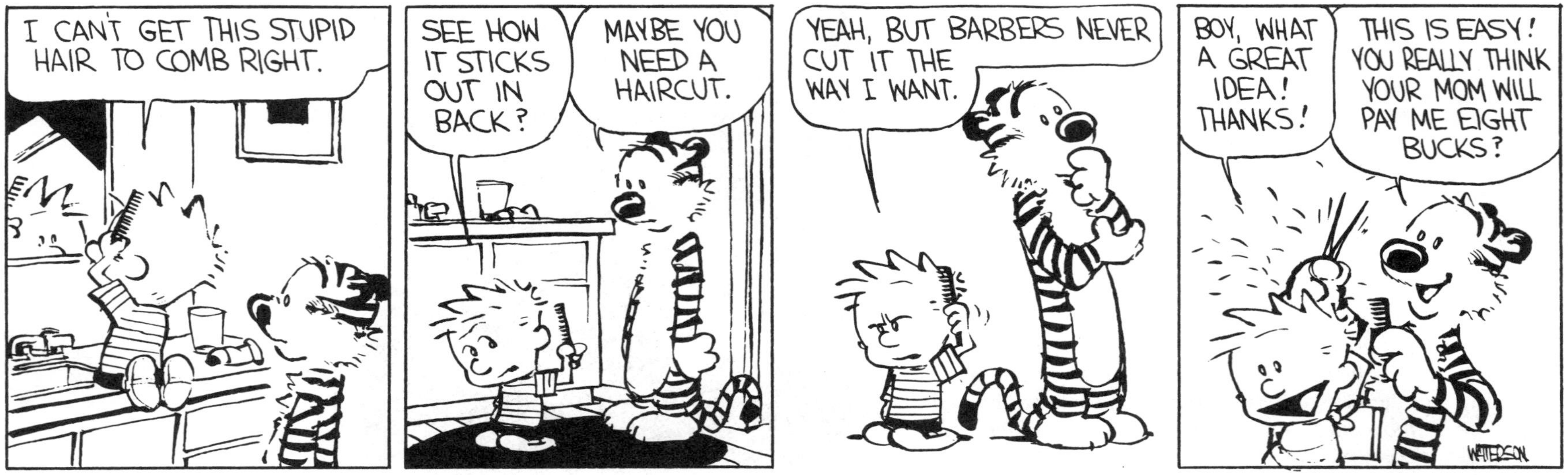
I CAN'T GET THIS STUPID HAIR TO COMB RIGHT.
SEE HOW IT STICKS OUT IN BACK?
MAYBE YOU NEED A HAIRCUT.
YEAH, BUT BARBERS NEVER CUT IT THE WAY I WANT.
BOY, WHAT A GREAT IDEA! THANKS!
THIS IS EASY! YOU REALLY THINK YOUR MOM WILL PAY ME EIGHT BUCKS?
WATTERSON

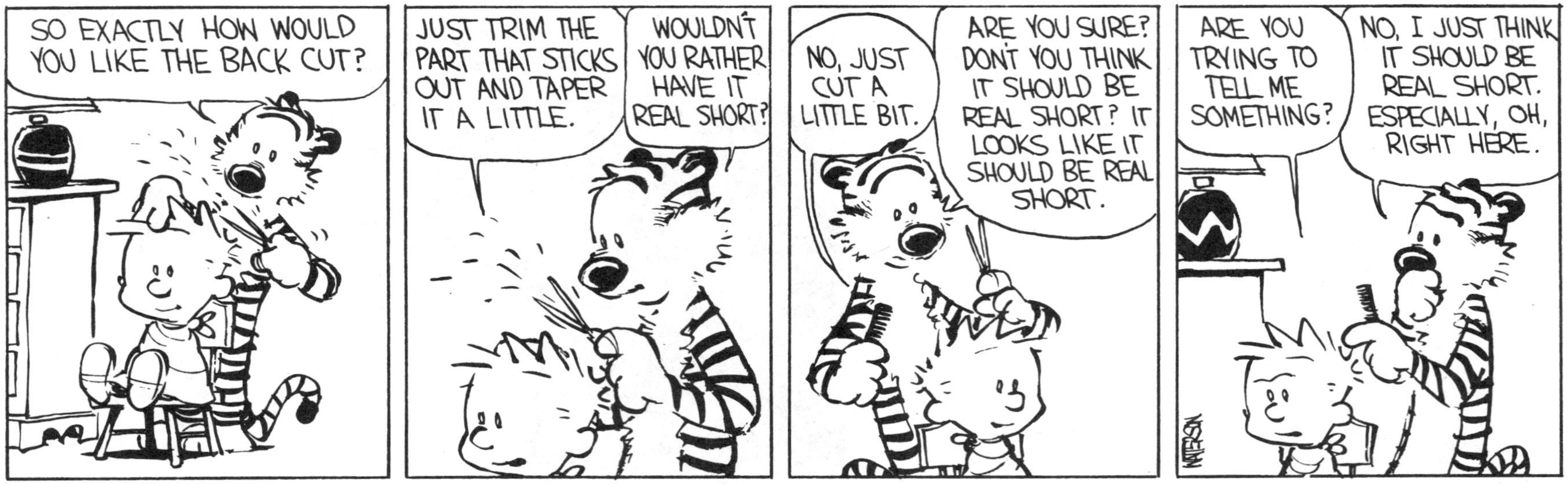
SO EXACTLY HOW WOULD YOU LIKE THE BACK CUT?
JUST TRIM THE PART THAT STICKS OUT AND TAPER IT A LITTLE.
WOULDN'T YOU RATHER HAVE IT REAL SHORT?
NO, JUST CUT A LITTLE BIT.
ARE YOU SURE? DON'T YOU THINK IT SHOULD BE REAL SHORT? IT LOOKS LIKE IT SHOULD BE REAL SHORT.
ARE YOU TRYING TO TELL ME SOMETHING?
NO, I JUST THINK IT SHOULD BE REAL SHORT. ESPECIALLY, OH, RIGHT HERE.
WATTERSON

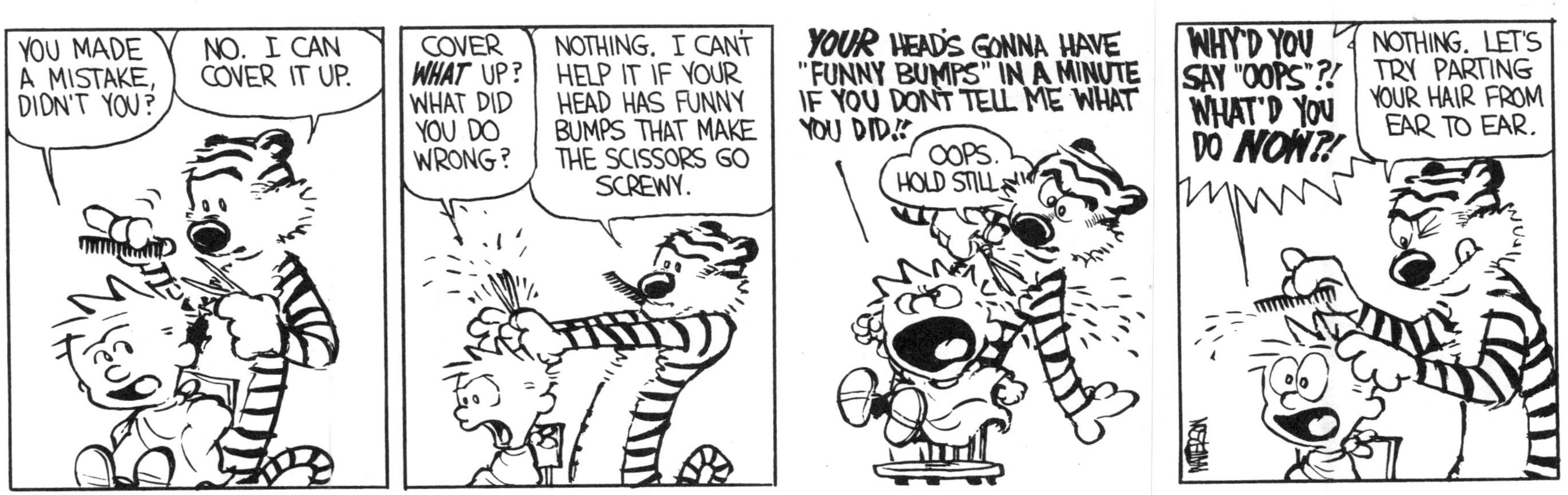
YOU MADE A MISTAKE, DIDN'T YOU?
NO. I CAN COVER IT UP.
COVER WHAT UP? WHAT DID YOU DO WRONG?
NOTHING. I CAN'T HELP IT IF YOUR HEAD HAS FUNNY BUMPS THAT MAKE THE SCISSORS GO SCREWY.
OOPS. HOLD STILL.
YOUR HEAD'S GONNA HAVE "FUNNY BUMPS" IN A MINUTE IF YOU DON'T TELL ME WHAT YOU DID!!
WHY'D YOU SAY "OOPS"?! WHAT'D YOU DO NOW?!
NOTHING. LET'S TRY PARTING YOUR HAIR FROM EAR TO EAR.
WATTERSON

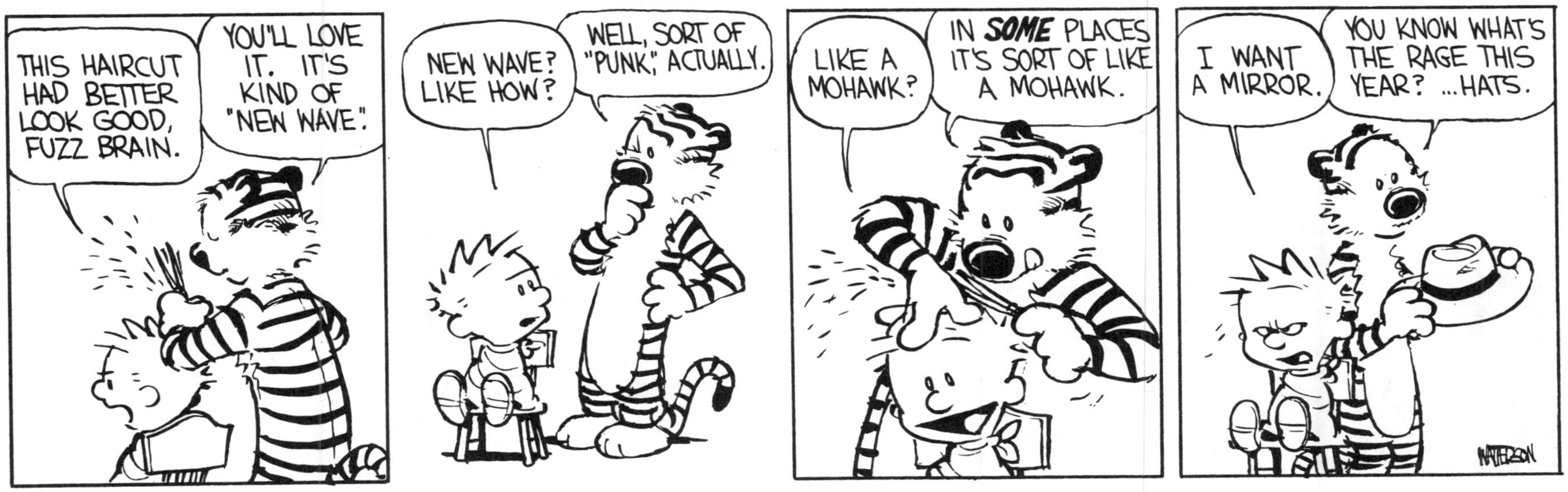
THIS HAIRCUT HAD BETTER LOOK GOOD, FUZZ BRAIN.
YOU'LL LOVE IT. IT'S KIND OF "NEW WAVE."
NEW WAVE? LIKE HOW?
WELL, SORT OF "PUNK," ACTUALLY.
LIKE A MOHAWK?
IN SOME PLACES IT'S SORT OF LIKE A MOHAWK.
I WANT A MIRROR.
YOU KNOW WHAT'S THE RAGE THIS YEAR? ...HATS.
WATTERSON

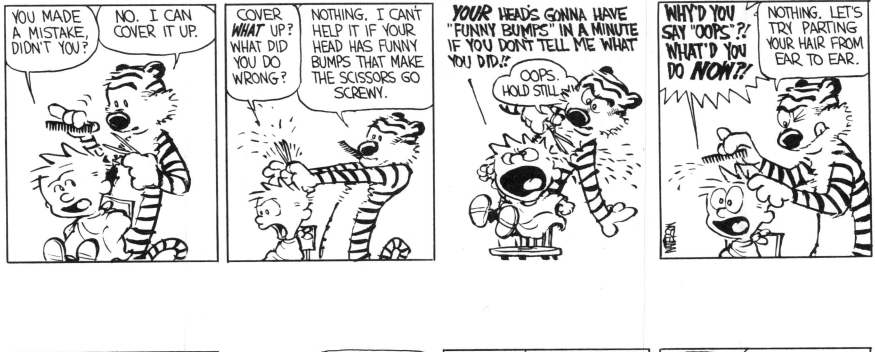

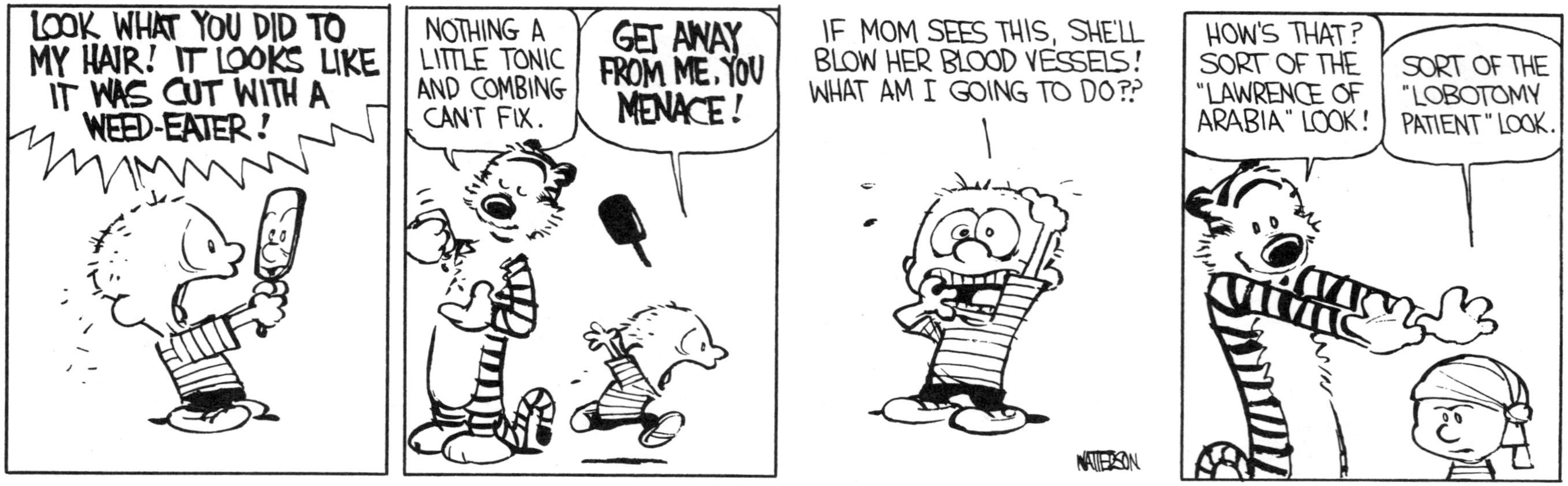
LOOK WHAT YOU DID TO MY HAIR! IT LOOKS LIKE IT WAS CUT WITH A WEED-EATER!
NOTHING A LITTLE TONIC AND COMBING CAN'T FIX.
GET AWAY FROM ME, YOU MENACE!
IF MOM SEES THIS, SHE'LL BLOW HER BLOOD VESSELS! WHAT AM I GOING TO DO?!?
WATTERSON
HOW'S THAT? SORT OF THE "LAWRENCE OF ARABIA" LOOK!
SORT OF THE "LOBOTOMY PATIENT" LOOK.

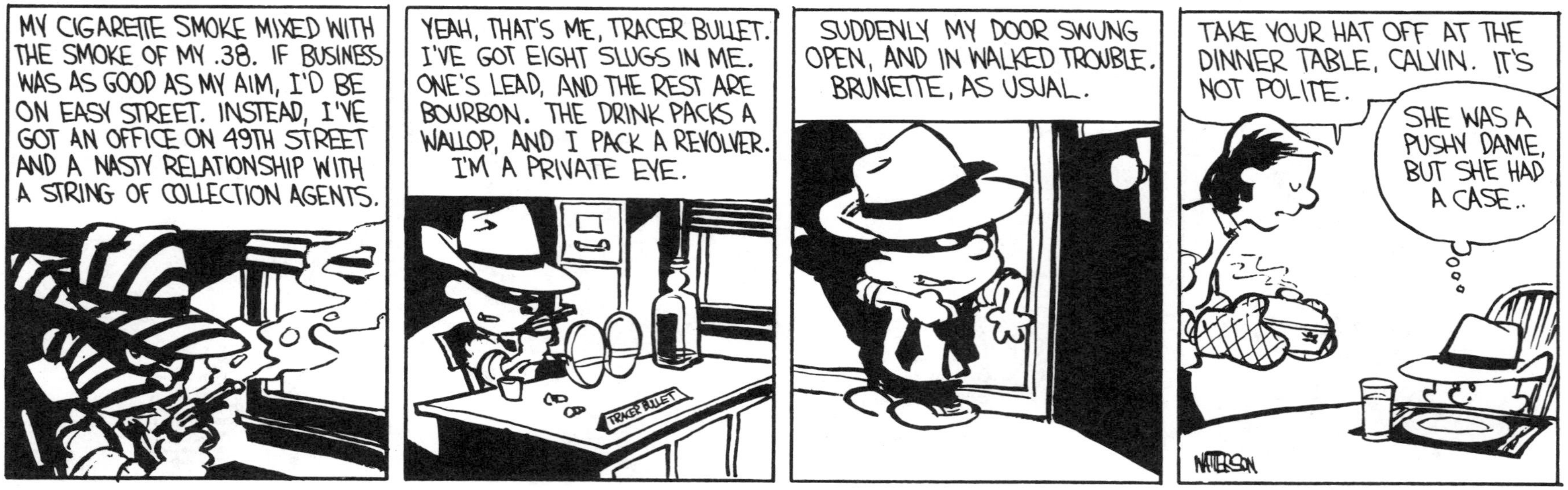
MY CIGARETTE SMOKE MIXED WITH THE SMOKE OF MY .38. IF BUSINESS WAS AS GOOD AS MY AIM, I'D BE ON EASY STREET. INSTEAD, I'VE GOT AN OFFICE ON 49TH STREET AND A NASTY RELATIONSHIP WITH A STRING OF COLLECTION AGENTS.
YEAH, THAT'S ME, TRACER BULLET. I'VE GOT EIGHT SLUGS IN ME. ONE'S LEAD, AND THE REST ARE BOURBON. THE DRINK PACKS A WALLOP, AND I PACK A REVOLVER. I'M A PRIVATE EYE.
TRACER BULLET
SUDDENLY MY DOOR SWUNG OPEN, AND IN WALKED TROUBLE. BRUNETTE, AS USUAL.
TAKE YOUR HAT OFF AT THE DINNER TABLE, CALVIN. IT'S NOT POLITE.
SHE WAS A PUSHY DAME, BUT SHE HAD A CASE..
WATTERSON

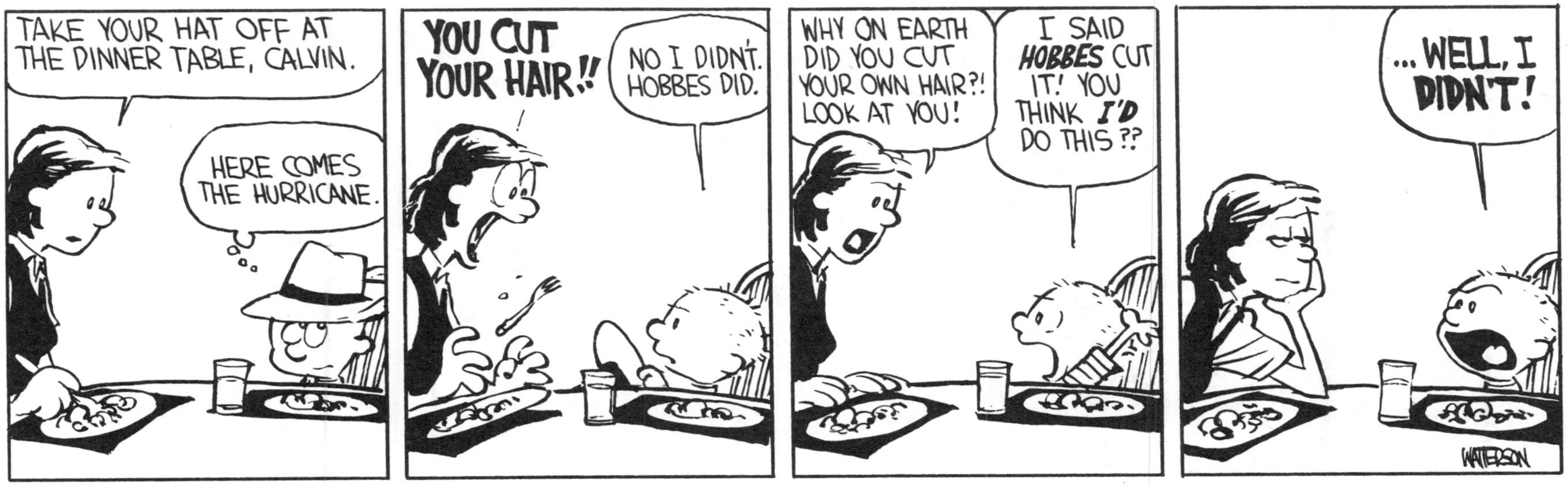
TAKE YOUR HAT OFF AT THE DINNER TABLE, CALVIN.
HERE COMES THE HURRICANE.
YOU CUT YOUR HAIR!!
NO I DIDN'T. HOBBES DID.
WHY ON EARTH DID YOU CUT YOUR OWN HAIR?! LOOK AT YOU!
I SAID HOBBES CUT IT! YOU THINK I'D DO THIS??
...WELL, I DIDN'T!
WATTERSON

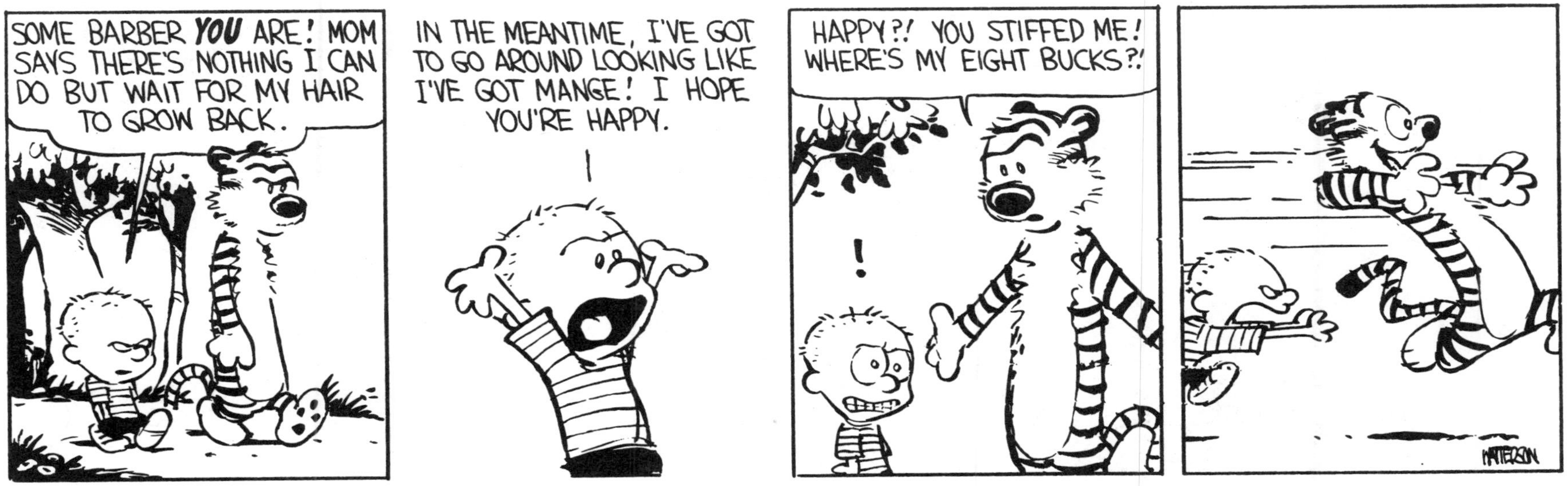
SOME BARBER YOU ARE! MOM SAYS THERE'S NOTHING I CAN DO BUT WAIT FOR MY HAIR TO GROW BACK.
IN THE MEANTIME, I'VE GOT TO GO AROUND LOOKING LIKE I'VE GOT MANGE! I HOPE YOU'RE HAPPY.
HAPPY?! YOU STIFFED ME! WHERE'S MY EIGHT BUCKS?!
!
WATTERSON

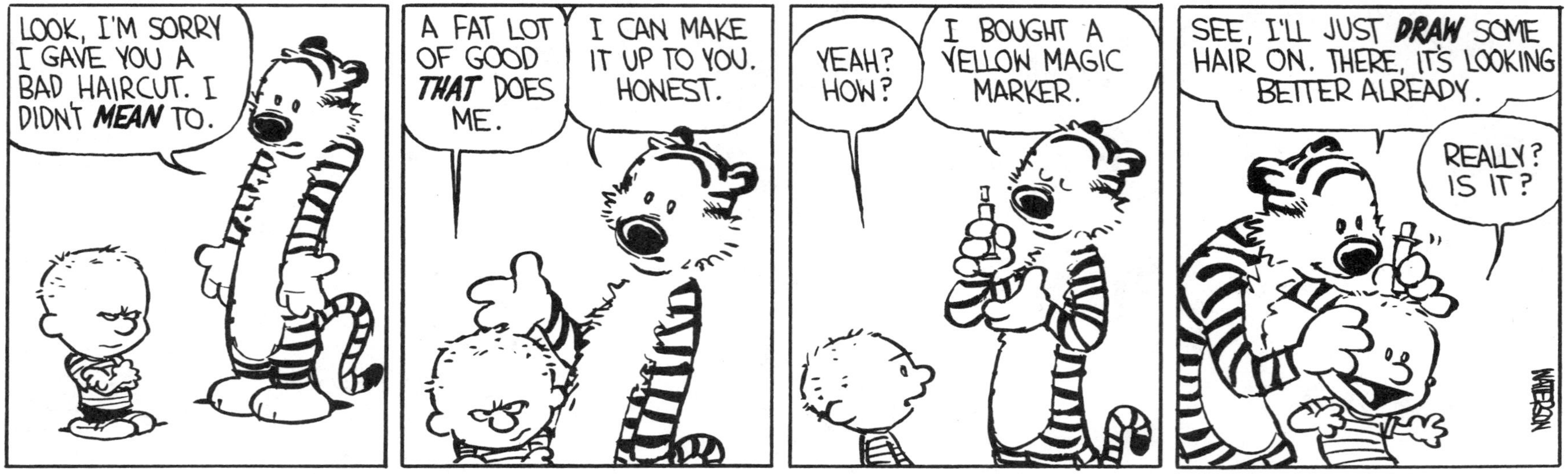
LOOK, I'M SORRY I GAVE YOU A BAD HAIRCUT. I DIDN'T **MEAN** TO.
A FAT LOT OF GOOD **THAT** DOES ME.
I CAN MAKE IT UP TO YOU. HONEST.
YEAH? HOW?
I BOUGHT A YELLOW MAGIC MARKER.
SEE, I'LL JUST **DRAW** SOME HAIR ON. THERE, IT'S LOOKING BETTER ALREADY.
REALLY? IS IT?
WATTERSON

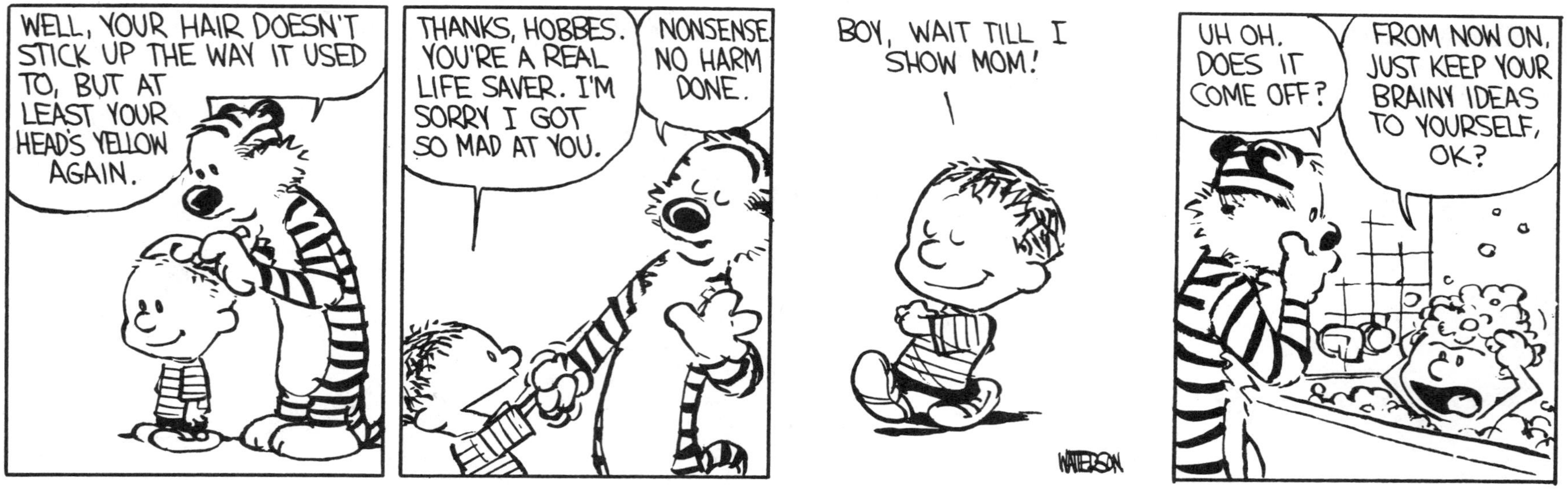
WELL, YOUR HAIR DOESN'T STICK UP THE WAY IT USED TO, BUT AT LEAST YOUR HEAD'S YELLOW AGAIN.
THANKS, HOBBES. YOU'RE A REAL LIFE SAVER. I'M SORRY I GOT SO MAD AT YOU.
NONSENSE. NO HARM DONE.
BOY, WAIT TILL I SHOW MOM!
WATTERSON
UH OH. DOES IT COME OFF?
FROM NOW ON, JUST KEEP YOUR BRAINY IDEAS TO YOURSELF, OK?

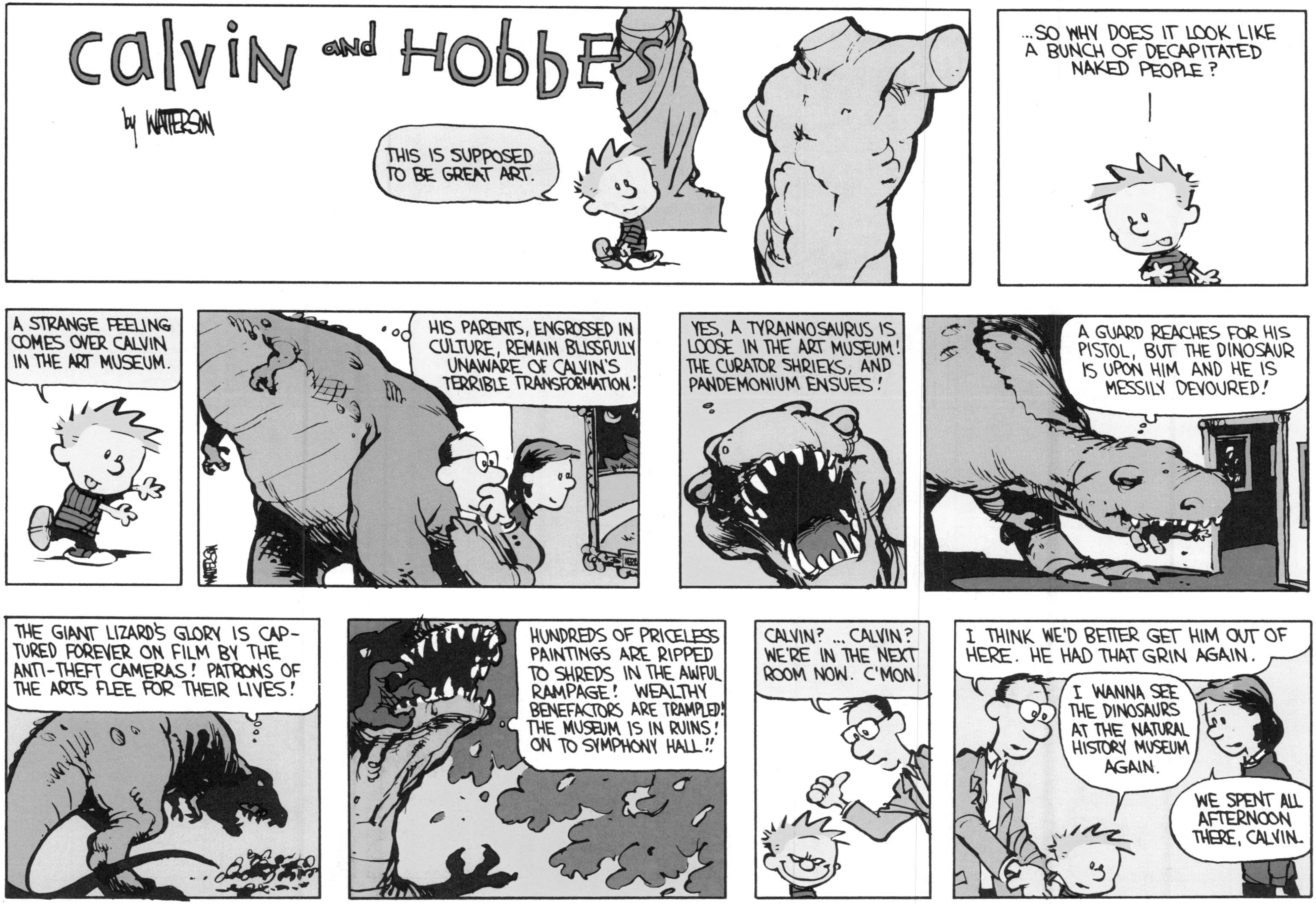
Calvin and HOBBES
by WATTERSON
THIS IS SUPPOSED TO BE GREAT ART.
...SO WHY DOES IT LOOK LIKE A BUNCH OF DECAPITATED NAKED PEOPLE?
A STRANGE FEELING COMES OVER CALVIN IN THE ART MUSEUM.
HIS PARENTS, ENGROSSED IN CULTURE, REMAIN BLISSFULLY UNAWARE OF CALVIN'S TERRIBLE TRANSFORMATION!
YES, A TYRANNOSAURUS IS LOOSE IN THE ART MUSEUM! THE CURATOR SHRIEKS, AND PANDEMONIUM ENSUES!
A GUARD REACHES FOR HIS PISTOL, BUT THE DINOSAUR IS UPON HIM AND HE IS MESSILY DEVOURED!
THE GIANT LIZARD'S GLORY IS CAPTURED FOREVER ON FILM BY THE ANTI-THEFT CAMERAS! PATRONS OF THE ARTS FLEE FOR THEIR LIVES!
HUNDREDS OF PRICELESS PAINTINGS ARE RIPPED TO SHREDS IN THE AWFUL RAMPAGE! WEALTHY BENEFACTORS ARE TRAMPLED! THE MUSEUM IS IN RUINS! ON TO SYMPHONY HALL!!
CALVIN? ... CALVIN? WE'RE IN THE NEXT ROOM NOW. C'MON.
I THINK WE'D BETTER GET HIM OUT OF HERE. HE HAD THAT GRIN AGAIN.
I WANNA SEE THE DINOSAURS AT THE NATURAL HISTORY MUSEUM AGAIN.
WE SPENT ALL AFTERNOON THERE, CALVIN.

This was an early tyrannosaur strip. The number of fingers, his alligator belly, the dragging tail, etc., are all wrong. Obviously, I did no research whatsoever. The parents are admiring a *Krazy Kat* landscape in the fourth panel.

Politics seems to be more and more poll driven, although I don't know that there's any connection between what we need and what we like. Calvin is not entirely clear on how his dad stays Dad, so he polls his own opinions and attempts to influence policy with the statistics. By the way, I think there should be a statute of limitations on yearbook photographs.

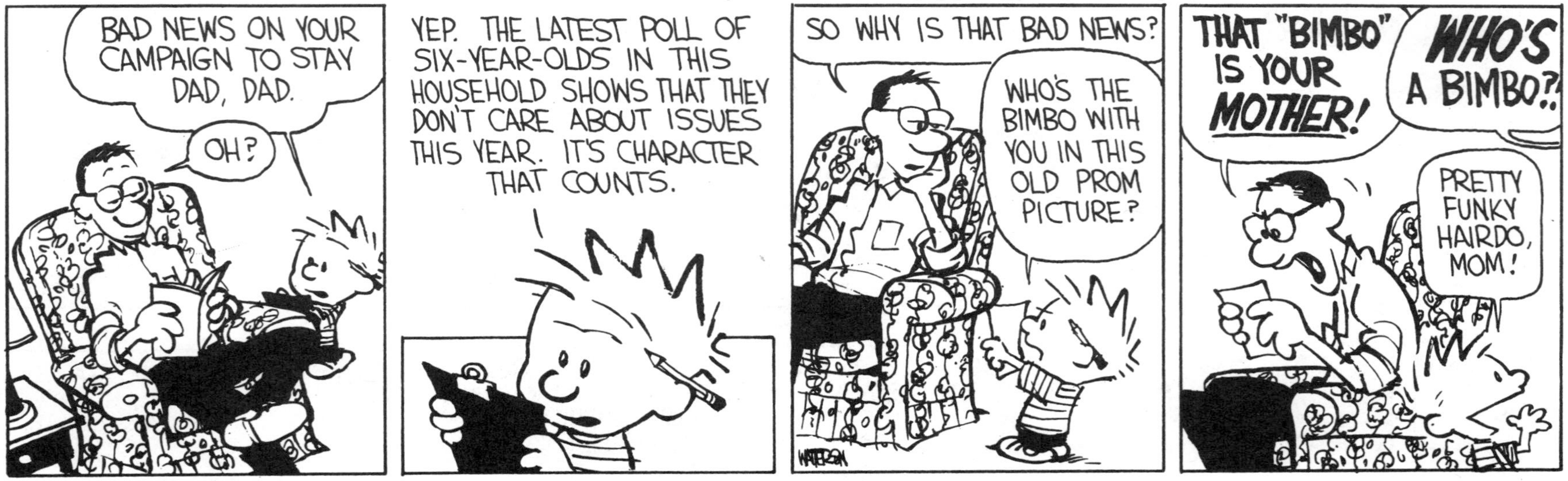

BAD NEWS ON YOUR CAMPAIGN TO STAY DAD, DAD.
OH?
YEP. THE LATEST POLL OF SIX-YEAR-OLDS IN THIS HOUSEHOLD SHOWS THAT THEY DON'T CARE ABOUT ISSUES THIS YEAR. IT'S CHARACTER THAT COUNTS.
SO WHY IS THAT BAD NEWS?
WHO'S THE BIMBO WITH YOU IN THIS OLD PROM PICTURE?
THAT "BIMBO" IS YOUR MOTHER!
WHO'S A BIMBO?!
PRETTY FUNKY HAIRDO, MOM!

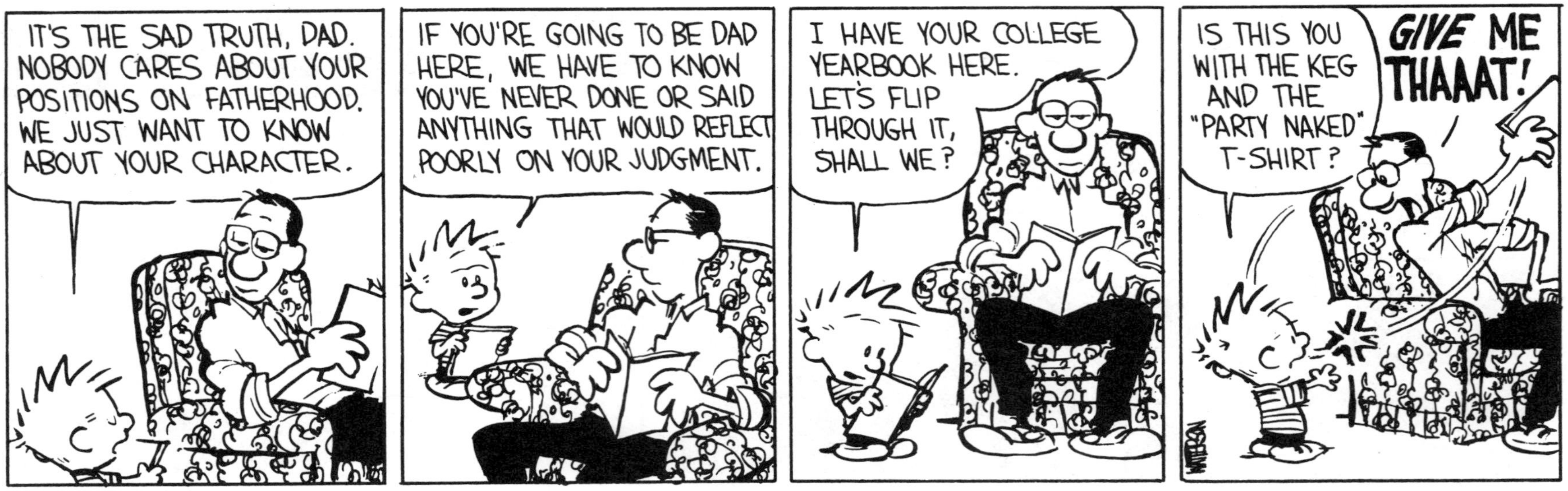

IT'S THE SAD TRUTH, DAD. NOBODY CARES ABOUT YOUR POSITIONS ON FATHERHOOD. WE JUST WANT TO KNOW ABOUT YOUR CHARACTER.
IF YOU'RE GOING TO BE DAD HERE, WE HAVE TO KNOW YOU'VE NEVER DONE OR SAID ANYTHING THAT WOULD REFLECT POORLY ON YOUR JUDGMENT.
I HAVE YOUR COLLEGE YEARBOOK HERE. LET'S FLIP THROUGH IT, SHALL WE?
IS THIS YOU WITH THE KEG AND THE "PARTY NAKED" T-SHIRT?
GIVE ME THAAAT!

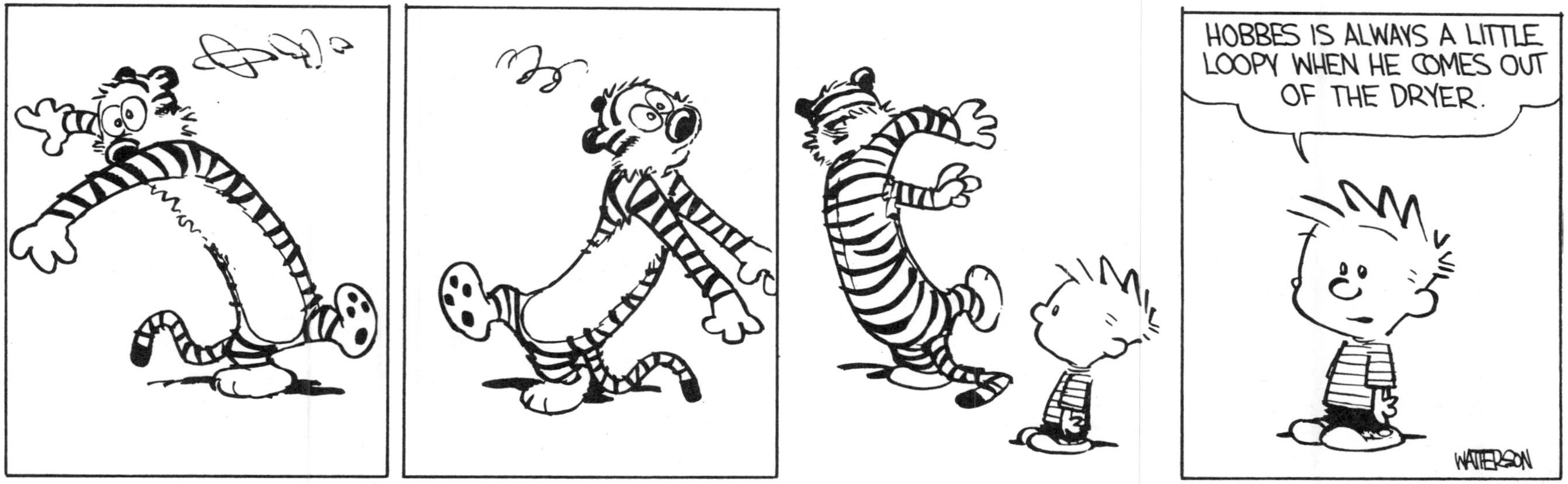
HOBBES IS ALWAYS A LITTLE LOOPY WHEN HE COMES OUT OF THE DRYER.
WATTERSON

Hobbes periodically gets washed in the washing machine. Calvin seems to take this in stride, but it's one of the stranger blurrings of what Hobbes is.

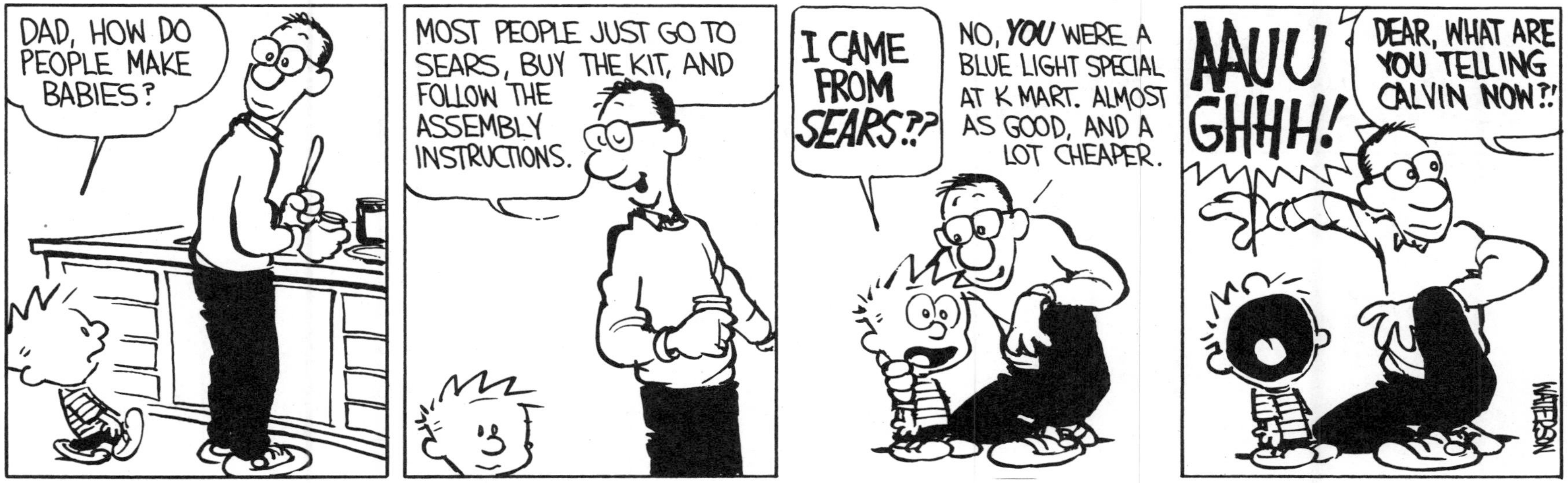
DAD, HOW DO PEOPLE MAKE BABIES?
MOST PEOPLE JUST GO TO SEARS, BUY THE KIT, AND FOLLOW THE ASSEMBLY INSTRUCTIONS.
I CAME FROM SEARS?!?
NO, YOU WERE A BLUE LIGHT SPECIAL AT K MART. ALMOST AS GOOD, AND A LOT CHEAPER.
AAUUGHHH!
DEAR, WHAT ARE YOU TELLING CALVIN NOW?!
WATTERSON

I imagine it must be a great temptation to misuse one's parental authority for private jokes.

Calvin's transmogrifier sums up the spirit of the strip. A cardboard box becomes a series of great inventions with a little imagination. The transmogrifier shows the kind of kid Calvin is, and it added a new dimension to the strip's world. This was an important story for *Calvin and Hobbes*, and I've used the transmogrifier several times since.

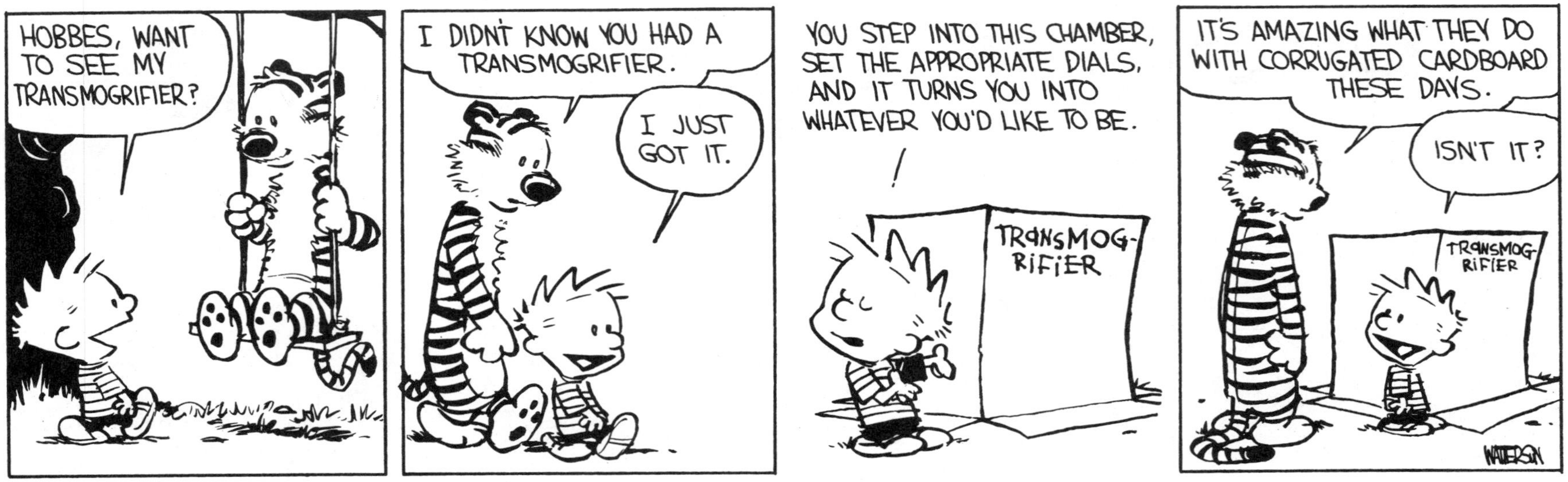

HOBBES, WANT TO SEE MY TRANSMOGRIFIER?
I DIDN'T KNOW YOU HAD A TRANSMOGRIFIER.
I JUST GOT IT.
YOU STEP INTO THIS CHAMBER, SET THE APPROPRIATE DIALS, AND IT TURNS YOU INTO WHATEVER YOU'D LIKE TO BE.
TRANSMOG-RIFIER
IT'S AMAZING WHAT THEY DO WITH CORRUGATED CARDBOARD THESE DAYS.
ISN'T IT?
TRANSMOG-RIFIER
WATTERSON

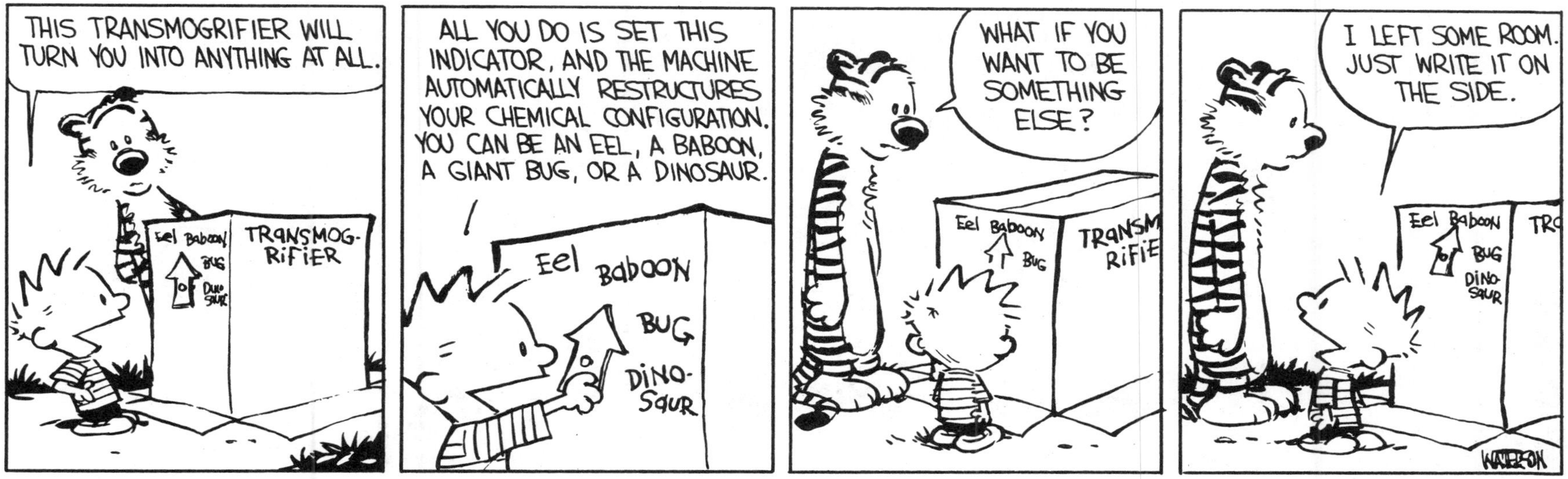
THIS TRANSMOGRIFIER WILL TURN YOU INTO ANYTHING AT ALL.
Eel Baboon Bug Dinosaur
TRANSMOGRIFIER
ALL YOU DO IS SET THIS INDICATOR, AND THE MACHINE AUTOMATICALLY RESTRUCTURES YOUR CHEMICAL CONFIGURATION. YOU CAN BE AN EEL, A BABOON, A GIANT BUG, OR A DINOSAUR.
Eel Baboon Bug Dino-saur
WHAT IF YOU WANT TO BE SOMETHING ELSE?
I LEFT SOME ROOM. JUST WRITE IT ON THE SIDE.
WATTERSON

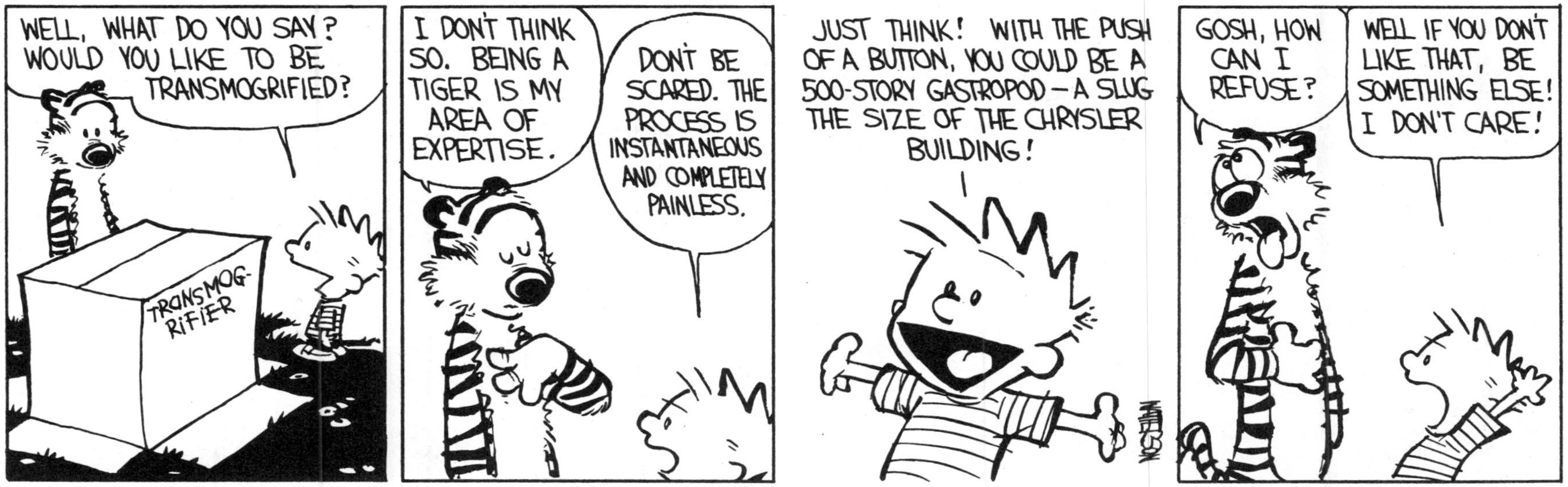
WELL, WHAT DO YOU SAY? WOULD YOU LIKE TO BE TRANSMOGRIFIED?
TRANSMOGRIFIER
I DON'T THINK SO. BEING A TIGER IS MY AREA OF EXPERTISE.
DON'T BE SCARED. THE PROCESS IS INSTANTANEOUS AND COMPLETELY PAINLESS.
JUST THINK! WITH THE PUSH OF A BUTTON, YOU COULD BE A 500-STORY GASTROPOD — A SLUG THE SIZE OF THE CHRYSLER BUILDING!
WATTERSON
GOSH, HOW CAN I REFUSE?
WELL IF YOU DON'T LIKE THAT, BE SOMETHING ELSE! I DON'T CARE!

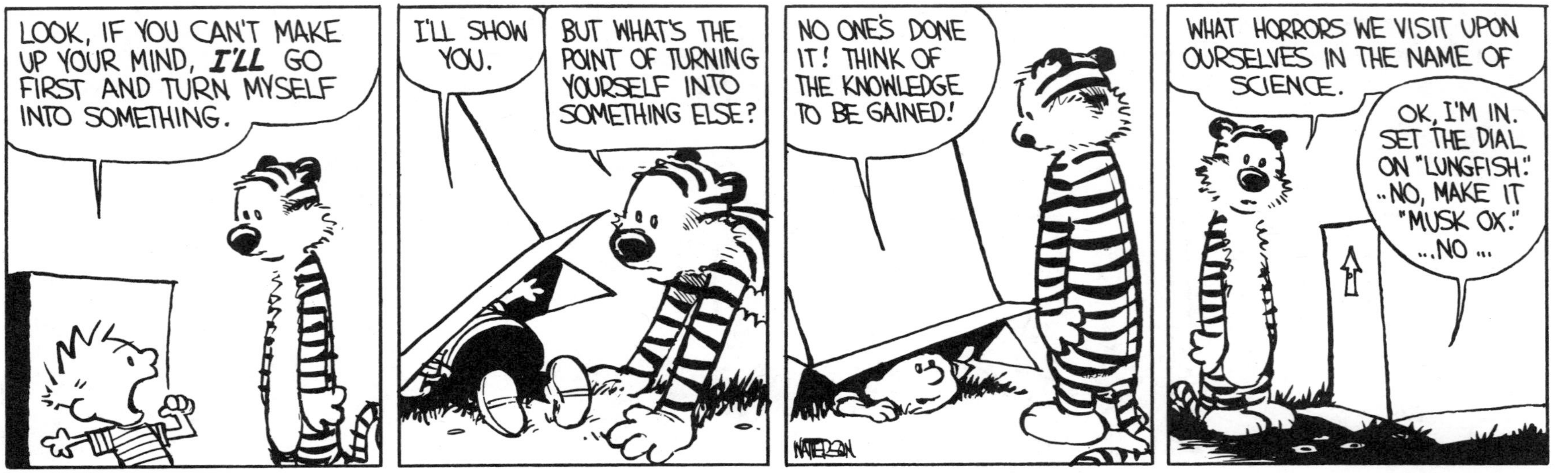
LOOK, IF YOU CAN'T MAKE UP YOUR MIND, *I'LL* GO FIRST AND TURN MYSELF INTO SOMETHING.
I'LL SHOW YOU.
BUT WHAT'S THE POINT OF TURNING YOURSELF INTO SOMETHING ELSE?
NO ONE'S DONE IT! THINK OF THE KNOWLEDGE TO BE GAINED!
WATTERSON
WHAT HORRORS WE VISIT UPON OURSELVES IN THE NAME OF SCIENCE.
OK, I'M IN. SET THE DIAL ON "LUNGFISH." ..NO, MAKE IT "MUSK OX." ...NO ...

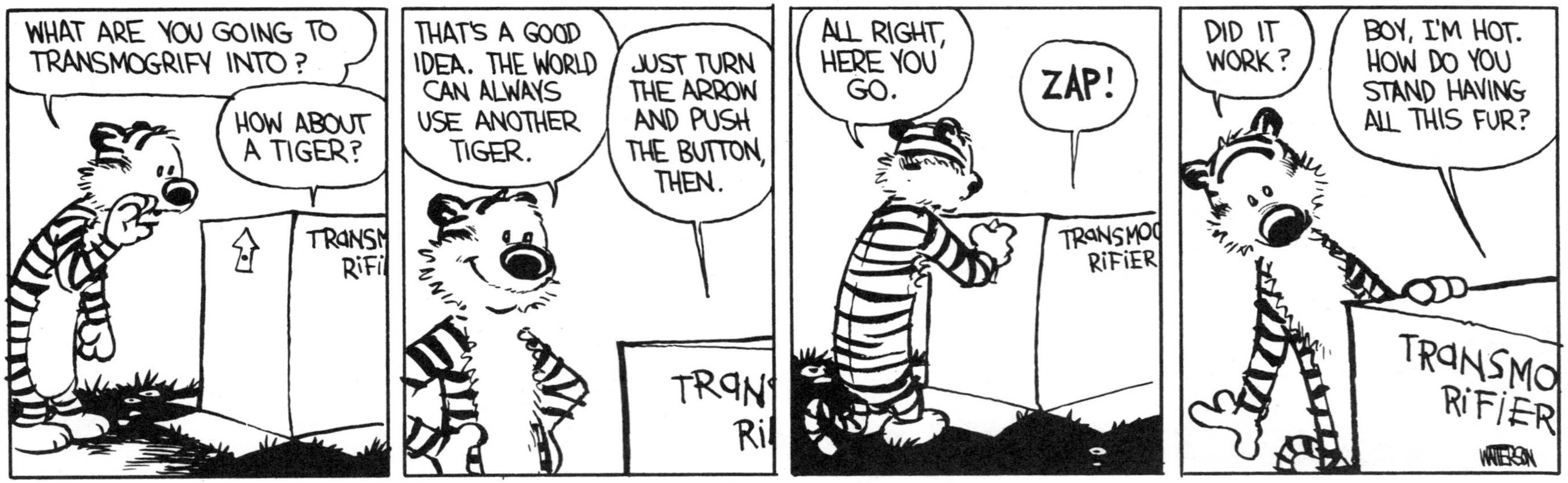
WHAT ARE YOU GOING TO TRANSMOGRIFY INTO?
HOW ABOUT A TIGER?
TRANSM RIFI
THAT'S A GOOD IDEA. THE WORLD CAN ALWAYS USE ANOTHER TIGER.
JUST TURN THE ARROW AND PUSH THE BUTTON, THEN.
TRAN RI
ALL RIGHT, HERE YOU GO.
ZAP!
TRANSMOG RIFIER
DID IT WORK?
BOY, I'M HOT. HOW DO YOU STAND HAVING ALL THIS FUR?
TRANSMO RIFIER
WATTERSON

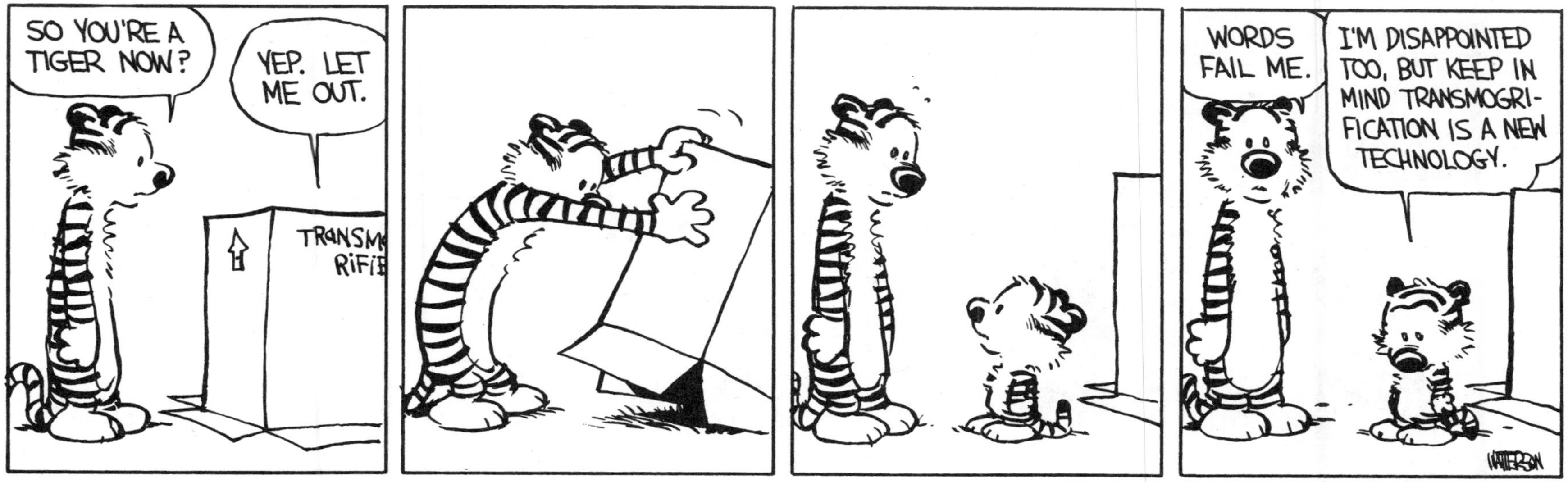
SO YOU'RE A TIGER NOW?
YEP. LET ME OUT.
WORDS FAIL ME.
I'M DISAPPOINTED TOO, BUT KEEP IN MIND TRANSMOGRI-FICATION IS A NEW TECHNOLOGY.

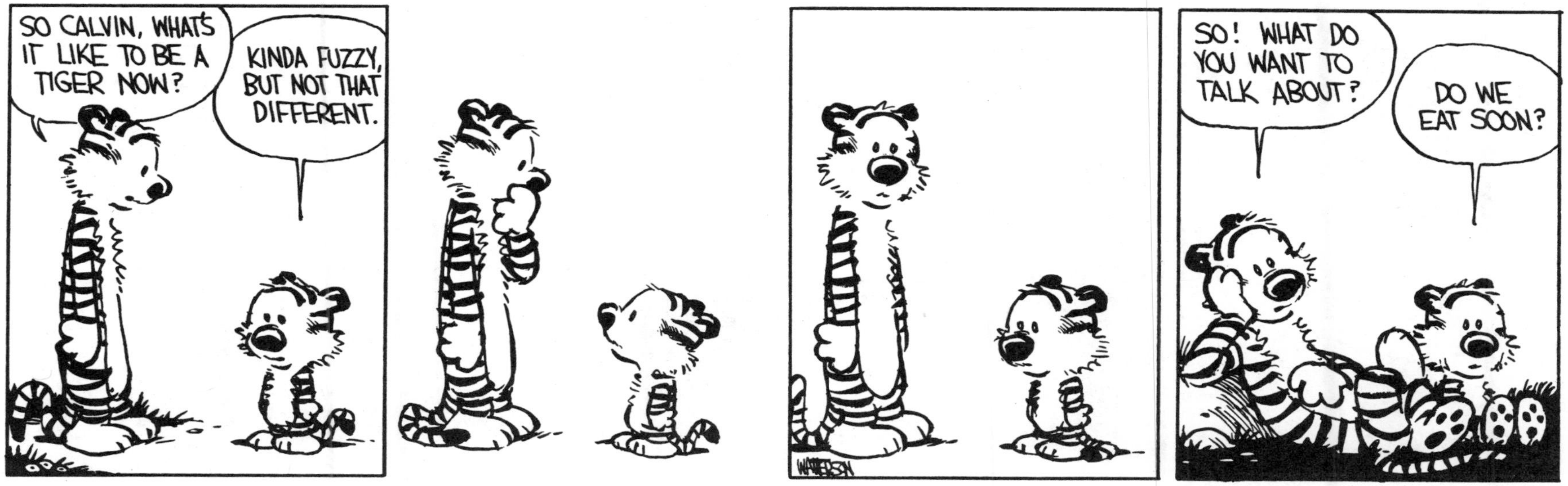
SO CALVIN, WHAT'S IT LIKE TO BE A TIGER NOW?
KINDA FUZZY, BUT NOT THAT DIFFERENT.
SO! WHAT DO YOU WANT TO TALK ABOUT?
DO WE EAT SOON?

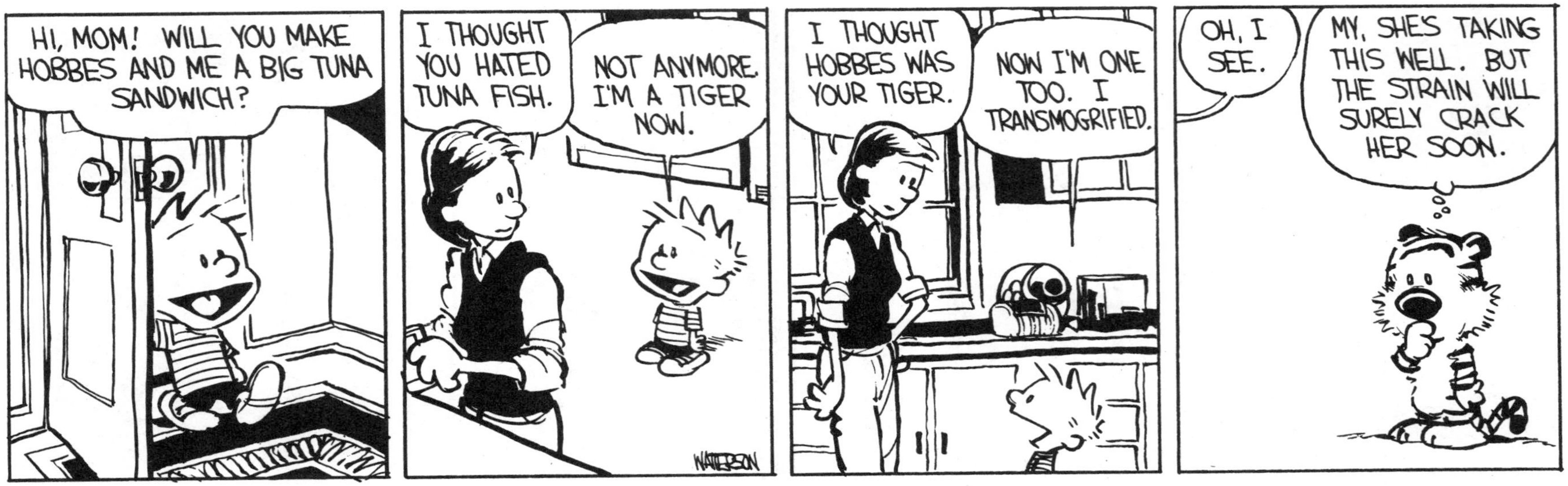
HI, MOM! WILL YOU MAKE HOBBES AND ME A BIG TUNA SANDWICH?
I THOUGHT YOU HATED TUNA FISH.
NOT ANYMORE. I'M A TIGER NOW.
I THOUGHT HOBBES WAS YOUR TIGER.
NOW I'M ONE TOO. I TRANSMOGRIFIED.
OH, I SEE.
MY, SHE'S TAKING THIS WELL. BUT THE STRAIN WILL SURELY CRACK HER SOON.

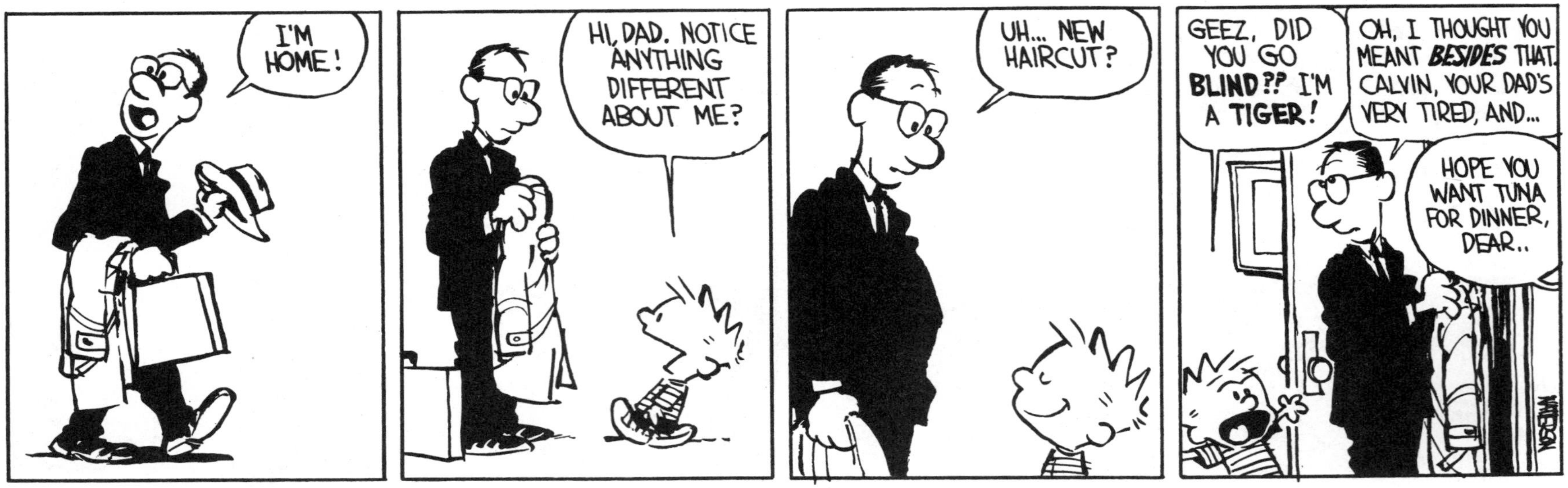
I'M HOME!
HI, DAD. NOTICE ANYTHING DIFFERENT ABOUT ME?
UH... NEW HAIRCUT?
GEEZ, DID YOU GO BLIND?? I'M A TIGER!
OH, I THOUGHT YOU MEANT BESIDES THAT. CALVIN, YOUR DAD'S VERY TIRED, AND...
HOPE YOU WANT TUNA FOR DINNER, DEAR..

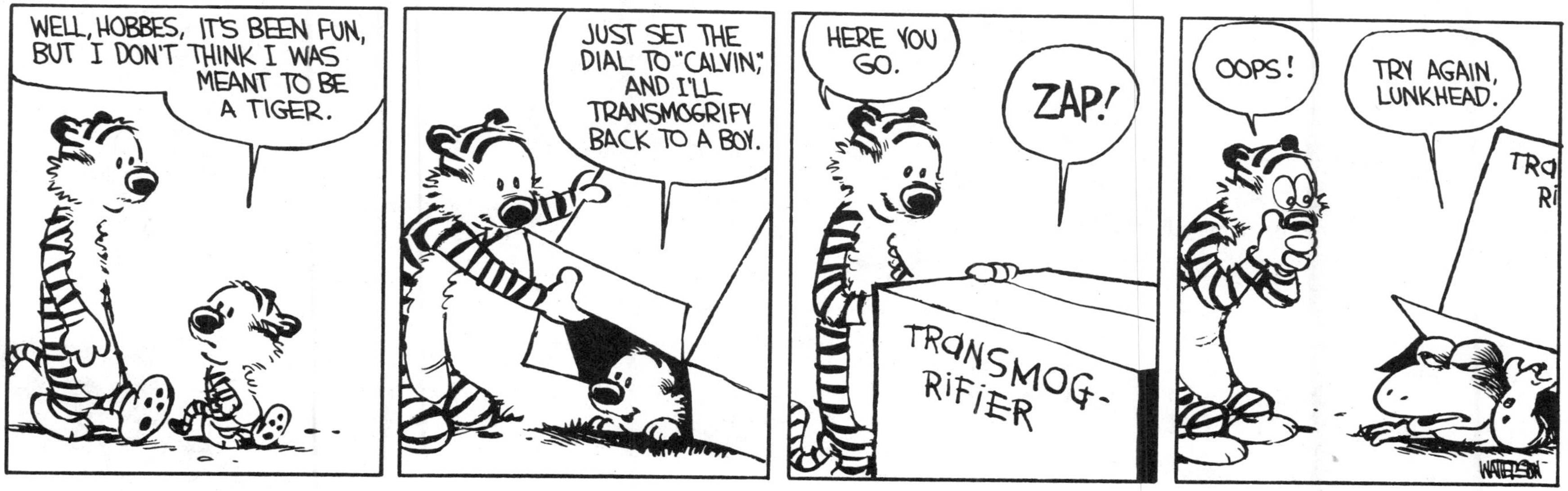
WELL, HOBBES, IT'S BEEN FUN, BUT I DON'T THINK I WAS MEANT TO BE A TIGER.
JUST SET THE DIAL TO "CALVIN," AND I'LL TRANSMOGRIFY BACK TO A BOY.
HERE YOU GO.
ZAP!
TRANSMOG-RIFIER
OOPS!
TRY AGAIN, LUNKHEAD.

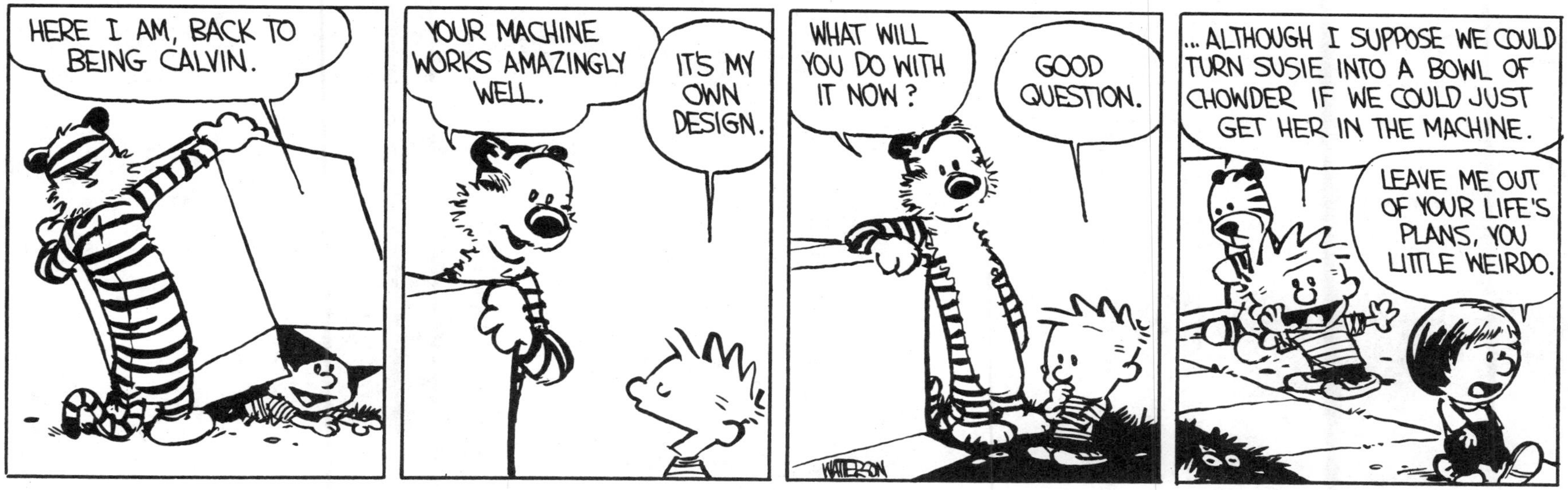
HERE I AM, BACK TO BEING CALVIN.
YOUR MACHINE WORKS AMAZINGLY WELL.
IT'S MY OWN DESIGN.
WHAT WILL YOU DO WITH IT NOW?
GOOD QUESTION.
...ALTHOUGH I SUPPOSE WE COULD TURN SUSIE INTO A BOWL OF CHOWDER IF WE COULD JUST GET HER IN THE MACHINE.
LEAVE ME OUT OF YOUR LIFE'S PLANS, YOU LITTLE WEIRDO.

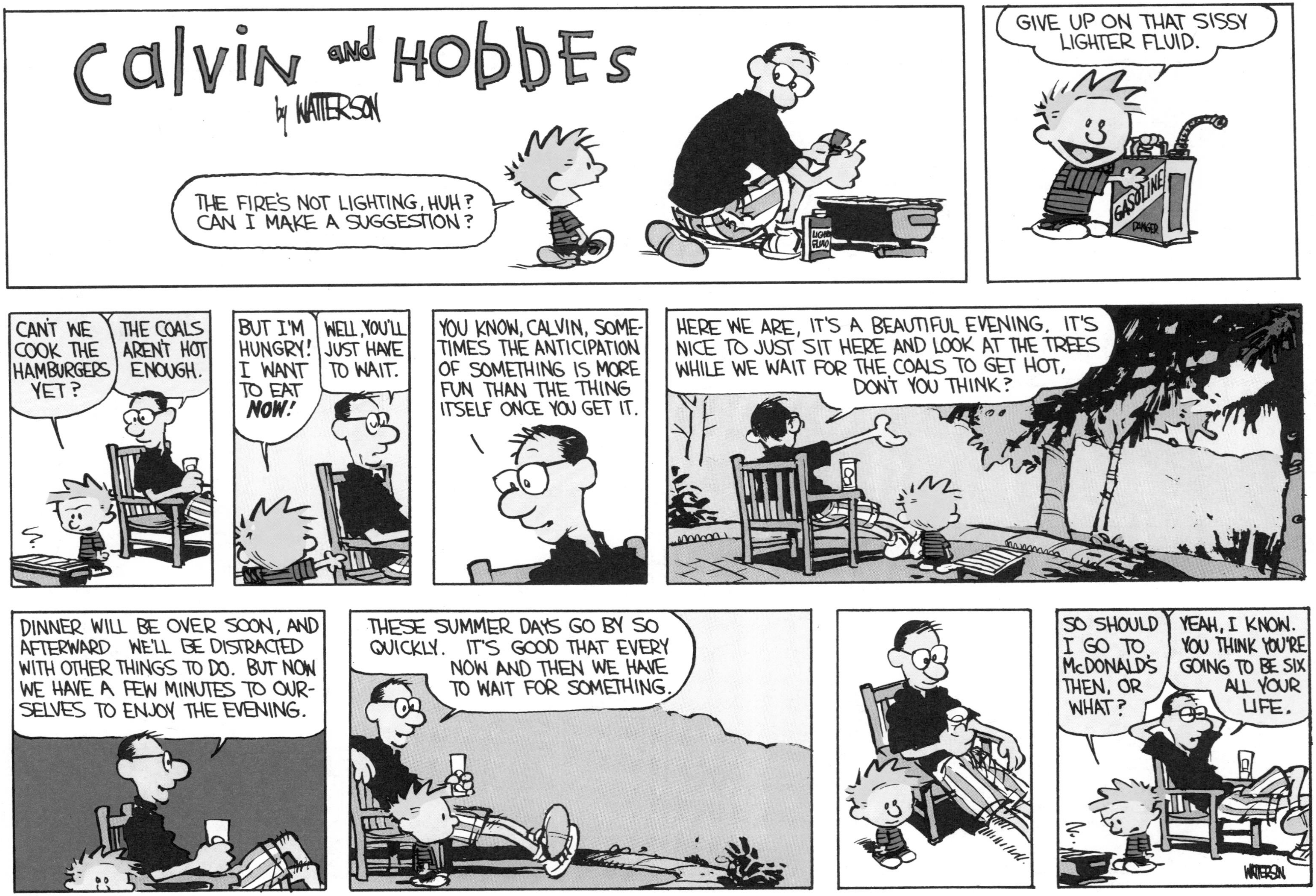
Calvin and HOBBES
by WATTERSON
THE FIRE'S NOT LIGHTING, HUH? CAN I MAKE A SUGGESTION?
LIGHTER FLUID
GIVE UP ON THAT SISSY LIGHTER FLUID.
GASOLINE
DANGER
CAN'T WE COOK THE HAMBURGERS YET?
THE COALS AREN'T HOT ENOUGH.
BUT I'M HUNGRY! I WANT TO EAT NOW!
WELL, YOU'LL JUST HAVE TO WAIT.
YOU KNOW, CALVIN, SOMETIMES THE ANTICIPATION OF SOMETHING IS MORE FUN THAN THE THING ITSELF ONCE YOU GET IT.
HERE WE ARE, IT'S A BEAUTIFUL EVENING. IT'S NICE TO JUST SIT HERE AND LOOK AT THE TREES WHILE WE WAIT FOR THE COALS TO GET HOT, DON'T YOU THINK?
DINNER WILL BE OVER SOON, AND AFTERWARD WE'LL BE DISTRACTED WITH OTHER THINGS TO DO. BUT NOW WE HAVE A FEW MINUTES TO OURSELVES TO ENJOY THE EVENING.
THESE SUMMER DAYS GO BY SO QUICKLY. IT'S GOOD THAT EVERY NOW AND THEN WE HAVE TO WAIT FOR SOMETHING.
SO SHOULD I GO TO McDONALD'S THEN, OR WHAT?
YEAH, I KNOW. YOU THINK YOU'RE GOING TO BE SIX ALL YOUR LIFE.
WATTERSON

You can lead people to truth, but you can't make them understand it: the story of my youth, as seen from the present.

For several years, I had Calvin's family go camping for vacation. The stories are mostly invented, but they're based on memories of trips my family took when I was a kid. Dried food looks pretty good after scaling, beheading, and gutting a gasping fish.

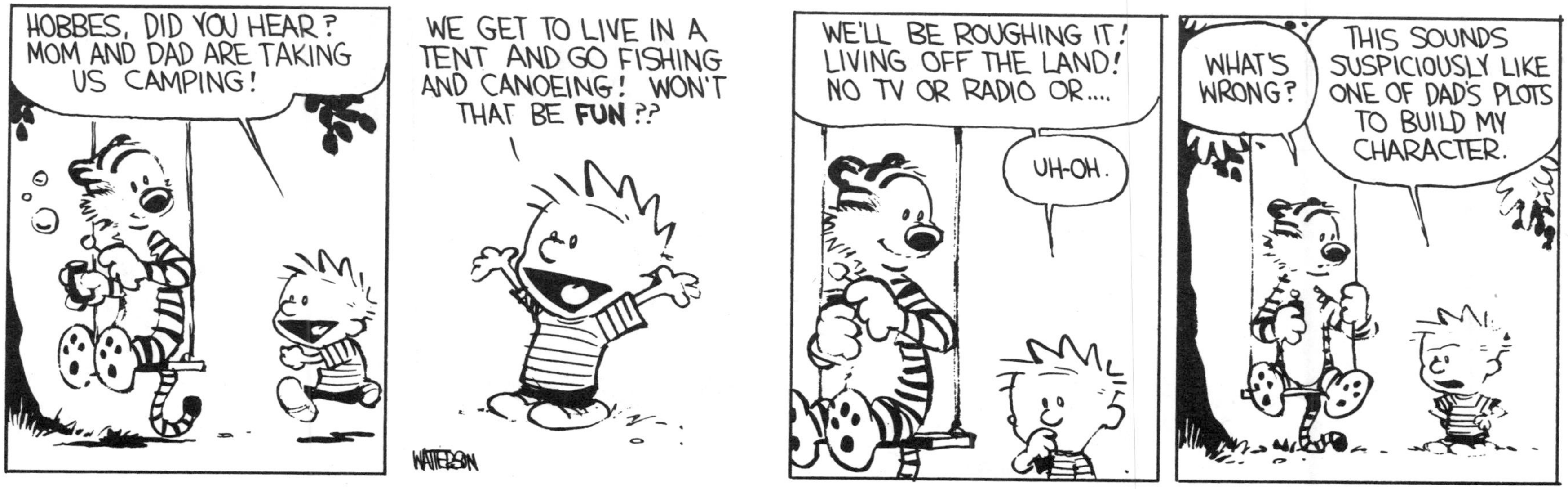

HOBBES, DID YOU HEAR? MOM AND DAD ARE TAKING US CAMPING!
WE GET TO LIVE IN A TENT AND GO FISHING AND CANOEING! WON'T THAT BE **FUN**??
WE'LL BE ROUGHING IT! LIVING OFF THE LAND! NO TV OR RADIO OR....
UH-OH.
WHAT'S WRONG?
THIS SOUNDS SUSPICIOUSLY LIKE ONE OF DAD'S PLOTS TO BUILD MY CHARACTER.

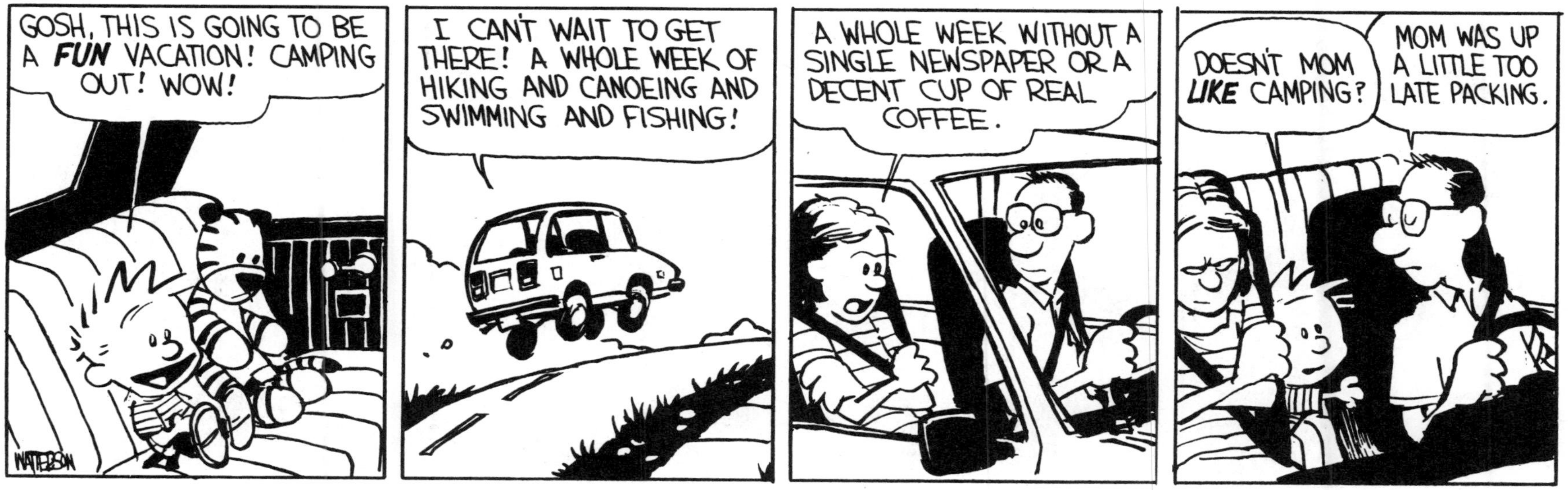

GOSH, THIS IS GOING TO BE A ***FUN*** VACATION! CAMPING OUT! WOW!
I CAN'T WAIT TO GET THERE! A WHOLE WEEK OF HIKING AND CANOEING AND SWIMMING AND FISHING!
A WHOLE WEEK WITHOUT A SINGLE NEWSPAPER OR A DECENT CUP OF REAL COFFEE.
DOESN'T MOM ***LIKE*** CAMPING?
MOM WAS UP A LITTLE TOO LATE PACKING.

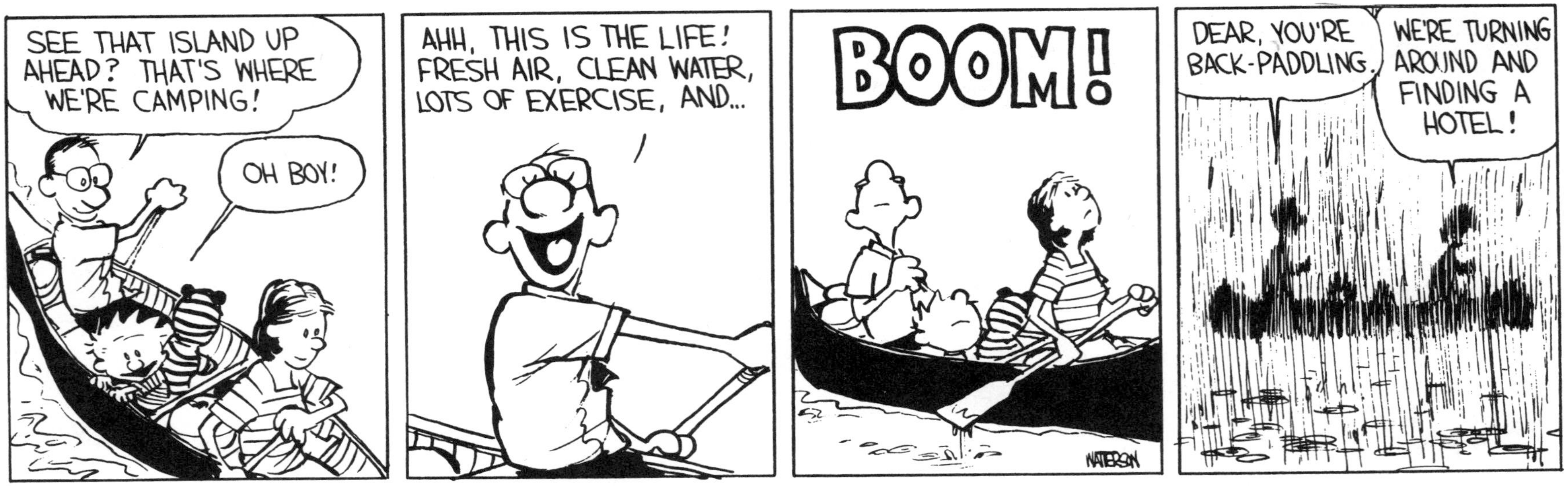
SEE THAT ISLAND UP AHEAD? THAT'S WHERE WE'RE CAMPING!
OH BOY!
AHH, THIS IS THE LIFE! FRESH AIR, CLEAN WATER, LOTS OF EXERCISE, AND...
BOOM!
DEAR, YOU'RE BACK-PADDLING.
WE'RE TURNING AROUND AND FINDING A HOTEL!
WATERSON

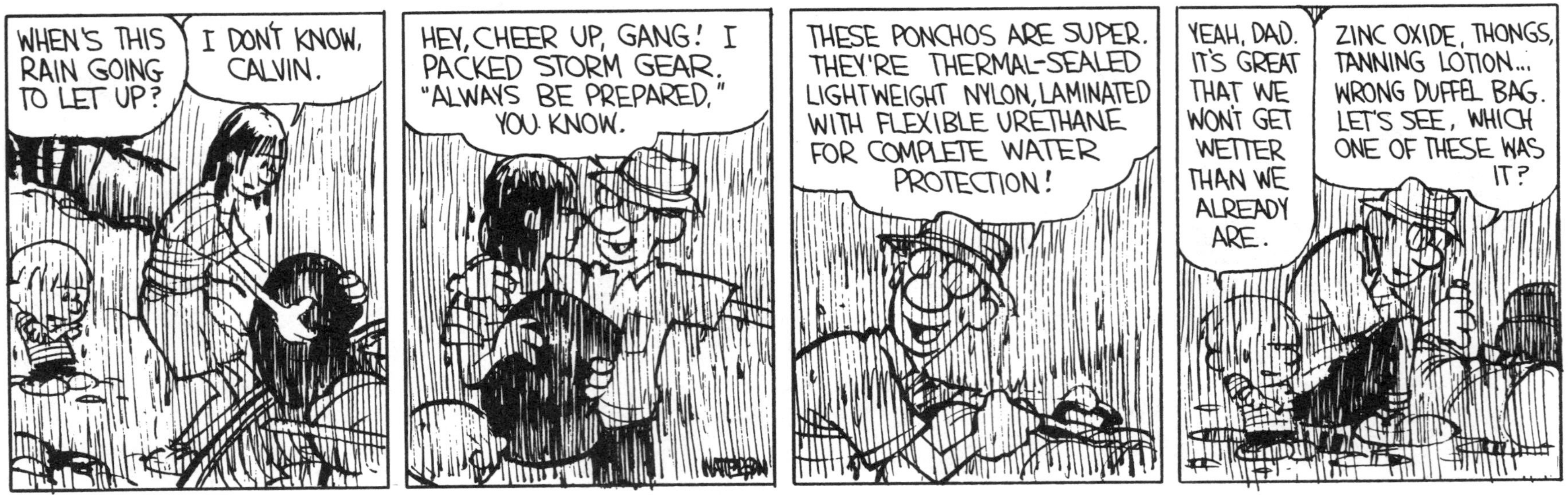
WHEN'S THIS RAIN GOING TO LET UP?
I DON'T KNOW, CALVIN.
HEY, CHEER UP, GANG! I PACKED STORM GEAR. "ALWAYS BE PREPARED," YOU KNOW.
THESE PONCHOS ARE SUPER. THEY'RE THERMAL-SEALED LIGHTWEIGHT NYLON, LAMINATED WITH FLEXIBLE URETHANE FOR COMPLETE WATER PROTECTION!
YEAH, DAD. IT'S GREAT THAT WE WON'T GET WETTER THAN WE ALREADY ARE.
ZINC OXIDE, THONGS, TANNING LOTION... WRONG DUFFEL BAG. LET'S SEE, WHICH ONE OF THESE WAS IT?
WATERSON

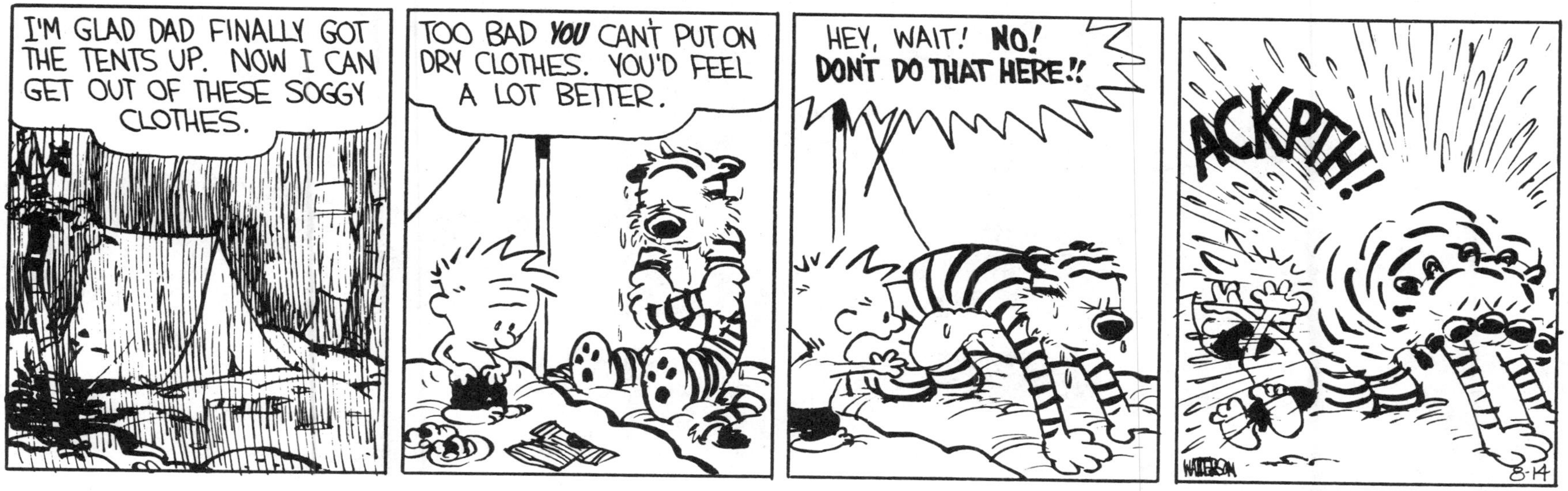
I'M GLAD DAD FINALLY GOT THE TENTS UP. NOW I CAN GET OUT OF THESE SOGGY CLOTHES.
TOO BAD **YOU** CAN'T PUT ON DRY CLOTHES. YOU'D FEEL A LOT BETTER.
HEY, WAIT! **NO! DON'T DO THAT HERE!!**
ACKPTH!
WATTERSON
8-14

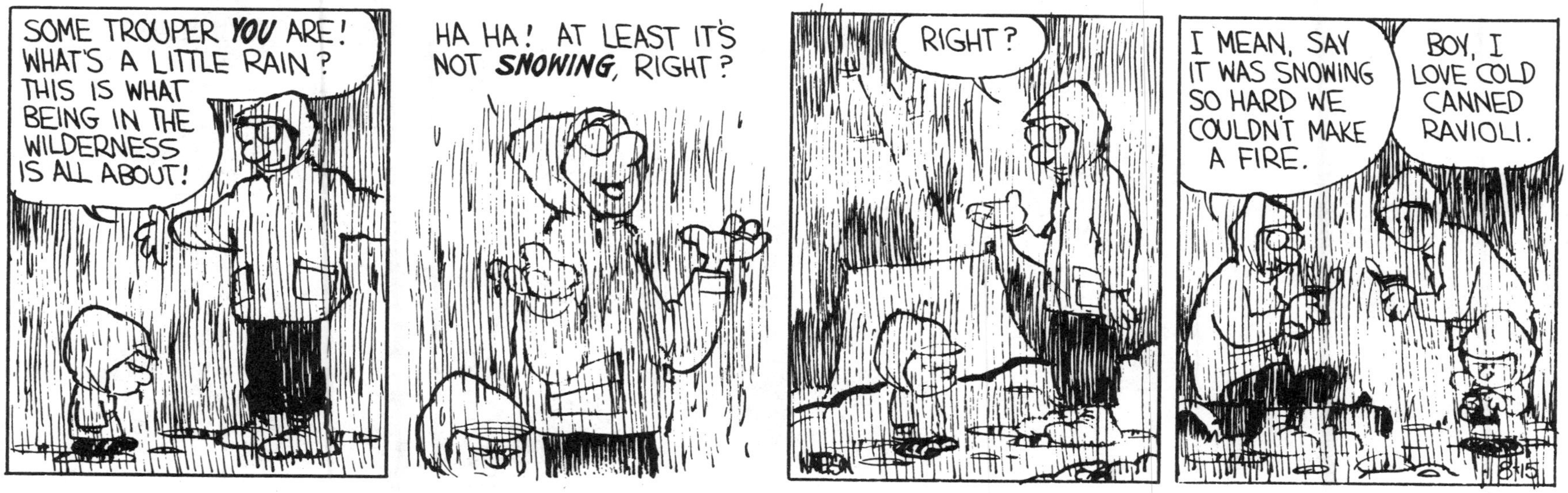
SOME TROUPER **YOU** ARE! WHAT'S A LITTLE RAIN? THIS IS WHAT BEING IN THE WILDERNESS IS ALL ABOUT!
HA HA! AT LEAST IT'S NOT **SNOWING**, RIGHT?
RIGHT?
I MEAN, SAY IT WAS SNOWING SO HARD WE COULDN'T MAKE A FIRE.
BOY, I LOVE COLD CANNED RAVIOLI.
WATTERSON
8-15

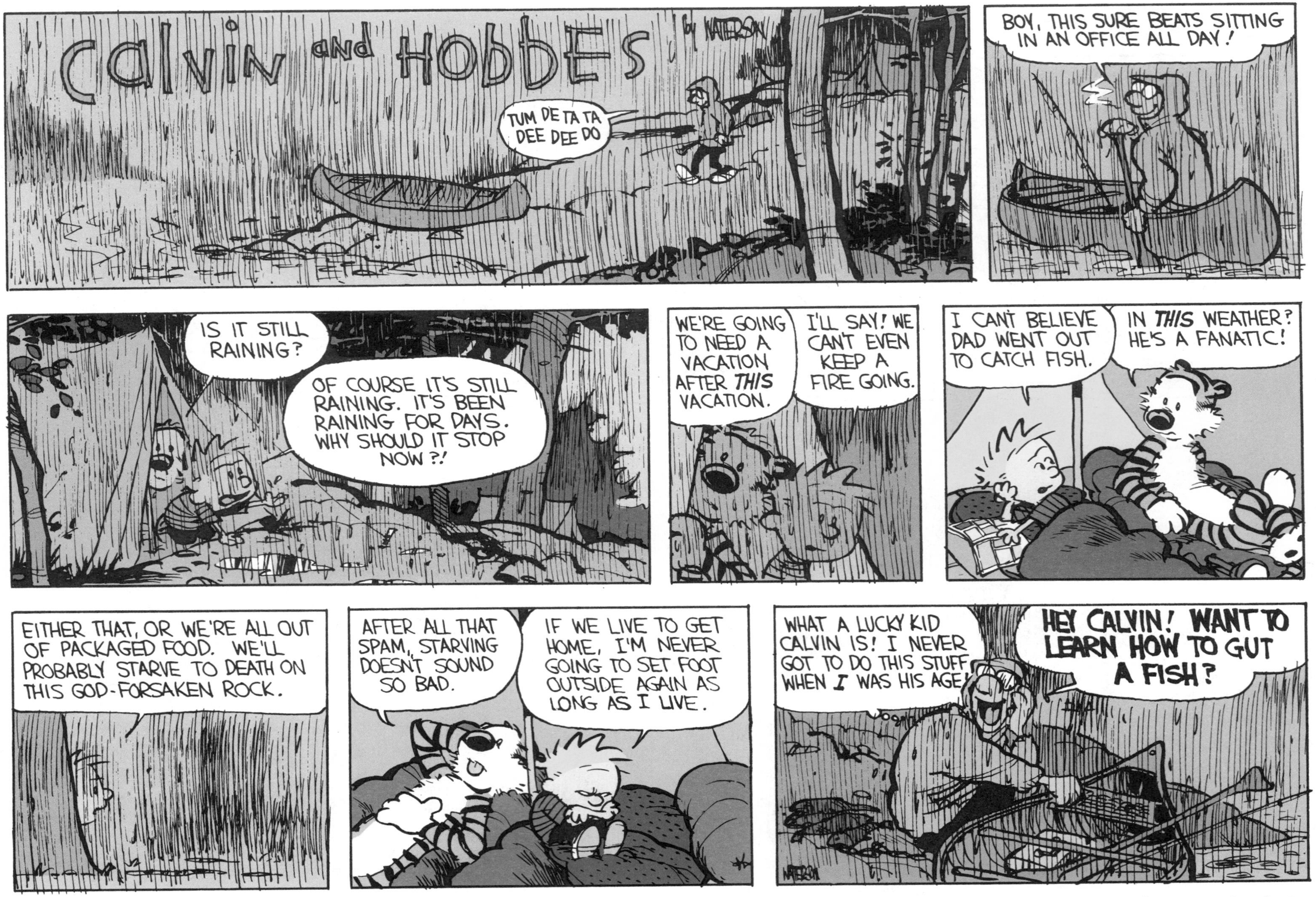
Calvin and HOBBES
by WATTERSON
TUM DE TA TA DEE DEE DO
BOY, THIS SURE BEATS SITTING IN AN OFFICE ALL DAY!
IS IT STILL RAINING?
OF COURSE IT'S STILL RAINING. IT'S BEEN RAINING FOR DAYS. WHY SHOULD IT STOP NOW?!
WE'RE GOING TO NEED A VACATION AFTER THIS VACATION.
I'LL SAY! WE CAN'T EVEN KEEP A FIRE GOING.
I CAN'T BELIEVE DAD WENT OUT TO CATCH FISH.
IN THIS WEATHER? HE'S A FANATIC!
EITHER THAT, OR WE'RE ALL OUT OF PACKAGED FOOD. WE'LL PROBABLY STARVE TO DEATH ON THIS GOD-FORSAKEN ROCK.
AFTER ALL THAT SPAM, STARVING DOESN'T SOUND SO BAD.
IF WE LIVE TO GET HOME, I'M NEVER GOING TO SET FOOT OUTSIDE AGAIN AS LONG AS I LIVE.
WHAT A LUCKY KID CALVIN IS! I NEVER GOT TO DO THIS STUFF WHEN I WAS HIS AGE!
HEY CALVIN! WANT TO LEARN HOW TO GUT A FISH?

Sunday strips must be drawn two months before publication to allow for color plates. To include a Sunday strip in a story, the entire story must be written that far in advance, and I'm almost never that far ahead on daily strips. Also, some papers don't have Sunday editions or they don't buy the Sunday strip, so a Sunday installment can't be crucial to the plot. For these reasons, it's rarely worth the trouble to coordinate Sundays and dailies.

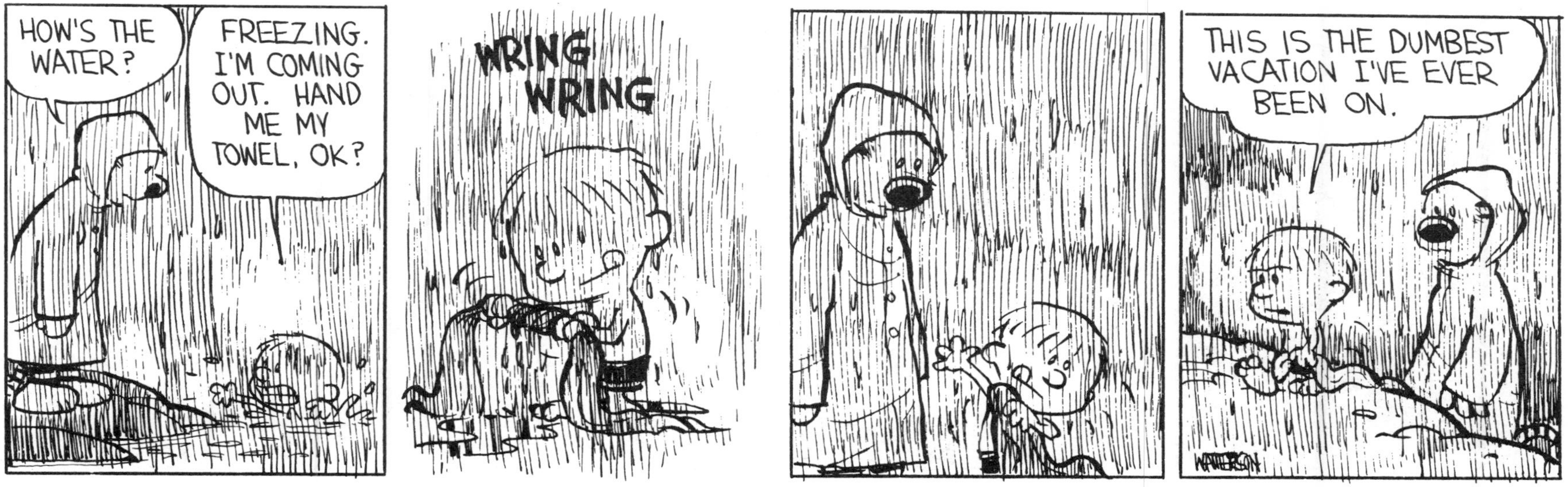
HOW'S THE WATER?
FREEZING. I'M COMING OUT. HAND ME MY TOWEL, OK?
WRING WRING
THIS IS THE DUMBEST VACATION I'VE EVER BEEN ON.
WATTERSON

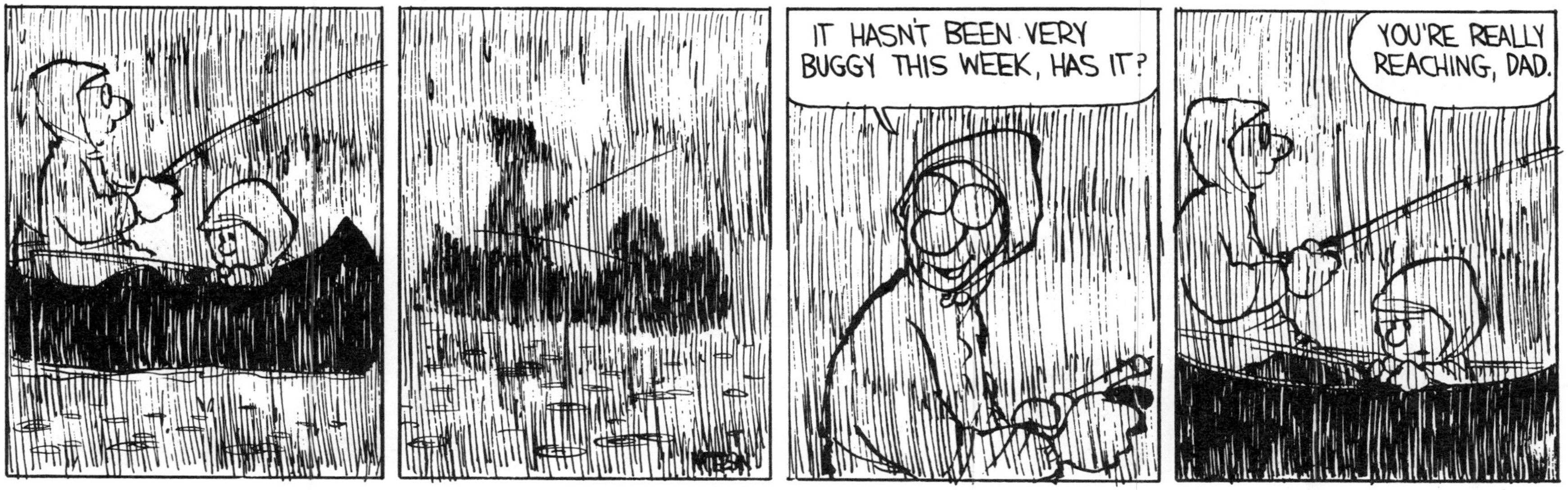
WATTERSON
IT HASN'T BEEN VERY BUGGY THIS WEEK, HAS IT?
YOU'RE REALLY REACHING, DAD.

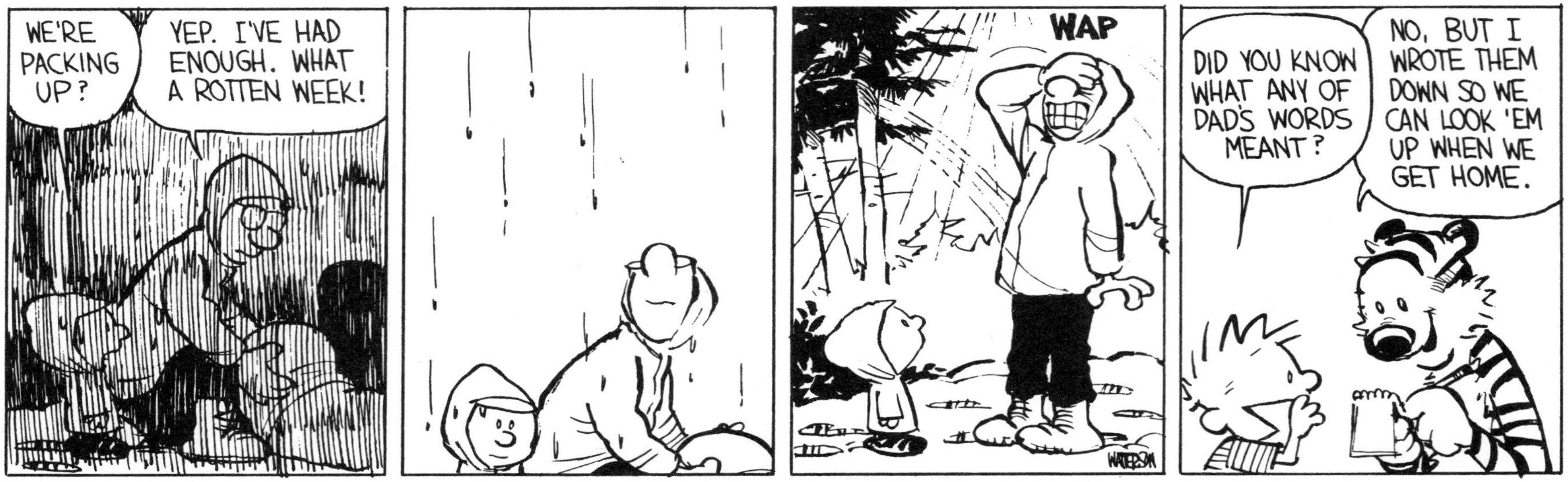
WE'RE PACKING UP?
YEP. I'VE HAD ENOUGH. WHAT A ROTTEN WEEK!
WAP
DID YOU KNOW WHAT ANY OF DAD'S WORDS MEANT?
NO, BUT I WROTE THEM DOWN SO WE CAN LOOK 'EM UP WHEN WE GET HOME.
WATERSON

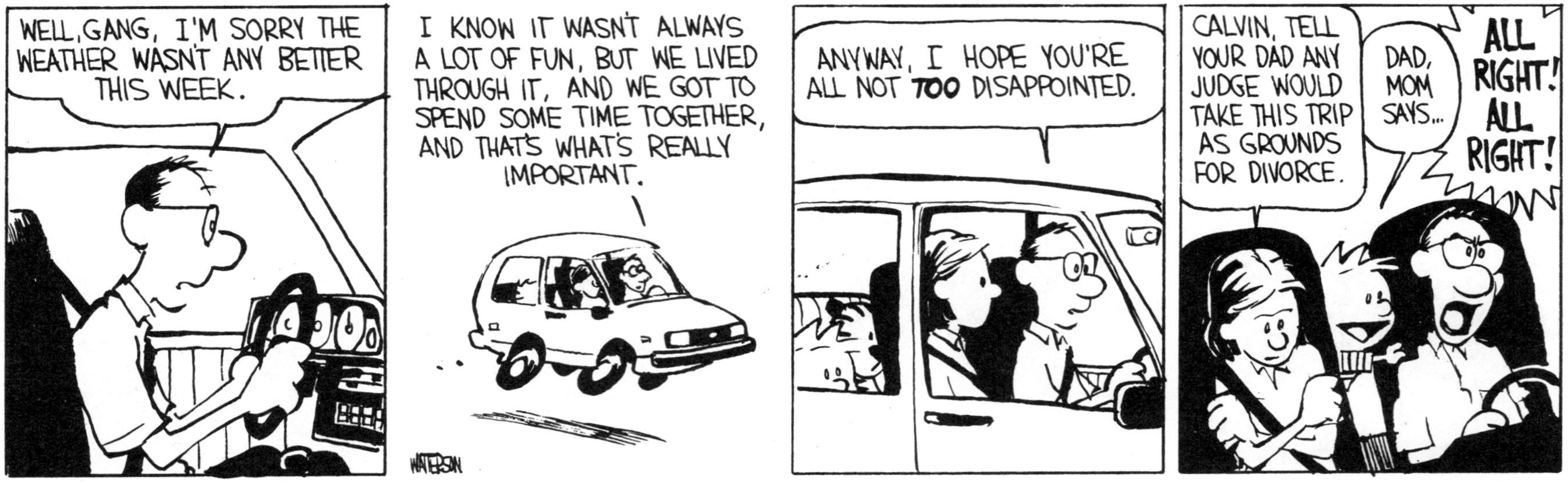
WELL, GANG, I'M SORRY THE WEATHER WASN'T ANY BETTER THIS WEEK.
I KNOW IT WASN'T ALWAYS A LOT OF FUN, BUT WE LIVED THROUGH IT, AND WE GOT TO SPEND SOME TIME TOGETHER, AND THAT'S WHAT'S REALLY IMPORTANT.
WATERSON
ANYWAY, I HOPE YOU'RE ALL NOT TOO DISAPPOINTED.
CALVIN, TELL YOUR DAD ANY JUDGE WOULD TAKE THIS TRIP AS GROUNDS FOR DIVORCE.
DAD, MOM SAYS...
ALL RIGHT! ALL RIGHT!

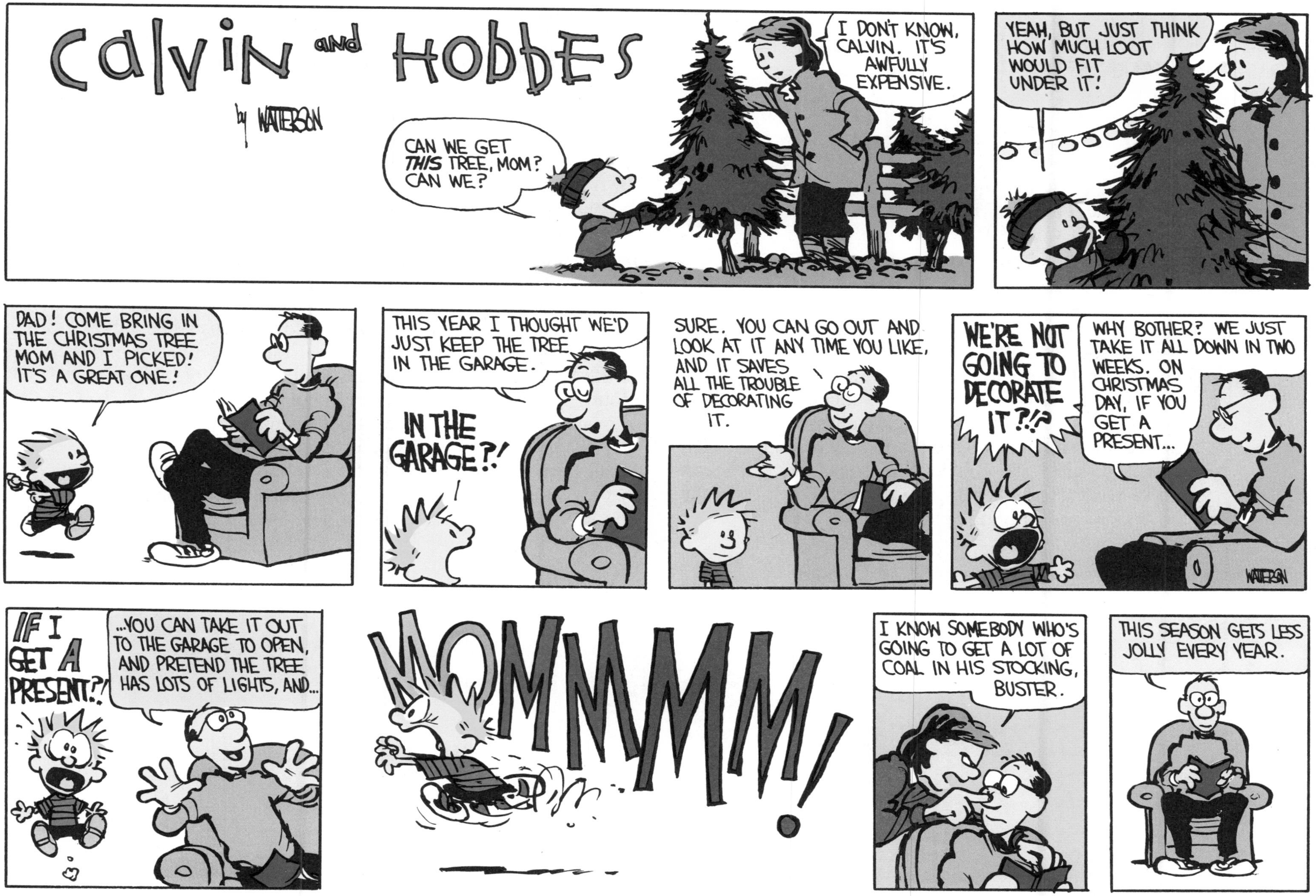
Calvin and HOBBES
by WATTERSON
CAN WE GET THIS TREE, MOM? CAN WE?
I DON'T KNOW, CALVIN. IT'S AWFULLY EXPENSIVE.
YEAH, BUT JUST THINK HOW MUCH LOOT WOULD FIT UNDER IT!
DAD! COME BRING IN THE CHRISTMAS TREE MOM AND I PICKED! IT'S A GREAT ONE!
THIS YEAR I THOUGHT WE'D JUST KEEP THE TREE IN THE GARAGE.
IN THE GARAGE?!
SURE. YOU CAN GO OUT AND LOOK AT IT ANY TIME YOU LIKE, AND IT SAVES ALL THE TROUBLE OF DECORATING IT.
WE'RE NOT GOING TO DECORATE IT?!?
WHY BOTHER? WE JUST TAKE IT ALL DOWN IN TWO WEEKS. ON CHRISTMAS DAY, IF YOU GET A PRESENT...
WATTERSON
IF I GET A PRESENT?!
...YOU CAN TAKE IT OUT TO THE GARAGE TO OPEN, AND PRETEND THE TREE HAS LOTS OF LIGHTS, AND...
MOMMMM!
I KNOW SOMEBODY WHO'S GOING TO GET A LOT OF COAL IN HIS STOCKING, BUSTER.
THIS SEASON GETS LESS JOLLY EVERY YEAR.

My dad used to say this.

SPACEMAN SPIFF

Spaceman Spiff predates *Calvin and Hobbes* by over a decade. I trace Spiff back to a comic strip I drew for a high school German class, called *Raumfahrer Rolf*. It was a pretty silly two-page comic in which the protagonist got eaten by a monster at the end, but it was written in some sort of German, and that was what counted. I reworked the character in college, calling him "Spaceman Mort," but the strip was conceived as a fairly elaborate, continuing project and that didn't seem like the best use of my academic time, so I never published it.

A year or so after college, the newly christened *Spaceman Spiff* was my first strip submission to newspaper syndicates. Spiff was a diminutive loudmouth, not unlike Calvin, albeit with a Chaplin mustache, flying goggles, and a cigar. He had a dimwitted assistant named Fargle, and they roamed through space in a dirigible. For obvious reasons, the syndicates rejected it. Years later, when I came up with Calvin, I finally had the opportunity to bring Spiff back.

When I was a kid, I followed the Apollo moon program with great interest, so Calvin shares that fascination with space travel. Spaceman Spiff is also a bit of a spoof on *Flash Gordon*. The narration in *Flash Gordon* is fairly overwrought, so I have Spiff describe his own exploits with a similar search for breathless superlatives.

The Spiff strips are limited in narrative potential, but I keep doing them because they're so much fun to draw. The planets and monsters offer great visual possibilities, especially in the Sunday strips. Most of the alien landscapes come from the canyons and deserts of southern Utah, a place more weird and spectacular than anything I'd previously been able to make up. The landscapes have become a significant part of the Spaceman Spiff sequences, and I often write the strip around the topography I feel like drawing.

Like all of Calvin's fantasies, Spaceman Spiff provides a way for me to draw some other comic strip when I want a break from *Calvin and Hobbes*. I can draw and write things that wouldn't fit in the strip otherwise, and this opens up opportunities to experiment with new interests.

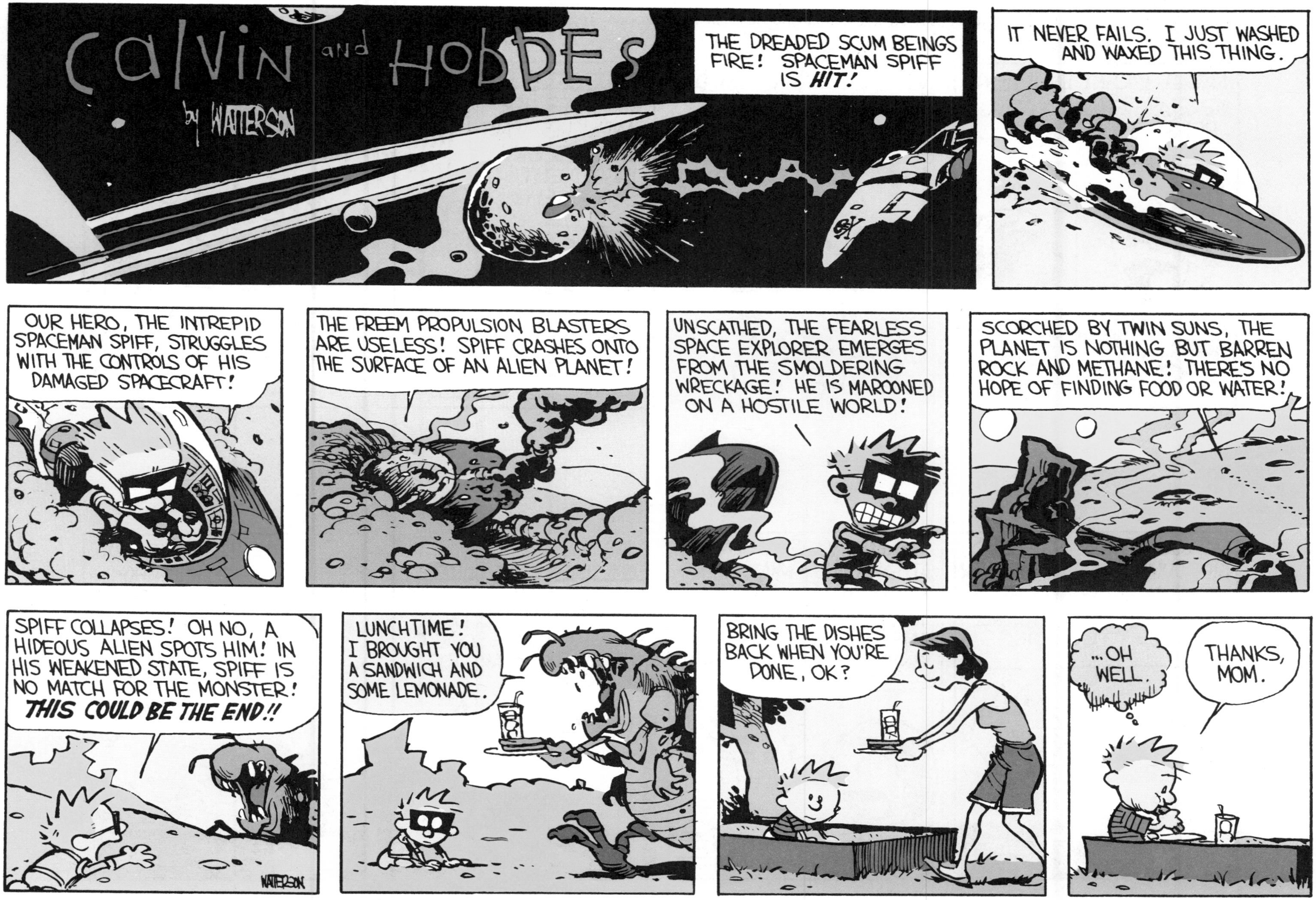
Calvin and HOBBES
by WATTERSON
THE DREADED SCUM BEINGS FIRE! SPACEMAN SPIFF IS HIT!
IT NEVER FAILS. I JUST WASHED AND WAXED THIS THING.
OUR HERO, THE INTREPID SPACEMAN SPIFF, STRUGGLES WITH THE CONTROLS OF HIS DAMAGED SPACECRAFT!
THE FREEM PROPULSION BLASTERS ARE USELESS! SPIFF CRASHES ONTO THE SURFACE OF AN ALIEN PLANET!
UNSCATHED, THE FEARLESS SPACE EXPLORER EMERGES FROM THE SMOLDERING WRECKAGE! HE IS MAROONED ON A HOSTILE WORLD!
SCORCHED BY TWIN SUNS, THE PLANET IS NOTHING BUT BARREN ROCK AND METHANE! THERE'S NO HOPE OF FINDING FOOD OR WATER!
SPIFF COLLAPSES! OH NO, A HIDEOUS ALIEN SPOTS HIM! IN HIS WEAKENED STATE, SPIFF IS NO MATCH FOR THE MONSTER! THIS COULD BE THE END!!
WATTERSON
LUNCHTIME! I BROUGHT YOU A SANDWICH AND SOME LEMONADE.
BRING THE DISHES BACK WHEN YOU'RE DONE, OK?
...OH WELL.
THANKS, MOM.

I overplayed the quasi-romantic tension between Calvin and Susie in early stories. This story was an improvement, because I just let the two personalities bounce off each other.

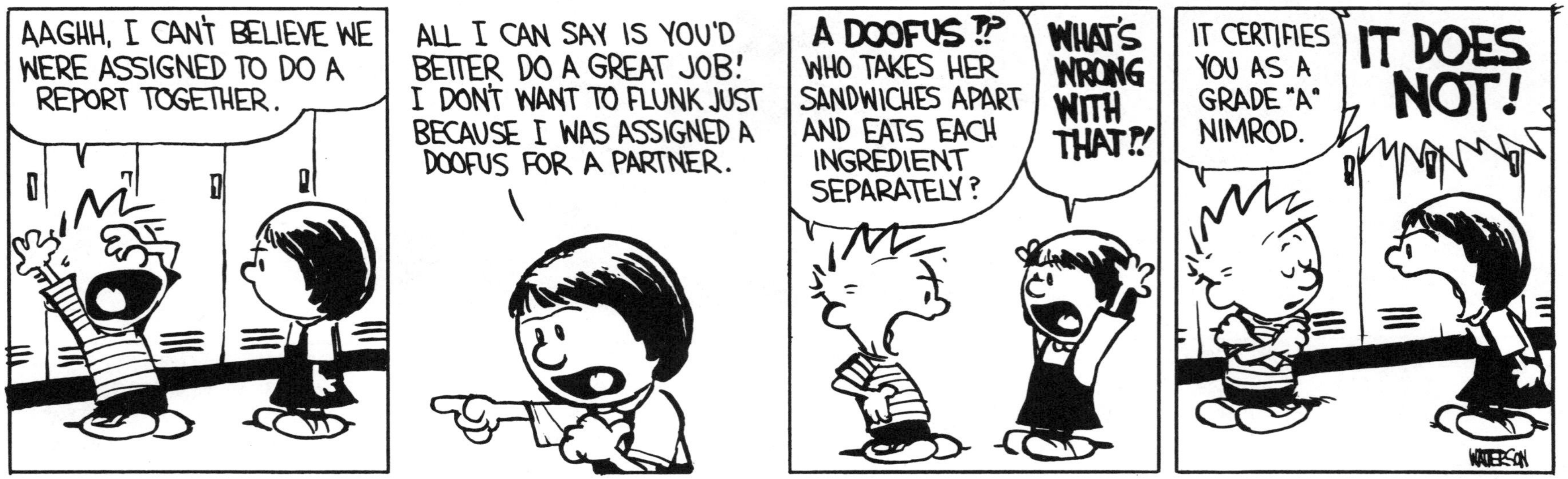
AAGHH, I CAN'T BELIEVE WE WERE ASSIGNED TO DO A REPORT TOGETHER.
ALL I CAN SAY IS YOU'D BETTER DO A GREAT JOB! I DON'T WANT TO FLUNK JUST BECAUSE I WAS ASSIGNED A DOOFUS FOR A PARTNER.
A DOOFUS ?! WHO TAKES HER SANDWICHES APART AND EATS EACH INGREDIENT SEPARATELY?
WHAT'S WRONG WITH THAT?!
IT CERTIFIES YOU AS A GRADE "A" NIMROD.
IT DOES NOT!
WATTERSON

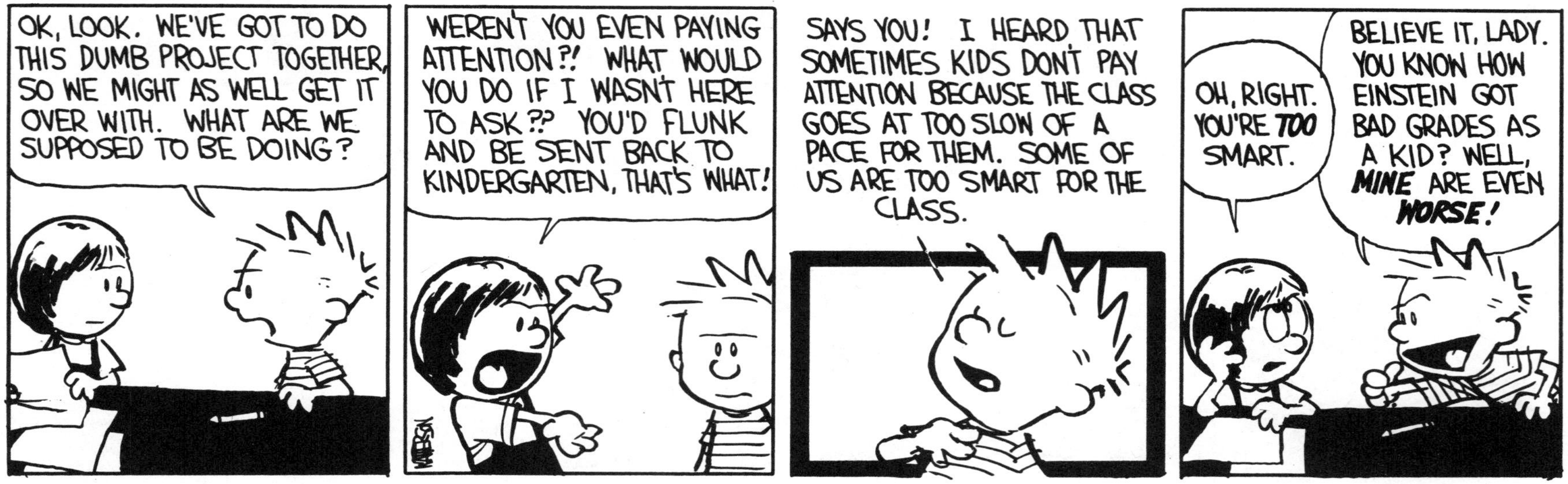
OK, LOOK. WE'VE GOT TO DO THIS DUMB PROJECT TOGETHER, SO WE MIGHT AS WELL GET IT OVER WITH. WHAT ARE WE SUPPOSED TO BE DOING?
WEREN'T YOU EVEN PAYING ATTENTION?! WHAT WOULD YOU DO IF I WASN'T HERE TO ASK?? YOU'D FLUNK AND BE SENT BACK TO KINDERGARTEN, THAT'S WHAT!
WATTERSON
SAYS YOU! I HEARD THAT SOMETIMES KIDS DON'T PAY ATTENTION BECAUSE THE CLASS GOES AT TOO SLOW OF A PACE FOR THEM. SOME OF US ARE TOO SMART FOR THE CLASS.
OH, RIGHT. YOU'RE TOO SMART.
BELIEVE IT, LADY. YOU KNOW HOW EINSTEIN GOT BAD GRADES AS A KID? WELL, MINE ARE EVEN WORSE!

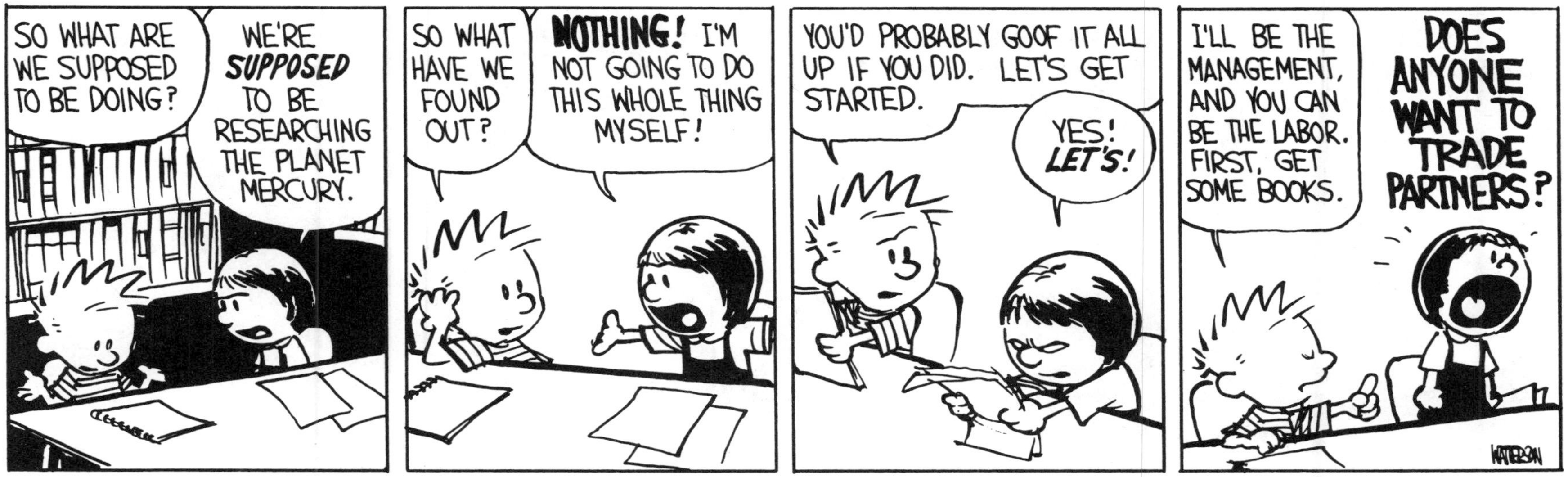
SO WHAT ARE WE SUPPOSED TO BE DOING?
WE'RE *SUPPOSED* TO BE RESEARCHING THE PLANET MERCURY.
SO WHAT HAVE WE FOUND OUT?
NOTHING! I'M NOT GOING TO DO THIS WHOLE THING MYSELF!
YOU'D PROBABLY GOOF IT ALL UP IF YOU DID. LET'S GET STARTED.
YES! *LET'S!*
I'LL BE THE MANAGEMENT, AND YOU CAN BE THE LABOR. FIRST, GET SOME BOOKS.
DOES ANYONE WANT TO TRADE PARTNERS?
WATTERSON

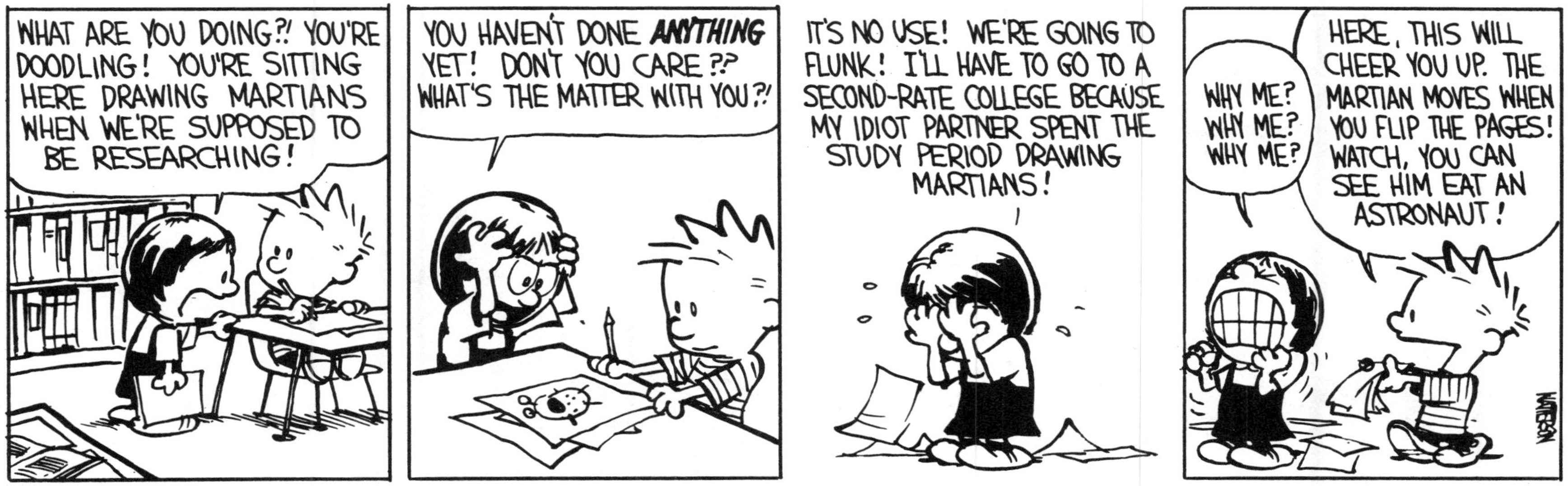
WHAT ARE YOU DOING?! YOU'RE DOODLING! YOU'RE SITTING HERE DRAWING MARTIANS WHEN WE'RE SUPPOSED TO BE RESEARCHING!
YOU HAVEN'T DONE *ANYTHING* YET! DON'T YOU CARE?? WHAT'S THE MATTER WITH YOU?!
IT'S NO USE! WE'RE GOING TO FLUNK! I'LL HAVE TO GO TO A SECOND-RATE COLLEGE BECAUSE MY IDIOT PARTNER SPENT THE STUDY PERIOD DRAWING MARTIANS!
WHY ME? WHY ME? WHY ME?
HERE, THIS WILL CHEER YOU UP. THE MARTIAN MOVES WHEN YOU FLIP THE PAGES! WATCH, YOU CAN SEE HIM EAT AN ASTRONAUT!
WATTERSON

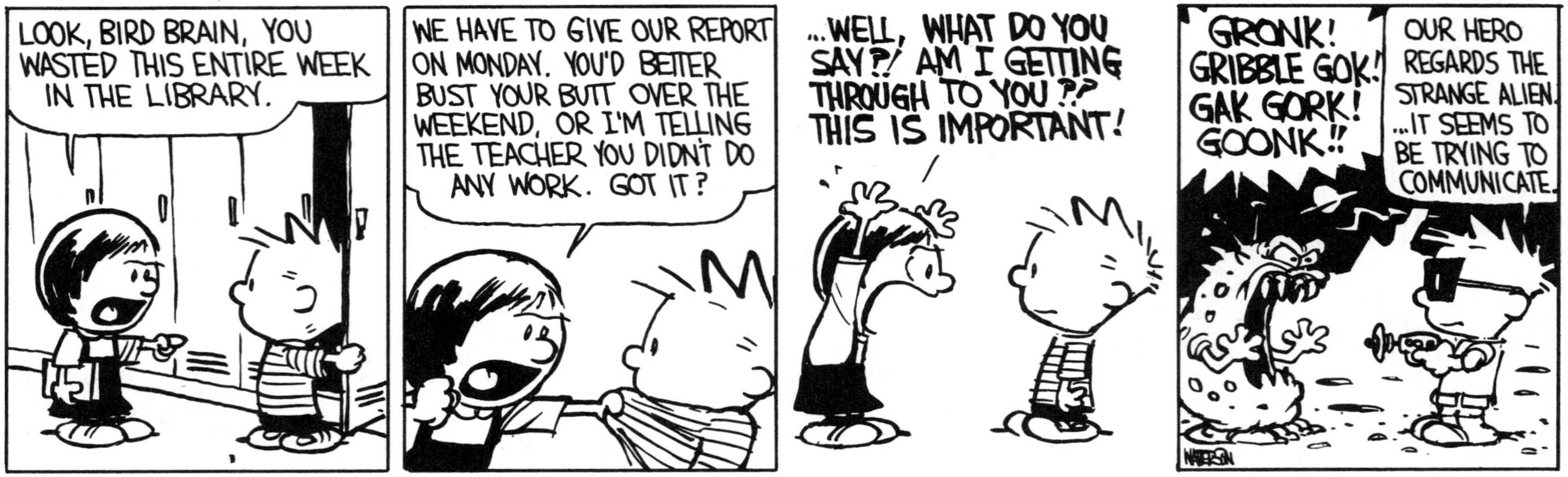
LOOK, BIRD BRAIN, YOU WASTED THIS ENTIRE WEEK IN THE LIBRARY.
WE HAVE TO GIVE OUR REPORT ON MONDAY. YOU'D BETTER BUST YOUR BUTT OVER THE WEEKEND, OR I'M TELLING THE TEACHER YOU DIDN'T DO ANY WORK. GOT IT?
...WELL, WHAT DO YOU SAY?! AM I GETTING THROUGH TO YOU?? THIS IS IMPORTANT!
GRONK! GRIBBLE GOK! GAK GORK! GOONK!!
OUR HERO REGARDS THE STRANGE ALIEN. ...IT SEEMS TO BE TRYING TO COMMUNICATE.
WATTERSON

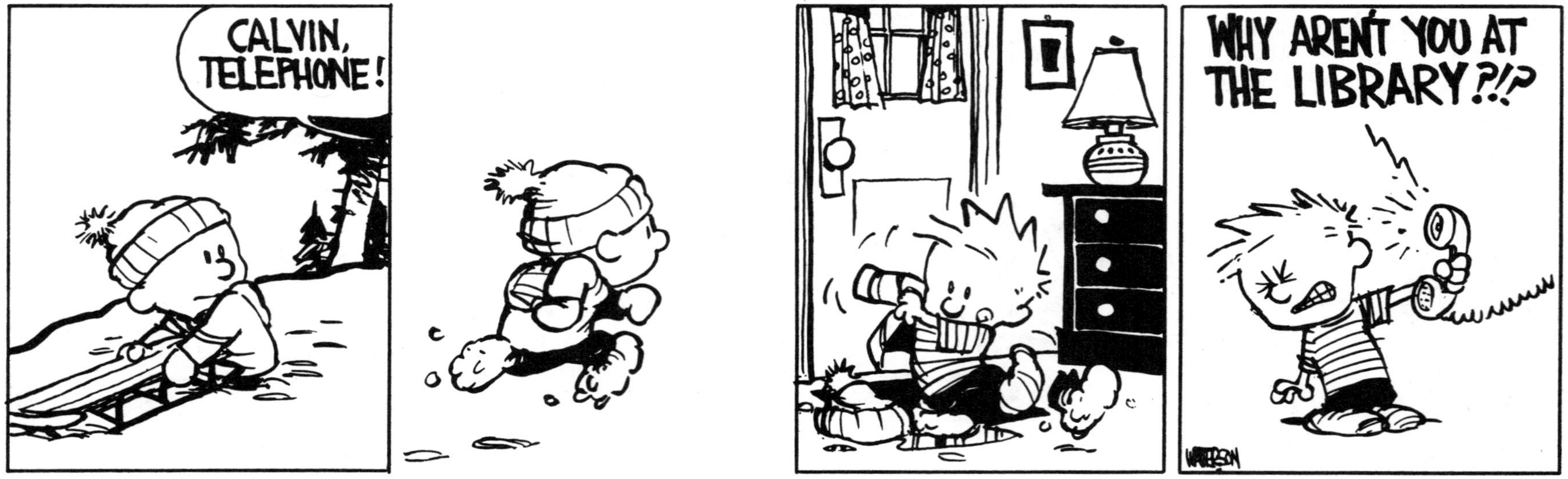
CALVIN, TELEPHONE!
WHY AREN'T YOU AT THE LIBRARY?!?
WATTERSON

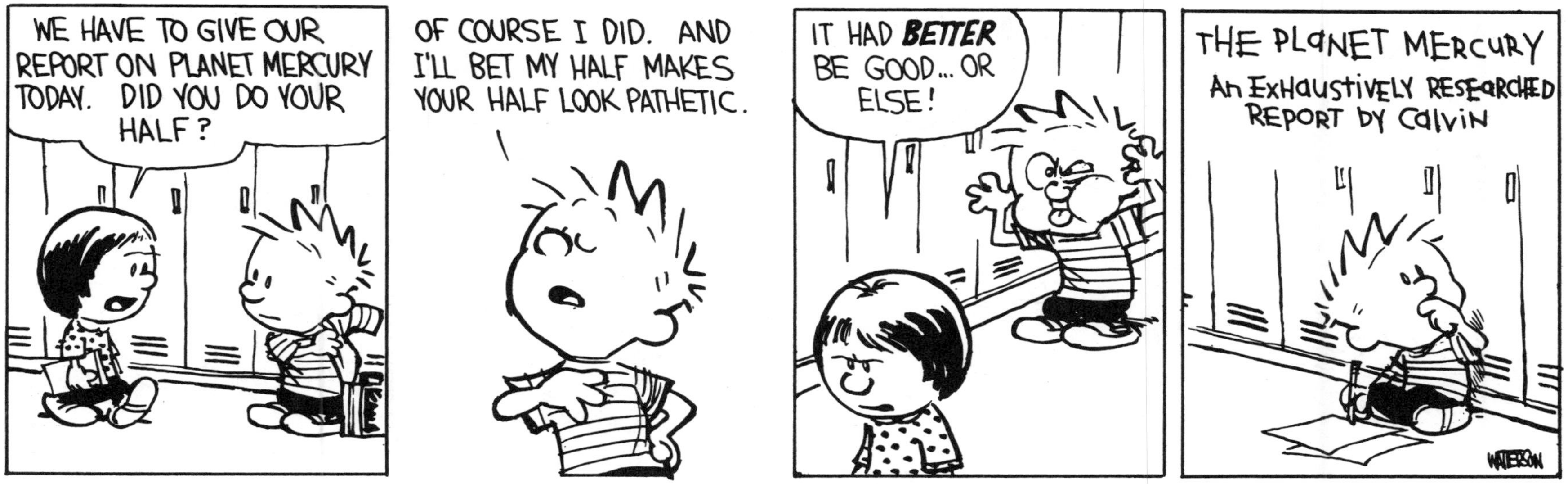
WE HAVE TO GIVE OUR REPORT ON PLANET MERCURY TODAY. DID YOU DO YOUR HALF?
OF COURSE I DID. AND I'LL BET MY HALF MAKES YOUR HALF LOOK PATHETIC.
IT HAD **BETTER** BE GOOD... OR ELSE!
THE PLANET MERCURY
An EXHAUSTIVELY RESEARCHED REPORT BY CALVIN

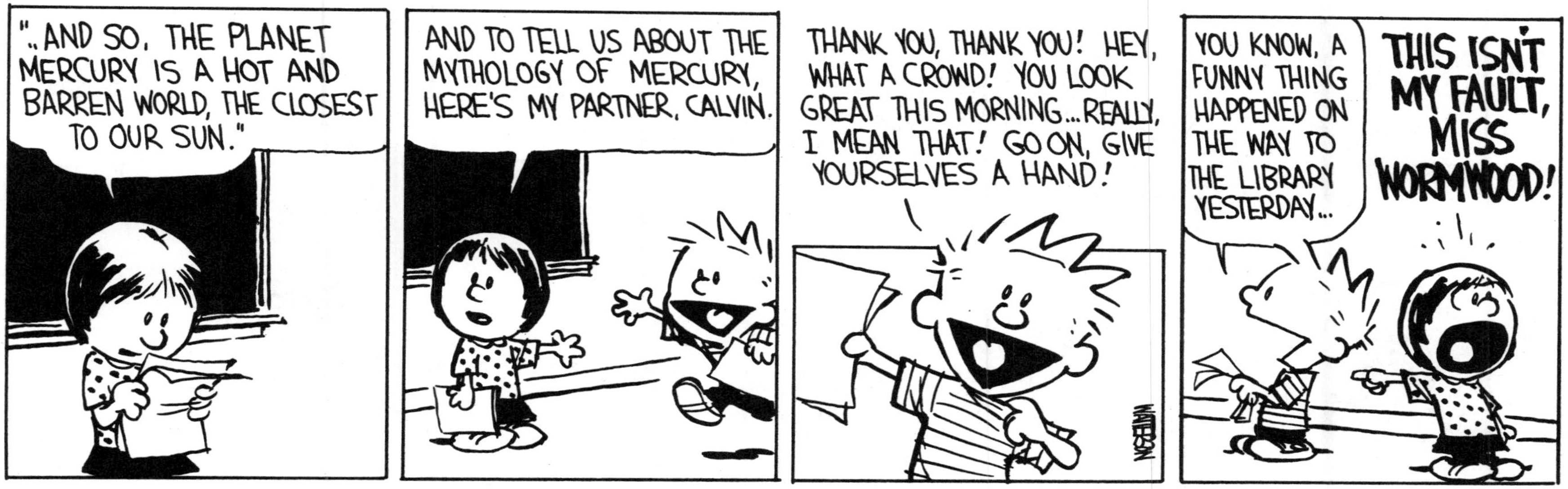
"..AND SO, THE PLANET MERCURY IS A HOT AND BARREN WORLD, THE CLOSEST TO OUR SUN."
AND TO TELL US ABOUT THE MYTHOLOGY OF MERCURY, HERE'S MY PARTNER, CALVIN.
THANK YOU, THANK YOU! HEY, WHAT A CROWD! YOU LOOK GREAT THIS MORNING... REALLY, I MEAN THAT! GO ON, GIVE YOURSELVES A HAND!
YOU KNOW, A FUNNY THING HAPPENED ON THE WAY TO THE LIBRARY YESTERDAY...
THIS ISN'T MY FAULT, MISS WORMWOOD!

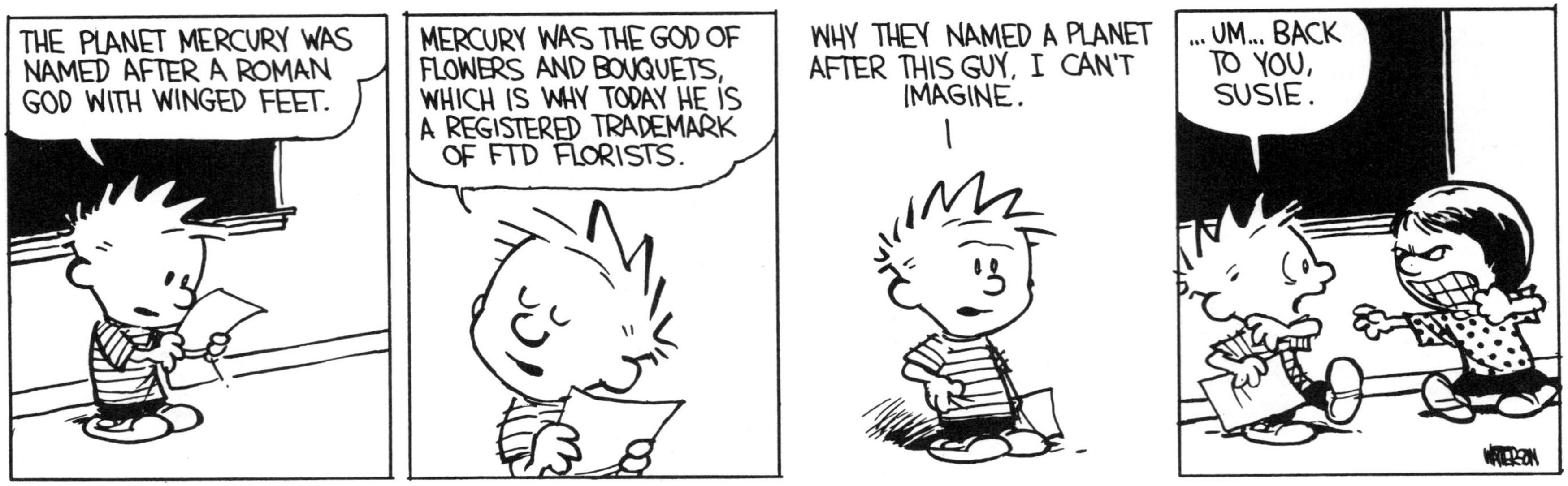
THE PLANET MERCURY WAS NAMED AFTER A ROMAN GOD WITH WINGED FEET.
MERCURY WAS THE GOD OF FLOWERS AND BOUQUETS, WHICH IS WHY TODAY HE IS A REGISTERED TRADEMARK OF FTD FLORISTS.
WHY THEY NAMED A PLANET AFTER THIS GUY, I CAN'T IMAGINE.
... UM... BACK TO YOU, SUSIE.
WATTERSON

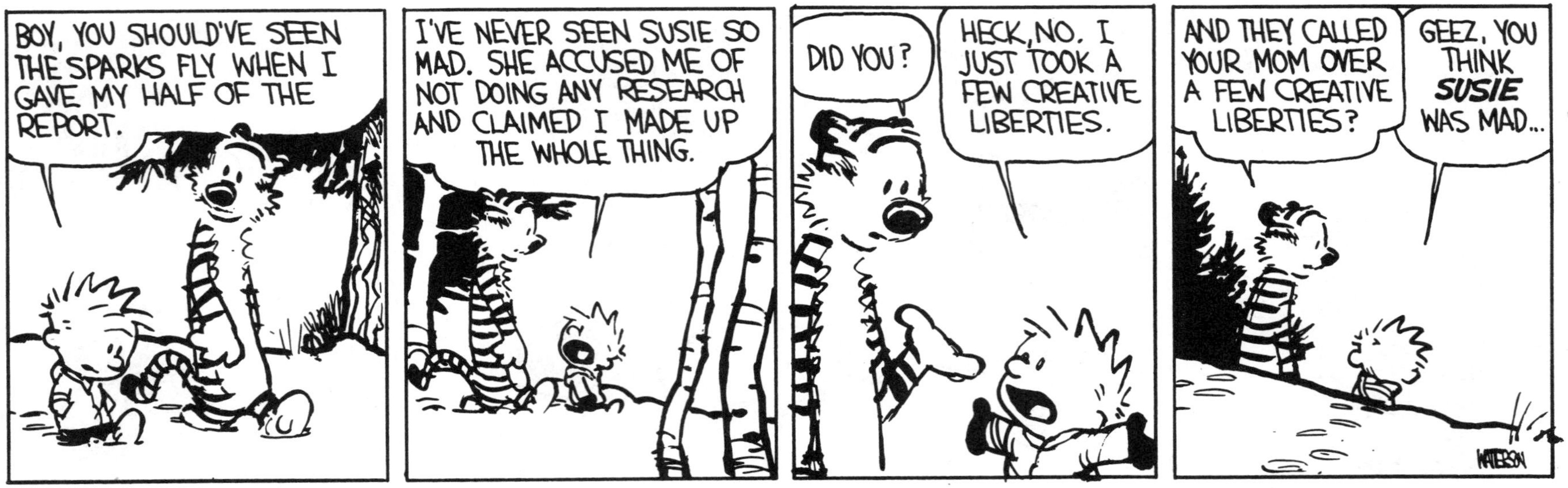
BOY, YOU SHOULD'VE SEEN THE SPARKS FLY WHEN I GAVE MY HALF OF THE REPORT.
I'VE NEVER SEEN SUSIE SO MAD. SHE ACCUSED ME OF NOT DOING ANY RESEARCH AND CLAIMED I MADE UP THE WHOLE THING.
DID YOU?
HECK, NO. I JUST TOOK A FEW CREATIVE LIBERTIES.
AND THEY CALLED YOUR MOM OVER A FEW CREATIVE LIBERTIES?
GEEZ, YOU THINK *SUSIE* WAS MAD...
WATTERSON

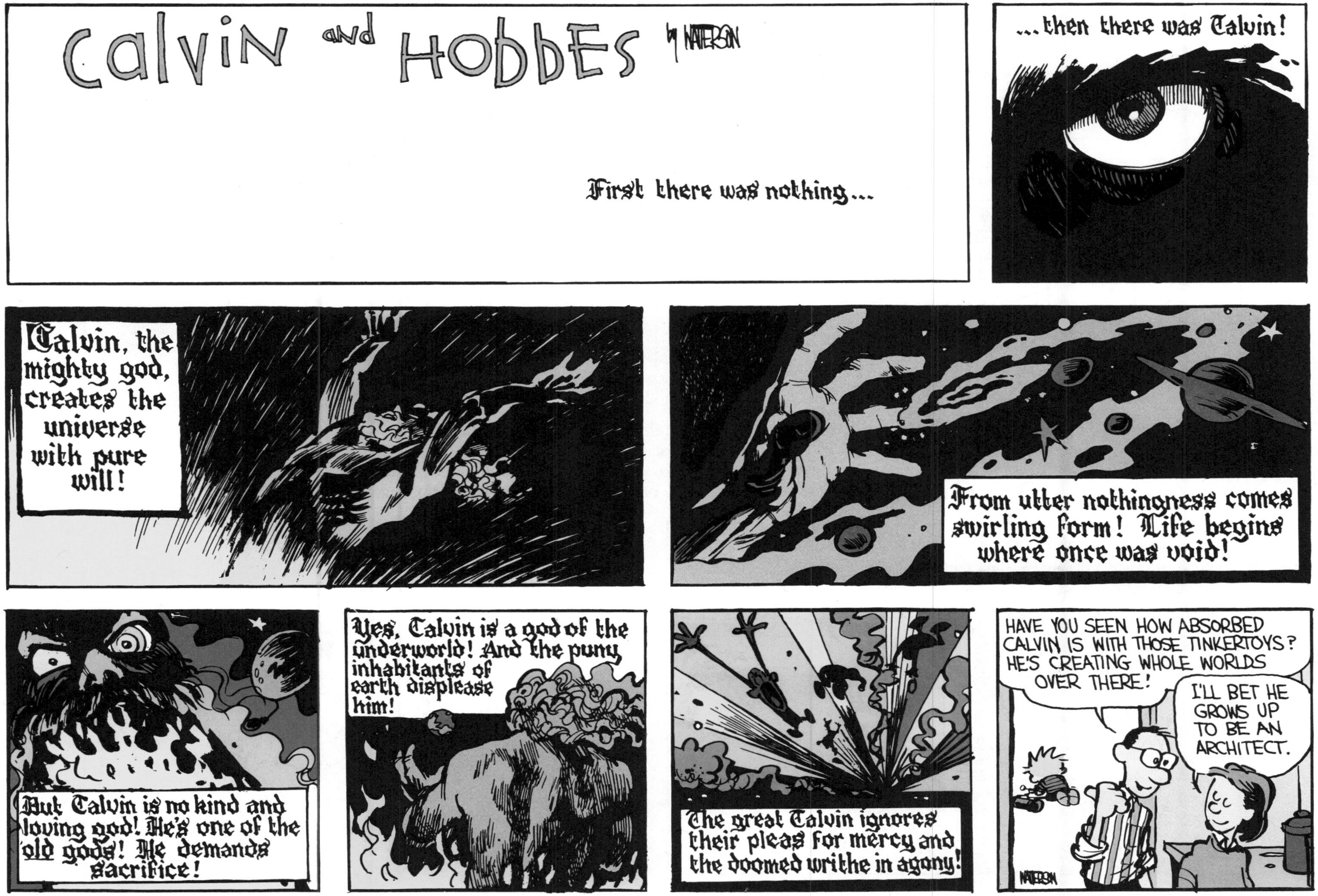
Calvin and Hobbes
by WATTERSON
First there was nothing...
...then there was Calvin!
Calvin, the mighty god, creates the universe with pure will!
From utter nothingness comes swirling form! Life begins where once was void!
But Calvin is no kind and loving god! He's one of the old gods! He demands sacrifice!
Yes, Calvin is a god of the underworld! And the puny inhabitants of earth displease him!
The great Calvin ignores their pleas for mercy and the doomed writhe in agony!
HAVE YOU SEEN HOW ABSORBED CALVIN IS WITH THOSE TINKERTOYS? HE'S CREATING WHOLE WORLDS OVER THERE!
I'LL BET HE GROWS UP TO BE AN ARCHITECT.
WATTERSON

This is not a great strip, but it was made worse by the Sunday format restrictions. Several of the panel divisions are mandatory, so I was forced to waste space in some panels (especially the first) and cram too much into panels elsewhere. I'd been frustrated before, but this time the format ruined what I had in mind.

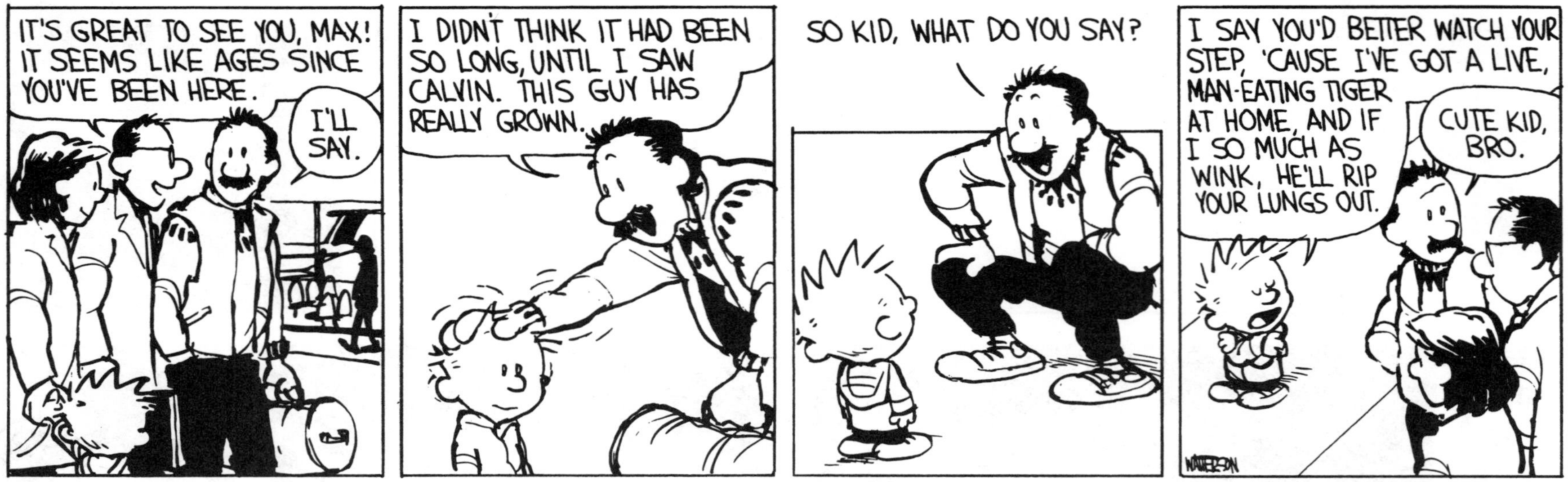
IT'S GREAT TO SEE YOU, MAX! IT SEEMS LIKE AGES SINCE YOU'VE BEEN HERE.
I'LL SAY.
I DIDN'T THINK IT HAD BEEN SO LONG, UNTIL I SAW CALVIN. THIS GUY HAS REALLY GROWN.
SO KID, WHAT DO YOU SAY?
I SAY YOU'D BETTER WATCH YOUR STEP, 'CAUSE I'VE GOT A LIVE, MAN-EATING TIGER AT HOME, AND IF I SO MUCH AS WINK, HE'LL RIP YOUR LUNGS OUT.
CUTE KID, BRO.
WATTERSON

I regret introducing Uncle Max into the strip. At the time, I thought a new character related to the family would open up story possibilities: the family could go visit Max, and so on. After the story ran, I realized that I hadn't established much identity for Max, and that he didn't bring out anything new in Calvin. The character, I concluded, was redundant. It was also very awkward that Max could not address Calvin's parents by name, and this should have tipped me off that the strip was not designed for the parents to have outside adult relationships. Max is gone.

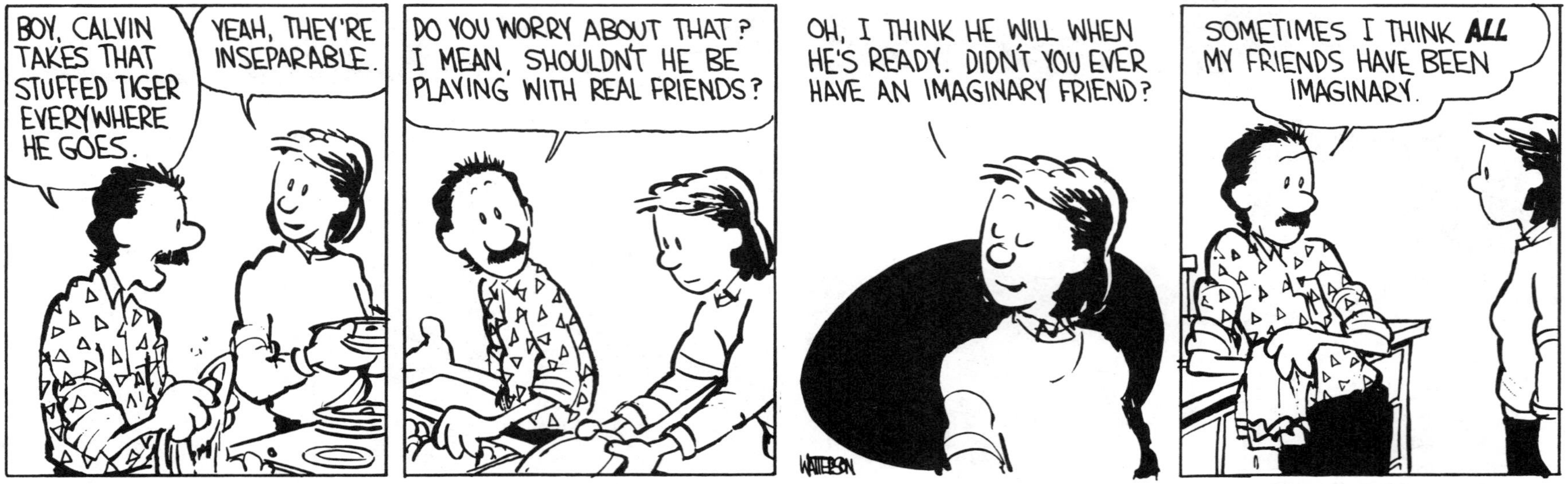
BOY, CALVIN TAKES THAT STUFFED TIGER EVERYWHERE HE GOES.
YEAH, THEY'RE INSEPARABLE.
DO YOU WORRY ABOUT THAT? I MEAN, SHOULDN'T HE BE PLAYING WITH REAL FRIENDS?
OH, I THINK HE WILL WHEN HE'S READY. DIDN'T YOU EVER HAVE AN IMAGINARY FRIEND?
SOMETIMES I THINK ALL MY FRIENDS HAVE BEEN IMAGINARY.
WATTERSON

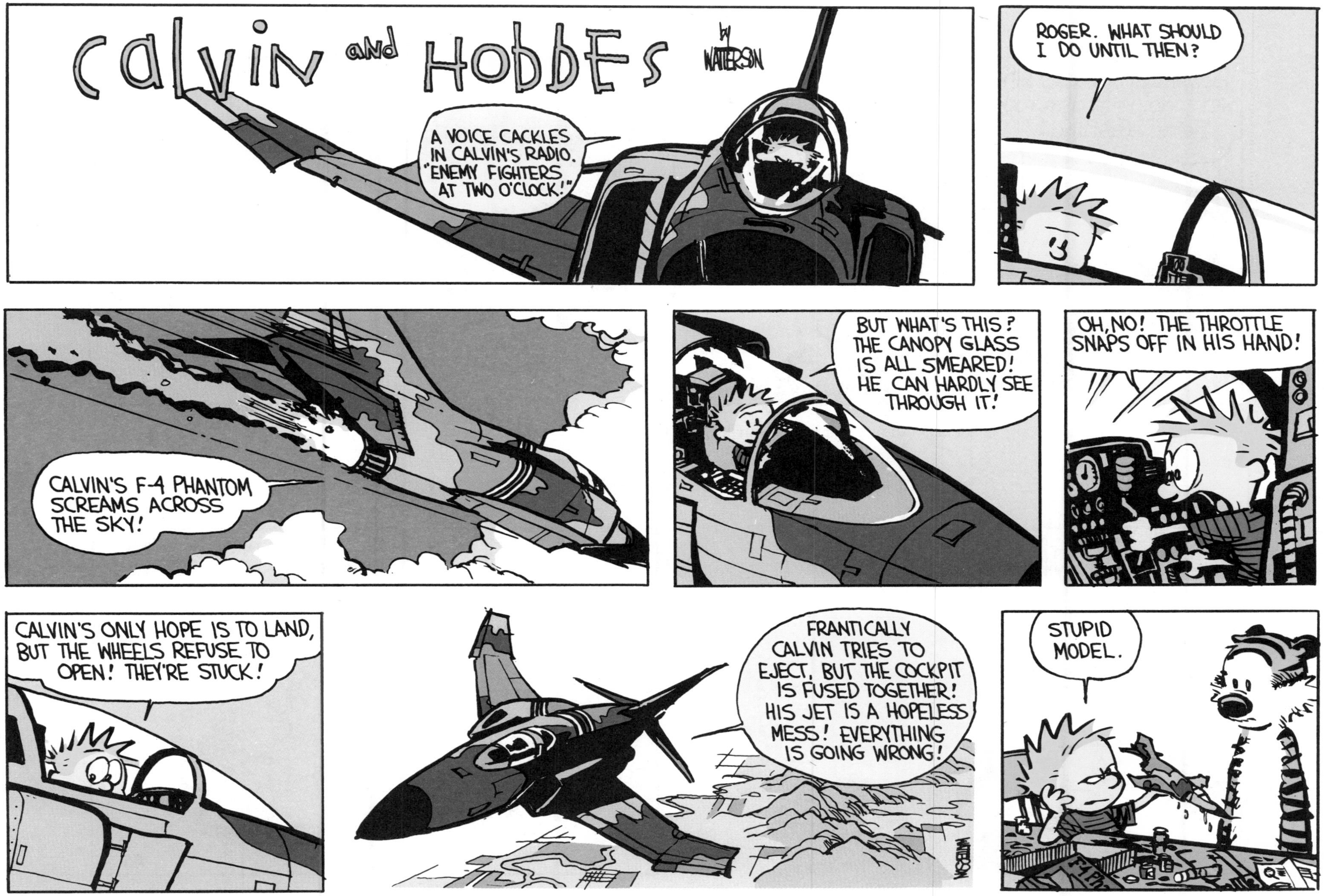
Calvin and HobbEs
by WATTERSON
A VOICE CACKLES IN CALVIN'S RADIO. "ENEMY FIGHTERS AT TWO O'CLOCK!"
ROGER. WHAT SHOULD I DO UNTIL THEN?
CALVIN'S F-4 PHANTOM SCREAMS ACROSS THE SKY!
BUT WHAT'S THIS? THE CANOPY GLASS IS ALL SMEARED! HE CAN HARDLY SEE THROUGH IT!
OH, NO! THE THROTTLE SNAPS OFF IN HIS HAND!
CALVIN'S ONLY HOPE IS TO LAND, BUT THE WHEELS REFUSE TO OPEN! THEY'RE STUCK!
FRANTICALLY CALVIN TRIES TO EJECT, BUT THE COCKPIT IS FUSED TOGETHER! HIS JET IS A HOPELESS MESS! EVERYTHING IS GOING WRONG!
STUPID MODEL.

Several years ago, on a whim, I bought a model airplane and built it. It's as frustrating now as when I was a kid. I got a few strips out of it though. In this one, I like the second panel "throwaway joke" more than the rest of the strip.

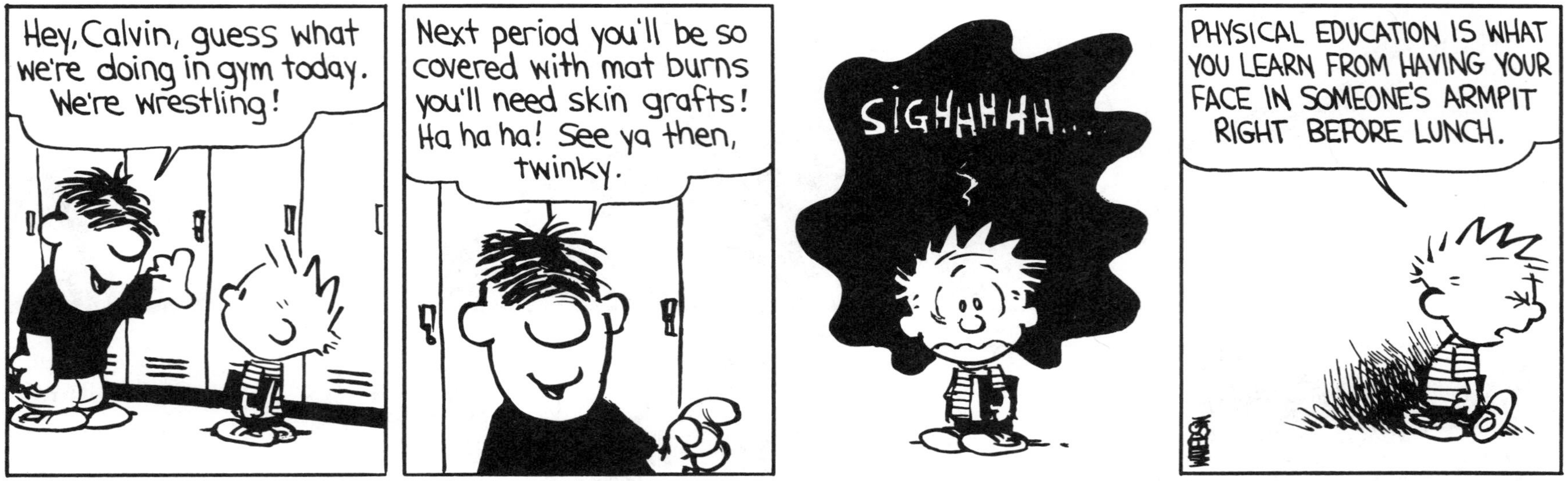
Hey, Calvin, guess what we're doing in gym today. We're wrestling!
Next period you'll be so covered with mat burns you'll need skin grafts! Ha ha ha! See ya then, twinky.
SIGHHHHH...
PHYSICAL EDUCATION IS WHAT YOU LEARN FROM HAVING YOUR FACE IN SOMEONE'S ARMPIT RIGHT BEFORE LUNCH.

High on my list of adulthood pleasures is the fact that nobody makes me wrestle sweaty guys anymore.

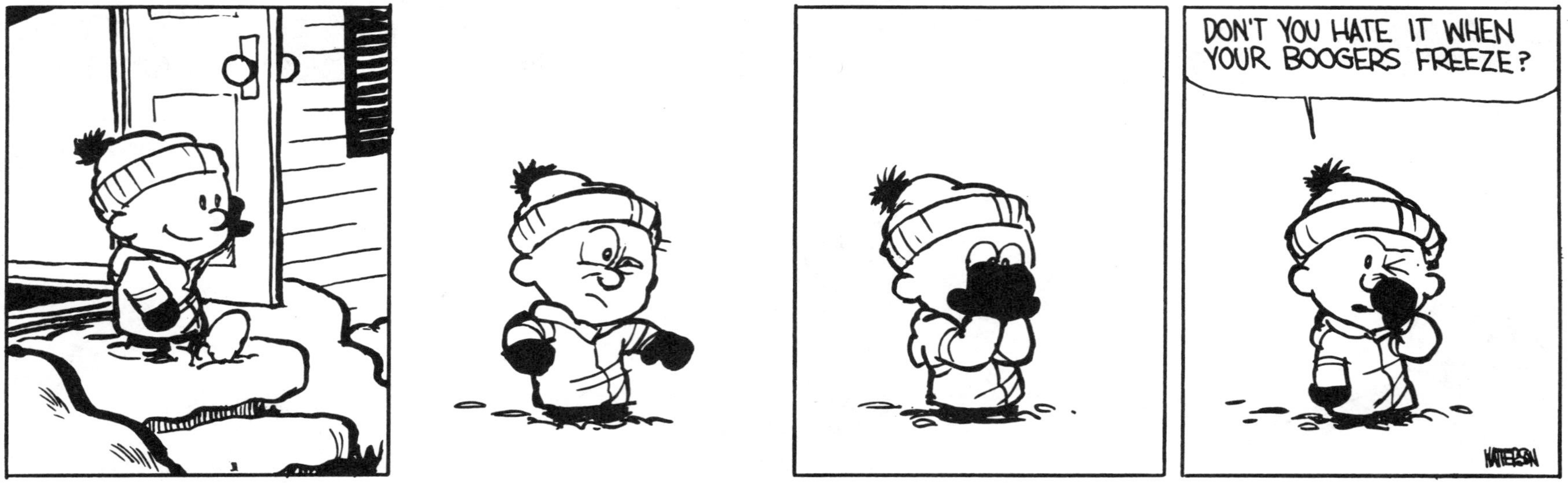
DON'T YOU HATE IT WHEN YOUR BOOGERS FREEZE?

I hope some historian will confirm that I was the first cartoonist to use the word "booger" in a newspaper comic strip.

I think we've all gone through something like this story. You die a thousand deaths before you even get in trouble.

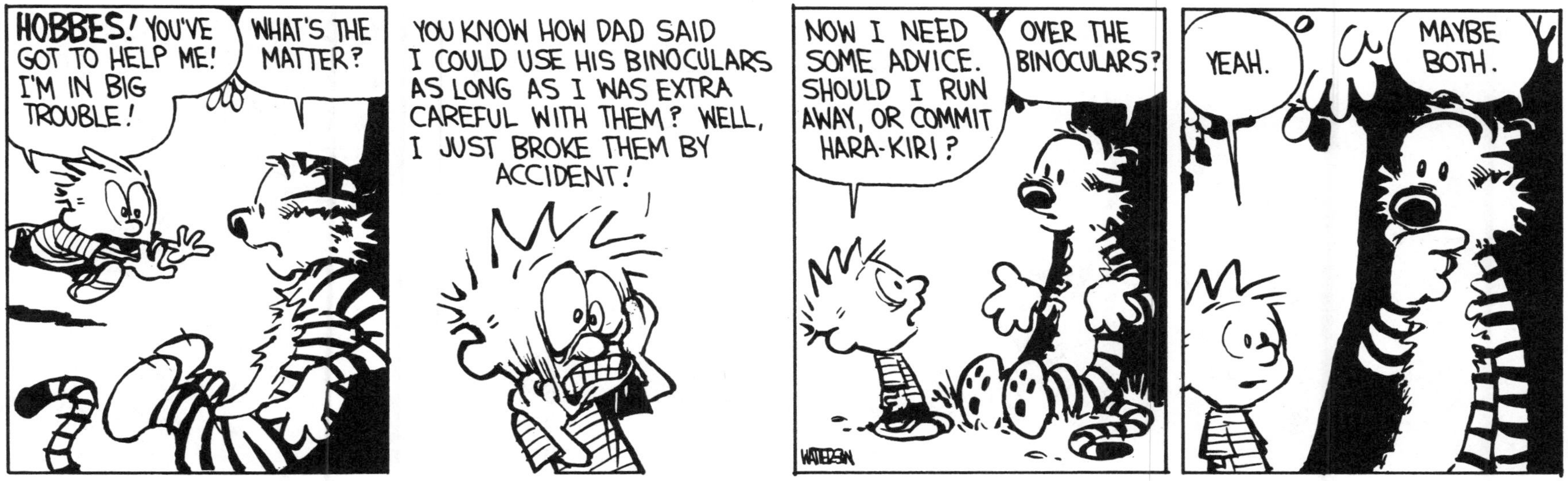
HOBBES! YOU'VE GOT TO HELP ME! I'M IN BIG TROUBLE!
WHAT'S THE MATTER?
YOU KNOW HOW DAD SAID I COULD USE HIS BINOCULARS AS LONG AS I WAS EXTRA CAREFUL WITH THEM? WELL, I JUST BROKE THEM BY ACCIDENT!
NOW I NEED SOME ADVICE. SHOULD I RUN AWAY, OR COMMIT HARA-KIRI?
OVER THE BINOCULARS?
YEAH.
MAYBE BOTH.

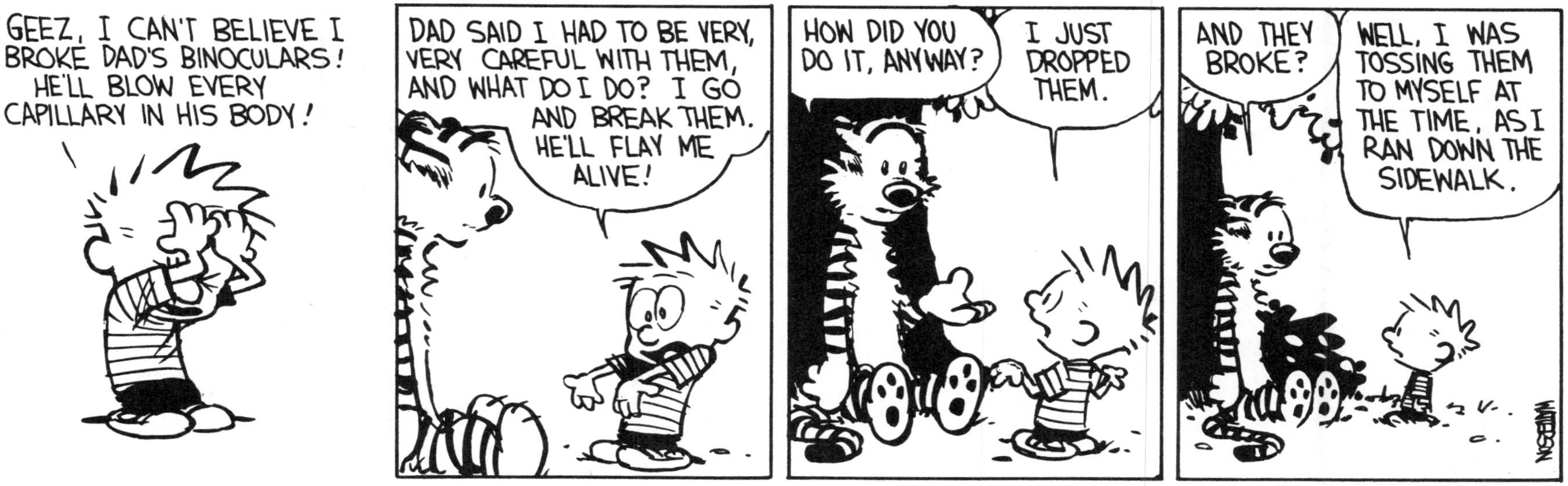
GEEZ, I CAN'T BELIEVE I BROKE DAD'S BINOCULARS! HE'LL BLOW EVERY CAPILLARY IN HIS BODY!
DAD SAID I HAD TO BE VERY, VERY CAREFUL WITH THEM, AND WHAT DO I DO? I GO AND BREAK THEM. HE'LL FLAY ME ALIVE!
HOW DID YOU DO IT, ANYWAY?
I JUST DROPPED THEM.
AND THEY BROKE?
WELL, I WAS TOSSING THEM TO MYSELF AT THE TIME, AS I RAN DOWN THE SIDEWALK.

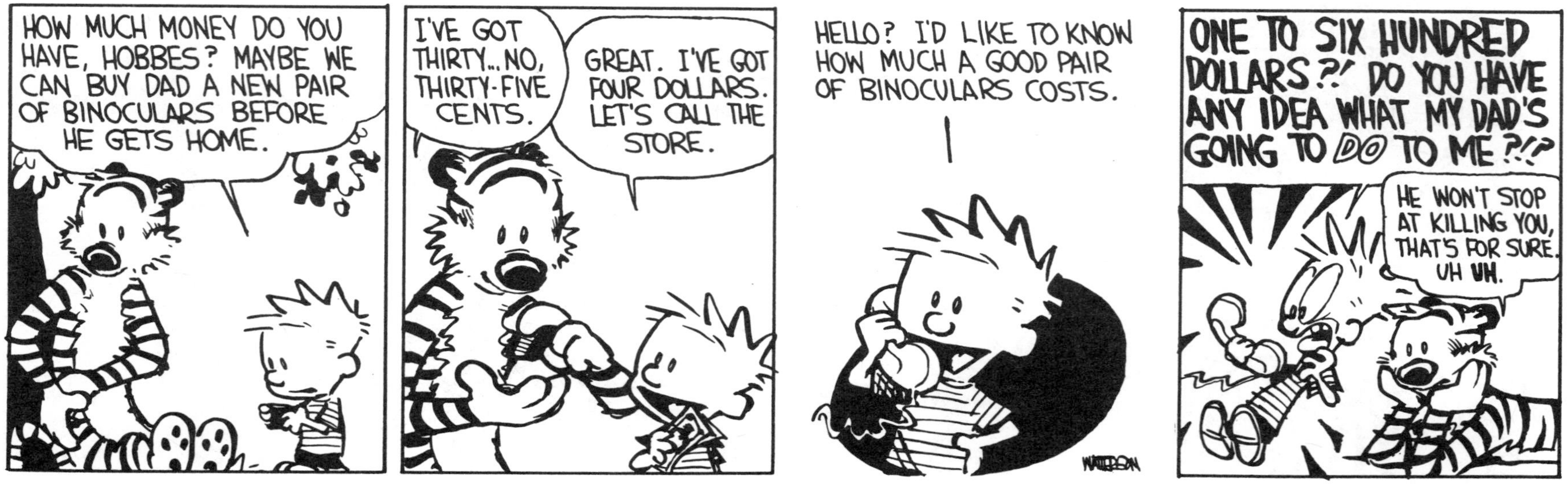
HOW MUCH MONEY DO YOU HAVE, HOBBES? MAYBE WE CAN BUY DAD A NEW PAIR OF BINOCULARS BEFORE HE GETS HOME.
I'VE GOT THIRTY... NO, THIRTY-FIVE CENTS.
GREAT. I'VE GOT FOUR DOLLARS. LET'S CALL THE STORE.
HELLO? I'D LIKE TO KNOW HOW MUCH A GOOD PAIR OF BINOCULARS COSTS.
ONE TO SIX HUNDRED DOLLARS?! DO YOU HAVE ANY IDEA WHAT MY DAD'S GOING TO DO TO ME?!?
HE WON'T STOP AT KILLING YOU, THAT'S FOR SURE. UH UH.

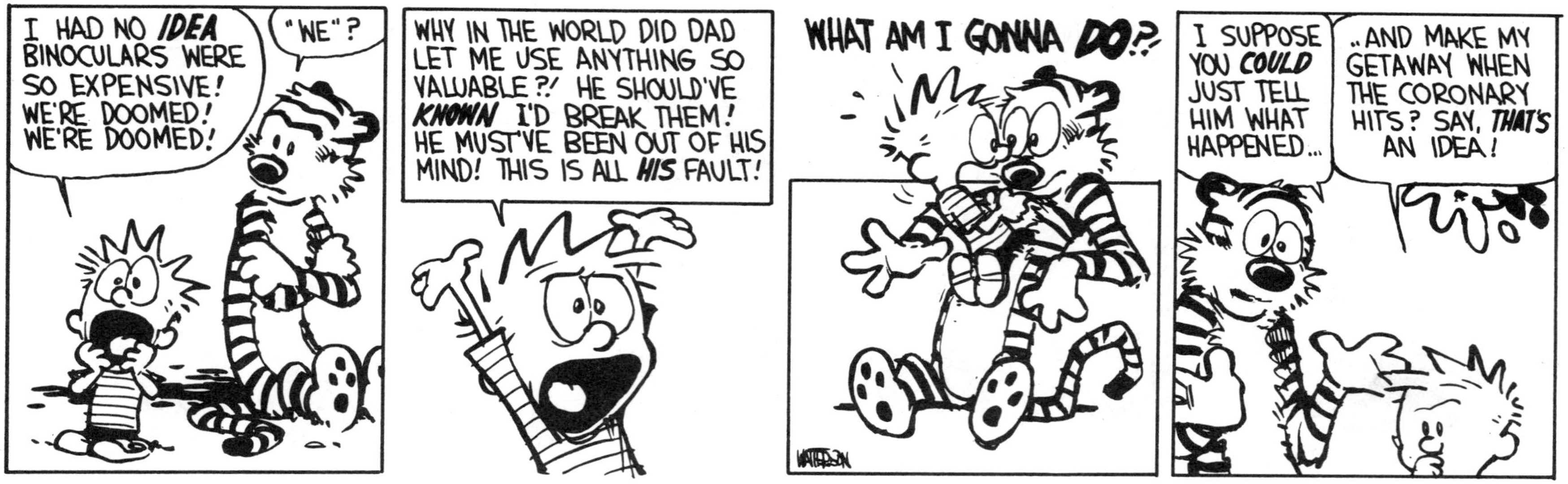
I HAD NO IDEA BINOCULARS WERE SO EXPENSIVE! WE'RE DOOMED! WE'RE DOOMED!
"WE"?
WHY IN THE WORLD DID DAD LET ME USE ANYTHING SO VALUABLE?! HE SHOULD'VE KNOWN I'D BREAK THEM! HE MUST'VE BEEN OUT OF HIS MIND! THIS IS ALL HIS FAULT!
WHAT AM I GONNA DO?!
I SUPPOSE YOU COULD JUST TELL HIM WHAT HAPPENED...
..AND MAKE MY GETAWAY WHEN THE CORONARY HITS? SAY, THAT'S AN IDEA!

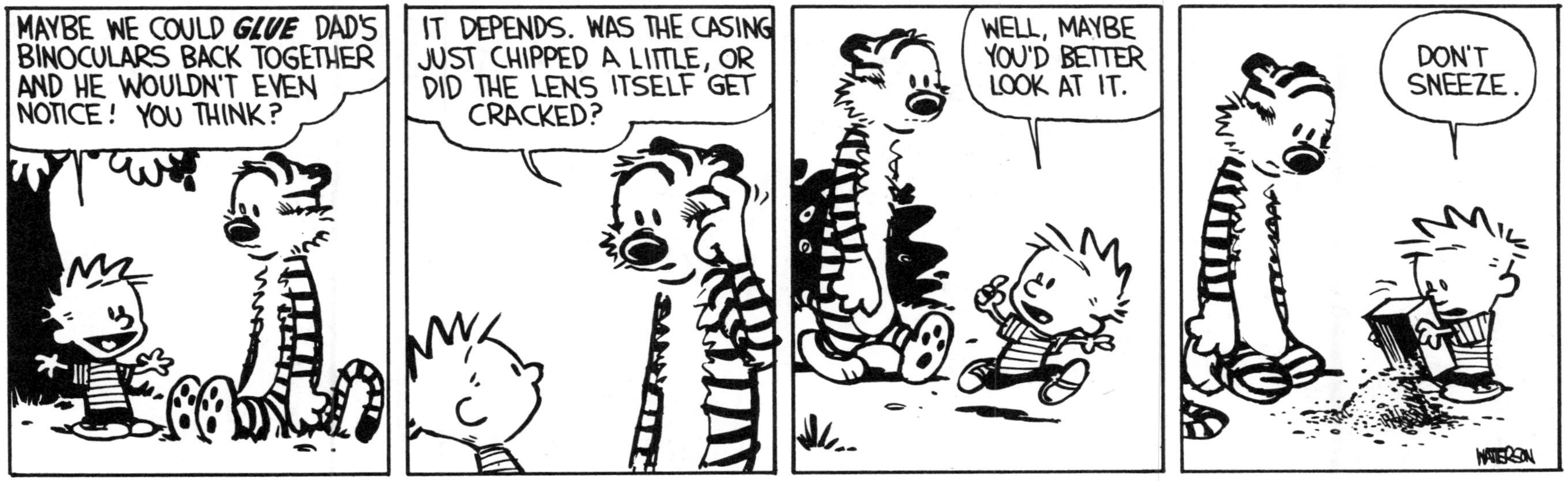
MAYBE WE COULD **GLUE** DAD'S BINOCULARS BACK TOGETHER AND HE WOULDN'T EVEN NOTICE! YOU THINK?
IT DEPENDS. WAS THE CASING JUST CHIPPED A LITTLE, OR DID THE LENS ITSELF GET CRACKED?
WELL, MAYBE YOU'D BETTER LOOK AT IT.
DON'T SNEEZE.
WATTERSON

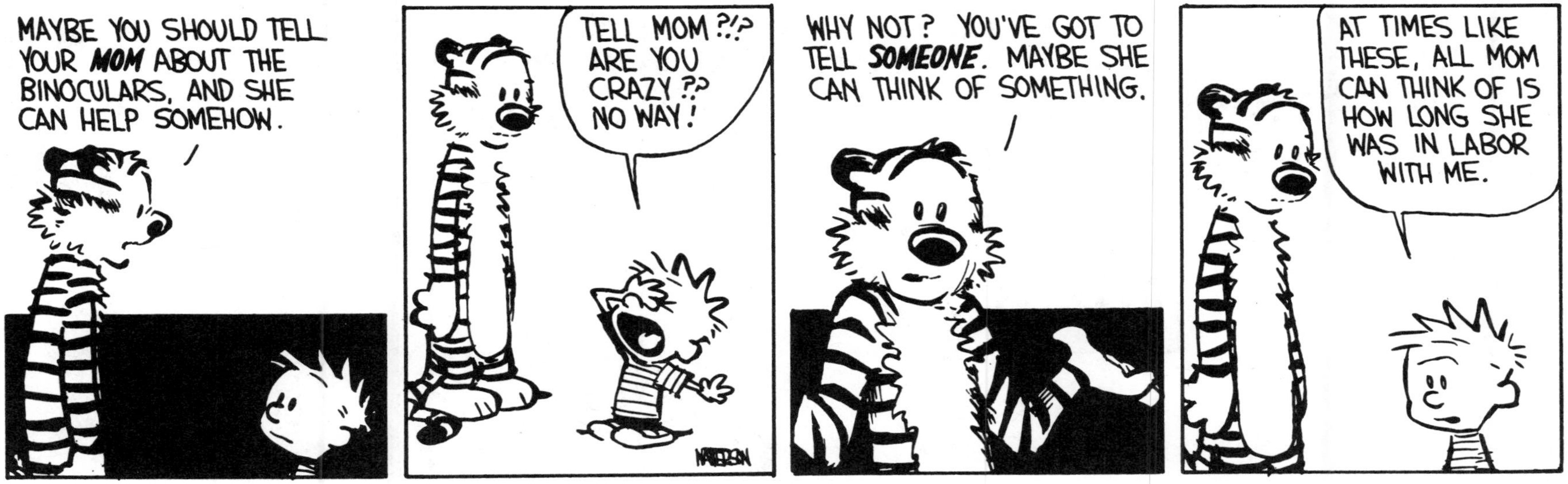
MAYBE YOU SHOULD TELL YOUR **MOM** ABOUT THE BINOCULARS, AND SHE CAN HELP SOMEHOW.
TELL MOM ?!? ARE YOU CRAZY ?? NO WAY!
WATTERSON
WHY NOT? YOU'VE GOT TO TELL **SOMEONE**. MAYBE SHE CAN THINK OF SOMETHING.
AT TIMES LIKE THESE, ALL MOM CAN THINK OF IS HOW LONG SHE WAS IN LABOR WITH ME.

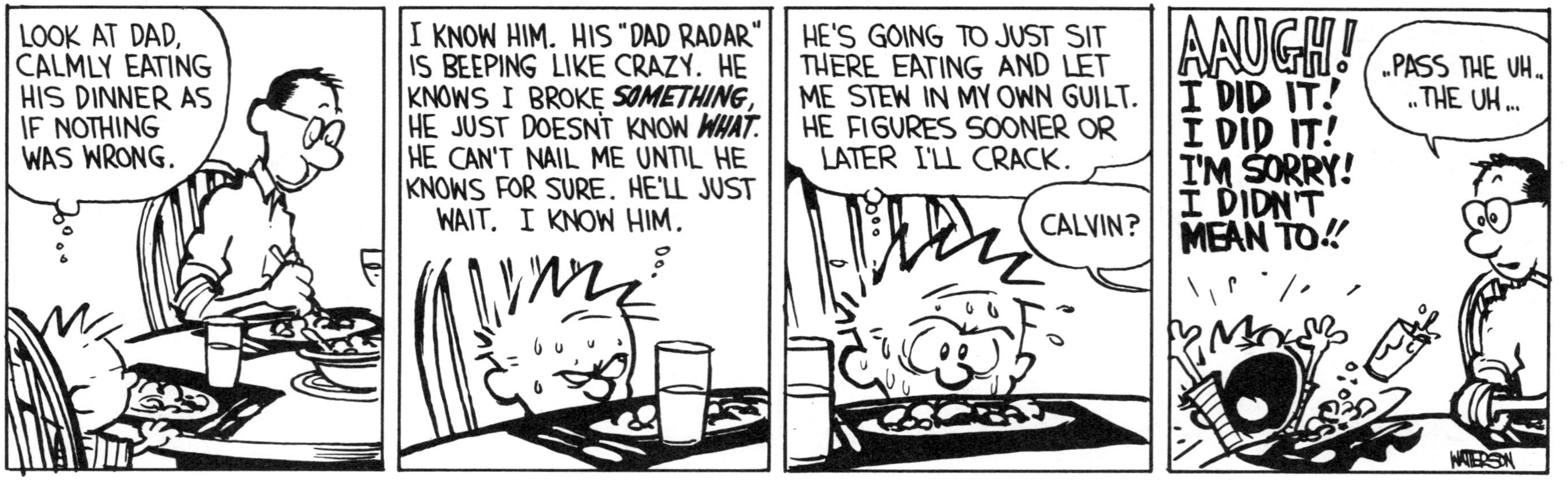
LOOK AT DAD, CALMLY EATING HIS DINNER AS IF NOTHING WAS WRONG.
I KNOW HIM. HIS "DAD RADAR" IS BEEPING LIKE CRAZY. HE KNOWS I BROKE SOMETHING, HE JUST DOESN'T KNOW WHAT. HE CAN'T NAIL ME UNTIL HE KNOWS FOR SURE. HE'LL JUST WAIT. I KNOW HIM.
HE'S GOING TO JUST SIT THERE EATING AND LET ME STEW IN MY OWN GUILT. HE FIGURES SOONER OR LATER I'LL CRACK.
CALVIN?
AAUGH! I DID IT! I DID IT! I'M SORRY! I DIDN'T MEAN TO!!
..PASS THE UH.. ..THE UH...
WATTERSON

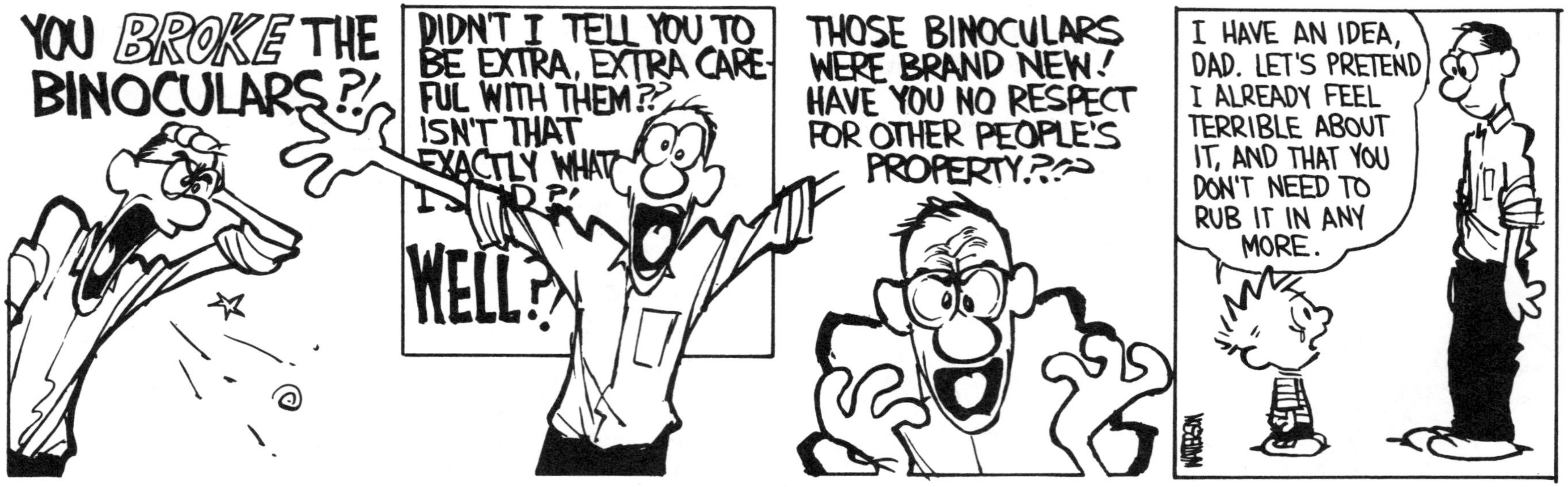
YOU BROKE THE BINOCULARS?!
DIDN'T I TELL YOU TO BE EXTRA, EXTRA CAREFUL WITH THEM??
ISN'T THAT EXACTLY WHAT
WELL?!
THOSE BINOCULARS WERE BRAND NEW! HAVE YOU NO RESPECT FOR OTHER PEOPLE'S PROPERTY?!?!
I HAVE AN IDEA, DAD. LET'S PRETEND I ALREADY FEEL TERRIBLE ABOUT IT, AND THAT YOU DON'T NEED TO RUB IT IN ANY MORE.
WATTERSON

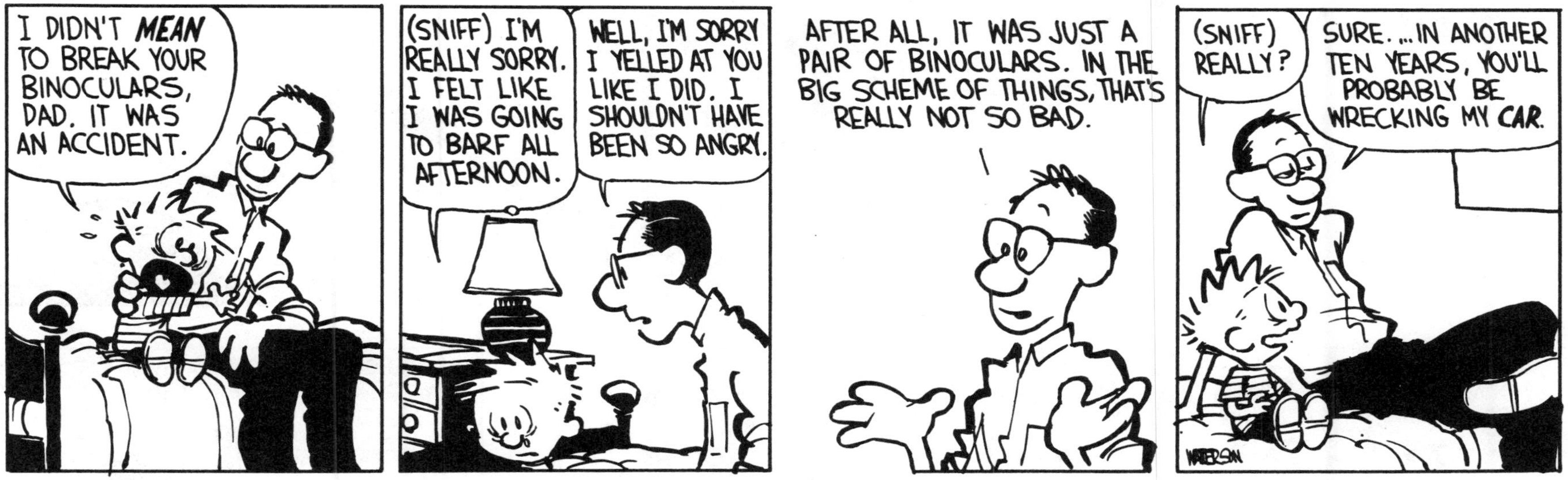
I DIDN'T **MEAN** TO BREAK YOUR BINOCULARS, DAD. IT WAS AN ACCIDENT.
(SNIFF) I'M REALLY SORRY. I FELT LIKE I WAS GOING TO BARF ALL AFTERNOON.
WELL, I'M SORRY I YELLED AT YOU LIKE I DID. I SHOULDN'T HAVE BEEN SO ANGRY.
AFTER ALL, IT WAS JUST A PAIR OF BINOCULARS. IN THE BIG SCHEME OF THINGS, THAT'S REALLY NOT SO BAD.
(SNIFF) REALLY?
SURE. ...IN ANOTHER TEN YEARS, YOU'LL PROBABLY BE WRECKING MY **CAR**.

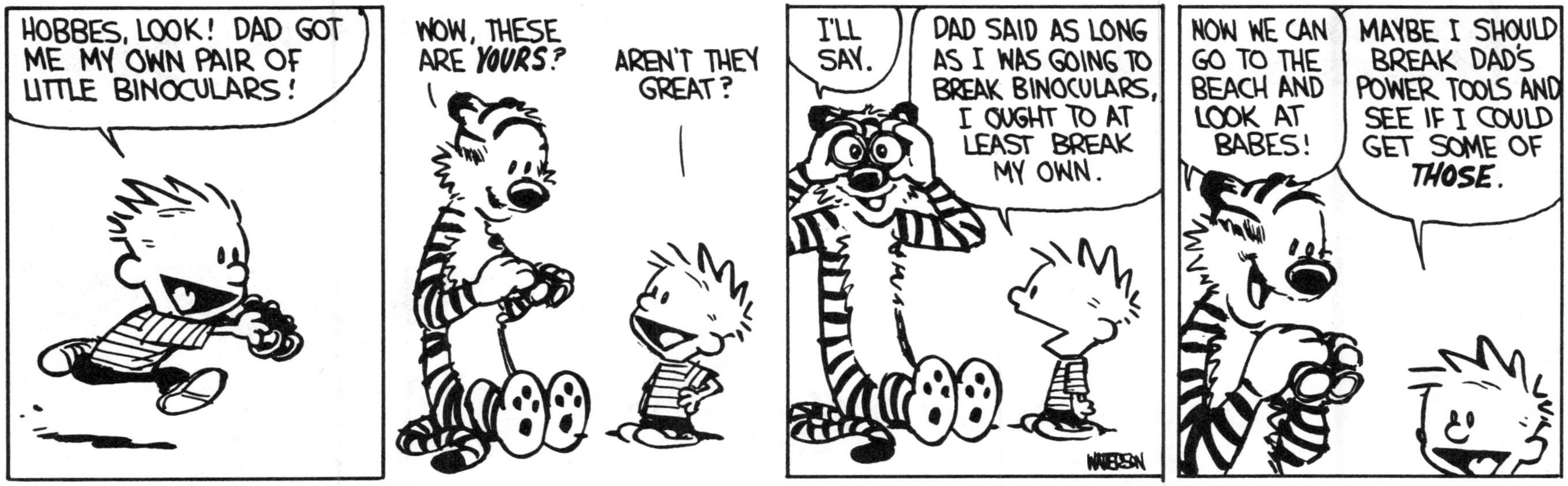
HOBBES, LOOK! DAD GOT ME MY OWN PAIR OF LITTLE BINOCULARS!
WOW, THESE ARE ***YOURS***?
AREN'T THEY GREAT?
I'LL SAY.
DAD SAID AS LONG AS I WAS GOING TO BREAK BINOCULARS, I OUGHT TO AT LEAST BREAK MY OWN.
NOW WE CAN GO TO THE BEACH AND LOOK AT BABES!
MAYBE I SHOULD BREAK DAD'S POWER TOOLS AND SEE IF I COULD GET SOME OF ***THOSE***.

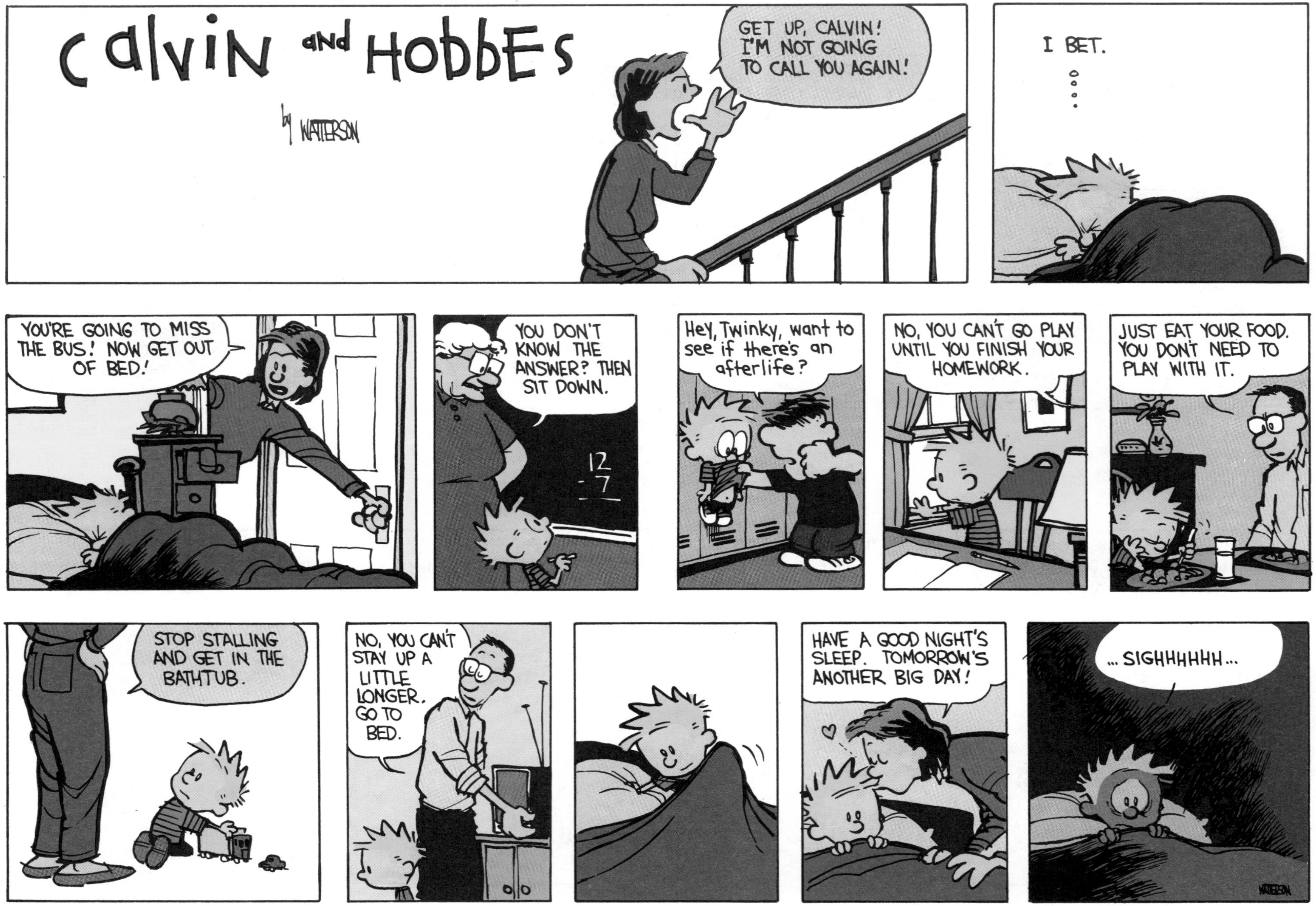
Calvin and HOBBES
by WATTERSON
GET UP, CALVIN! I'M NOT GOING TO CALL YOU AGAIN!
I BET.
YOU'RE GOING TO MISS THE BUS! NOW GET OUT OF BED!
YOU DON'T KNOW THE ANSWER? THEN SIT DOWN.
12
- 7
Hey, Twinky, want to see if there's an afterlife?
NO, YOU CAN'T GO PLAY UNTIL YOU FINISH YOUR HOMEWORK.
JUST EAT YOUR FOOD. YOU DON'T NEED TO PLAY WITH IT.
STOP STALLING AND GET IN THE BATHTUB.
NO, YOU CAN'T STAY UP A LITTLE LONGER. GO TO BED.
HAVE A GOOD NIGHT'S SLEEP. TOMORROW'S ANOTHER BIG DAY!
... SIGHHHHHH ...
WATTERSON

I've never understood people who remember childhood as an idyllic time.

I think this is one of the better Rosalyn stories. With each one, it gets harder to top the previous conflict, so this time I added Stupendous Man to the mix.

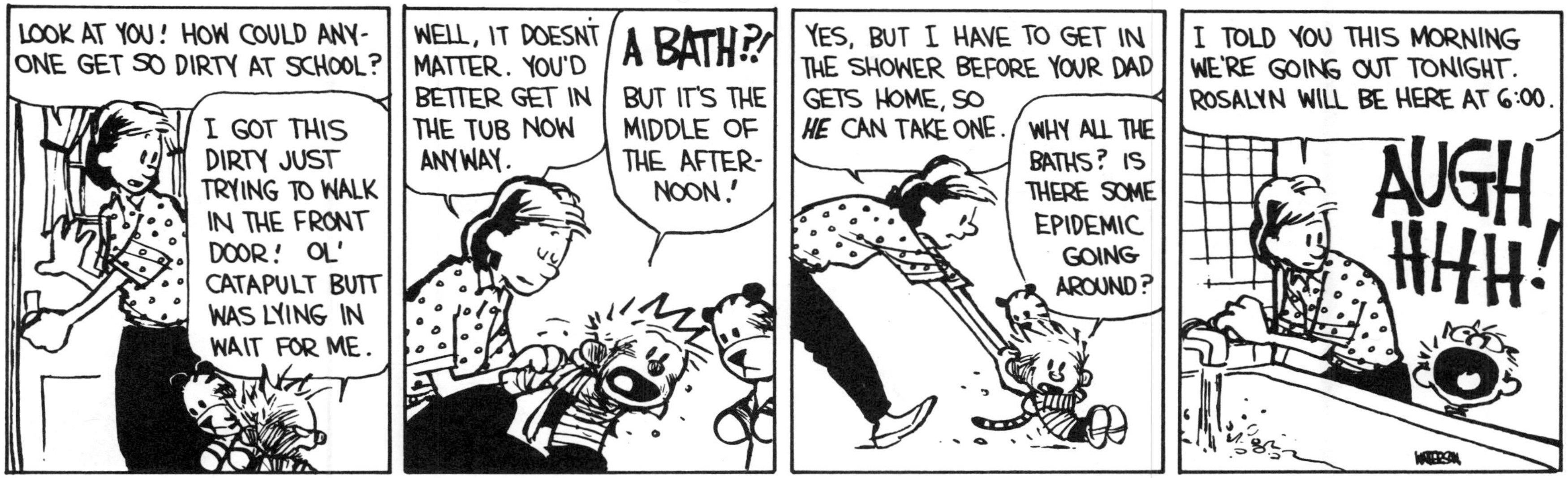
LOOK AT YOU! HOW COULD ANYONE GET SO DIRTY AT SCHOOL?
I GOT THIS DIRTY JUST TRYING TO WALK IN THE FRONT DOOR! OL' CATAPULT BUTT WAS LYING IN WAIT FOR ME.
WELL, IT DOESN'T MATTER. YOU'D BETTER GET IN THE TUB NOW ANYWAY.
A BATH?!
BUT IT'S THE MIDDLE OF THE AFTERNOON!
YES, BUT I HAVE TO GET IN THE SHOWER BEFORE YOUR DAD GETS HOME, SO *HE* CAN TAKE ONE.
WHY ALL THE BATHS? IS THERE SOME EPIDEMIC GOING AROUND?
I TOLD YOU THIS MORNING WE'RE GOING OUT TONIGHT. ROSALYN WILL BE HERE AT 6:00.
AUGHHHH!

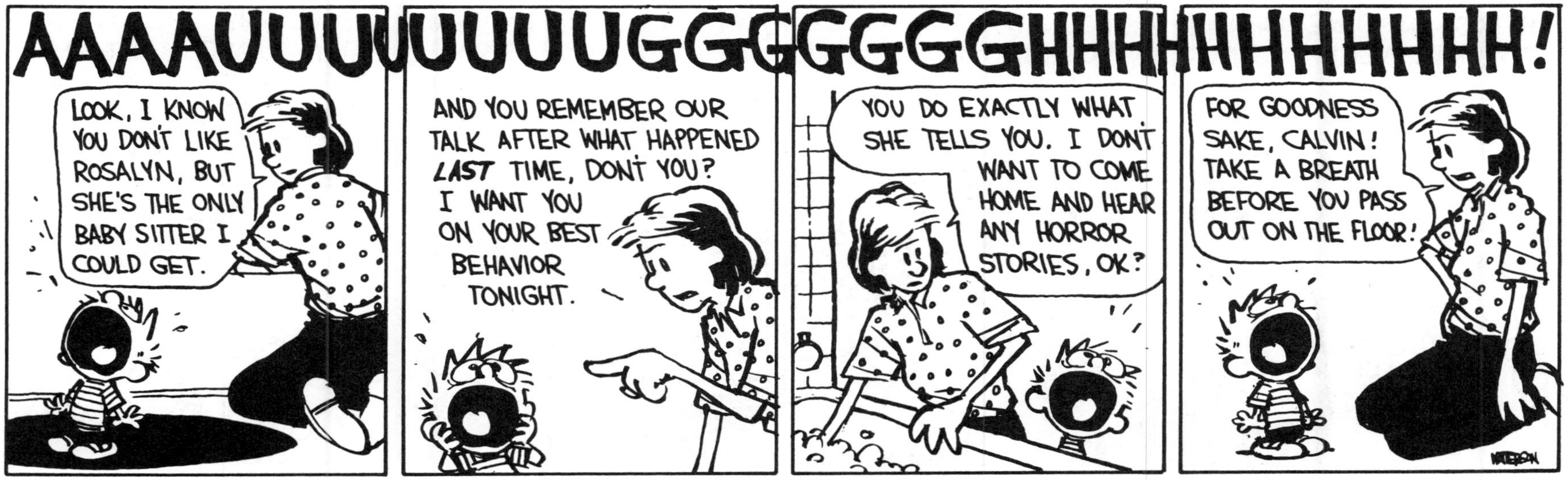
AAAAUUUUUUUUUGGGGGGGHHHHHHHHHHH!
LOOK, I KNOW YOU DON'T LIKE ROSALYN, BUT SHE'S THE ONLY BABY SITTER I COULD GET.
AND YOU REMEMBER OUR TALK AFTER WHAT HAPPENED *LAST* TIME, DON'T YOU? I WANT YOU ON YOUR BEST BEHAVIOR TONIGHT.
YOU DO EXACTLY WHAT SHE TELLS YOU. I DON'T WANT TO COME HOME AND HEAR ANY HORROR STORIES, OK?
FOR GOODNESS SAKE, CALVIN! TAKE A BREATH BEFORE YOU PASS OUT ON THE FLOOR!

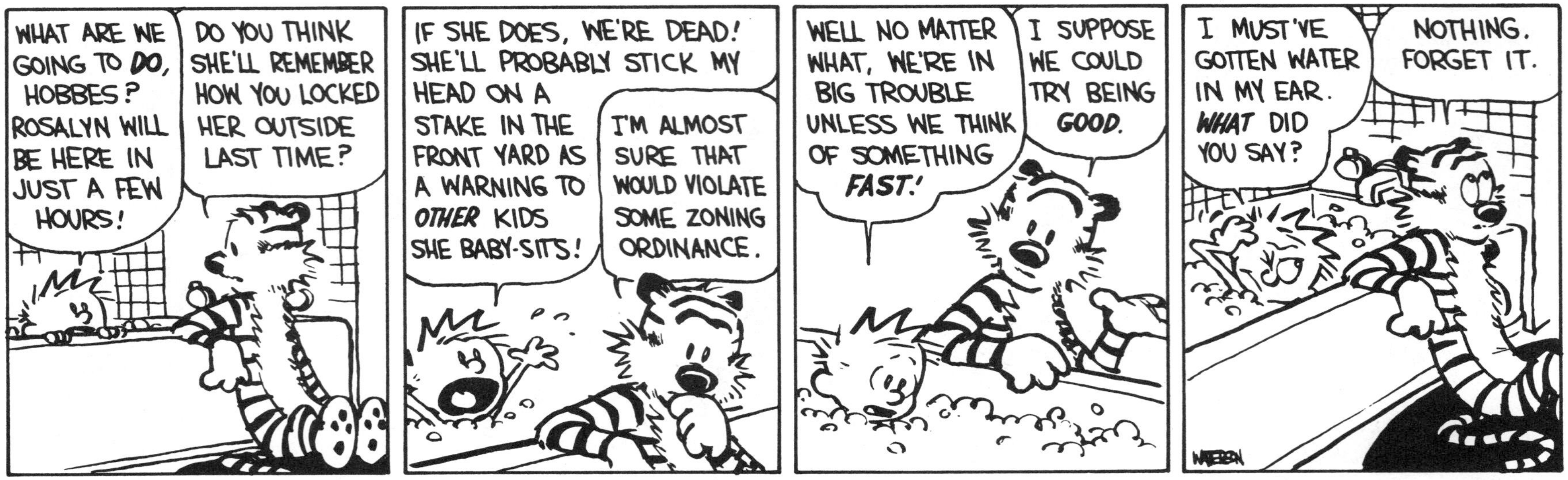
WHAT ARE WE GOING TO DO, HOBBES? ROSALYN WILL BE HERE IN JUST A FEW HOURS!
DO YOU THINK SHE'LL REMEMBER HOW YOU LOCKED HER OUTSIDE LAST TIME?
IF SHE DOES, WE'RE DEAD! SHE'LL PROBABLY STICK MY HEAD ON A STAKE IN THE FRONT YARD AS A WARNING TO OTHER KIDS SHE BABY-SITS!
I'M ALMOST SURE THAT WOULD VIOLATE SOME ZONING ORDINANCE.
WELL NO MATTER WHAT, WE'RE IN BIG TROUBLE UNLESS WE THINK OF SOMETHING FAST!
I SUPPOSE WE COULD TRY BEING GOOD.
I MUST'VE GOTTEN WATER IN MY EAR. WHAT DID YOU SAY?
NOTHING. FORGET IT.

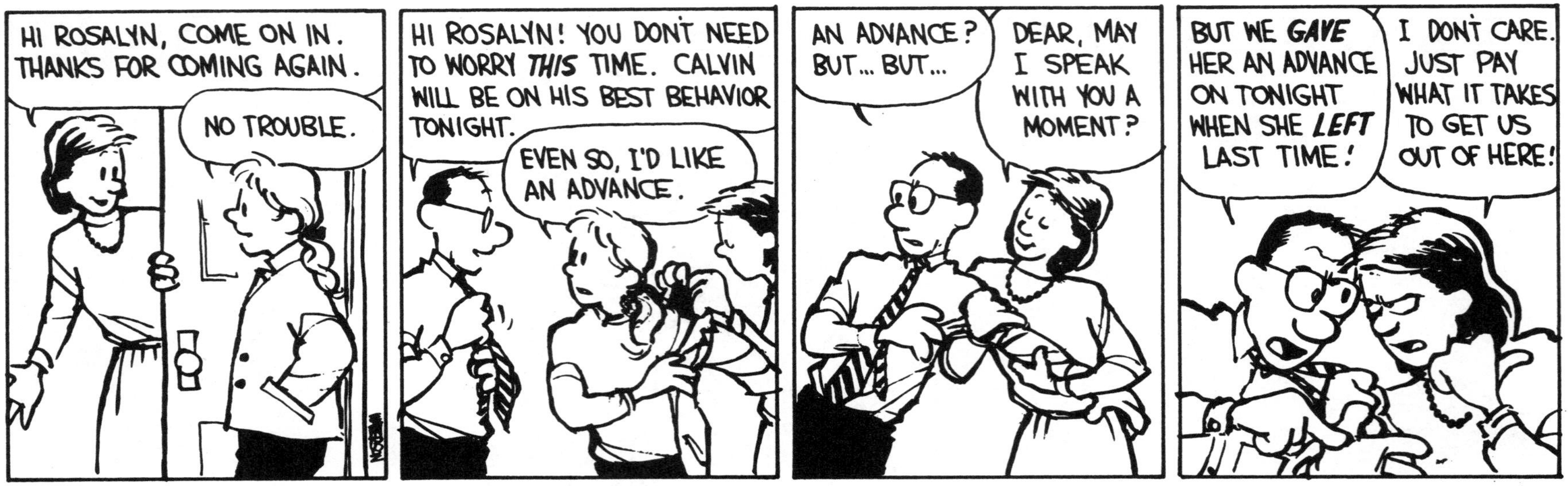
HI ROSALYN, COME ON IN. THANKS FOR COMING AGAIN.
NO TROUBLE.
HI ROSALYN! YOU DON'T NEED TO WORRY THIS TIME. CALVIN WILL BE ON HIS BEST BEHAVIOR TONIGHT.
EVEN SO, I'D LIKE AN ADVANCE.
AN ADVANCE? BUT... BUT...
DEAR, MAY I SPEAK WITH YOU A MOMENT?
BUT WE GAVE HER AN ADVANCE ON TONIGHT WHEN SHE LEFT LAST TIME!
I DON'T CARE. JUST PAY WHAT IT TAKES TO GET US OUT OF HERE!

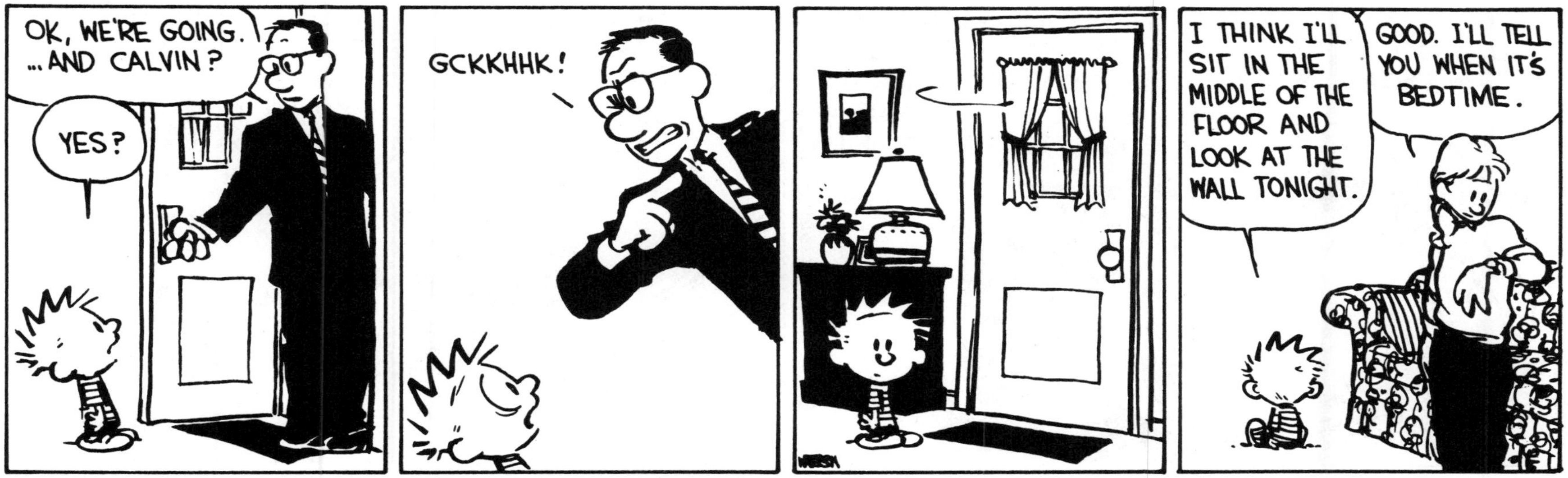
OK, WE'RE GOING. ...AND CALVIN?
YES?
GCKKHHK!
I THINK I'LL SIT IN THE MIDDLE OF THE FLOOR AND LOOK AT THE WALL TONIGHT.
GOOD. I'LL TELL YOU WHEN IT'S BEDTIME.

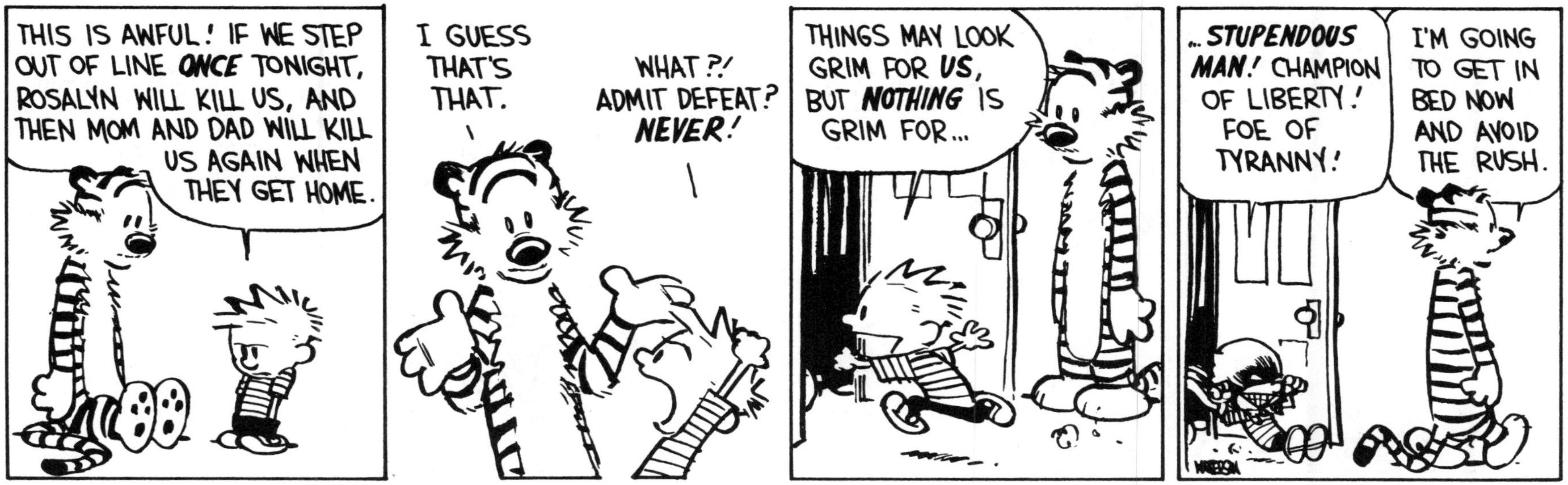
THIS IS AWFUL! IF WE STEP OUT OF LINE ONCE TONIGHT, ROSALYN WILL KILL US, AND THEN MOM AND DAD WILL KILL US AGAIN WHEN THEY GET HOME.
I GUESS THAT'S THAT.
WHAT?! ADMIT DEFEAT? NEVER!
THINGS MAY LOOK GRIM FOR US, BUT NOTHING IS GRIM FOR...
...STUPENDOUS MAN! CHAMPION OF LIBERTY! FOE OF TYRANNY!
I'M GOING TO GET IN BED NOW AND AVOID THE RUSH.

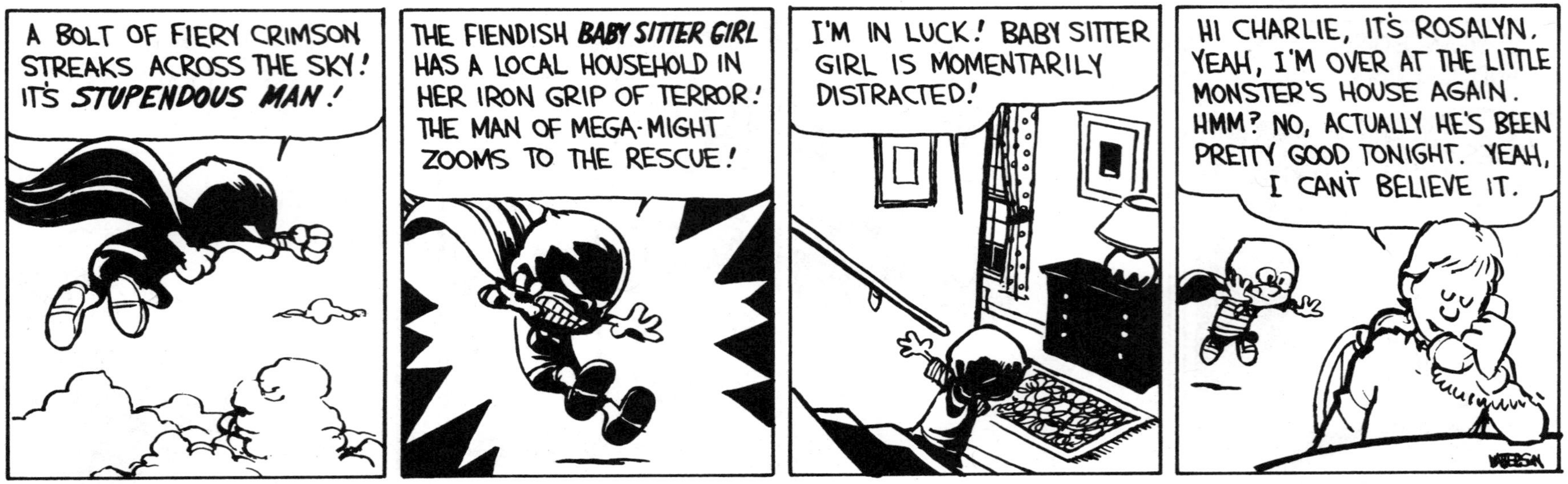
A BOLT OF FIERY CRIMSON STREAKS ACROSS THE SKY! IT'S STUPENDOUS MAN!
THE FIENDISH BABY SITTER GIRL HAS A LOCAL HOUSEHOLD IN HER IRON GRIP OF TERROR! THE MAN OF MEGA-MIGHT ZOOMS TO THE RESCUE!
I'M IN LUCK! BABY SITTER GIRL IS MOMENTARILY DISTRACTED!
HI CHARLIE, IT'S ROSALYN. YEAH, I'M OVER AT THE LITTLE MONSTER'S HOUSE AGAIN. HMM? NO, ACTUALLY HE'S BEEN PRETTY GOOD TONIGHT. YEAH, I CAN'T BELIEVE IT.

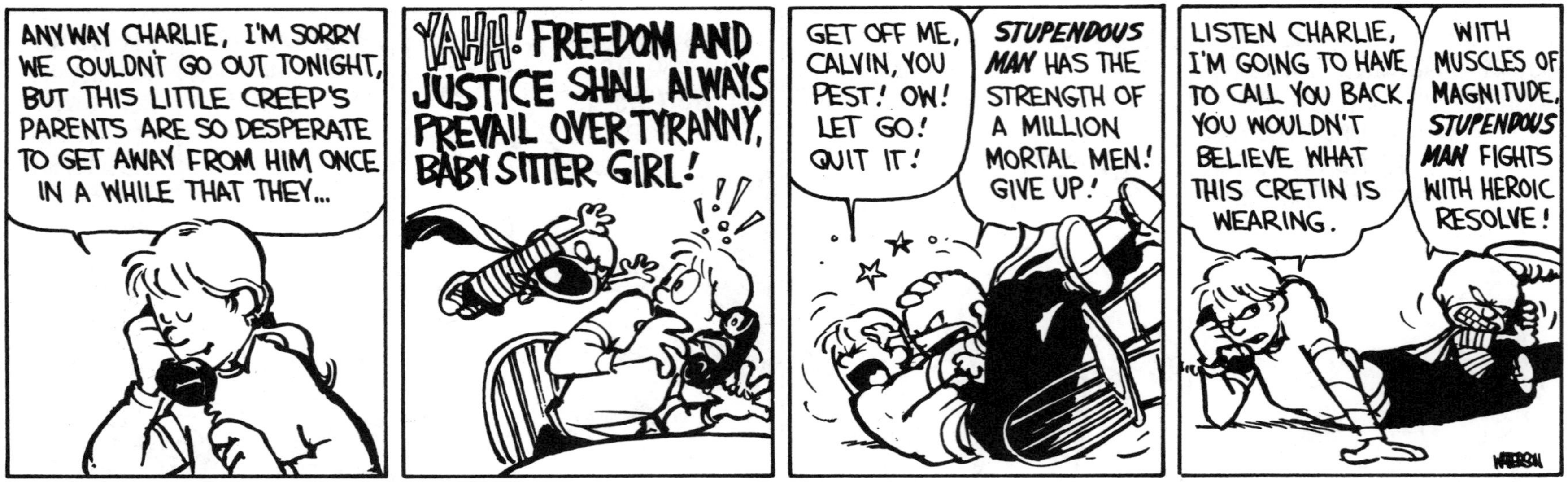
ANYWAY CHARLIE, I'M SORRY WE COULDN'T GO OUT TONIGHT, BUT THIS LITTLE CREEP'S PARENTS ARE SO DESPERATE TO GET AWAY FROM HIM ONCE IN A WHILE THAT THEY...
YAHH! FREEDOM AND JUSTICE SHALL ALWAYS PREVAIL OVER TYRANNY, BABY SITTER GIRL!
!!
GET OFF ME, CALVIN, YOU PEST! OW! LET GO! QUIT IT!
STUPENDOUS MAN HAS THE STRENGTH OF A MILLION MORTAL MEN! GIVE UP!
LISTEN CHARLIE, I'M GOING TO HAVE TO CALL YOU BACK. YOU WOULDN'T BELIEVE WHAT THIS CRETIN IS WEARING.
WITH MUSCLES OF MAGNITUDE, STUPENDOUS MAN FIGHTS WITH HEROIC RESOLVE!

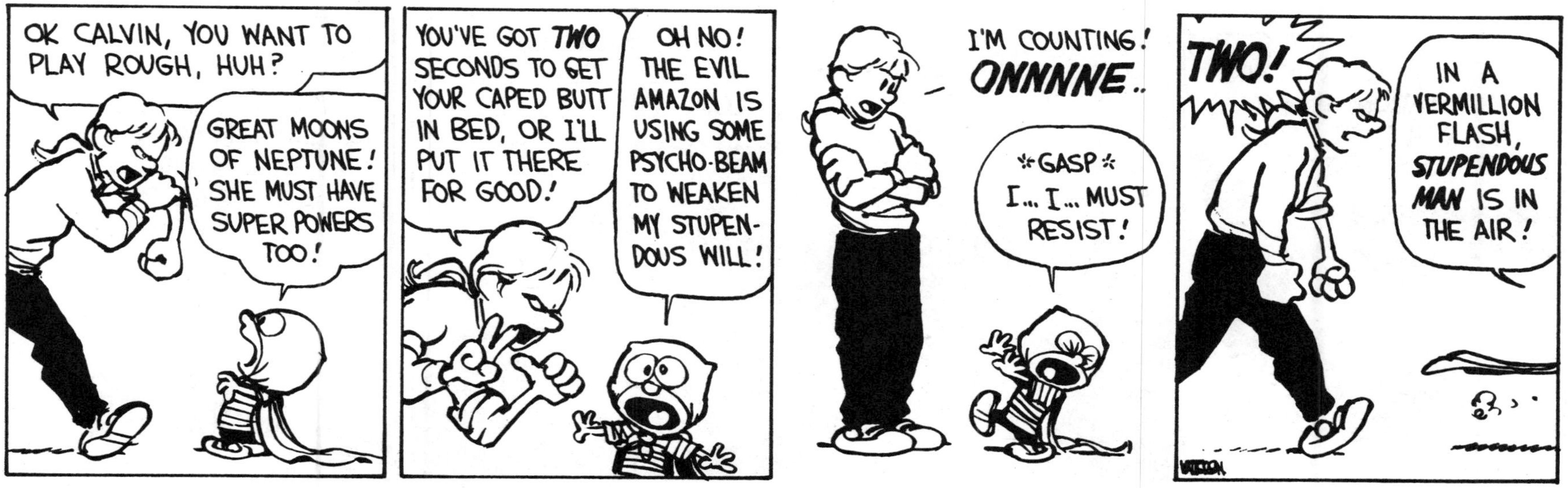
OK CALVIN, YOU WANT TO PLAY ROUGH, HUH?
GREAT MOONS OF NEPTUNE! SHE MUST HAVE SUPER POWERS TOO!
YOU'VE GOT **TWO** SECONDS TO GET YOUR CAPED BUTT IN BED, OR I'LL PUT IT THERE FOR GOOD!
OH NO! THE EVIL AMAZON IS USING SOME PSYCHO-BEAM TO WEAKEN MY STUPENDOUS WILL!
I'M COUNTING! **ONNNNE**..
GASP I... I... MUST RESIST!
TWO!
IN A VERMILLION FLASH, ***STUPENDOUS MAN*** IS IN THE AIR!

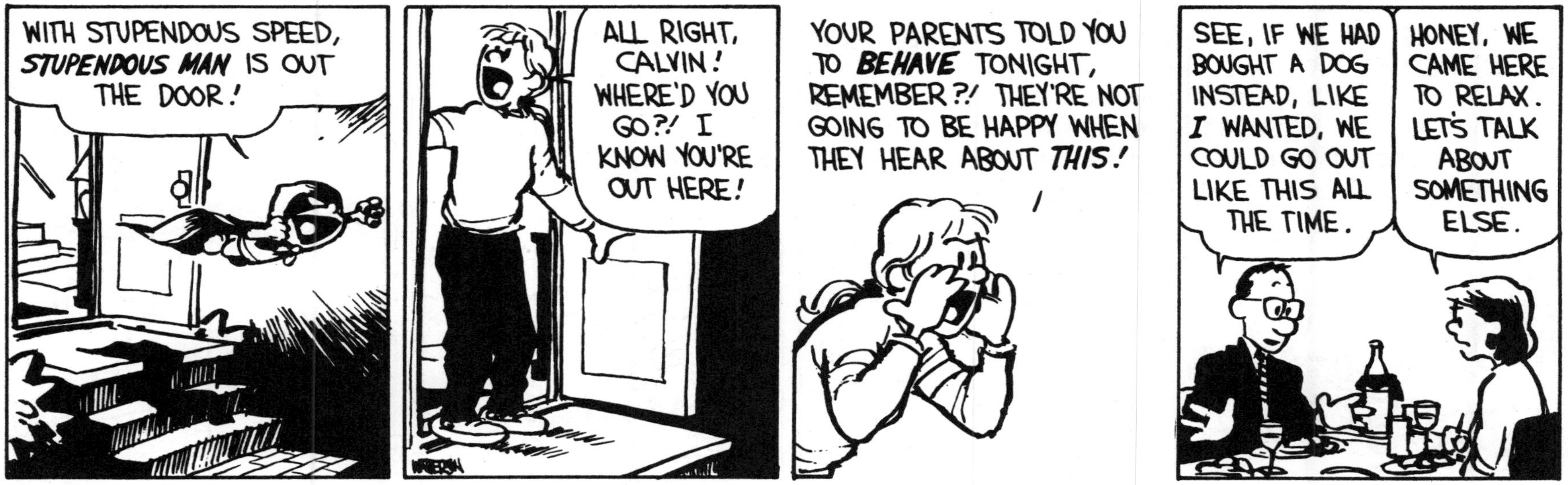
WITH STUPENDOUS SPEED, ***STUPENDOUS MAN*** IS OUT THE DOOR!
ALL RIGHT, CALVIN! WHERE'D YOU GO?! I KNOW YOU'RE OUT HERE!
YOUR PARENTS TOLD YOU TO ***BEHAVE*** TONIGHT, REMEMBER?! THEY'RE NOT GOING TO BE HAPPY WHEN THEY HEAR ABOUT ***THIS***!
SEE, IF WE HAD BOUGHT A DOG INSTEAD, LIKE ***I*** WANTED, WE COULD GO OUT LIKE THIS ALL THE TIME.
HONEY, WE CAME HERE TO RELAX. LET'S TALK ABOUT SOMETHING ELSE.

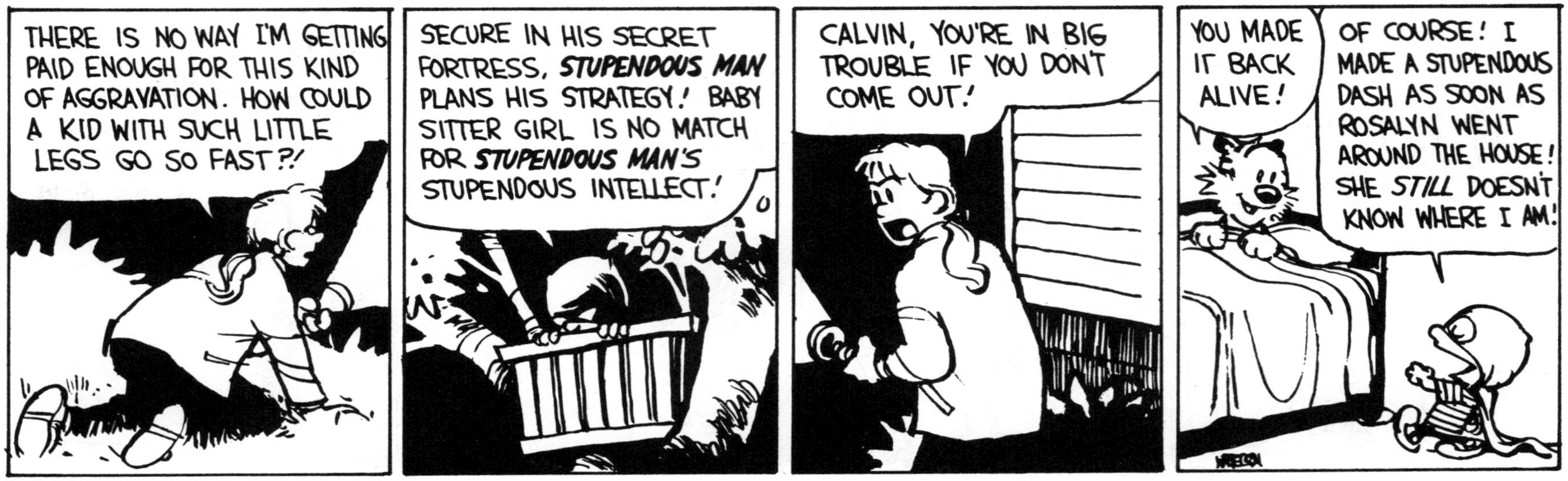
THERE IS NO WAY I'M GETTING PAID ENOUGH FOR THIS KIND OF AGGRAVATION. HOW COULD A KID WITH SUCH LITTLE LEGS GO SO FAST?!
SECURE IN HIS SECRET FORTRESS, STUPENDOUS MAN PLANS HIS STRATEGY! BABY SITTER GIRL IS NO MATCH FOR STUPENDOUS MAN'S STUPENDOUS INTELLECT!
CALVIN, YOU'RE IN BIG TROUBLE IF YOU DON'T COME OUT!
YOU MADE IT BACK ALIVE!
OF COURSE! I MADE A STUPENDOUS DASH AS SOON AS ROSALYN WENT AROUND THE HOUSE! SHE STILL DOESN'T KNOW WHERE I AM!

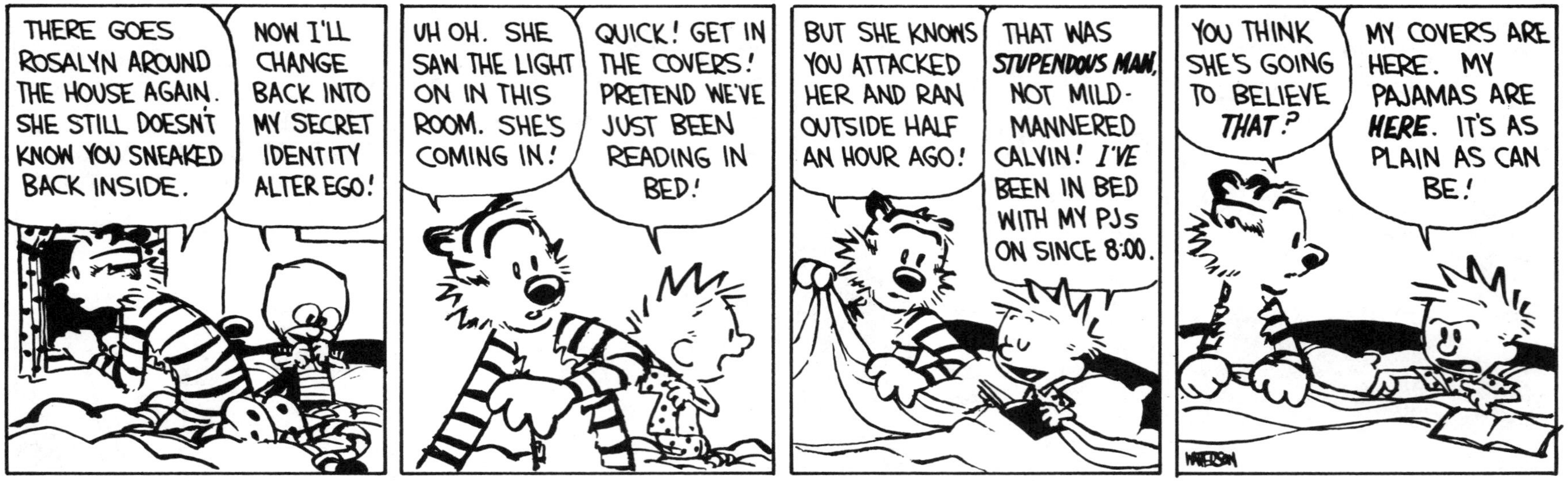
THERE GOES ROSALYN AROUND THE HOUSE AGAIN. SHE STILL DOESN'T KNOW YOU SNEAKED BACK INSIDE.
NOW I'LL CHANGE BACK INTO MY SECRET IDENTITY ALTER EGO!
UH OH. SHE SAW THE LIGHT ON IN THIS ROOM. SHE'S COMING IN!
QUICK! GET IN THE COVERS! PRETEND WE'VE JUST BEEN READING IN BED!
BUT SHE KNOWS YOU ATTACKED HER AND RAN OUTSIDE HALF AN HOUR AGO!
THAT WAS STUPENDOUS MAN, NOT MILD-MANNERED CALVIN! I'VE BEEN IN BED WITH MY PJs ON SINCE 8:00.
YOU THINK SHE'S GOING TO BELIEVE THAT?
MY COVERS ARE HERE. MY PAJAMAS ARE HERE. IT'S AS PLAIN AS CAN BE!

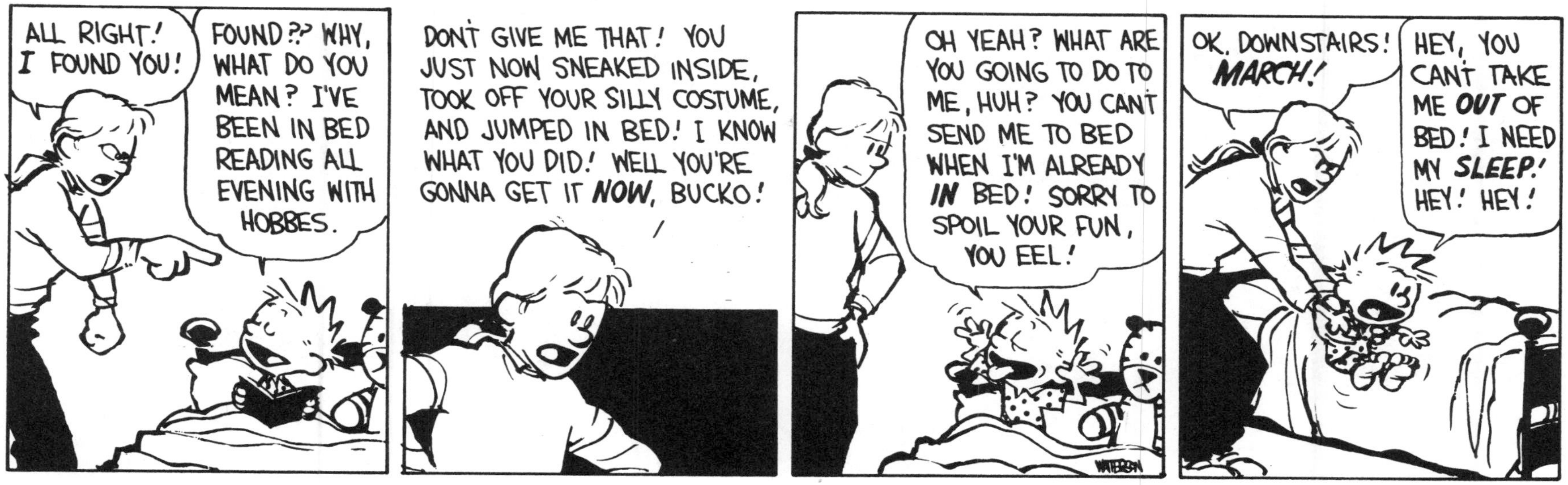
ALL RIGHT! I FOUND YOU!
FOUND?? WHY, WHAT DO YOU MEAN? I'VE BEEN IN BED READING ALL EVENING WITH HOBBES.
DON'T GIVE ME THAT! YOU JUST NOW SNEAKED INSIDE, TOOK OFF YOUR SILLY COSTUME, AND JUMPED IN BED! I KNOW WHAT YOU DID! WELL YOU'RE GONNA GET IT NOW, BUCKO!
OH YEAH? WHAT ARE YOU GOING TO DO TO ME, HUH? YOU CAN'T SEND ME TO BED WHEN I'M ALREADY IN BED! SORRY TO SPOIL YOUR FUN, YOU EEL!
OK. DOWNSTAIRS! MARCH!
HEY, YOU CAN'T TAKE ME OUT OF BED! I NEED MY SLEEP! HEY! HEY!

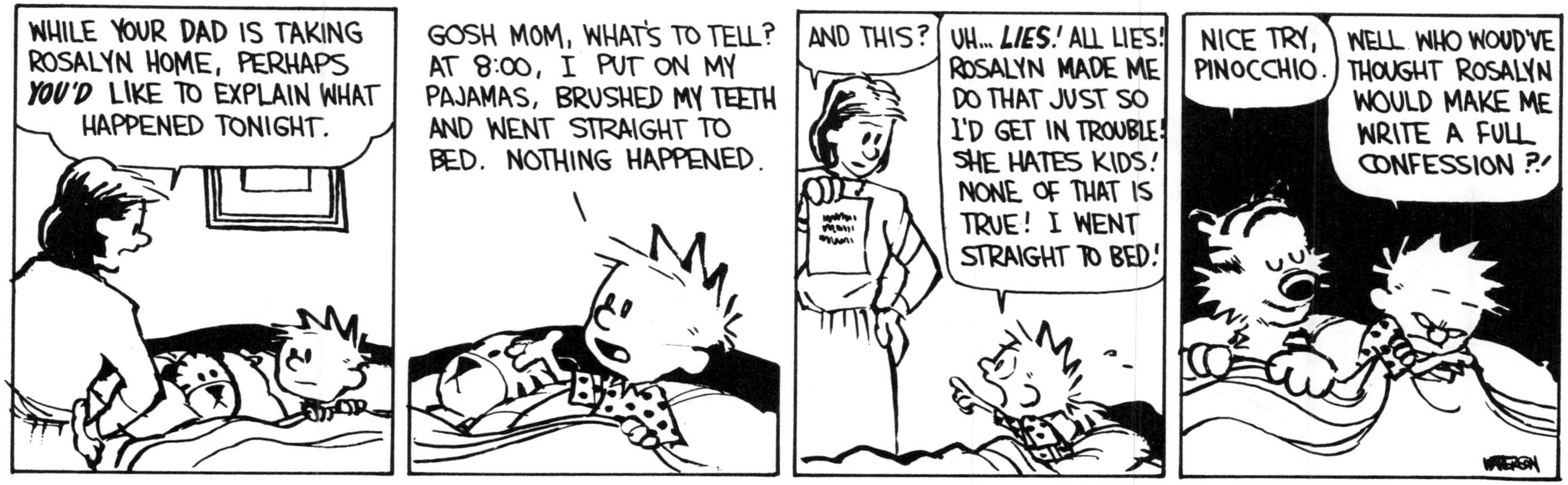
WHILE YOUR DAD IS TAKING ROSALYN HOME, PERHAPS YOU'D LIKE TO EXPLAIN WHAT HAPPENED TONIGHT.
GOSH MOM, WHAT'S TO TELL? AT 8:00, I PUT ON MY PAJAMAS, BRUSHED MY TEETH AND WENT STRAIGHT TO BED. NOTHING HAPPENED.
AND THIS?
UH... LIES! ALL LIES! ROSALYN MADE ME DO THAT JUST SO I'D GET IN TROUBLE! SHE HATES KIDS! NONE OF THAT IS TRUE! I WENT STRAIGHT TO BED!
NICE TRY, PINOCCHIO.
WELL WHO WOUD'VE THOUGHT ROSALYN WOULD MAKE ME WRITE A FULL CONFESSION ?!

The strips of these two pages are part of a story where Calvin goes to Mars. It was an early attempt to write something with an environmental message, and the story was pretty heavy-handed. The cartoony backgrounds are a bit overdone too. Working on deadline, I have to go with story ideas as they come, but this one needed a few more rewrites.

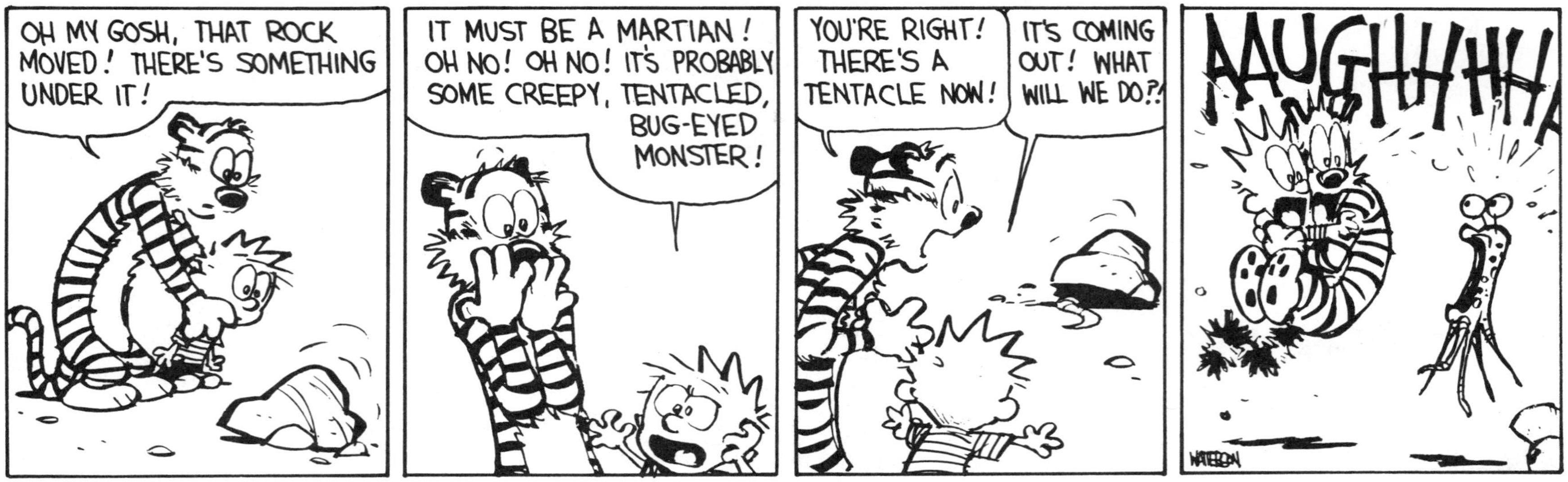
OH MY GOSH, THAT ROCK MOVED! THERE'S SOMETHING UNDER IT!
IT MUST BE A MARTIAN! OH NO! OH NO! IT'S PROBABLY SOME CREEPY, TENTACLED, BUG-EYED MONSTER!
YOU'RE RIGHT! THERE'S A TENTACLE NOW!
IT'S COMING OUT! WHAT WILL WE DO?!
AAUGHHHHH
WATTERSON

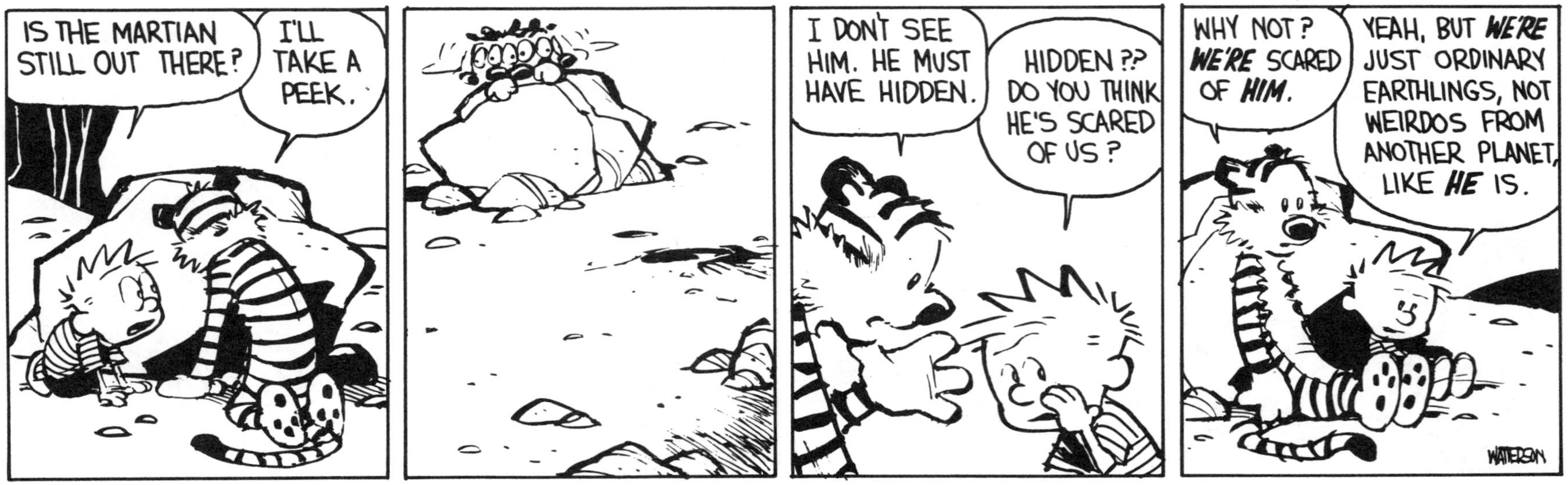
IS THE MARTIAN STILL OUT THERE?
I'LL TAKE A PEEK.
I DON'T SEE HIM. HE MUST HAVE HIDDEN.
HIDDEN?? DO YOU THINK HE'S SCARED OF US?
WHY NOT? WE'RE SCARED OF HIM.
YEAH, BUT WE'RE JUST ORDINARY EARTHLINGS, NOT WEIRDOS FROM ANOTHER PLANET, LIKE HE IS.
WATTERSON

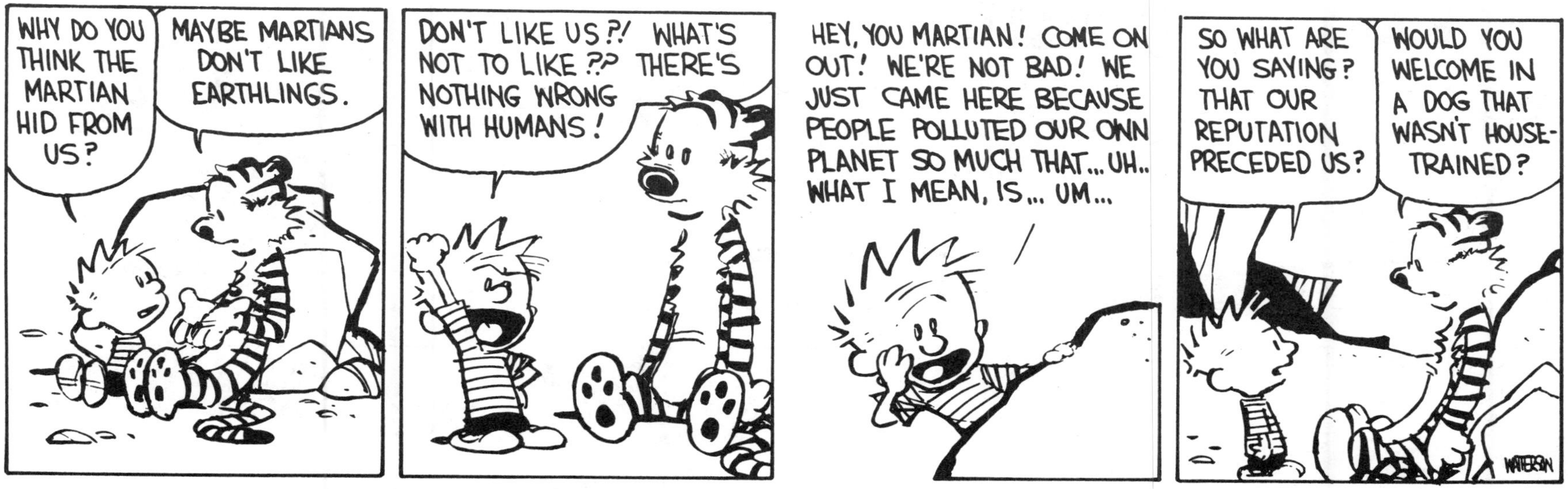
WHY DO YOU THINK THE MARTIAN HID FROM US?
MAYBE MARTIANS DON'T LIKE EARTHLINGS.
DON'T LIKE US?! WHAT'S NOT TO LIKE?? THERE'S NOTHING WRONG WITH HUMANS!
HEY, YOU MARTIAN! COME ON OUT! WE'RE NOT BAD! WE JUST CAME HERE BECAUSE PEOPLE POLLUTED OUR OWN PLANET SO MUCH THAT... UH.. WHAT I MEAN, IS... UM...
SO WHAT ARE YOU SAYING? THAT OUR REPUTATION PRECEDED US?
WOULD YOU WELCOME IN A DOG THAT WASN'T HOUSE-TRAINED?
WATTERSON

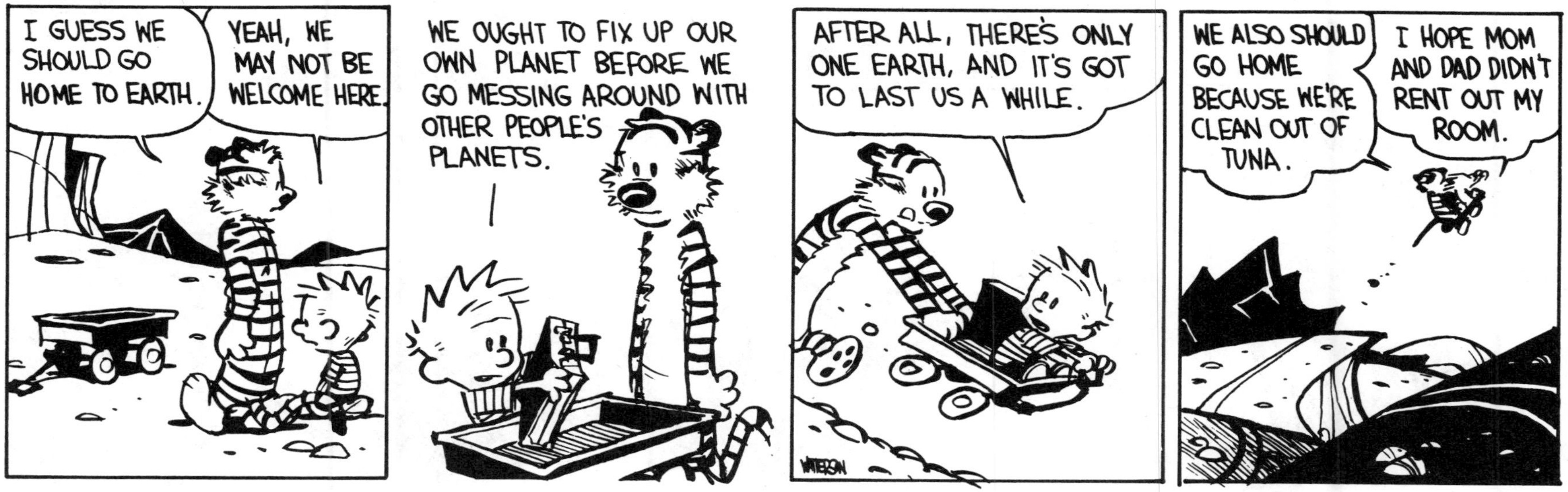
I GUESS WE SHOULD GO HOME TO EARTH.
YEAH, WE MAY NOT BE WELCOME HERE.
WE OUGHT TO FIX UP OUR OWN PLANET BEFORE WE GO MESSING AROUND WITH OTHER PEOPLE'S PLANETS.
AFTER ALL, THERE'S ONLY ONE EARTH, AND IT'S GOT TO LAST US A WHILE.
WE ALSO SHOULD GO HOME BECAUSE WE'RE CLEAN OUT OF TUNA.
I HOPE MOM AND DAD DIDN'T RENT OUT MY ROOM.
WATTERSON

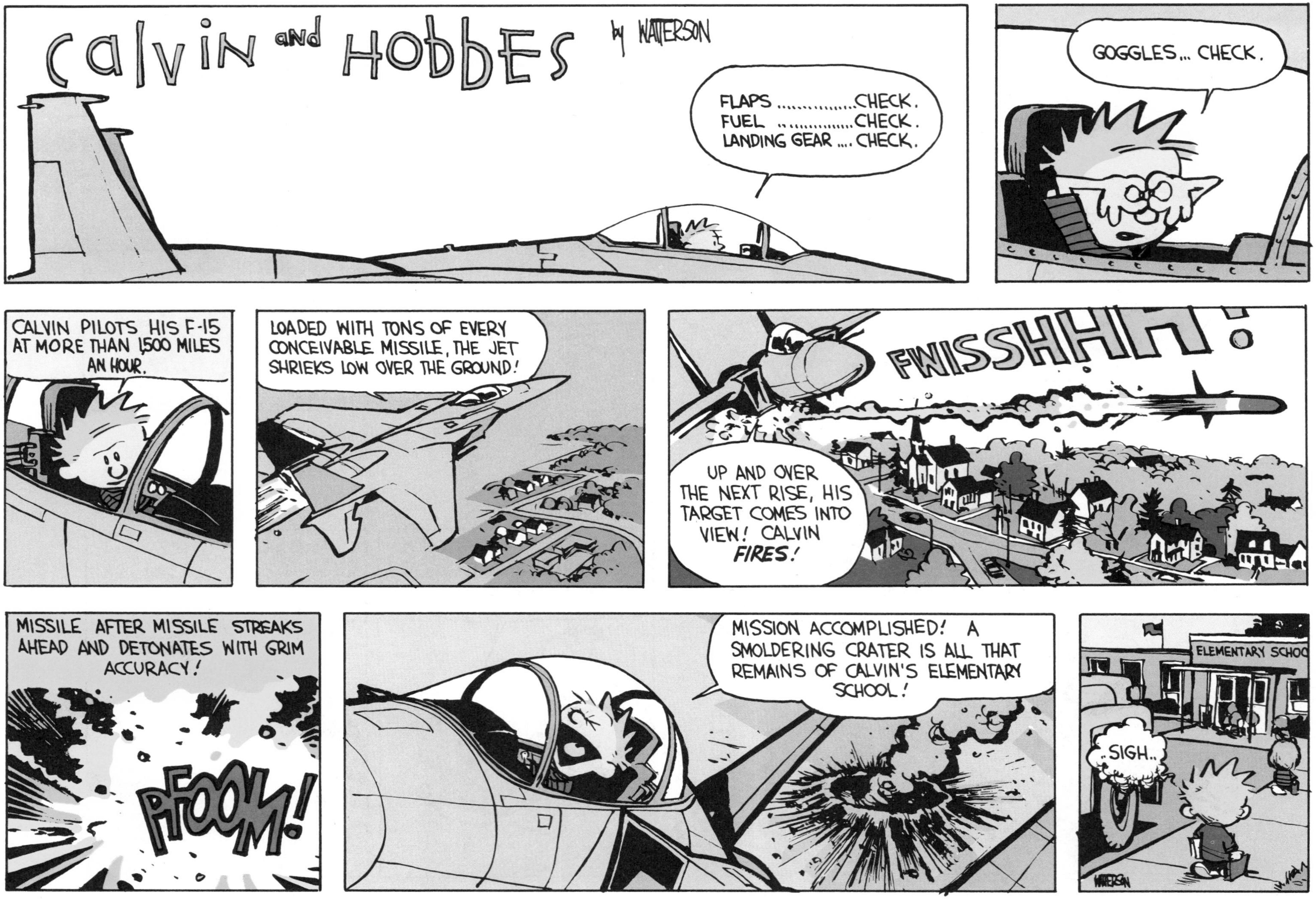
Calvin and HOBBES
by WATTERSON
FLAPS ....CHECK.
FUEL ....CHECK.
LANDING GEAR .... CHECK.
GOGGLES... CHECK.
CALVIN PILOTS HIS F-15 AT MORE THAN 1,500 MILES AN HOUR.
LOADED WITH TONS OF EVERY CONCEIVABLE MISSILE, THE JET SHRIEKS LOW OVER THE GROUND!
FWISSHHH!
UP AND OVER THE NEXT RISE, HIS TARGET COMES INTO VIEW! CALVIN FIRES!
MISSILE AFTER MISSILE STREAKS AHEAD AND DETONATES WITH GRIM ACCURACY!
PFOOM!
MISSION ACCOMPLISHED! A SMOLDERING CRATER IS ALL THAT REMAINS OF CALVIN'S ELEMENTARY SCHOOL!
ELEMENTARY SCHO
..SIGH..
WATTERSON

I got some nasty mail about this strip. Some readers thought it was inexcusable to show a kid fantasize about bombing his school off the face of the earth. Apparently some of my readers were never kids themselves.

Calvin is a great character to write for, because I only need to know as much as a lazy six-year-old. After this story ran, I received more information on bats than I ever cared to know.

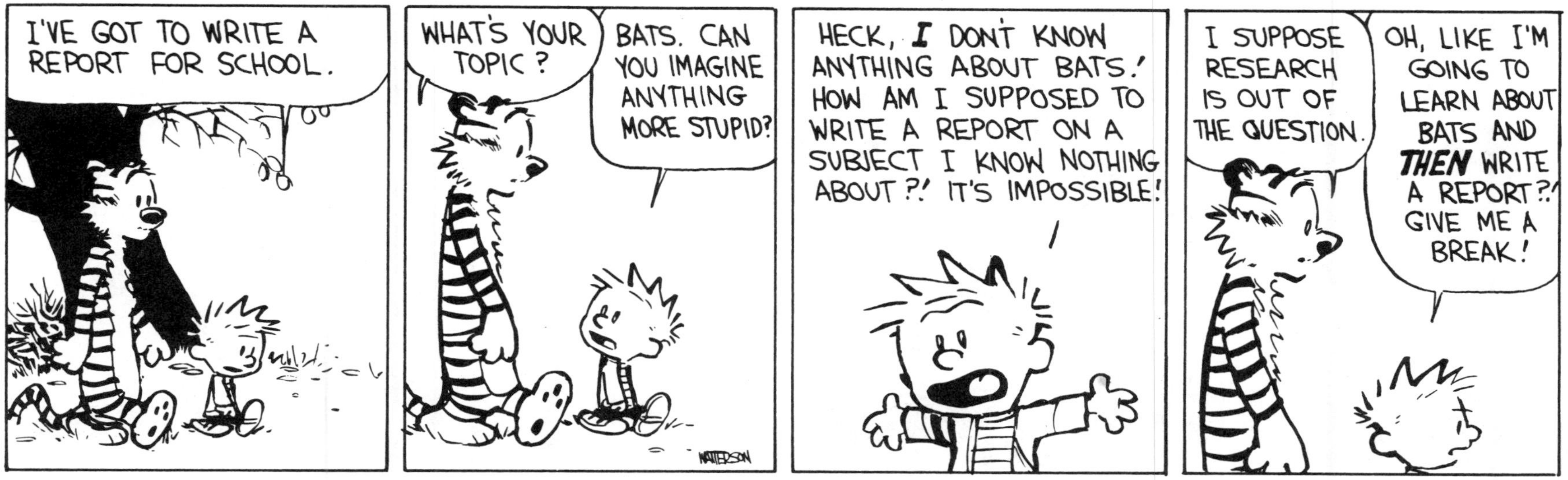
I'VE GOT TO WRITE A REPORT FOR SCHOOL.
WHAT'S YOUR TOPIC?
BATS. CAN YOU IMAGINE ANYTHING MORE STUPID?
HECK, I DON'T KNOW ANYTHING ABOUT BATS! HOW AM I SUPPOSED TO WRITE A REPORT ON A SUBJECT I KNOW NOTHING ABOUT?! IT'S IMPOSSIBLE!
I SUPPOSE RESEARCH IS OUT OF THE QUESTION.
OH, LIKE I'M GOING TO LEARN ABOUT BATS AND THEN WRITE A REPORT?! GIVE ME A BREAK!
WATTERSON

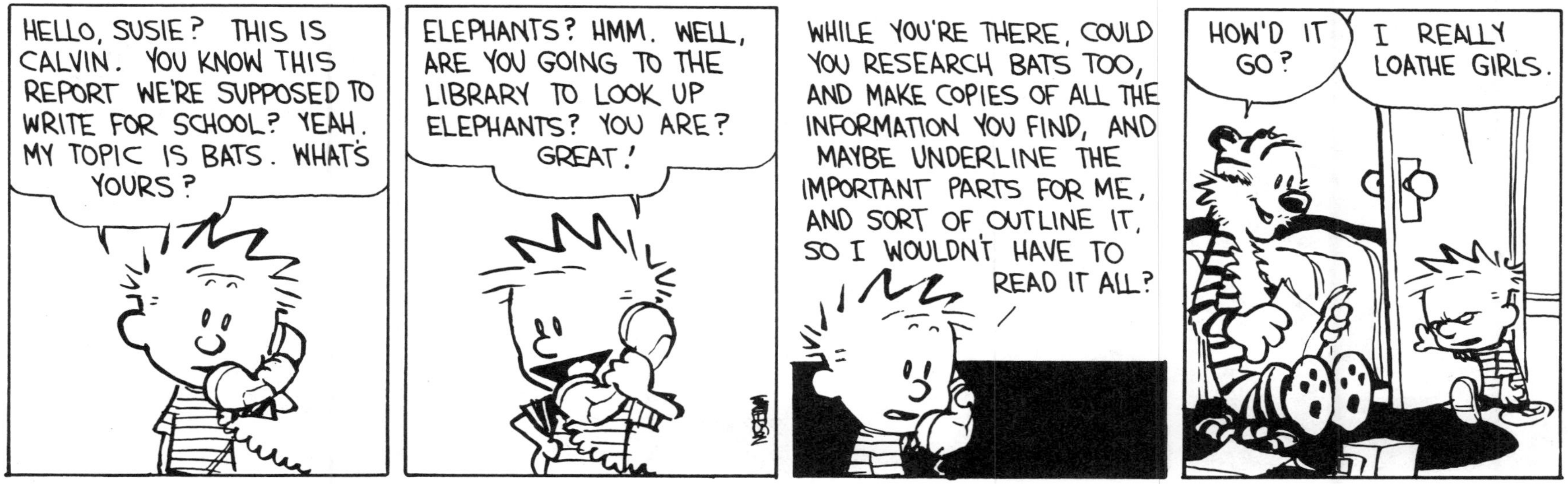
HELLO, SUSIE? THIS IS CALVIN. YOU KNOW THIS REPORT WE'RE SUPPOSED TO WRITE FOR SCHOOL? YEAH. MY TOPIC IS BATS. WHAT'S YOURS?
ELEPHANTS? HMM. WELL, ARE YOU GOING TO THE LIBRARY TO LOOK UP ELEPHANTS? YOU ARE? GREAT!
WHILE YOU'RE THERE, COULD YOU RESEARCH BATS TOO, AND MAKE COPIES OF ALL THE INFORMATION YOU FIND, AND MAYBE UNDERLINE THE IMPORTANT PARTS FOR ME, AND SORT OF OUTLINE IT, SO I WOULDN'T HAVE TO READ IT ALL?
HOW'D IT GO?
I REALLY LOATHE GIRLS.

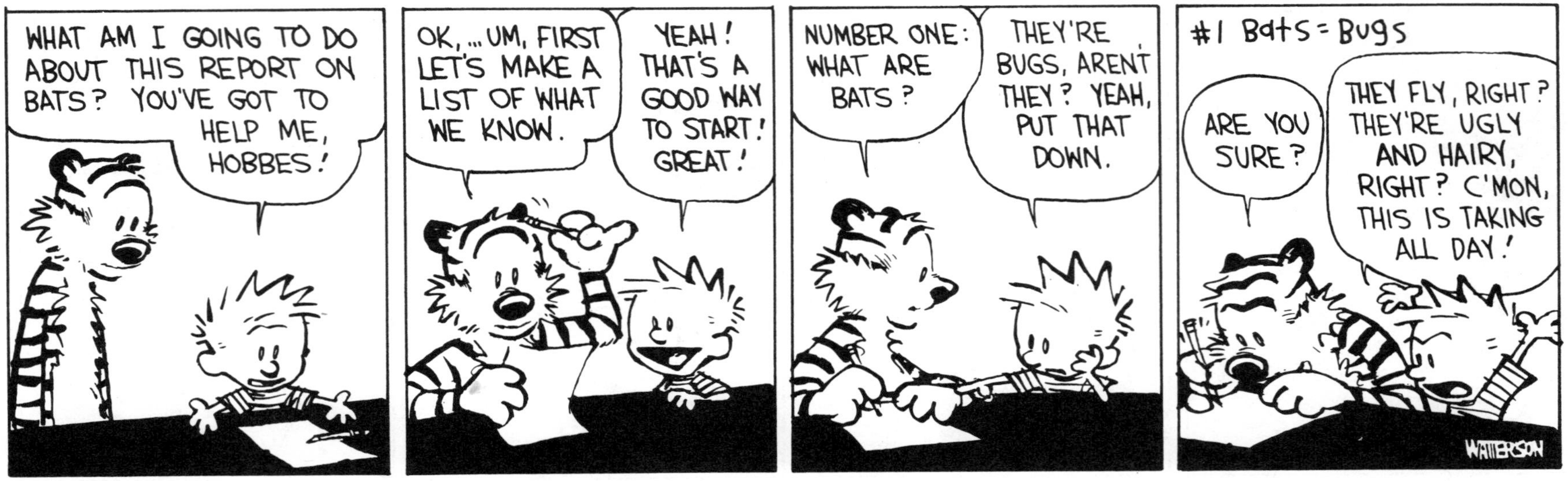
WHAT AM I GOING TO DO ABOUT THIS REPORT ON BATS? YOU'VE GOT TO HELP ME, HOBBES!
OK, ... UM, FIRST LET'S MAKE A LIST OF WHAT WE KNOW.
YEAH! THAT'S A GOOD WAY TO START! GREAT!
NUMBER ONE: WHAT ARE BATS?
THEY'RE BUGS, AREN'T THEY? YEAH, PUT THAT DOWN.
#1 Bats = Bugs
ARE YOU SURE?
THEY FLY, RIGHT? THEY'RE UGLY AND HAIRY, RIGHT? C'MON, THIS IS TAKING ALL DAY!
WATTERSON

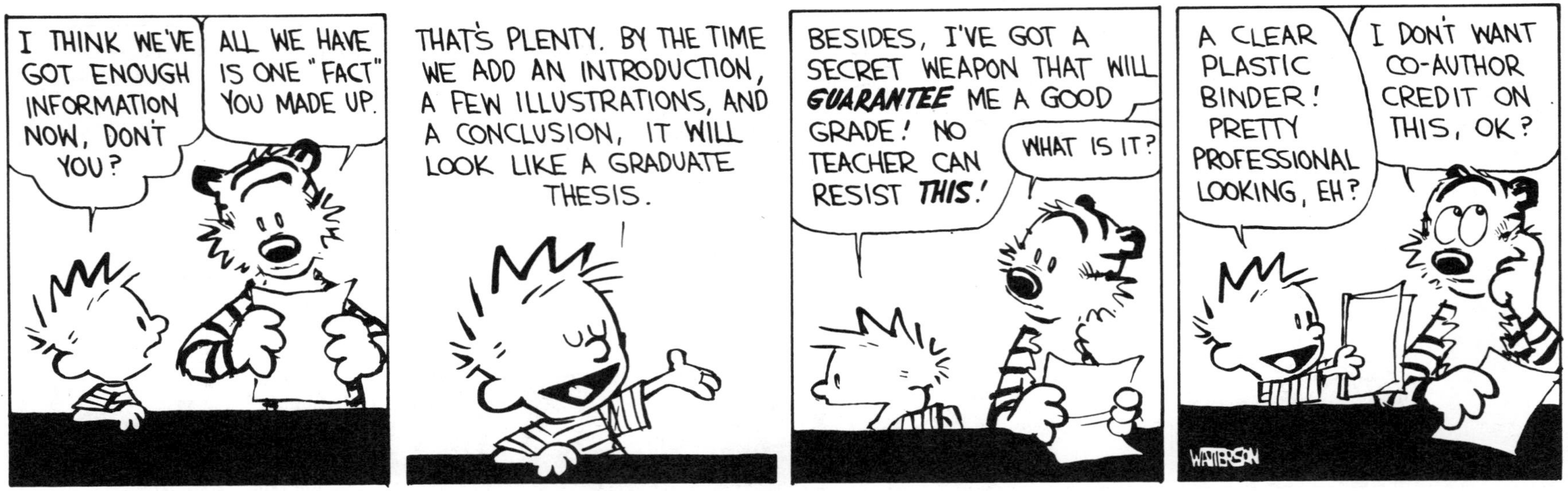
I THINK WE'VE GOT ENOUGH INFORMATION NOW, DON'T YOU?
ALL WE HAVE IS ONE "FACT" YOU MADE UP.
THAT'S PLENTY. BY THE TIME WE ADD AN INTRODUCTION, A FEW ILLUSTRATIONS, AND A CONCLUSION, IT WILL LOOK LIKE A GRADUATE THESIS.
BESIDES, I'VE GOT A SECRET WEAPON THAT WILL GUARANTEE ME A GOOD GRADE! NO TEACHER CAN RESIST THIS!
WHAT IS IT?
A CLEAR PLASTIC BINDER! PRETTY PROFESSIONAL LOOKING, EH?
I DON'T WANT CO-AUTHOR CREDIT ON THIS, OK?
WATTERSON

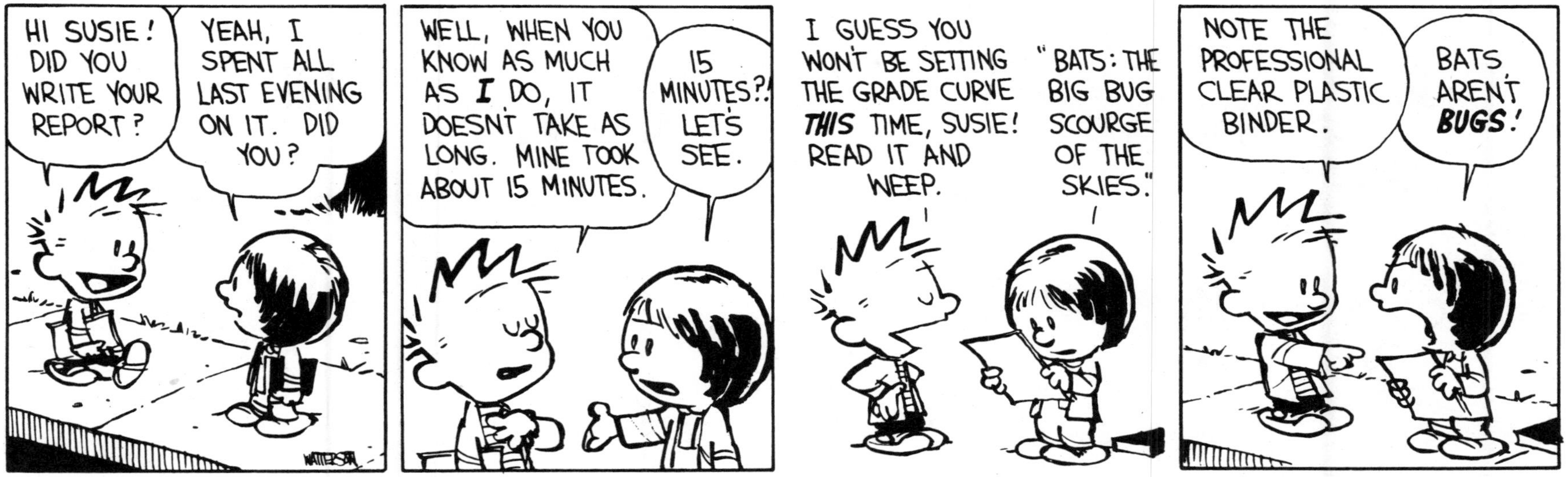
HI SUSIE! DID YOU WRITE YOUR REPORT?
YEAH, I SPENT ALL LAST EVENING ON IT. DID YOU?
WELL, WHEN YOU KNOW AS MUCH AS **I** DO, IT DOESN'T TAKE AS LONG. MINE TOOK ABOUT 15 MINUTES.
15 MINUTES?! LET'S SEE.
I GUESS YOU WON'T BE SETTING THE GRADE CURVE **THIS** TIME, SUSIE! READ IT AND WEEP.
"BATS: THE BIG BUG SCOURGE OF THE SKIES."
NOTE THE PROFESSIONAL CLEAR PLASTIC BINDER.
BATS AREN'T **BUGS**!

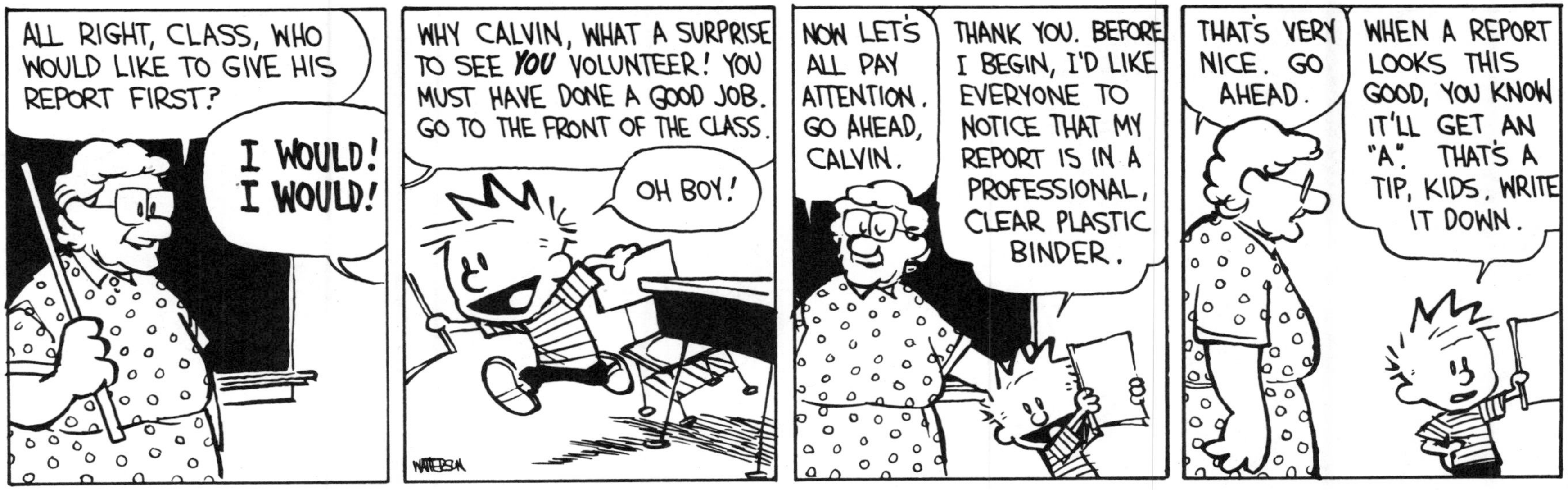
ALL RIGHT, CLASS, WHO WOULD LIKE TO GIVE HIS REPORT FIRST?
I WOULD! I WOULD!
WHY CALVIN, WHAT A SURPRISE TO SEE **YOU** VOLUNTEER! YOU MUST HAVE DONE A GOOD JOB. GO TO THE FRONT OF THE CLASS.
OH BOY!
NOW LET'S ALL PAY ATTENTION. GO AHEAD, CALVIN.
THANK YOU. BEFORE I BEGIN, I'D LIKE EVERYONE TO NOTICE THAT MY REPORT IS IN A PROFESSIONAL, CLEAR PLASTIC BINDER.
THAT'S VERY NICE. GO AHEAD.
WHEN A REPORT LOOKS THIS GOOD, YOU KNOW IT'LL GET AN "A". THAT'S A TIP, KIDS. WRITE IT DOWN.

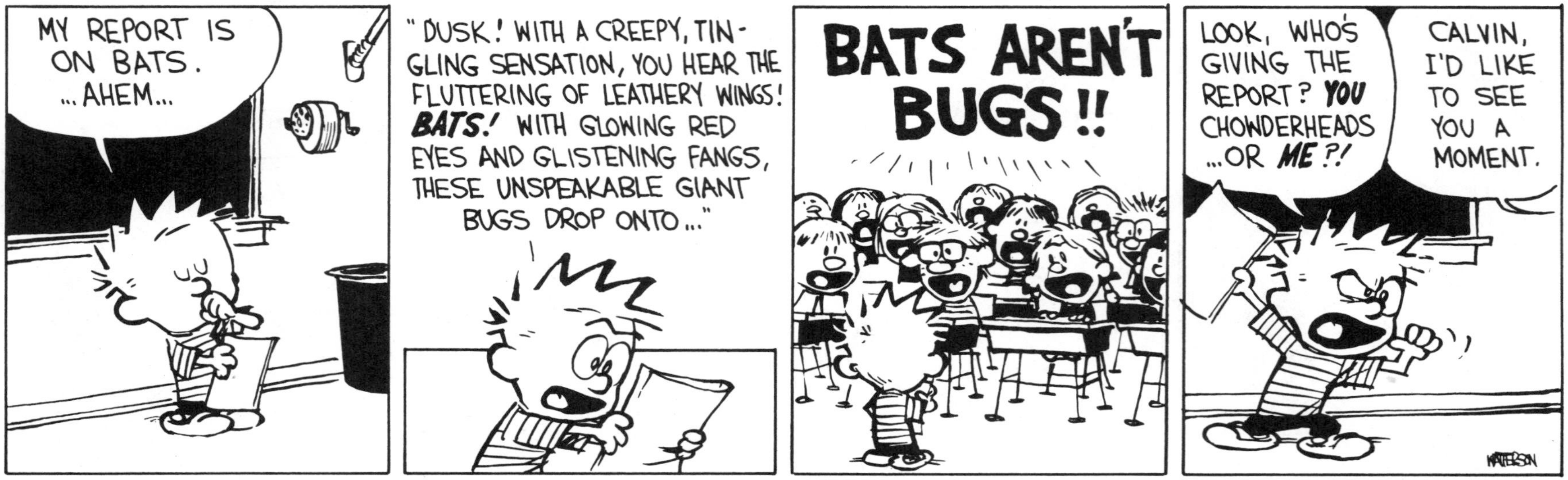
MY REPORT IS ON BATS. ...AHEM...
"DUSK! WITH A CREEPY, TINGLING SENSATION, YOU HEAR THE FLUTTERING OF LEATHERY WINGS! BATS! WITH GLOWING RED EYES AND GLISTENING FANGS, THESE UNSPEAKABLE GIANT BUGS DROP ONTO..."
BATS AREN'T BUGS!!
LOOK, WHO'S GIVING THE REPORT? YOU CHOWDERHEADS ...OR ME?!
CALVIN, I'D LIKE TO SEE YOU A MOMENT.
WATTERSON

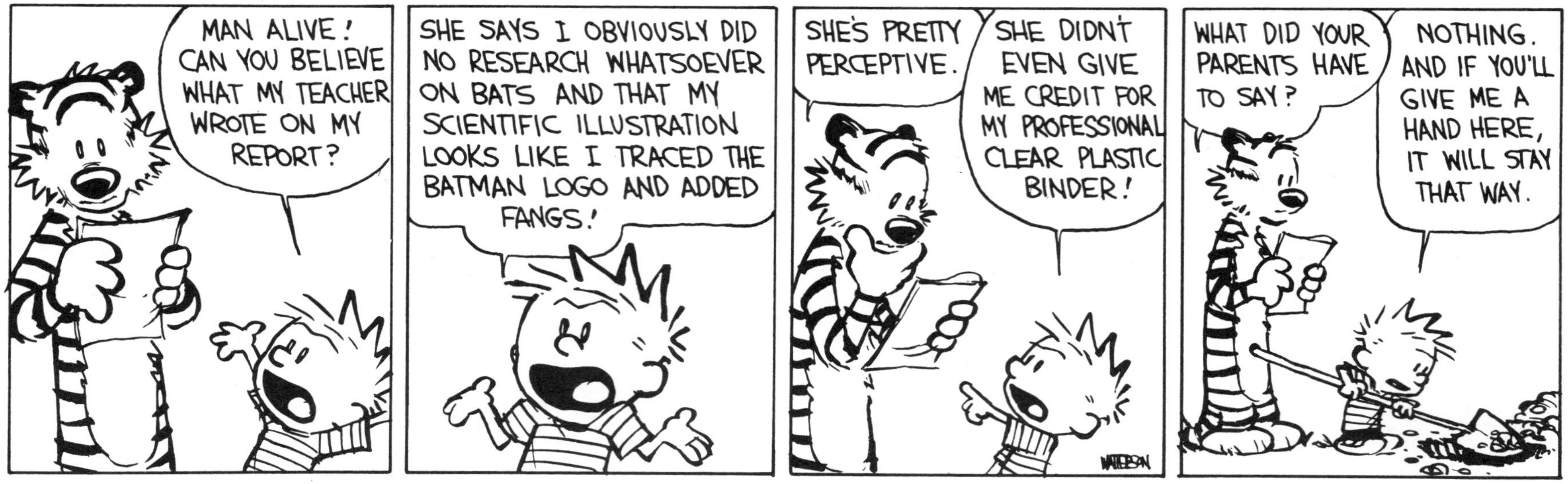
MAN ALIVE! CAN YOU BELIEVE WHAT MY TEACHER WROTE ON MY REPORT?
SHE SAYS I OBVIOUSLY DID NO RESEARCH WHATSOEVER ON BATS AND THAT MY SCIENTIFIC ILLUSTRATION LOOKS LIKE I TRACED THE BATMAN LOGO AND ADDED FANGS!
SHE'S PRETTY PERCEPTIVE.
SHE DIDN'T EVEN GIVE ME CREDIT FOR MY PROFESSIONAL CLEAR PLASTIC BINDER!
WATTERSON
WHAT DID YOUR PARENTS HAVE TO SAY?
NOTHING. AND IF YOU'LL GIVE ME A HAND HERE, IT WILL STAY THAT WAY.

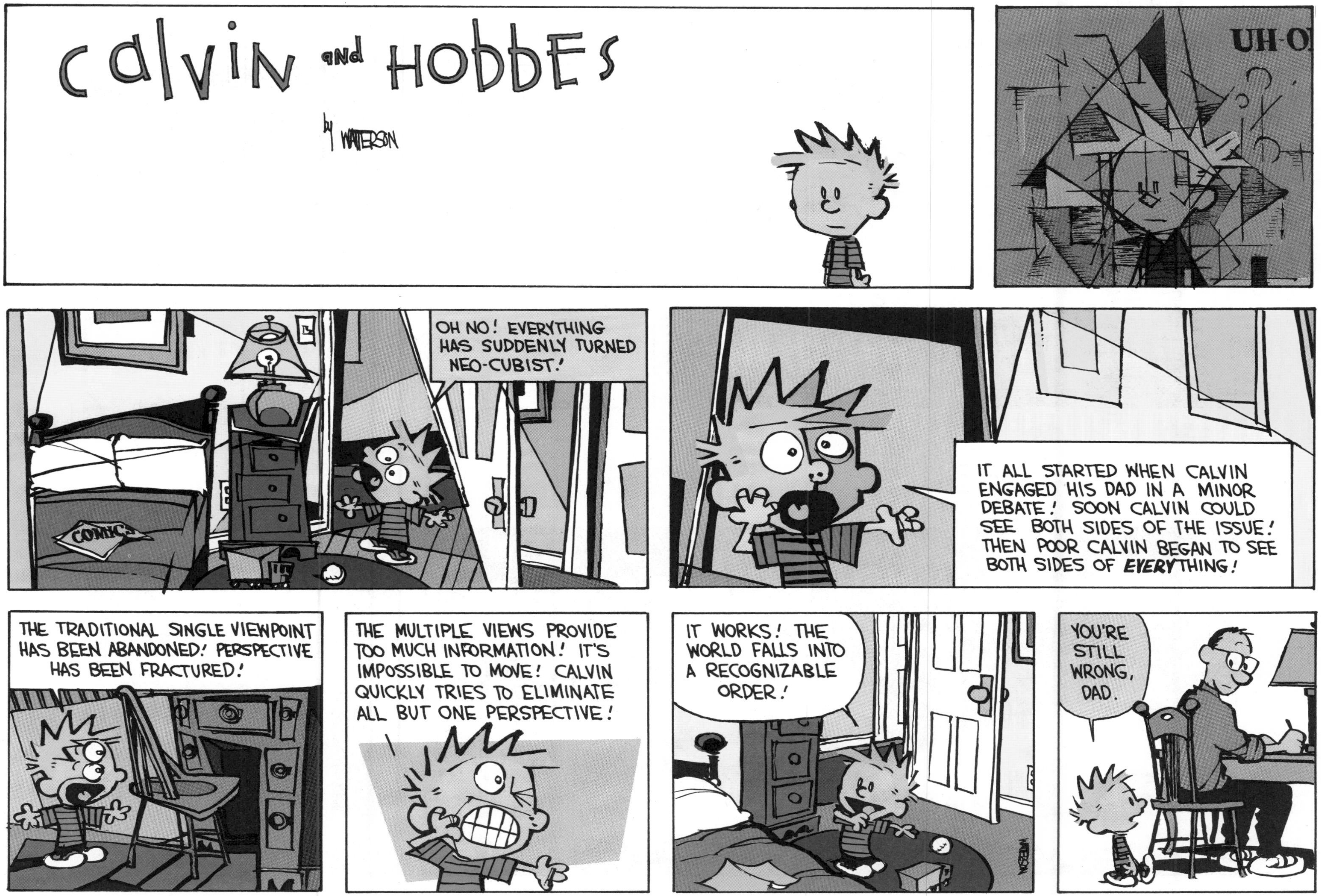
Calvin and HOBBES
by WATTERSON
UH-O
OH NO! EVERYTHING HAS SUDDENLY TURNED NEO-CUBIST!
COMICS
IT ALL STARTED WHEN CALVIN ENGAGED HIS DAD IN A MINOR DEBATE! SOON CALVIN COULD SEE BOTH SIDES OF THE ISSUE! THEN POOR CALVIN BEGAN TO SEE BOTH SIDES OF EVERYTHING!
THE TRADITIONAL SINGLE VIEWPOINT HAS BEEN ABANDONED! PERSPECTIVE HAS BEEN FRACTURED!
THE MULTIPLE VIEWS PROVIDE TOO MUCH INFORMATION! IT'S IMPOSSIBLE TO MOVE! CALVIN QUICKLY TRIES TO ELIMINATE ALL BUT ONE PERSPECTIVE!
IT WORKS! THE WORLD FALLS INTO A RECOGNIZABLE ORDER!
WATTERSON
YOU'RE STILL WRONG, DAD.

I'm often paralyzed by being able to see all sides of an issue. I worked that into my interest in art for this strip, which was a lot of fun to draw.

This is part of a story where Calvin keeps getting bigger. At this point, I stopped trying to put in humorous dialogue, and just let the pictures advance the plot. My original idea was to do this for a month and see how long readers would put up with it. I wisely chickened out, since the idea wasn't all that interesting to begin with. It's just weird for weirdness's sake, and I don't think it holds up very well.

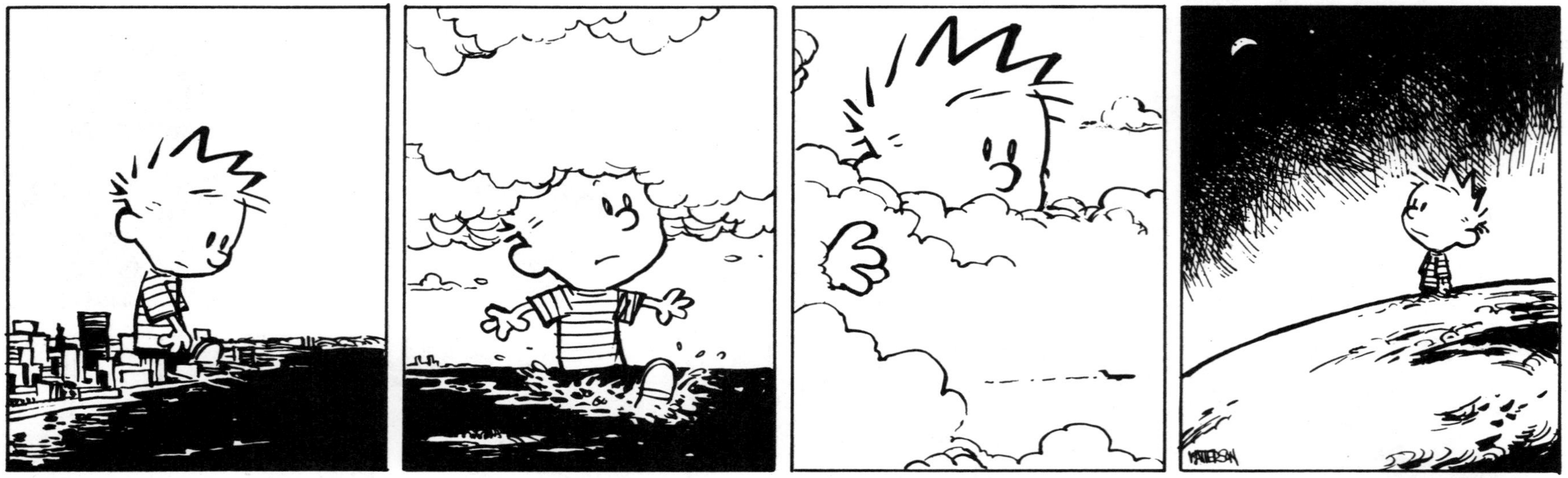

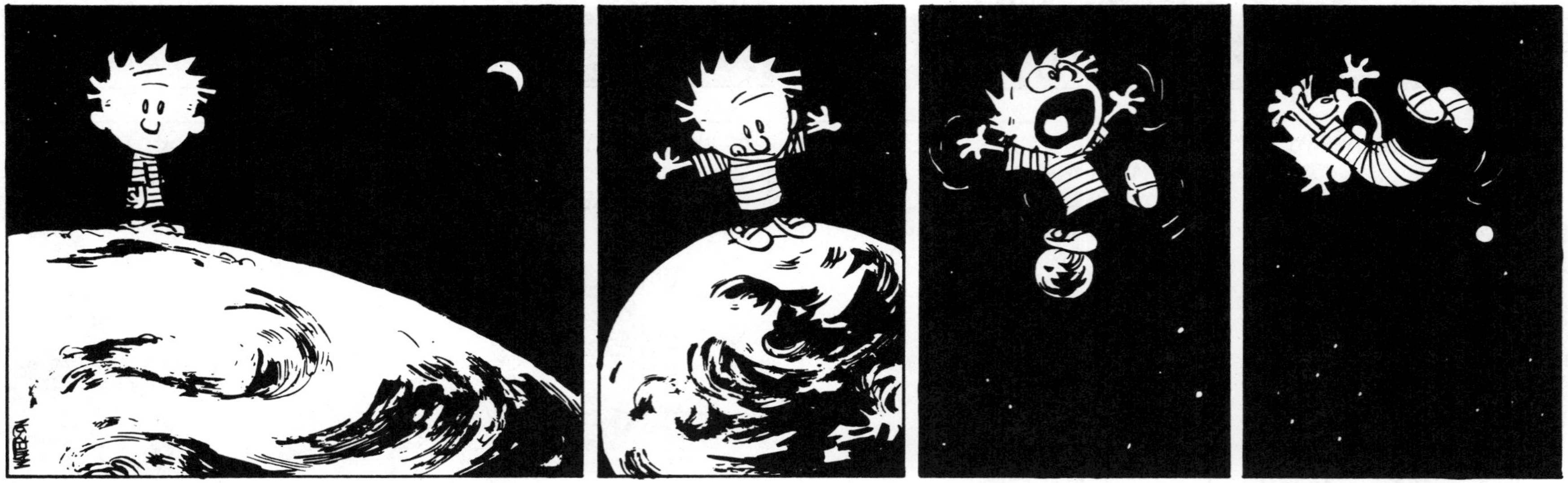

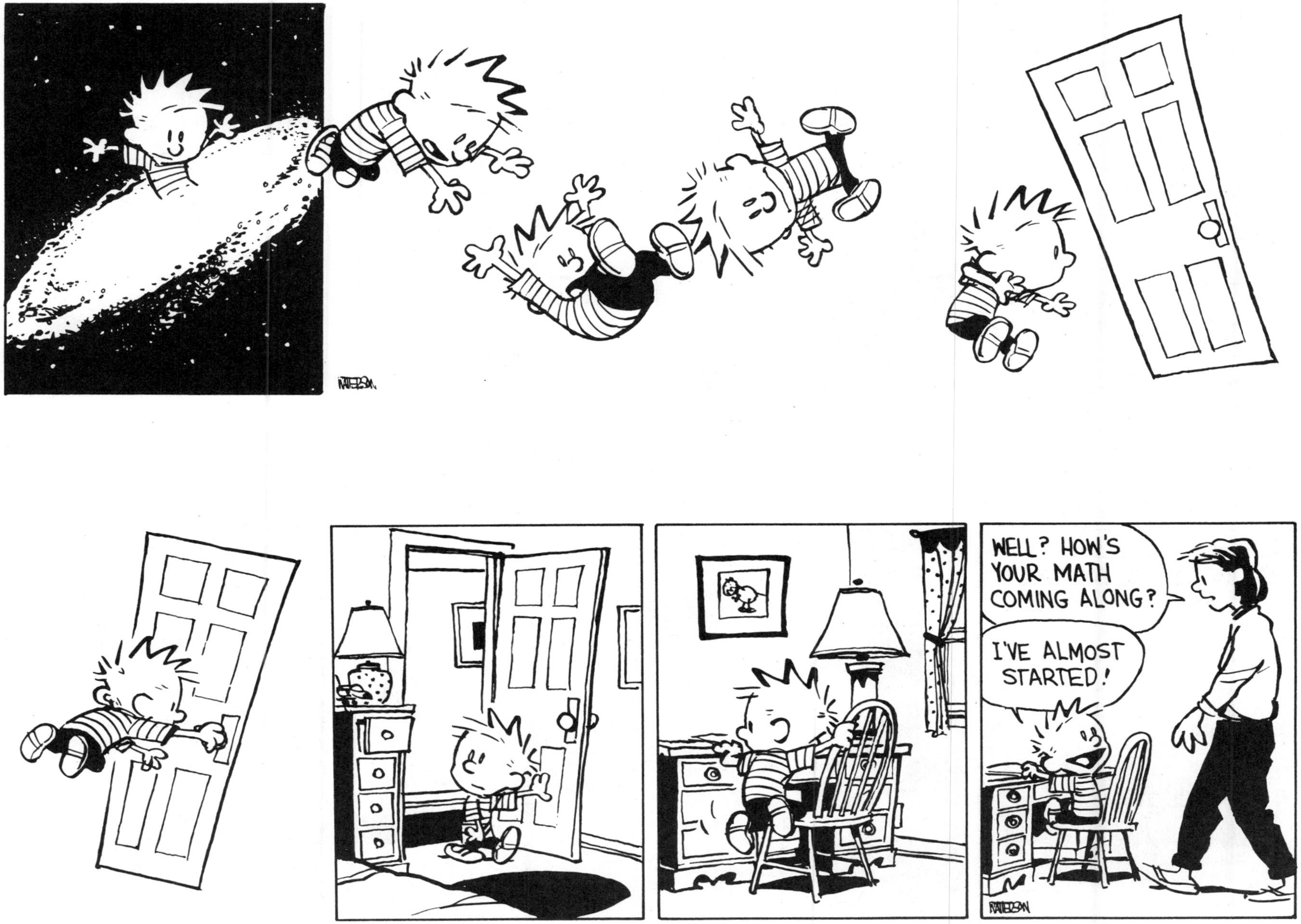
WELL? HOW'S YOUR MATH COMING ALONG?
I'VE ALMOST STARTED!

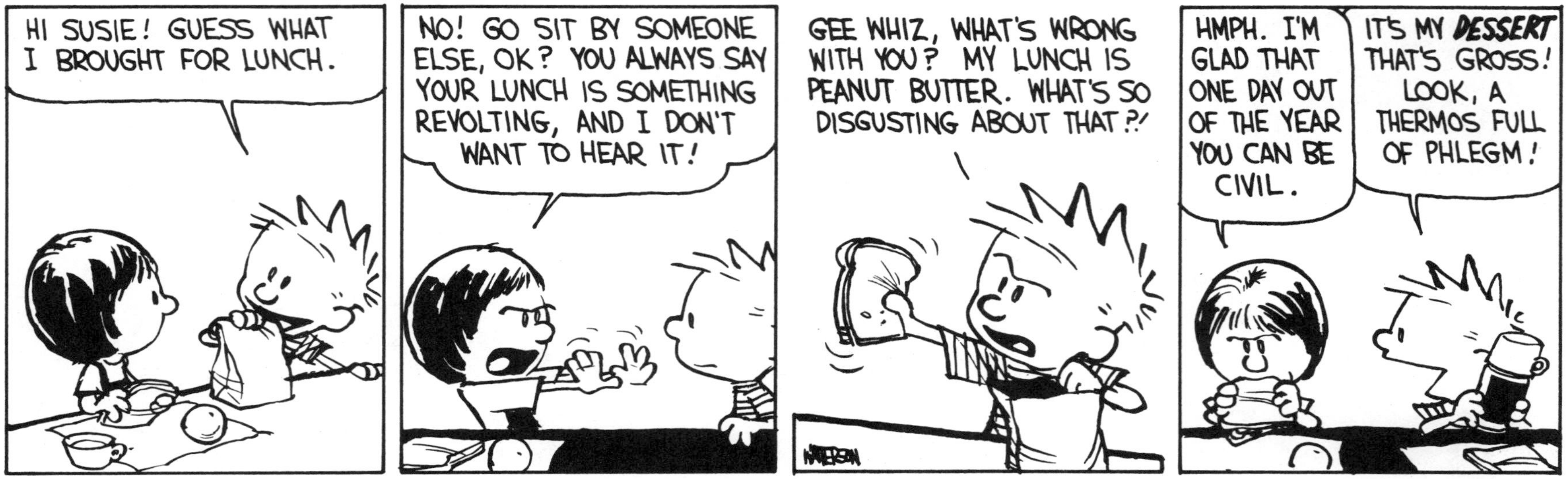
HI SUSIE! GUESS WHAT I BROUGHT FOR LUNCH.
NO! GO SIT BY SOMEONE ELSE, OK? YOU ALWAYS SAY YOUR LUNCH IS SOMETHING REVOLTING, AND I DON'T WANT TO HEAR IT!
GEE WHIZ, WHAT'S WRONG WITH YOU? MY LUNCH IS PEANUT BUTTER. WHAT'S SO DISGUSTING ABOUT THAT?!
HMPH. I'M GLAD THAT ONE DAY OUT OF THE YEAR YOU CAN BE CIVIL.
IT'S MY DESSERT THAT'S GROSS! LOOK, A THERMOS FULL OF PHLEGM!
WATTERSON

This strip got *Calvin and Hobbes* canceled from one newspaper. The paper had just picked up the strip when this example of disgusting juvenile humor appeared. Generally, I've been able to keep Calvin in newspapers longer than a week, but not this time.

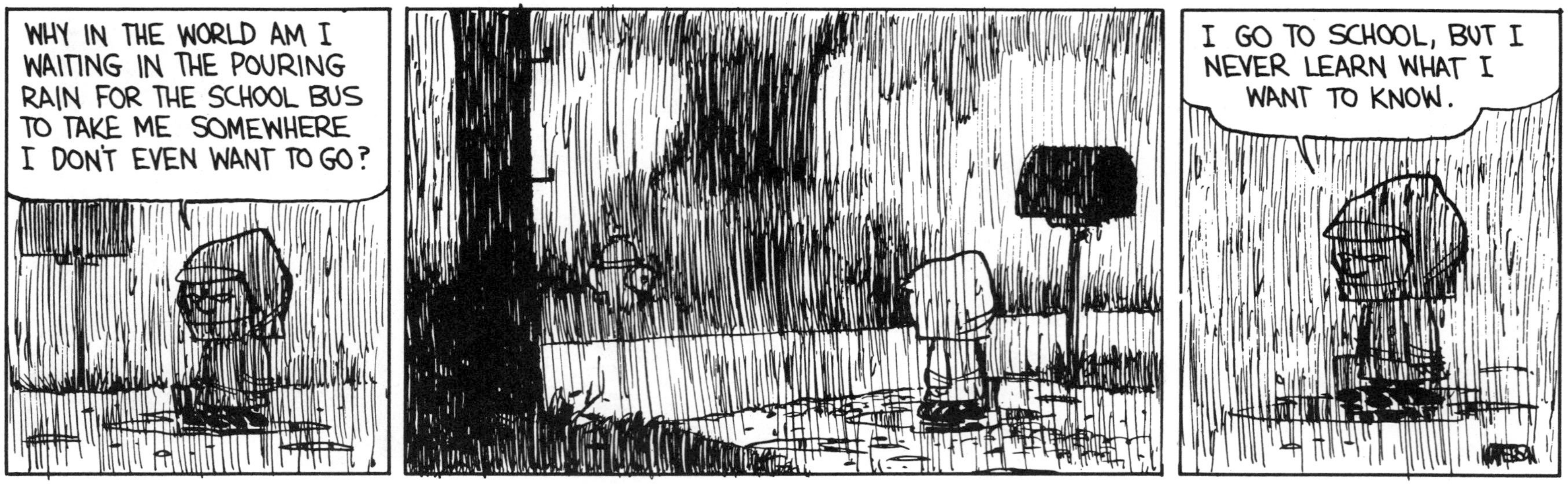
WHY IN THE WORLD AM I WAITING IN THE POURING RAIN FOR THE SCHOOL BUS TO TAKE ME SOMEWHERE I DON'T EVEN WANT TO GO?
I GO TO SCHOOL, BUT I NEVER LEARN WHAT I WANT TO KNOW.
WATTERSON

Pen and ink is not a great medium for suggesting atmospherics, but the second panel here works pretty well. Waiting for the bus in bad weather, whether going to school or a job, always seemed like adding insult to injury. Rainy days should be spent at home with a cup of tea and a good book.

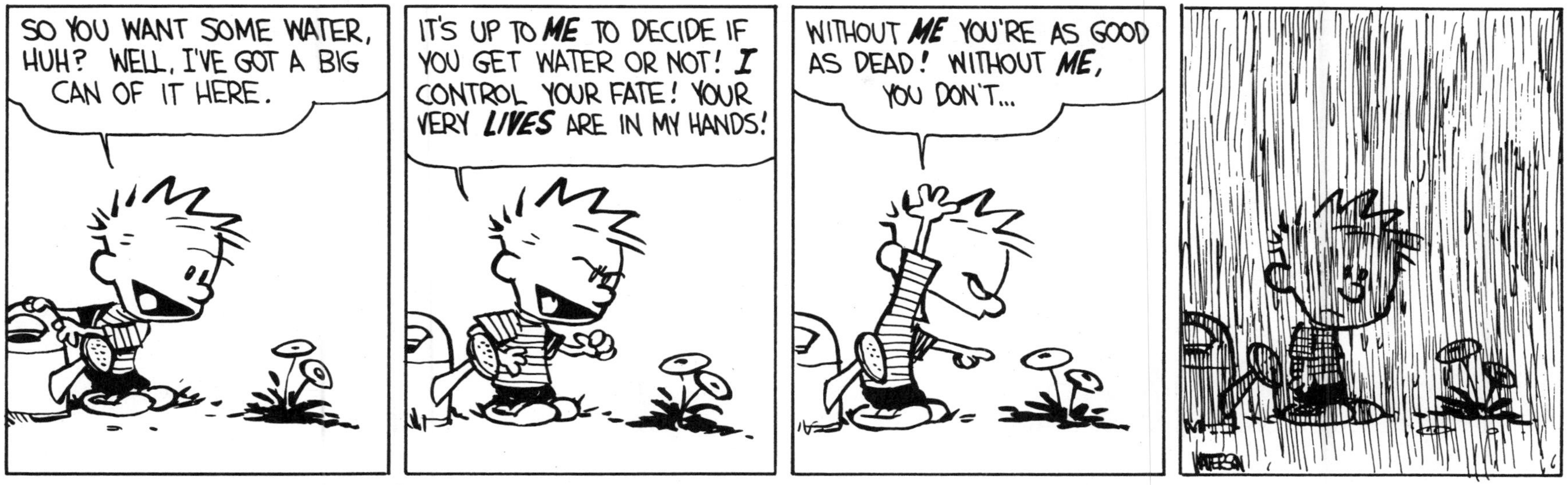
SO YOU WANT SOME WATER, HUH? WELL, I'VE GOT A BIG CAN OF IT HERE.
IT'S UP TO ME TO DECIDE IF YOU GET WATER OR NOT! I CONTROL YOUR FATE! YOUR VERY LIVES ARE IN MY HANDS!
WITHOUT ME YOU'RE AS GOOD AS DEAD! WITHOUT ME, YOU DON'T...
WATTERSON

The illusion of control.

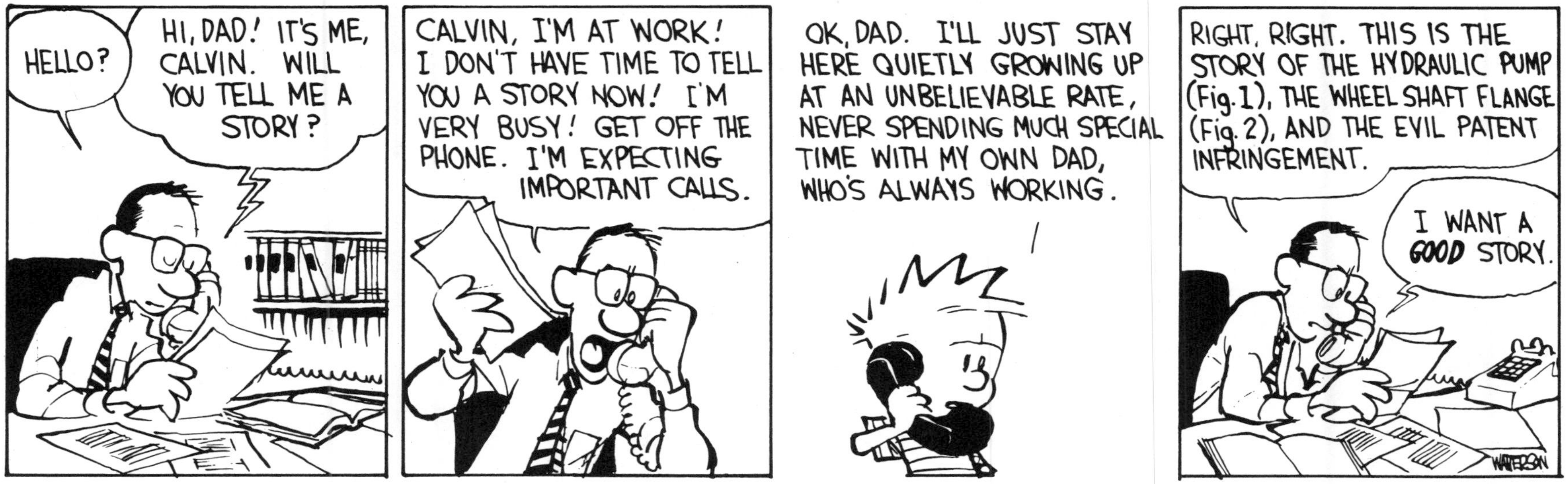
HELLO?
HI, DAD! IT'S ME, CALVIN. WILL YOU TELL ME A STORY?
CALVIN, I'M AT WORK! I DON'T HAVE TIME TO TELL YOU A STORY NOW! I'M VERY BUSY! GET OFF THE PHONE. I'M EXPECTING IMPORTANT CALLS.
OK, DAD. I'LL JUST STAY HERE QUIETLY GROWING UP AT AN UNBELIEVABLE RATE, NEVER SPENDING MUCH SPECIAL TIME WITH MY OWN DAD, WHO'S ALWAYS WORKING.
RIGHT, RIGHT. THIS IS THE STORY OF THE HYDRAULIC PUMP (Fig. 1), THE WHEEL SHAFT FLANGE (Fig. 2), AND THE EVIL PATENT INFRINGEMENT.
I WANT A GOOD STORY.
WATTERSON

Most cartoon characters have a generic white collar job, but eventually I decided that Calvin's dad, like my dad, is a patent attorney. I think it's funnier when things are specific, rather than generalized.

CALVIN'S WAGON

Calvin's wagon is a simple device to add some physical comedy to the strip, and I most often use it when Calvin gets longwinded or philosophical. I think the action lends a silly counterpoint to the text, and it's a lot more interesting to draw than talking heads. Sometimes the wagon ride even acts as a visual metaphor for Calvin's topic of discussion.

Calvin rides the wagon through the woods, bouncing off rocks and flying over ravines. When I was a kid, our backyard dropped off into a big woods, but it was brambly and swampy, not like Calvin's, which seems to be more like a national forest. I was not a real outdoorsy kid, but occasionally I'd tramp out through the brush to map a pond, or to try to see unusual birds and animals. Calvin's woods is important to the strip, because it's the place where Calvin and Hobbes can get away from everyone and be themselves. The solitude of the woods brings out Calvin's small, but redeeming, contemplative side.

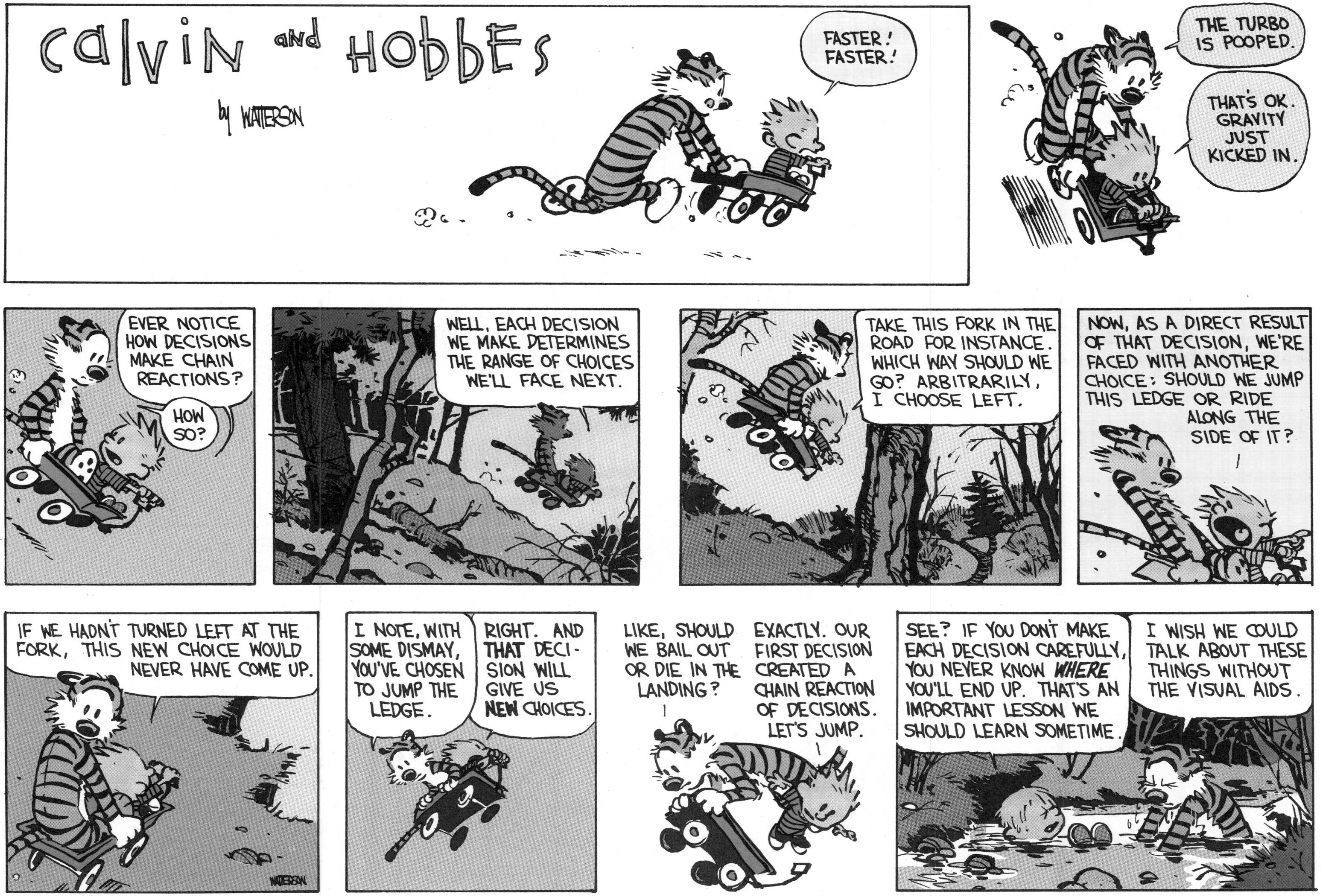

Calvin and HOBBES
by WATTERSON
FASTER! FASTER!
THE TURBO IS POOPED.
THAT'S OK. GRAVITY JUST KICKED IN.
EVER NOTICE HOW DECISIONS MAKE CHAIN REACTIONS?
HOW SO?
WELL, EACH DECISION WE MAKE DETERMINES THE RANGE OF CHOICES WE'LL FACE NEXT.
TAKE THIS FORK IN THE ROAD FOR INSTANCE. WHICH WAY SHOULD WE GO? ARBITRARILY, I CHOOSE LEFT.
NOW, AS A DIRECT RESULT OF THAT DECISION, WE'RE FACED WITH ANOTHER CHOICE: SHOULD WE JUMP THIS LEDGE OR RIDE ALONG THE SIDE OF IT?
IF WE HADN'T TURNED LEFT AT THE FORK, THIS NEW CHOICE WOULD NEVER HAVE COME UP.
WATTERSON
I NOTE, WITH SOME DISMAY, YOU'VE CHOSEN TO JUMP THE LEDGE.
RIGHT. AND **THAT** DECI-SION WILL GIVE US **NEW** CHOICES.
LIKE, SHOULD WE BAIL OUT OR DIE IN THE LANDING?
EXACTLY. OUR FIRST DECISION CREATED A CHAIN REACTION OF DECISIONS. LET'S JUMP.
SEE? IF YOU DON'T MAKE EACH DECISION CAREFULLY, YOU NEVER KNOW ***WHERE*** YOU'LL END UP. THAT'S AN IMPORTANT LESSON WE SHOULD LEARN SOMETIME.
I WISH WE COULD TALK ABOUT THESE THINGS WITHOUT THE VISUAL AIDS.

For some reason, when I watch my cats sleep, poems spring to mind.

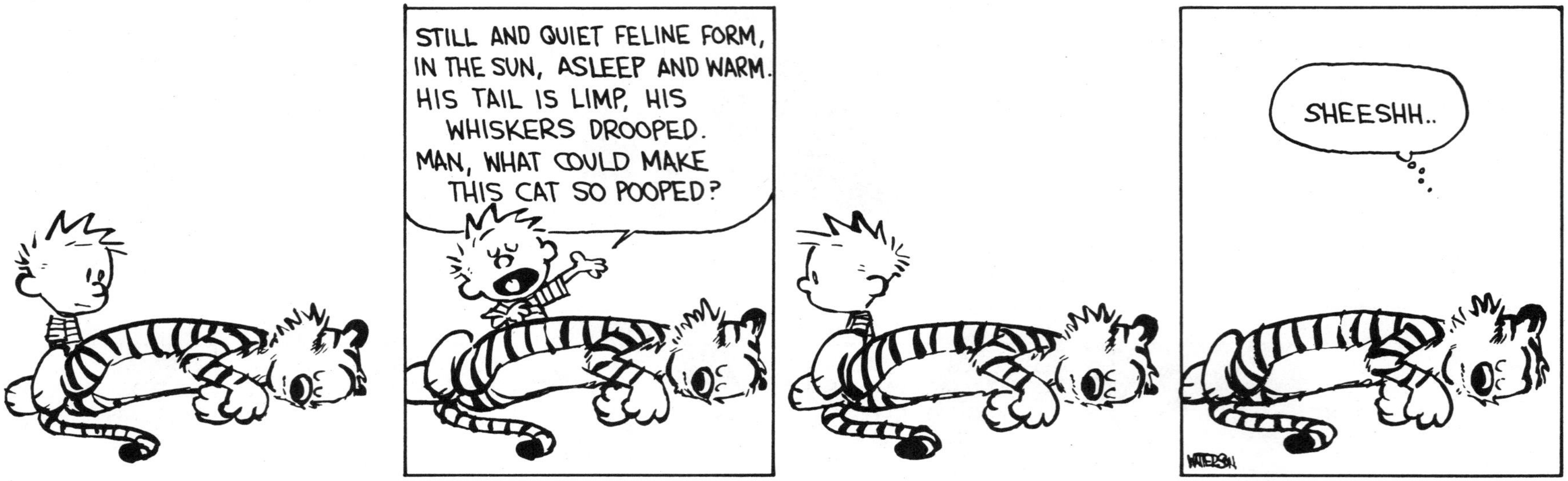

STILL AND QUIET FELINE FORM,
IN THE SUN, ASLEEP AND WARM.
HIS TAIL IS LIMP, HIS WHISKERS DROOPED.
MAN, WHAT COULD MAKE THIS CAT SO POOPED?
SHEESHH..

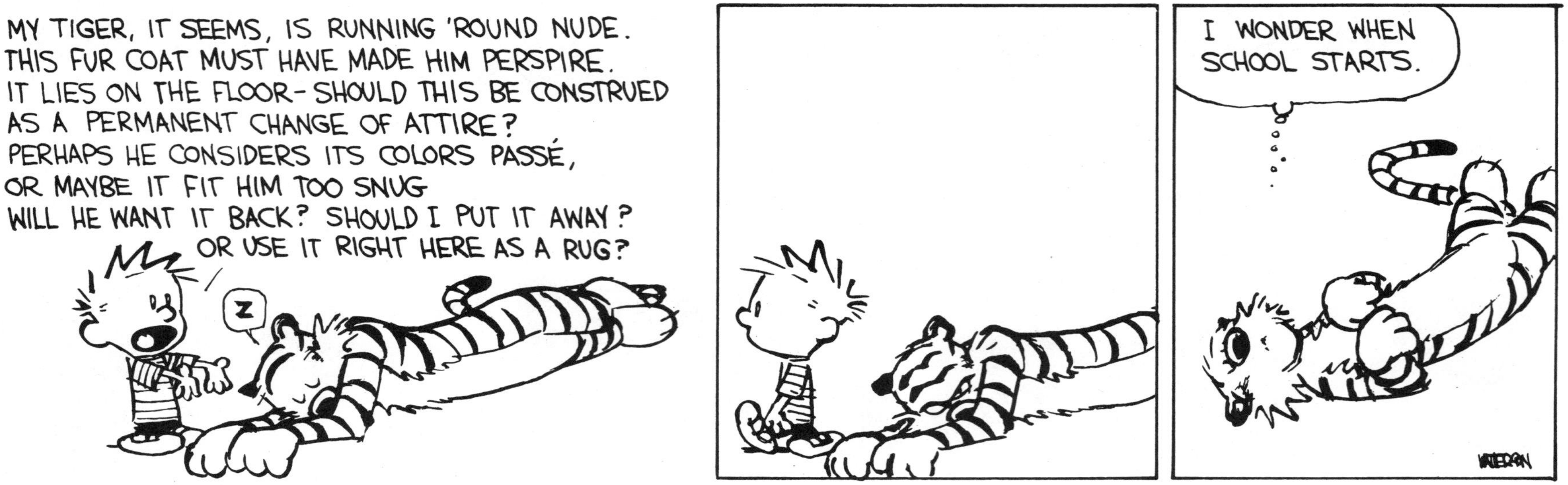

MY TIGER, IT SEEMS, IS RUNNING 'ROUND NUDE.
THIS FUR COAT MUST HAVE MADE HIM PERSPIRE.
IT LIES ON THE FLOOR- SHOULD THIS BE CONSTRUED
AS A PERMANENT CHANGE OF ATTIRE?
PERHAPS HE CONSIDERS ITS COLORS PASSÉ,
OR MAYBE IT FIT HIM TOO SNUG
WILL HE WANT IT BACK? SHOULD I PUT IT AWAY?
OR USE IT RIGHT HERE AS A RUG?
Z
I WONDER WHEN SCHOOL STARTS.

My dad and I still have this relationship, but I like to think I go a little easier on my mom now.

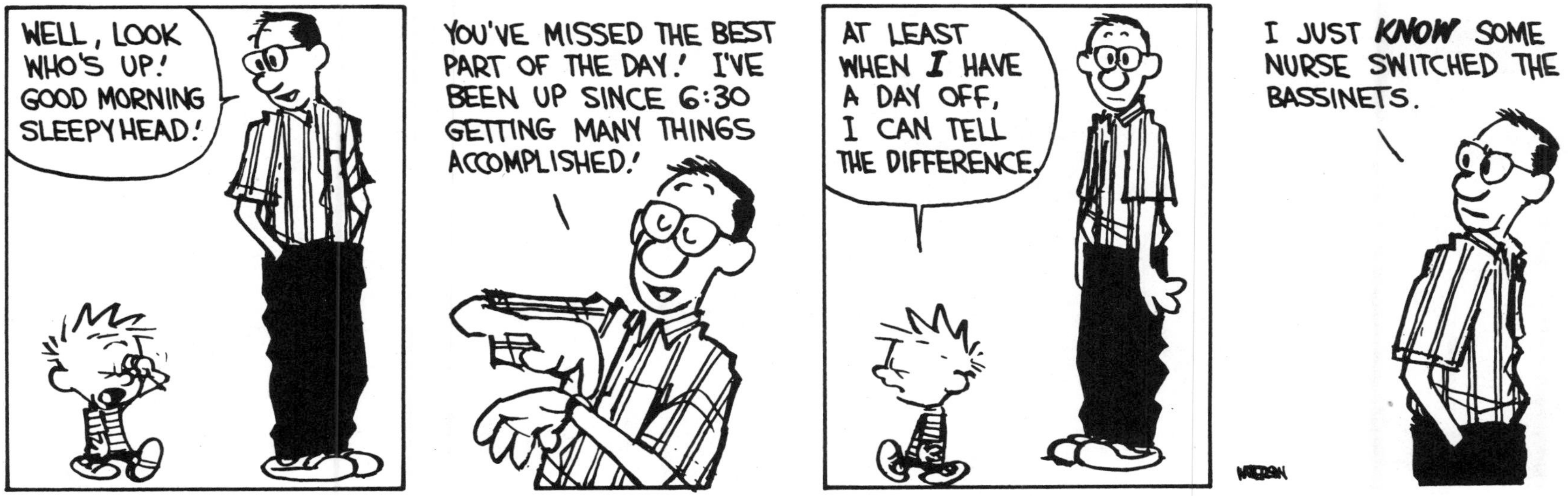
WELL, LOOK WHO'S UP! GOOD MORNING SLEEPYHEAD!
YOU'VE MISSED THE BEST PART OF THE DAY! I'VE BEEN UP SINCE 6:30 GETTING MANY THINGS ACCOMPLISHED!
AT LEAST WHEN I HAVE A DAY OFF, I CAN TELL THE DIFFERENCE.
I JUST KNOW SOME NURSE SWITCHED THE BASSINETS.

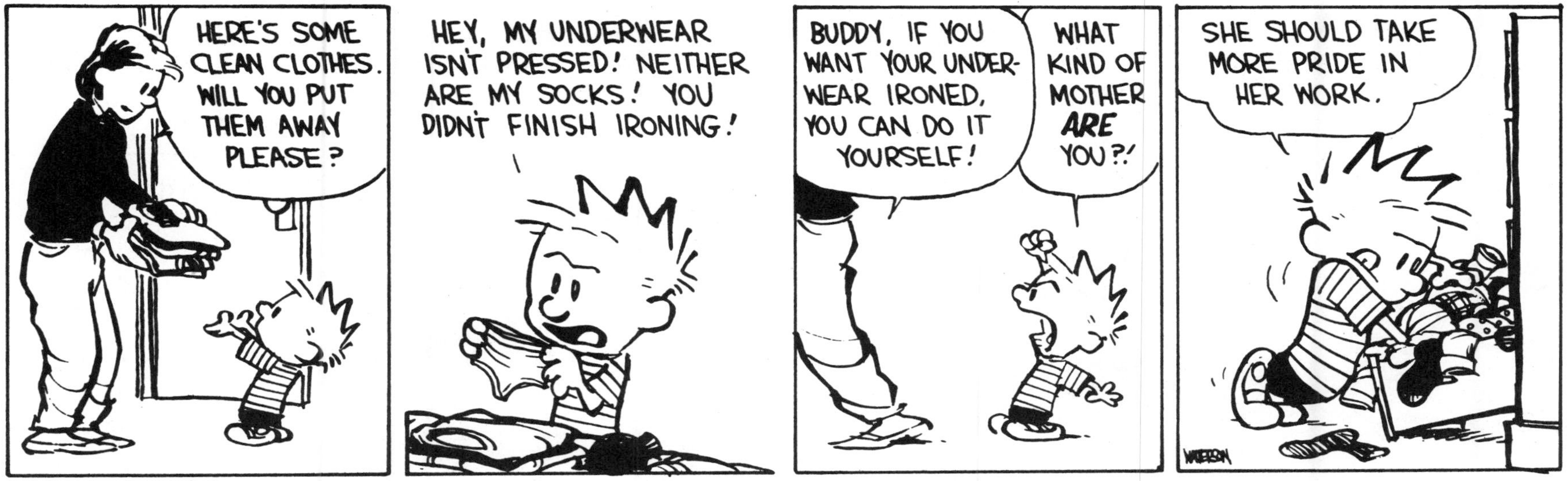
HERE'S SOME CLEAN CLOTHES. WILL YOU PUT THEM AWAY PLEASE?
HEY, MY UNDERWEAR ISN'T PRESSED! NEITHER ARE MY SOCKS! YOU DIDN'T FINISH IRONING!
BUDDY, IF YOU WANT YOUR UNDERWEAR IRONED, YOU CAN DO IT YOURSELF!
WHAT KIND OF MOTHER ARE YOU?!
SHE SHOULD TAKE MORE PRIDE IN HER WORK.

I never write stories with the ending in mind, because I want the story to develop a life of its own, and I want the resolution of the dilemma to surprise me. Sometimes I really get myself stuck that way. This story spun completely out of control and surprised me throughout, so it's one of my favorites. I think most of us would be horrified to meet ourselves and discover what everyone else already knows about us.

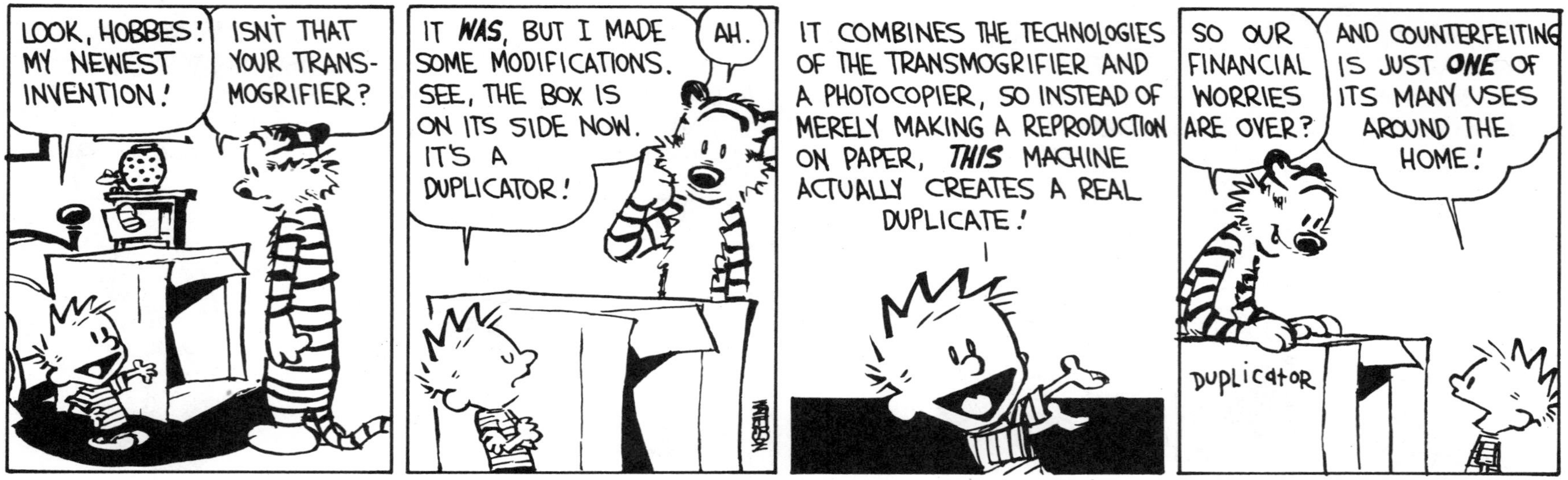
LOOK, HOBBES! MY NEWEST INVENTION!
ISN'T THAT YOUR TRANSMOGRIFIER?
IT WAS, BUT I MADE SOME MODIFICATIONS. SEE, THE BOX IS ON ITS SIDE NOW. IT'S A DUPLICATOR!
AH.
IT COMBINES THE TECHNOLOGIES OF THE TRANSMOGRIFIER AND A PHOTOCOPIER, SO INSTEAD OF MERELY MAKING A REPRODUCTION ON PAPER, THIS MACHINE ACTUALLY CREATES A REAL DUPLICATE!
SO OUR FINANCIAL WORRIES ARE OVER?
AND COUNTERFEITING IS JUST ONE OF ITS MANY USES AROUND THE HOME!
DUPLICATOR

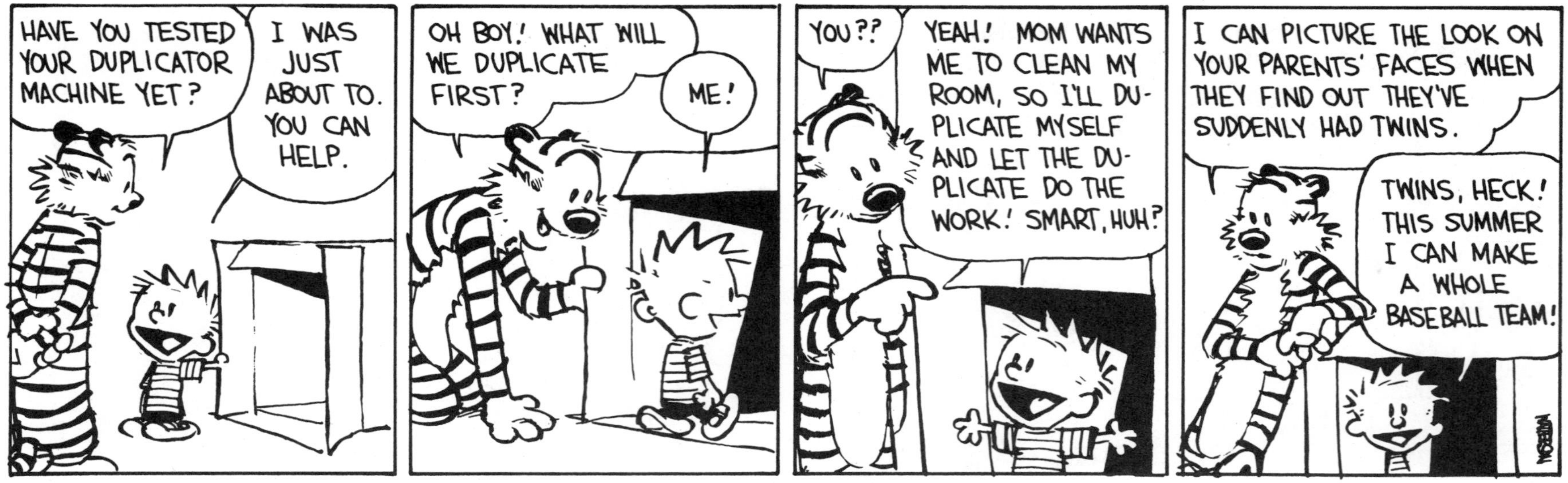
HAVE YOU TESTED YOUR DUPLICATOR MACHINE YET?
I WAS JUST ABOUT TO. YOU CAN HELP.
OH BOY! WHAT WILL WE DUPLICATE FIRST?
ME!
YOU??
YEAH! MOM WANTS ME TO CLEAN MY ROOM, SO I'LL DUPLICATE MYSELF AND LET THE DUPLICATE DO THE WORK! SMART, HUH?
I CAN PICTURE THE LOOK ON YOUR PARENTS' FACES WHEN THEY FIND OUT THEY'VE SUDDENLY HAD TWINS.
TWINS, HECK! THIS SUMMER I CAN MAKE A WHOLE BASEBALL TEAM!

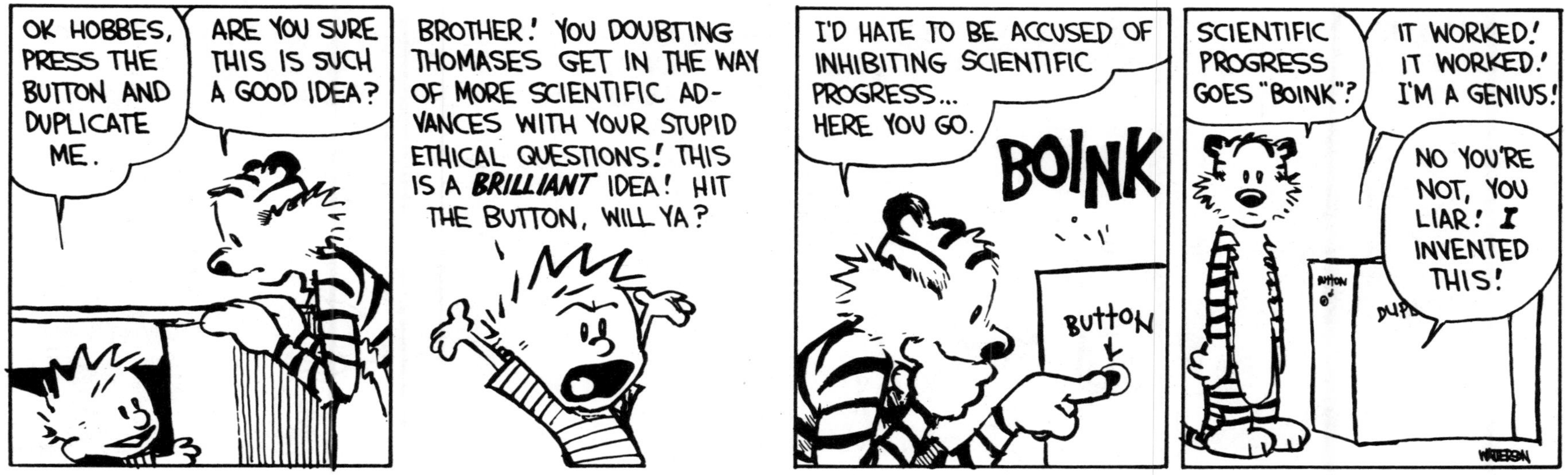
OK HOBBES, PRESS THE BUTTON AND DUPLICATE ME.
ARE YOU SURE THIS IS SUCH A GOOD IDEA?
BROTHER! YOU DOUBTING THOMASES GET IN THE WAY OF MORE SCIENTIFIC ADVANCES WITH YOUR STUPID ETHICAL QUESTIONS! THIS IS A **BRILLIANT** IDEA! HIT THE BUTTON, WILL YA?
I'D HATE TO BE ACCUSED OF INHIBITING SCIENTIFIC PROGRESS... HERE YOU GO.
BOINK
BUTTON
SCIENTIFIC PROGRESS GOES "BOINK"?
IT WORKED! IT WORKED! I'M A GENIUS!
NO YOU'RE NOT, YOU LIAR! **I** INVENTED THIS!

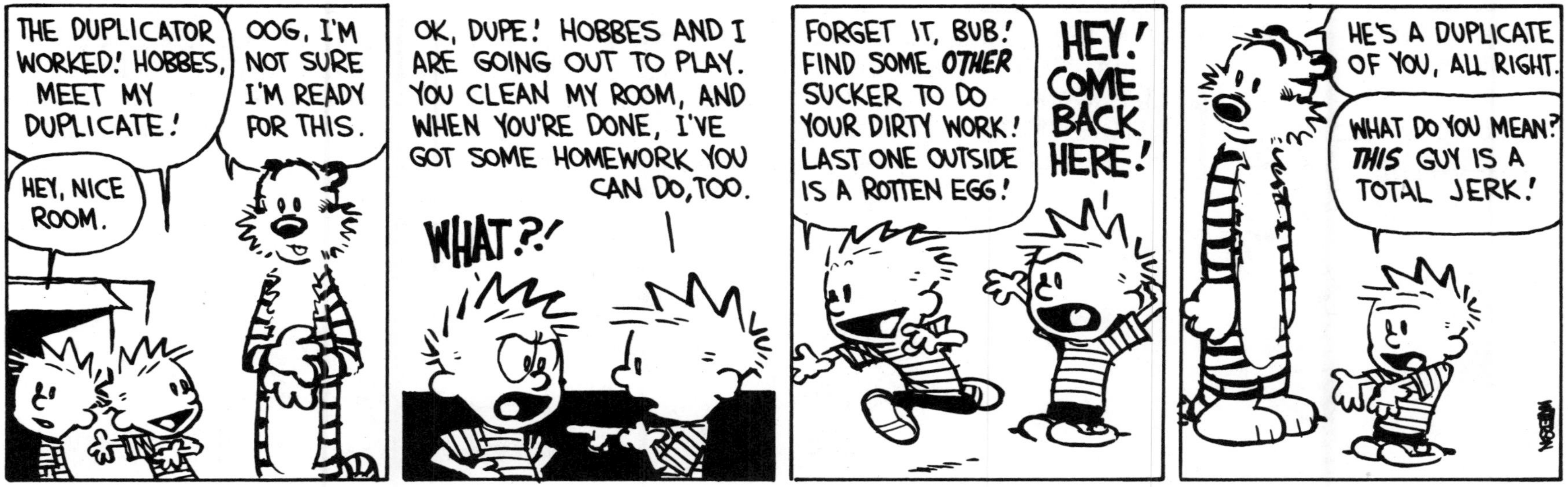
THE DUPLICATOR WORKED! HOBBES, MEET MY DUPLICATE!
OOG. I'M NOT SURE I'M READY FOR THIS.
HEY, NICE ROOM.
OK, DUPE! HOBBES AND I ARE GOING OUT TO PLAY. YOU CLEAN MY ROOM, AND WHEN YOU'RE DONE, I'VE GOT SOME HOMEWORK YOU CAN DO, TOO.
WHAT?!
FORGET IT, BUB! FIND SOME **OTHER** SUCKER TO DO YOUR DIRTY WORK! LAST ONE OUTSIDE IS A ROTTEN EGG!
HEY! COME BACK HERE!
HE'S A DUPLICATE OF YOU, ALL RIGHT.
WHAT DO YOU MEAN? **THIS** GUY IS A TOTAL JERK!

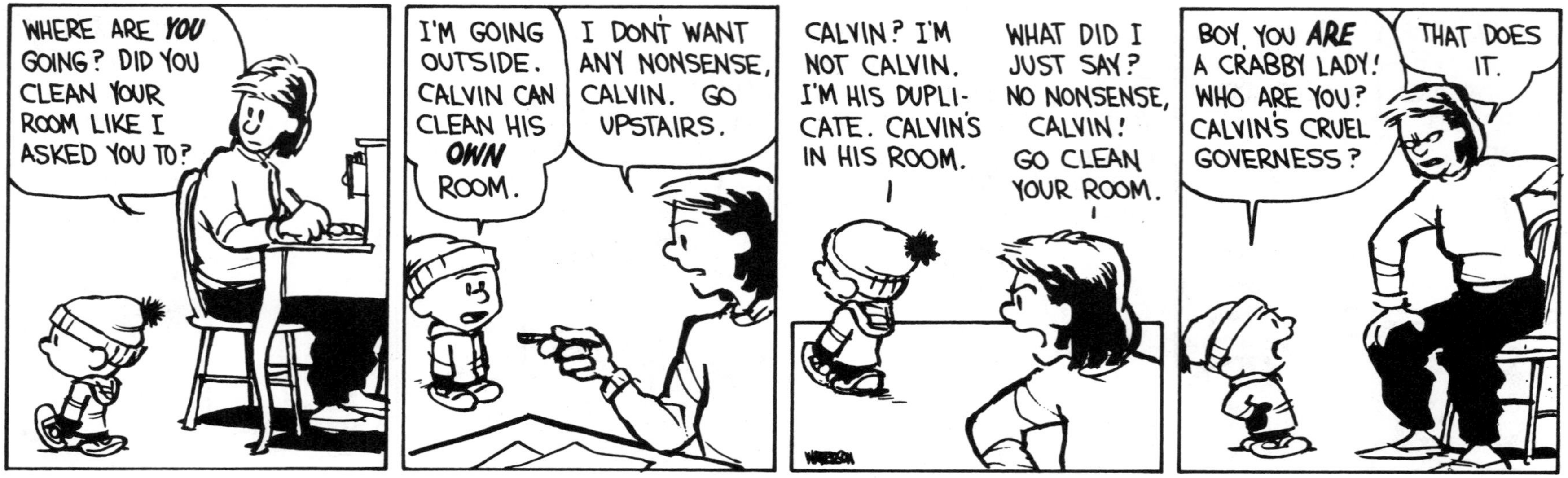
WHERE ARE **YOU** GOING? DID YOU CLEAN YOUR ROOM LIKE I ASKED YOU TO?
I'M GOING OUTSIDE. CALVIN CAN CLEAN HIS **OWN** ROOM.
I DON'T WANT ANY NONSENSE, CALVIN. GO UPSTAIRS.
CALVIN? I'M NOT CALVIN. I'M HIS DUPLICATE. CALVIN'S IN HIS ROOM.
WHAT DID I JUST SAY? NO NONSENSE, CALVIN! GO CLEAN YOUR ROOM.
BOY, YOU **ARE** A CRABBY LADY! WHO ARE YOU? CALVIN'S CRUEL GOVERNESS?
THAT DOES IT.

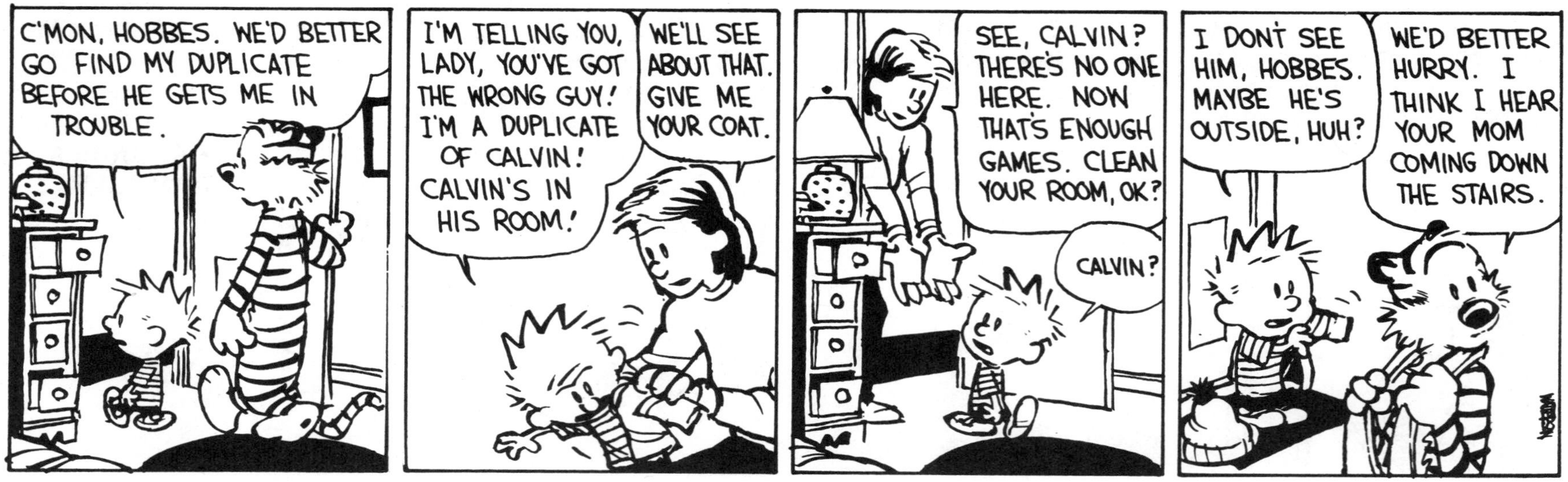
C'MON, HOBBES. WE'D BETTER GO FIND MY DUPLICATE BEFORE HE GETS ME IN TROUBLE.
I'M TELLING YOU, LADY, YOU'VE GOT THE WRONG GUY! I'M A DUPLICATE OF CALVIN! CALVIN'S IN HIS ROOM!
WE'LL SEE ABOUT THAT. GIVE ME YOUR COAT.
SEE, CALVIN? THERE'S NO ONE HERE. NOW THAT'S ENOUGH GAMES. CLEAN YOUR ROOM, OK?
CALVIN?
I DON'T SEE HIM, HOBBES. MAYBE HE'S OUTSIDE, HUH?
WE'D BETTER HURRY. I THINK I HEAR YOUR MOM COMING DOWN THE STAIRS.

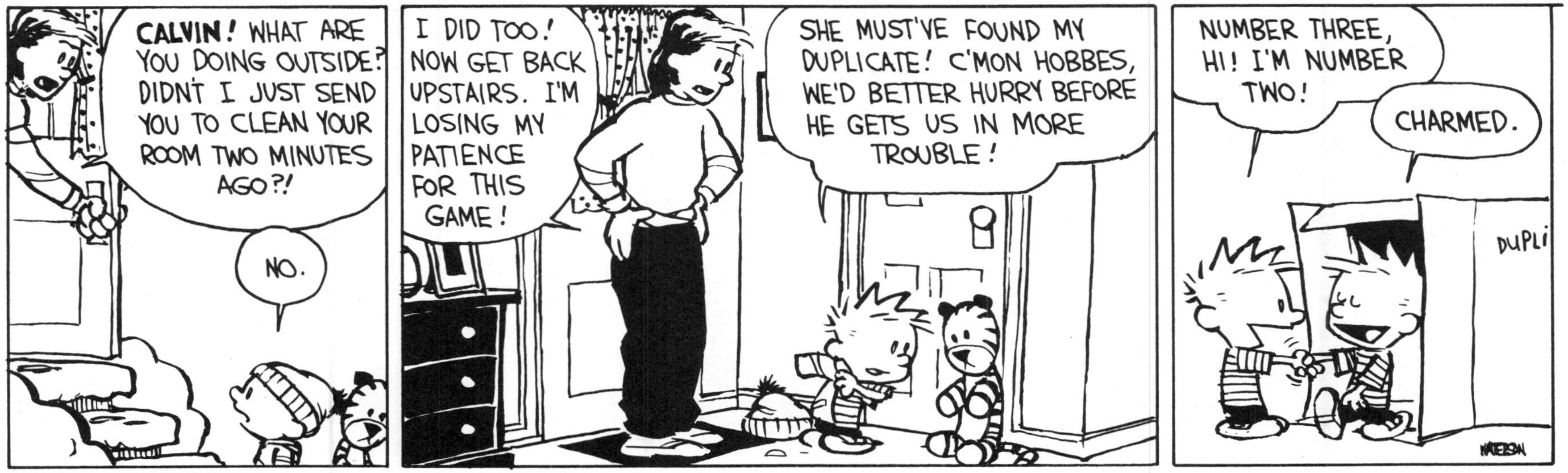
CALVIN! WHAT ARE YOU DOING OUTSIDE? DIDN'T I JUST SEND YOU TO CLEAN YOUR ROOM TWO MINUTES AGO?!
NO.
I DID TOO! NOW GET BACK UPSTAIRS. I'M LOSING MY PATIENCE FOR THIS GAME!
SHE MUST'VE FOUND MY DUPLICATE! C'MON HOBBES, WE'D BETTER HURRY BEFORE HE GETS US IN MORE TROUBLE!
NUMBER THREE, HI! I'M NUMBER TWO!
CHARMED.
DUPLI
WATERSON

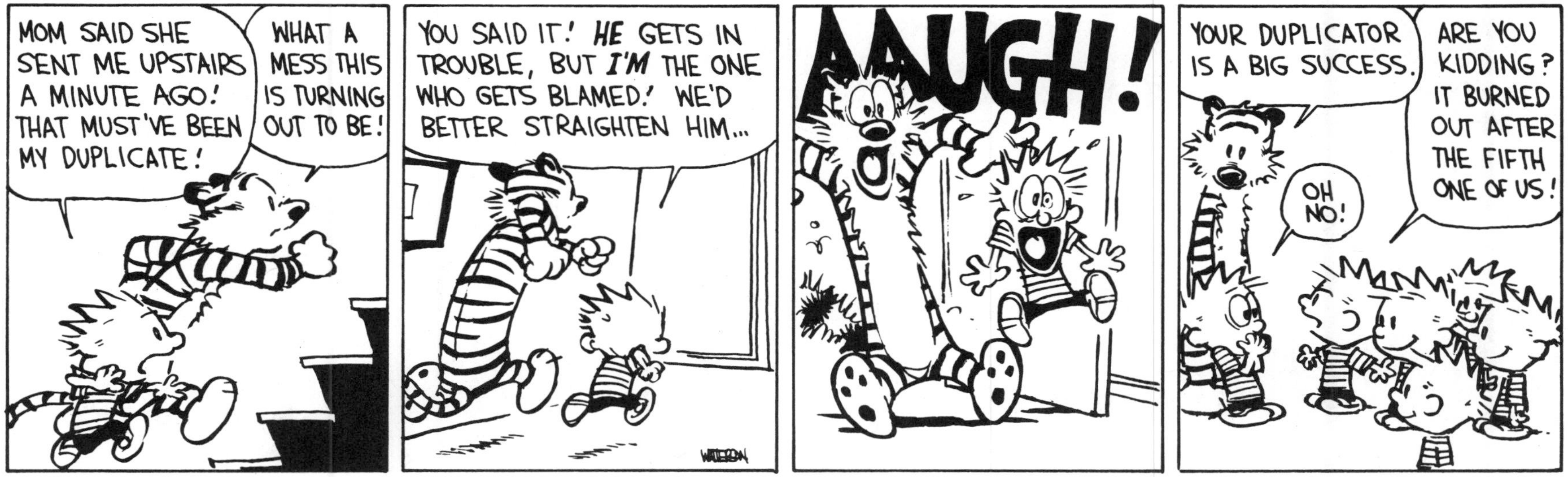
MOM SAID SHE SENT ME UPSTAIRS A MINUTE AGO! THAT MUST'VE BEEN MY DUPLICATE!
WHAT A MESS THIS IS TURNING OUT TO BE!
YOU SAID IT! HE GETS IN TROUBLE, BUT I'M THE ONE WHO GETS BLAMED! WE'D BETTER STRAIGHTEN HIM...
WATERSON
AAUGH!
YOUR DUPLICATOR IS A BIG SUCCESS.
ARE YOU KIDDING? IT BURNED OUT AFTER THE FIFTH ONE OF US!
OH NO!

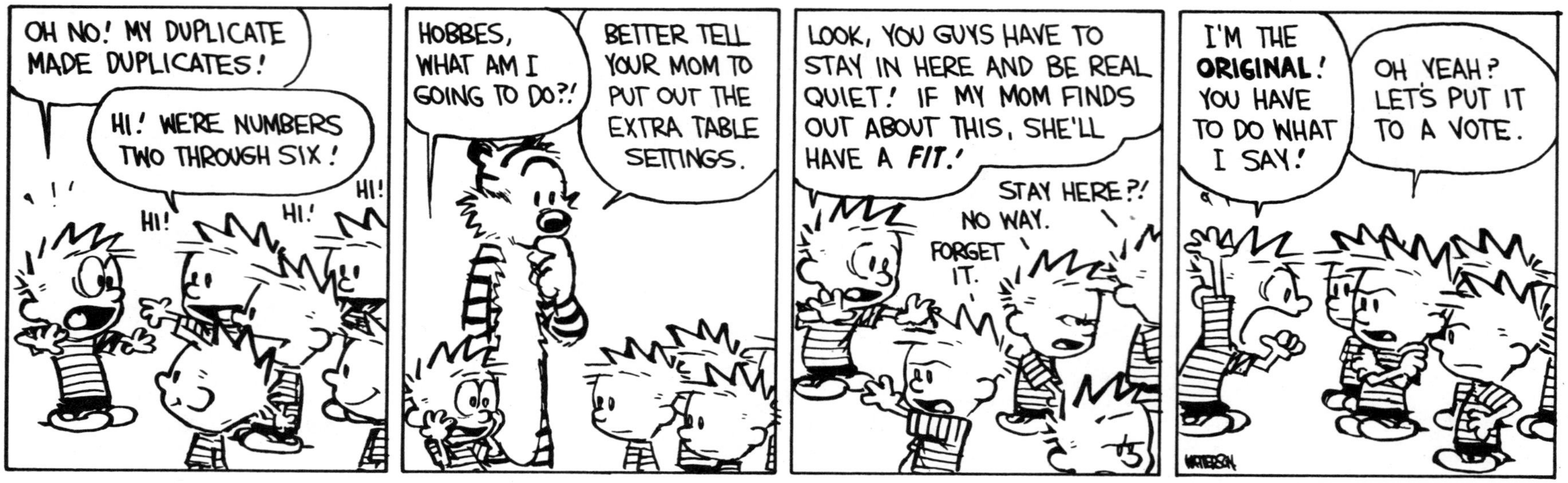
OH NO! MY DUPLICATE MADE DUPLICATES!
HI! WE'RE NUMBERS TWO THROUGH SIX!
HI!
HI!
HI!
HOBBES, WHAT AM I GOING TO DO?!
BETTER TELL YOUR MOM TO PUT OUT THE EXTRA TABLE SETTINGS.
LOOK, YOU GUYS HAVE TO STAY IN HERE AND BE REAL QUIET! IF MY MOM FINDS OUT ABOUT THIS, SHE'LL HAVE A **FIT**!
STAY HERE?!
NO WAY.
FORGET IT.
I'M THE **ORIGINAL**! YOU HAVE TO DO WHAT I SAY!
OH YEAH? LET'S PUT IT TO A VOTE.

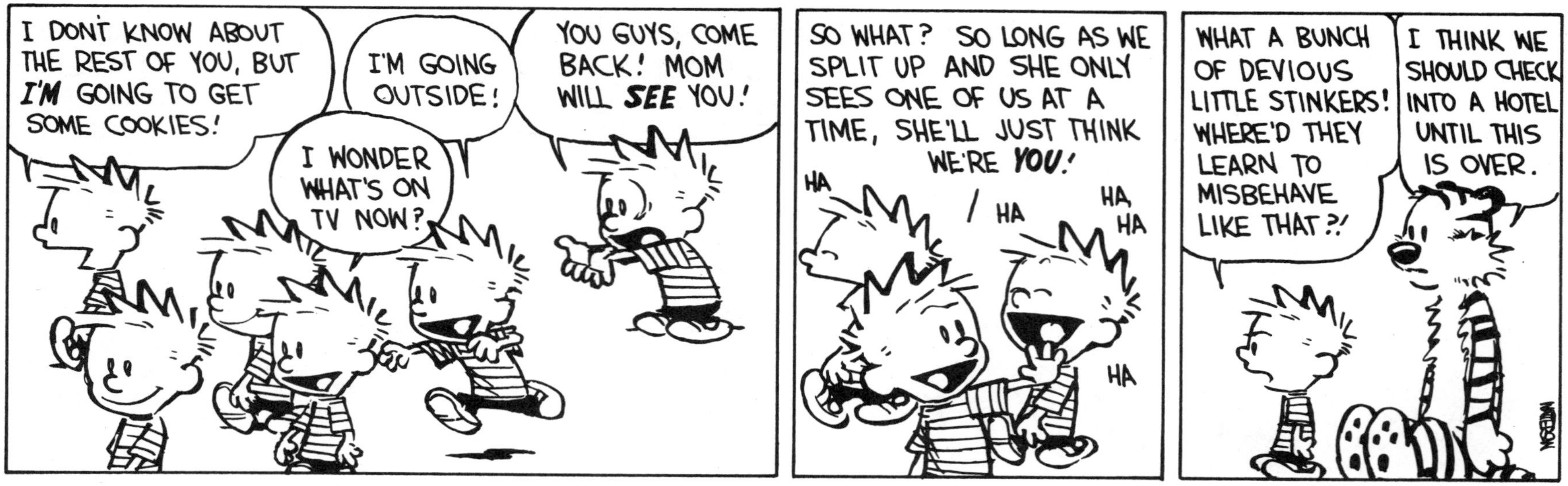
I DON'T KNOW ABOUT THE REST OF YOU, BUT ***I'M*** GOING TO GET SOME COOKIES!
I'M GOING OUTSIDE!
I WONDER WHAT'S ON TV NOW?
YOU GUYS, COME BACK! MOM WILL ***SEE*** YOU!
SO WHAT? SO LONG AS WE SPLIT UP AND SHE ONLY SEES ONE OF US AT A TIME, SHE'LL JUST THINK WE'RE ***YOU***!
HA
HA
HA
HA
HA
WHAT A BUNCH OF DEVIOUS LITTLE STINKERS! WHERE'D THEY LEARN TO MISBEHAVE LIKE THAT?!
I THINK WE SHOULD CHECK INTO A HOTEL UNTIL THIS IS OVER.

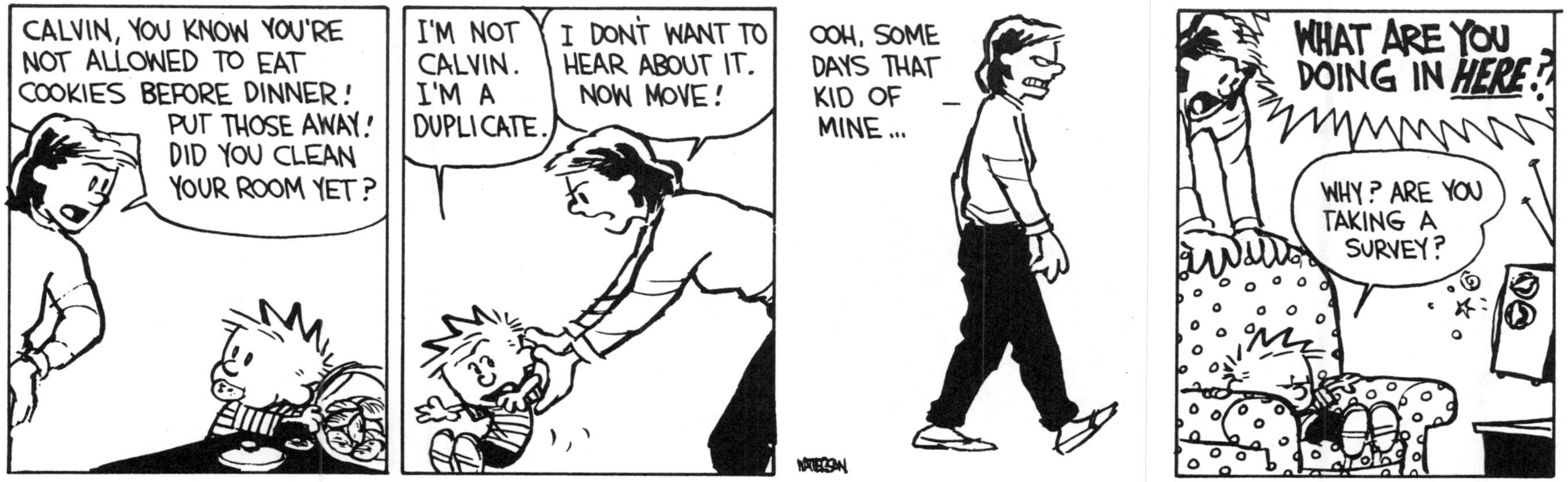
CALVIN, YOU KNOW YOU'RE NOT ALLOWED TO EAT COOKIES BEFORE DINNER!
PUT THOSE AWAY! DID YOU CLEAN YOUR ROOM YET?
I'M NOT CALVIN. I'M A DUPLICATE.
I DON'T WANT TO HEAR ABOUT IT. NOW MOVE!
OOH, SOME DAYS THAT KID OF MINE... —
WATTERSON
WHAT ARE YOU DOING IN HERE?!
WHY? ARE YOU TAKING A SURVEY?

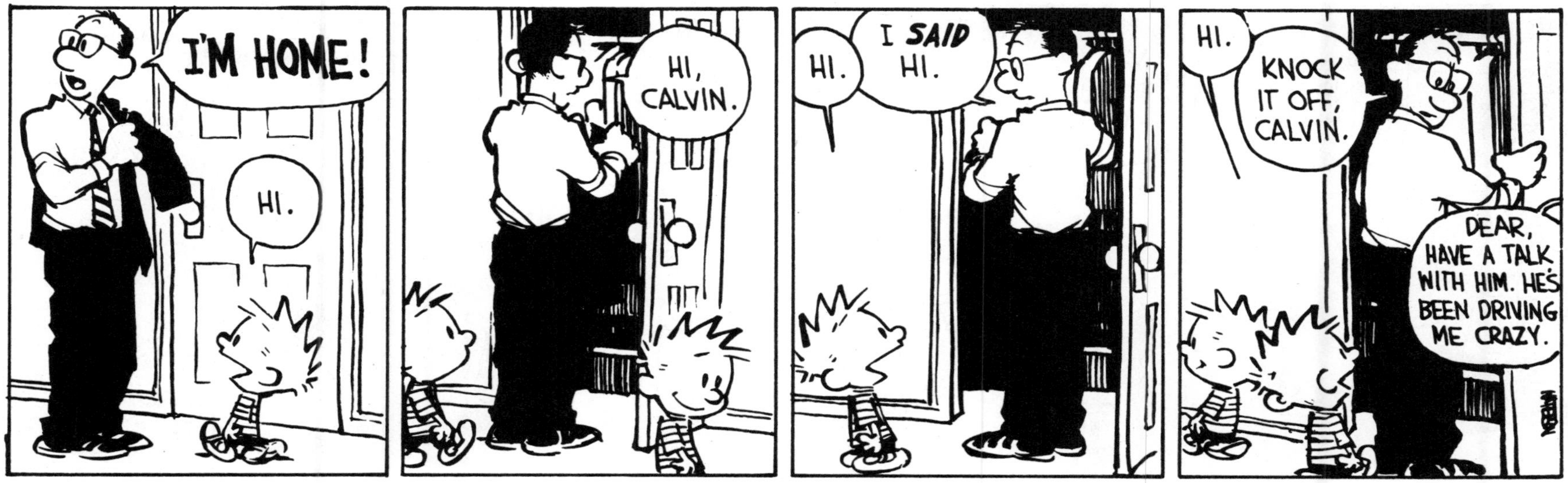
I'M HOME!
HI.
HI, CALVIN.
HI.
I SAID HI.
HI.
KNOCK IT OFF, CALVIN.
DEAR, HAVE A TALK WITH HIM. HE'S BEEN DRIVING ME CRAZY.

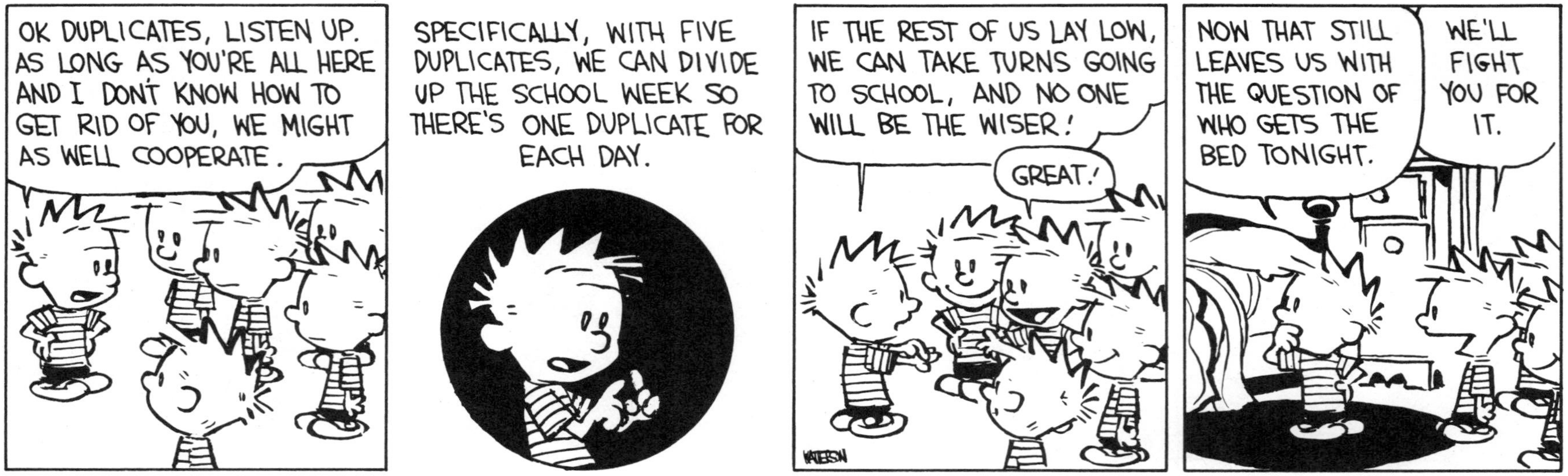

OK DUPLICATES, LISTEN UP. AS LONG AS YOU'RE ALL HERE AND I DON'T KNOW HOW TO GET RID OF YOU, WE MIGHT AS WELL COOPERATE.
SPECIFICALLY, WITH FIVE DUPLICATES, WE CAN DIVIDE UP THE SCHOOL WEEK SO THERE'S ONE DUPLICATE FOR EACH DAY.
IF THE REST OF US LAY LOW, WE CAN TAKE TURNS GOING TO SCHOOL, AND NO ONE WILL BE THE WISER!
GREAT!
NOW THAT STILL LEAVES US WITH THE QUESTION OF WHO GETS THE BED TONIGHT.
WE'LL FIGHT YOU FOR IT.

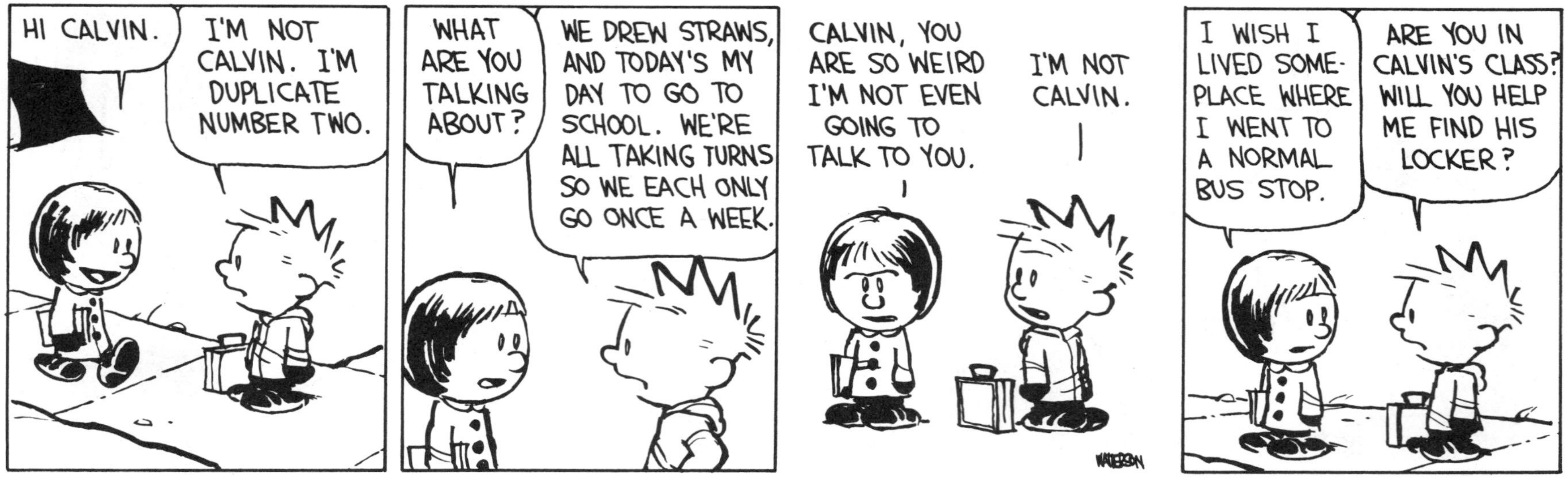

HI CALVIN.
I'M NOT CALVIN. I'M DUPLICATE NUMBER TWO.
WHAT ARE YOU TALKING ABOUT?
WE DREW STRAWS, AND TODAY'S MY DAY TO GO TO SCHOOL. WE'RE ALL TAKING TURNS SO WE EACH ONLY GO ONCE A WEEK.
CALVIN, YOU ARE SO WEIRD I'M NOT EVEN GOING TO TALK TO YOU.
I'M NOT CALVIN.
I WISH I LIVED SOME-PLACE WHERE I WENT TO A NORMAL BUS STOP.
ARE YOU IN CALVIN'S CLASS? WILL YOU HELP ME FIND HIS LOCKER?

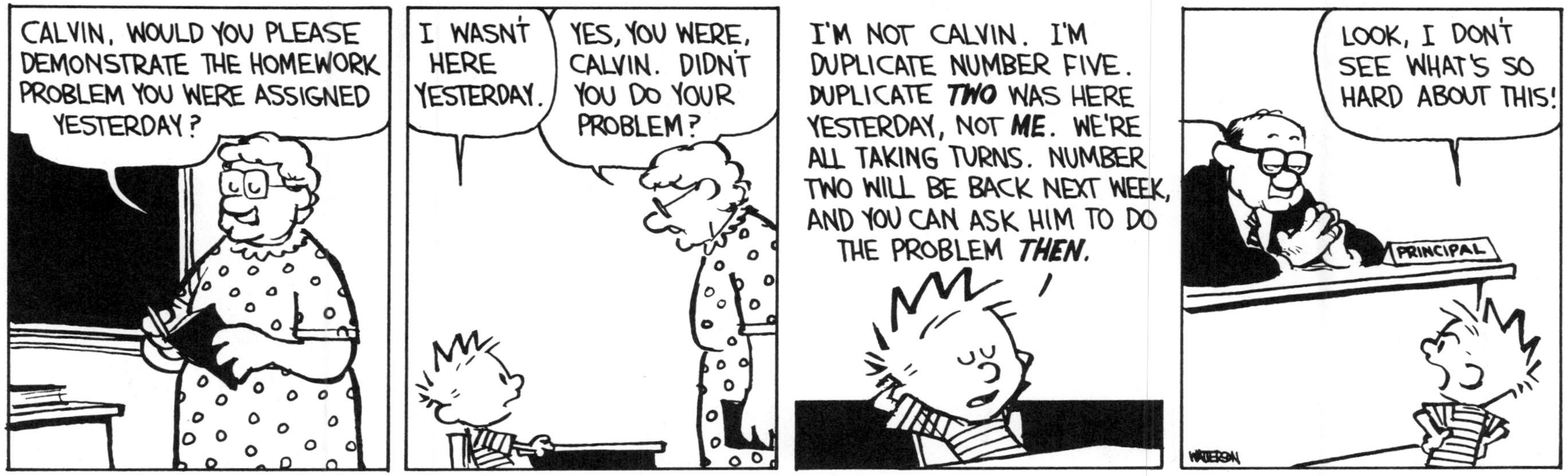
CALVIN, WOULD YOU PLEASE DEMONSTRATE THE HOMEWORK PROBLEM YOU WERE ASSIGNED YESTERDAY?
I WASN'T HERE YESTERDAY.
YES, YOU WERE, CALVIN. DIDN'T YOU DO YOUR PROBLEM?
I'M NOT CALVIN. I'M DUPLICATE NUMBER FIVE. DUPLICATE **TWO** WAS HERE YESTERDAY, NOT **ME**. WE'RE ALL TAKING TURNS. NUMBER TWO WILL BE BACK NEXT WEEK, AND YOU CAN ASK HIM TO DO THE PROBLEM **THEN**.
PRINCIPAL
LOOK, I DON'T SEE WHAT'S SO HARD ABOUT THIS!

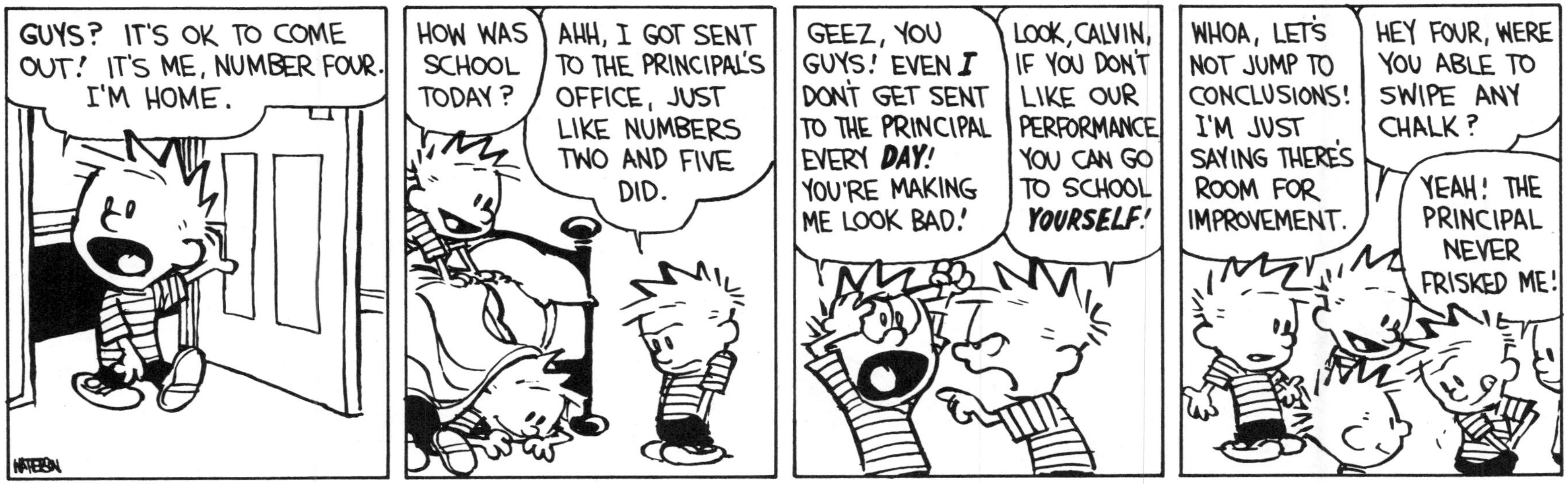
GUYS? IT'S OK TO COME OUT! IT'S ME, NUMBER FOUR. I'M HOME.
HOW WAS SCHOOL TODAY?
AHH, I GOT SENT TO THE PRINCIPAL'S OFFICE, JUST LIKE NUMBERS TWO AND FIVE DID.
GEEZ, YOU GUYS! EVEN ***I*** DON'T GET SENT TO THE PRINCIPAL EVERY ***DAY***! YOU'RE MAKING ME LOOK BAD!
LOOK, CALVIN, IF YOU DON'T LIKE OUR PERFORMANCE YOU CAN GO TO SCHOOL ***YOURSELF***!
WHOA, LET'S NOT JUMP TO CONCLUSIONS! I'M JUST SAYING THERE'S ROOM FOR IMPROVEMENT.
HEY FOUR, WERE YOU ABLE TO SWIPE ANY CHALK?
YEAH! THE PRINCIPAL NEVER FRISKED ME!

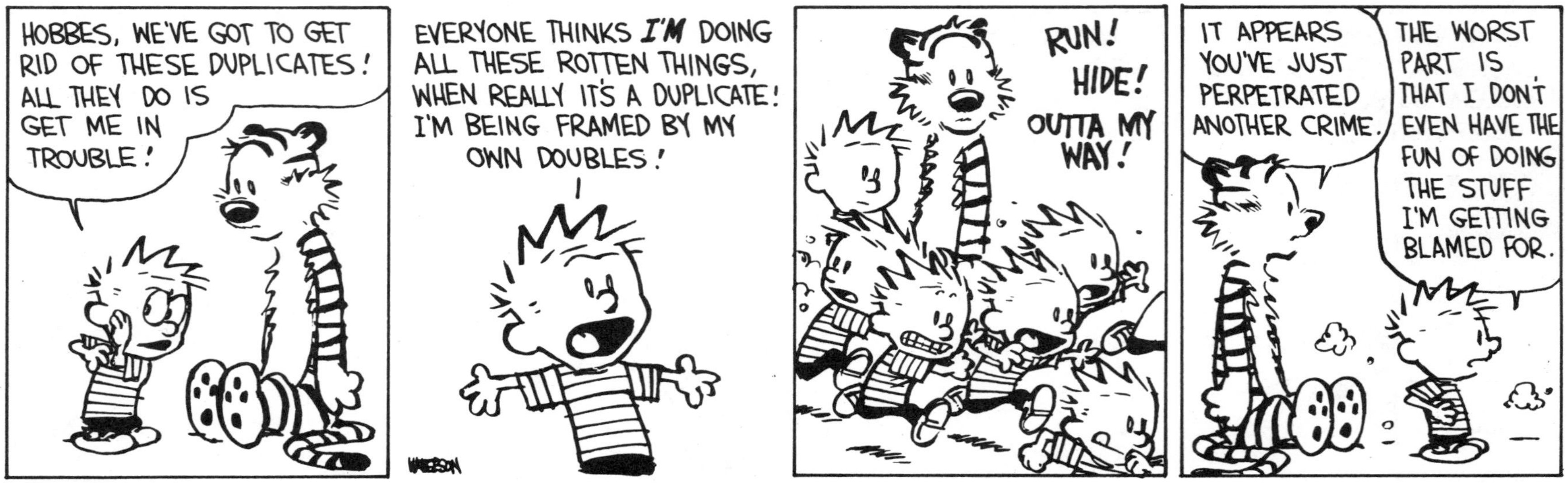
HOBBES, WE'VE GOT TO GET RID OF THESE DUPLICATES! ALL THEY DO IS GET ME IN TROUBLE!
EVERYONE THINKS I'M DOING ALL THESE ROTTEN THINGS, WHEN REALLY IT'S A DUPLICATE! I'M BEING FRAMED BY MY OWN DOUBLES!
RUN!
HIDE!
OUTTA MY WAY!
IT APPEARS YOU'VE JUST PERPETRATED ANOTHER CRIME.
THE WORST PART IS THAT I DON'T EVEN HAVE THE FUN OF DOING THE STUFF I'M GETTING BLAMED FOR.

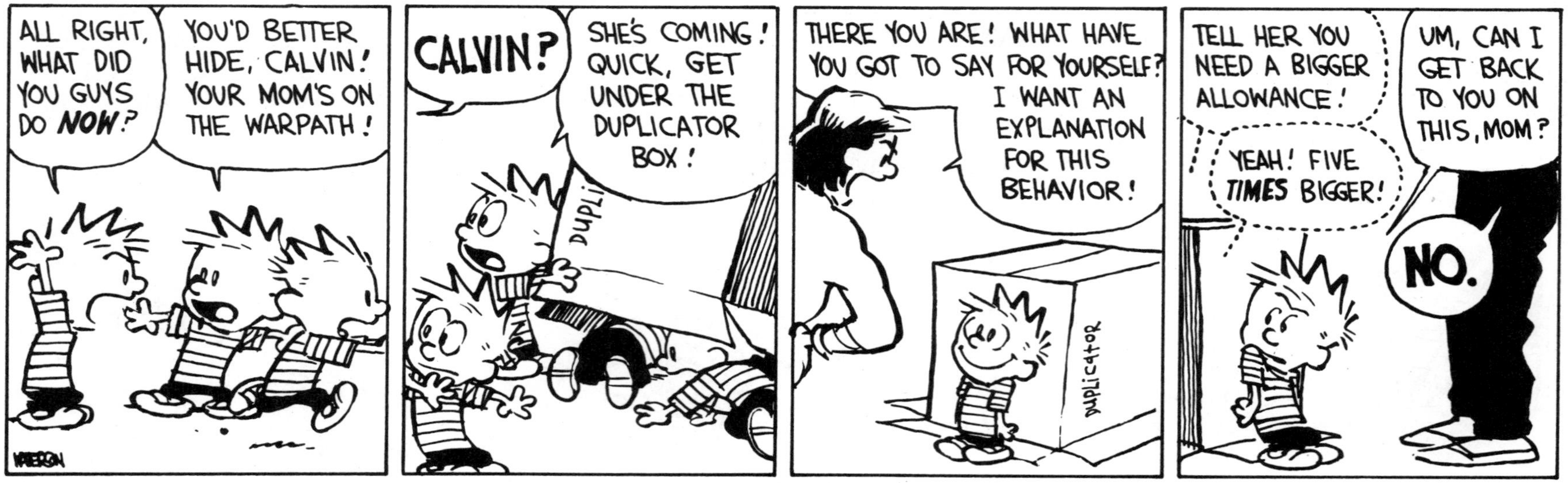
ALL RIGHT, WHAT DID YOU GUYS DO NOW?
YOU'D BETTER HIDE, CALVIN! YOUR MOM'S ON THE WARPATH!
CALVIN?
SHE'S COMING! QUICK, GET UNDER THE DUPLICATOR BOX!
DUPLI
THERE YOU ARE! WHAT HAVE YOU GOT TO SAY FOR YOURSELF? I WANT AN EXPLANATION FOR THIS BEHAVIOR!
DUPLICATOR
TELL HER YOU NEED A BIGGER ALLOWANCE!
YEAH! FIVE TIMES BIGGER!
UM, CAN I GET BACK TO YOU ON THIS, MOM?
NO.

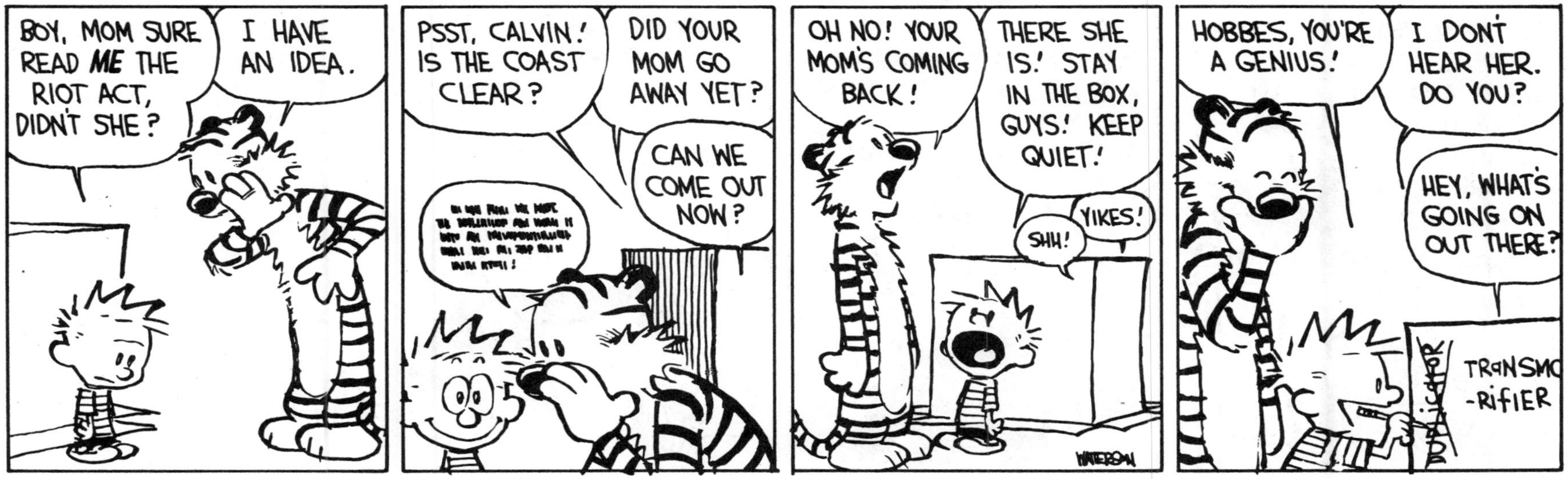
BOY, MOM SURE READ ***ME*** THE RIOT ACT, DIDN'T SHE?
I HAVE AN IDEA.
PSST, CALVIN! IS THE COAST CLEAR?
DID YOUR MOM GO AWAY YET?
CAN WE COME OUT NOW?
OH NO! YOUR MOM'S COMING BACK!
THERE SHE IS! STAY IN THE BOX, GUYS! KEEP QUIET!
SHH!
YIKES!
HOBBES, YOU'RE A GENIUS!
I DON'T HEAR HER. DO YOU?
HEY, WHAT'S GOING ON OUT THERE?
DUPLICATOR
TRANSM
-RIFIER

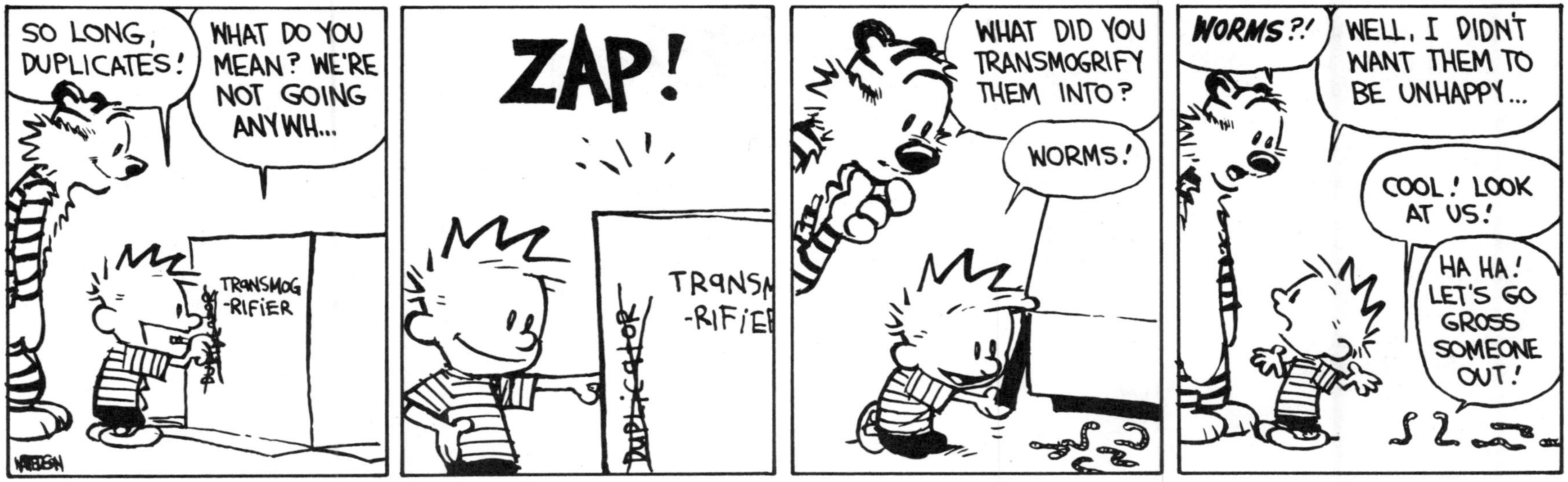
SO LONG, DUPLICATES!
WHAT DO YOU MEAN? WE'RE NOT GOING ANYWH...
TRANSMOG -RIFIER
ZAP!
TRANSM
-RIFIE
DUPLICATOR
WHAT DID YOU TRANSMOGRIFY THEM INTO?
WORMS!
WORMS?!
WELL, I DIDN'T WANT THEM TO BE UNHAPPY...
COOL! LOOK AT US!
HA HA! LET'S GO GROSS SOMEONE OUT!

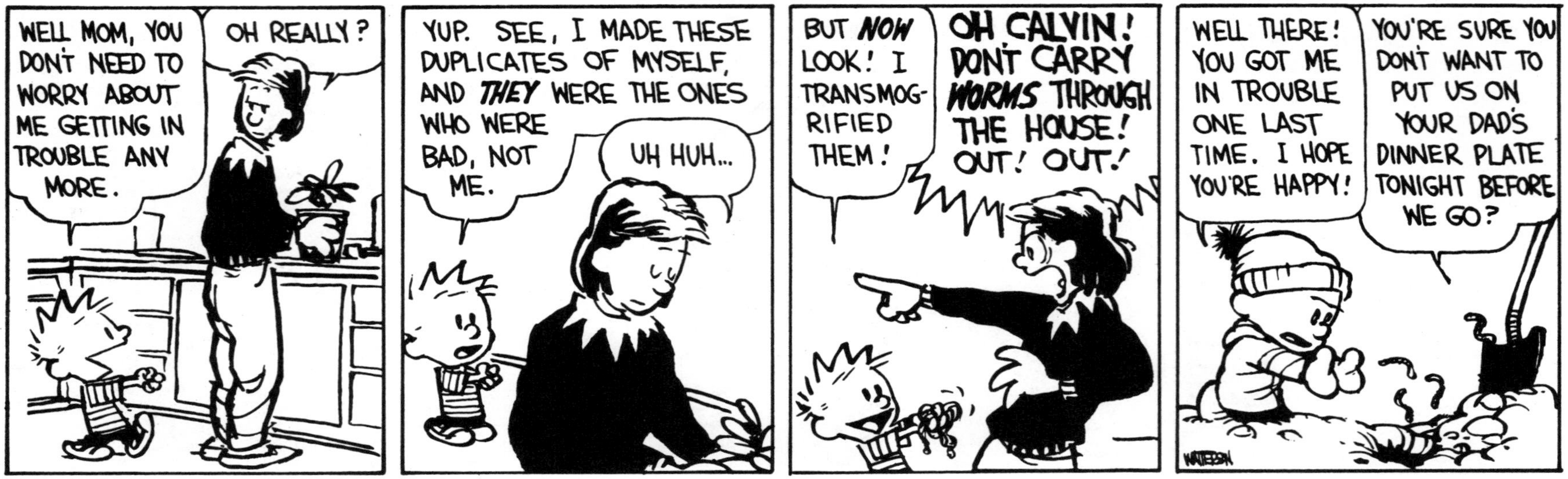
WELL MOM, YOU DON'T NEED TO WORRY ABOUT ME GETTING IN TROUBLE ANY MORE.
OH REALLY?
YUP. SEE, I MADE THESE DUPLICATES OF MYSELF, AND *THEY* WERE THE ONES WHO WERE BAD, NOT ME.
UH HUH...
BUT *NOW* LOOK! I TRANSMOGRIFIED THEM!
OH CALVIN! DON'T CARRY *WORMS* THROUGH THE HOUSE! OUT! OUT!
WELL THERE! YOU GOT ME IN TROUBLE ONE LAST TIME. I HOPE YOU'RE HAPPY!
YOU'RE SURE YOU DON'T WANT TO PUT US ON YOUR DAD'S DINNER PLATE TONIGHT BEFORE WE GO?

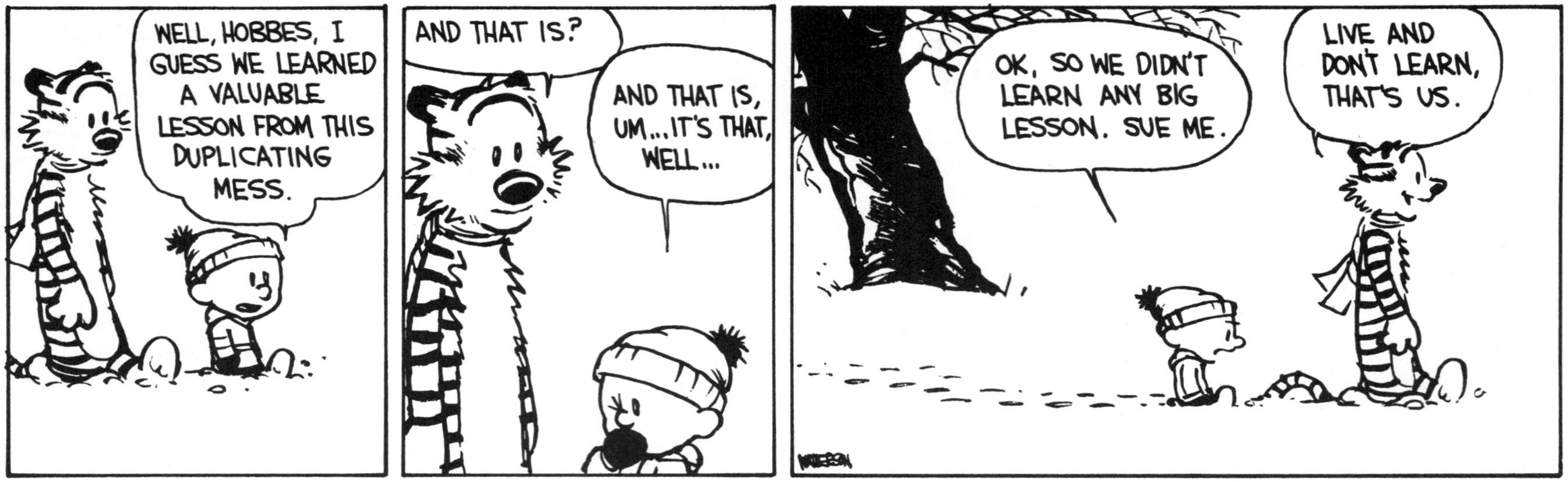
WELL, HOBBES, I GUESS WE LEARNED A VALUABLE LESSON FROM THIS DUPLICATING MESS.
AND THAT IS?
AND THAT IS, UM...IT'S THAT, WELL...
OK, SO WE DIDN'T LEARN ANY BIG LESSON. SUE ME.
LIVE AND DON'T LEARN, THAT'S US.

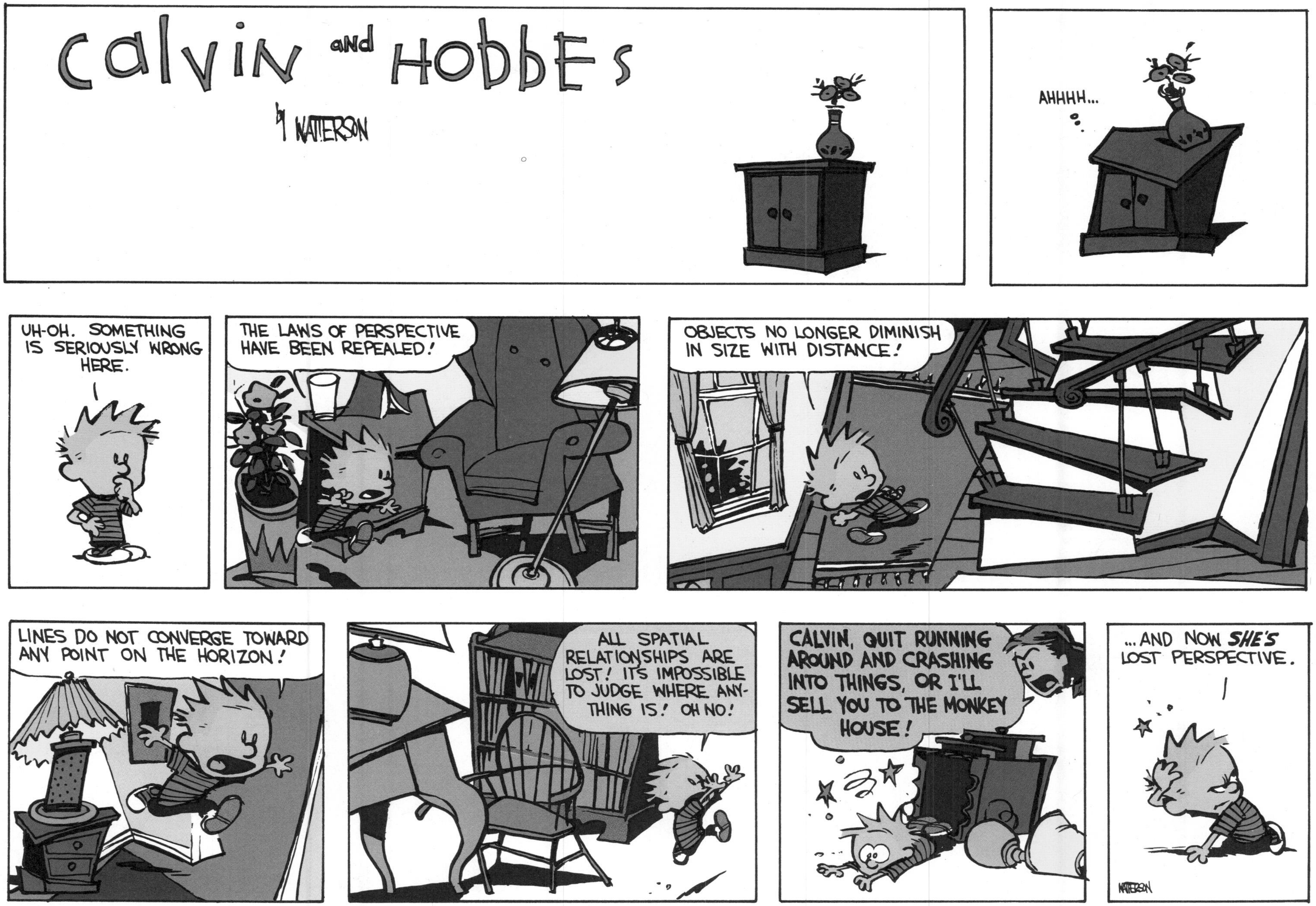
Calvin and HOBBES
by WATTERSON
AHHHH...
UH-OH. SOMETHING IS SERIOUSLY WRONG HERE.
THE LAWS OF PERSPECTIVE HAVE BEEN REPEALED!
OBJECTS NO LONGER DIMINISH IN SIZE WITH DISTANCE!
LINES DO NOT CONVERGE TOWARD ANY POINT ON THE HORIZON!
ALL SPATIAL RELATIONSHIPS ARE LOST! ITS IMPOSSIBLE TO JUDGE WHERE ANYTHING IS! OH NO!
CALVIN, QUIT RUNNING AROUND AND CRASHING INTO THINGS, OR I'LL SELL YOU TO THE MONKEY HOUSE!
...AND NOW SHE'S LOST PERSPECTIVE.
WATTERSON

This strip was a lot of fun to draw. It was surprising how often I had to "correct" the perspective to make it wrong.

Much of this story is based on actual memories, and I think it nicely touches on a number of issues. I still have no use for organized sports of any kind. This story also introduced Calvinball, another idea that captures the spirit of the strip.

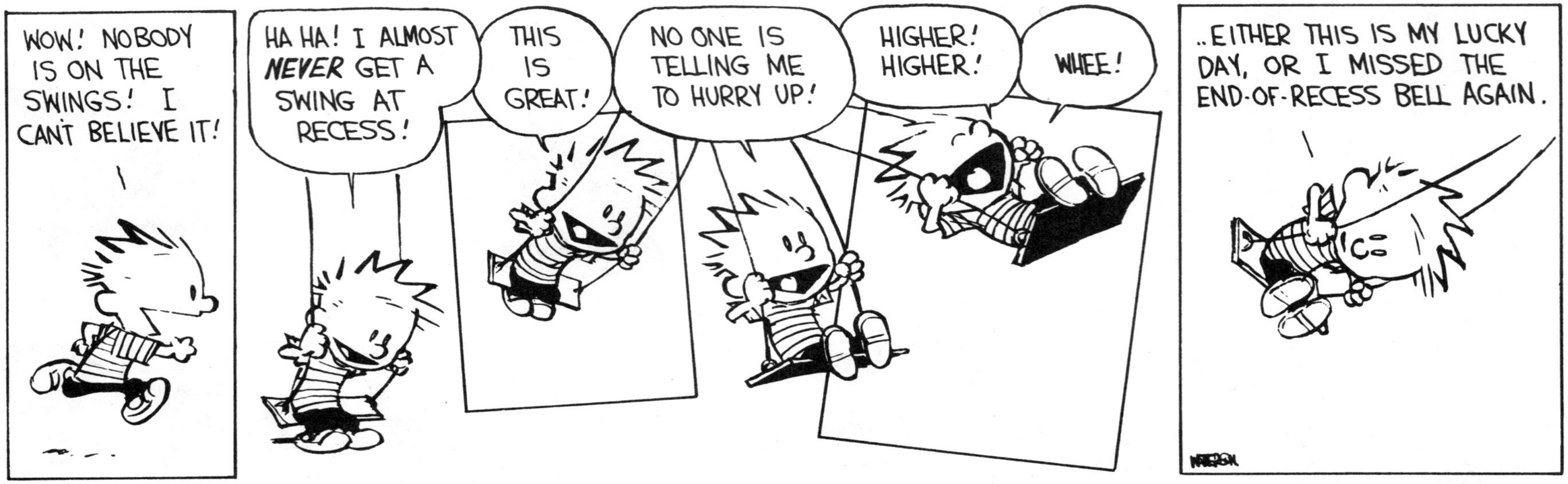
WOW! NOBODY IS ON THE SWINGS! I CAN'T BELIEVE IT!
HA HA! I ALMOST NEVER GET A SWING AT RECESS!
THIS IS GREAT!
NO ONE IS TELLING ME TO HURRY UP!
HIGHER! HIGHER!
WHEE!
..EITHER THIS IS MY LUCKY DAY, OR I MISSED THE END-OF-RECESS BELL AGAIN.

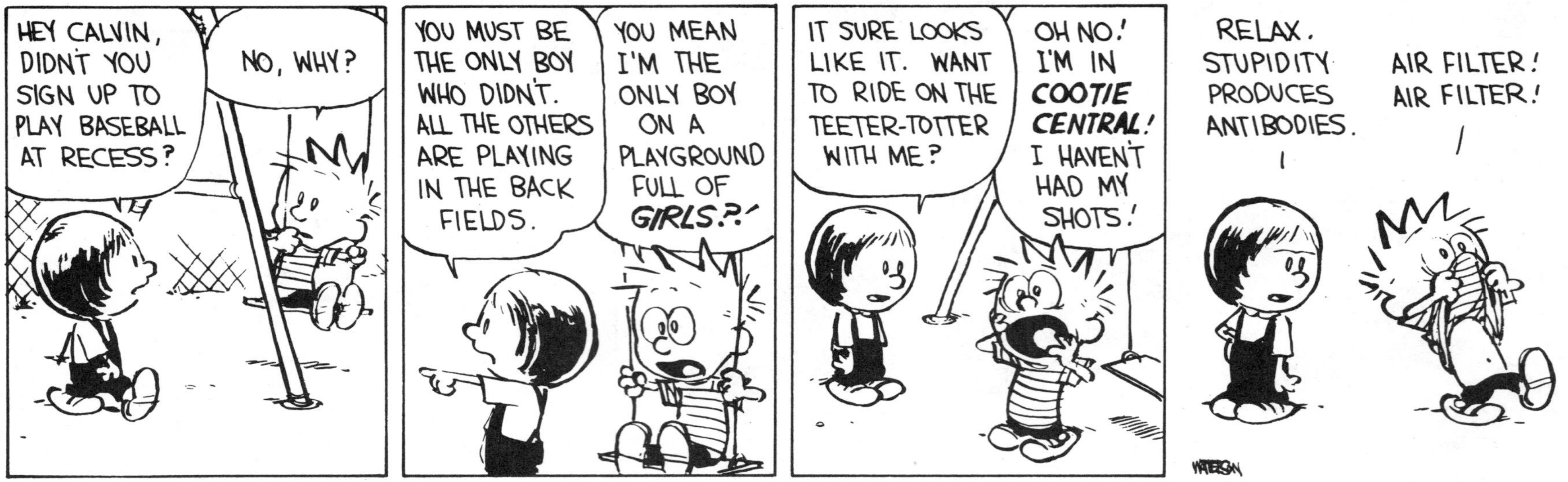
HEY CALVIN, DIDN'T YOU SIGN UP TO PLAY BASEBALL AT RECESS?
NO, WHY?
YOU MUST BE THE ONLY BOY WHO DIDN'T. ALL THE OTHERS ARE PLAYING IN THE BACK FIELDS.
YOU MEAN I'M THE ONLY BOY ON A PLAYGROUND FULL OF GIRLS?!
IT SURE LOOKS LIKE IT. WANT TO RIDE ON THE TEETER-TOTTER WITH ME?
OH NO! I'M IN COOTIE CENTRAL! I HAVEN'T HAD MY SHOTS!
RELAX. STUPIDITY PRODUCES ANTIBODIES.
AIR FILTER! AIR FILTER!

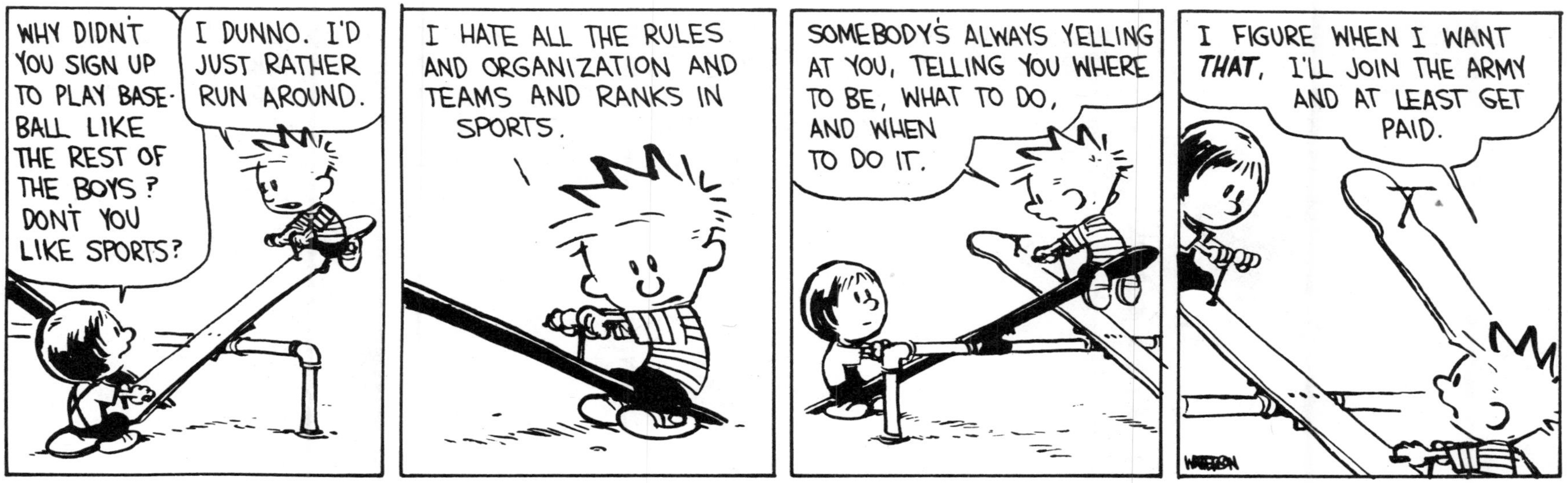
WHY DIDN'T YOU SIGN UP TO PLAY BASE-BALL LIKE THE REST OF THE BOYS? DON'T YOU LIKE SPORTS?
I DUNNO. I'D JUST RATHER RUN AROUND.
I HATE ALL THE RULES AND ORGANIZATION AND TEAMS AND RANKS IN SPORTS.
SOMEBODY'S ALWAYS YELLING AT YOU, TELLING YOU WHERE TO BE, WHAT TO DO, AND WHEN TO DO IT.
I FIGURE WHEN I WANT *THAT*, I'LL JOIN THE ARMY AND AT LEAST GET PAID.

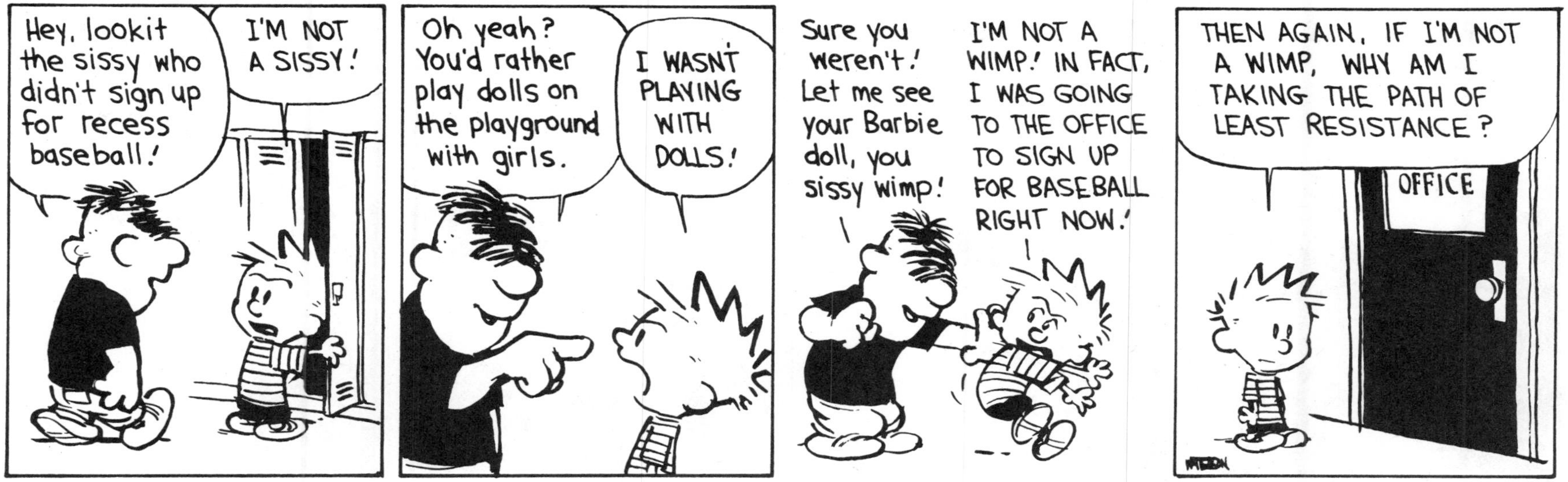
Hey, lookit the sissy who didn't sign up for recess baseball!
I'M NOT A SISSY!
Oh yeah? You'd rather play dolls on the playground with girls.
I WASN'T PLAYING WITH DOLLS!
Sure you weren't! Let me see your Barbie doll, you sissy wimp!
I'M NOT A WIMP! IN FACT, I WAS GOING TO THE OFFICE TO SIGN UP FOR BASEBALL RIGHT NOW!
THEN AGAIN, IF I'M NOT A WIMP, WHY AM I TAKING THE PATH OF LEAST RESISTANCE?
OFFICE

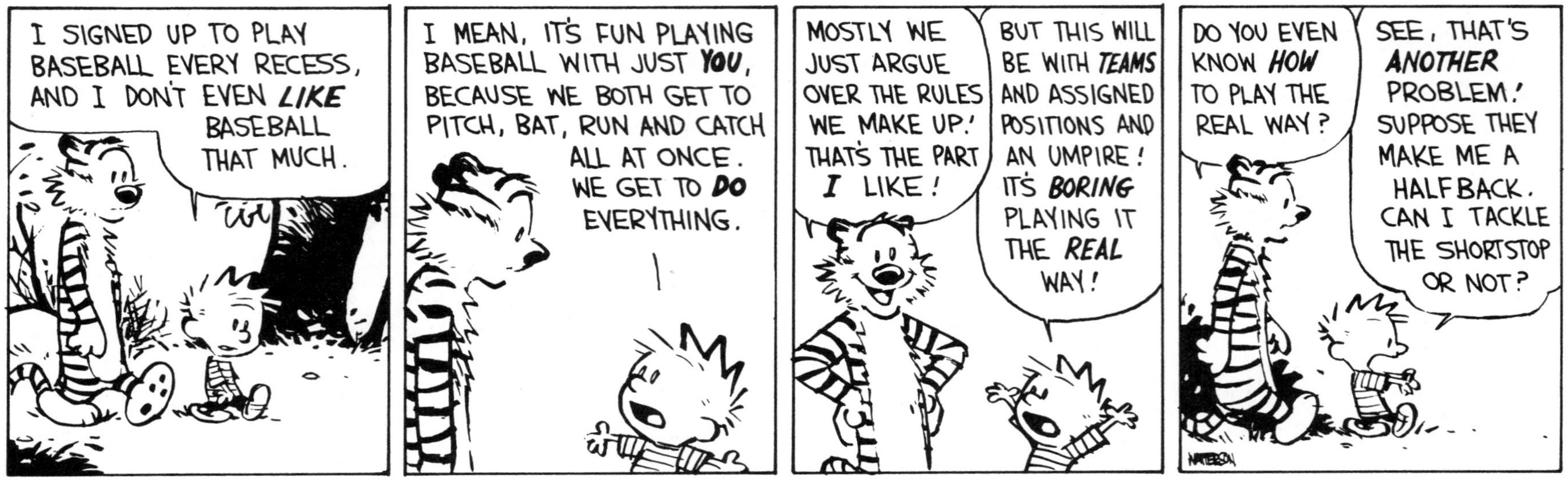
I SIGNED UP TO PLAY BASEBALL EVERY RECESS, AND I DON'T EVEN LIKE BASEBALL THAT MUCH.
I MEAN, IT'S FUN PLAYING BASEBALL WITH JUST YOU, BECAUSE WE BOTH GET TO PITCH, BAT, RUN AND CATCH ALL AT ONCE. WE GET TO DO EVERYTHING.
MOSTLY WE JUST ARGUE OVER THE RULES WE MAKE UP! THAT'S THE PART I LIKE!
BUT THIS WILL BE WITH TEAMS AND ASSIGNED POSITIONS AND AN UMPIRE! IT'S BORING PLAYING IT THE REAL WAY!
DO YOU EVEN KNOW HOW TO PLAY THE REAL WAY?
SEE, THAT'S ANOTHER PROBLEM! SUPPOSE THEY MAKE ME A HALFBACK. CAN I TACKLE THE SHORTSTOP OR NOT?

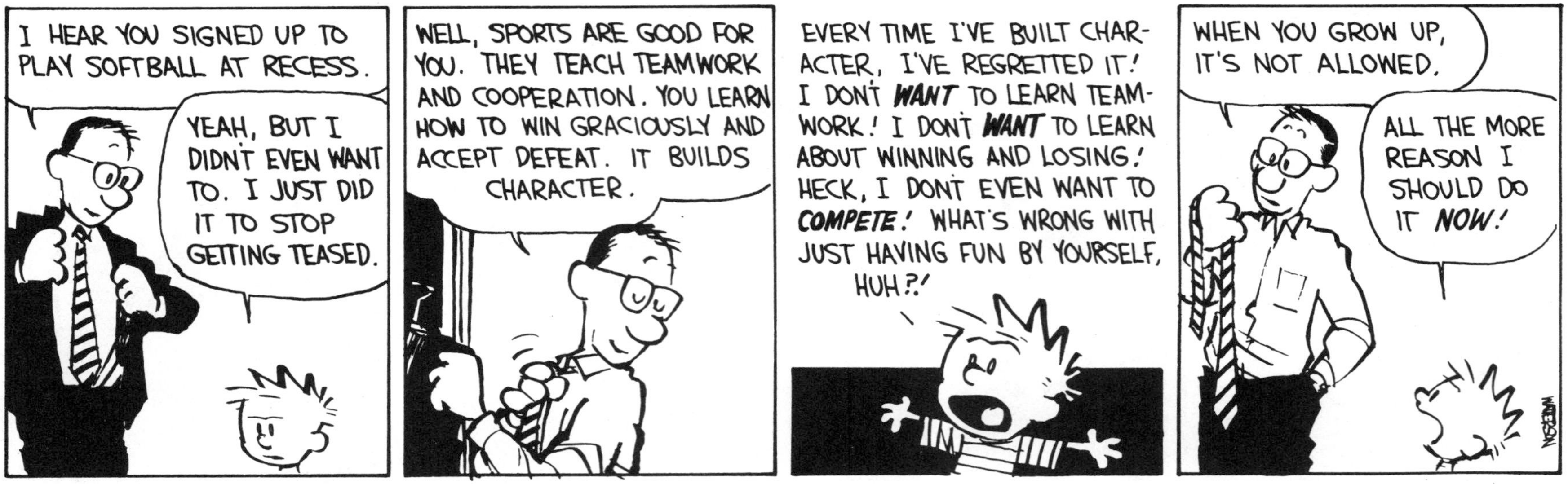
I HEAR YOU SIGNED UP TO PLAY SOFTBALL AT RECESS.
YEAH, BUT I DIDN'T EVEN WANT TO. I JUST DID IT TO STOP GETTING TEASED.
WELL, SPORTS ARE GOOD FOR YOU. THEY TEACH TEAMWORK AND COOPERATION. YOU LEARN HOW TO WIN GRACIOUSLY AND ACCEPT DEFEAT. IT BUILDS CHARACTER.
EVERY TIME I'VE BUILT CHARACTER, I'VE REGRETTED IT! I DON'T WANT TO LEARN TEAMWORK! I DON'T WANT TO LEARN ABOUT WINNING AND LOSING! HECK, I DON'T EVEN WANT TO COMPETE! WHAT'S WRONG WITH JUST HAVING FUN BY YOURSELF, HUH?!
WHEN YOU GROW UP, IT'S NOT ALLOWED.
ALL THE MORE REASON I SHOULD DO IT NOW!

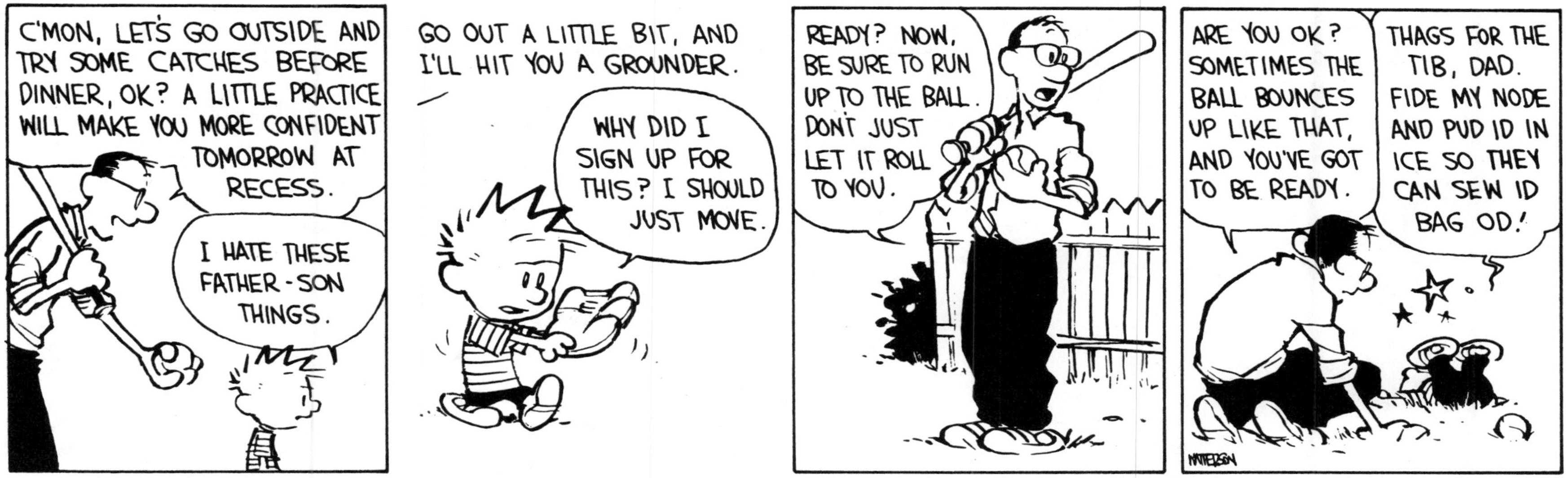
C'MON, LET'S GO OUTSIDE AND TRY SOME CATCHES BEFORE DINNER, OK? A LITTLE PRACTICE WILL MAKE YOU MORE CONFIDENT TOMORROW AT RECESS.
I HATE THESE FATHER-SON THINGS.
GO OUT A LITTLE BIT, AND I'LL HIT YOU A GROUNDER.
WHY DID I SIGN UP FOR THIS? I SHOULD JUST MOVE.
READY? NOW, BE SURE TO RUN UP TO THE BALL. DON'T JUST LET IT ROLL TO YOU.
ARE YOU OK? SOMETIMES THE BALL BOUNCES UP LIKE THAT, AND YOU'VE GOT TO BE READY.
THAGS FOR THE TIB, DAD. FIDE MY NODE AND PUD ID IN ICE SO THEY CAN SEW ID BAG OD!

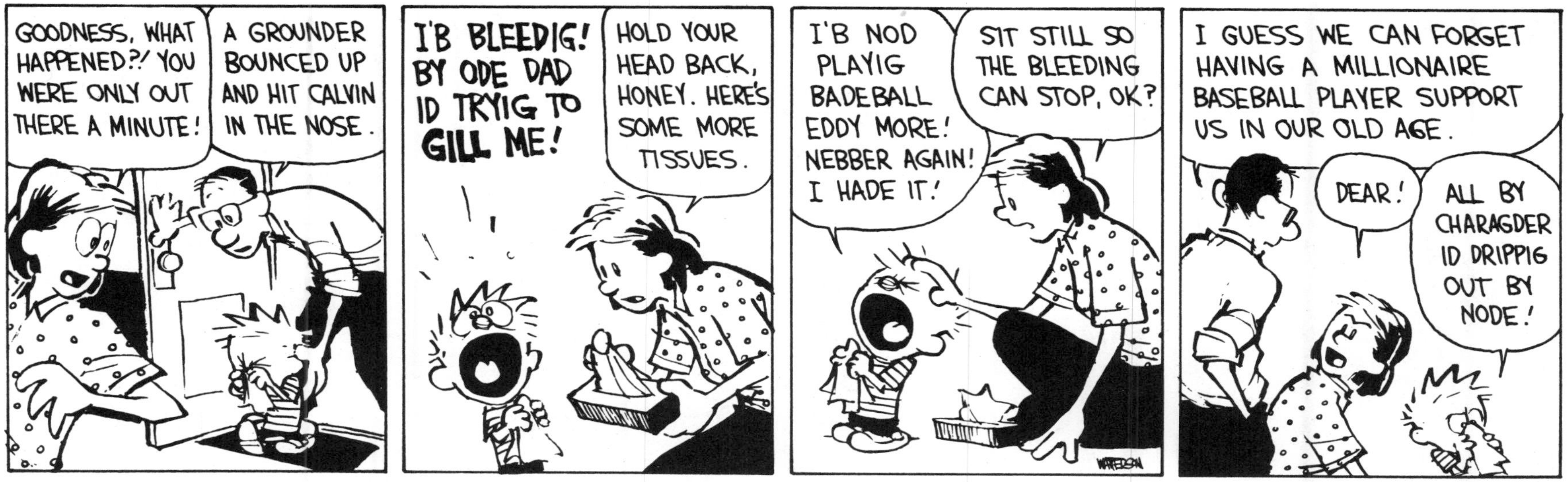
GOODNESS, WHAT HAPPENED?! YOU WERE ONLY OUT THERE A MINUTE!
A GROUNDER BOUNCED UP AND HIT CALVIN IN THE NOSE.
I'B BLEEDIG! BY ODE DAD ID TRYIG TO GILL ME!
HOLD YOUR HEAD BACK, HONEY. HERE'S SOME MORE TISSUES.
I'B NOD PLAYIG BADEBALL EDDY MORE! NEBBER AGAIN! I HADE IT!
SIT STILL SO THE BLEEDING CAN STOP, OK?
I GUESS WE CAN FORGET HAVING A MILLIONAIRE BASEBALL PLAYER SUPPORT US IN OUR OLD AGE.
DEAR!
ALL BY CHARAGDER ID DRIPPIG OUT BY NODE!

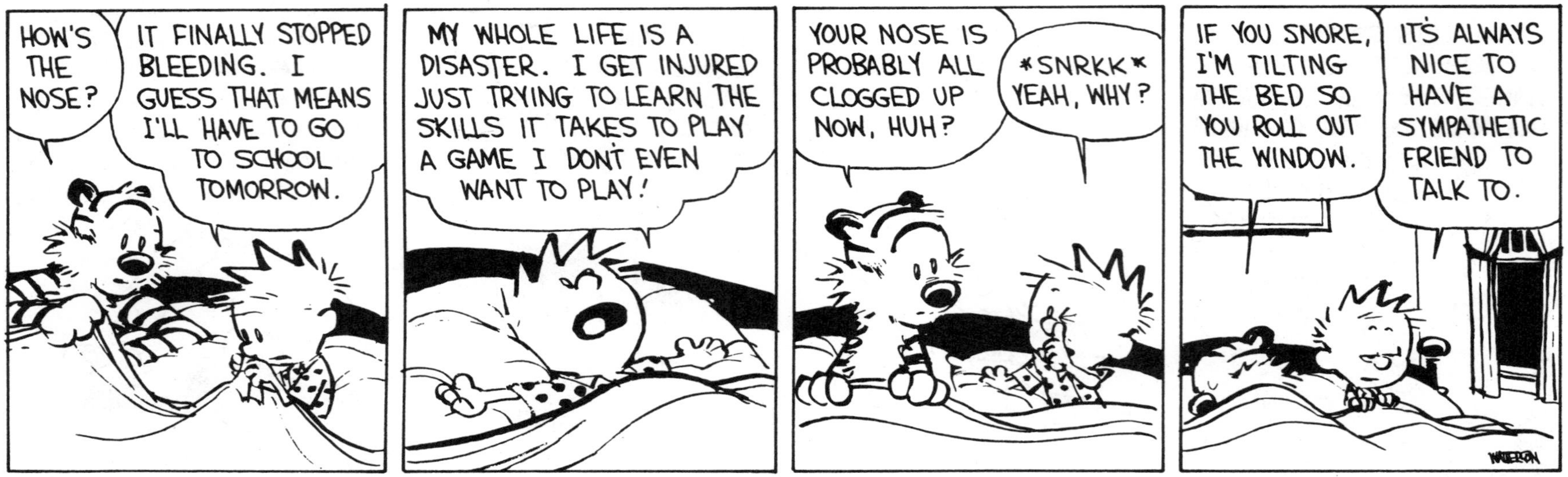
HOW'S THE NOSE?
IT FINALLY STOPPED BLEEDING. I GUESS THAT MEANS I'LL HAVE TO GO TO SCHOOL TOMORROW.
MY WHOLE LIFE IS A DISASTER. I GET INJURED JUST TRYING TO LEARN THE SKILLS IT TAKES TO PLAY A GAME I DON'T EVEN WANT TO PLAY!
YOUR NOSE IS PROBABLY ALL CLOGGED UP NOW, HUH?
SNRKK YEAH, WHY?
IF YOU SNORE, I'M TILTING THE BED SO YOU ROLL OUT THE WINDOW.
IT'S ALWAYS NICE TO HAVE A SYMPATHETIC FRIEND TO TALK TO.
WATTERSON

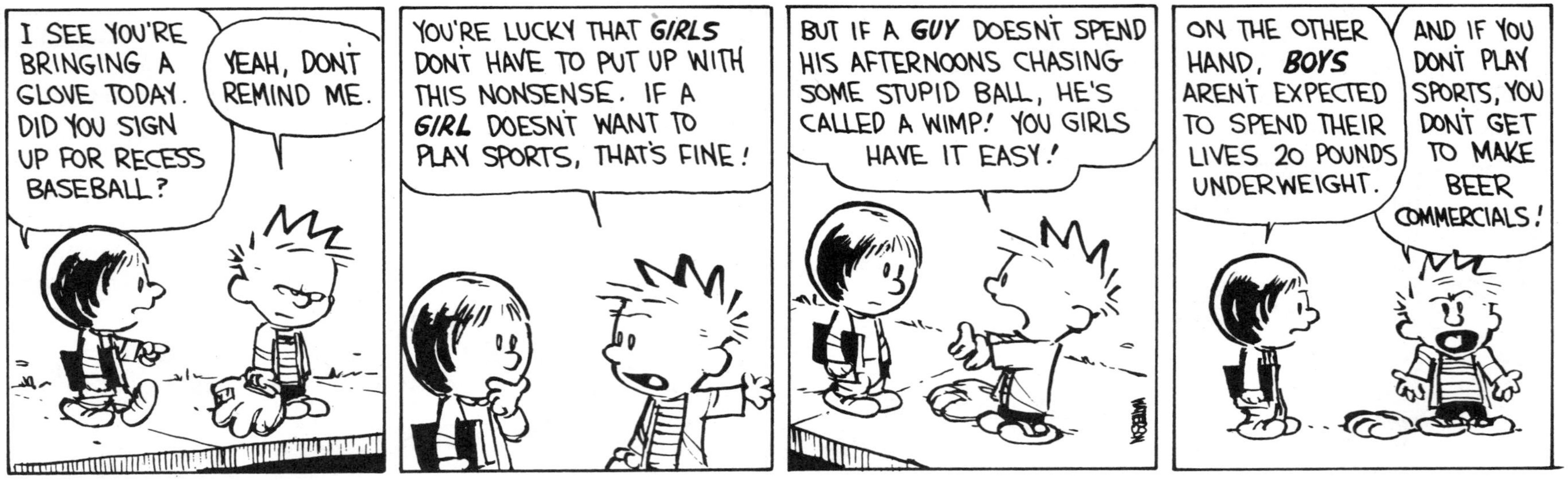
I SEE YOU'RE BRINGING A GLOVE TODAY. DID YOU SIGN UP FOR RECESS BASEBALL?
YEAH, DON'T REMIND ME.
YOU'RE LUCKY THAT GIRLS DON'T HAVE TO PUT UP WITH THIS NONSENSE. IF A GIRL DOESN'T WANT TO PLAY SPORTS, THAT'S FINE!
BUT IF A GUY DOESN'T SPEND HIS AFTERNOONS CHASING SOME STUPID BALL, HE'S CALLED A WIMP! YOU GIRLS HAVE IT EASY!
WATTERSON
ON THE OTHER HAND, BOYS AREN'T EXPECTED TO SPEND THEIR LIVES 20 POUNDS UNDERWEIGHT.
AND IF YOU DON'T PLAY SPORTS, YOU DON'T GET TO MAKE BEER COMMERCIALS!

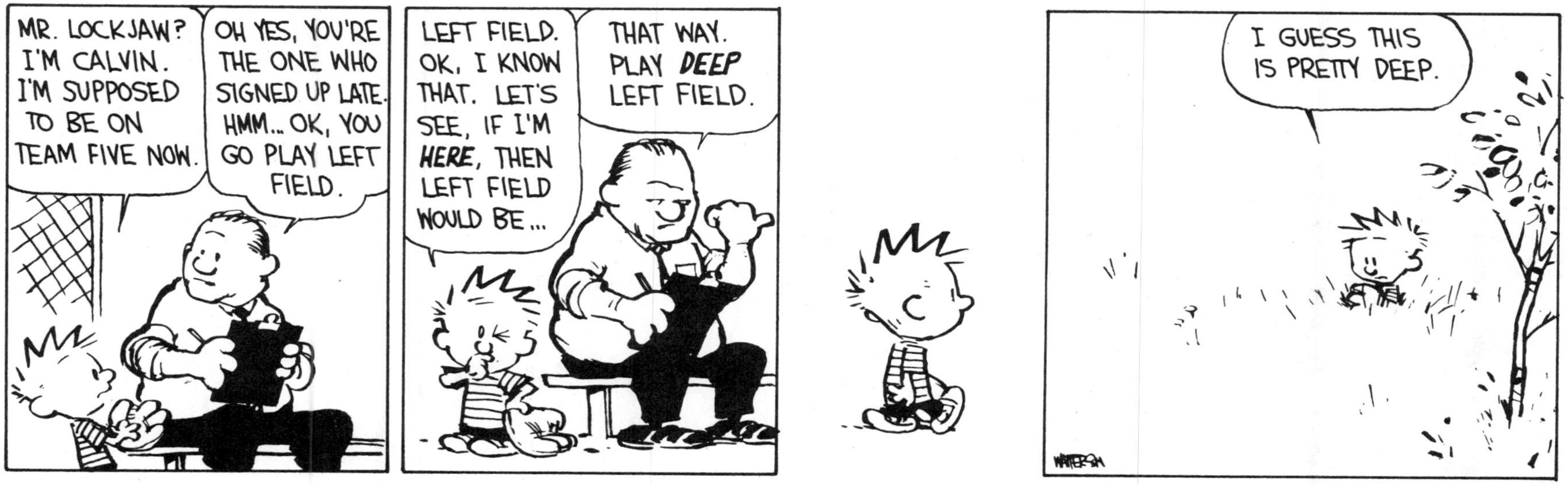
MR. LOCKJAW? I'M CALVIN. I'M SUPPOSED TO BE ON TEAM FIVE NOW.
OH YES, YOU'RE THE ONE WHO SIGNED UP LATE. HMM... OK, YOU GO PLAY LEFT FIELD.
LEFT FIELD. OK, I KNOW THAT. LET'S SEE, IF I'M HERE, THEN LEFT FIELD WOULD BE...
THAT WAY. PLAY DEEP LEFT FIELD.
I GUESS THIS IS PRETTY DEEP.

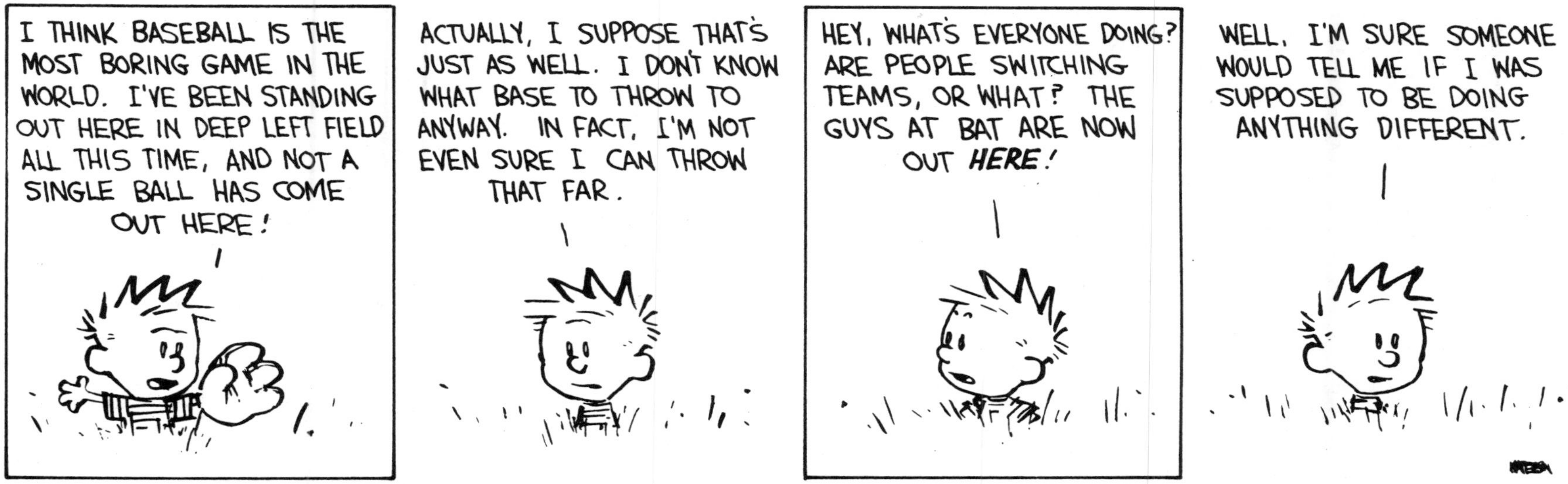
I THINK BASEBALL IS THE MOST BORING GAME IN THE WORLD. I'VE BEEN STANDING OUT HERE IN DEEP LEFT FIELD ALL THIS TIME, AND NOT A SINGLE BALL HAS COME OUT HERE!
ACTUALLY, I SUPPOSE THAT'S JUST AS WELL. I DON'T KNOW WHAT BASE TO THROW TO ANYWAY. IN FACT, I'M NOT EVEN SURE I CAN THROW THAT FAR.
HEY, WHAT'S EVERYONE DOING? ARE PEOPLE SWITCHING TEAMS, OR WHAT? THE GUYS AT BAT ARE NOW OUT HERE!
WELL, I'M SURE SOMEONE WOULD TELL ME IF I WAS SUPPOSED TO BE DOING ANYTHING DIFFERENT.

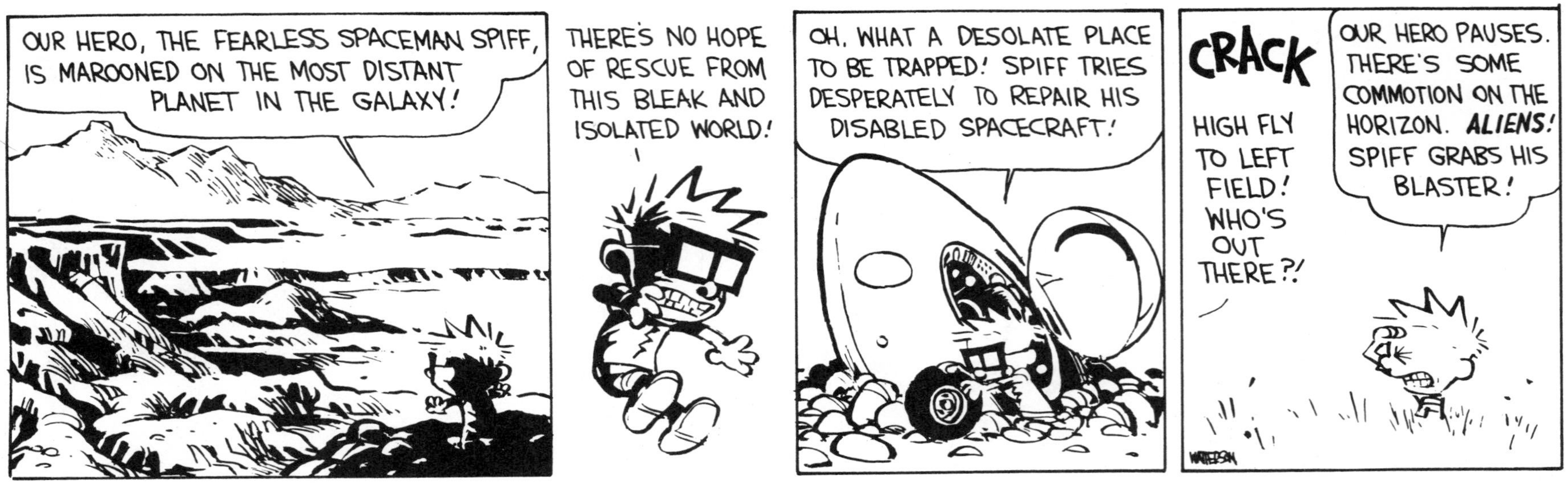
OUR HERO, THE FEARLESS SPACEMAN SPIFF, IS MAROONED ON THE MOST DISTANT PLANET IN THE GALAXY!
THERE'S NO HOPE OF RESCUE FROM THIS BLEAK AND ISOLATED WORLD!
OH, WHAT A DESOLATE PLACE TO BE TRAPPED! SPIFF TRIES DESPERATELY TO REPAIR HIS DISABLED SPACECRAFT!
CRACK
HIGH FLY TO LEFT FIELD! WHO'S OUT THERE?!
OUR HERO PAUSES. THERE'S SOME COMMOTION ON THE HORIZON. ALIENS! SPIFF GRABS HIS BLASTER!

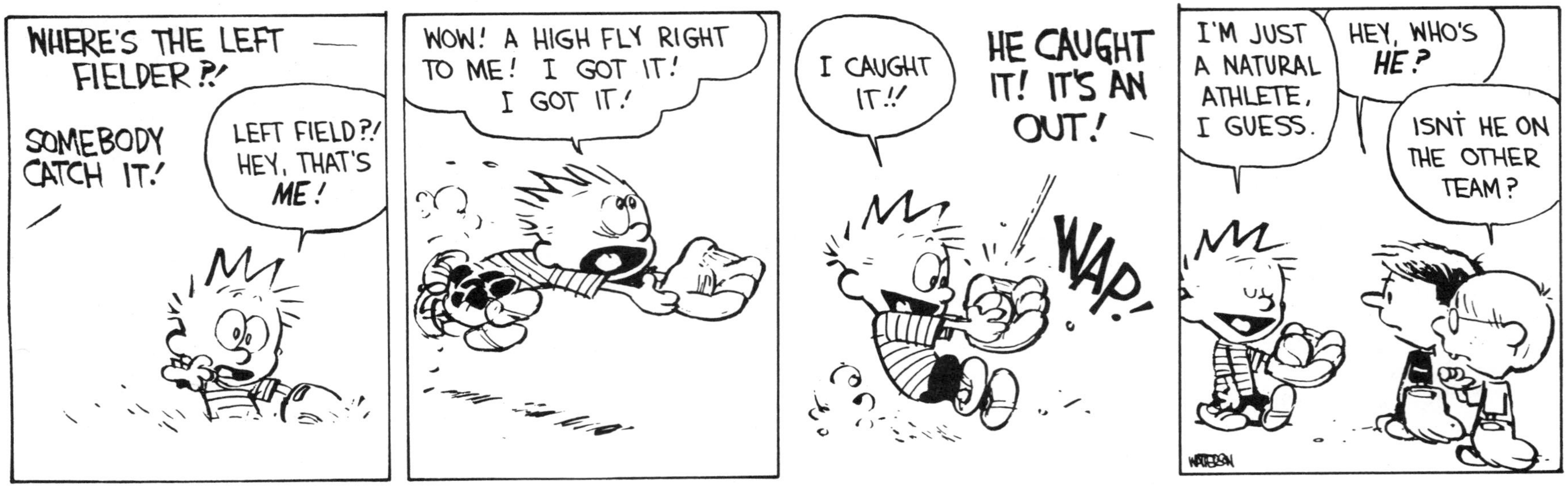
WHERE'S THE LEFT FIELDER?!
SOMEBODY CATCH IT!
LEFT FIELD?! HEY, THAT'S ME!
WOW! A HIGH FLY RIGHT TO ME! I GOT IT! I GOT IT!
I CAUGHT IT!!
HE CAUGHT IT! IT'S AN OUT!
WAP!
I'M JUST A NATURAL ATHLETE, I GUESS.
HEY, WHO'S HE?
ISN'T HE ON THE OTHER TEAM?

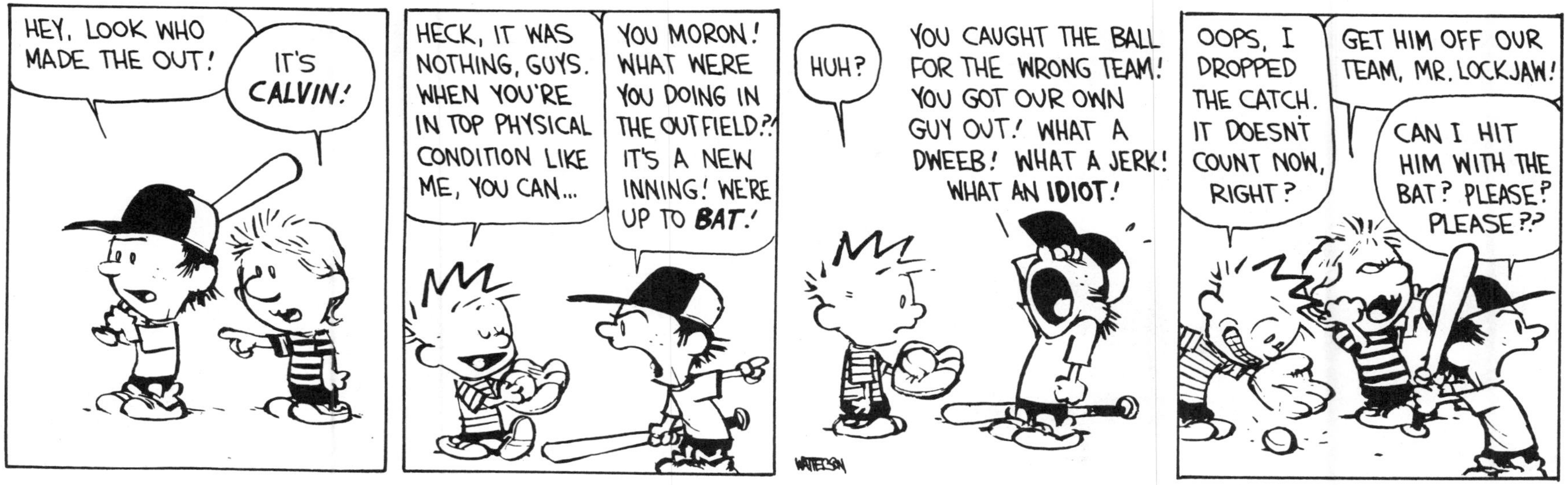
HEY, LOOK WHO MADE THE OUT!
IT'S CALVIN!
HECK, IT WAS NOTHING, GUYS. WHEN YOU'RE IN TOP PHYSICAL CONDITION LIKE ME, YOU CAN...
YOU MORON! WHAT WERE YOU DOING IN THE OUTFIELD?! IT'S A NEW INNING! WE'RE UP TO BAT!
HUH?
YOU CAUGHT THE BALL FOR THE WRONG TEAM! YOU GOT OUR OWN GUY OUT! WHAT A DWEEB! WHAT A JERK! WHAT AN IDIOT!
WATTERSON
OOPS, I DROPPED THE CATCH. IT DOESN'T COUNT NOW, RIGHT?
GET HIM OFF OUR TEAM, MR. LOCKJAW!
CAN I HIT HIM WITH THE BAT? PLEASE? PLEASE??

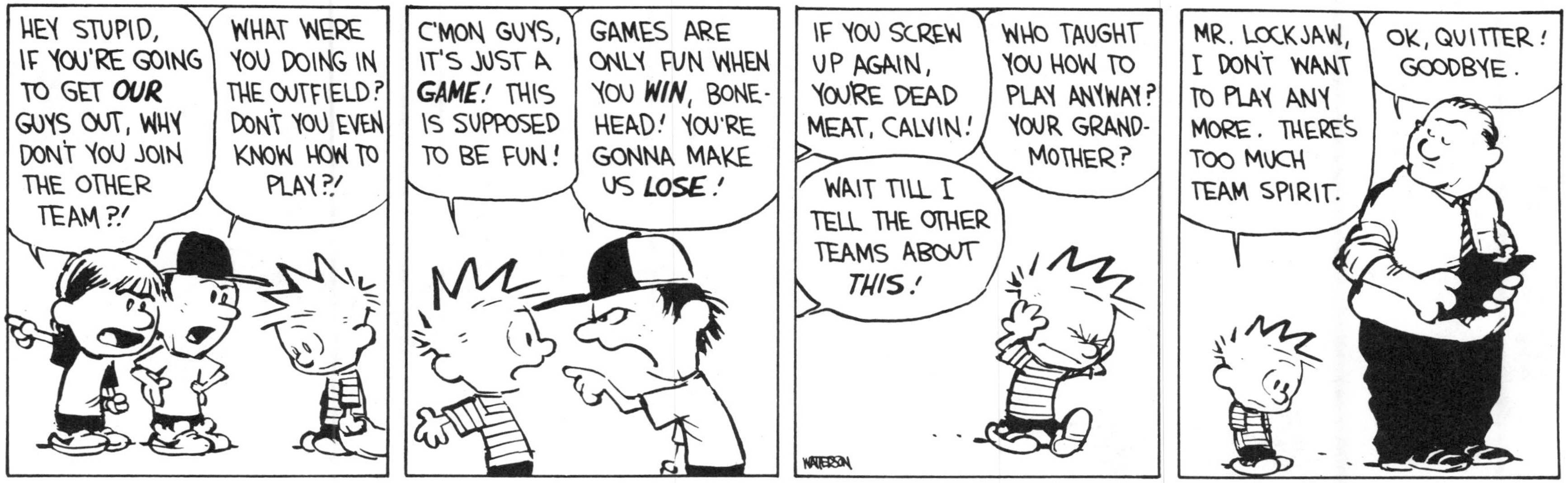
HEY STUPID, IF YOU'RE GOING TO GET OUR GUYS OUT, WHY DON'T YOU JOIN THE OTHER TEAM?!
WHAT WERE YOU DOING IN THE OUTFIELD? DON'T YOU EVEN KNOW HOW TO PLAY?!
C'MON GUYS, IT'S JUST A GAME! THIS IS SUPPOSED TO BE FUN!
GAMES ARE ONLY FUN WHEN YOU WIN, BONEHEAD! YOU'RE GONNA MAKE US LOSE!
IF YOU SCREW UP AGAIN, YOU'RE DEAD MEAT, CALVIN!
WHO TAUGHT YOU HOW TO PLAY ANYWAY? YOUR GRANDMOTHER?
WAIT TILL I TELL THE OTHER TEAMS ABOUT THIS!
WATTERSON
MR. LOCKJAW, I DON'T WANT TO PLAY ANY MORE. THERE'S TOO MUCH TEAM SPIRIT.
OK, QUITTER! GOODBYE.

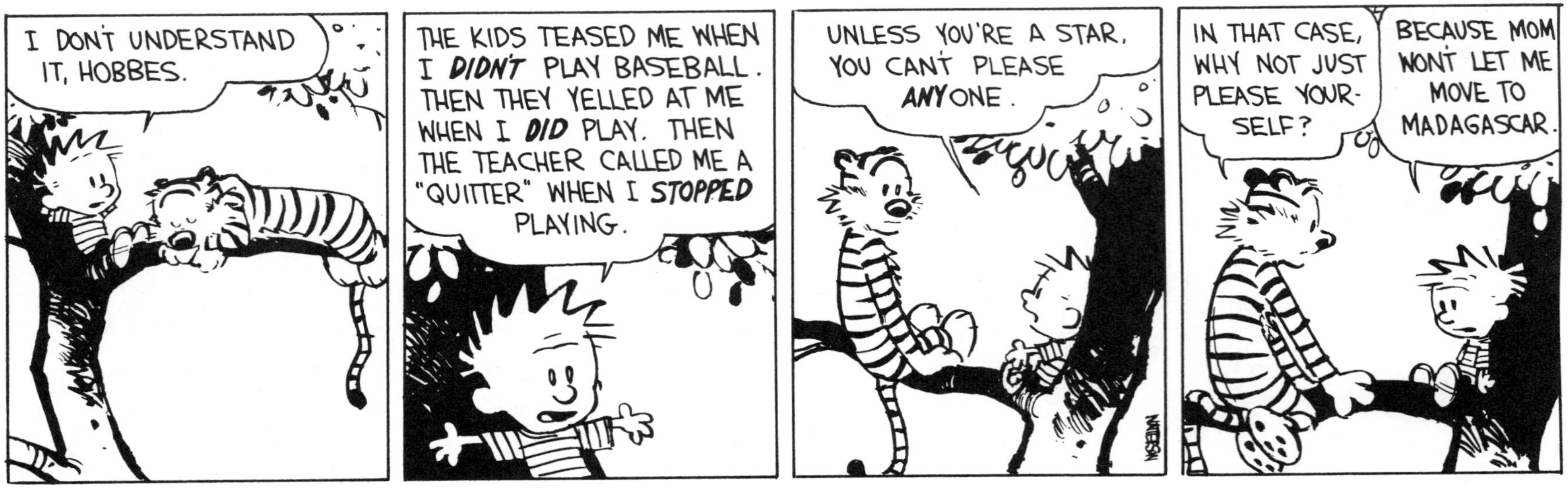
I DON'T UNDERSTAND IT, HOBBES.
THE KIDS TEASED ME WHEN I **DIDN'T** PLAY BASEBALL. THEN THEY YELLED AT ME WHEN I **DID** PLAY. THEN THE TEACHER CALLED ME A "QUITTER" WHEN I **STOPPED** PLAYING.
UNLESS YOU'RE A STAR, YOU CAN'T PLEASE **ANY**ONE.
IN THAT CASE, WHY NOT JUST PLEASE YOURSELF?
BECAUSE MOM WON'T LET ME MOVE TO MADAGASCAR.
WATTERSON

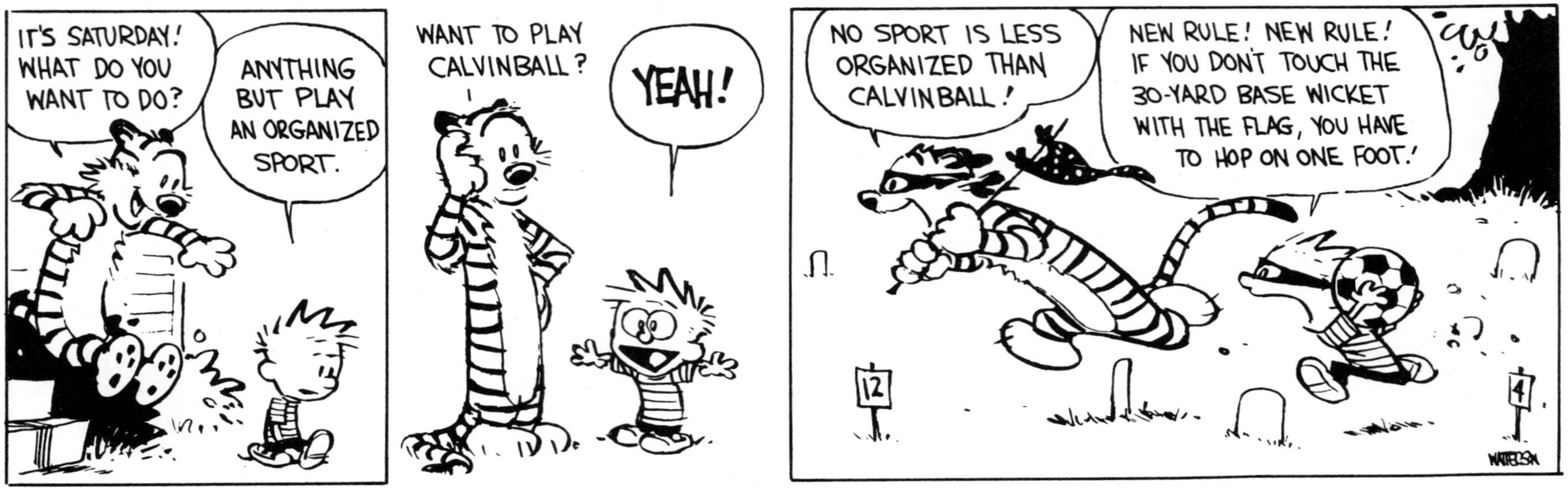
IT'S SATURDAY! WHAT DO YOU WANT TO DO?
ANYTHING BUT PLAY AN ORGANIZED SPORT.
WANT TO PLAY CALVINBALL?
YEAH!
NO SPORT IS LESS ORGANIZED THAN CALVINBALL!
NEW RULE! NEW RULE! IF YOU DON'T TOUCH THE 30-YARD BASE WICKET WITH THE FLAG, YOU HAVE TO HOP ON ONE FOOT!
12
4
WATTERSON

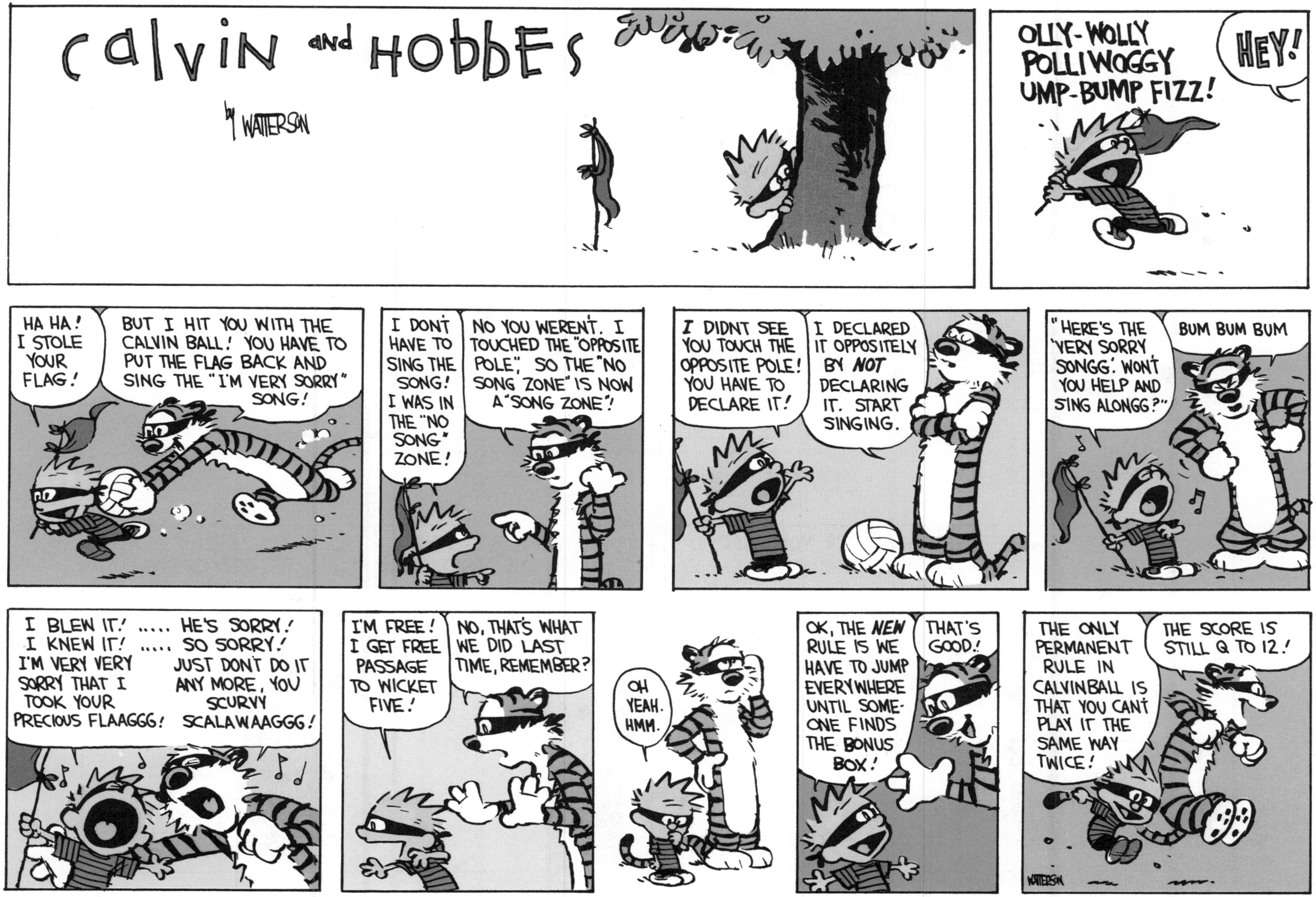
Calvin and Hobbes
by WATTERSON
OLLY-WOLLY POLLIWOGGY UMP-BUMP FIZZ!
HEY!
HA HA! I STOLE YOUR FLAG!
BUT I HIT YOU WITH THE CALVIN BALL! YOU HAVE TO PUT THE FLAG BACK AND SING THE "I'M VERY SORRY" SONG!
I DON'T HAVE TO SING THE SONG! I WAS IN THE "NO SONG" ZONE!
NO YOU WEREN'T. I TOUCHED THE "OPPOSITE POLE", SO THE "NO SONG ZONE" IS NOW A "SONG ZONE"!
I DIDN'T SEE YOU TOUCH THE OPPOSITE POLE! YOU HAVE TO DECLARE IT!
I DECLARED IT OPPOSITELY BY NOT DECLARING IT. START SINGING.
"HERE'S THE 'VERY SORRY SONGG'. WON'T YOU HELP AND SING ALONGG?"
BUM BUM BUM
I BLEW IT! I KNEW IT! I'M VERY VERY SORRY THAT I TOOK YOUR PRECIOUS FLAAGGG!
..... HE'S SORRY! ..... SO SORRY! JUST DON'T DO IT ANY MORE, YOU SCURVY SCALAWAAGGG!
I'M FREE! I GET FREE PASSAGE TO WICKET FIVE!
NO, THAT'S WHAT WE DID LAST TIME, REMEMBER?
OH YEAH. HMM.
OK, THE NEW RULE IS WE HAVE TO JUMP EVERYWHERE UNTIL SOMEONE FINDS THE BONUS BOX!
THAT'S GOOD!
THE ONLY PERMANENT RULE IN CALVINBALL IS THAT YOU CAN'T PLAY IT THE SAME WAY TWICE!
THE SCORE IS STILL Q TO 12!
WATTERSON

People have asked how to play Calvinball. It's pretty simple: you make up the rules as you go.

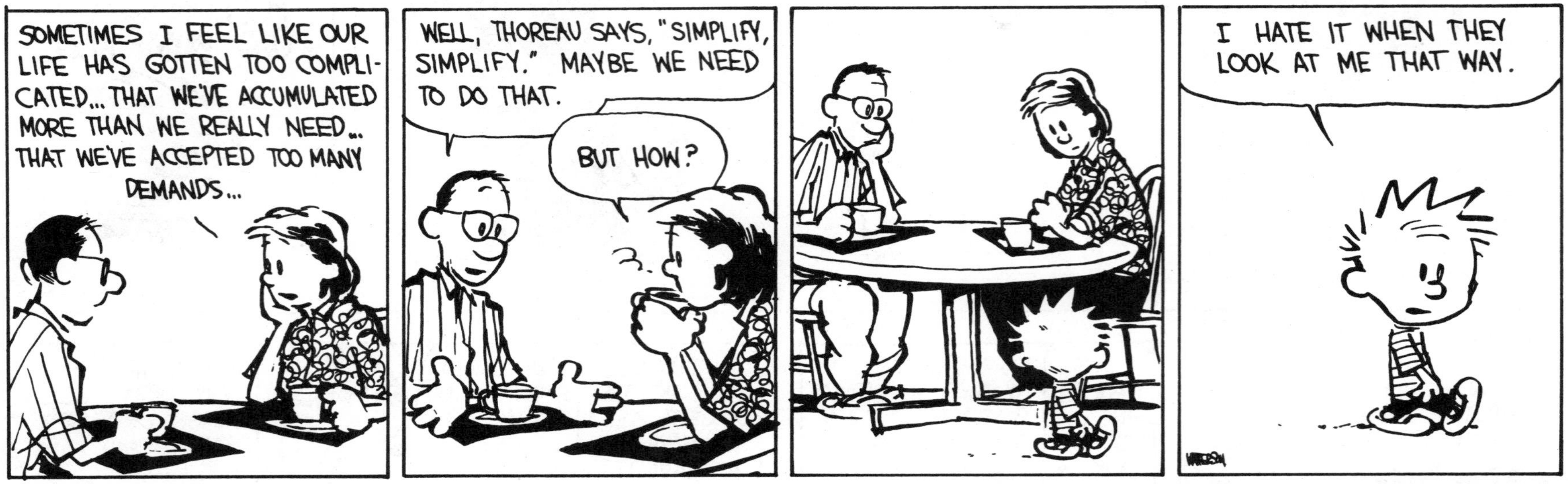
SOMETIMES I FEEL LIKE OUR LIFE HAS GOTTEN TOO COMPLICATED... THAT WE'VE ACCUMULATED MORE THAN WE REALLY NEED... THAT WE'VE ACCEPTED TOO MANY DEMANDS...
WELL, THOREAU SAYS, "SIMPLIFY, SIMPLIFY." MAYBE WE NEED TO DO THAT.
BUT HOW?
I HATE IT WHEN THEY LOOK AT ME THAT WAY.

Calvin's parents are sometimes ambivalent about their child's effect on their lives, as I imagine any sane parent would be. Depicting that used to disturb some readers, who expected family strips to be highly sanitized. Now that television sitcoms are commonly a half-hour volley of vicious insults, this sort of strip looks positively heartwarming.

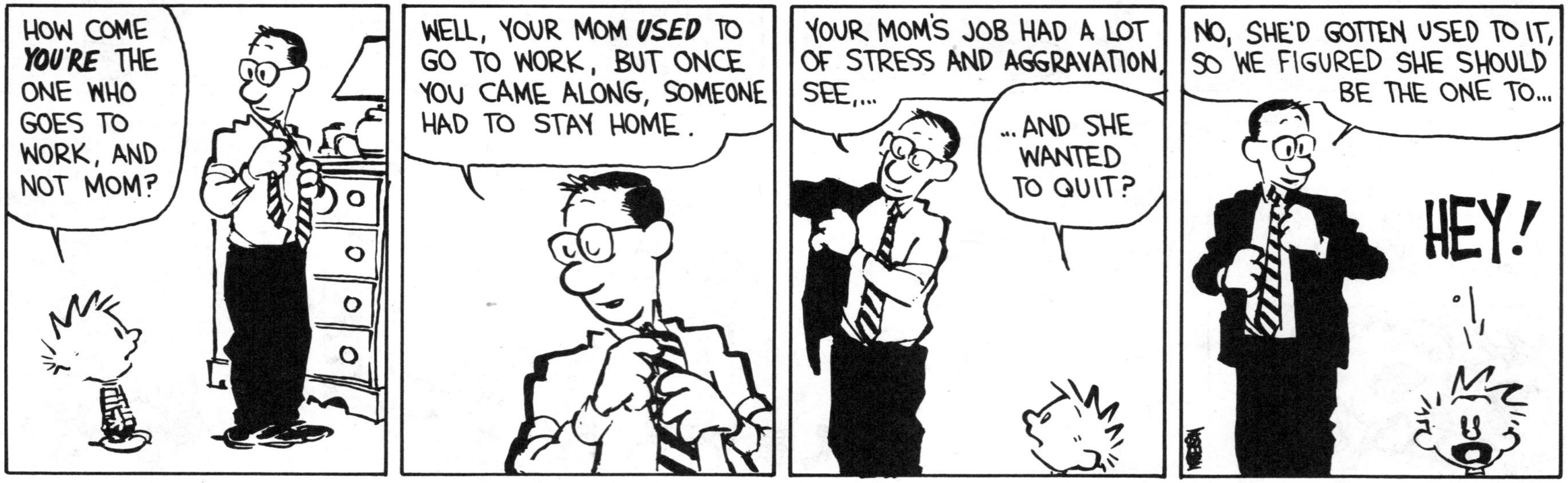
HOW COME ***YOU'RE*** THE ONE WHO GOES TO WORK, AND NOT MOM?
WELL, YOUR MOM ***USED*** TO GO TO WORK, BUT ONCE YOU CAME ALONG, SOMEONE HAD TO STAY HOME.
YOUR MOM'S JOB HAD A LOT OF STRESS AND AGGRAVATION, SEE,...
...AND SHE WANTED TO QUIT?
NO, SHE'D GOTTEN USED TO IT, SO WE FIGURED SHE SHOULD BE THE ONE TO...
HEY!

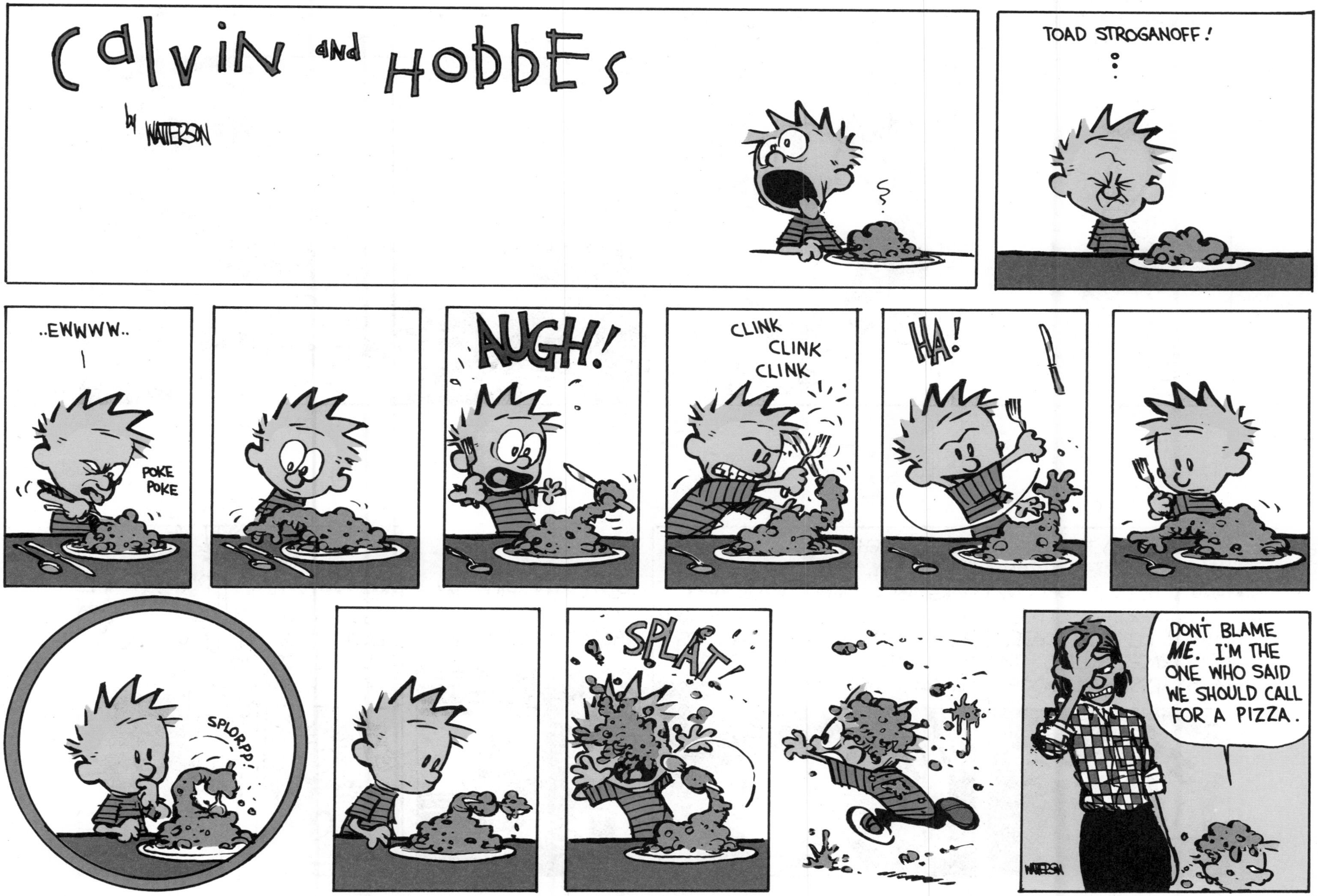
Calvin and HOBBES
by WATTERSON
TOAD STROGANOFF!
..EWWWW..
POKE POKE
AUGH!
CLINK CLINK CLINK
HA!
SPLORPP!
SPLAT!
DON'T BLAME *ME*. I'M THE ONE WHO SAID WE SHOULD CALL FOR A PIZZA.
WATTERSON

When I was a kid, I drew a comic strip about oatmeal that was alive. At the time, I thought that was absolutely hilarious, so I suppose that's where this comes from. Calvin's adversarial relationship with his mom's cooking is a slight exaggeration of my own fussy eating habits as a kid.

Tracer Bullet stories are extremely time-consuming to write, so I don't attempt them often. I'm not at all familiar with *film noir* or detective novels, so these are just spoofs on the clichés of the genre. Cartoonists don't use black much anymore (the eye, being lazy, is attracted to empty white space, especially when the panels are so small), and we miss some dramatic possibilities that way.

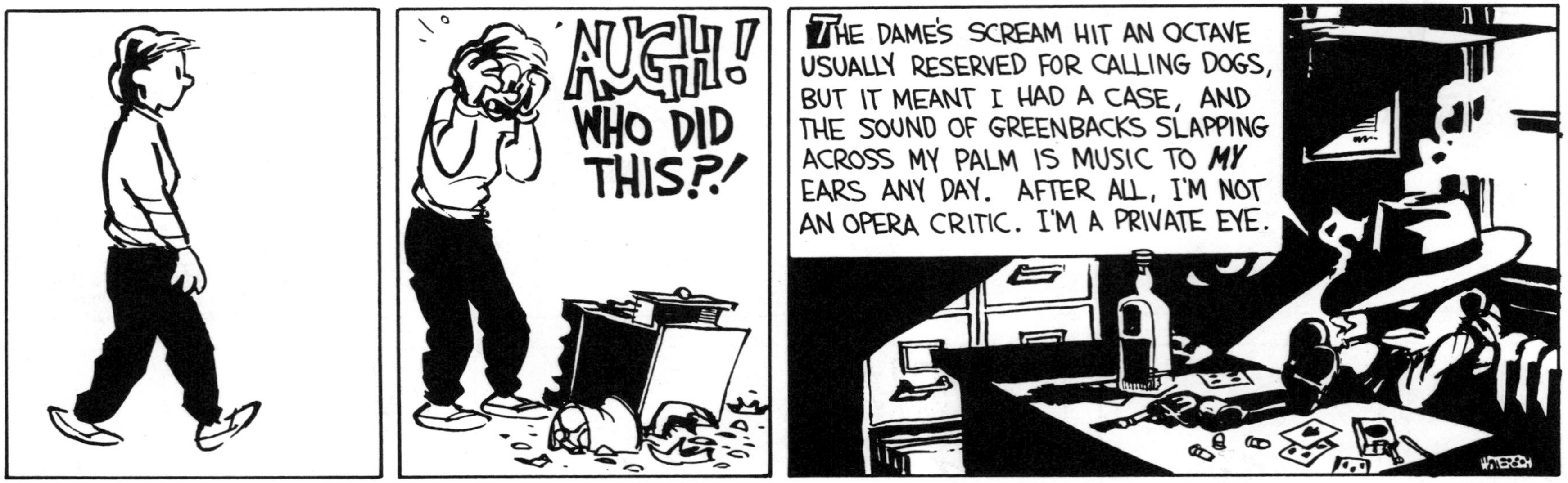

AUGH! WHO DID THIS?!
THE DAME'S SCREAM HIT AN OCTAVE USUALLY RESERVED FOR CALLING DOGS, BUT IT MEANT I HAD A CASE, AND THE SOUND OF GREENBACKS SLAPPING ACROSS MY PALM IS MUSIC TO MY EARS ANY DAY. AFTER ALL, I'M NOT AN OPERA CRITIC. I'M A PRIVATE EYE.
WATTERSON

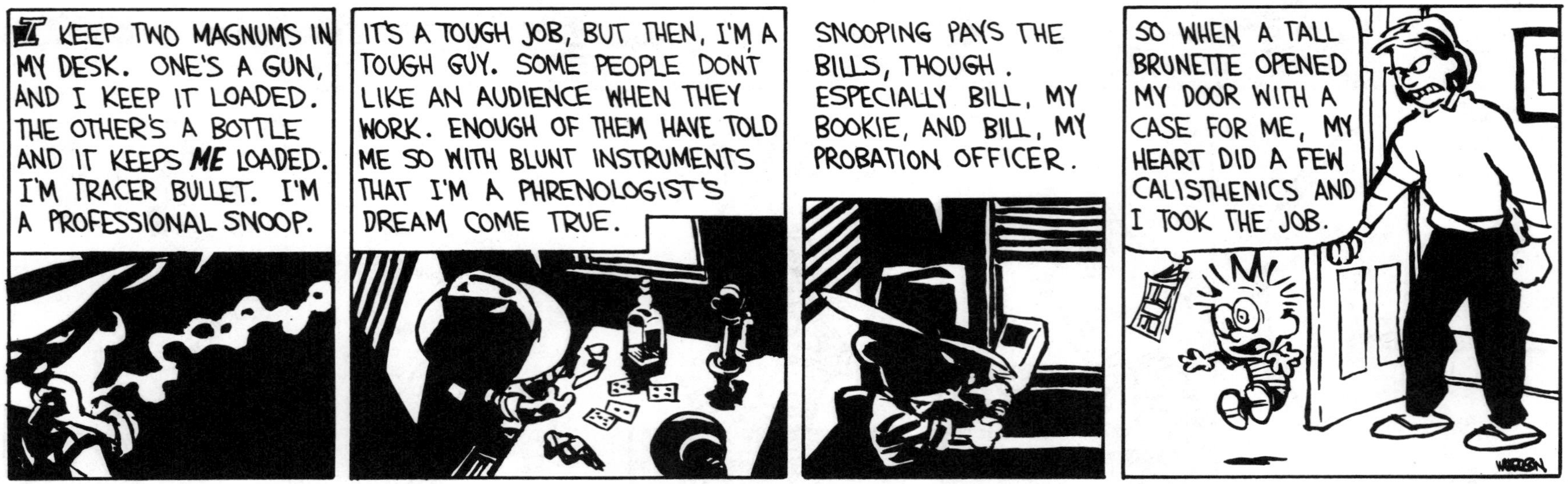

I KEEP TWO MAGNUMS IN MY DESK. ONE'S A GUN, AND I KEEP IT LOADED. THE OTHER'S A BOTTLE AND IT KEEPS ME LOADED. I'M TRACER BULLET. I'M A PROFESSIONAL SNOOP.
IT'S A TOUGH JOB, BUT THEN, I'M A TOUGH GUY. SOME PEOPLE DON'T LIKE AN AUDIENCE WHEN THEY WORK. ENOUGH OF THEM HAVE TOLD ME SO WITH BLUNT INSTRUMENTS THAT I'M A PHRENOLOGIST'S DREAM COME TRUE.
SNOOPING PAYS THE BILLS, THOUGH. ESPECIALLY BILL, MY BOOKIE, AND BILL, MY PROBATION OFFICER.
SO WHEN A TALL BRUNETTE OPENED MY DOOR WITH A CASE FOR ME, MY HEART DID A FEW CALISTHENICS AND I TOOK THE JOB.
WATTERSON

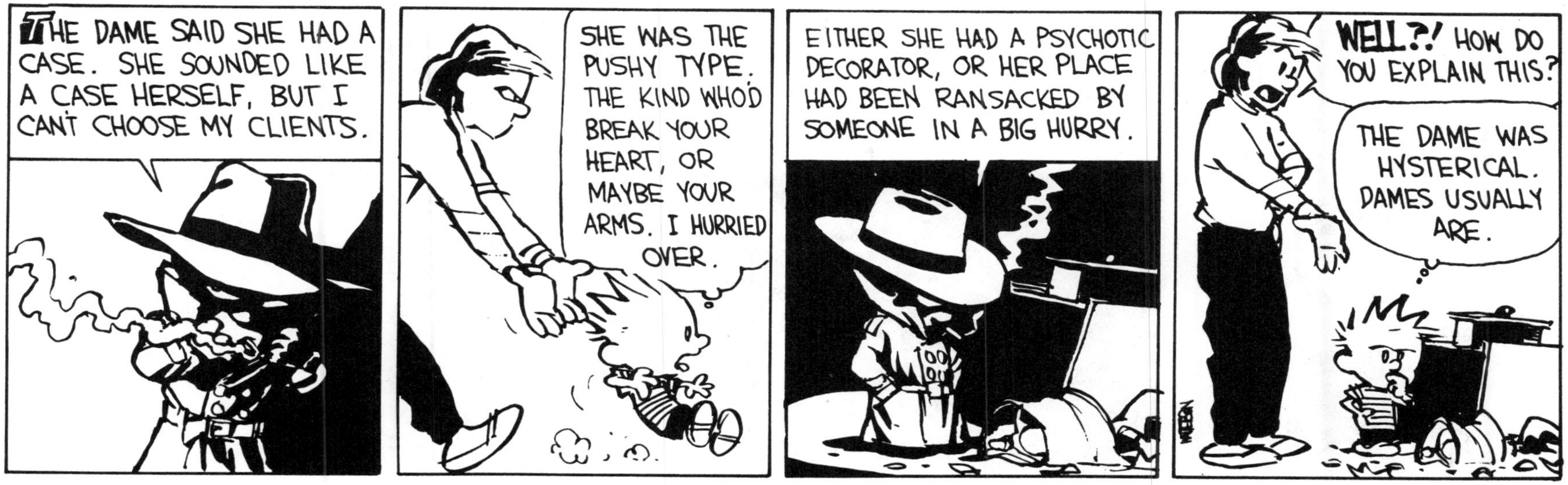
THE DAME SAID SHE HAD A CASE. SHE SOUNDED LIKE A CASE HERSELF, BUT I CAN'T CHOOSE MY CLIENTS.
SHE WAS THE PUSHY TYPE. THE KIND WHO'D BREAK YOUR HEART, OR MAYBE YOUR ARMS. I HURRIED OVER.
EITHER SHE HAD A PSYCHOTIC DECORATOR, OR HER PLACE HAD BEEN RANSACKED BY SOMEONE IN A BIG HURRY.
WELL?! HOW DO YOU EXPLAIN THIS?
THE DAME WAS HYSTERICAL. DAMES USUALLY ARE.

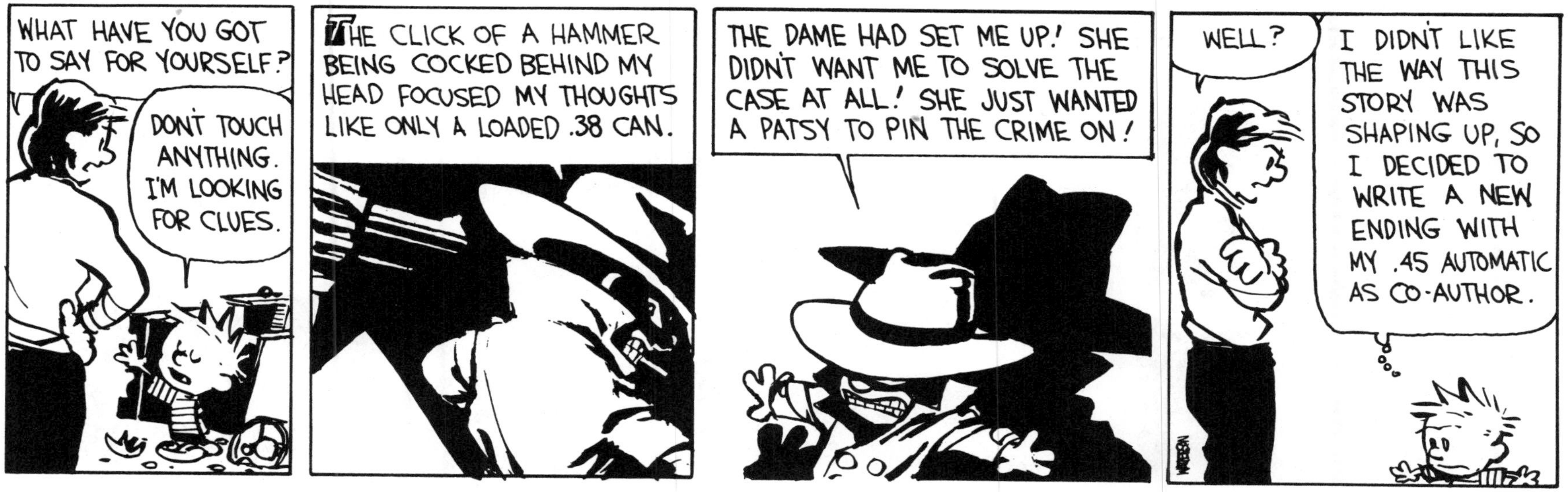
WHAT HAVE YOU GOT TO SAY FOR YOURSELF?
DON'T TOUCH ANYTHING. I'M LOOKING FOR CLUES.
THE CLICK OF A HAMMER BEING COCKED BEHIND MY HEAD FOCUSED MY THOUGHTS LIKE ONLY A LOADED .38 CAN.
THE DAME HAD SET ME UP! SHE DIDN'T WANT ME TO SOLVE THE CASE AT ALL! SHE JUST WANTED A PATSY TO PIN THE CRIME ON!
WELL?
I DIDN'T LIKE THE WAY THIS STORY WAS SHAPING UP, SO I DECIDED TO WRITE A NEW ENDING WITH MY .45 AUTOMATIC AS CO-AUTHOR.

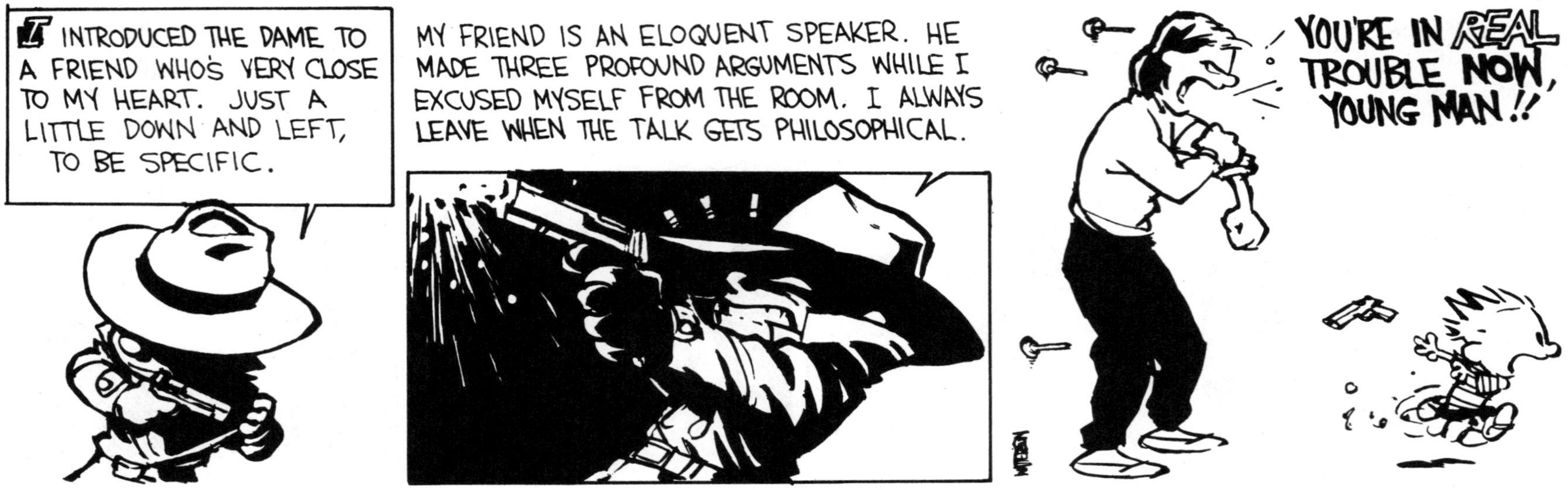
I INTRODUCED THE DAME TO A FRIEND WHO'S VERY CLOSE TO MY HEART. JUST A LITTLE DOWN AND LEFT, TO BE SPECIFIC.
MY FRIEND IS AN ELOQUENT SPEAKER. HE MADE THREE PROFOUND ARGUMENTS WHILE I EXCUSED MYSELF FROM THE ROOM. I ALWAYS LEAVE WHEN THE TALK GETS PHILOSOPHICAL.
YOU'RE IN REAL TROUBLE NOW, YOUNG MAN!!

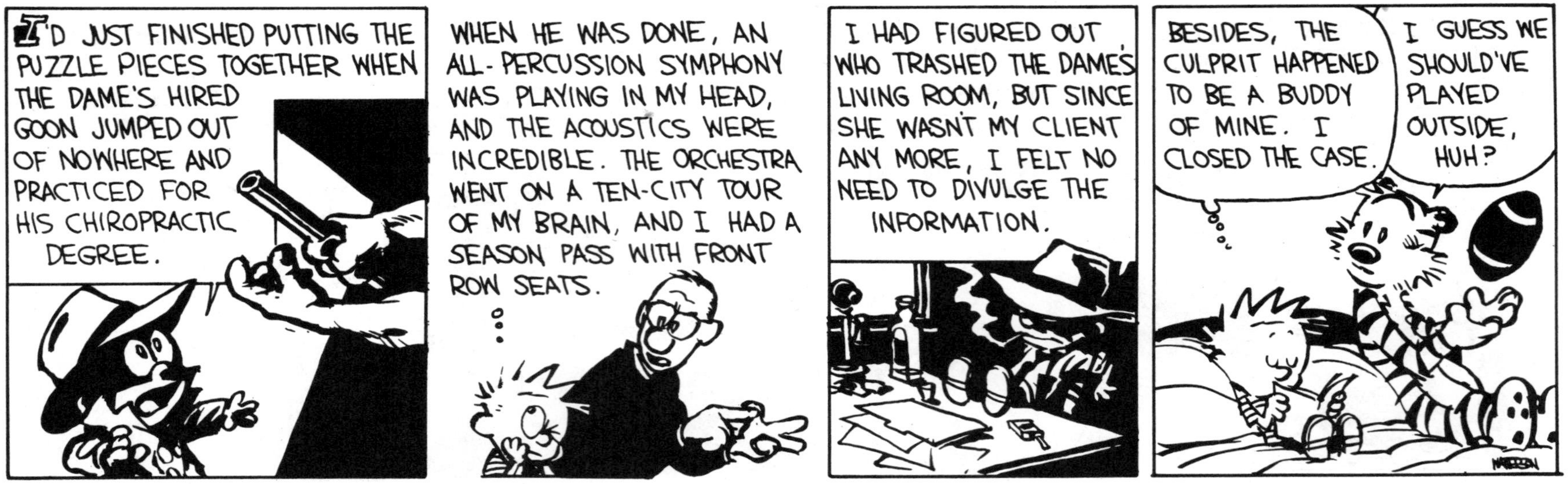
I'D JUST FINISHED PUTTING THE PUZZLE PIECES TOGETHER WHEN THE DAME'S HIRED GOON JUMPED OUT OF NOWHERE AND PRACTICED FOR HIS CHIROPRACTIC DEGREE.
WHEN HE WAS DONE, AN ALL-PERCUSSION SYMPHONY WAS PLAYING IN MY HEAD, AND THE ACOUSTICS WERE INCREDIBLE. THE ORCHESTRA WENT ON A TEN-CITY TOUR OF MY BRAIN, AND I HAD A SEASON PASS WITH FRONT ROW SEATS.
I HAD FIGURED OUT WHO TRASHED THE DAME'S LIVING ROOM, BUT SINCE SHE WASN'T MY CLIENT ANY MORE, I FELT NO NEED TO DIVULGE THE INFORMATION.
BESIDES, THE CULPRIT HAPPENED TO BE A BUDDY OF MINE. I CLOSED THE CASE.
I GUESS WE SHOULD'VE PLAYED OUTSIDE, HUH?

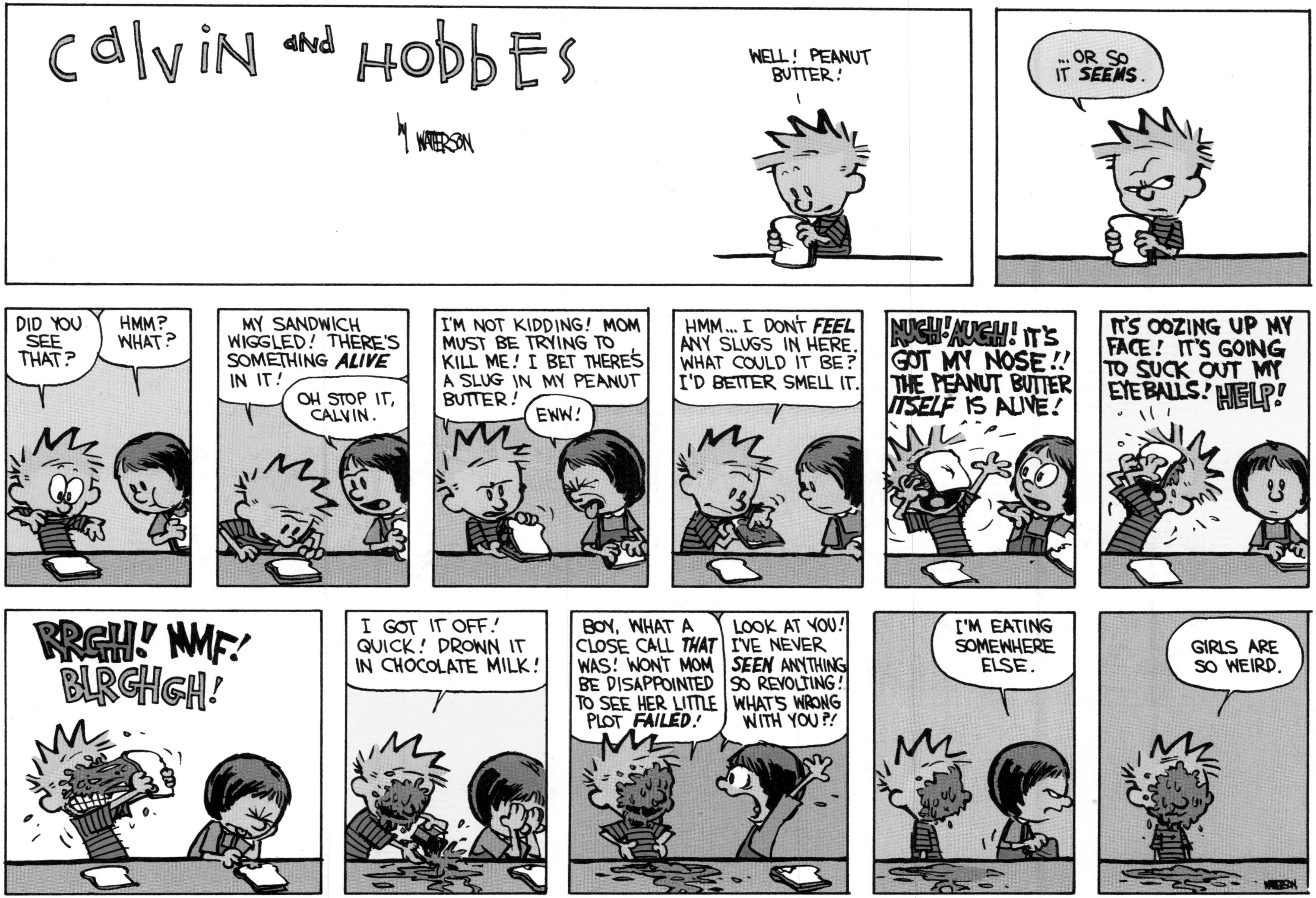
Calvin and Hobbes
by WATTERSON
WELL! PEANUT BUTTER!
...OR SO IT SEEMS.
DID YOU SEE THAT?
HMM? WHAT?
MY SANDWICH WIGGLED! THERE'S SOMETHING ALIVE IN IT!
OH STOP IT, CALVIN.
I'M NOT KIDDING! MOM MUST BE TRYING TO KILL ME! I BET THERE'S A SLUG IN MY PEANUT BUTTER!
EWW!
HMM... I DON'T FEEL ANY SLUGS IN HERE. WHAT COULD IT BE? I'D BETTER SMELL IT.
AUGH! AUGH! IT'S GOT MY NOSE!! THE PEANUT BUTTER ITSELF IS ALIVE!
IT'S OOZING UP MY FACE! IT'S GOING TO SUCK OUT MY EYEBALLS! HELP!
RRGH! NMF! BLRGHGH!
I GOT IT OFF! QUICK! DROWN IT IN CHOCOLATE MILK!
BOY, WHAT A CLOSE CALL THAT WAS! WON'T MOM BE DISAPPOINTED TO SEE HER LITTLE PLOT FAILED!
LOOK AT YOU! I'VE NEVER SEEN ANYTHING SO REVOLTING! WHAT'S WRONG WITH YOU?!
I'M EATING SOMEWHERE ELSE.
GIRLS ARE SO WEIRD.
WATTERSON
Calvin will probably have trouble getting dates when he's older.

The Get Rid Of Slimy girlS club is based on similar clubs my next-door neighbor and I formed when we were kids. Our mission was to harass neighborhood girls, but if they wouldn't come out, we'd often settle for harassing my brother. We prepared for a lot of great struggles that never happened. Once we gathered big hickory nuts, loaded them into a suitcase, locked it so nobody else could open it, and stashed it up high in a tree. When the Critical Moment came, we planned to scramble up the tree and unleash a hail of nuts upon our astonished pursuers. Six months later, when the leaves were down, we looked up and discovered the suitcase was still in the tree. The hinges had rusted, the nuts had rotted, and the suitcase was ruined. Our great plans often had this kind of boring anticlimax, which is why fiction comes in so handy.

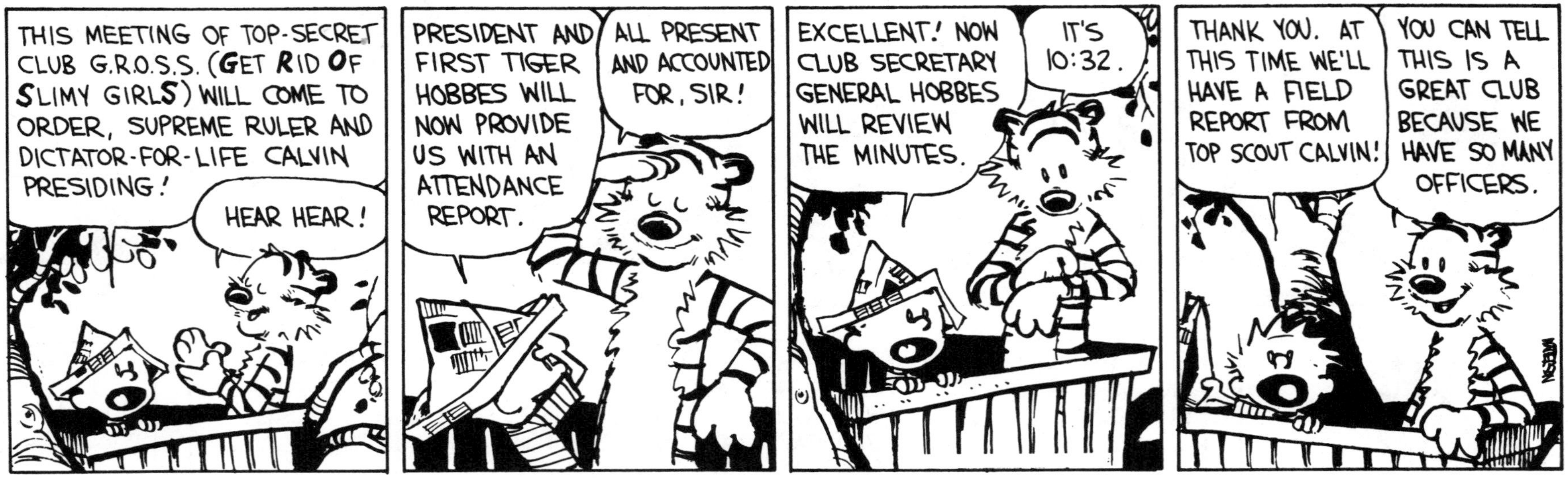

THIS MEETING OF TOP-SECRET CLUB G.R.O.S.S. (GET RID OF SLIMY GIRLS) WILL COME TO ORDER, SUPREME RULER AND DICTATOR-FOR-LIFE CALVIN PRESIDING!
HEAR HEAR!
PRESIDENT AND FIRST TIGER HOBBES WILL NOW PROVIDE US WITH AN ATTENDANCE REPORT.
ALL PRESENT AND ACCOUNTED FOR, SIR!
EXCELLENT! NOW CLUB SECRETARY GENERAL HOBBES WILL REVIEW THE MINUTES.
IT'S 10:32.
THANK YOU. AT THIS TIME WE'LL HAVE A FIELD REPORT FROM TOP SCOUT CALVIN!
YOU CAN TELL THIS IS A GREAT CLUB BECAUSE WE HAVE SO MANY OFFICERS.

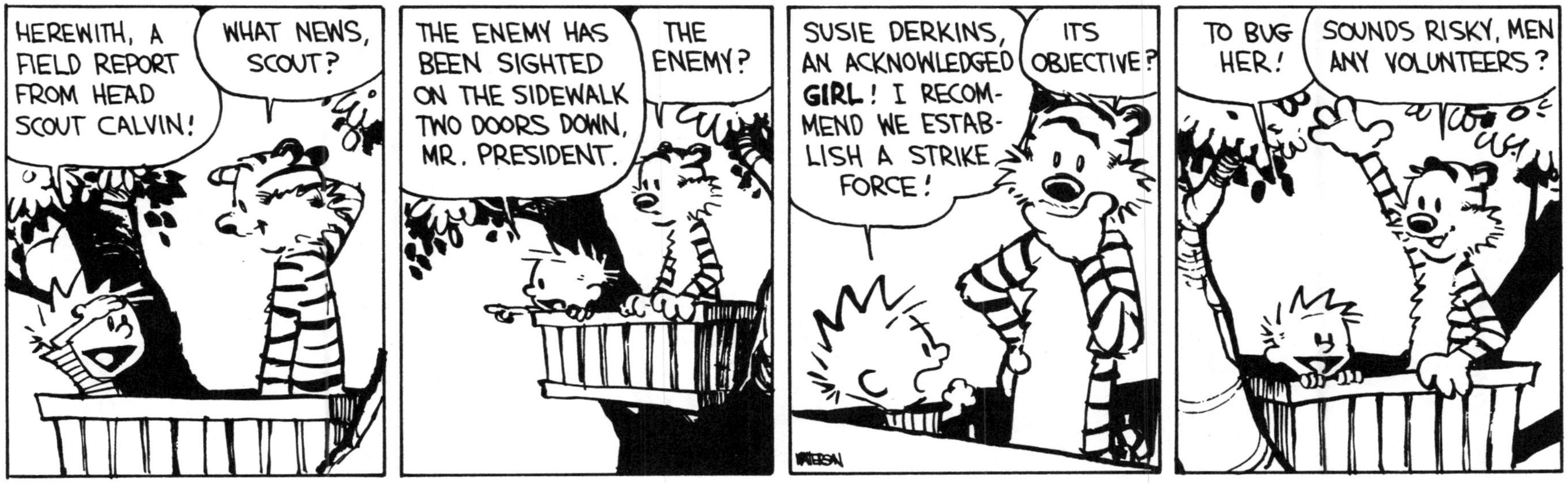
HEREWITH, A FIELD REPORT FROM HEAD SCOUT CALVIN!
WHAT NEWS, SCOUT?
THE ENEMY HAS BEEN SIGHTED ON THE SIDEWALK TWO DOORS DOWN, MR. PRESIDENT.
THE ENEMY?
SUSIE DERKINS, AN ACKNOWLEDGED GIRL! I RECOMMEND WE ESTABLISH A STRIKE FORCE!
ITS OBJECTIVE?
TO BUG HER!
SOUNDS RISKY, MEN ANY VOLUNTEERS?
WATTERSON

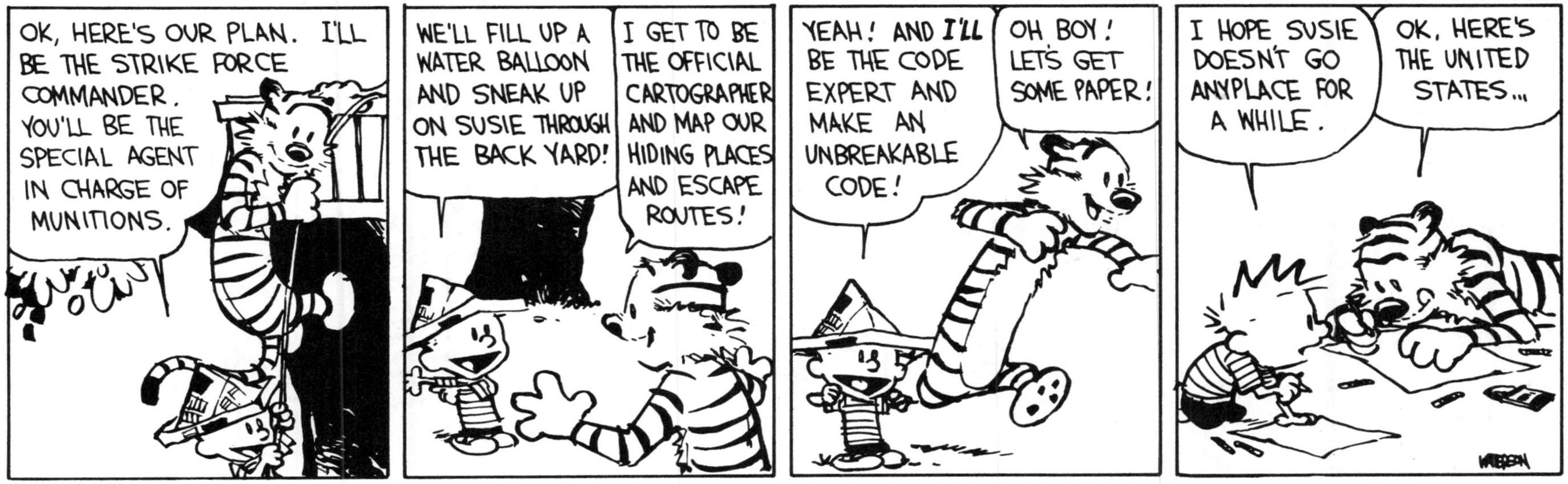
OK, HERE'S OUR PLAN. I'LL BE THE STRIKE FORCE COMMANDER. YOU'LL BE THE SPECIAL AGENT IN CHARGE OF MUNITIONS.
WE'LL FILL UP A WATER BALLOON AND SNEAK UP ON SUSIE THROUGH THE BACK YARD!
I GET TO BE THE OFFICIAL CARTOGRAPHER AND MAP OUR HIDING PLACES AND ESCAPE ROUTES!
YEAH! AND I'LL BE THE CODE EXPERT AND MAKE AN UNBREAKABLE CODE!
OH BOY! LET'S GET SOME PAPER!
I HOPE SUSIE DOESN'T GO ANYPLACE FOR A WHILE.
OK, HERE'S THE UNITED STATES...
WATTERSON

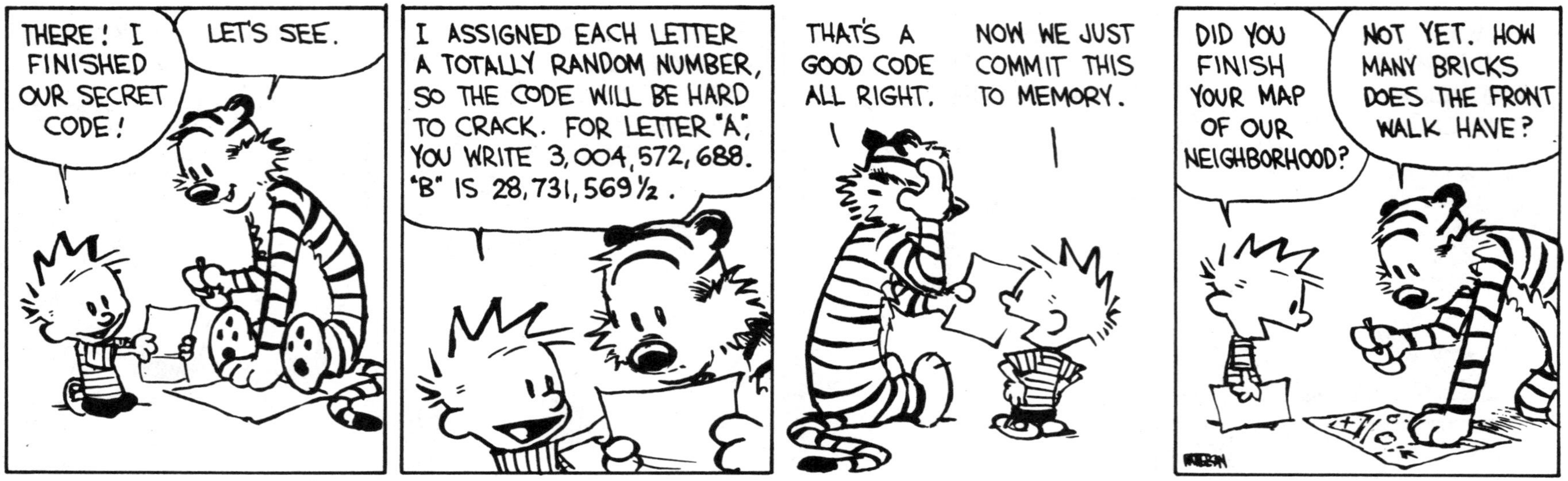
THERE! I FINISHED OUR SECRET CODE!
LET'S SEE.
I ASSIGNED EACH LETTER A TOTALLY RANDOM NUMBER, SO THE CODE WILL BE HARD TO CRACK. FOR LETTER "A", YOU WRITE 3,004,572,688. "B" IS 28,731,569½.
THAT'S A GOOD CODE ALL RIGHT.
NOW WE JUST COMMIT THIS TO MEMORY.
DID YOU FINISH YOUR MAP OF OUR NEIGHBORHOOD?
NOT YET. HOW MANY BRICKS DOES THE FRONT WALK HAVE?

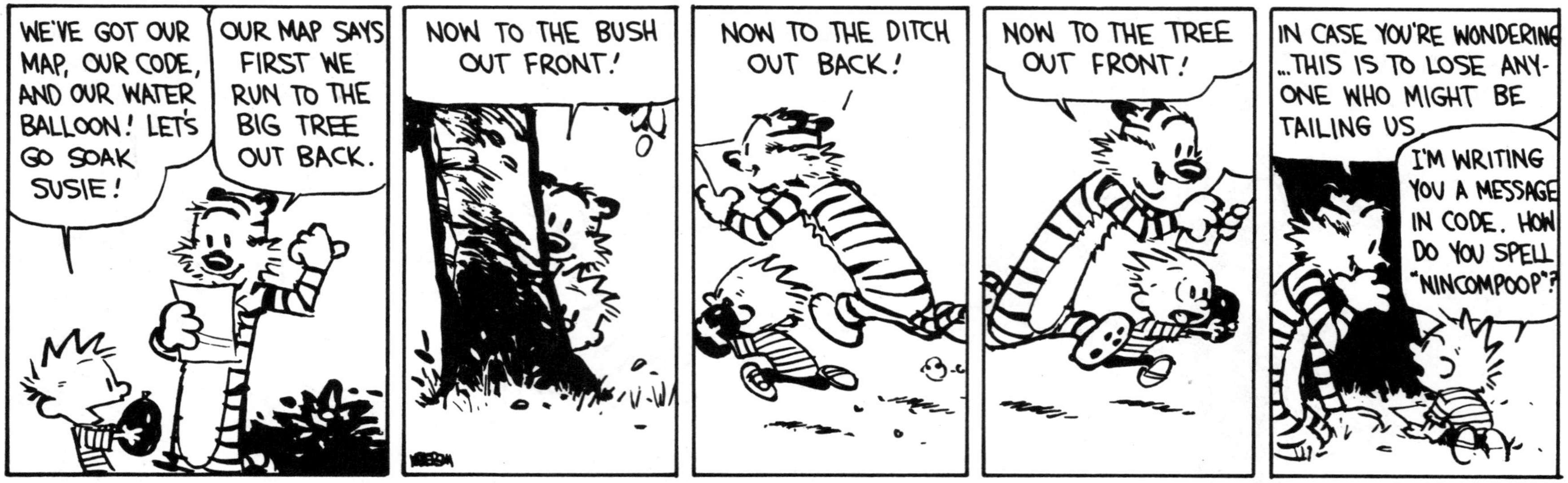
WE'VE GOT OUR MAP, OUR CODE, AND OUR WATER BALLOON! LET'S GO SOAK SUSIE!
OUR MAP SAYS FIRST WE RUN TO THE BIG TREE OUT BACK.
NOW TO THE BUSH OUT FRONT!
NOW TO THE DITCH OUT BACK!
NOW TO THE TREE OUT FRONT!
IN CASE YOU'RE WONDERING ...THIS IS TO LOSE ANYONE WHO MIGHT BE TAILING US.
I'M WRITING YOU A MESSAGE IN CODE. HOW DO YOU SPELL "NINCOMPOOP"?

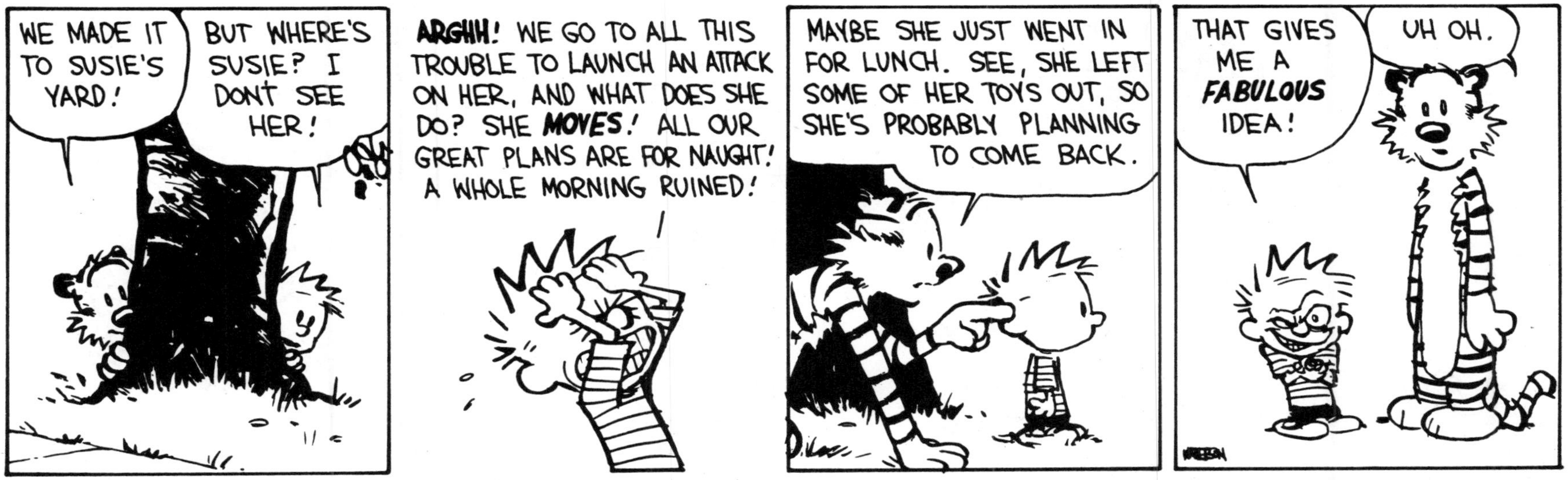
WE MADE IT TO SUSIE'S YARD!
BUT WHERE'S SUSIE? I DON'T SEE HER!
ARGHH! WE GO TO ALL THIS TROUBLE TO LAUNCH AN ATTACK ON HER, AND WHAT DOES SHE DO? SHE MOVES! ALL OUR GREAT PLANS ARE FOR NAUGHT! A WHOLE MORNING RUINED!
MAYBE SHE JUST WENT IN FOR LUNCH. SEE, SHE LEFT SOME OF HER TOYS OUT, SO SHE'S PROBABLY PLANNING TO COME BACK.
THAT GIVES ME A FABULOUS IDEA!
UH OH.

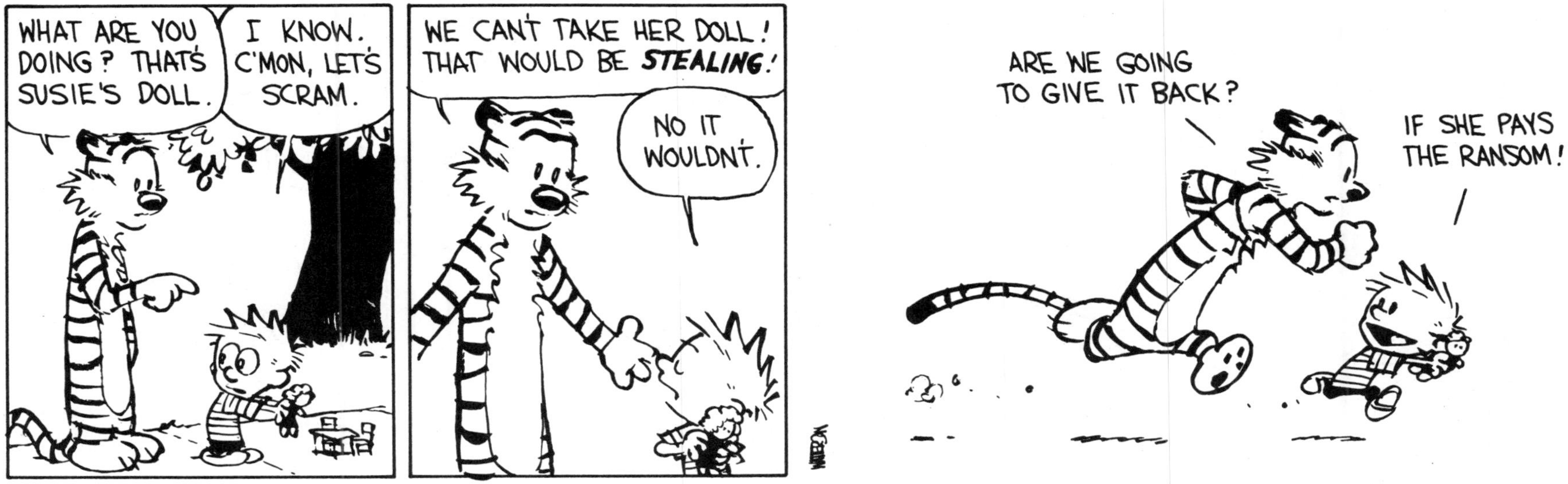
WHAT ARE YOU DOING? THAT'S SUSIE'S DOLL.
I KNOW. C'MON, LET'S SCRAM.
WE CAN'T TAKE HER DOLL! THAT WOULD BE STEALING!
NO IT WOULDN'T.
ARE WE GOING TO GIVE IT BACK?
IF SHE PAYS THE RANSOM!

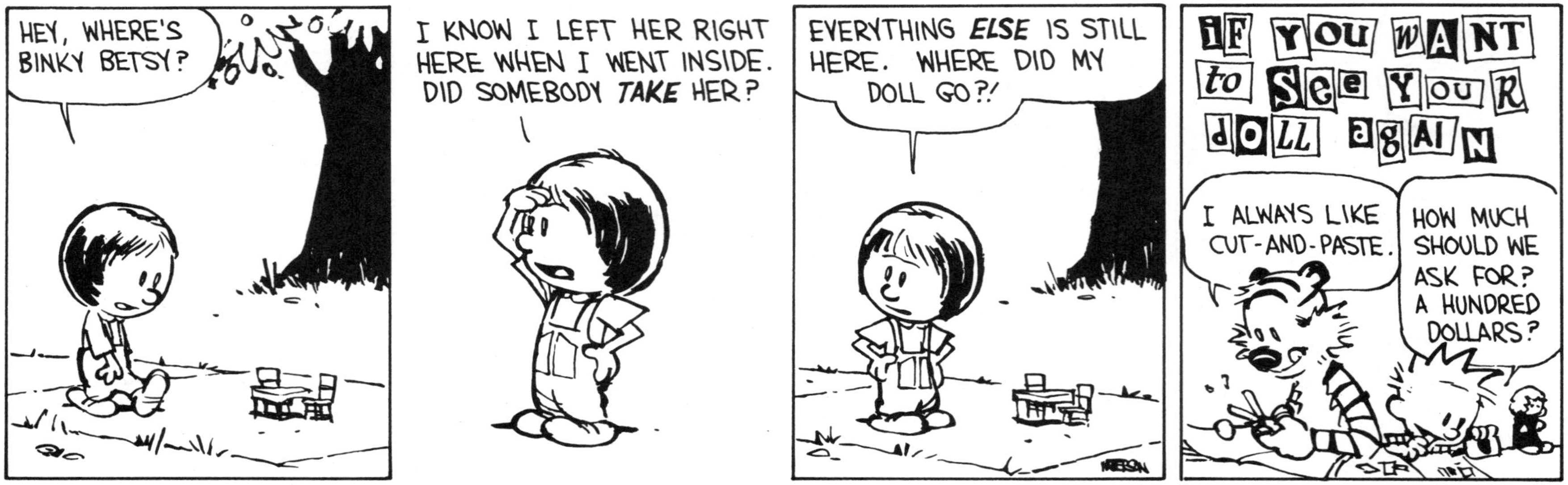
HEY, WHERE'S BINKY BETSY?
I KNOW I LEFT HER RIGHT HERE WHEN I WENT INSIDE. DID SOMEBODY *TAKE* HER?
EVERYTHING *ELSE* IS STILL HERE. WHERE DID MY DOLL GO?!
IF YOU WANT to SEE YOUR doll again
I ALWAYS LIKE CUT-AND-PASTE.
HOW MUCH SHOULD WE ASK FOR? A HUNDRED DOLLARS?

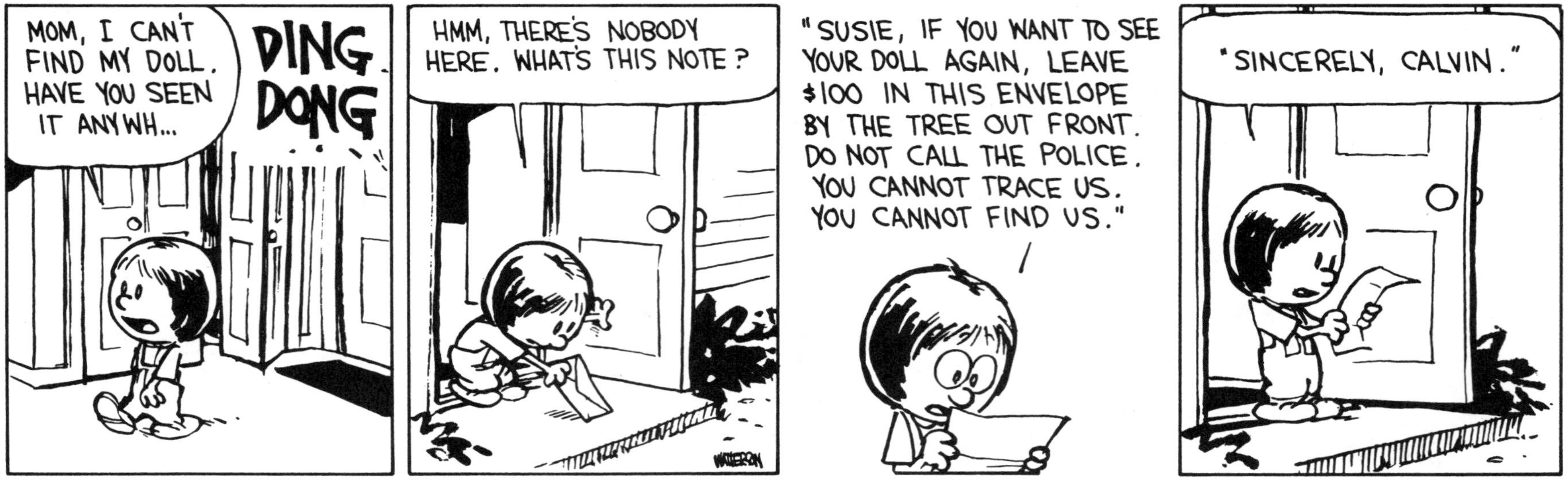
MOM, I CAN'T FIND MY DOLL. HAVE YOU SEEN IT ANYWH...
DING DONG
HMM, THERE'S NOBODY HERE. WHAT'S THIS NOTE?
"SUSIE, IF YOU WANT TO SEE YOUR DOLL AGAIN, LEAVE $100 IN THIS ENVELOPE BY THE TREE OUT FRONT. DO NOT CALL THE POLICE. YOU CANNOT TRACE US. YOU CANNOT FIND US."
"SINCERELY, CALVIN."

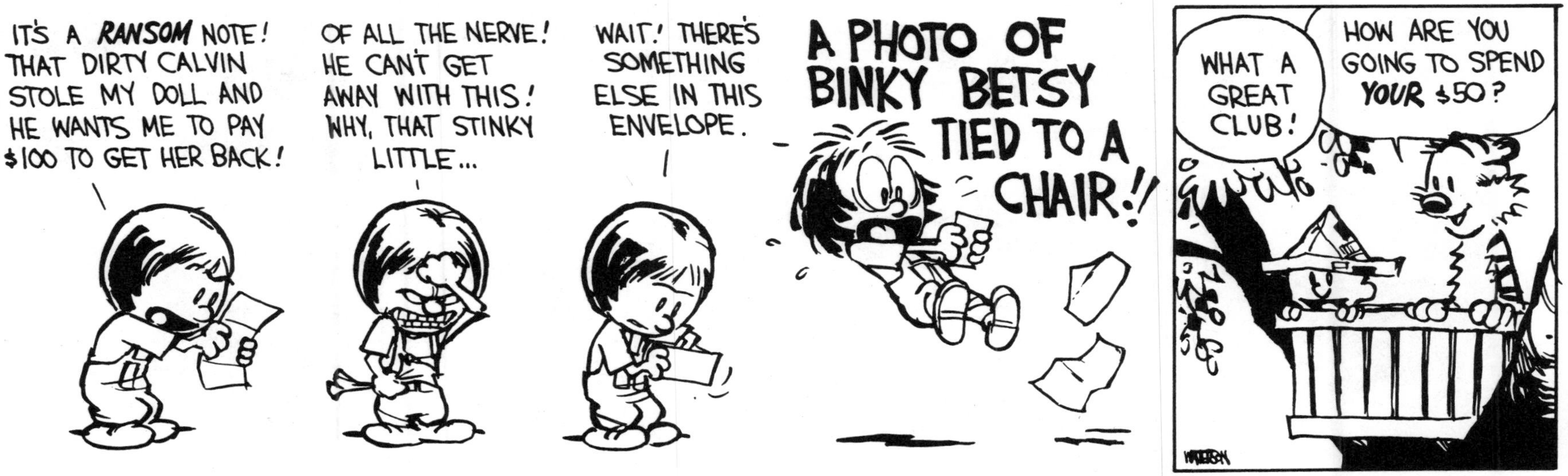
IT'S A RANSOM NOTE! THAT DIRTY CALVIN STOLE MY DOLL AND HE WANTS ME TO PAY $100 TO GET HER BACK!
OF ALL THE NERVE! HE CAN'T GET AWAY WITH THIS! WHY, THAT STINKY LITTLE...
WAIT! THERE'S SOMETHING ELSE IN THIS ENVELOPE.
A PHOTO OF BINKY BETSY TIED TO A CHAIR!!
WHAT A GREAT CLUB!
HOW ARE YOU GOING TO SPEND YOUR $50?

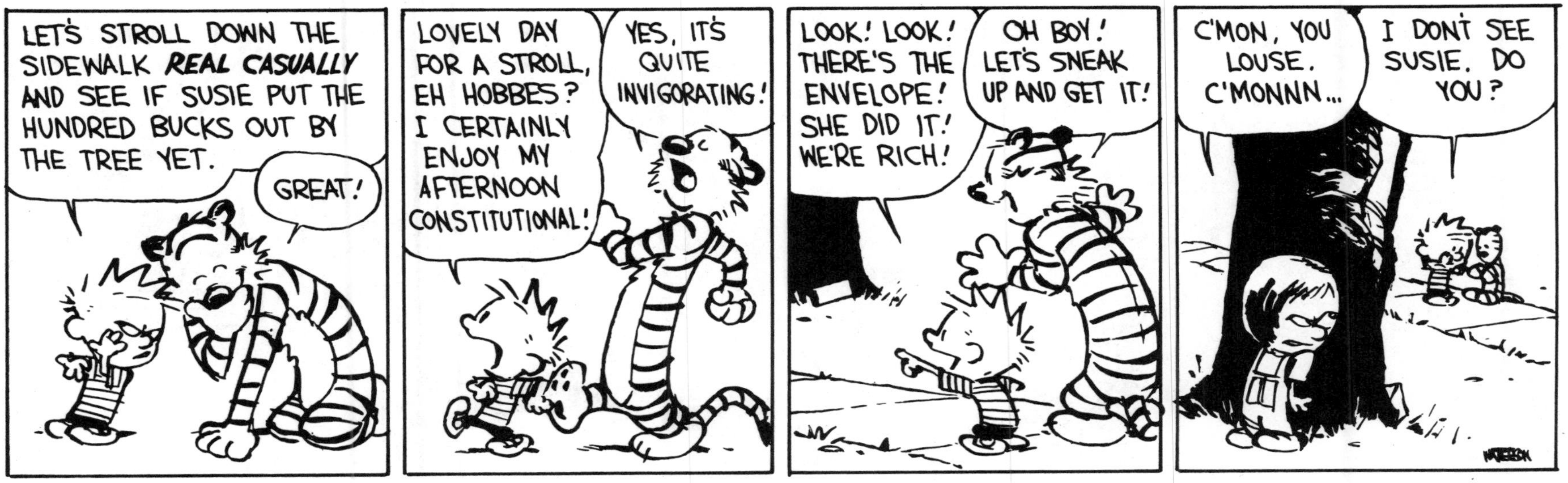
LET'S STROLL DOWN THE SIDEWALK REAL CASUALLY AND SEE IF SUSIE PUT THE HUNDRED BUCKS OUT BY THE TREE YET.
GREAT!
LOVELY DAY FOR A STROLL, EH HOBBES? I CERTAINLY ENJOY MY AFTERNOON CONSTITUTIONAL!
YES, IT'S QUITE INVIGORATING!
LOOK! LOOK! THERE'S THE ENVELOPE! SHE DID IT! WE'RE RICH!
OH BOY! LET'S SNEAK UP AND GET IT!
C'MON, YOU LOUSE. C'MONNN...
I DON'T SEE SUSIE. DO YOU?

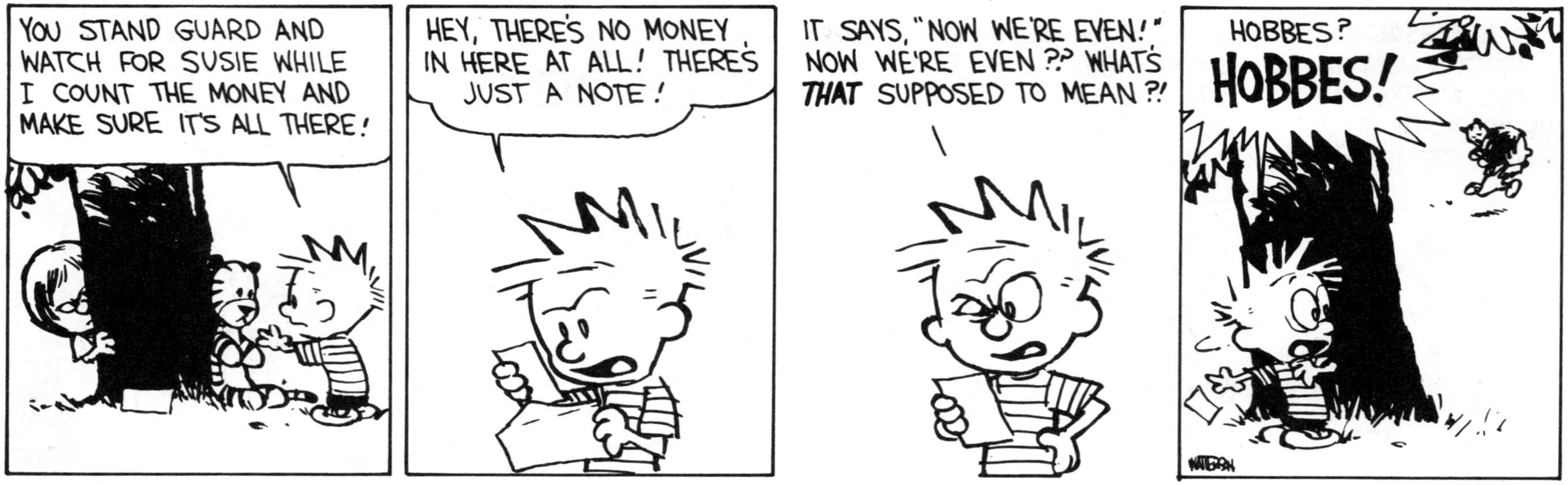
YOU STAND GUARD AND WATCH FOR SUSIE WHILE I COUNT THE MONEY AND MAKE SURE IT'S ALL THERE!
HEY, THERE'S NO MONEY IN HERE AT ALL! THERE'S JUST A NOTE!
IT SAYS, "NOW WE'RE EVEN!" NOW WE'RE EVEN ?? WHAT'S THAT SUPPOSED TO MEAN ?!
HOBBES?
HOBBES!
WATTERSON

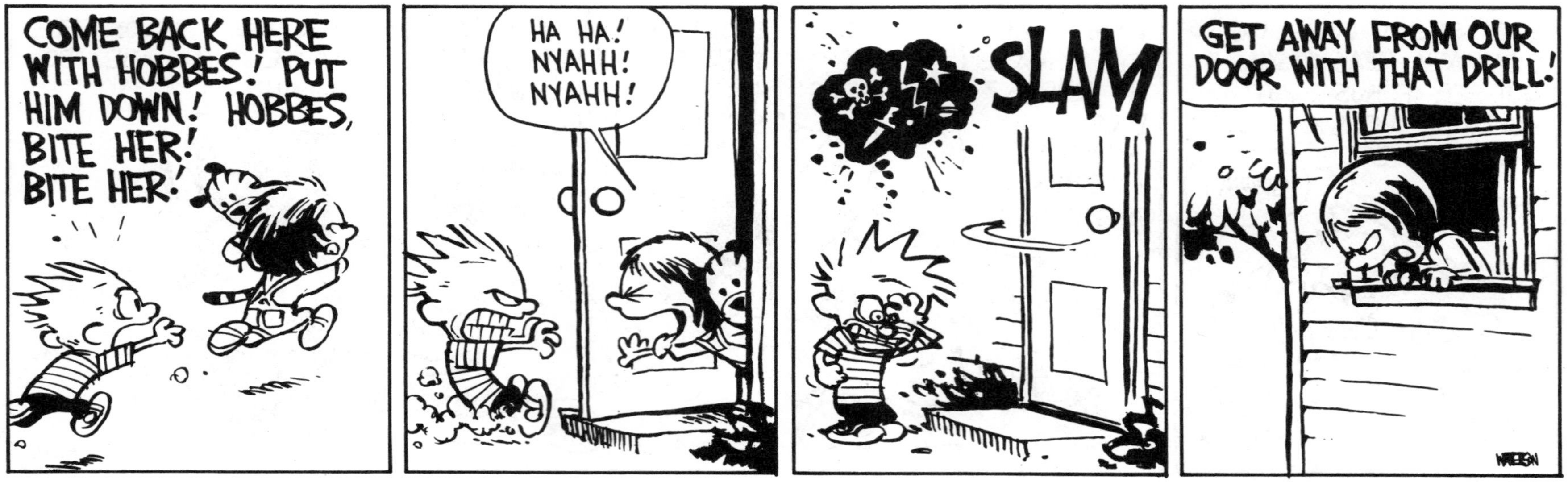
COME BACK HERE WITH HOBBES! PUT HIM DOWN! HOBBES, BITE HER! BITE HER!
HA HA! NYAHH! NYAHH!
SLAM
GET AWAY FROM OUR DOOR WITH THAT DRILL!
WATTERSON

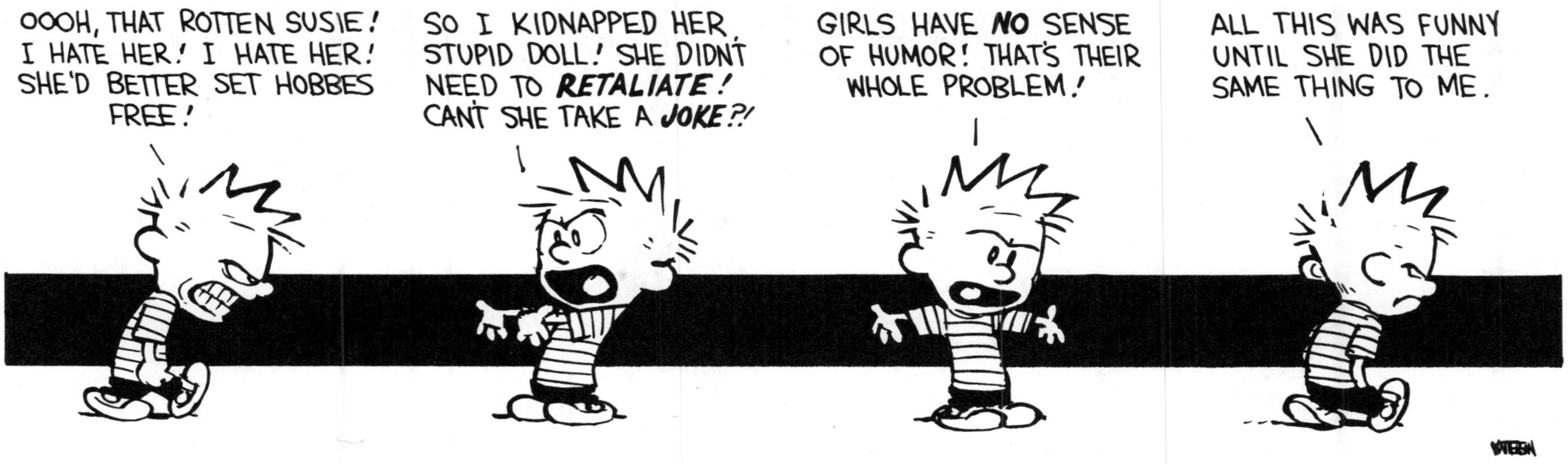
OOOH, THAT ROTTEN SUSIE! I HATE HER! I HATE HER! SHE'D BETTER SET HOBBES FREE!
SO I KIDNAPPED HER STUPID DOLL! SHE DIDN'T NEED TO RETALIATE! CAN'T SHE TAKE A JOKE?!
GIRLS HAVE NO SENSE OF HUMOR! THAT'S THEIR WHOLE PROBLEM!
ALL THIS WAS FUNNY UNTIL SHE DID THE SAME THING TO ME.

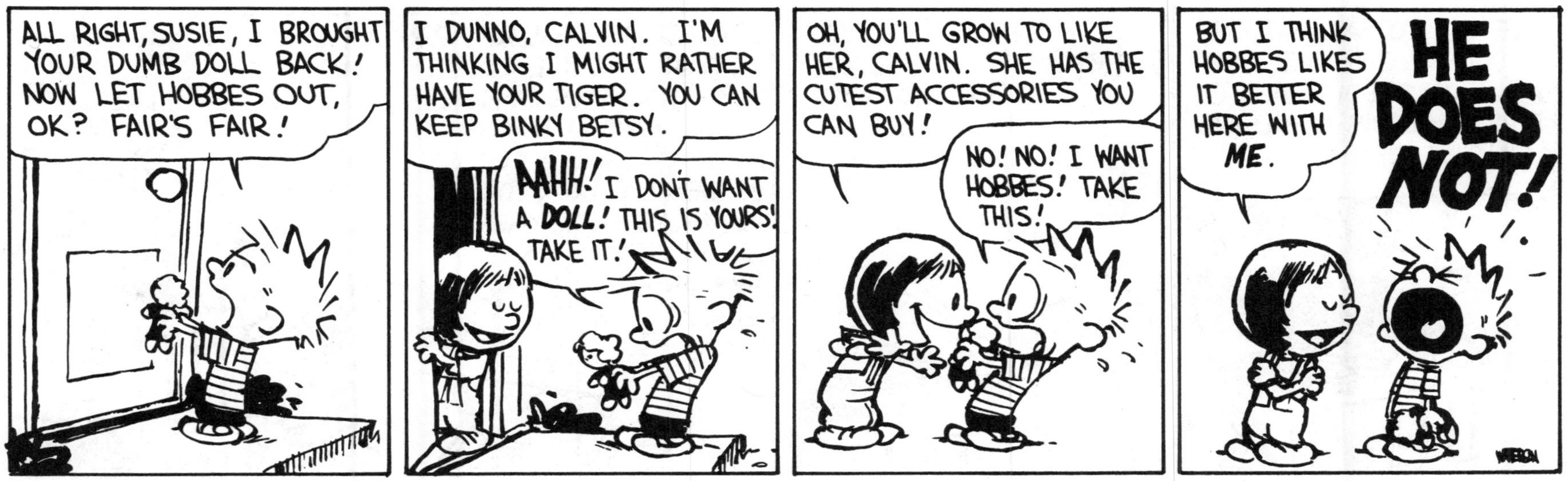
ALL RIGHT, SUSIE, I BROUGHT YOUR DUMB DOLL BACK! NOW LET HOBBES OUT, OK? FAIR'S FAIR!
I DUNNO, CALVIN. I'M THINKING I MIGHT RATHER HAVE YOUR TIGER. YOU CAN KEEP BINKY BETSY.
AAHH! I DON'T WANT A DOLL! THIS IS YOURS! TAKE IT!
OH, YOU'LL GROW TO LIKE HER, CALVIN. SHE HAS THE CUTEST ACCESSORIES YOU CAN BUY!
NO! NO! I WANT HOBBES! TAKE THIS!
BUT I THINK HOBBES LIKES IT BETTER HERE WITH ME.
HE DOES NOT!

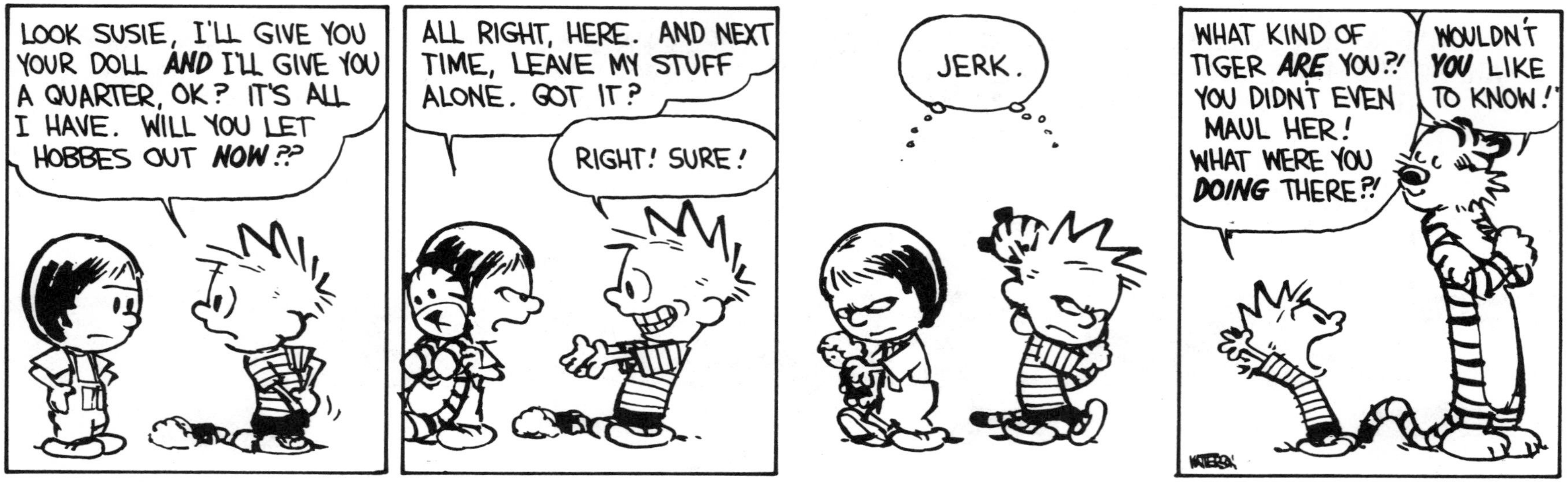
LOOK SUSIE, I'LL GIVE YOU YOUR DOLL AND I'LL GIVE YOU A QUARTER, OK? IT'S ALL I HAVE. WILL YOU LET HOBBES OUT NOW ?!?
ALL RIGHT, HERE. AND NEXT TIME, LEAVE MY STUFF ALONE. GOT IT?
RIGHT! SURE!
JERK.
WHAT KIND OF TIGER ARE YOU ?! YOU DIDN'T EVEN MAUL HER! WHAT WERE YOU DOING THERE ?!
WOULDN'T YOU LIKE TO KNOW!

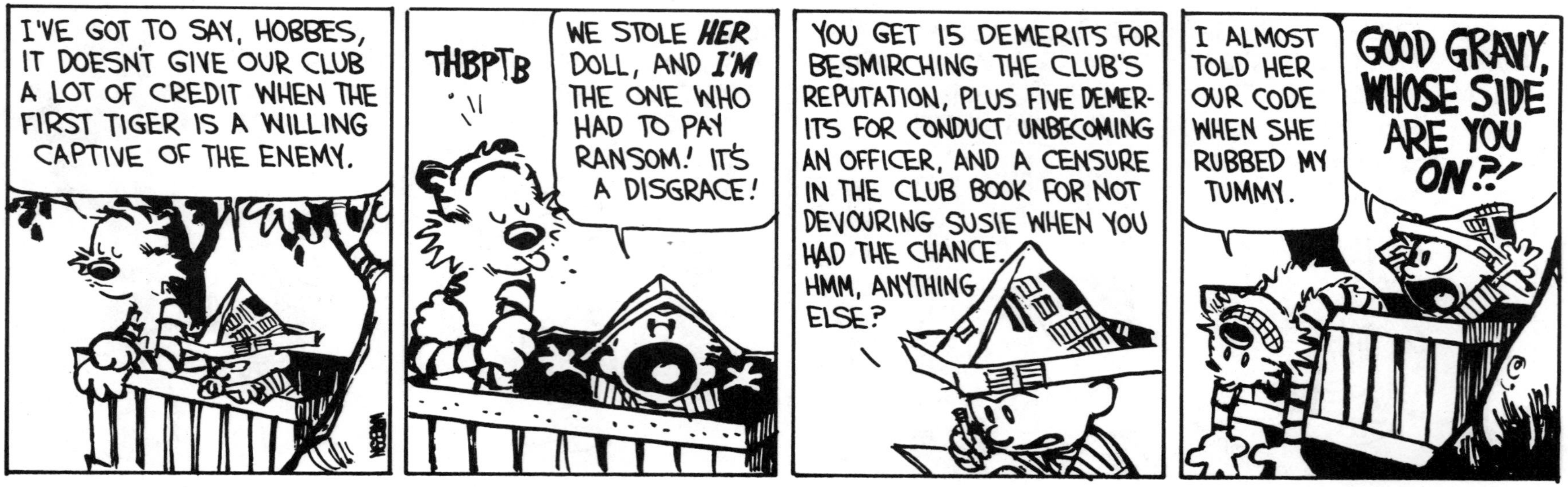
I'VE GOT TO SAY, HOBBES, IT DOESN'T GIVE OUR CLUB A LOT OF CREDIT WHEN THE FIRST TIGER IS A WILLING CAPTIVE OF THE ENEMY.
THBPTB
WE STOLE HER DOLL, AND I'M THE ONE WHO HAD TO PAY RANSOM! IT'S A DISGRACE!
YOU GET 15 DEMERITS FOR BESMIRCHING THE CLUB'S REPUTATION, PLUS FIVE DEMERITS FOR CONDUCT UNBECOMING AN OFFICER, AND A CENSURE IN THE CLUB BOOK FOR NOT DEVOURING SUSIE WHEN YOU HAD THE CHANCE. HMM, ANYTHING ELSE?
I ALMOST TOLD HER OUR CODE WHEN SHE RUBBED MY TUMMY.
GOOD GRAVY, WHOSE SIDE ARE YOU ON ?!

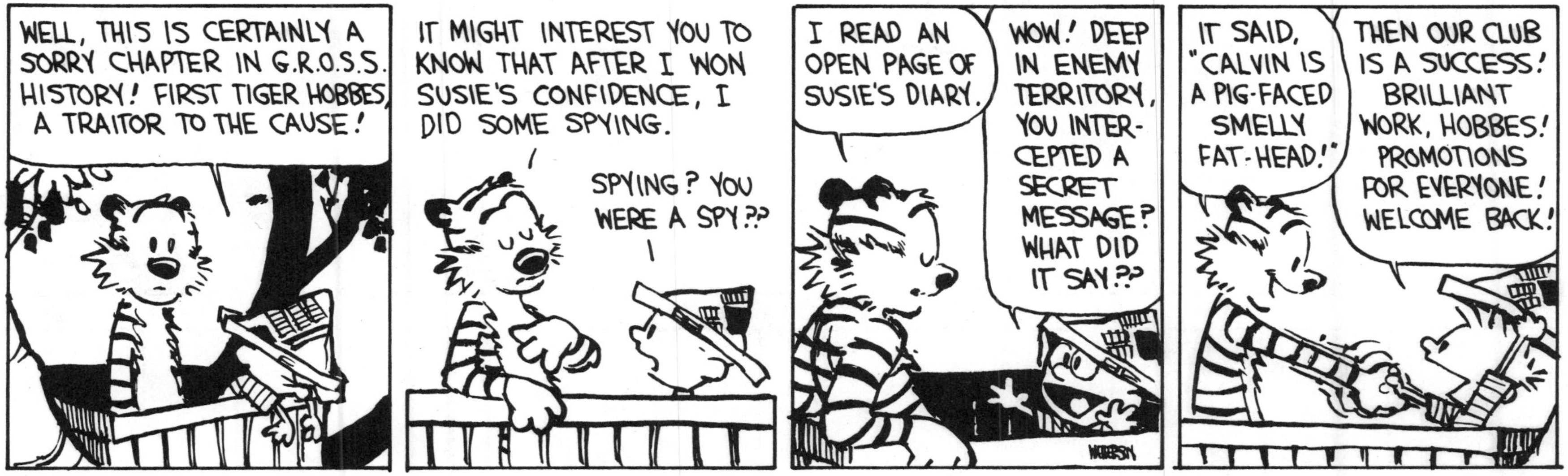

WELL, THIS IS CERTAINLY A SORRY CHAPTER IN G.R.O.S.S. HISTORY! FIRST TIGER HOBBES, A TRAITOR TO THE CAUSE!
IT MIGHT INTEREST YOU TO KNOW THAT AFTER I WON SUSIE'S CONFIDENCE, I DID SOME SPYING.
SPYING? YOU WERE A SPY??
I READ AN OPEN PAGE OF SUSIE'S DIARY.
WOW! DEEP IN ENEMY TERRITORY, YOU INTERCEPTED A SECRET MESSAGE? WHAT DID IT SAY??
IT SAID, "CALVIN IS A PIG-FACED SMELLY FAT-HEAD!"
THEN OUR CLUB IS A SUCCESS! BRILLIANT WORK, HOBBES! PROMOTIONS FOR EVERYONE! WELCOME BACK!

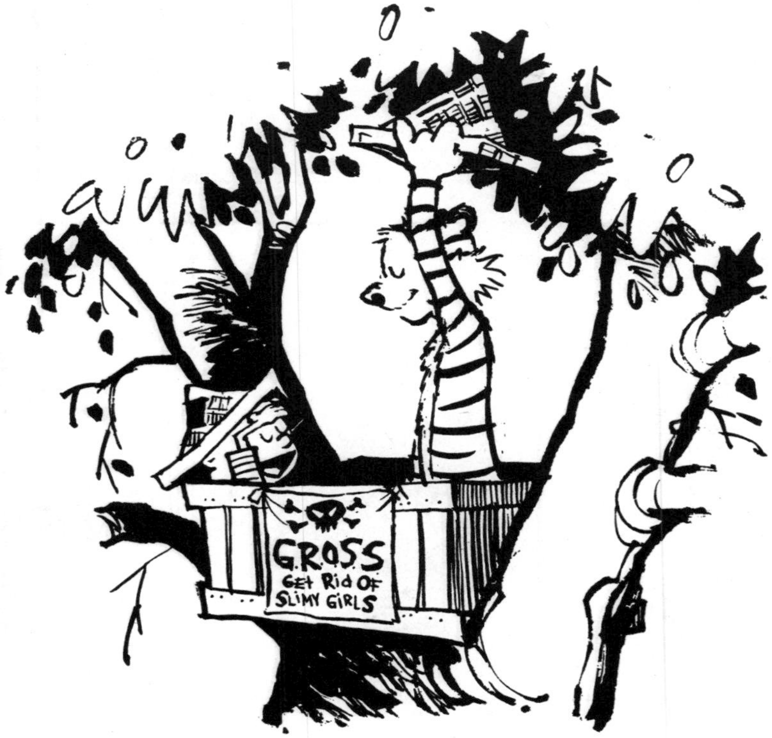

G.R.O.S.S
GET RID OF SLIMY GIRLS

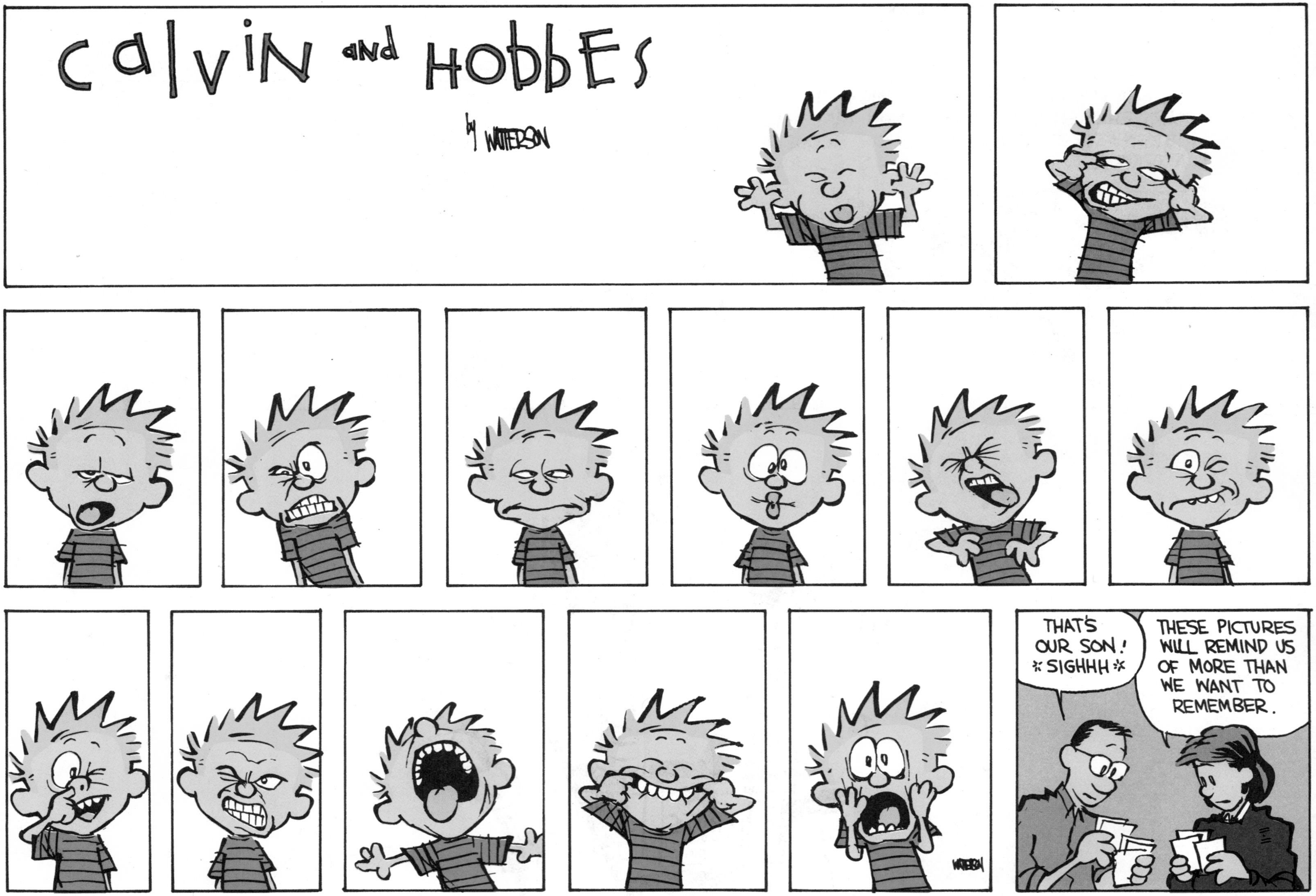
Calvin and HOBBES
by WATTERSON
THAT'S OUR SON! *SIGHHH*
THESE PICTURES WILL REMIND US OF MORE THAN WE WANT TO REMEMBER.
WATTERSON

Standing in front of the mirror to sketch in this strip, I was glad I work in the privacy of my own home.

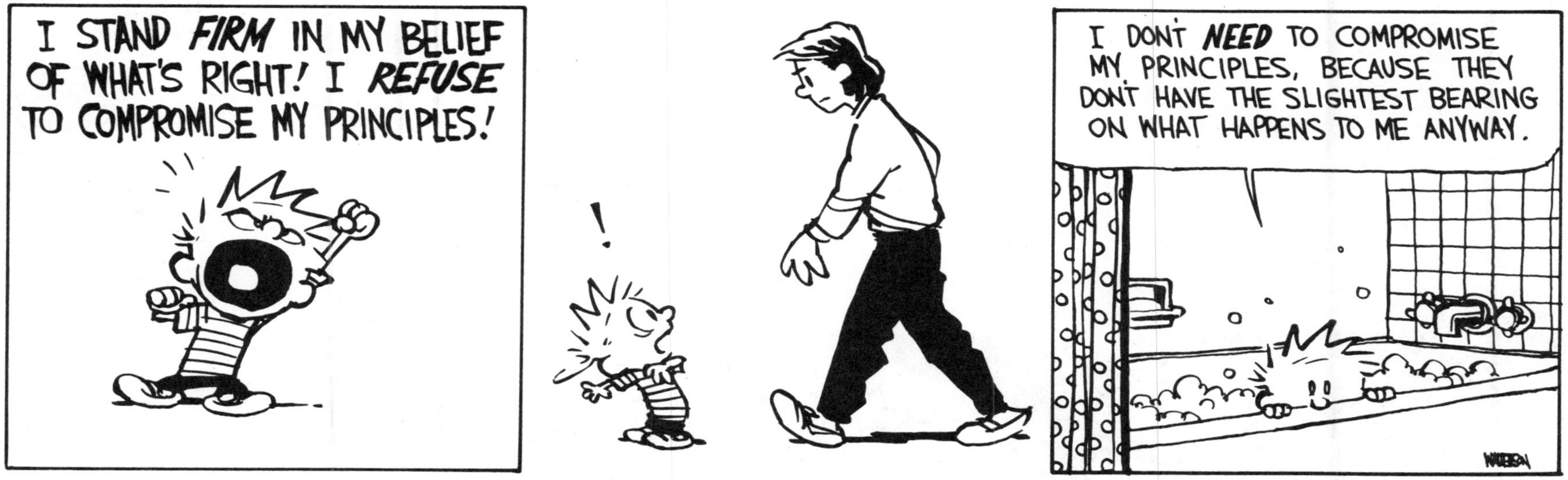
I STAND FIRM IN MY BELIEF OF WHAT'S RIGHT! I REFUSE TO COMPROMISE MY PRINCIPLES!
!
I DON'T NEED TO COMPROMISE MY PRINCIPLES, BECAUSE THEY DON'T HAVE THE SLIGHTEST BEARING ON WHAT HAPPENS TO ME ANYWAY.

During my fight to keep the syndicate from licensing my work, I sometimes drew strips that had additional private meanings for myself. The cartoon above mocked my ability to argue with the syndicate, and the cartoon below is how I interpreted the syndicate's position. I wouldn't have drawn these if the material didn't stand on its own, or if it was in any way inconsistent with the characters, but cartoons such as these helped me laugh at my predicament at a time when very little about it seemed funny.

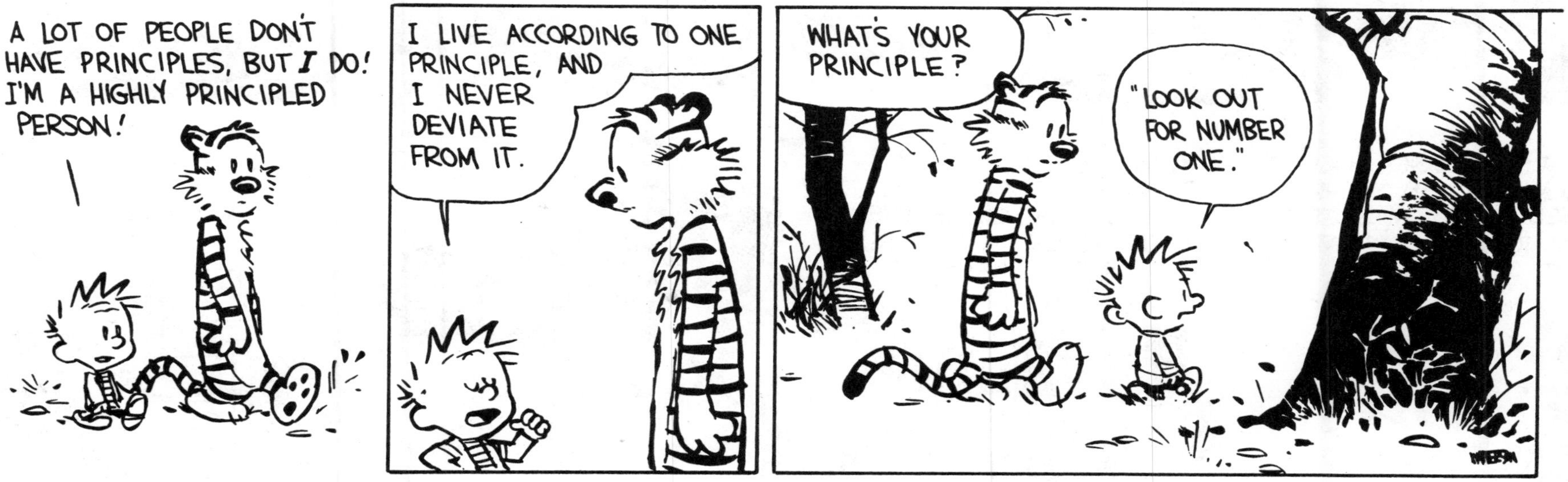
A LOT OF PEOPLE DON'T HAVE PRINCIPLES, BUT I DO! I'M A HIGHLY PRINCIPLED PERSON!
I LIVE ACCORDING TO ONE PRINCIPLE, AND I NEVER DEVIATE FROM IT.
WHAT'S YOUR PRINCIPLE?
"LOOK OUT FOR NUMBER ONE."

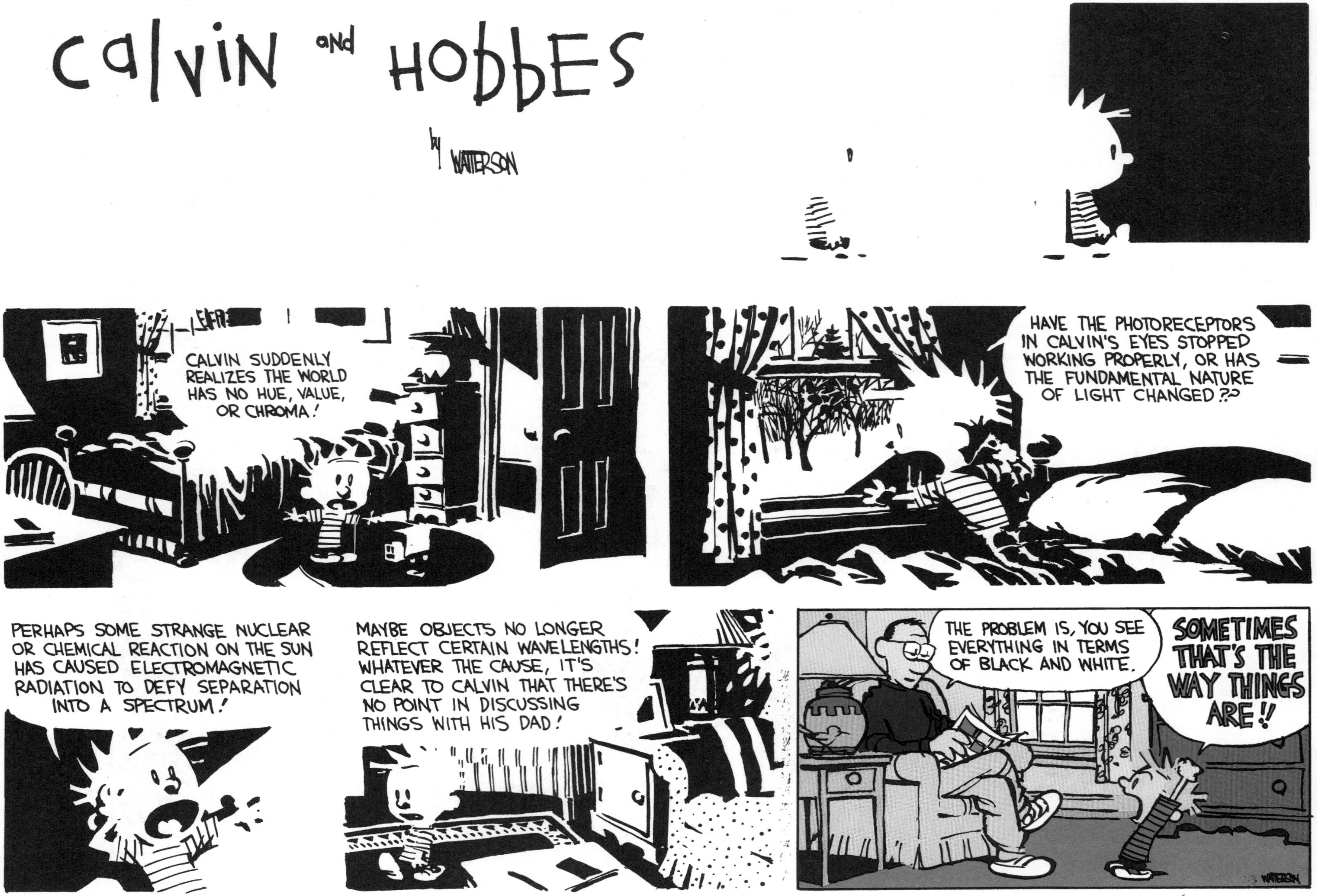
Calvin and Hobbes
by Watterson
CALVIN SUDDENLY REALIZES THE WORLD HAS NO HUE, VALUE, OR CHROMA!
HAVE THE PHOTORECEPTORS IN CALVIN'S EYES STOPPED WORKING PROPERLY, OR HAS THE FUNDAMENTAL NATURE OF LIGHT CHANGED ??
PERHAPS SOME STRANGE NUCLEAR OR CHEMICAL REACTION ON THE SUN HAS CAUSED ELECTROMAGNETIC RADIATION TO DEFY SEPARATION INTO A SPECTRUM!
MAYBE OBJECTS NO LONGER REFLECT CERTAIN WAVELENGTHS! WHATEVER THE CAUSE, IT'S CLEAR TO CALVIN THAT THERE'S NO POINT IN DISCUSSING THINGS WITH HIS DAD!
THE PROBLEM IS, YOU SEE EVERYTHING IN TERMS OF BLACK AND WHITE.
SOMETIMES THAT'S THE WAY THINGS ARE!!
WATTERSON

During the licensing fight, I was often accused of seeing issues in black and white, so I illustrated it literally for the strip. Calvin's retort is my own. It was a fun challenge to make the pictures intelligible without any outlines. Best of all, I only needed to color one panel.

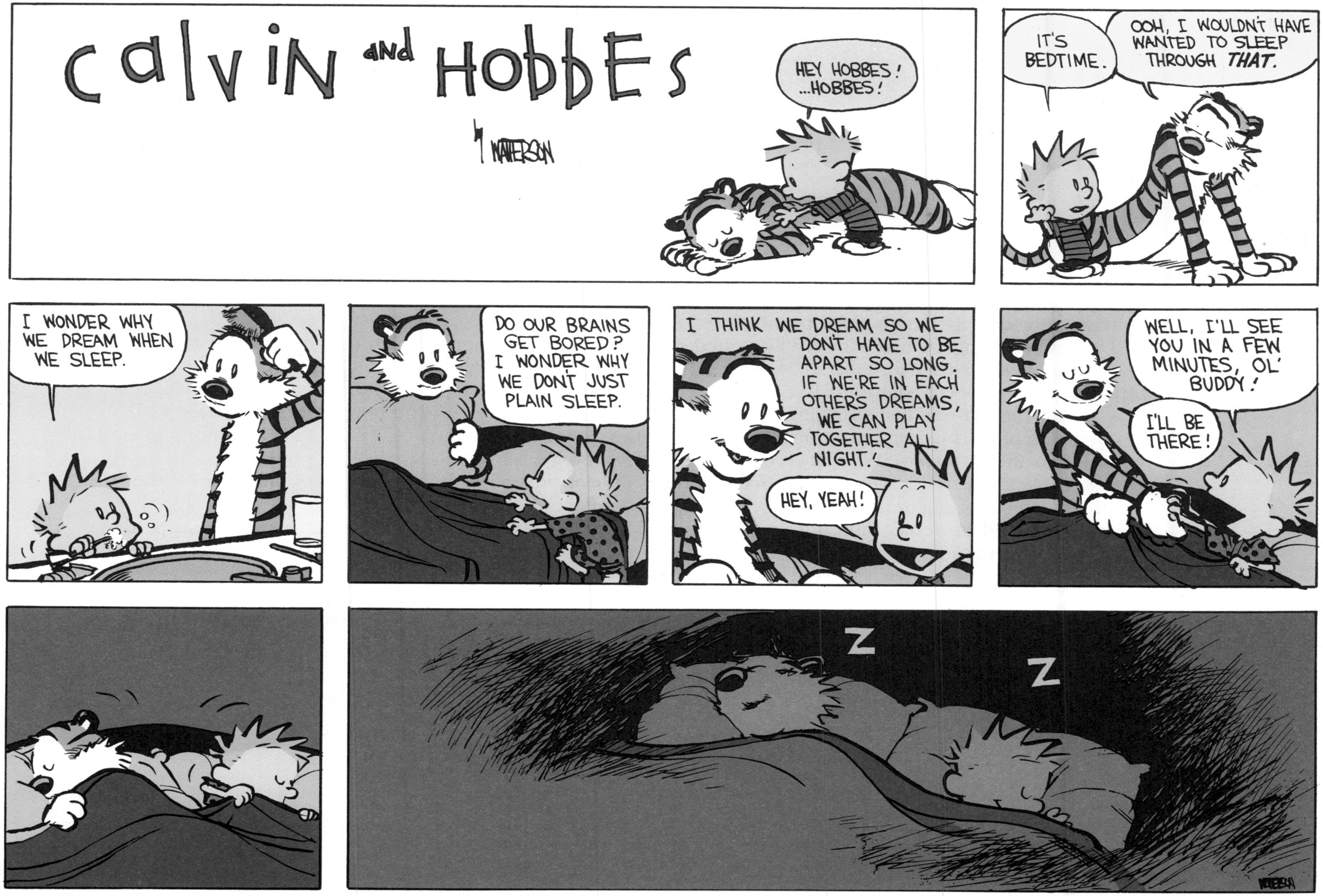
Calvin and Hobbes
by Watterson
HEY HOBBES! ...HOBBES!
IT'S BEDTIME.
OOH, I WOULDN'T HAVE WANTED TO SLEEP THROUGH *THAT*.
I WONDER WHY WE DREAM WHEN WE SLEEP.
DO OUR BRAINS GET BORED? I WONDER WHY WE DON'T JUST PLAIN SLEEP.
I THINK WE DREAM SO WE DON'T HAVE TO BE APART SO LONG. IF WE'RE IN EACH OTHER'S DREAMS, WE CAN PLAY TOGETHER ALL NIGHT.
HEY, YEAH!
WELL, I'LL SEE YOU IN A FEW MINUTES, OL' BUDDY!
I'LL BE THERE!
Z
Z

Our cat Sprite was often a model for Hobbes, both in looks and personality. When she died, I drew this cartoon. We can always meet again in dreams.

DINOSAURS

The dinosaurs I put in *Calvin and Hobbes* have become one of my favorite additions to the strip. Dinosaurs have appeared in many strips before mine, but I like to think I've treated them with a little more respect than they've often received at the hands of cartoonists.

When I was Calvin's age, I had a nicely illustrated dinosaur book and some dinosaur models, so it was a natural step to have Calvin share that interest. The first dinosaurs I put in the strip were based on my childhood memories of them. Back in the '60s, dinosaurs were imagined as lumbering, dim-witted, cold-blooded, oversized lizards. That's how I drew them in the first strips, and these drawings are now pretty embarrassing to look at. When I realized that dinosaurs offered Calvin interesting story possibilities, I started searching for books to rekindle my interest in them. It was then I discovered what I'd missed in paleontology during the last twenty years.

Dinosaurs, I quickly learned, were wilder than anything I'd ever imagined. Tails up, with birdlike agility, these were truly the creatures of nightmares. My drawings began to reflect the new information, and with each strip, I've tried to learn more and to depict dinosaurs more accurately. I do this partly for my own amusement, and partly because, for Calvin, dinosaurs are very, very real.

Dinosaurs have expanded Calvin's world and opened up some exciting graphic possibilities. The biggest reward for me, however, has been the fun I've had exploring a new interest. I enjoy dinosaurs more now than I did as a kid, and much of the job of being a cartoonist lies in keeping alive a sense of curiosity and wonder. Sometimes the best way to generate new ideas is to go out and learn something.

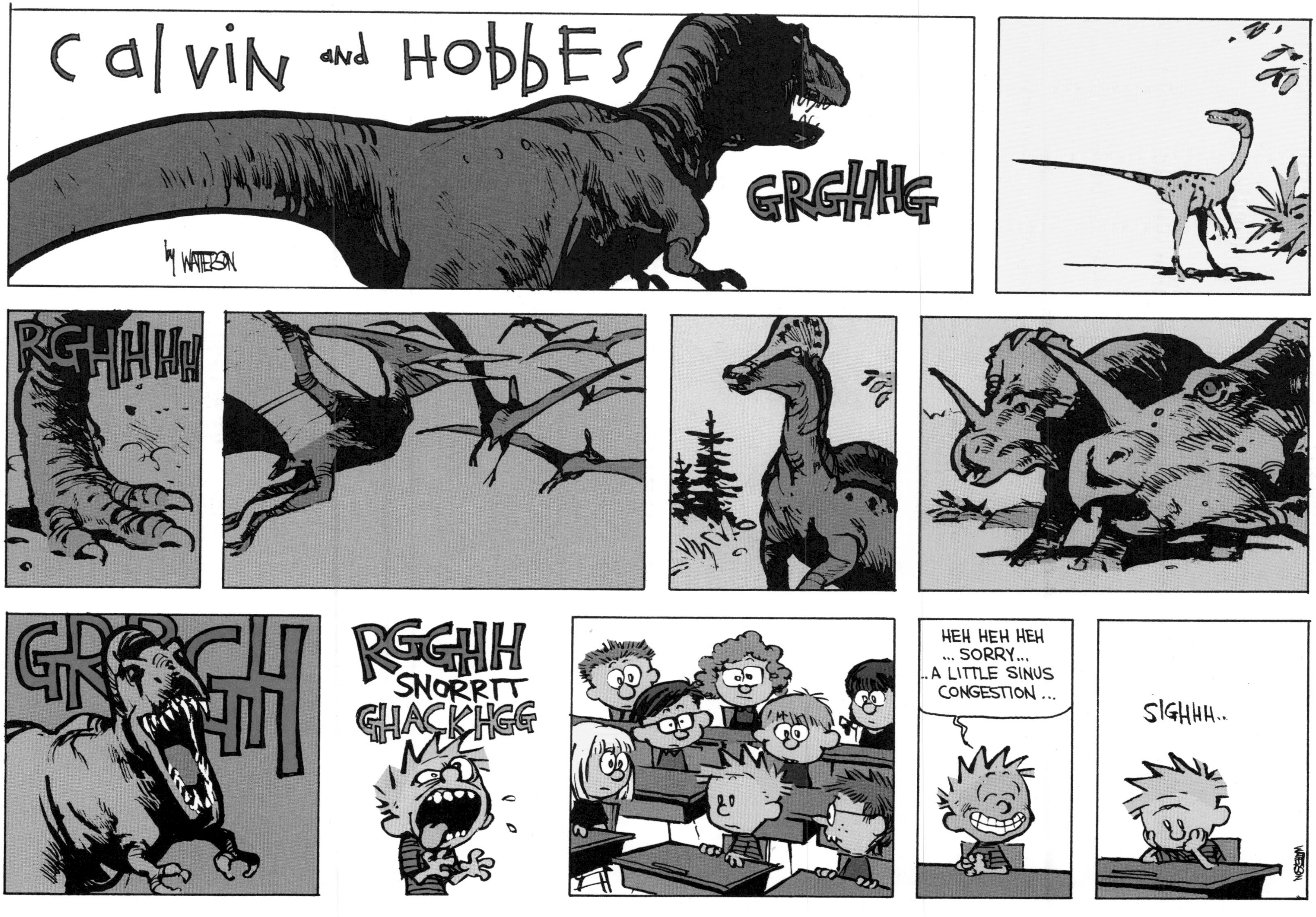
Calvin and HOBBES
by WATTERSON
GRGHHG
RGHHHH
GRRRCH
RGGHH
SNORRTT
GHACKHGG
HEH HEH HEH ... SORRY... ..A LITTLE SINUS CONGESTION ...
SIGHHH..

Here is another story with Calvin and his cardboard box. Unlike most stories I write, this one creates some suspense at the beginning by dropping the reader into events without explaining what's going on. The humor of this story depends on the reader being familiar with Calvin's personality, so I could only do this sort of thing after the strip was established. Writing is most fun after readers are willing to enter the strip's world on its own terms.

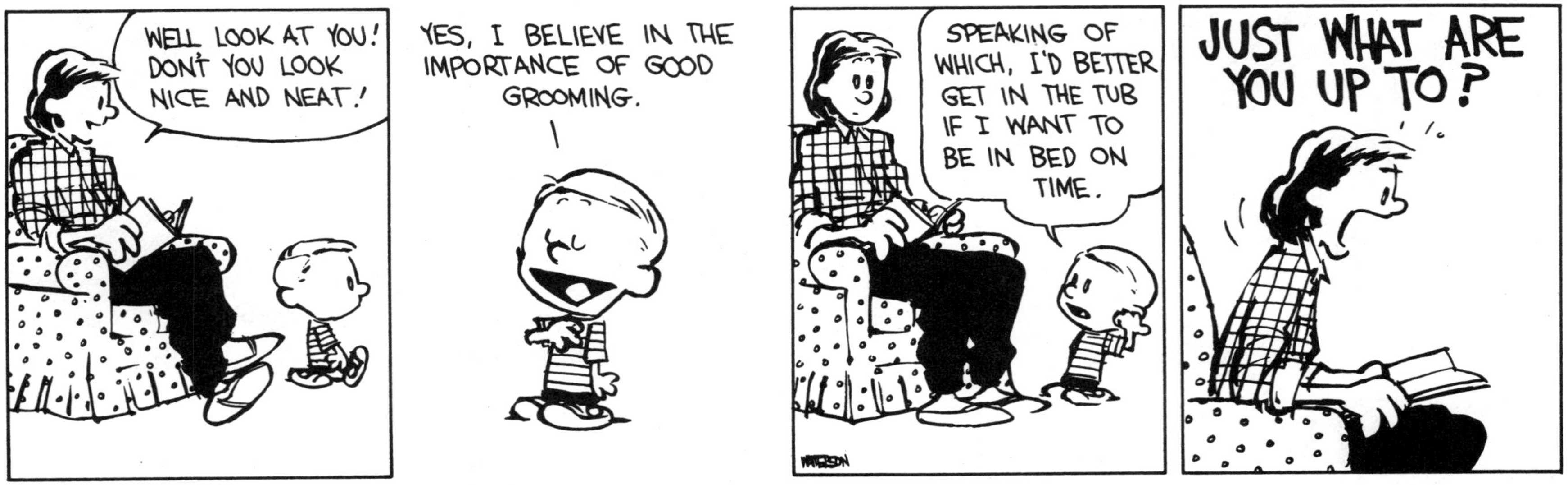
WELL LOOK AT YOU! DON'T YOU LOOK NICE AND NEAT!
YES, I BELIEVE IN THE IMPORTANCE OF GOOD GROOMING.
SPEAKING OF WHICH, I'D BETTER GET IN THE TUB IF I WANT TO BE IN BED ON TIME.
JUST WHAT ARE YOU UP TO?

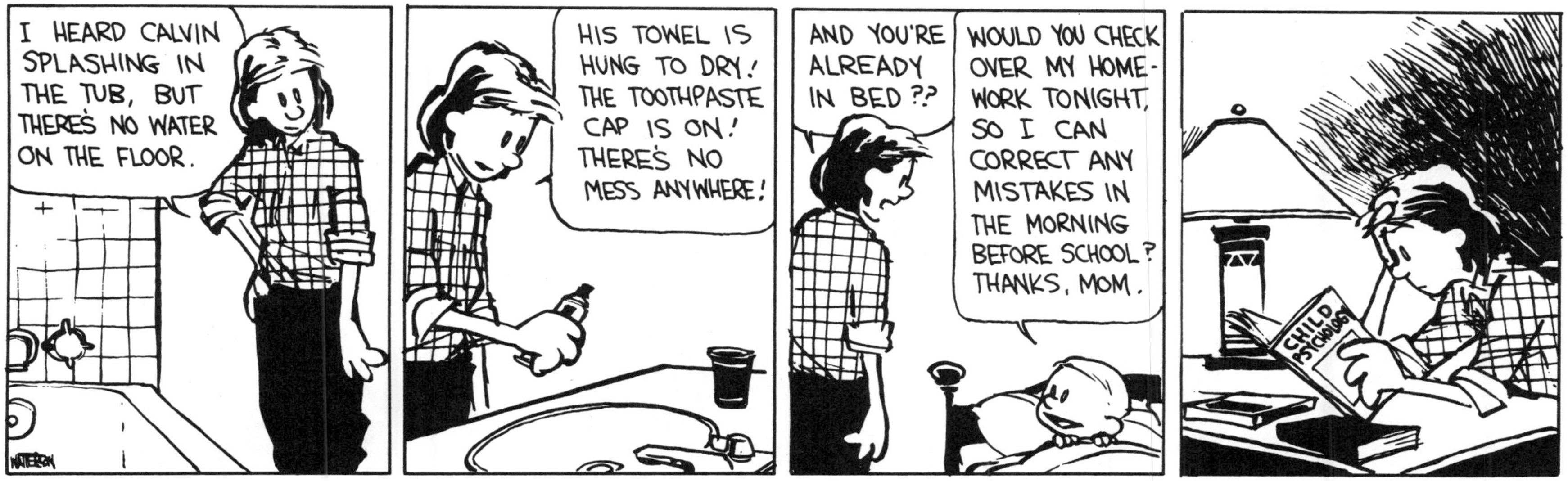
I HEARD CALVIN SPLASHING IN THE TUB, BUT THERE'S NO WATER ON THE FLOOR.
HIS TOWEL IS HUNG TO DRY! THE TOOTHPASTE CAP IS ON! THERE'S NO MESS ANYWHERE!
AND YOU'RE ALREADY IN BED ??
WOULD YOU CHECK OVER MY HOME-WORK TONIGHT, SO I CAN CORRECT ANY MISTAKES IN THE MORNING BEFORE SCHOOL? THANKS, MOM.
CHILD PSYCHOLOGY

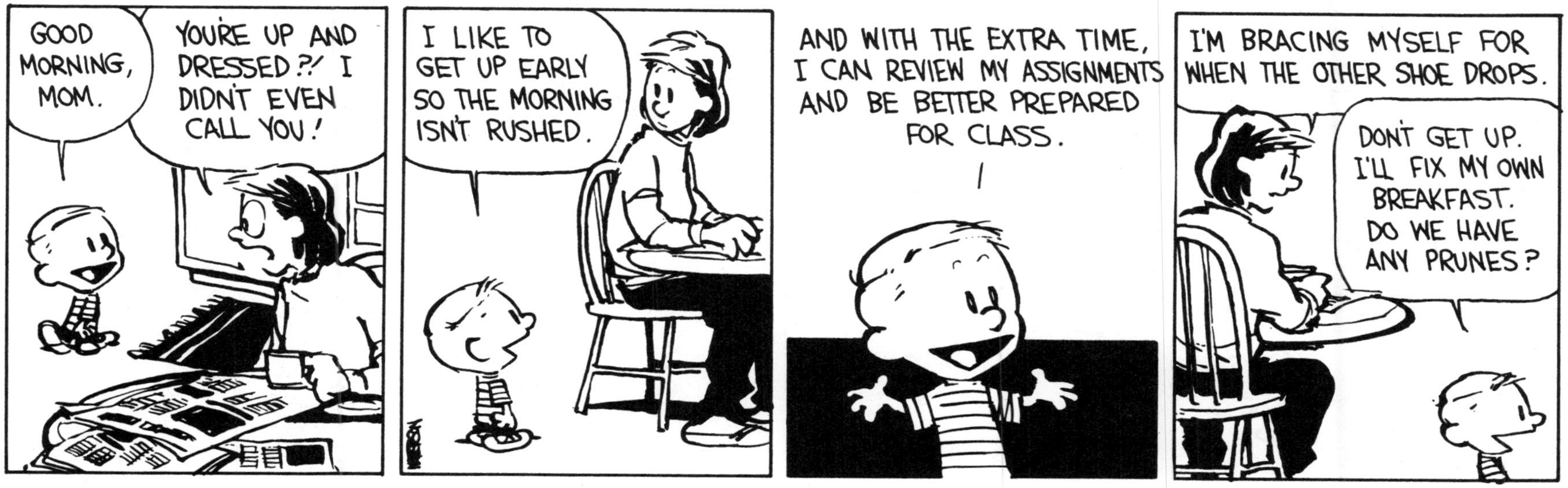
GOOD MORNING, MOM.
YOU'RE UP AND DRESSED?! I DIDN'T EVEN CALL YOU!
I LIKE TO GET UP EARLY SO THE MORNING ISN'T RUSHED.
AND WITH THE EXTRA TIME, I CAN REVIEW MY ASSIGNMENTS AND BE BETTER PREPARED FOR CLASS.
I'M BRACING MYSELF FOR WHEN THE OTHER SHOE DROPS.
DON'T GET UP. I'LL FIX MY OWN BREAKFAST. DO WE HAVE ANY PRUNES?

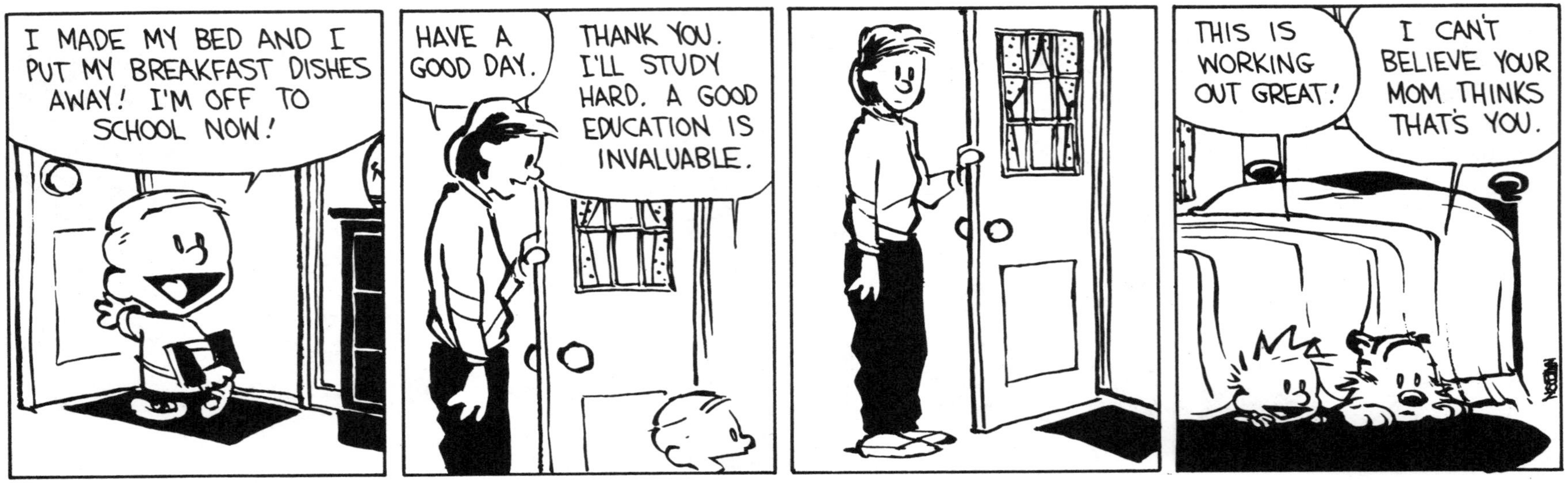
I MADE MY BED AND I PUT MY BREAKFAST DISHES AWAY! I'M OFF TO SCHOOL NOW!
HAVE A GOOD DAY.
THANK YOU. I'LL STUDY HARD. A GOOD EDUCATION IS INVALUABLE.
THIS IS WORKING OUT GREAT!
I CAN'T BELIEVE YOUR MOM THINKS THAT'S YOU.

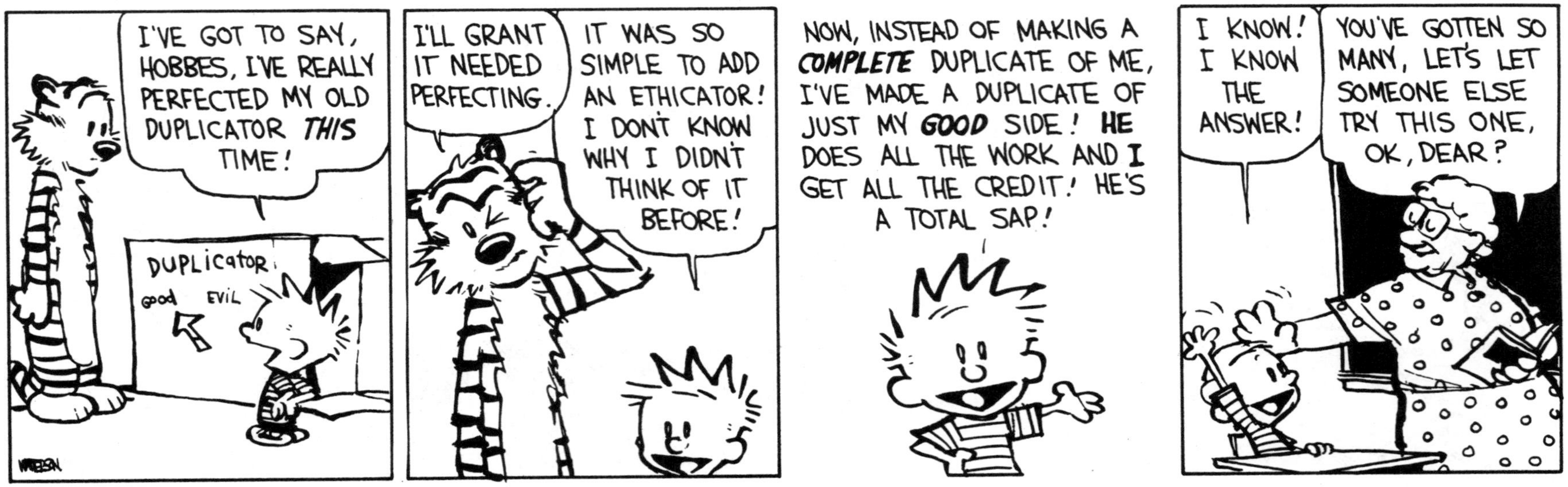
I'VE GOT TO SAY, HOBBES, I'VE REALLY PERFECTED MY OLD DUPLICATOR THIS TIME!
DUPLICATOR
GOOD
EVIL
I'LL GRANT IT NEEDED PERFECTING.
IT WAS SO SIMPLE TO ADD AN ETHICATOR! I DON'T KNOW WHY I DIDN'T THINK OF IT BEFORE!
NOW, INSTEAD OF MAKING A COMPLETE DUPLICATE OF ME, I'VE MADE A DUPLICATE OF JUST MY GOOD SIDE! HE DOES ALL THE WORK AND I GET ALL THE CREDIT! HE'S A TOTAL SAP!
I KNOW! I KNOW THE ANSWER!
YOU'VE GOTTEN SO MANY, LET'S LET SOMEONE ELSE TRY THIS ONE, OK, DEAR?

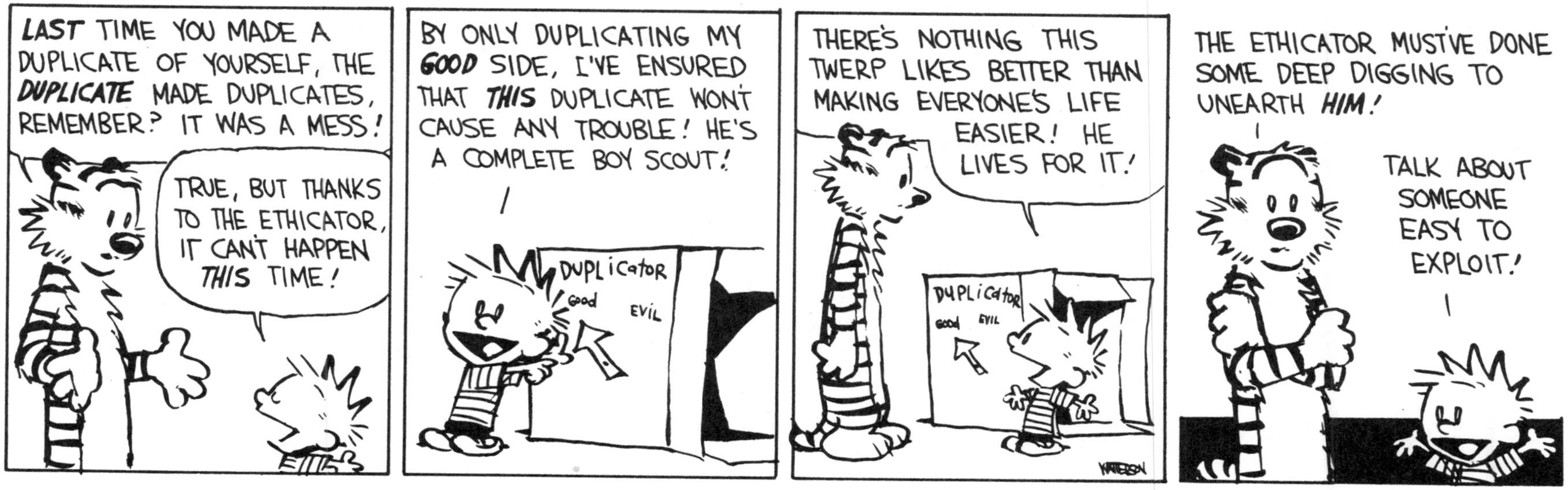
LAST TIME YOU MADE A DUPLICATE OF YOURSELF, THE DUPLICATE MADE DUPLICATES, REMEMBER? IT WAS A MESS!
TRUE, BUT THANKS TO THE ETHICATOR, IT CAN'T HAPPEN THIS TIME!
BY ONLY DUPLICATING MY GOOD SIDE, I'VE ENSURED THAT THIS DUPLICATE WON'T CAUSE ANY TROUBLE! HE'S A COMPLETE BOY SCOUT!
DUPLicator
Good
EVIL
THERE'S NOTHING THIS TWERP LIKES BETTER THAN MAKING EVERYONE'S LIFE EASIER! HE LIVES FOR IT!
DUPLicator
Good
EVIL
THE ETHICATOR MUST'VE DONE SOME DEEP DIGGING TO UNEARTH HIM!
TALK ABOUT SOMEONE EASY TO EXPLOIT!

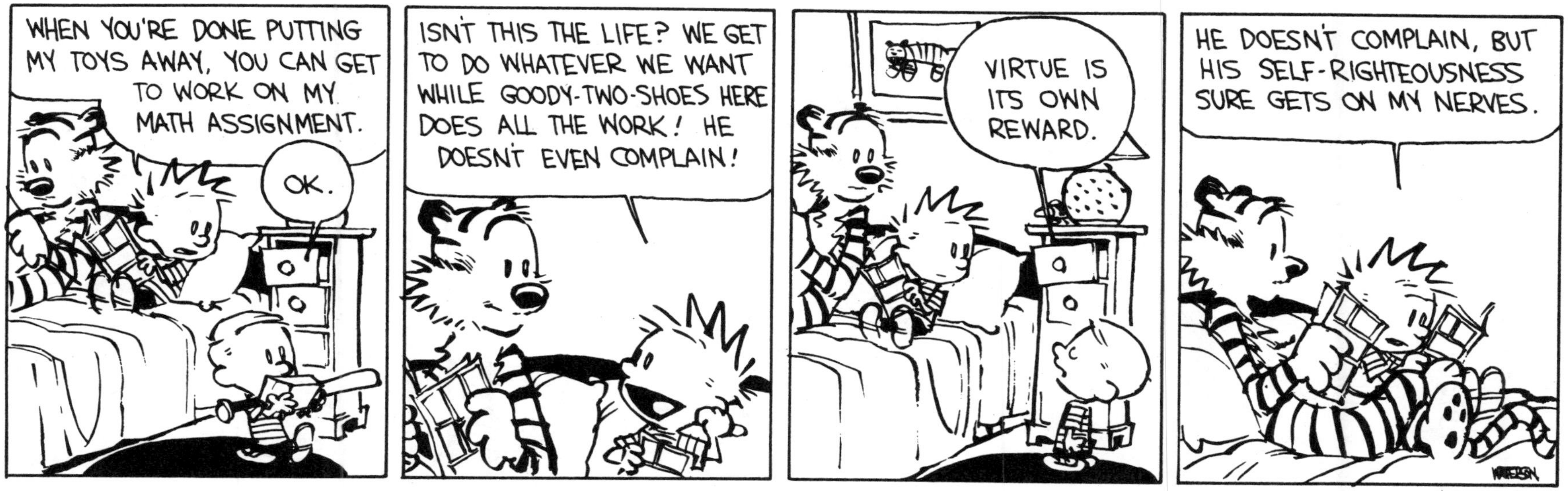
WHEN YOU'RE DONE PUTTING MY TOYS AWAY, YOU CAN GET TO WORK ON MY MATH ASSIGNMENT.
OK.
ISN'T THIS THE LIFE? WE GET TO DO WHATEVER WE WANT WHILE GOODY-TWO-SHOES HERE DOES ALL THE WORK! HE DOESN'T EVEN COMPLAIN!
VIRTUE IS ITS OWN REWARD.
HE DOESN'T COMPLAIN, BUT HIS SELF-RIGHTEOUSNESS SURE GETS ON MY NERVES.

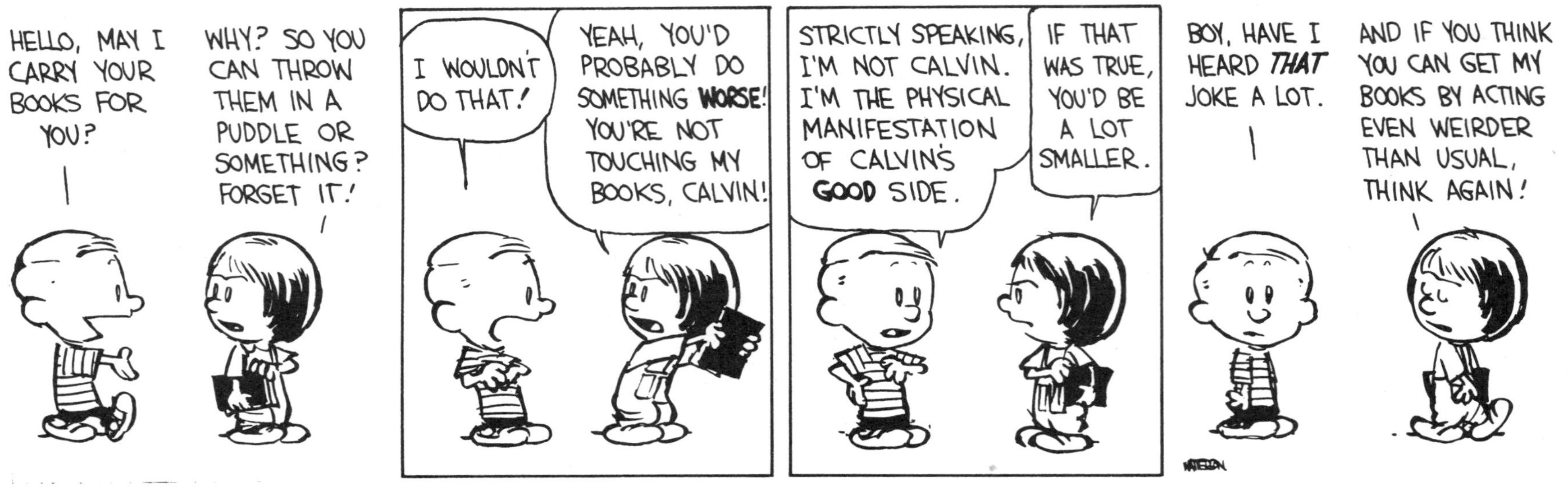
HELLO, MAY I CARRY YOUR BOOKS FOR YOU?
WHY? SO YOU CAN THROW THEM IN A PUDDLE OR SOMETHING? FORGET IT!
I WOULDN'T DO THAT!
YEAH, YOU'D PROBABLY DO SOMETHING WORSE! YOU'RE NOT TOUCHING MY BOOKS, CALVIN!
STRICTLY SPEAKING, I'M NOT CALVIN. I'M THE PHYSICAL MANIFESTATION OF CALVIN'S GOOD SIDE.
IF THAT WAS TRUE, YOU'D BE A LOT SMALLER.
BOY, HAVE I HEARD THAT JOKE A LOT.
AND IF YOU THINK YOU CAN GET MY BOOKS BY ACTING EVEN WEIRDER THAN USUAL, THINK AGAIN!

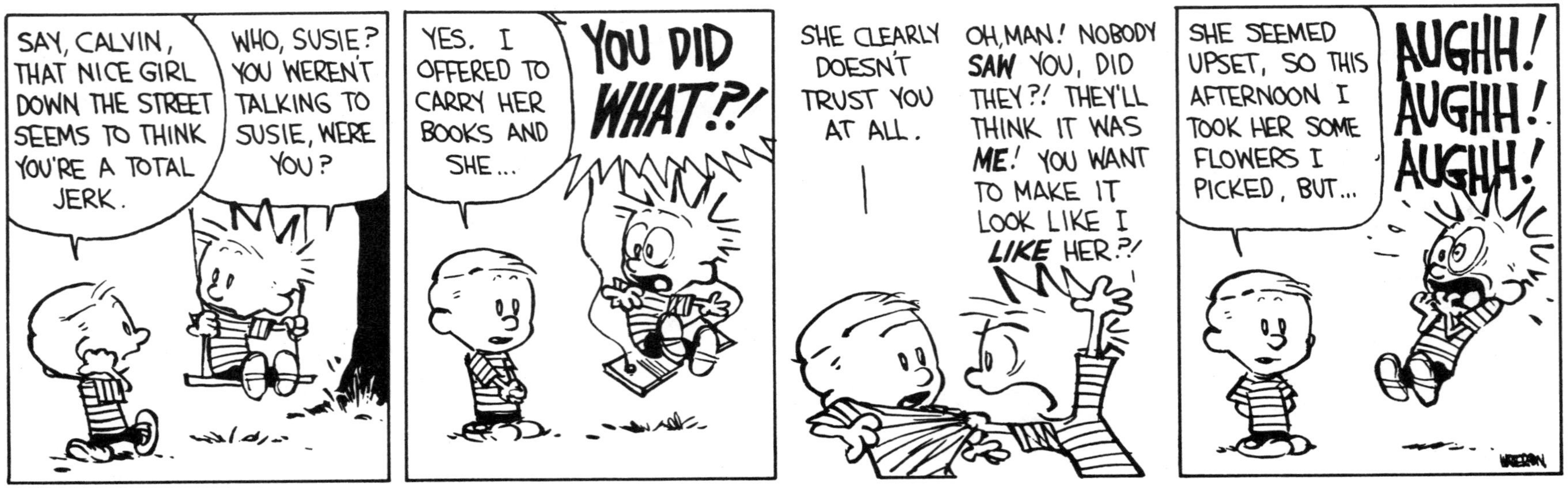
SAY, CALVIN, THAT NICE GIRL DOWN THE STREET SEEMS TO THINK YOU'RE A TOTAL JERK.
WHO, SUSIE? YOU WEREN'T TALKING TO SUSIE, WERE YOU?
YES. I OFFERED TO CARRY HER BOOKS AND SHE...
YOU DID WHAT?!
SHE CLEARLY DOESN'T TRUST YOU AT ALL.
OH, MAN! NOBODY SAW YOU, DID THEY?! THEY'LL THINK IT WAS ME! YOU WANT TO MAKE IT LOOK LIKE I LIKE HER?!
SHE SEEMED UPSET, SO THIS AFTERNOON I TOOK HER SOME FLOWERS I PICKED, BUT...
AUGHH! AUGHH! AUGHH!

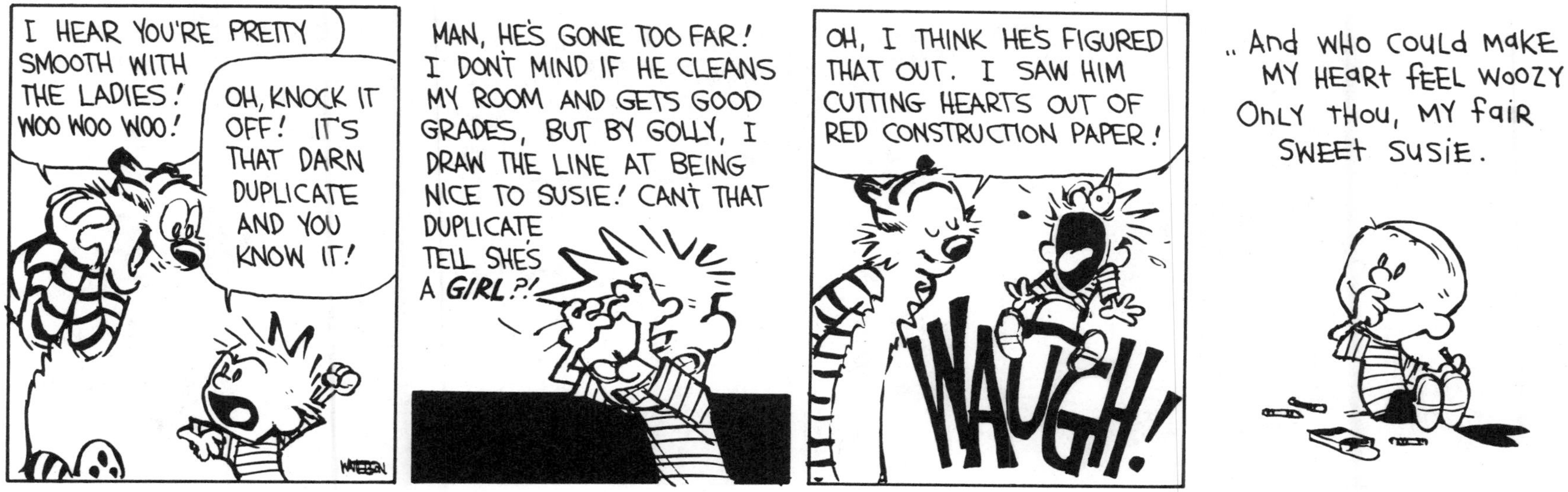
I HEAR YOU'RE PRETTY SMOOTH WITH THE LADIES! WOO WOO WOO!
OH, KNOCK IT OFF! IT'S THAT DARN DUPLICATE AND YOU KNOW IT!
MAN, HE'S GONE TOO FAR! I DON'T MIND IF HE CLEANS MY ROOM AND GETS GOOD GRADES, BUT BY GOLLY, I DRAW THE LINE AT BEING NICE TO SUSIE! CAN'T THAT DUPLICATE TELL SHE'S A GIRL?!
OH, I THINK HE'S FIGURED THAT OUT. I SAW HIM CUTTING HEARTS OUT OF RED CONSTRUCTION PAPER!
WAUGH!
.. And who could make my heart feel woozy? Only thou, my fair sweet Susie.

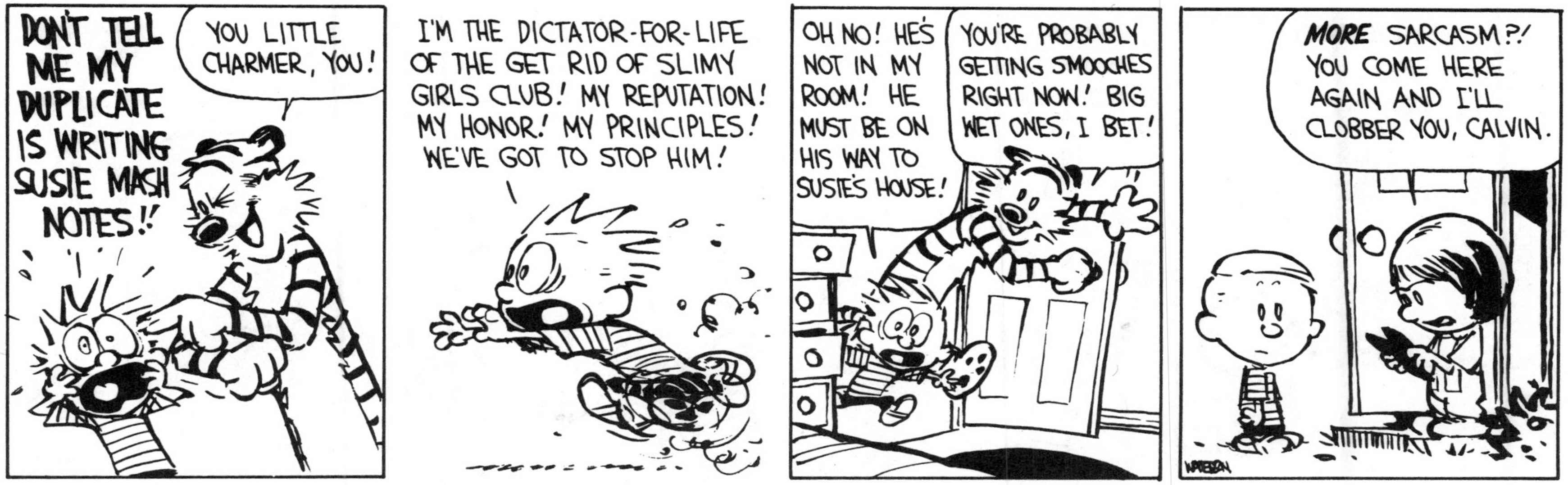
DON'T TELL ME MY DUPLICATE IS WRITING SUSIE MASH NOTES!!
YOU LITTLE CHARMER, YOU!
I'M THE DICTATOR-FOR-LIFE OF THE GET RID OF SLIMY GIRLS CLUB! MY REPUTATION! MY HONOR! MY PRINCIPLES! WE'VE GOT TO STOP HIM!
OH NO! HE'S NOT IN MY ROOM! HE MUST BE ON HIS WAY TO SUSIE'S HOUSE!
YOU'RE PROBABLY GETTING SMOOCHES RIGHT NOW! BIG WET ONES, I BET!
MORE SARCASM?! YOU COME HERE AGAIN AND I'LL CLOBBER YOU, CALVIN.

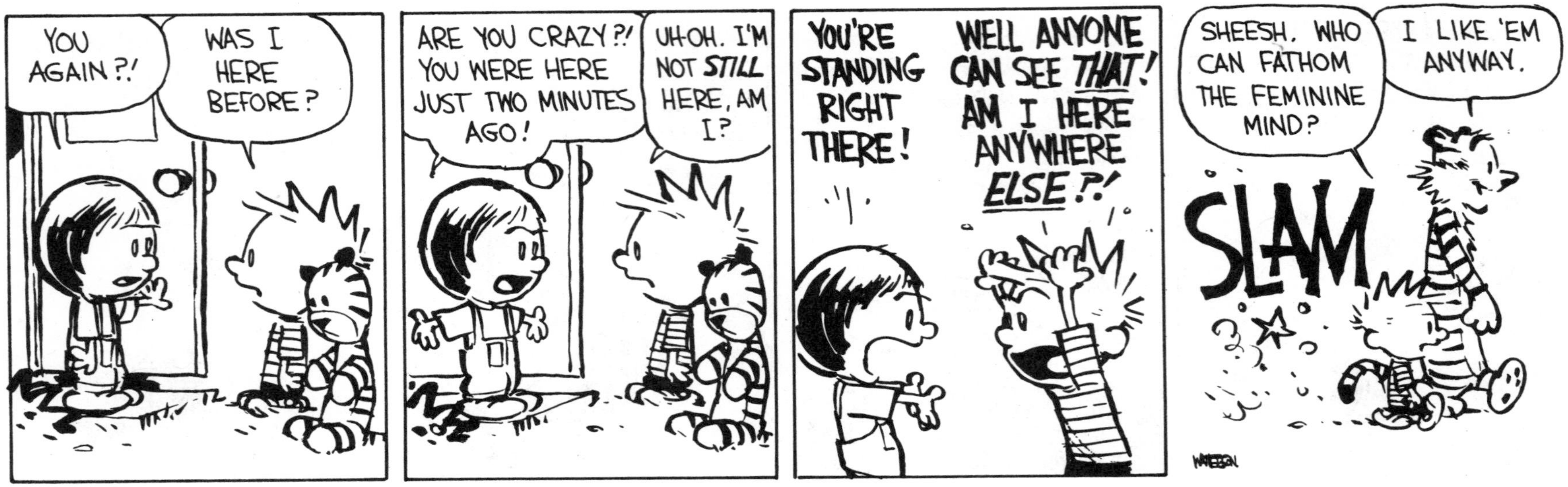
YOU AGAIN?!
WAS I HERE BEFORE?
ARE YOU CRAZY?! YOU WERE HERE JUST TWO MINUTES AGO!
UH-OH. I'M NOT STILL HERE, AM I?
YOU'RE STANDING RIGHT THERE!
WELL ANYONE CAN SEE THAT! AM I HERE ANYWHERE ELSE?!
SHEESH. WHO CAN FATHOM THE FEMININE MIND?
I LIKE 'EM ANYWAY.
SLAM
WATTERSON

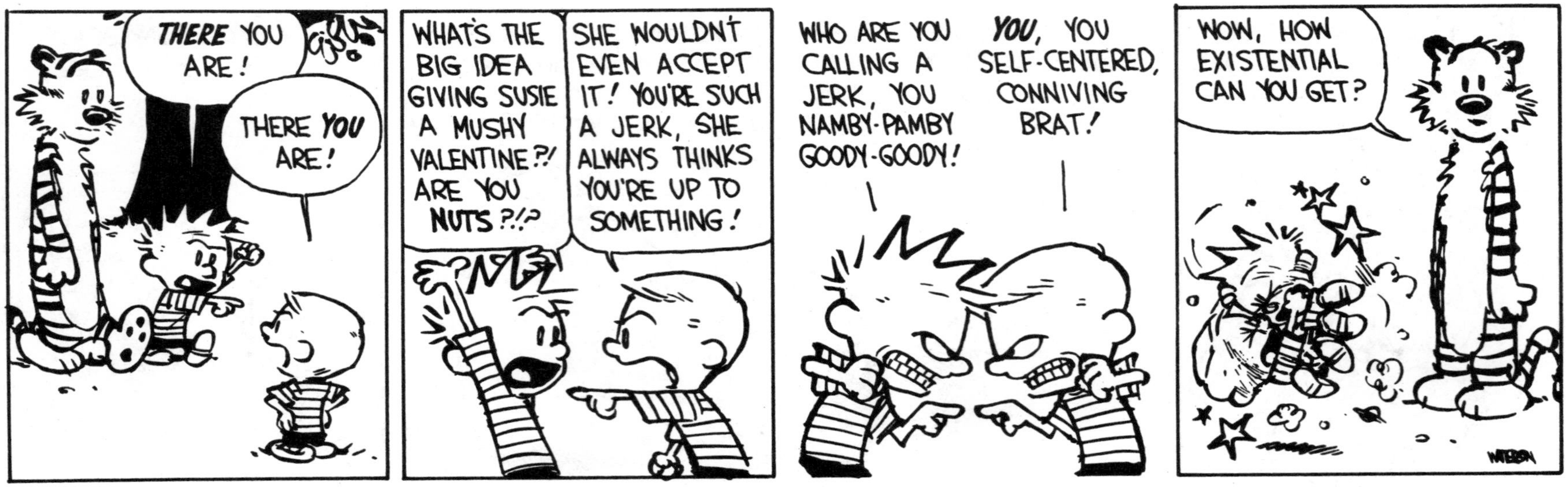
THERE YOU ARE!
THERE YOU ARE!
WHAT'S THE BIG IDEA GIVING SUSIE A MUSHY VALENTINE?! ARE YOU NUTS?!?
SHE WOULDN'T EVEN ACCEPT IT! YOU'RE SUCH A JERK, SHE ALWAYS THINKS YOU'RE UP TO SOMETHING!
WHO ARE YOU CALLING A JERK, YOU NAMBY-PAMBY GOODY-GOODY!
YOU, YOU SELF-CENTERED, CONNIVING BRAT!
WOW, HOW EXISTENTIAL CAN YOU GET?
WATTERSON

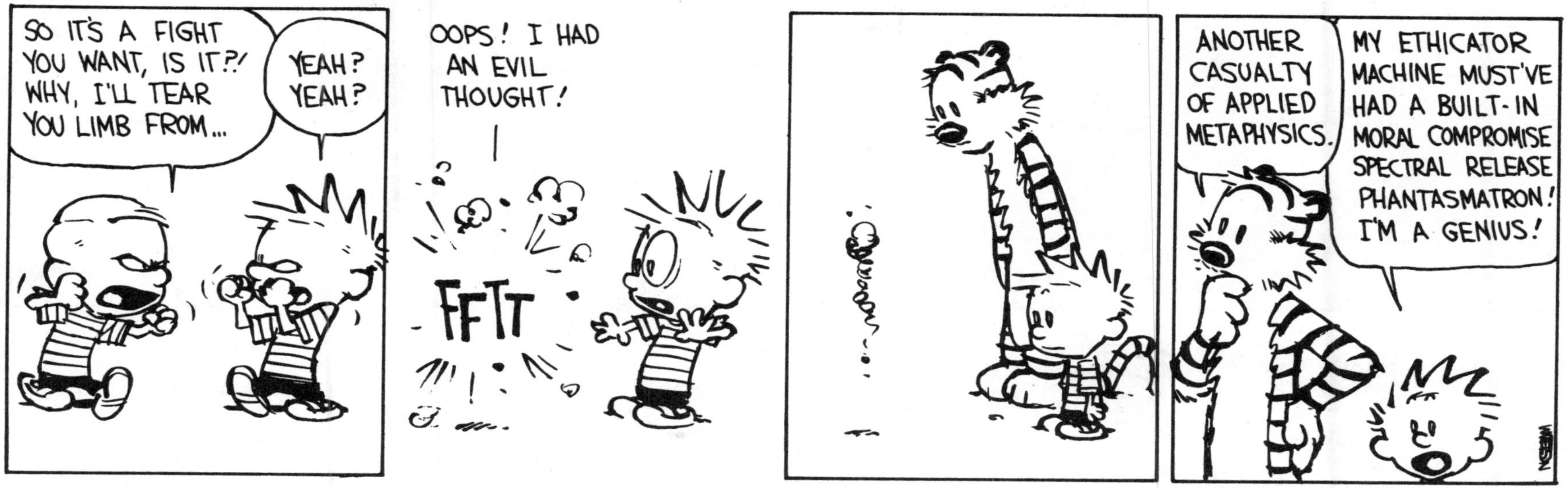
SO IT'S A FIGHT YOU WANT, IS IT?! WHY, I'LL TEAR YOU LIMB FROM...
YEAH? YEAH?
OOPS! I HAD AN EVIL THOUGHT!
FFTT
ANOTHER CASUALTY OF APPLIED METAPHYSICS.
MY ETHICATOR MACHINE MUST'VE HAD A BUILT-IN MORAL COMPROMISE SPECTRAL RELEASE PHANTASMATRON! I'M A GENIUS!

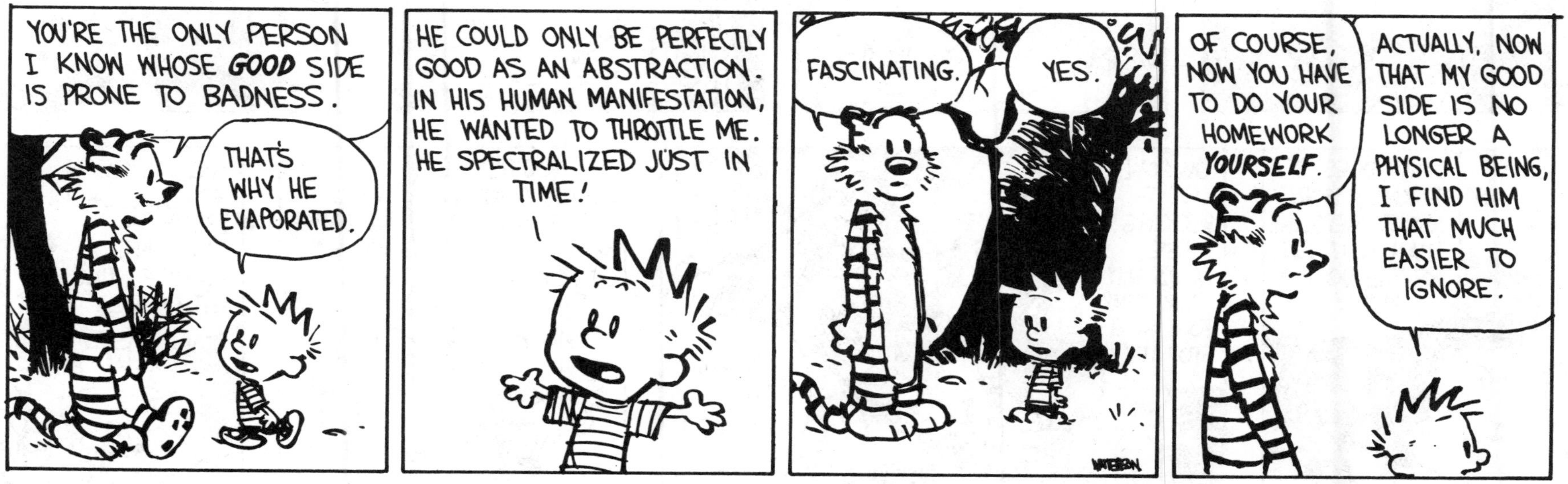
YOU'RE THE ONLY PERSON I KNOW WHOSE **GOOD** SIDE IS PRONE TO BADNESS.
THAT'S WHY HE EVAPORATED.
HE COULD ONLY BE PERFECTLY GOOD AS AN ABSTRACTION. IN HIS HUMAN MANIFESTATION, HE WANTED TO THROTTLE ME. HE SPECTRALIZED JUST IN TIME!
FASCINATING.
YES.
OF COURSE, NOW YOU HAVE TO DO YOUR HOMEWORK **YOURSELF**.
ACTUALLY, NOW THAT MY GOOD SIDE IS NO LONGER A PHYSICAL BEING, I FIND HIM THAT MUCH EASIER TO IGNORE.

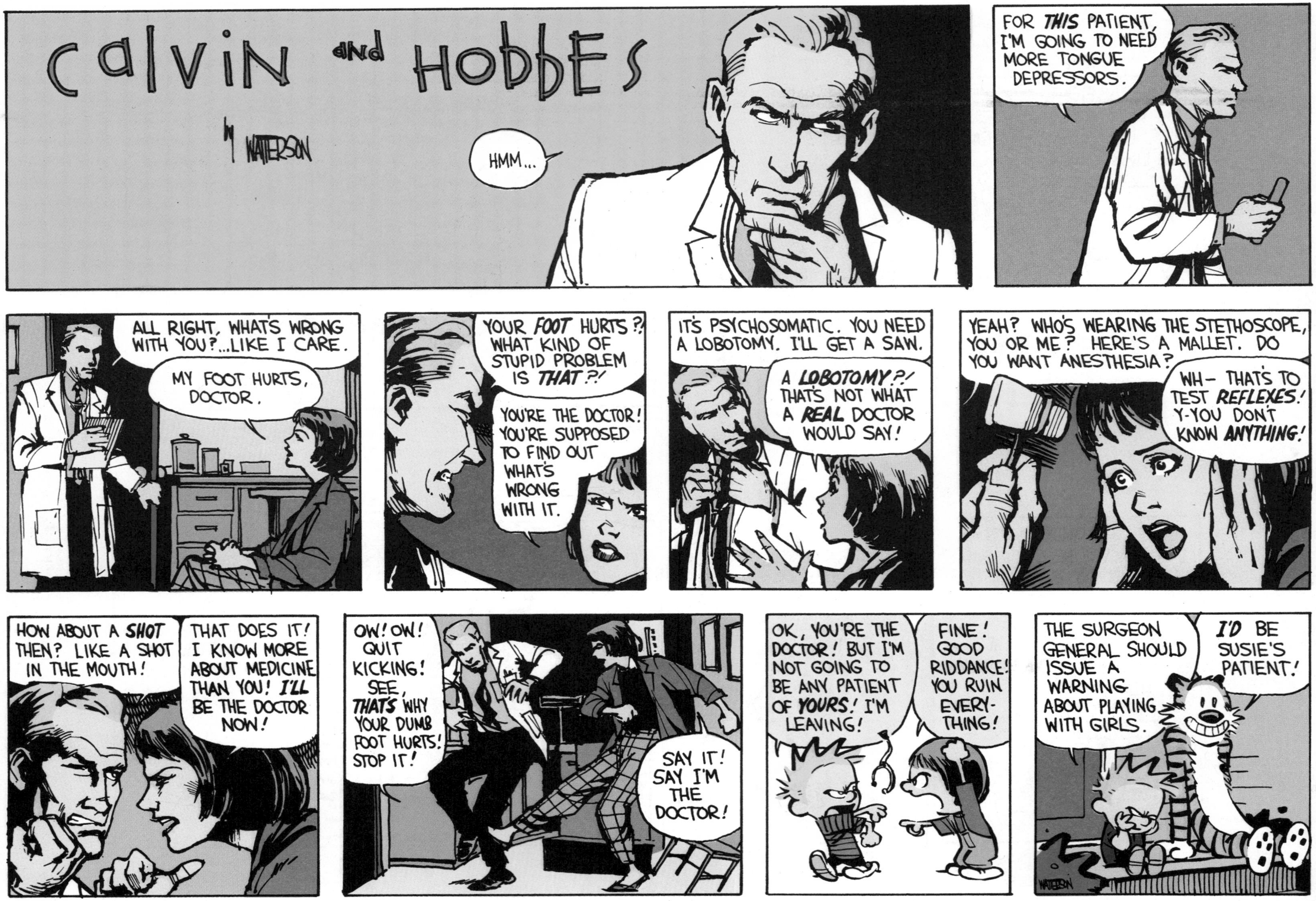
Calvin and Hobbes
by Watterson
HMM...
FOR THIS PATIENT, I'M GOING TO NEED MORE TONGUE DEPRESSORS.
ALL RIGHT, WHAT'S WRONG WITH YOU?...LIKE I CARE.
MY FOOT HURTS, DOCTOR.
YOUR FOOT HURTS?! WHAT KIND OF STUPID PROBLEM IS THAT?!
YOU'RE THE DOCTOR! YOU'RE SUPPOSED TO FIND OUT WHAT'S WRONG WITH IT.
IT'S PSYCHOSOMATIC. YOU NEED A LOBOTOMY. I'LL GET A SAW.
A LOBOTOMY?! THAT'S NOT WHAT A REAL DOCTOR WOULD SAY!
YEAH? WHO'S WEARING THE STETHOSCOPE, YOU OR ME? HERE'S A MALLET. DO YOU WANT ANESTHESIA?
WH- THAT'S TO TEST REFLEXES! Y-YOU DON'T KNOW ANYTHING!
HOW ABOUT A SHOT THEN? LIKE A SHOT IN THE MOUTH!
THAT DOES IT! I KNOW MORE ABOUT MEDICINE THAN YOU! I'LL BE THE DOCTOR NOW!
OW! OW! QUIT KICKING! SEE, THAT'S WHY YOUR DUMB FOOT HURTS! STOP IT!
SAY IT! SAY I'M THE DOCTOR!
OK, YOU'RE THE DOCTOR! BUT I'M NOT GOING TO BE ANY PATIENT OF YOURS! I'M LEAVING!
FINE! GOOD RIDDANCE! YOU RUIN EVERY-THING!
THE SURGEON GENERAL SHOULD ISSUE A WARNING ABOUT PLAYING WITH GIRLS.
I'D BE SUSIE'S PATIENT!
WATTERSON

Drawing the strip as if it were a soap opera strip is a fun visual surprise, and the "serious" pictures make the dialogue even more ludicrous. For the sake of the satire, I wish I'd drawn this more stylishly, the way the best cartoonists of those strips did.

An animal perspective sheds some light on religious questions.

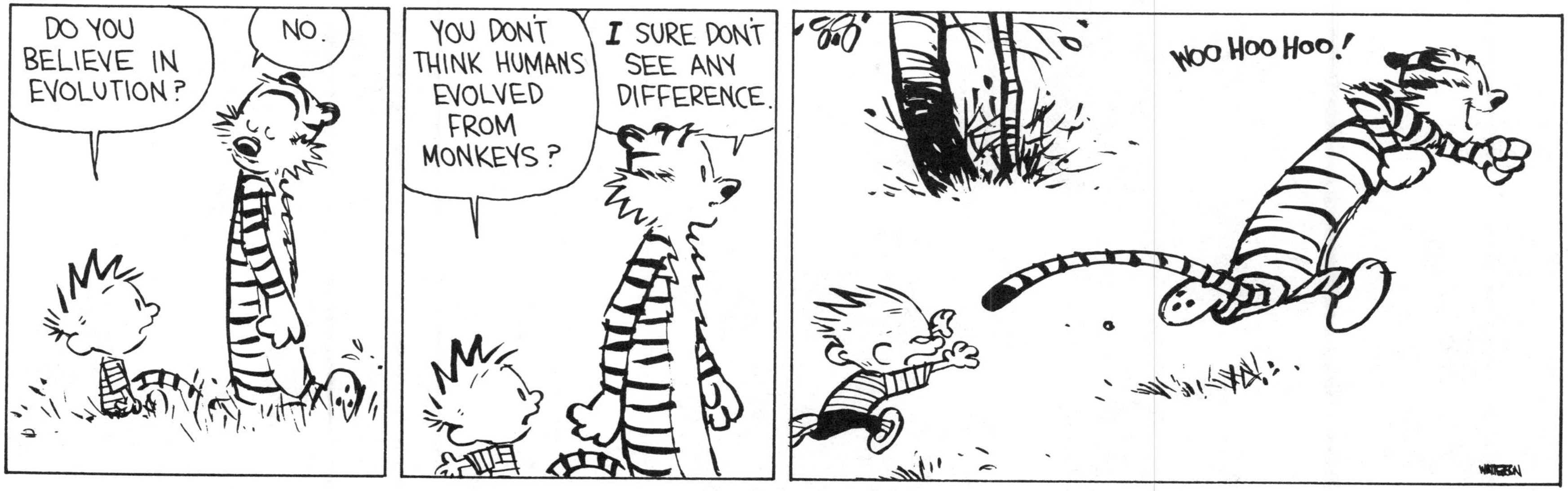
DO YOU BELIEVE IN EVOLUTION?
NO.
YOU DON'T THINK HUMANS EVOLVED FROM MONKEYS?
I SURE DON'T SEE ANY DIFFERENCE.
WOO HOO HOO!

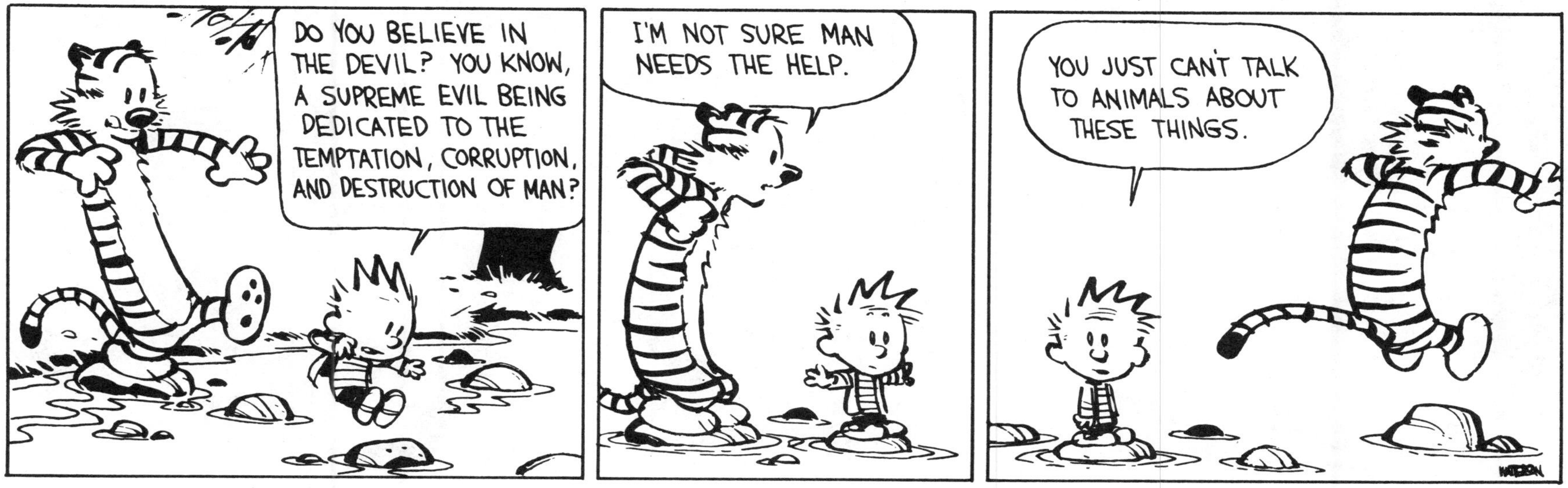
DO YOU BELIEVE IN THE DEVIL? YOU KNOW, A SUPREME EVIL BEING DEDICATED TO THE TEMPTATION, CORRUPTION, AND DESTRUCTION OF MAN?
I'M NOT SURE MAN NEEDS THE HELP.
YOU JUST CAN'T TALK TO ANIMALS ABOUT THESE THINGS.

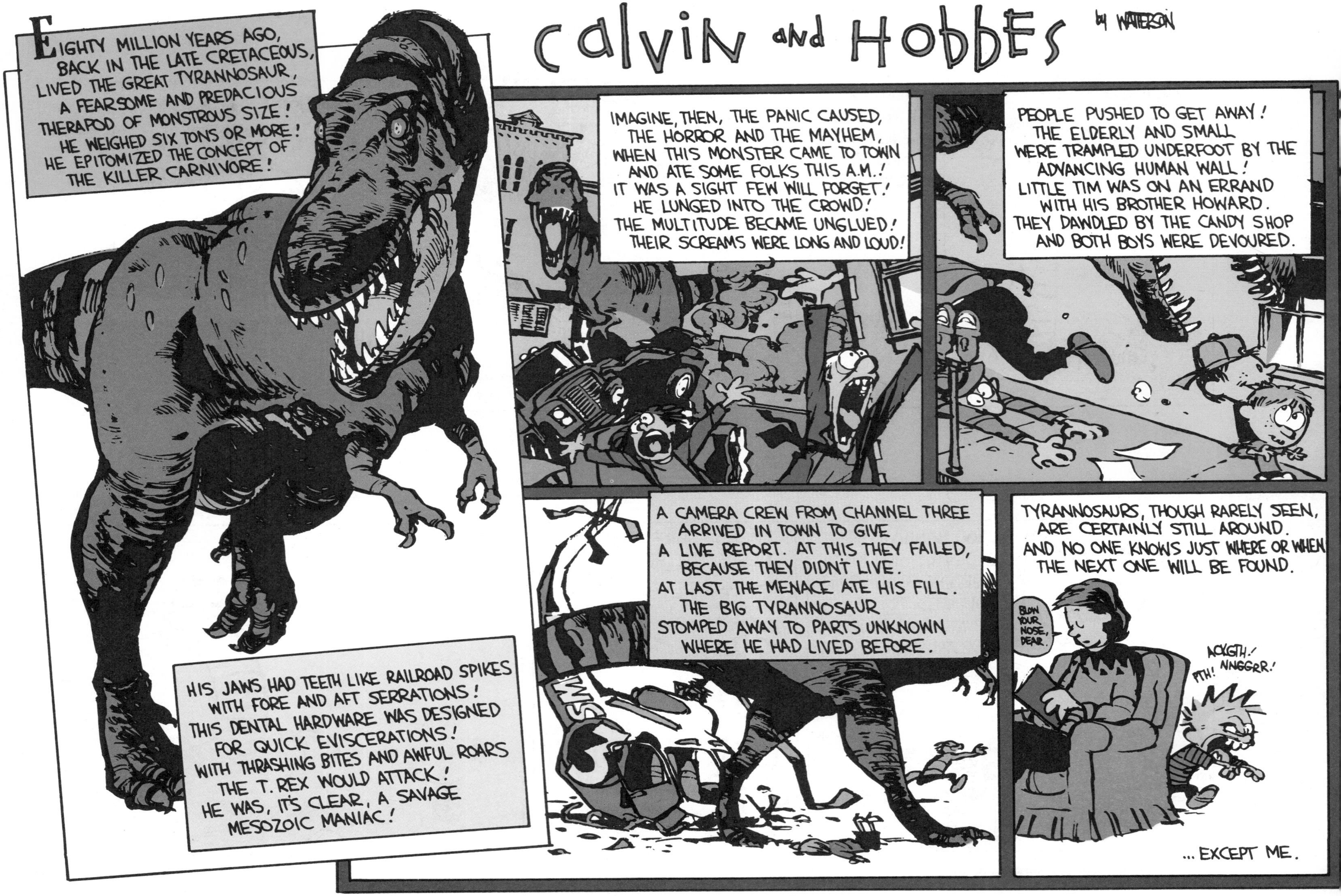
Calvin and Hobbes
by WATTERSON
EIGHTY MILLION YEARS AGO, BACK IN THE LATE CRETACEOUS, LIVED THE GREAT TYRANNOSAUR, A FEARSOME AND PREDACIOUS THERAPOD OF MONSTROUS SIZE! HE WEIGHED SIX TONS OR MORE! HE EPITOMIZED THE CONCEPT OF THE KILLER CARNIVORE!
HIS JAWS HAD TEETH LIKE RAILROAD SPIKES WITH FORE AND AFT SERRATIONS! THIS DENTAL HARDWARE WAS DESIGNED FOR QUICK EVISCERATIONS! WITH THRASHING BITES AND AWFUL ROARS THE T. REX WOULD ATTACK! HE WAS, IT'S CLEAR, A SAVAGE MESOZOIC MANIAC!
IMAGINE, THEN, THE PANIC CAUSED, THE HORROR AND THE MAYHEM, WHEN THIS MONSTER CAME TO TOWN AND ATE SOME FOLKS THIS A.M.! IT WAS A SIGHT FEW WILL FORGET! HE LUNGED INTO THE CROWD! THE MULTITUDE BECAME UNGLUED! THEIR SCREAMS WERE LONG AND LOUD!
PEOPLE PUSHED TO GET AWAY! THE ELDERLY AND SMALL WERE TRAMPLED UNDERFOOT BY THE ADVANCING HUMAN WALL! LITTLE TIM WAS ON AN ERRAND WITH HIS BROTHER HOWARD. THEY DAWDLED BY THE CANDY SHOP AND BOTH BOYS WERE DEVOURED.
A CAMERA CREW FROM CHANNEL THREE ARRIVED IN TOWN TO GIVE A LIVE REPORT. AT THIS THEY FAILED, BECAUSE THEY DIDN'T LIVE. AT LAST THE MENACE ATE HIS FILL. THE BIG TYRANNOSAUR STOMPED AWAY TO PARTS UNKNOWN WHERE HE HAD LIVED BEFORE.
TYRANNOSAURS, THOUGH RARELY SEEN, ARE CERTAINLY STILL AROUND. AND NO ONE KNOWS JUST WHERE OR WHEN THE NEXT ONE WILL BE FOUND.
BLOW YOUR NOSE, DEAR.
ACKGTH! NNGGRR!
PTH!
... EXCEPT ME.

I worked on various versions of this poem, off and on, for several months. Originally I intended to illustrate the poem lavishly and use it for a book, but I never had the time. When I got the new Sunday format, I was eager to try things I couldn't previously do, so I drew up this version for a Sunday strip.

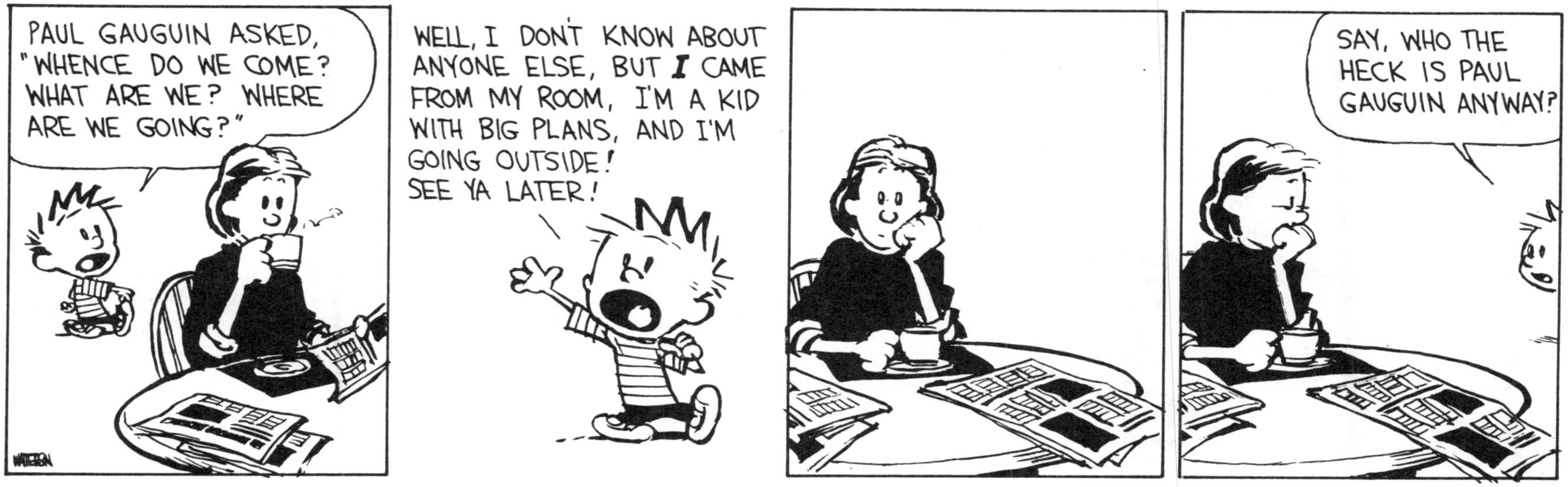
PAUL GAUGUIN ASKED, "WHENCE DO WE COME? WHAT ARE WE? WHERE ARE WE GOING?"
WELL, I DON'T KNOW ABOUT ANYONE ELSE, BUT I CAME FROM MY ROOM, I'M A KID WITH BIG PLANS, AND I'M GOING OUTSIDE! SEE YA LATER!
SAY, WHO THE HECK IS PAUL GAUGUIN ANYWAY?

I still think this strip is funny.

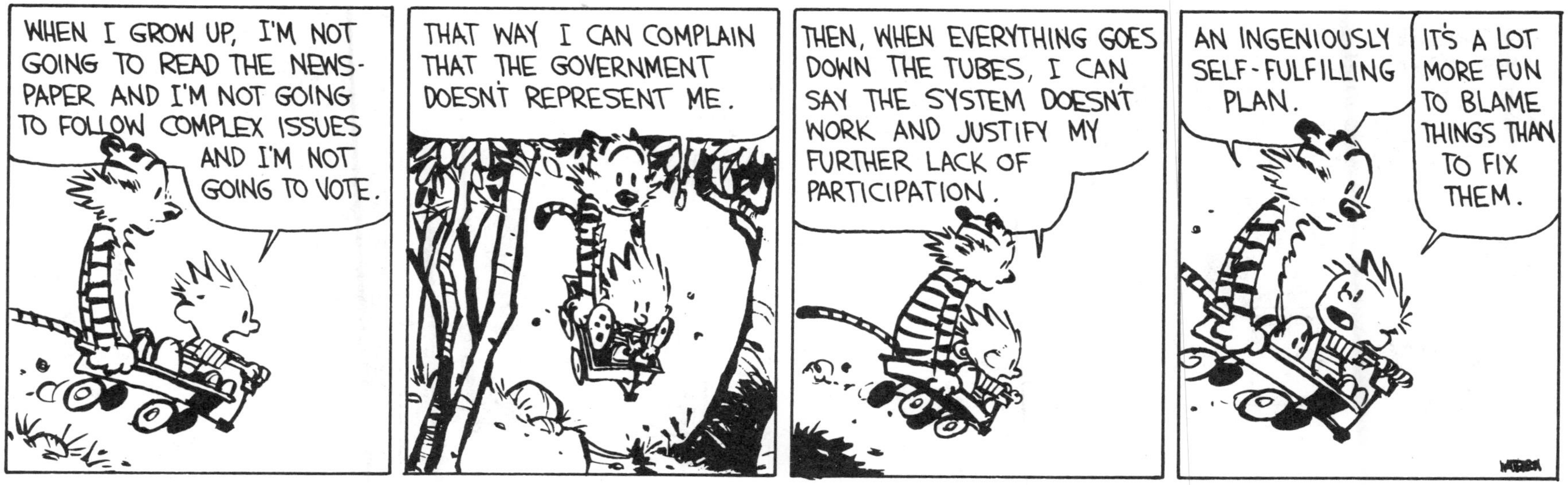
WHEN I GROW UP, I'M NOT GOING TO READ THE NEWSPAPER AND I'M NOT GOING TO FOLLOW COMPLEX ISSUES
AND I'M NOT GOING TO VOTE.
THAT WAY I CAN COMPLAIN THAT THE GOVERNMENT DOESN'T REPRESENT ME.
THEN, WHEN EVERYTHING GOES DOWN THE TUBES, I CAN SAY THE SYSTEM DOESN'T WORK AND JUSTIFY MY FURTHER LACK OF PARTICIPATION.
AN INGENIOUSLY SELF-FULFILLING PLAN.
IT'S A LOT MORE FUN TO BLAME THINGS THAN TO FIX THEM.

A political cartoon does not have to have labels written across everything, or make its point with a sledgehammer.

The late twentieth-century drug of choice.

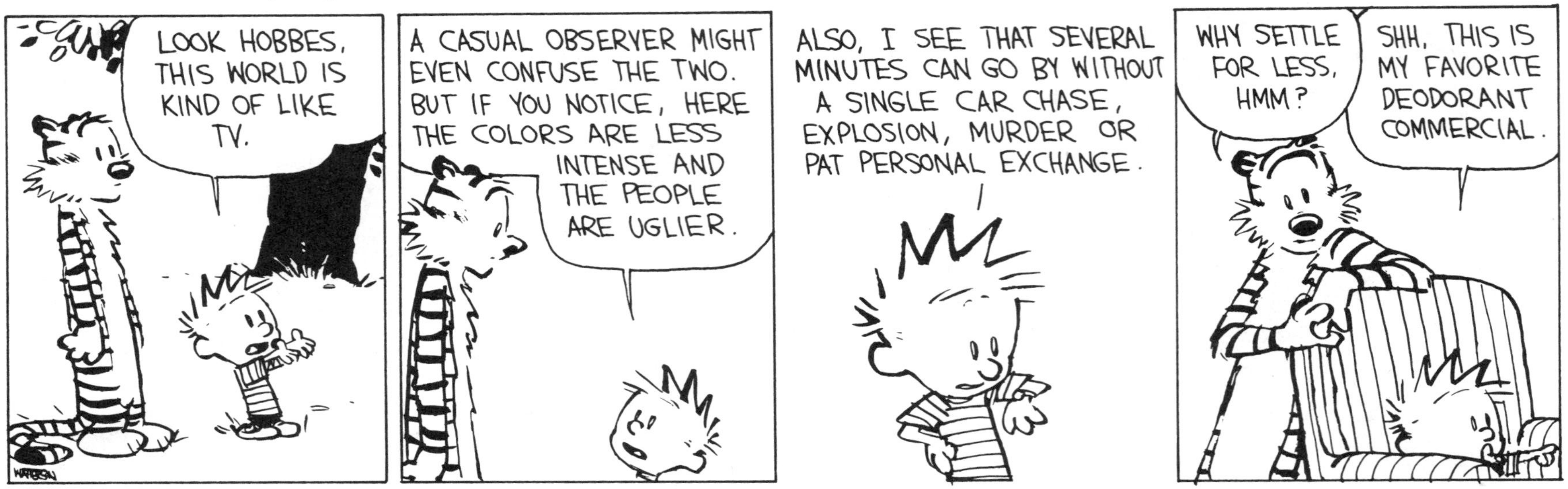
LOOK HOBBES, THIS WORLD IS KIND OF LIKE TV.
A CASUAL OBSERVER MIGHT EVEN CONFUSE THE TWO. BUT IF YOU NOTICE, HERE THE COLORS ARE LESS INTENSE AND THE PEOPLE ARE UGLIER.
ALSO, I SEE THAT SEVERAL MINUTES CAN GO BY WITHOUT A SINGLE CAR CHASE, EXPLOSION, MURDER OR PAT PERSONAL EXCHANGE.
WHY SETTLE FOR LESS, HMM?
SHH, THIS IS MY FAVORITE DEODORANT COMMERCIAL.

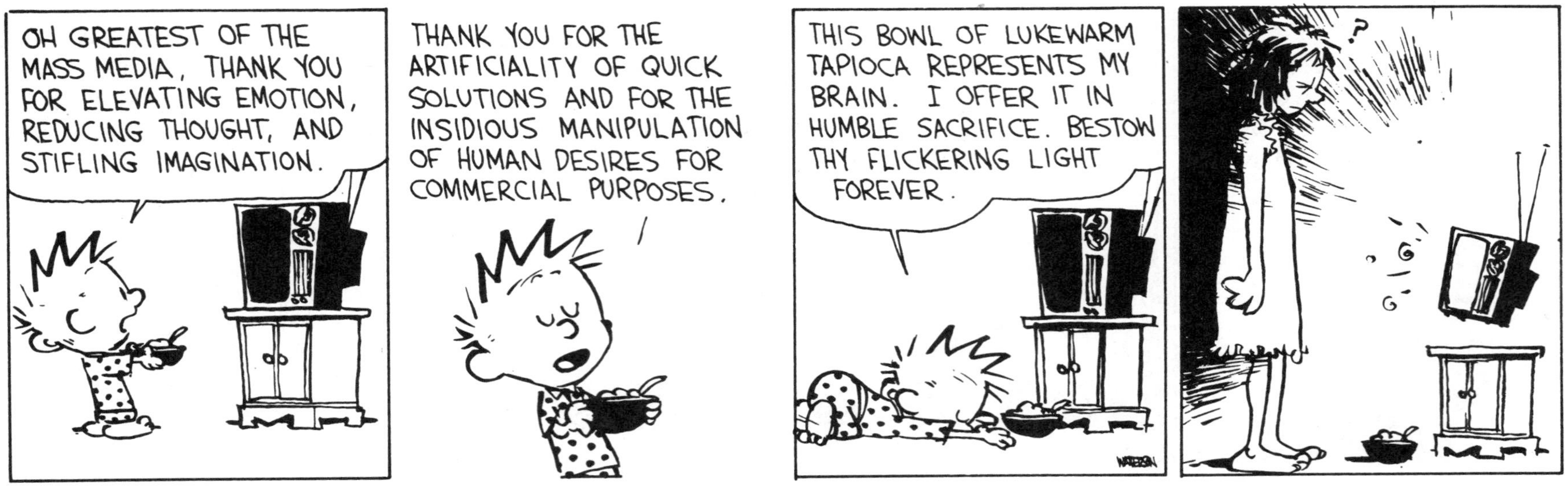
OH GREATEST OF THE MASS MEDIA, THANK YOU FOR ELEVATING EMOTION, REDUCING THOUGHT, AND STIFLING IMAGINATION.
THANK YOU FOR THE ARTIFICIALITY OF QUICK SOLUTIONS AND FOR THE INSIDIOUS MANIPULATION OF HUMAN DESIRES FOR COMMERCIAL PURPOSES.
THIS BOWL OF LUKEWARM TAPIOCA REPRESENTS MY BRAIN. I OFFER IT IN HUMBLE SACRIFICE. BESTOW THY FLICKERING LIGHT FOREVER.
?

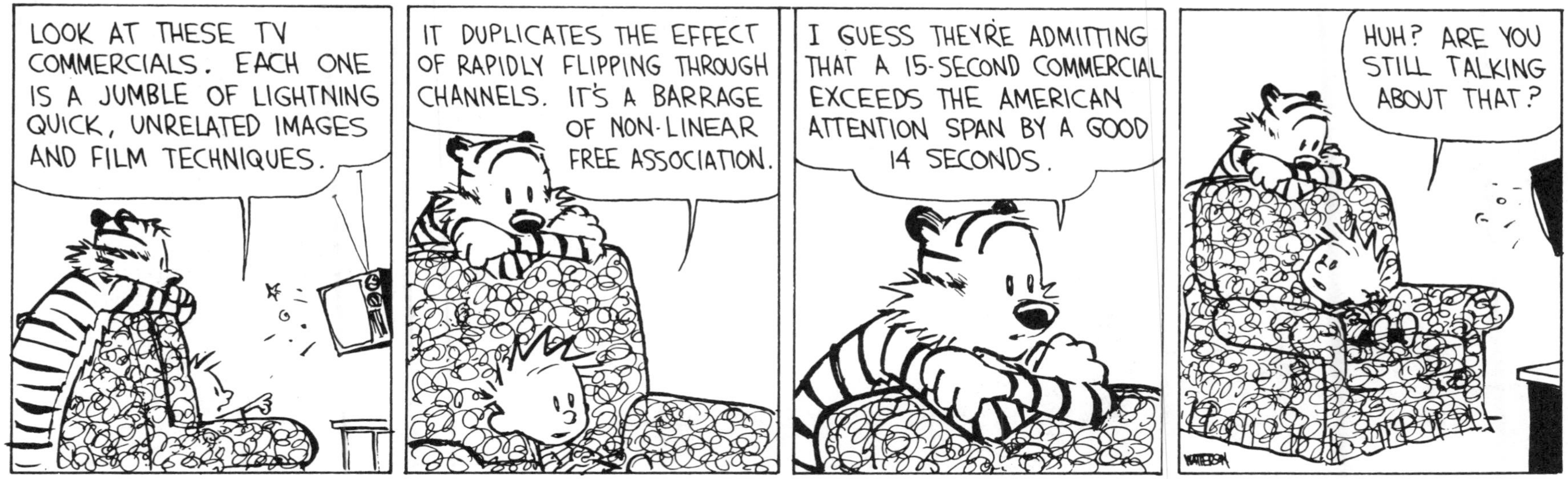
LOOK AT THESE TV COMMERCIALS. EACH ONE IS A JUMBLE OF LIGHTNING QUICK, UNRELATED IMAGES AND FILM TECHNIQUES.
IT DUPLICATES THE EFFECT OF RAPIDLY FLIPPING THROUGH CHANNELS. IT'S A BARRAGE OF NON-LINEAR FREE ASSOCIATION.
I GUESS THEY'RE ADMITTING THAT A 15-SECOND COMMERCIAL EXCEEDS THE AMERICAN ATTENTION SPAN BY A GOOD 14 SECONDS.
HUH? ARE YOU STILL TALKING ABOUT THAT?

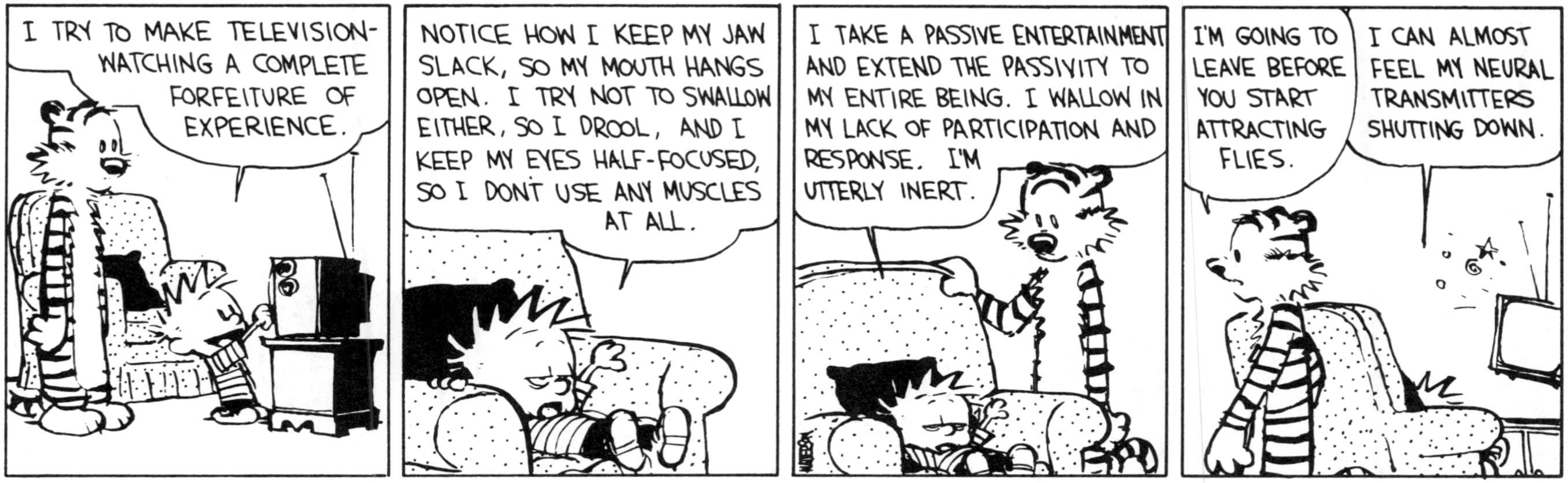
I TRY TO MAKE TELEVISION-WATCHING A COMPLETE FORFEITURE OF EXPERIENCE.
NOTICE HOW I KEEP MY JAW SLACK, SO MY MOUTH HANGS OPEN. I TRY NOT TO SWALLOW EITHER, SO I DROOL, AND I KEEP MY EYES HALF-FOCUSED, SO I DON'T USE ANY MUSCLES AT ALL.
I TAKE A PASSIVE ENTERTAINMENT AND EXTEND THE PASSIVITY TO MY ENTIRE BEING. I WALLOW IN MY LACK OF PARTICIPATION AND RESPONSE. I'M UTTERLY INERT.
I'M GOING TO LEAVE BEFORE YOU START ATTRACTING FLIES.
I CAN ALMOST FEEL MY NEURAL TRANSMITTERS SHUTTING DOWN.

For some time, I've used Calvin's snowmen as a way to make fun of the art world. I enjoy studying art, but the field certainly attracts its share of pretentious blowhards.

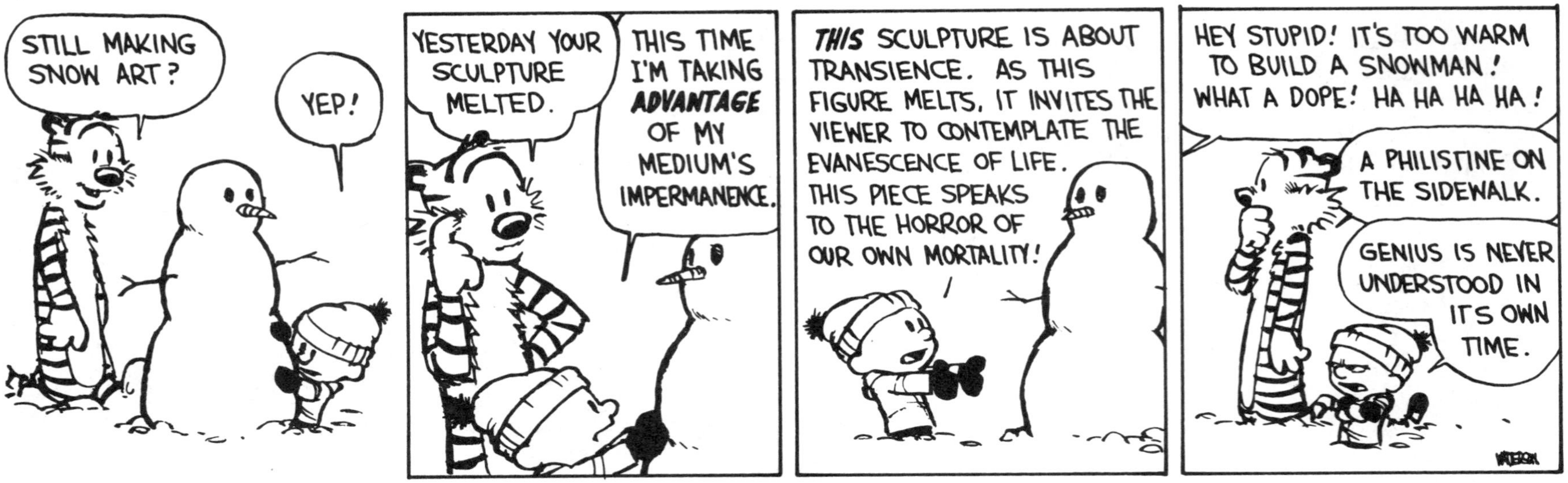
STILL MAKING SNOW ART?
YEP!
YESTERDAY YOUR SCULPTURE MELTED.
THIS TIME I'M TAKING **ADVANTAGE** OF MY MEDIUM'S IMPERMANENCE.
THIS SCULPTURE IS ABOUT TRANSIENCE. AS THIS FIGURE MELTS, IT INVITES THE VIEWER TO CONTEMPLATE THE EVANESCENCE OF LIFE. THIS PIECE SPEAKS TO THE HORROR OF OUR OWN MORTALITY!
HEY STUPID! IT'S TOO WARM TO BUILD A SNOWMAN! WHAT A DOPE! HA HA HA HA!
A PHILISTINE ON THE SIDEWALK.
GENIUS IS NEVER UNDERSTOOD IN ITS OWN TIME.

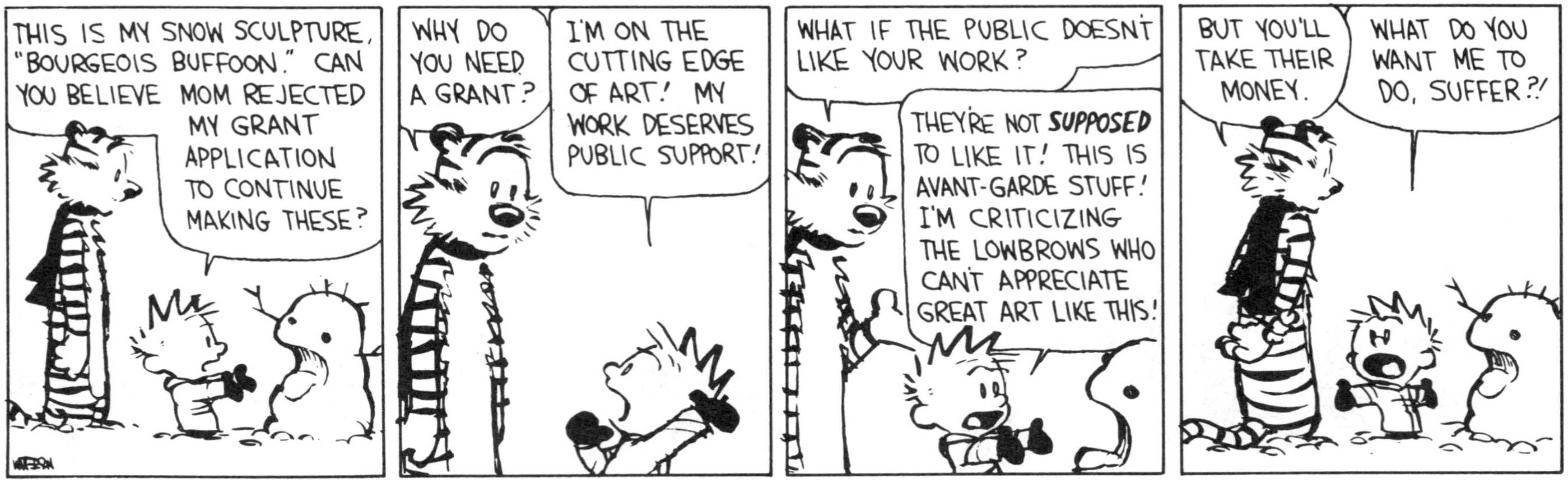
THIS IS MY SNOW SCULPTURE, "BOURGEOIS BUFFOON." CAN YOU BELIEVE MOM REJECTED MY GRANT APPLICATION TO CONTINUE MAKING THESE?
WHY DO YOU NEED A GRANT?
I'M ON THE CUTTING EDGE OF ART! MY WORK DESERVES PUBLIC SUPPORT!
WHAT IF THE PUBLIC DOESN'T LIKE YOUR WORK?
THEY'RE NOT **SUPPOSED** TO LIKE IT! THIS IS AVANT-GARDE STUFF! I'M CRITICIZING THE LOWBROWS WHO CAN'T APPRECIATE GREAT ART LIKE THIS!
BUT YOU'LL TAKE THEIR MONEY.
WHAT DO YOU WANT ME TO DO, SUFFER?!

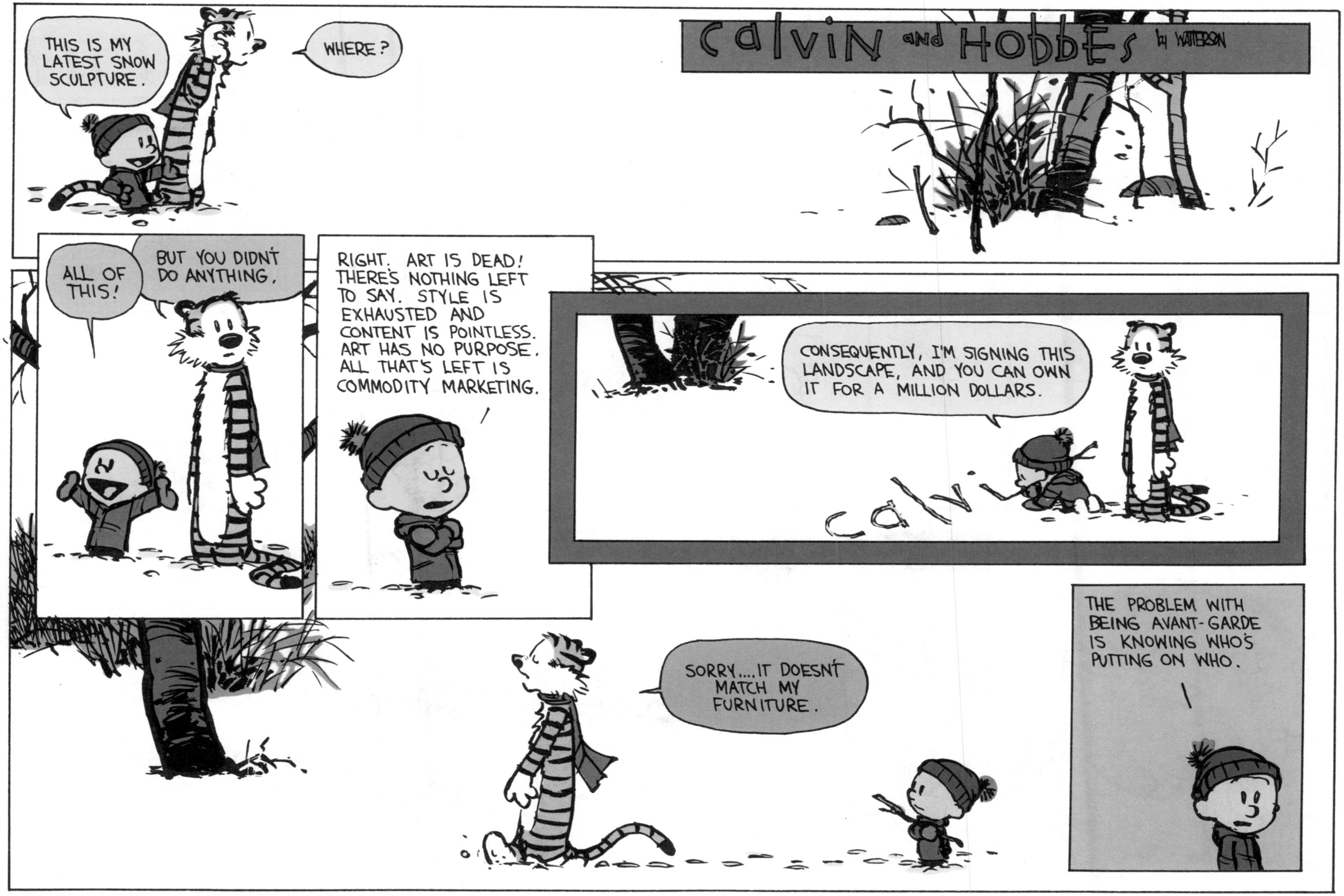
Calvin and HOBBES by WATTERSON
THIS IS MY LATEST SNOW SCULPTURE.
WHERE?
ALL OF THIS!
BUT YOU DIDN'T DO ANYTHING.
RIGHT. ART IS DEAD! THERE'S NOTHING LEFT TO SAY. STYLE IS EXHAUSTED AND CONTENT IS POINTLESS. ART HAS NO PURPOSE. ALL THAT'S LEFT IS COMMODITY MARKETING.
CONSEQUENTLY, I'M SIGNING THIS LANDSCAPE, AND YOU CAN OWN IT FOR A MILLION DOLLARS.
CALV
SORRY.... IT DOESN'T MATCH MY FURNITURE.
THE PROBLEM WITH BEING AVANT-GARDE IS KNOWING WHO'S PUTTING ON WHO.

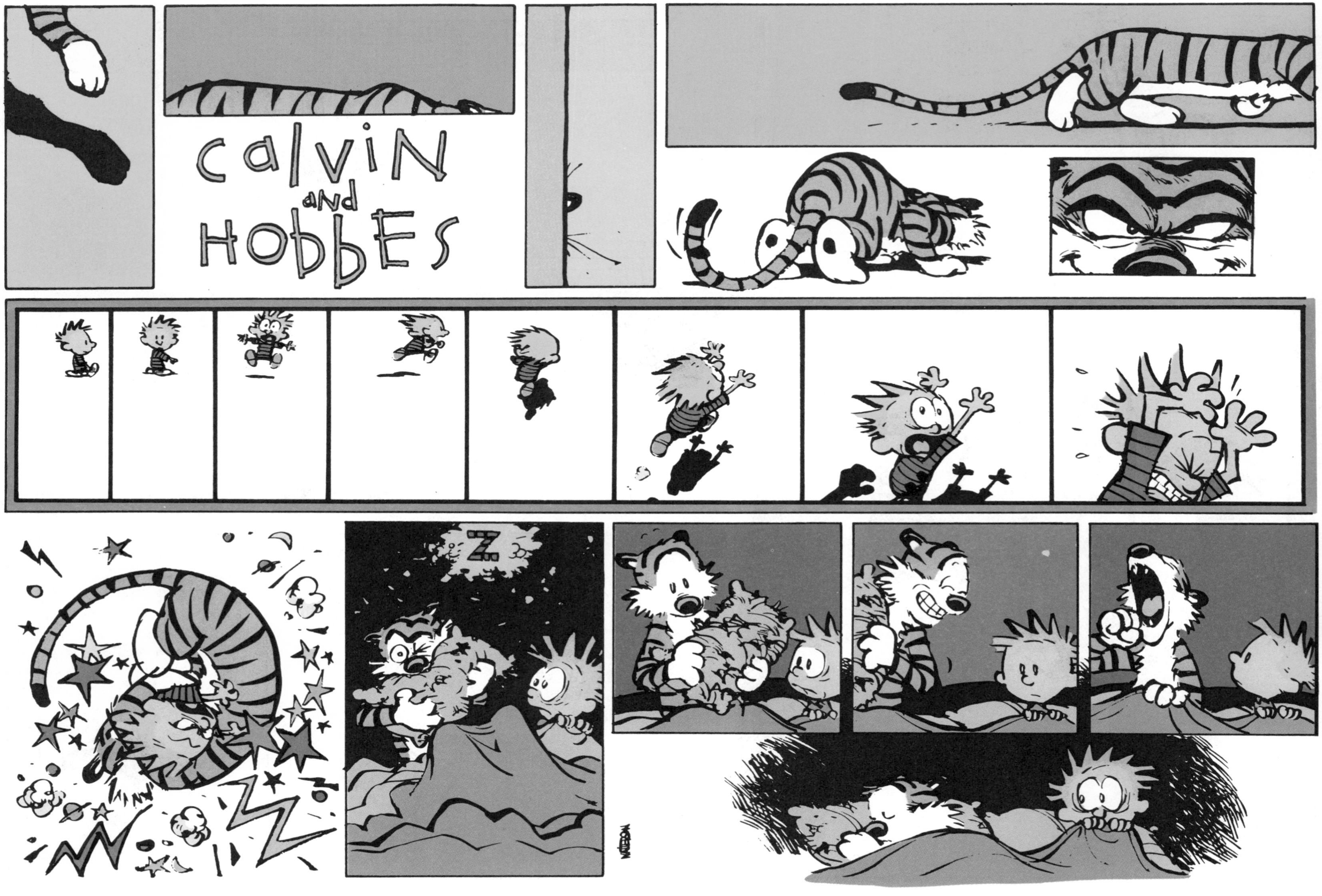
Calvin and HOBBES
Z
WATTERSON

The initial thrill of being able to design my Sunday strip layouts was soon tempered by the difficulty of it. A confusing layout will obstruct the flow of the story, so it's important that the design provides a logical path for the eye. The new Sunday strips take two or three times as long to draw as the old Sunday strips.

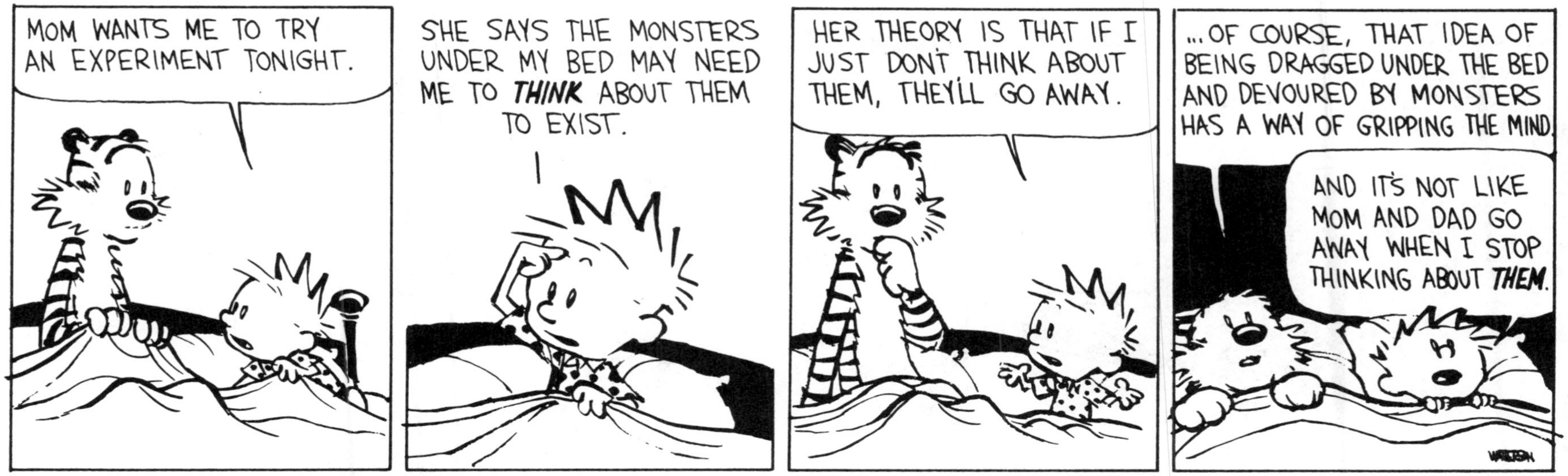
MOM WANTS ME TO TRY AN EXPERIMENT TONIGHT.
SHE SAYS THE MONSTERS UNDER MY BED MAY NEED ME TO *THINK* ABOUT THEM TO EXIST.
HER THEORY IS THAT IF I JUST DON'T THINK ABOUT THEM, THEY'LL GO AWAY.
...OF COURSE, THAT IDEA OF BEING DRAGGED UNDER THE BED AND DEVOURED BY MONSTERS HAS A WAY OF GRIPPING THE MIND.
AND IT'S NOT LIKE MOM AND DAD GO AWAY WHEN I STOP THINKING ABOUT *THEM*.

Several months after returning from my first sabbatical, I found myself behind on deadlines and sending out material I wasn't satisfied with. This happens occasionally, and it always sends me into a tailspin, because I get discouraged and write even worse material. The strip can be a monster sometimes, and I illustrated my situation in a story where Calvin quiets his monsters by throwing them garbage.

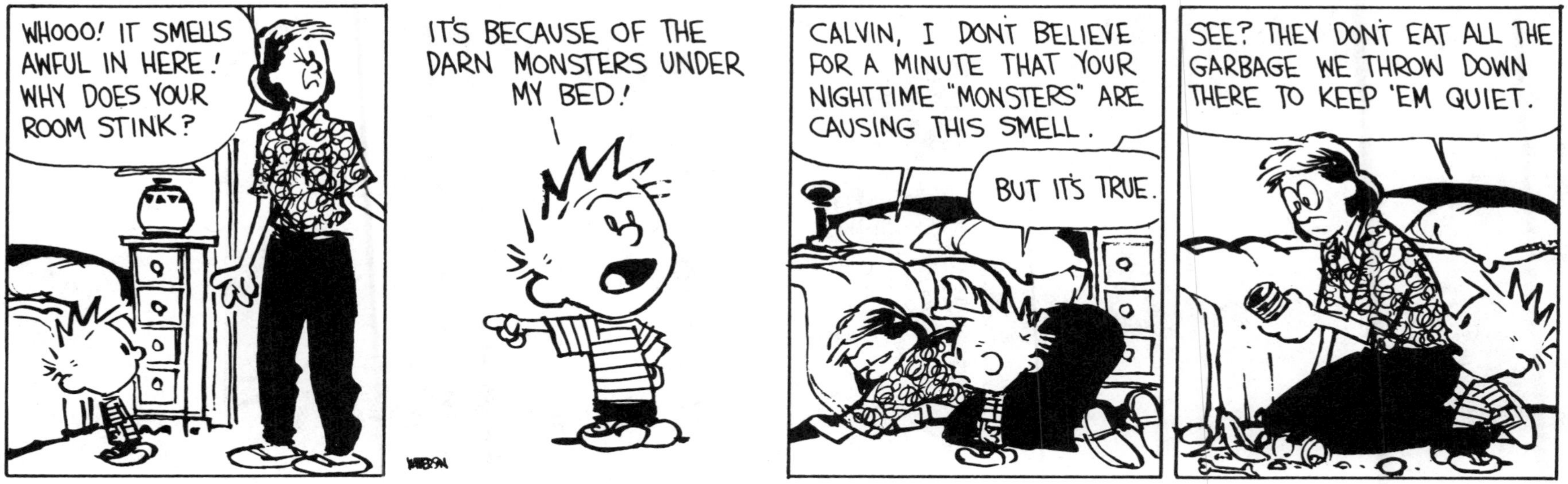
WHOOO! IT SMELLS AWFUL IN HERE! WHY DOES YOUR ROOM STINK?
IT'S BECAUSE OF THE DARN MONSTERS UNDER MY BED!
CALVIN, I DON'T BELIEVE FOR A MINUTE THAT YOUR NIGHTTIME "MONSTERS" ARE CAUSING THIS SMELL.
BUT IT'S TRUE.
SEE? THEY DON'T EAT ALL THE GARBAGE WE THROW DOWN THERE TO KEEP 'EM QUIET.

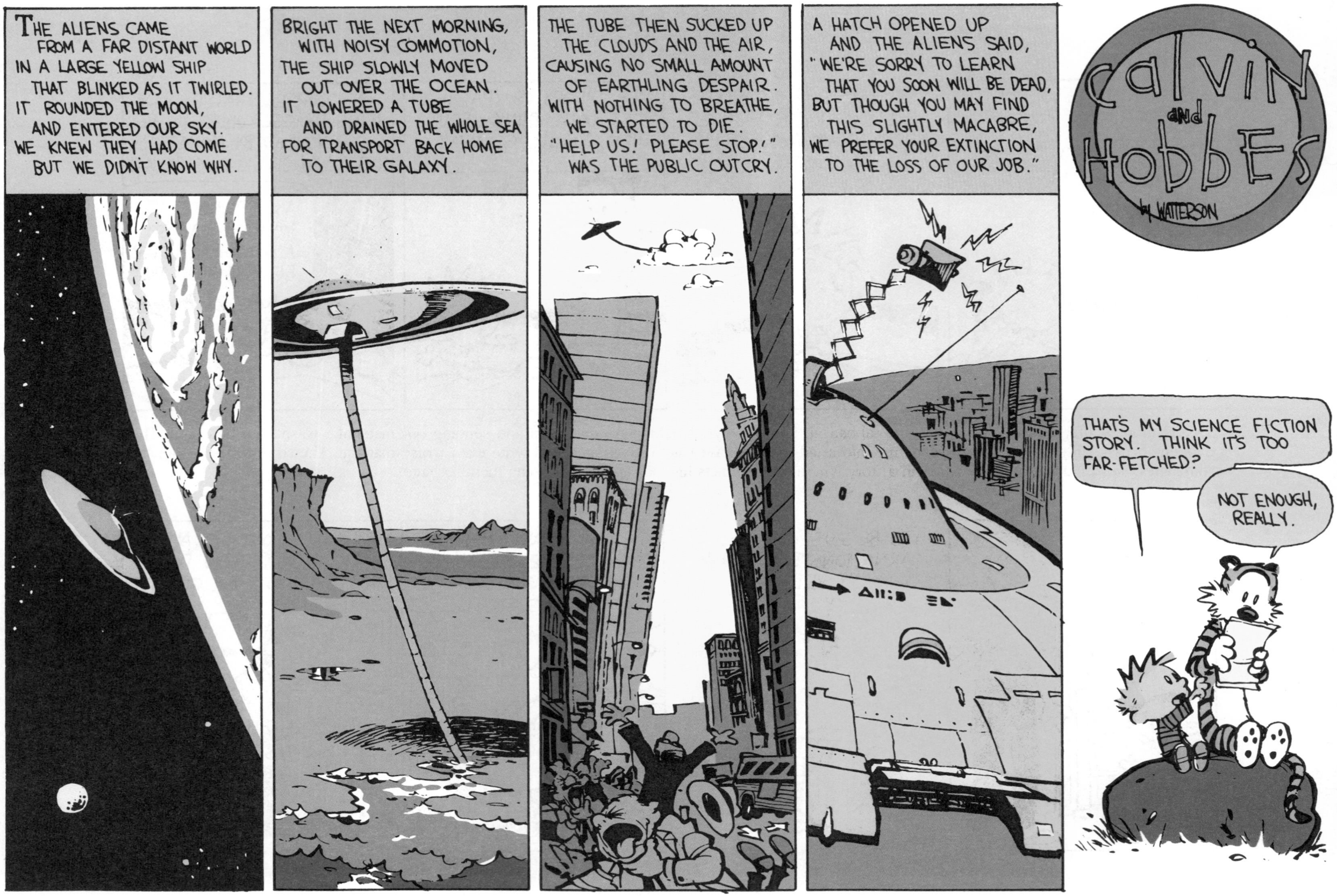
THE ALIENS CAME FROM A FAR DISTANT WORLD IN A LARGE YELLOW SHIP THAT BLINKED AS IT TWIRLED. IT ROUNDED THE MOON, AND ENTERED OUR SKY. WE KNEW THEY HAD COME BUT WE DIDN'T KNOW WHY.
BRIGHT THE NEXT MORNING, WITH NOISY COMMOTION, THE SHIP SLOWLY MOVED OUT OVER THE OCEAN. IT LOWERED A TUBE AND DRAINED THE WHOLE SEA FOR TRANSPORT BACK HOME TO THEIR GALAXY.
THE TUBE THEN SUCKED UP THE CLOUDS AND THE AIR, CAUSING NO SMALL AMOUNT OF EARTHLING DESPAIR. WITH NOTHING TO BREATHE, WE STARTED TO DIE. "HELP US! PLEASE STOP!" WAS THE PUBLIC OUTCRY.
A HATCH OPENED UP AND THE ALIENS SAID, "WE'RE SORRY TO LEARN THAT YOU SOON WILL BE DEAD, BUT THOUGH YOU MAY FIND THIS SLIGHTLY MACABRE, WE PREFER YOUR EXTINCTION TO THE LOSS OF OUR JOB."
Calvin and Hobbes
by WATTERSON
THAT'S MY SCIENCE FICTION STORY. THINK IT'S TOO FAR-FETCHED?
NOT ENOUGH, REALLY.

In recent years, the strip has had more overt commentary to it. I didn't set out with that as a goal, but I guess that's where my mind is. I always try to keep the strip funny and true to the characters, because preachy cartoons get tiresome quickly.

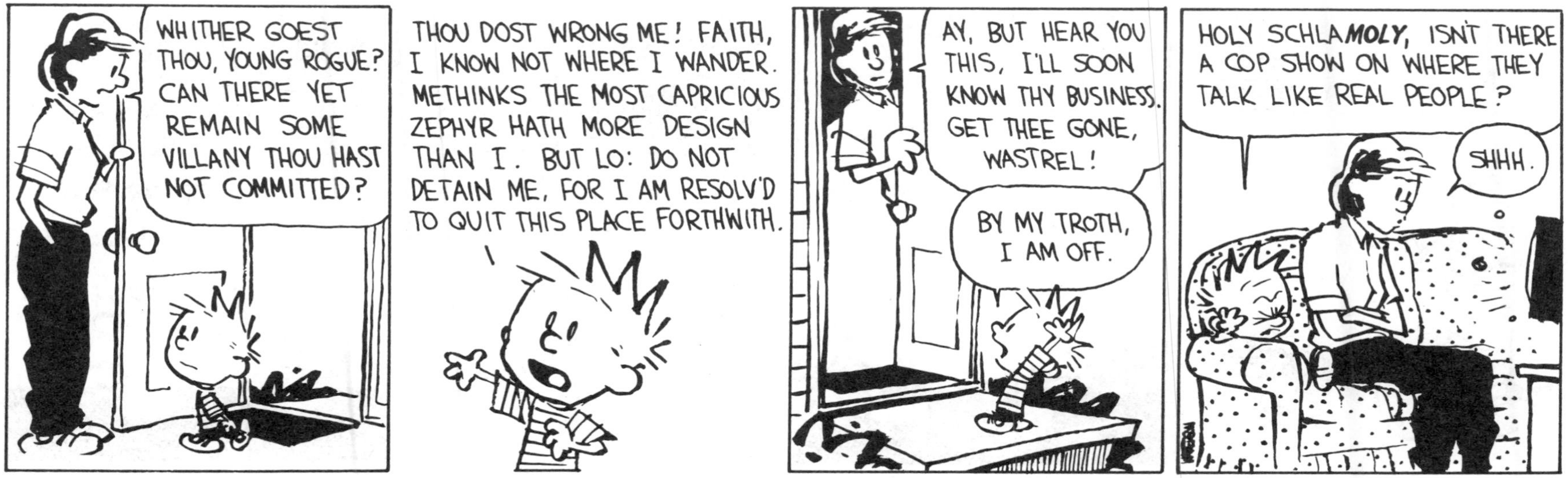

WHITHER GOEST THOU, YOUNG ROGUE? CAN THERE YET REMAIN SOME VILLANY THOU HAST NOT COMMITTED?
THOU DOST WRONG ME! FAITH, I KNOW NOT WHERE I WANDER. METHINKS THE MOST CAPRICIOUS ZEPHYR HATH MORE DESIGN THAN I. BUT LO: DO NOT DETAIN ME, FOR I AM RESOLV'D TO QUIT THIS PLACE FORTHWITH.
AY, BUT HEAR YOU THIS, I'LL SOON KNOW THY BUSINESS. GET THEE GONE, WASTREL!
BY MY TROTH, I AM OFF.
HOLY SCHLA**MOLY**, ISN'T THERE A COP SHOW ON WHERE THEY TALK LIKE REAL PEOPLE?
SHHH.

I watched a Shakespeare play on TV without understanding a word of it. It gave me an idea for a strip, though.

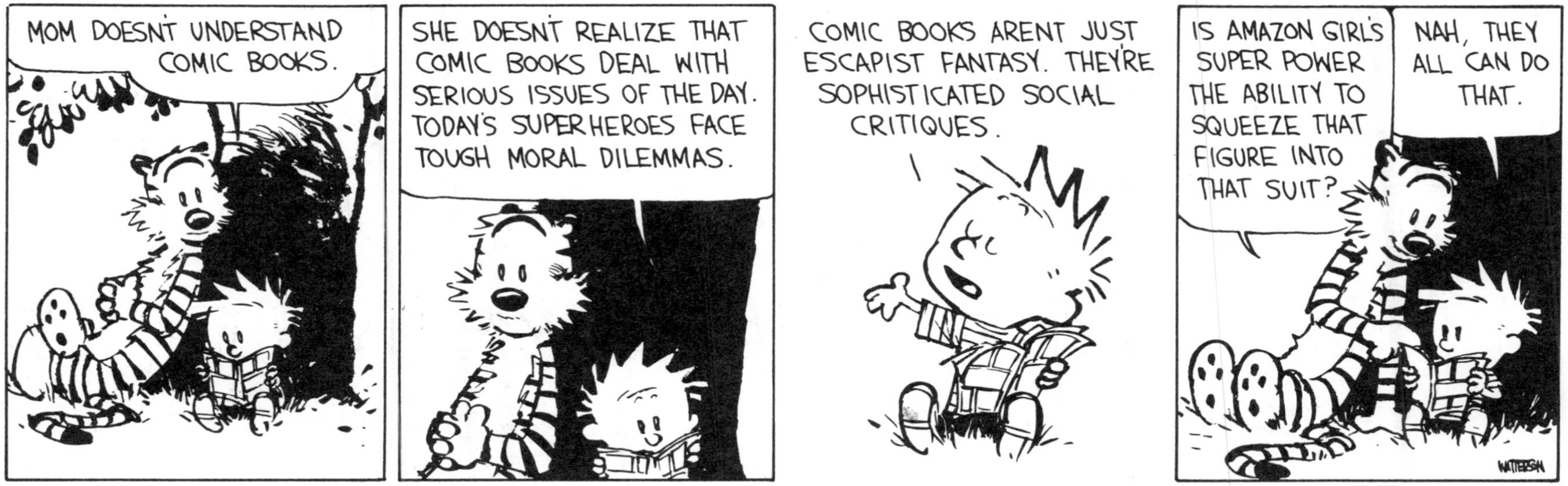

MOM DOESN'T UNDERSTAND COMIC BOOKS.
SHE DOESN'T REALIZE THAT COMIC BOOKS DEAL WITH SERIOUS ISSUES OF THE DAY. TODAY'S SUPERHEROES FACE TOUGH MORAL DILEMMAS.
COMIC BOOKS AREN'T JUST ESCAPIST FANTASY. THEY'RE SOPHISTICATED SOCIAL CRITIQUES.
IS AMAZON GIRL'S SUPER POWER THE ABILITY TO SQUEEZE THAT FIGURE INTO THAT SUIT?
NAH, THEY ALL CAN DO THAT.
WATTERSON

You can make your superhero a psychopath, you can draw gut-splattering violence, and you can call it a "graphic novel," but comic books are still incredibly stupid.

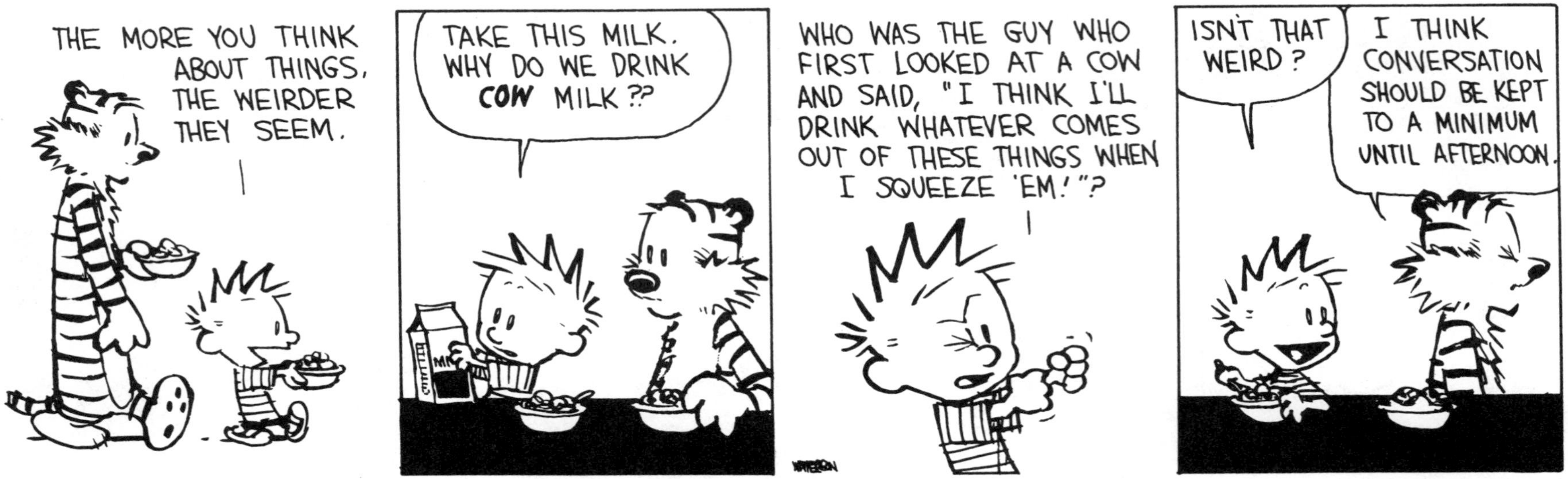
THE MORE YOU THINK ABOUT THINGS, THE WEIRDER THEY SEEM.
TAKE THIS MILK. WHY DO WE DRINK COW MILK ??
WHO WAS THE GUY WHO FIRST LOOKED AT A COW AND SAID, "I THINK I'LL DRINK WHATEVER COMES OUT OF THESE THINGS WHEN I SQUEEZE 'EM!"?
ISN'T THAT WEIRD?
I THINK CONVERSATION SHOULD BE KEPT TO A MINIMUM UNTIL AFTERNOON.

It's sometimes sort of frightening where my mind will go if I let it. Who *was* that guy?!

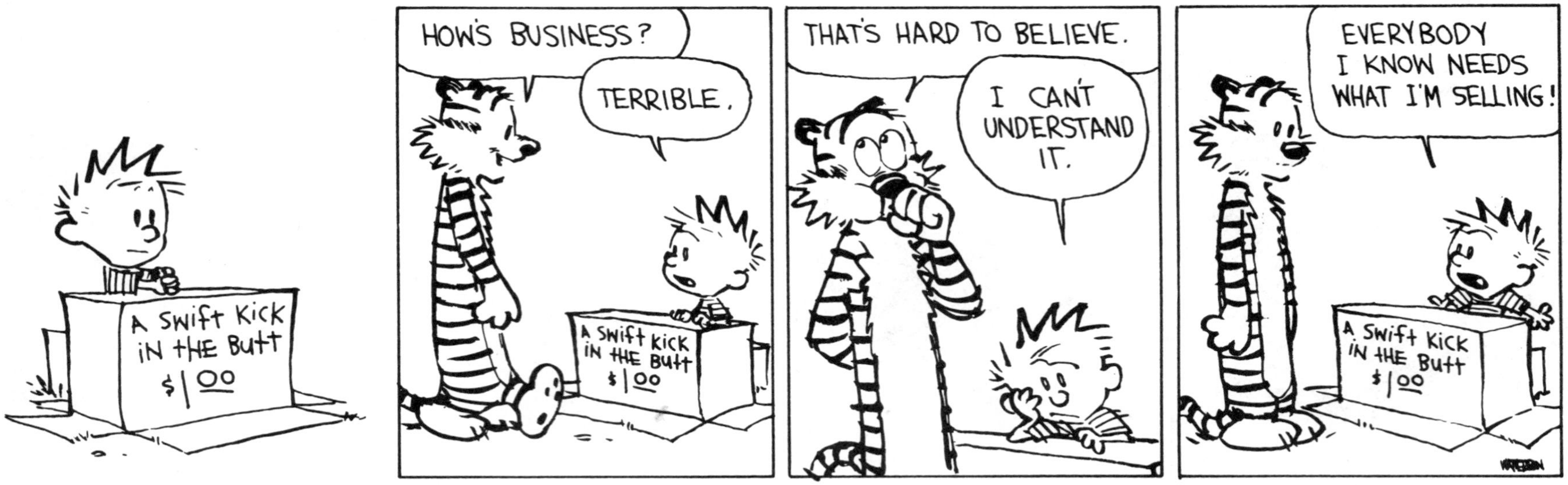
A SWIFT KICK IN THE BUTT $1.00
HOW'S BUSINESS?
TERRIBLE.
THAT'S HARD TO BELIEVE.
I CAN'T UNDERSTAND IT.
EVERYBODY I KNOW NEEDS WHAT I'M SELLING!

People will pay for what they want, but not for what they need.

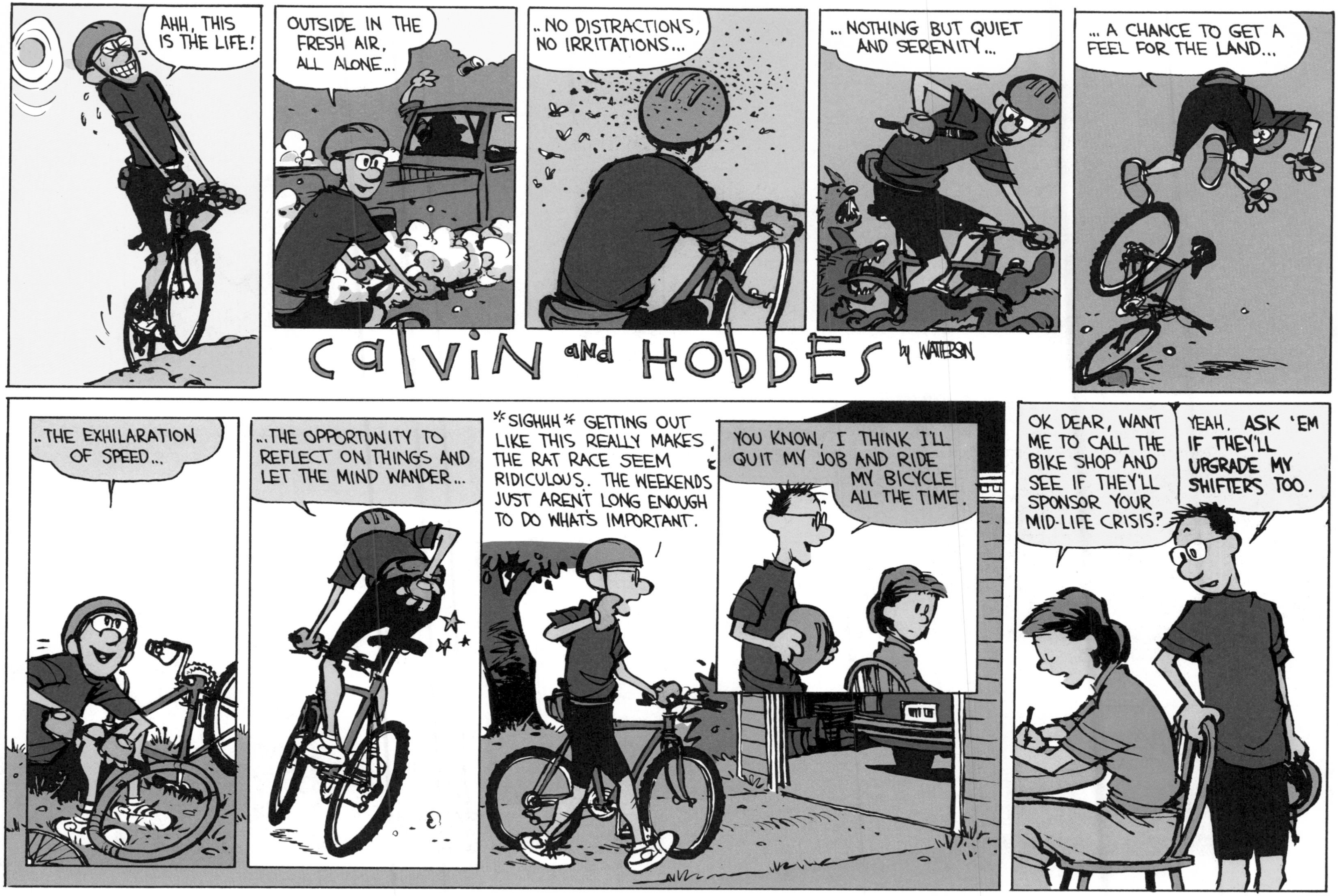
AHH, THIS IS THE LIFE!
OUTSIDE IN THE FRESH AIR, ALL ALONE...
..NO DISTRACTIONS, NO IRRITATIONS...
...NOTHING BUT QUIET AND SERENITY...
...A CHANCE TO GET A FEEL FOR THE LAND...
CALVIN AND HOBBES by WATTERSON
..THE EXHILARATION OF SPEED...
...THE OPPORTUNITY TO REFLECT ON THINGS AND LET THE MIND WANDER...
SIGHHH GETTING OUT LIKE THIS REALLY MAKES THE RAT RACE SEEM RIDICULOUS. THE WEEKENDS JUST AREN'T LONG ENOUGH TO DO WHAT'S IMPORTANT.
YOU KNOW, I THINK I'LL QUIT MY JOB AND RIDE MY BICYCLE ALL THE TIME.
OK DEAR, WANT ME TO CALL THE BIKE SHOP AND SEE IF THEY'LL SPONSOR YOUR MID-LIFE CRISIS?
YEAH. ASK 'EM IF THEY'LL UPGRADE MY SHIFTERS TOO.

I enjoy cycling, so I occasionally do some bike strips. Other cyclists seem to enjoy them, so it's tempting to do more of them, but bike strips risk being self-indulgent. A lot of cartoonists do golf strips, and I find those insufferable. When I do a bike strip, I always try to focus on Calvin's dad's personality, so it's not just a joke for particular hobbyists.

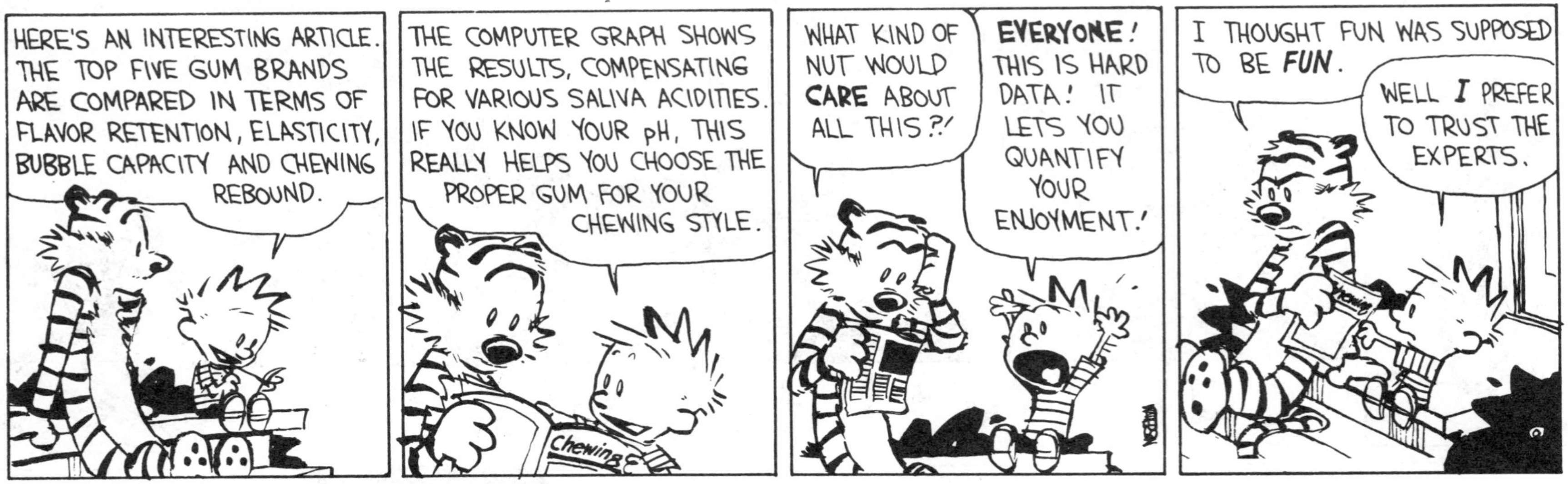
HERE'S AN INTERESTING ARTICLE. THE TOP FIVE GUM BRANDS ARE COMPARED IN TERMS OF FLAVOR RETENTION, ELASTICITY, BUBBLE CAPACITY AND CHEWING REBOUND.
THE COMPUTER GRAPH SHOWS THE RESULTS, COMPENSATING FOR VARIOUS SALIVA ACIDITIES. IF YOU KNOW YOUR pH, THIS REALLY HELPS YOU CHOOSE THE PROPER GUM FOR YOUR CHEWING STYLE.
Chewing
WHAT KIND OF NUT WOULD CARE ABOUT ALL THIS?!
EVERYONE! THIS IS HARD DATA! IT LETS YOU QUANTIFY YOUR ENJOYMENT!
I THOUGHT FUN WAS SUPPOSED TO BE FUN.
WELL I PREFER TO TRUST THE EXPERTS.

There are magazines now for every hobby and obsession, and they're all the same. Calvin's *Chewing* magazine is based on the cycling magazines I read. The silly articles I make up are so close to the real thing, it's hardly satire.

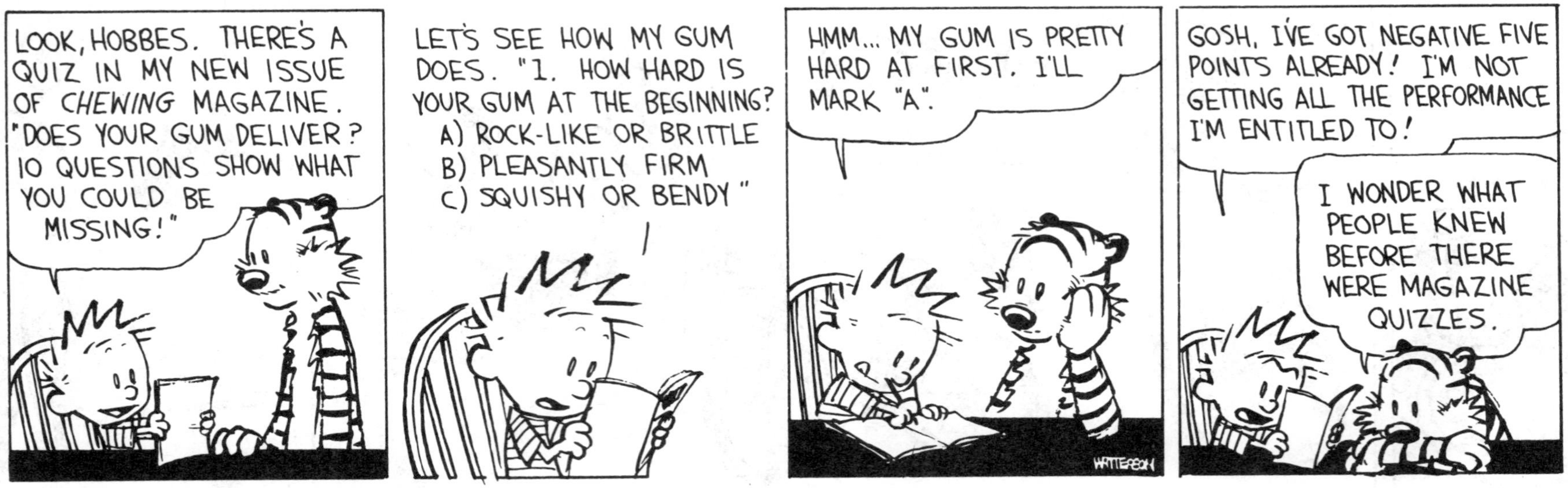
LOOK, HOBBES. THERE'S A QUIZ IN MY NEW ISSUE OF CHEWING MAGAZINE. "DOES YOUR GUM DELIVER? 10 QUESTIONS SHOW WHAT YOU COULD BE MISSING!"
LET'S SEE HOW MY GUM DOES. "1. HOW HARD IS YOUR GUM AT THE BEGINNING? A) ROCK-LIKE OR BRITTLE B) PLEASANTLY FIRM C) SQUISHY OR BENDY"
HMM... MY GUM IS PRETTY HARD AT FIRST. I'LL MARK "A".
WATTERSON
GOSH, I'VE GOT NEGATIVE FIVE POINTS ALREADY! I'M NOT GETTING ALL THE PERFORMANCE I'M ENTITLED TO!
I WONDER WHAT PEOPLE KNEW BEFORE THERE WERE MAGAZINE QUIZZES.

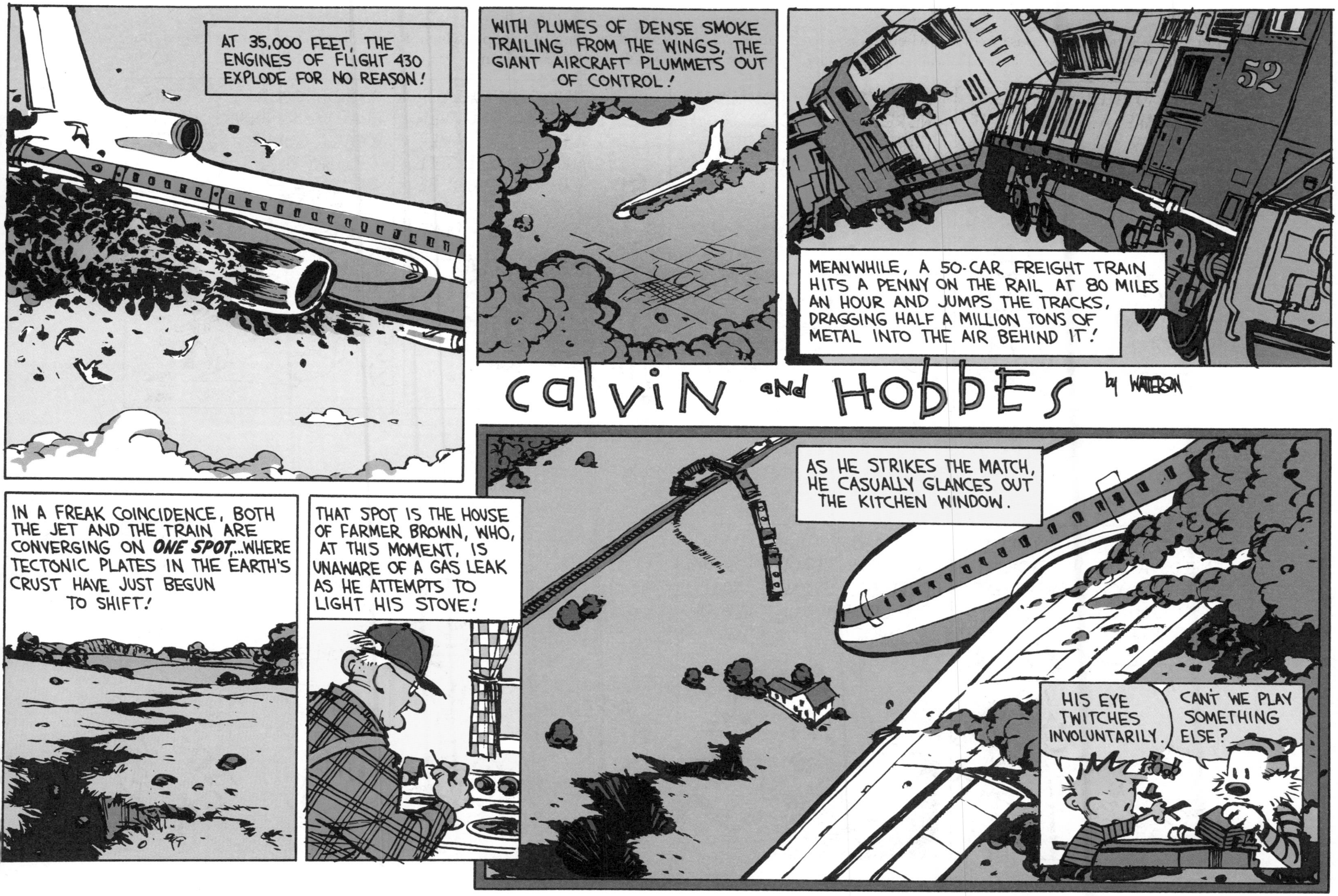
AT 35,000 FEET, THE ENGINES OF FLIGHT 430 EXPLODE FOR NO REASON!
WITH PLUMES OF DENSE SMOKE TRAILING FROM THE WINGS, THE GIANT AIRCRAFT PLUMMETS OUT OF CONTROL!
52
MEANWHILE, A 50-CAR FREIGHT TRAIN HITS A PENNY ON THE RAIL AT 80 MILES AN HOUR AND JUMPS THE TRACKS, DRAGGING HALF A MILLION TONS OF METAL INTO THE AIR BEHIND IT!
CALVIN AND HOBBES
by WATTERSON
IN A FREAK COINCIDENCE, BOTH THE JET AND THE TRAIN ARE CONVERGING ON ONE SPOT...WHERE TECTONIC PLATES IN THE EARTH'S CRUST HAVE JUST BEGUN TO SHIFT!
THAT SPOT IS THE HOUSE OF FARMER BROWN, WHO, AT THIS MOMENT, IS UNAWARE OF A GAS LEAK AS HE ATTEMPTS TO LIGHT HIS STOVE!
AS HE STRIKES THE MATCH, HE CASUALLY GLANCES OUT THE KITCHEN WINDOW.
HIS EYE TWITCHES INVOLUNTARILY.
CAN'T WE PLAY SOMETHING ELSE?

One of Calvin's better build-ups.

I entered a school safety poster contest when I was a kid. I labored over a careful drawing of Snoopy, which got me disqualified. I was crushed, but it was a pretty good lesson about the value of originality. Calvin, of course, has the opposite problem.

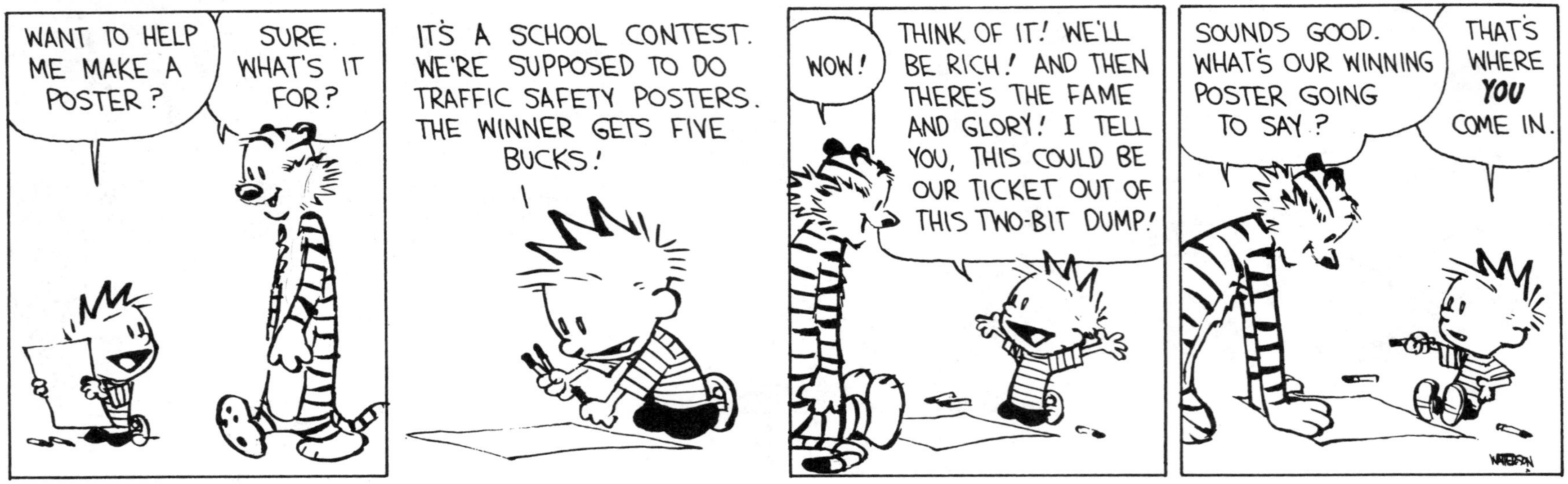
WANT TO HELP ME MAKE A POSTER?
SURE. WHAT'S IT FOR?
IT'S A SCHOOL CONTEST. WE'RE SUPPOSED TO DO TRAFFIC SAFETY POSTERS. THE WINNER GETS FIVE BUCKS!
WOW!
THINK OF IT! WE'LL BE RICH! AND THEN THERE'S THE FAME AND GLORY! I TELL YOU, THIS COULD BE OUR TICKET OUT OF THIS TWO-BIT DUMP!
SOUNDS GOOD. WHAT'S OUR WINNING POSTER GOING TO SAY?
THAT'S WHERE **YOU** COME IN.

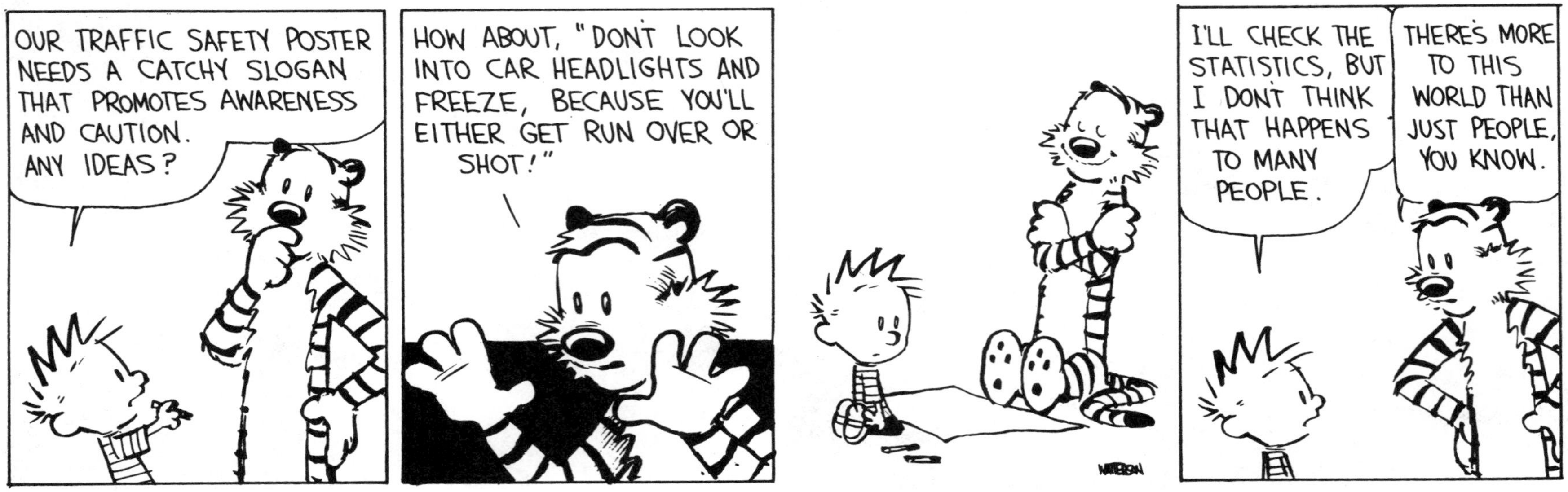
OUR TRAFFIC SAFETY POSTER NEEDS A CATCHY SLOGAN THAT PROMOTES AWARENESS AND CAUTION. ANY IDEAS?
HOW ABOUT, "DON'T LOOK INTO CAR HEADLIGHTS AND FREEZE, BECAUSE YOU'LL EITHER GET RUN OVER OR SHOT!"
I'LL CHECK THE STATISTICS, BUT I DON'T THINK THAT HAPPENS TO MANY PEOPLE.
THERE'S MORE TO THIS WORLD THAN JUST PEOPLE, YOU KNOW.

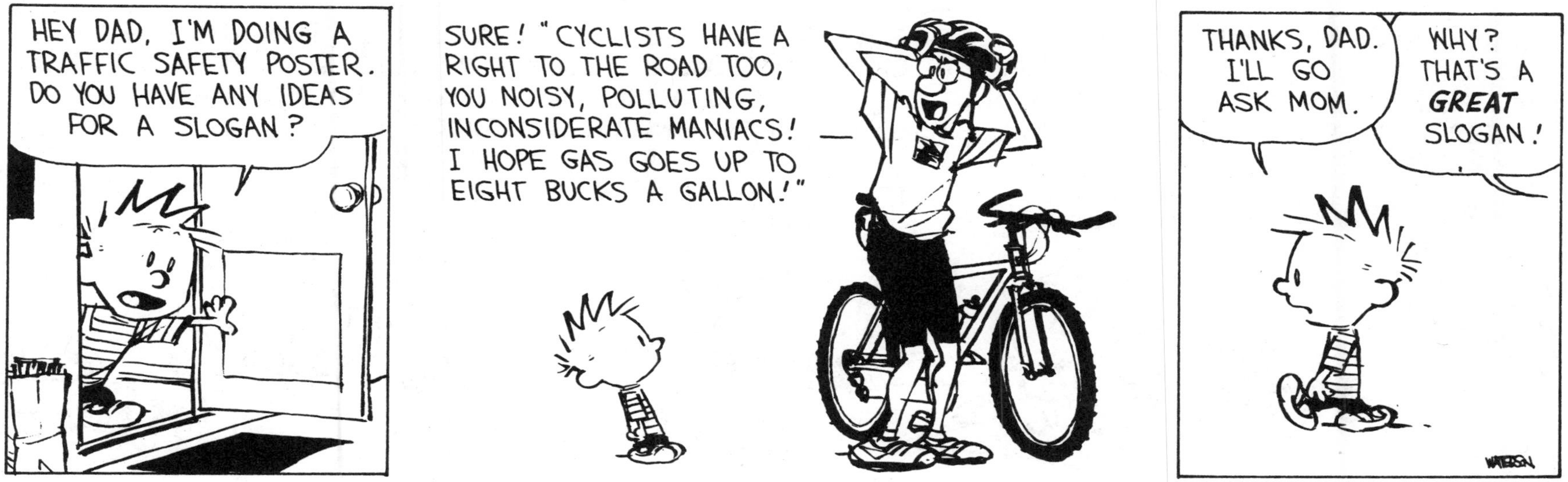
HEY DAD, I'M DOING A TRAFFIC SAFETY POSTER. DO YOU HAVE ANY IDEAS FOR A SLOGAN?
SURE! "CYCLISTS HAVE A RIGHT TO THE ROAD TOO, YOU NOISY, POLLUTING, INCONSIDERATE MANIACS! I HOPE GAS GOES UP TO EIGHT BUCKS A GALLON!"
THANKS, DAD. I'LL GO ASK MOM.
WHY? THAT'S A **GREAT** SLOGAN!
WATTERSON

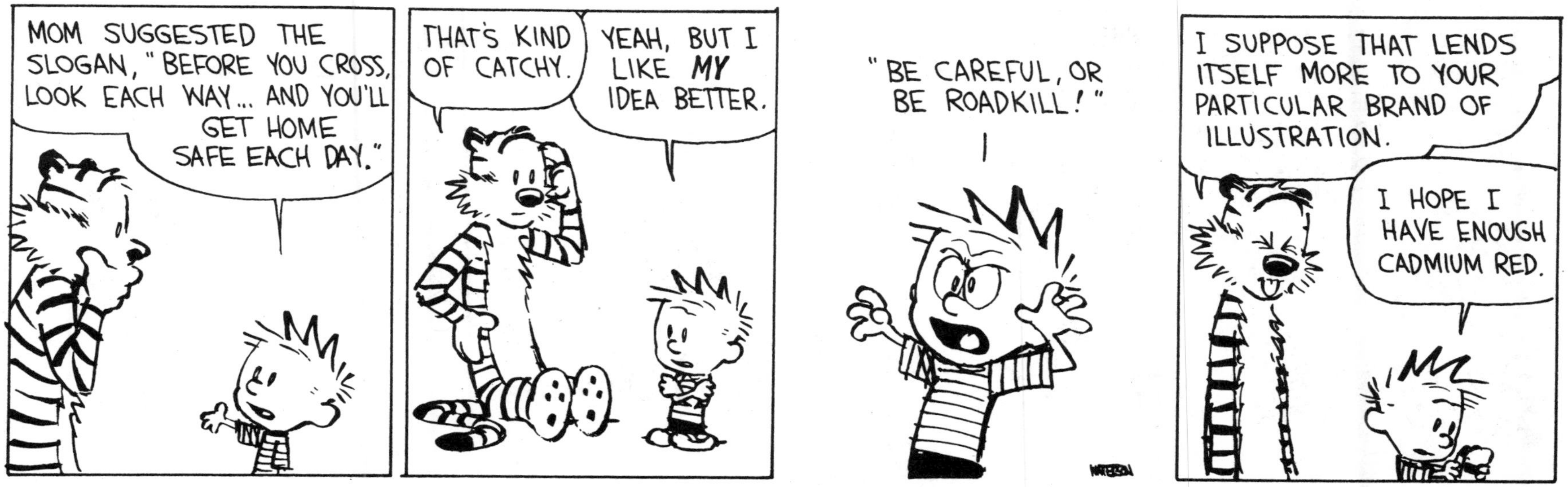
MOM SUGGESTED THE SLOGAN, "BEFORE YOU CROSS, LOOK EACH WAY... AND YOU'LL GET HOME SAFE EACH DAY."
THAT'S KIND OF CATCHY.
YEAH, BUT I LIKE **MY** IDEA BETTER.
"BE CAREFUL, OR BE ROADKILL!"
WATTERSON
I SUPPOSE THAT LENDS ITSELF MORE TO YOUR PARTICULAR BRAND OF ILLUSTRATION.
I HOPE I HAVE ENOUGH CADMIUM RED.

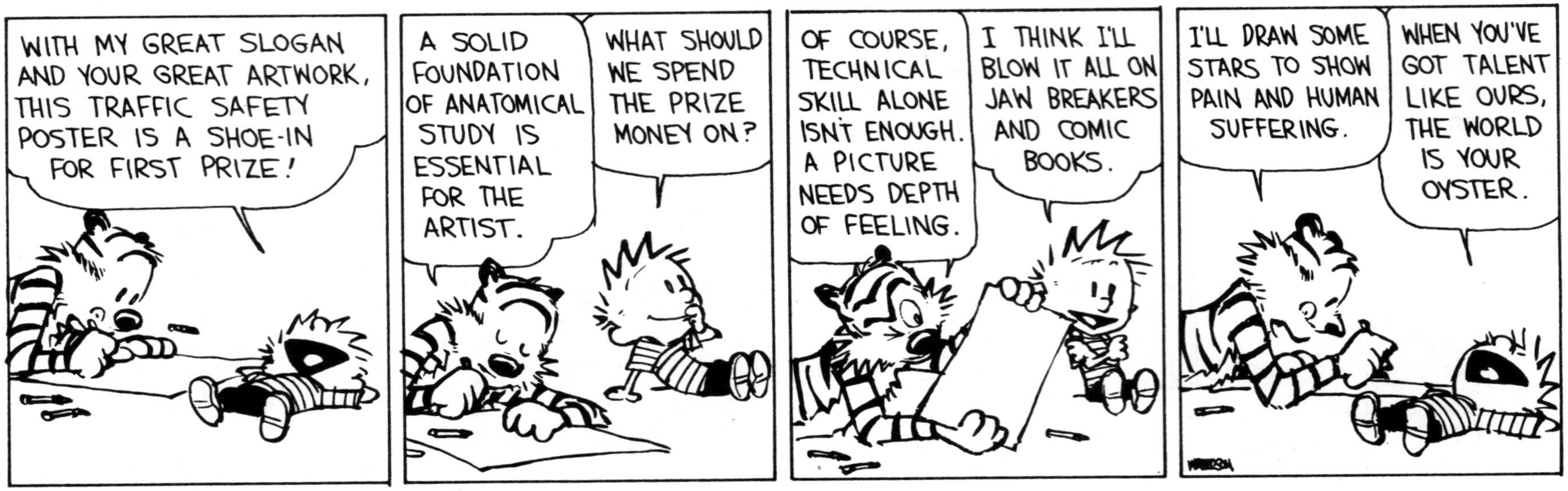
WITH MY GREAT SLOGAN AND YOUR GREAT ARTWORK, THIS TRAFFIC SAFETY POSTER IS A SHOE-IN FOR FIRST PRIZE!
A SOLID FOUNDATION OF ANATOMICAL STUDY IS ESSENTIAL FOR THE ARTIST.
WHAT SHOULD WE SPEND THE PRIZE MONEY ON?
OF COURSE, TECHNICAL SKILL ALONE ISN'T ENOUGH. A PICTURE NEEDS DEPTH OF FEELING.
I THINK I'LL BLOW IT ALL ON JAW BREAKERS AND COMIC BOOKS.
I'LL DRAW SOME STARS TO SHOW PAIN AND HUMAN SUFFERING.
WHEN YOU'VE GOT TALENT LIKE OURS, THE WORLD IS YOUR OYSTER.

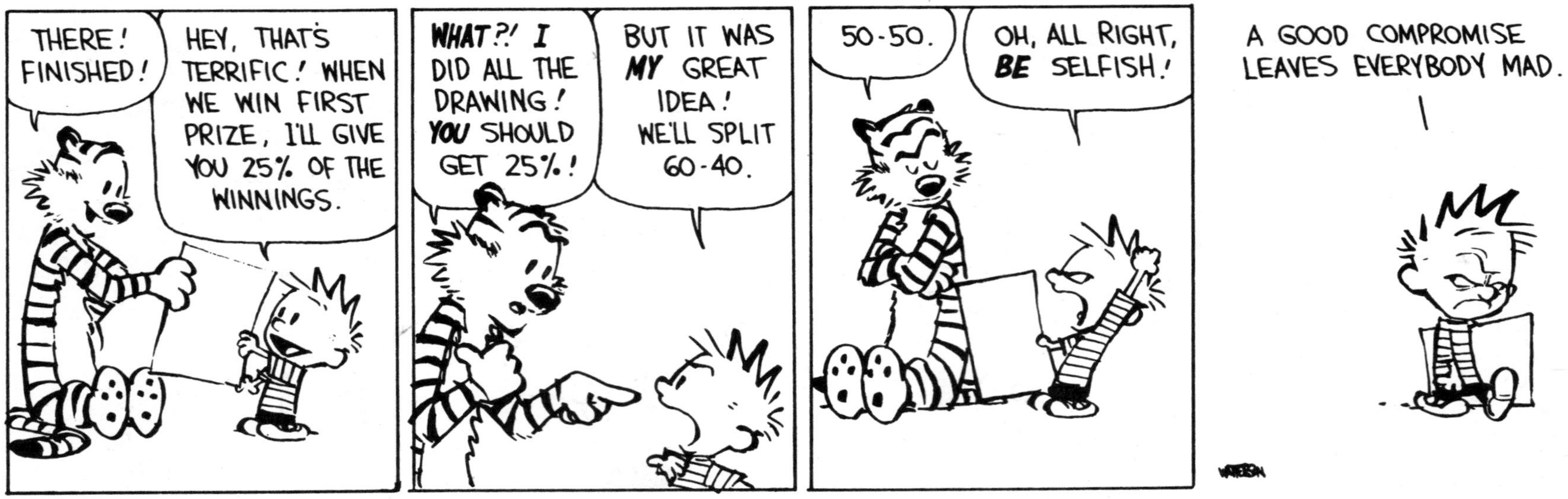
THERE! FINISHED!
HEY, THAT'S TERRIFIC! WHEN WE WIN FIRST PRIZE, I'LL GIVE YOU 25% OF THE WINNINGS.
WHAT?! **I** DID ALL THE DRAWING! **YOU** SHOULD GET 25%!
BUT IT WAS **MY** GREAT IDEA! WE'LL SPLIT 60-40.
50-50.
OH, ALL RIGHT, **BE** SELFISH!
A GOOD COMPROMISE LEAVES EVERYBODY MAD.

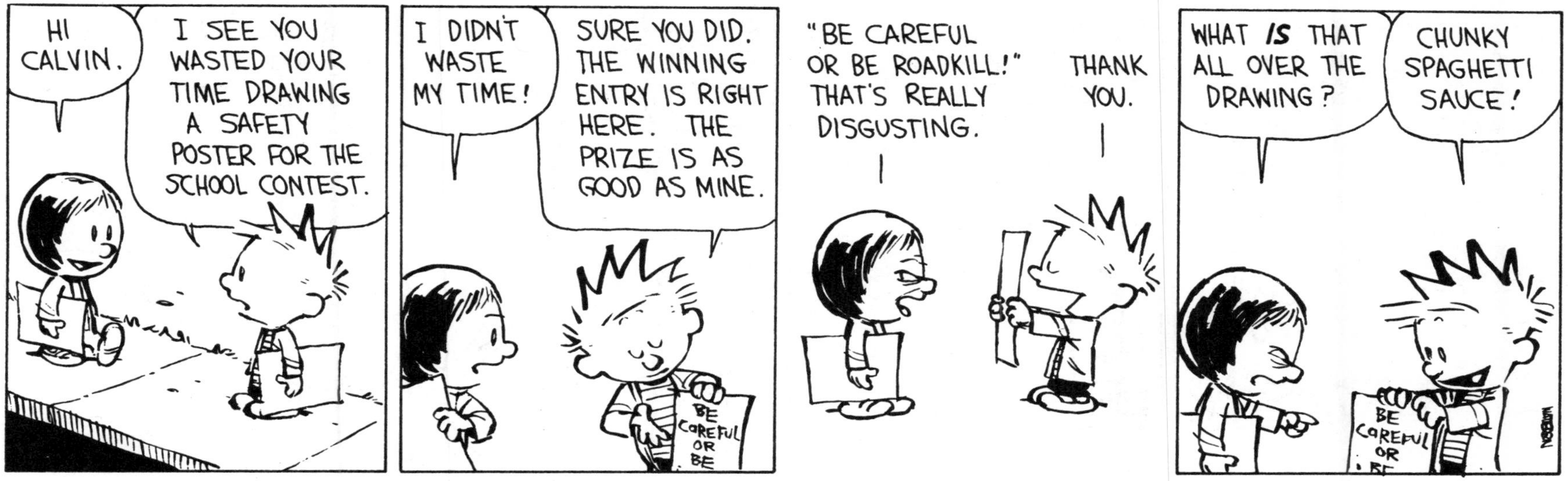
HI CALVIN.
I SEE YOU WASTED YOUR TIME DRAWING A SAFETY POSTER FOR THE SCHOOL CONTEST.
I DIDN'T WASTE MY TIME!
SURE YOU DID. THE WINNING ENTRY IS RIGHT HERE. THE PRIZE IS AS GOOD AS MINE.
BE CAREFUL OR BE
"BE CAREFUL OR BE ROADKILL!" THAT'S REALLY DISGUSTING.
THANK YOU.
WHAT **IS** THAT ALL OVER THE DRAWING?
CHUNKY SPAGHETTI SAUCE!
BE CAREFUL OR

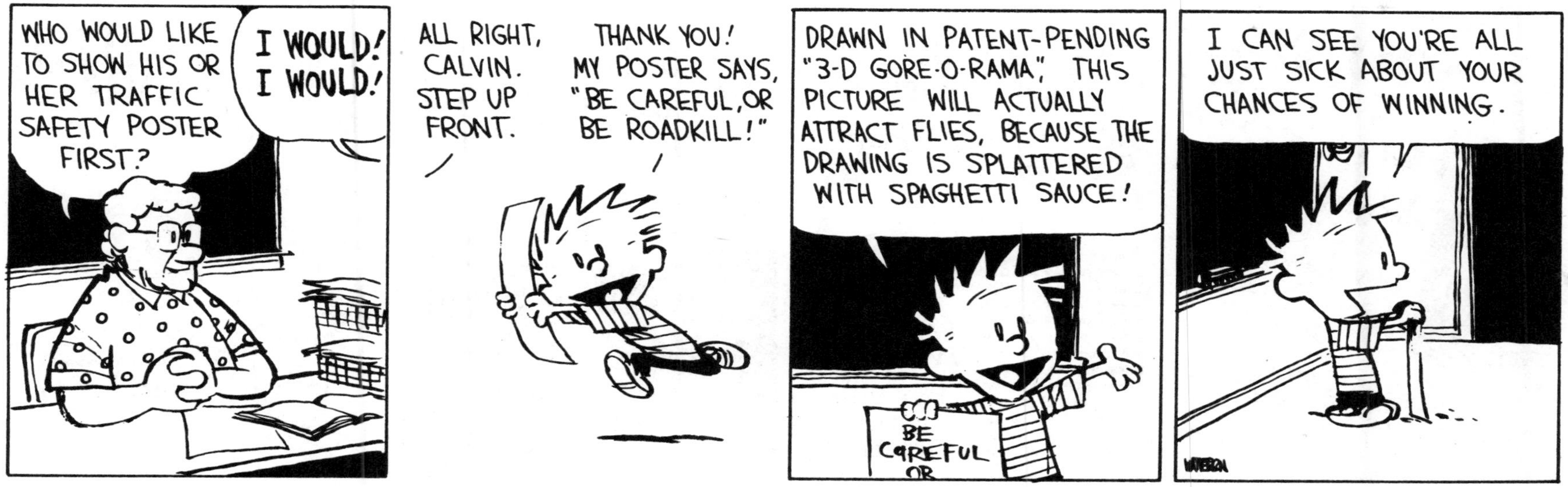
WHO WOULD LIKE TO SHOW HIS OR HER TRAFFIC SAFETY POSTER FIRST?
I WOULD! I WOULD!
ALL RIGHT, CALVIN. STEP UP FRONT.
THANK YOU! MY POSTER SAYS, "BE CAREFUL, OR BE ROADKILL!"
DRAWN IN PATENT-PENDING "3-D GORE-O-RAMA," THIS PICTURE WILL ACTUALLY ATTRACT FLIES, BECAUSE THE DRAWING IS SPLATTERED WITH SPAGHETTI SAUCE!
BE CAREFUL
I CAN SEE YOU'RE ALL JUST SICK ABOUT YOUR CHANCES OF WINNING.

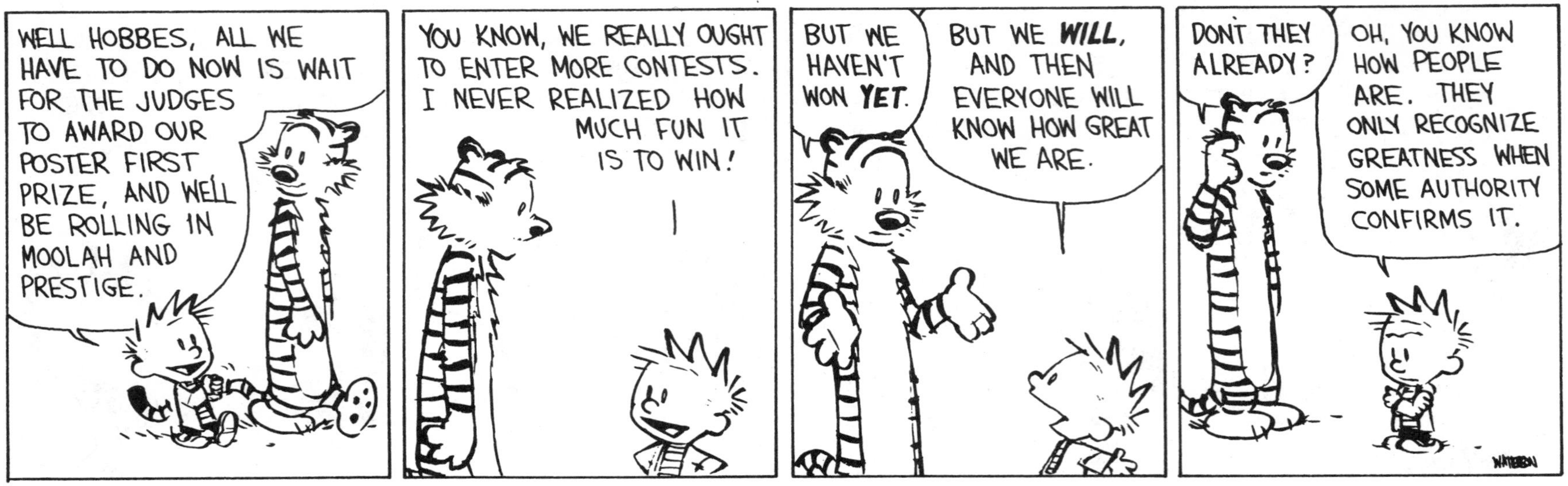
WELL HOBBES, ALL WE HAVE TO DO NOW IS WAIT FOR THE JUDGES TO AWARD OUR POSTER FIRST PRIZE, AND WE'LL BE ROLLING IN MOOLAH AND PRESTIGE.
YOU KNOW, WE REALLY OUGHT TO ENTER MORE CONTESTS. I NEVER REALIZED HOW MUCH FUN IT IS TO WIN!
BUT WE HAVEN'T WON **YET**.
BUT WE **WILL**, AND THEN EVERYONE WILL KNOW HOW GREAT WE ARE.
DON'T THEY ALREADY?
OH, YOU KNOW HOW PEOPLE ARE. THEY ONLY RECOGNIZE GREATNESS WHEN SOME AUTHORITY CONFIRMS IT.

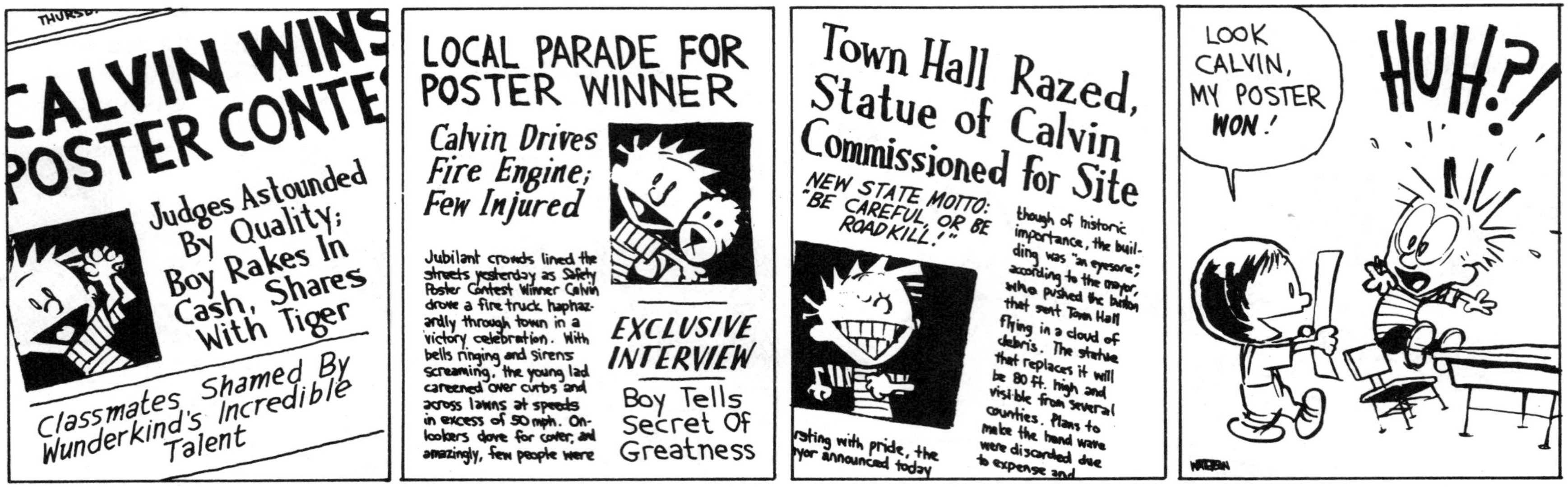
CALVIN WINS POSTER CONTE
Judges Astounded By Quality; Boy Rakes In Cash, Shares With Tiger
Classmates Shamed By Wunderkind's Incredible Talent
LOCAL PARADE FOR POSTER WINNER
Calvin Drives Fire Engine; Few Injured
Jubilant crowds lined the streets yesterday as Safety Poster Contest Winner Calvin drove a fire truck haphazardly through town in a victory celebration. With bells ringing and sirens screaming, the young lad careened over curbs and across lawns at speeds in excess of 50 mph. Onlookers dove for cover, and amazingly, few people were
EXCLUSIVE INTERVIEW
Boy Tells Secret Of Greatness
Town Hall Razed, Statue of Calvin Commissioned for Site
NEW STATE MOTTO: "BE CAREFUL, OR BE ROADKILL!"
rsting with pride, the yor announced today
though of historic importance, the building was "an eyesore," according to the mayor, who pushed the button that sent Town Hall flying in a cloud of debris. The statue that replaces it will be 80 ft. high and visible from several counties. Plans to make the hand wave were discarded due to expense and
LOOK CALVIN, MY POSTER **WON**!
HUH?!

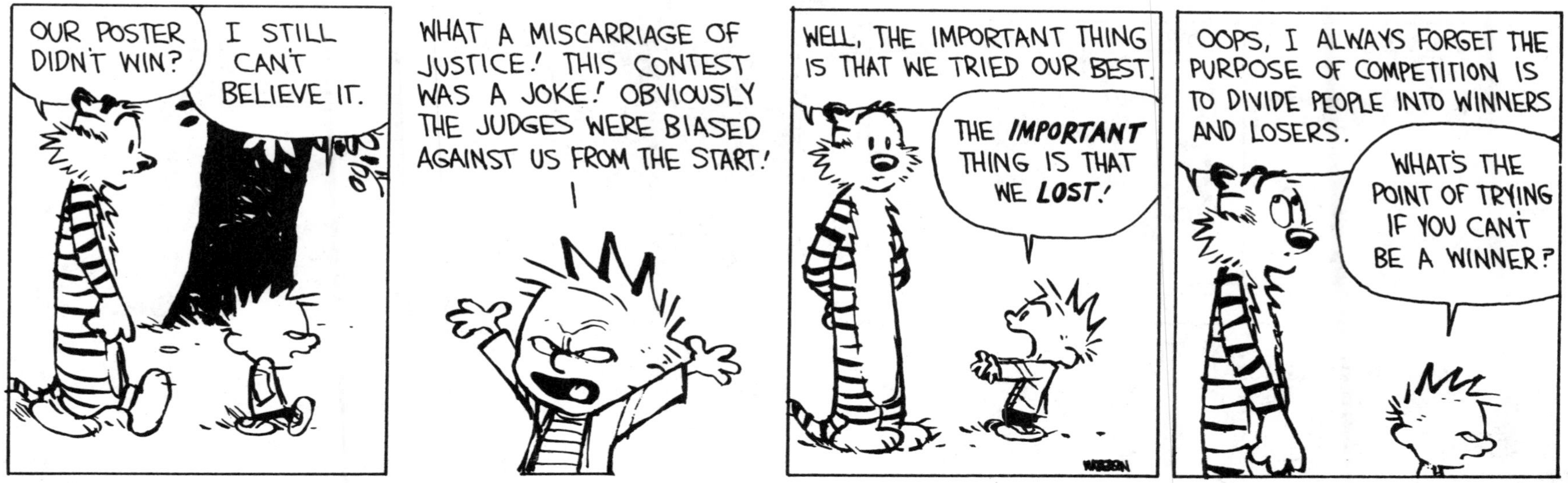
OUR POSTER DIDN'T WIN?
I STILL CAN'T BELIEVE IT.
WHAT A MISCARRIAGE OF JUSTICE! THIS CONTEST WAS A JOKE! OBVIOUSLY THE JUDGES WERE BIASED AGAINST US FROM THE START!
WELL, THE IMPORTANT THING IS THAT WE TRIED OUR BEST.
THE IMPORTANT THING IS THAT WE LOST!
OOPS, I ALWAYS FORGET THE PURPOSE OF COMPETITION IS TO DIVIDE PEOPLE INTO WINNERS AND LOSERS.
WHAT'S THE POINT OF TRYING IF YOU CAN'T BE A WINNER?

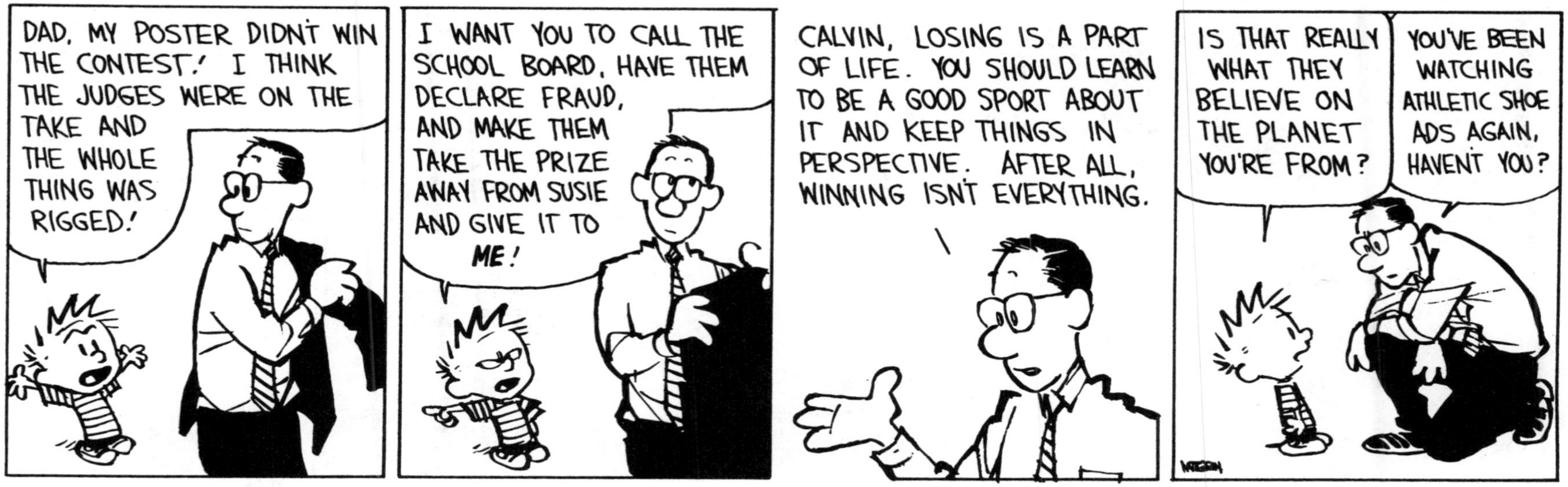
DAD, MY POSTER DIDN'T WIN THE CONTEST! I THINK THE JUDGES WERE ON THE TAKE AND THE WHOLE THING WAS RIGGED!
I WANT YOU TO CALL THE SCHOOL BOARD, HAVE THEM DECLARE FRAUD, AND MAKE THEM TAKE THE PRIZE AWAY FROM SUSIE AND GIVE IT TO ME!
CALVIN, LOSING IS A PART OF LIFE. YOU SHOULD LEARN TO BE A GOOD SPORT ABOUT IT AND KEEP THINGS IN PERSPECTIVE. AFTER ALL, WINNING ISN'T EVERYTHING.
IS THAT REALLY WHAT THEY BELIEVE ON THE PLANET YOU'RE FROM?
YOU'VE BEEN WATCHING ATHLETIC SHOE ADS AGAIN, HAVEN'T YOU?

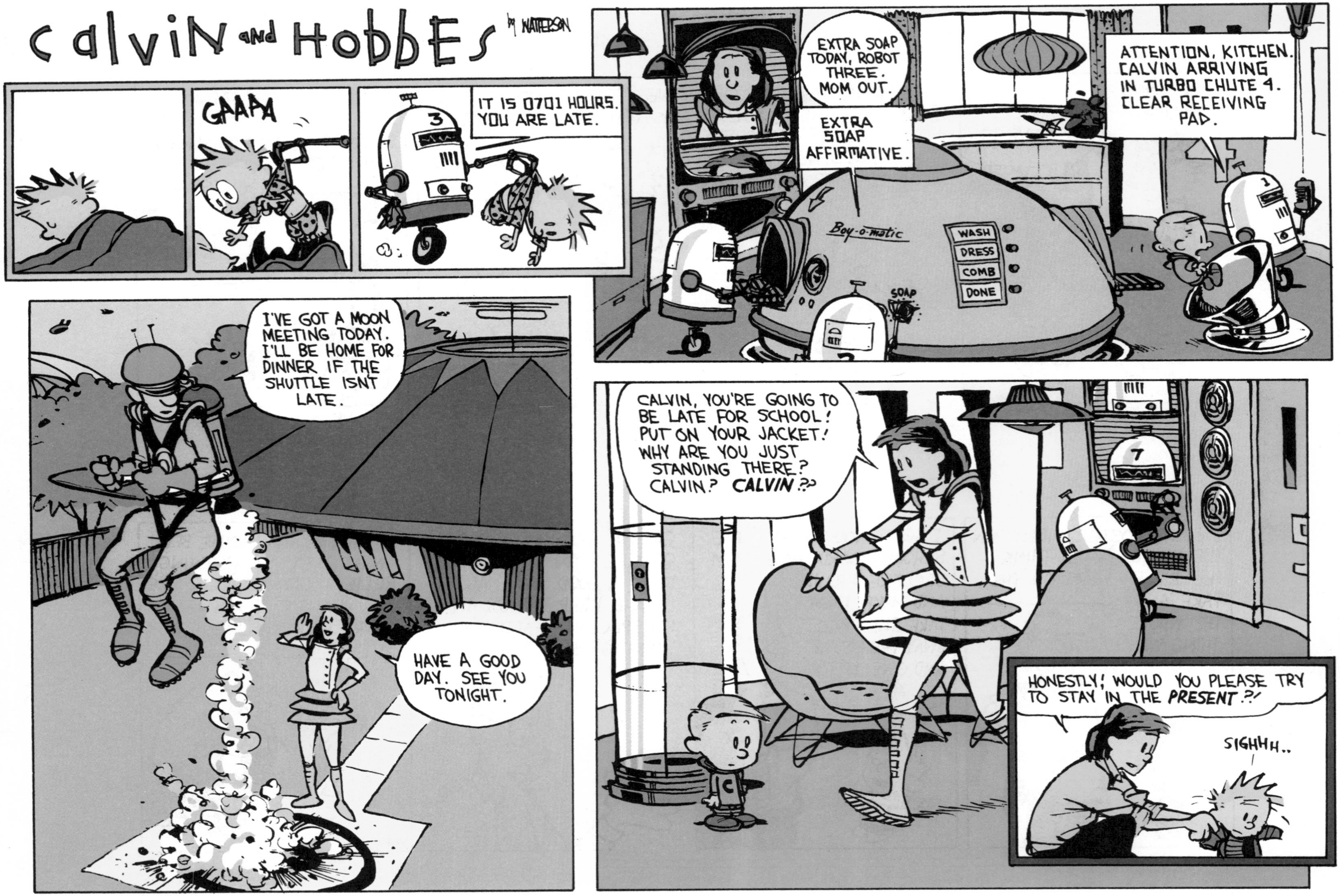
Calvin and Hobbes
by WATTERSON
GAAAA
IT IS 0701 HOURS. YOU ARE LATE.
EXTRA SOAP TODAY, ROBOT THREE. MOM OUT.
EXTRA SOAP AFFIRMATIVE.
Boy-o-matic
WASH
DRESS
COMB
DONE
SOAP
ATTENTION, KITCHEN. CALVIN ARRIVING IN TURBO CHUTE 4. CLEAR RECEIVING PAD.
I'VE GOT A MOON MEETING TODAY. I'LL BE HOME FOR DINNER IF THE SHUTTLE ISN'T LATE.
HAVE A GOOD DAY. SEE YOU TONIGHT.
CALVIN, YOU'RE GOING TO BE LATE FOR SCHOOL! PUT ON YOUR JACKET! WHY ARE YOU JUST STANDING THERE? CALVIN? CALVIN?!
HONESTLY! WOULD YOU PLEASE TRY TO STAY IN THE PRESENT?!
SIGHHH..

I'd like a suit like Calvin's dad wears.

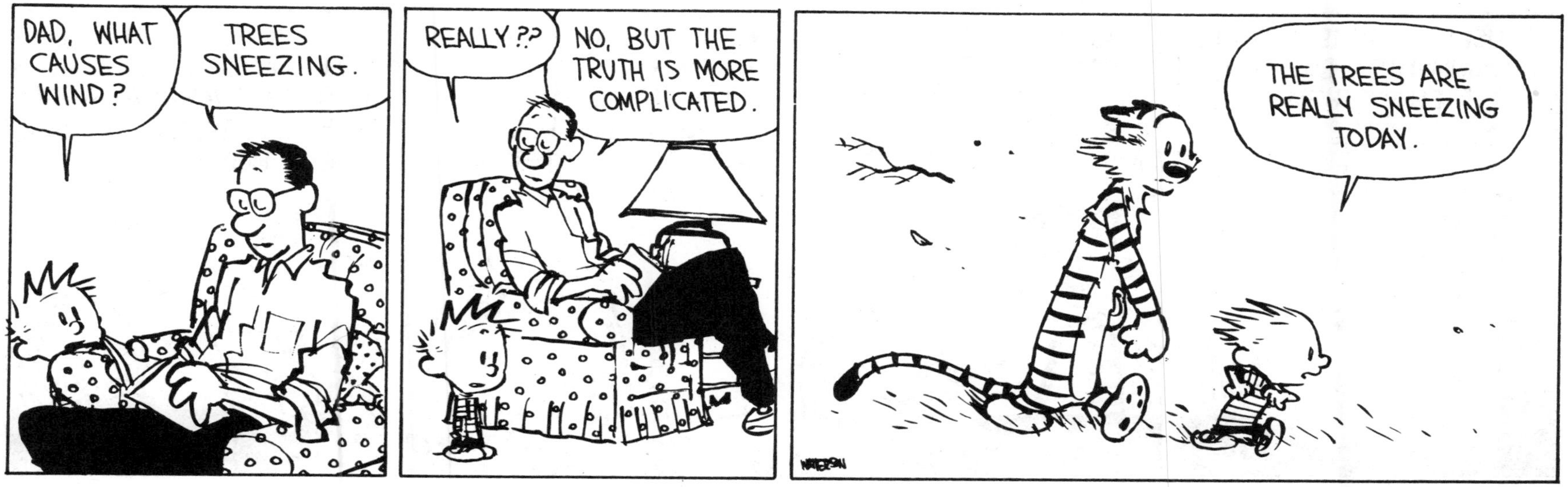
DAD, WHAT CAUSES WIND?
TREES SNEEZING.
REALLY??
NO, BUT THE TRUTH IS MORE COMPLICATED.
THE TREES ARE REALLY SNEEZING TODAY.

Most ignorance is willful.

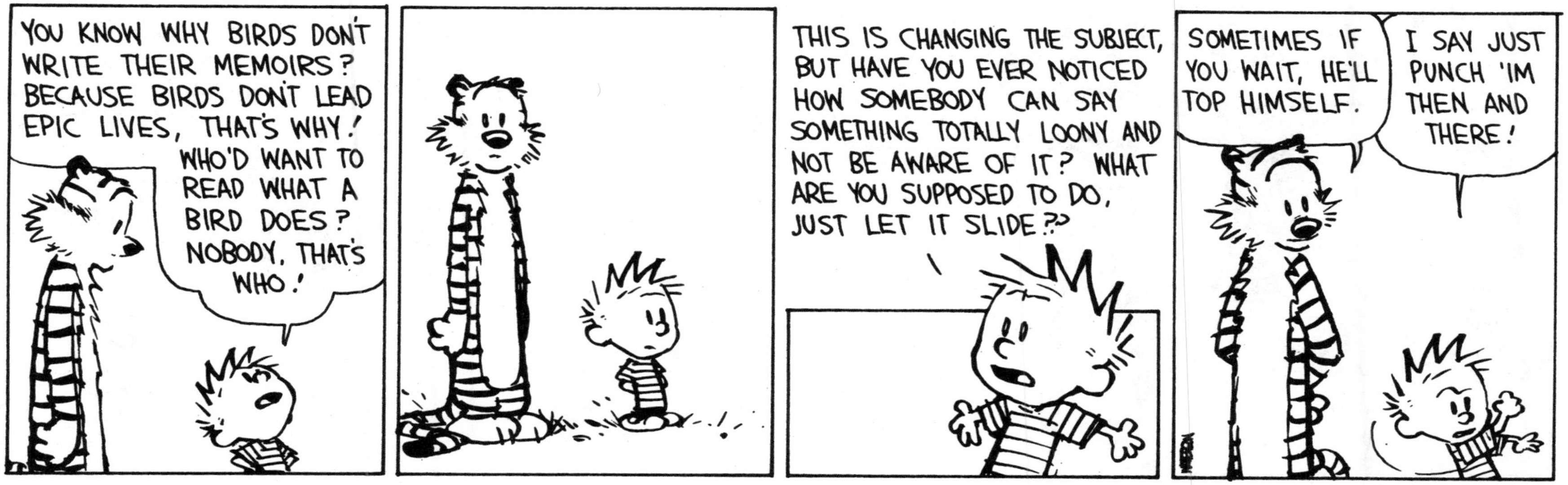
YOU KNOW WHY BIRDS DON'T WRITE THEIR MEMOIRS? BECAUSE BIRDS DON'T LEAD EPIC LIVES, THAT'S WHY! WHO'D WANT TO READ WHAT A BIRD DOES? NOBODY, THAT'S WHO!
THIS IS CHANGING THE SUBJECT, BUT HAVE YOU EVER NOTICED HOW SOMEBODY CAN SAY SOMETHING TOTALLY LOONY AND NOT BE AWARE OF IT? WHAT ARE YOU SUPPOSED TO DO, JUST LET IT SLIDE??
SOMETIMES IF YOU WAIT, HE'LL TOP HIMSELF.
I SAY JUST PUNCH 'IM THEN AND THERE!

My wife is very funny, although sometimes unintentionally. I exaggerated one of her abrupt subject shifts for this strip.

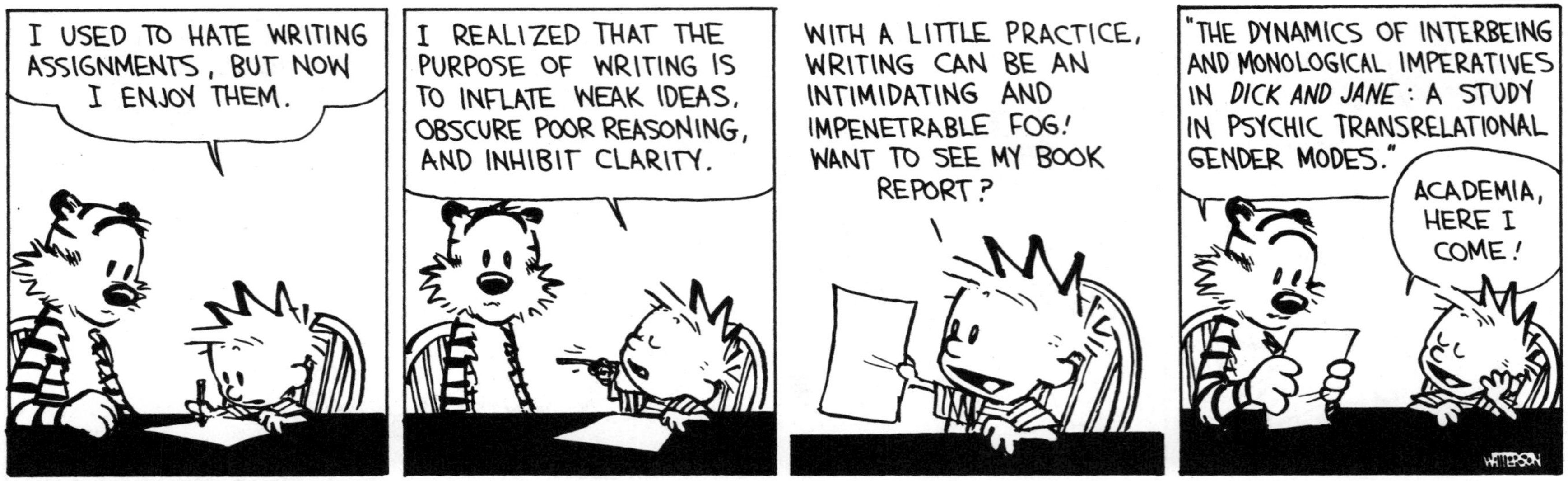
I USED TO HATE WRITING ASSIGNMENTS, BUT NOW I ENJOY THEM.
I REALIZED THAT THE PURPOSE OF WRITING IS TO INFLATE WEAK IDEAS, OBSCURE POOR REASONING, AND INHIBIT CLARITY.
WITH A LITTLE PRACTICE, WRITING CAN BE AN INTIMIDATING AND IMPENETRABLE FOG! WANT TO SEE MY BOOK REPORT?
"THE DYNAMICS OF INTERBEING AND MONOLOGICAL IMPERATIVES IN *DICK AND JANE*: A STUDY IN PSYCHIC TRANSRELATIONAL GENDER MODES."
ACADEMIA, HERE I COME!
WATTERSON

I read a book of art criticism that was an avalanche of politically correct, New Age, academic jargon and art-speak. The writing so annoyed me that I started underlining the worst passages of gibberish for future reference, and I've adapted it for several strips. Calvin, of course, quickly grasps the purpose of such writing.

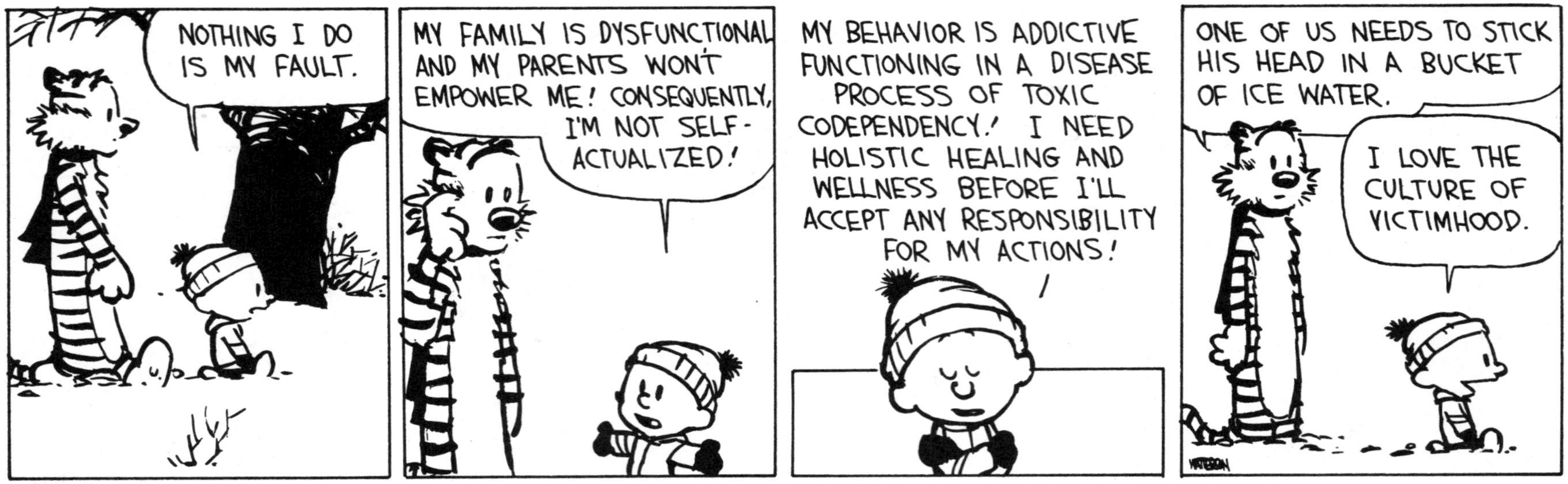
NOTHING I DO IS MY FAULT.
MY FAMILY IS DYSFUNCTIONAL AND MY PARENTS WON'T EMPOWER ME! CONSEQUENTLY, I'M NOT SELF-ACTUALIZED!
MY BEHAVIOR IS ADDICTIVE FUNCTIONING IN A DISEASE PROCESS OF TOXIC CODEPENDENCY! I NEED HOLISTIC HEALING AND WELLNESS BEFORE I'LL ACCEPT ANY RESPONSIBILITY FOR MY ACTIONS!
ONE OF US NEEDS TO STICK HIS HEAD IN A BUCKET OF ICE WATER.
I LOVE THE CULTURE OF VICTIMHOOD.
WATTERSON

I also hate pop psychobabble.

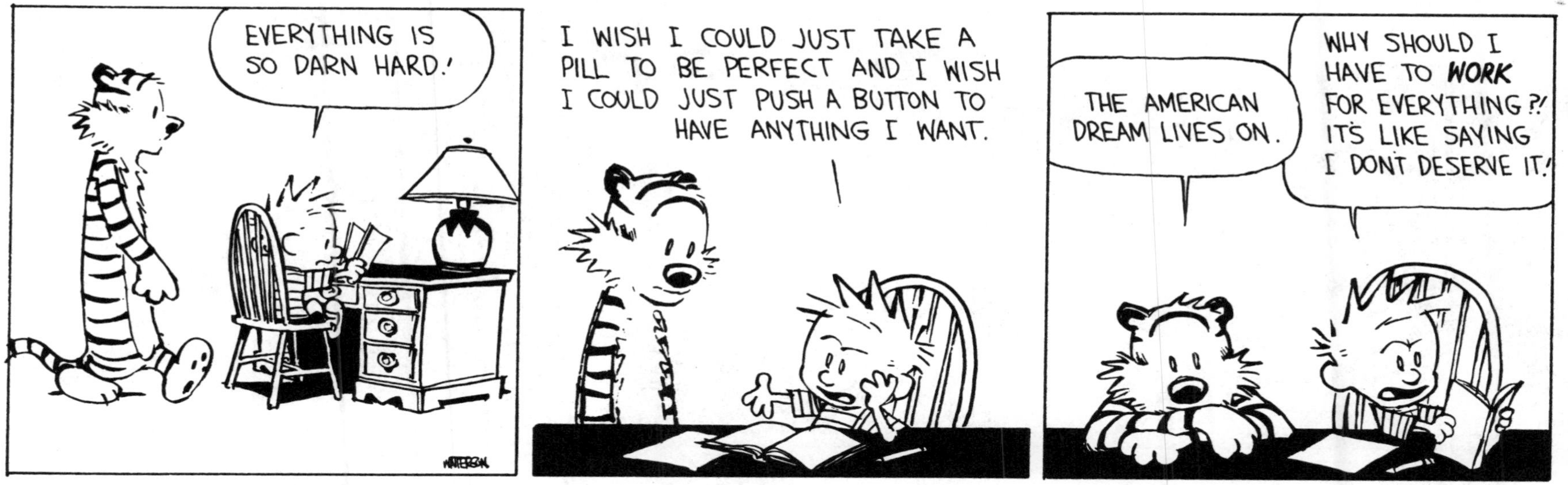
EVERYTHING IS SO DARN HARD!
I WISH I COULD JUST TAKE A PILL TO BE PERFECT AND I WISH I COULD JUST PUSH A BUTTON TO HAVE ANYTHING I WANT.
WHY SHOULD I HAVE TO **WORK** FOR EVERYTHING?! IT'S LIKE SAYING I DON'T DESERVE IT!
THE AMERICAN DREAM LIVES ON.

As somebody said, we all want to go to heaven, but nobody wants to do what it takes to get there.

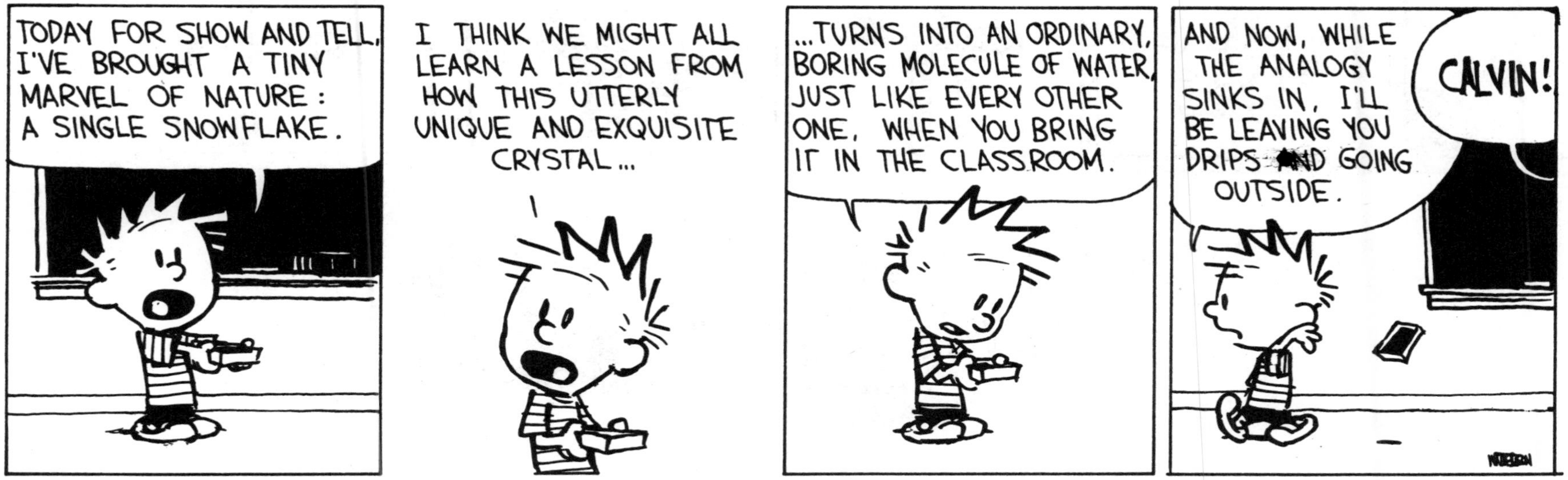
TODAY FOR SHOW AND TELL, I'VE BROUGHT A TINY MARVEL OF NATURE: A SINGLE SNOWFLAKE.
I THINK WE MIGHT ALL LEARN A LESSON FROM HOW THIS UTTERLY UNIQUE AND EXQUISITE CRYSTAL...
...TURNS INTO AN ORDINARY, BORING MOLECULE OF WATER, JUST LIKE EVERY OTHER ONE, WHEN YOU BRING IT IN THE CLASSROOM.
AND NOW, WHILE THE ANALOGY SINKS IN, I'LL BE LEAVING YOU DRIPS AND GOING OUTSIDE.
CALVIN!

I did pretty well at school, but I don't remember it with much fondness.

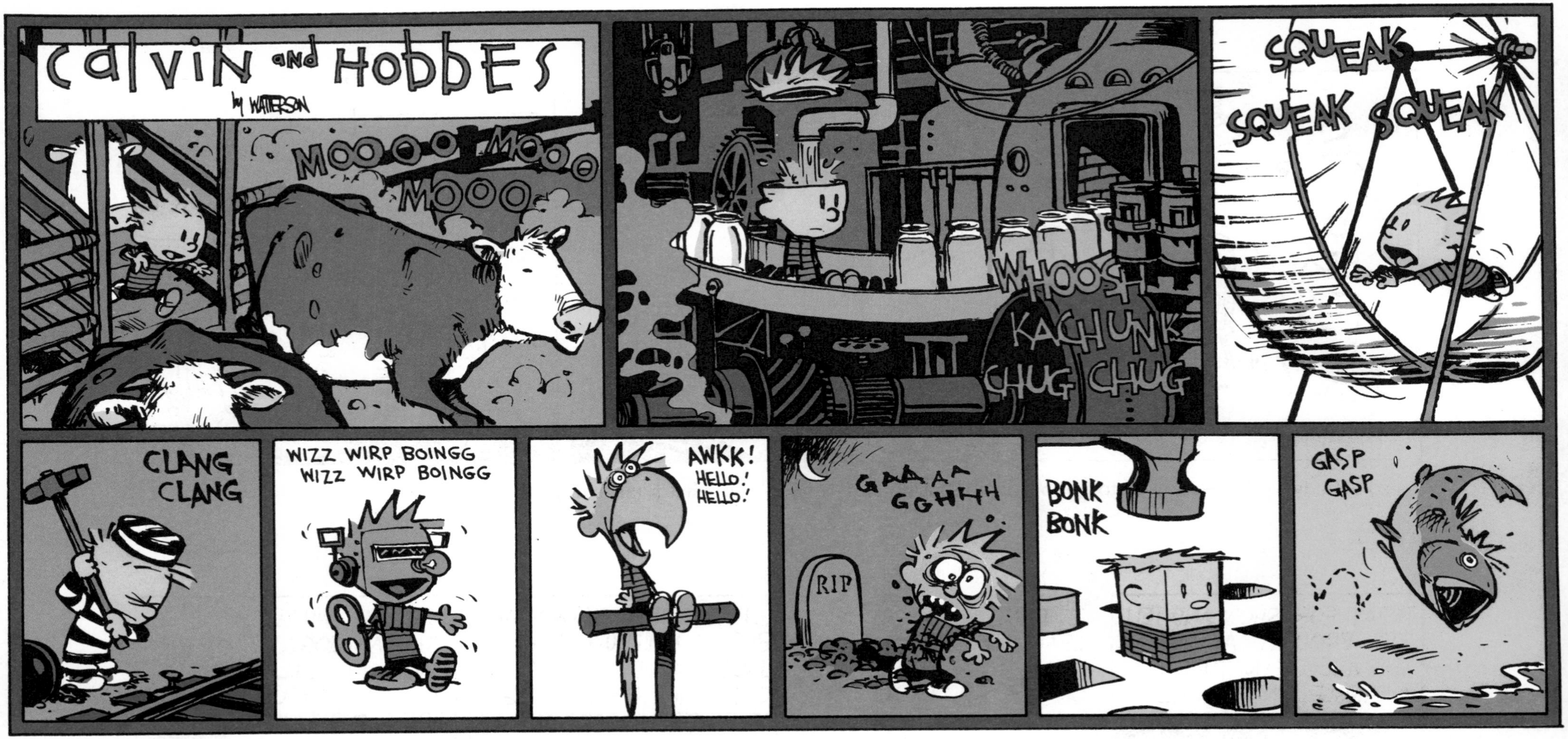
Calvin and HOBBES
by WATTERSON
MOOOOO MOOO
MOOO
WHOOSH
KACHUNK
CHUG CHUG
SQUEAK
SQUEAK SQUEAK
CLANG
CLANG
WIZZ WIRP BOINGG
WIZZ WIRP BOINGG
AWKK!
HELLO!
HELLO!
GAAAA
GGHHH
RIP
BONK
BONK
GASP
GASP

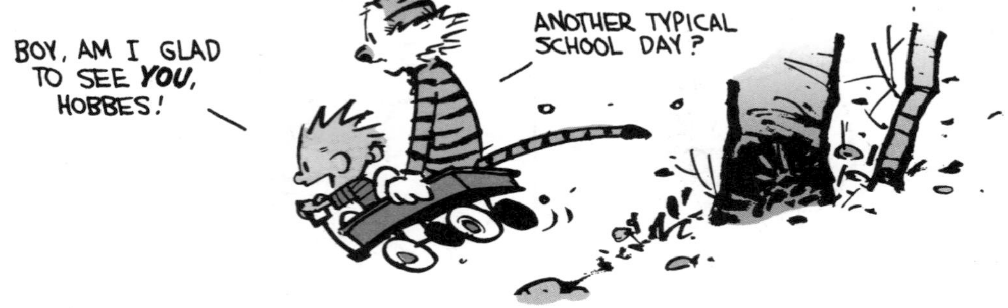
BOY, AM I GLAD TO SEE **YOU**, HOBBES!
ANOTHER TYPICAL SCHOOL DAY?

If Calvin thinks school is like this, wait until he gets his first job.

Stupendous Man hasn't given me as many ideas as I hoped, but I like this story because of the various viewpoints it juggles.

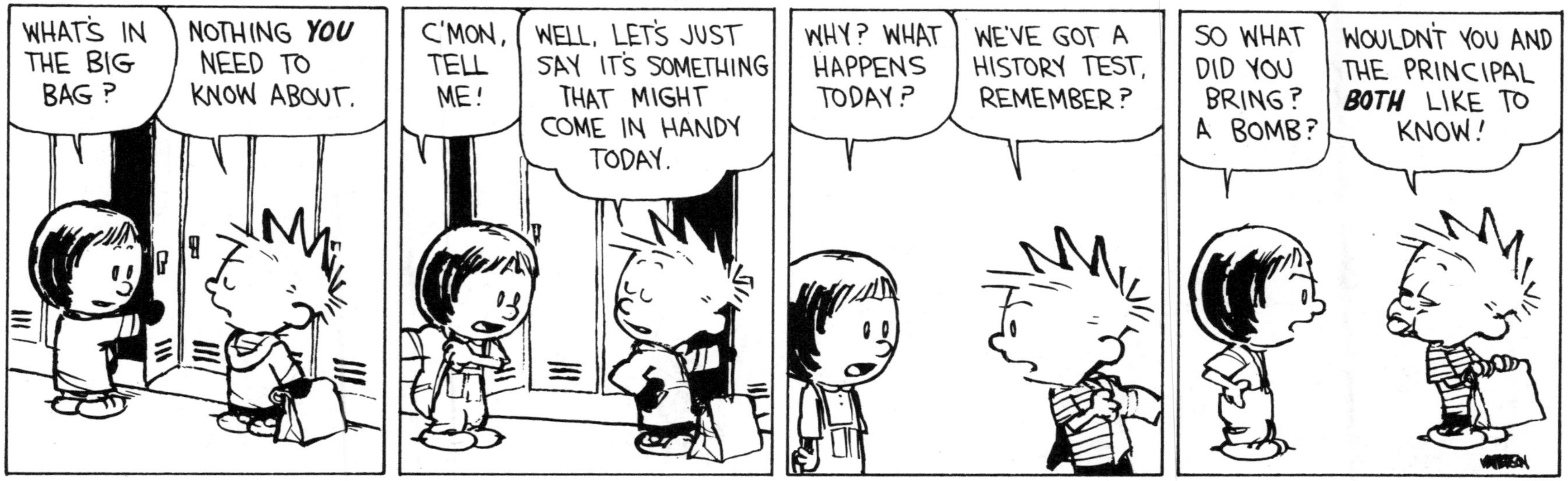
WHAT'S IN THE BIG BAG?
NOTHING *YOU* NEED TO KNOW ABOUT.
C'MON, TELL ME!
WELL, LET'S JUST SAY IT'S SOMETHING THAT MIGHT COME IN HANDY TODAY.
WHY? WHAT HAPPENS TODAY?
WE'VE GOT A HISTORY TEST, REMEMBER?
SO WHAT DID YOU BRING? A BOMB?
WOULDN'T YOU AND THE PRINCIPAL *BOTH* LIKE TO KNOW!

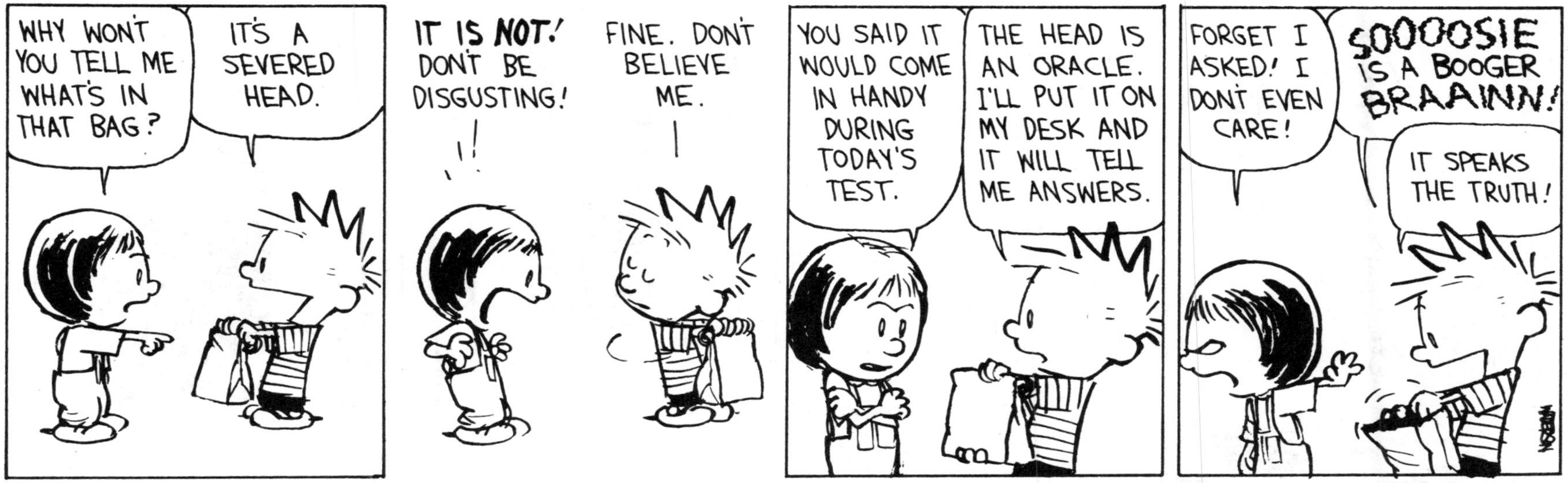
WHY WON'T YOU TELL ME WHAT'S IN THAT BAG?
IT'S A SEVERED HEAD.
IT IS *NOT*! DON'T BE DISGUSTING!
FINE. DON'T BELIEVE ME.
YOU SAID IT WOULD COME IN HANDY DURING TODAY'S TEST.
THE HEAD IS AN ORACLE. I'LL PUT IT ON MY DESK AND IT WILL TELL ME ANSWERS.
FORGET I ASKED! I DON'T EVEN CARE!
SOOOOSIE IS A BOOGER BRAAINN!
IT SPEAKS THE TRUTH!

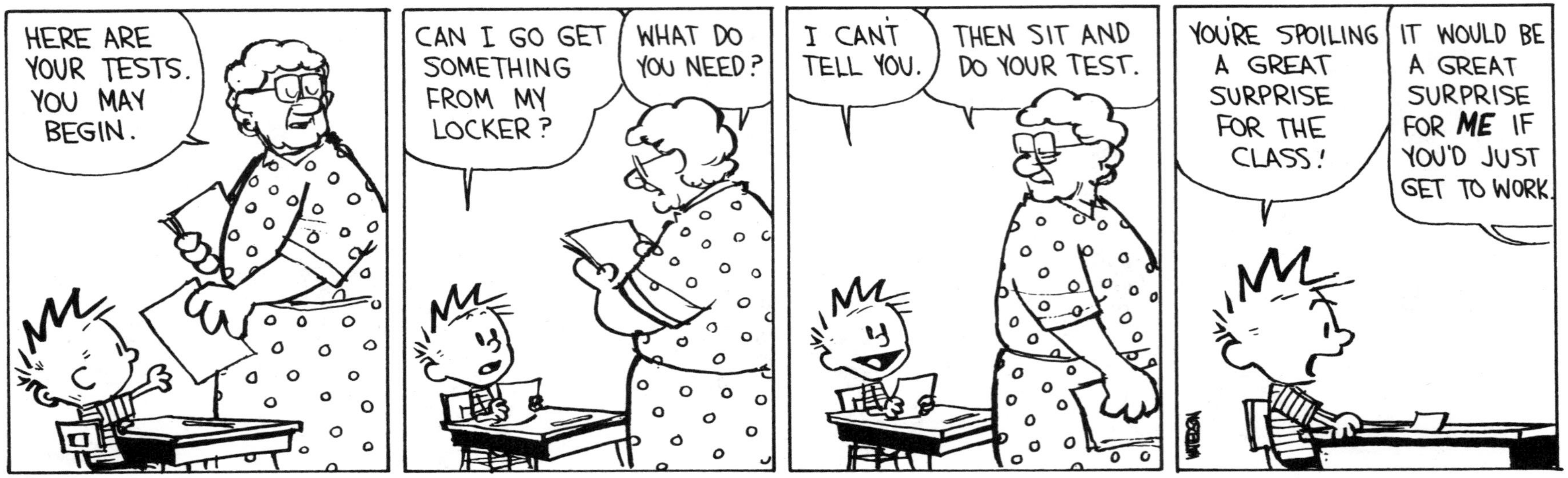
HERE ARE YOUR TESTS. YOU MAY BEGIN.
CAN I GO GET SOMETHING FROM MY LOCKER?
WHAT DO YOU NEED?
I CAN'T TELL YOU.
THEN SIT AND DO YOUR TEST.
YOU'RE SPOILING A GREAT SURPRISE FOR THE CLASS!
IT WOULD BE A GREAT SURPRISE FOR ME IF YOU'D JUST GET TO WORK.
WATTERSON

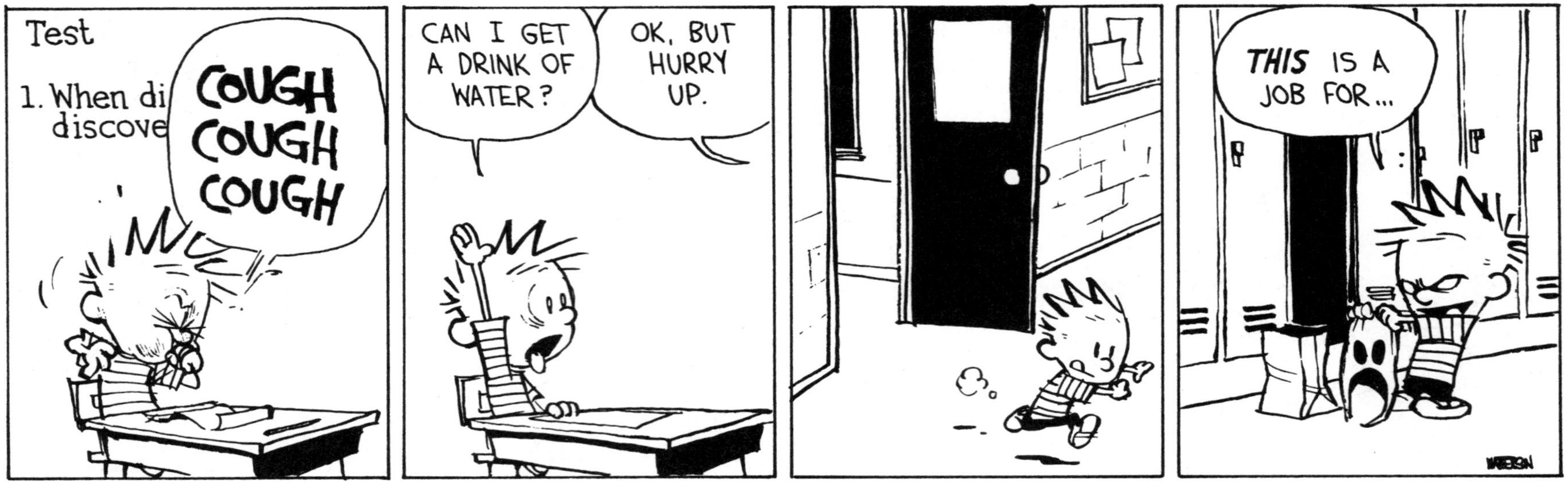
Test
1. When di
discove
COUGH COUGH COUGH
CAN I GET A DRINK OF WATER?
OK, BUT HURRY UP.
THIS IS A JOB FOR...
WATTERSON

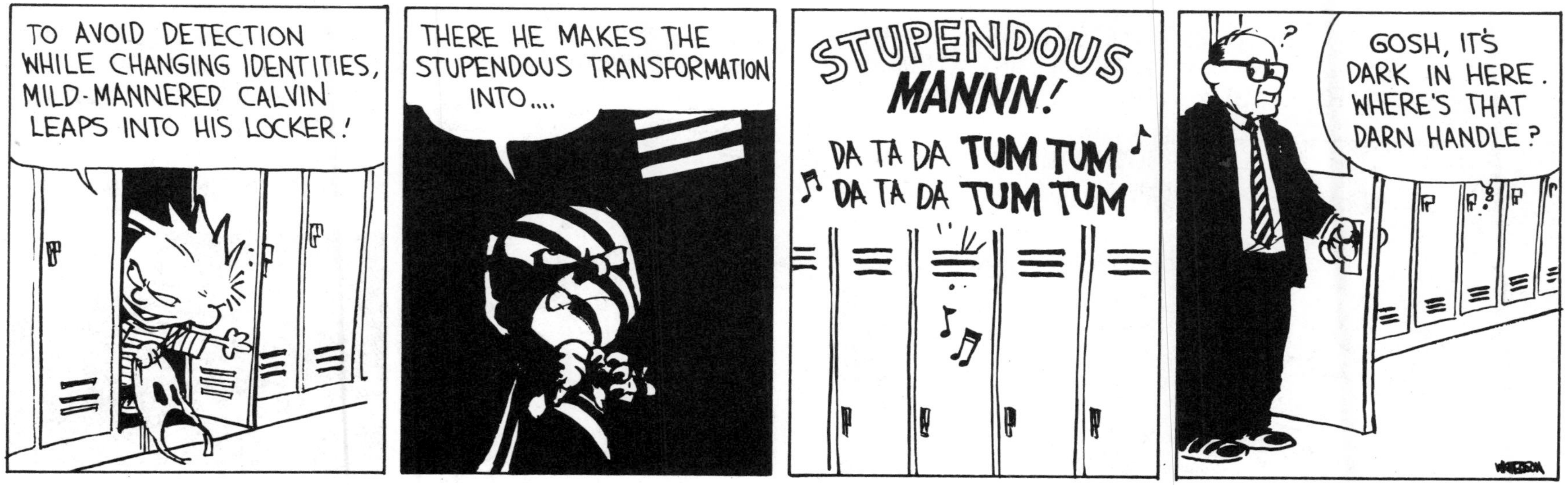
TO AVOID DETECTION WHILE CHANGING IDENTITIES, MILD-MANNERED CALVIN LEAPS INTO HIS LOCKER!
THERE HE MAKES THE STUPENDOUS TRANSFORMATION INTO....
STUPENDOUS MANNN!
DA TA DA TUM TUM DA TA DA TUM TUM
?
GOSH, IT'S DARK IN HERE. WHERE'S THAT DARN HANDLE?

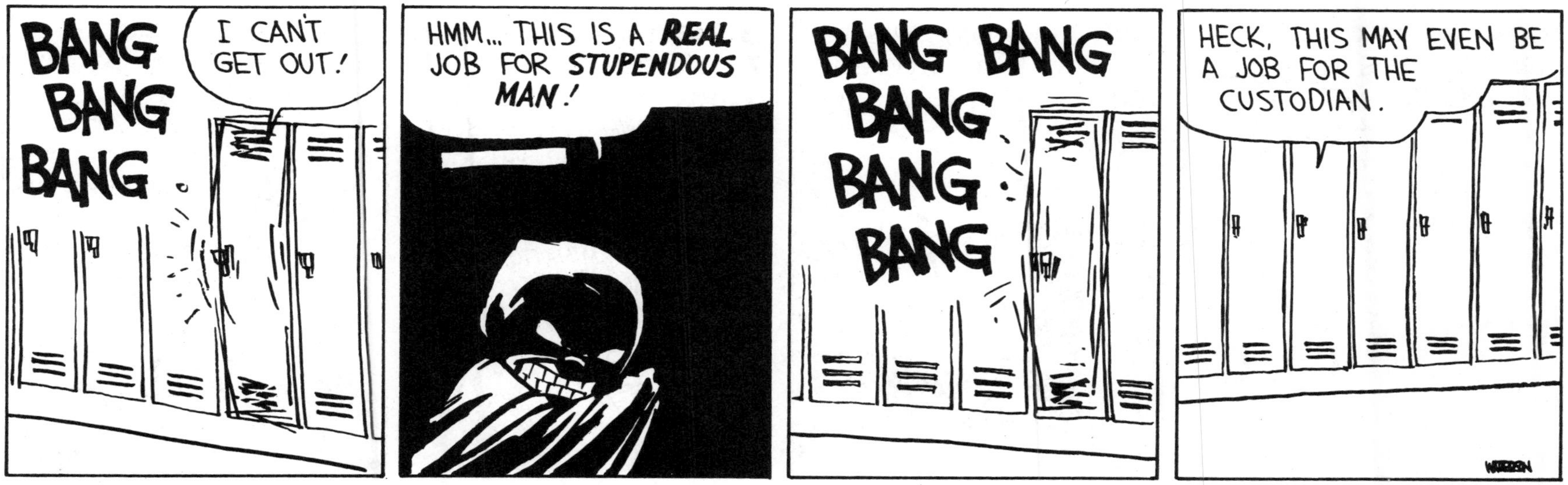
BANG BANG BANG
I CAN'T GET OUT!
HMM... THIS IS A REAL JOB FOR STUPENDOUS MAN!
BANG BANG BANG BANG BANG
HECK, THIS MAY EVEN BE A JOB FOR THE CUSTODIAN.

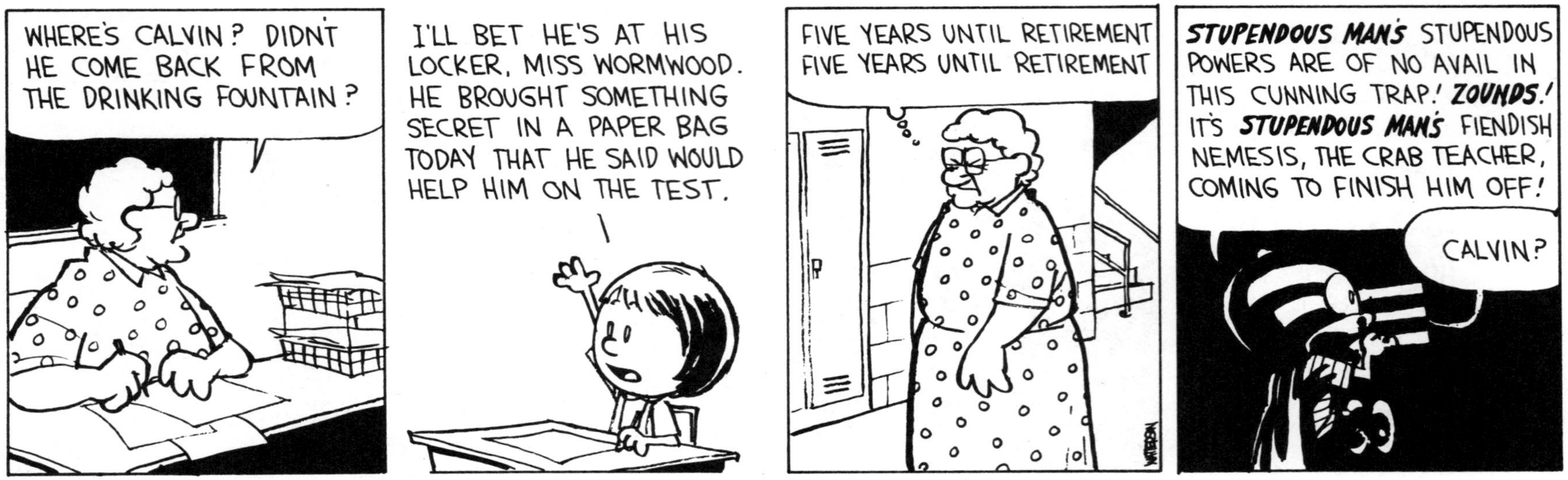
WHERE'S CALVIN? DIDN'T HE COME BACK FROM THE DRINKING FOUNTAIN?
I'LL BET HE'S AT HIS LOCKER, MISS WORMWOOD. HE BROUGHT SOMETHING SECRET IN A PAPER BAG TODAY THAT HE SAID WOULD HELP HIM ON THE TEST.
FIVE YEARS UNTIL RETIREMENT FIVE YEARS UNTIL RETIREMENT
STUPENDOUS MAN'S STUPENDOUS POWERS ARE OF NO AVAIL IN THIS CUNNING TRAP! ZOUNDS! IT'S STUPENDOUS MAN'S FIENDISH NEMESIS, THE CRAB TEACHER, COMING TO FINISH HIM OFF!
CALVIN?

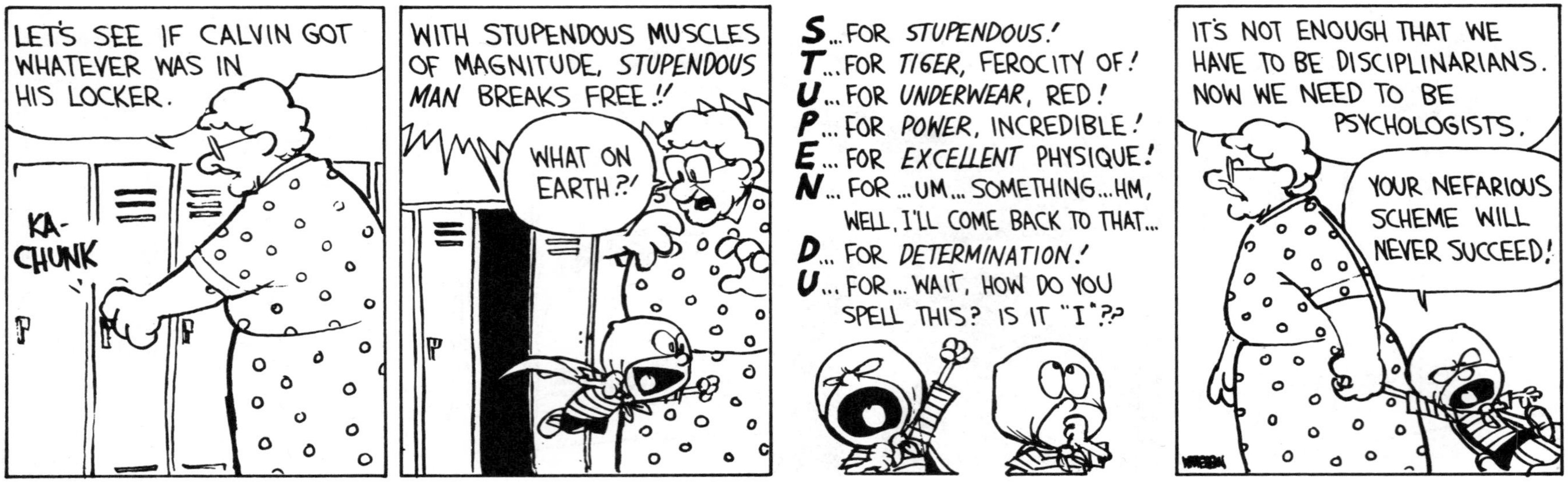
LET'S SEE IF CALVIN GOT WHATEVER WAS IN HIS LOCKER.
KA-CHUNK
WITH STUPENDOUS MUSCLES OF MAGNITUDE, STUPENDOUS MAN BREAKS FREE!!
WHAT ON EARTH?!
S... FOR STUPENDOUS!
T... FOR TIGER, FEROCITY OF!
U... FOR UNDERWEAR, RED!
P... FOR POWER, INCREDIBLE!
E... FOR EXCELLENT PHYSIQUE!
N... FOR ... UM... SOMETHING... HM, WELL, I'LL COME BACK TO THAT...
D... FOR DETERMINATION!
U... FOR... WAIT, HOW DO YOU SPELL THIS? IS IT "I"??
IT'S NOT ENOUGH THAT WE HAVE TO BE DISCIPLINARIANS. NOW WE NEED TO BE PSYCHOLOGISTS.
YOUR NEFARIOUS SCHEME WILL NEVER SUCCEED!

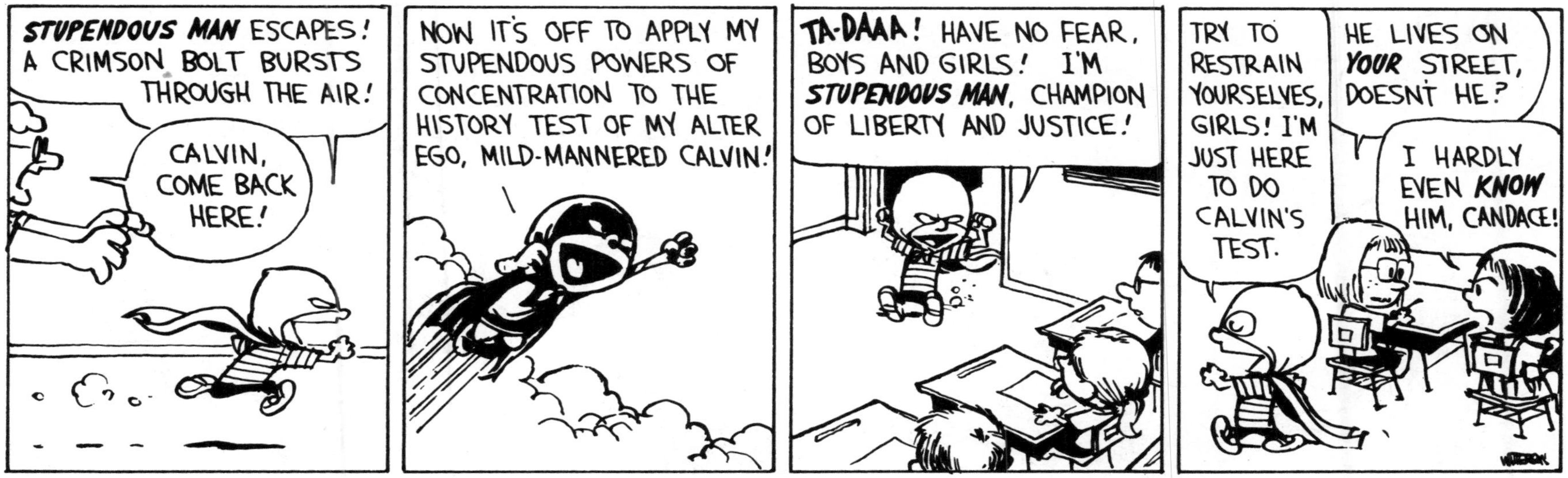
STUPENDOUS MAN ESCAPES! A CRIMSON BOLT BURSTS THROUGH THE AIR!
CALVIN, COME BACK HERE!
NOW IT'S OFF TO APPLY MY STUPENDOUS POWERS OF CONCENTRATION TO THE HISTORY TEST OF MY ALTER EGO, MILD-MANNERED CALVIN!
TA-DAAA! HAVE NO FEAR, BOYS AND GIRLS! I'M STUPENDOUS MAN, CHAMPION OF LIBERTY AND JUSTICE!
TRY TO RESTRAIN YOURSELVES, GIRLS! I'M JUST HERE TO DO CALVIN'S TEST.
HE LIVES ON YOUR STREET, DOESN'T HE?
I HARDLY EVEN KNOW HIM, CANDACE!

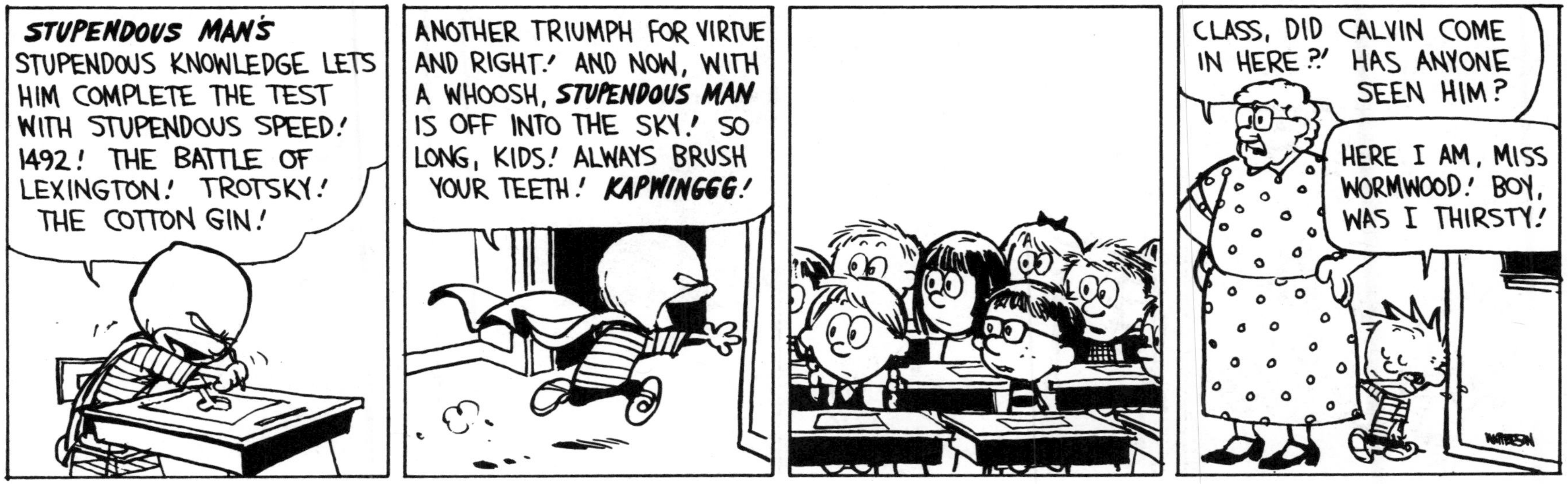
STUPENDOUS MAN'S STUPENDOUS KNOWLEDGE LETS HIM COMPLETE THE TEST WITH STUPENDOUS SPEED! 1492! THE BATTLE OF LEXINGTON! TROTSKY! THE COTTON GIN!
ANOTHER TRIUMPH FOR VIRTUE AND RIGHT! AND NOW, WITH A WHOOSH, STUPENDOUS MAN IS OFF INTO THE SKY! SO LONG, KIDS! ALWAYS BRUSH YOUR TEETH! KAPWINGGG!
CLASS, DID CALVIN COME IN HERE?! HAS ANYONE SEEN HIM?
HERE I AM, MISS WORMWOOD! BOY, WAS I THIRSTY!

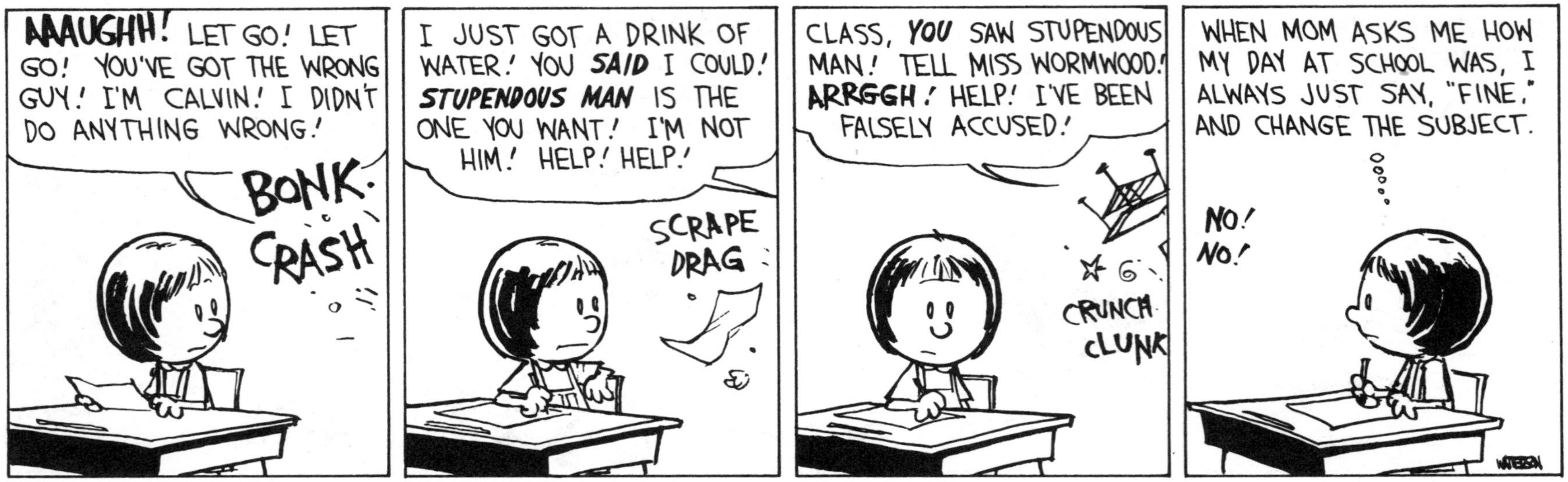
AAAUGHH! LET GO! LET GO! YOU'VE GOT THE WRONG GUY! I'M CALVIN! I DIDN'T DO ANYTHING WRONG!
BONK
CRASH
I JUST GOT A DRINK OF WATER! YOU SAID I COULD! STUPENDOUS MAN IS THE ONE YOU WANT! I'M NOT HIM! HELP! HELP!
SCRAPE
DRAG
CLASS, YOU SAW STUPENDOUS MAN! TELL MISS WORMWOOD! ARRGGH! HELP! I'VE BEEN FALSELY ACCUSED!
CRUNCH
CLUNK
WHEN MOM ASKS ME HOW MY DAY AT SCHOOL WAS, I ALWAYS JUST SAY, "FINE," AND CHANGE THE SUBJECT.
NO!
NO!

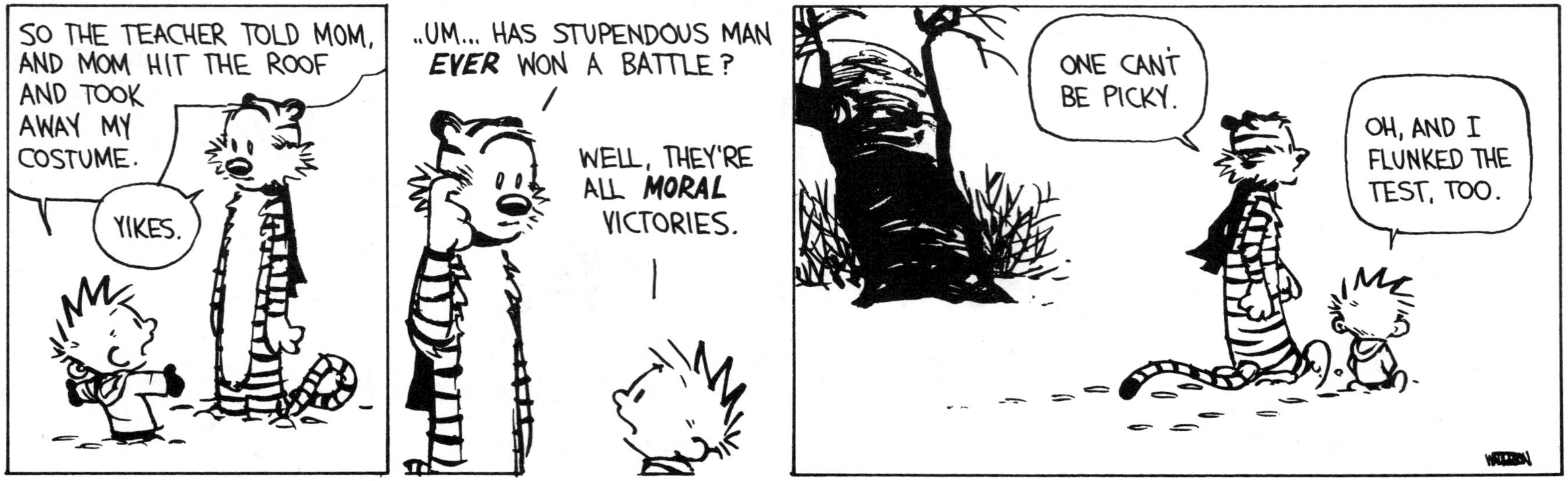
SO THE TEACHER TOLD MOM, AND MOM HIT THE ROOF AND TOOK AWAY MY COSTUME.
YIKES.
..UM... HAS STUPENDOUS MAN EVER WON A BATTLE?
WELL, THEY'RE ALL MORAL VICTORIES.
ONE CAN'T BE PICKY.
OH, AND I FLUNKED THE TEST, TOO.

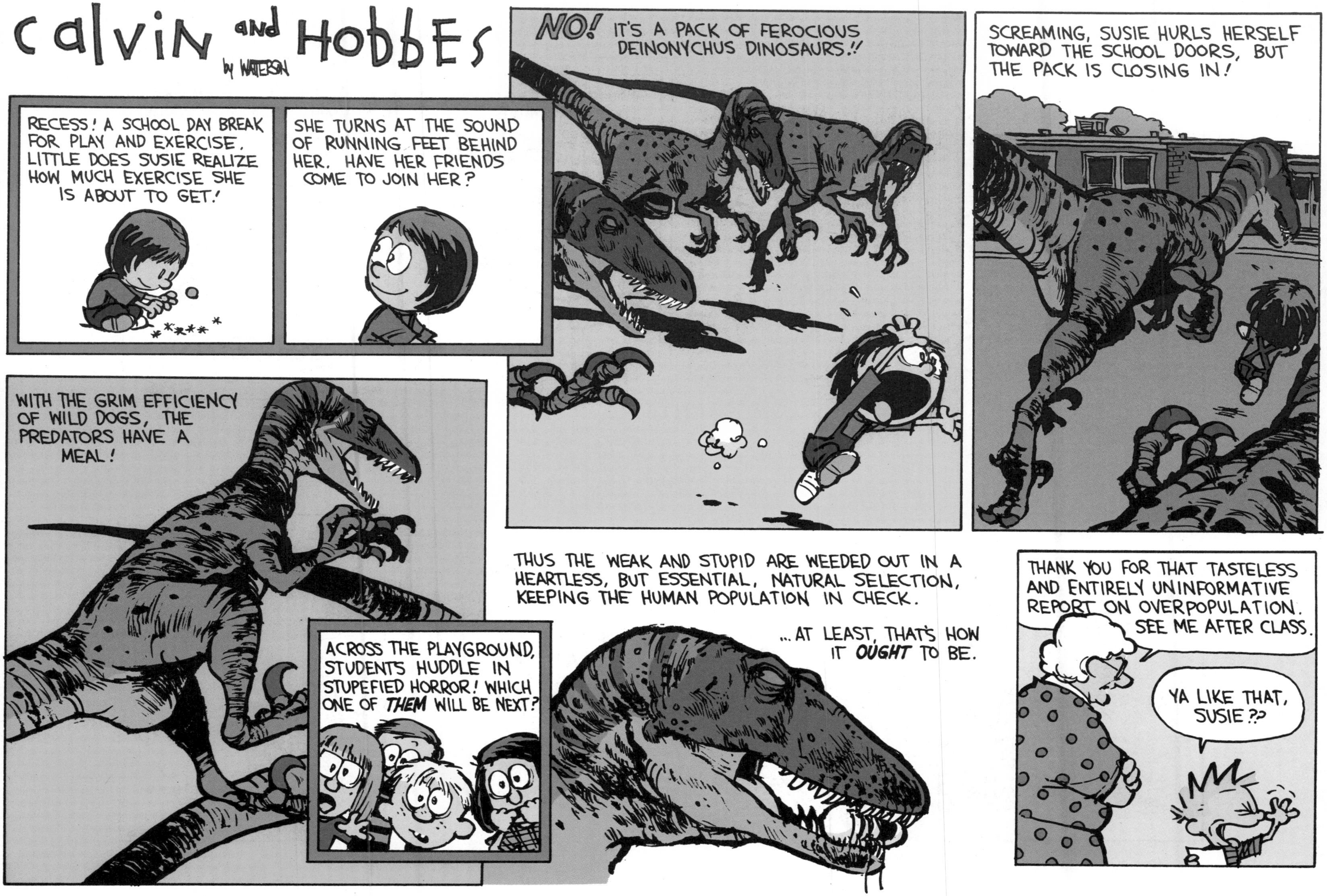
Calvin and HOBBES
by WATTERSON
RECESS! A SCHOOL DAY BREAK FOR PLAY AND EXERCISE. LITTLE DOES SUSIE REALIZE HOW MUCH EXERCISE SHE IS ABOUT TO GET!
SHE TURNS AT THE SOUND OF RUNNING FEET BEHIND HER. HAVE HER FRIENDS COME TO JOIN HER?
NO! IT'S A PACK OF FEROCIOUS DEINONYCHUS DINOSAURS!!
SCREAMING, SUSIE HURLS HERSELF TOWARD THE SCHOOL DOORS, BUT THE PACK IS CLOSING IN!
WITH THE GRIM EFFICIENCY OF WILD DOGS, THE PREDATORS HAVE A MEAL!
ACROSS THE PLAYGROUND, STUDENTS HUDDLE IN STUPEFIED HORROR! WHICH ONE OF THEM WILL BE NEXT?
THUS THE WEAK AND STUPID ARE WEEDED OUT IN A HEARTLESS, BUT ESSENTIAL, NATURAL SELECTION, KEEPING THE HUMAN POPULATION IN CHECK.
...AT LEAST, THAT'S HOW IT OUGHT TO BE.
THANK YOU FOR THAT TASTELESS AND ENTIRELY UNINFORMATIVE REPORT ON OVERPOPULATION. SEE ME AFTER CLASS.
YA LIKE THAT, SUSIE?!

This strip was drawn before the movie *Jurassic Park* came out, and the deinonychus here is a smaller relative of the velociraptors in the film. I stopped doing dinosaur strips for about six months when the movie was released. A few little drawings can't create the visceral response of large-screen computer special effects, and I didn't want Calvin's imagination to look less vivid for the comparison.

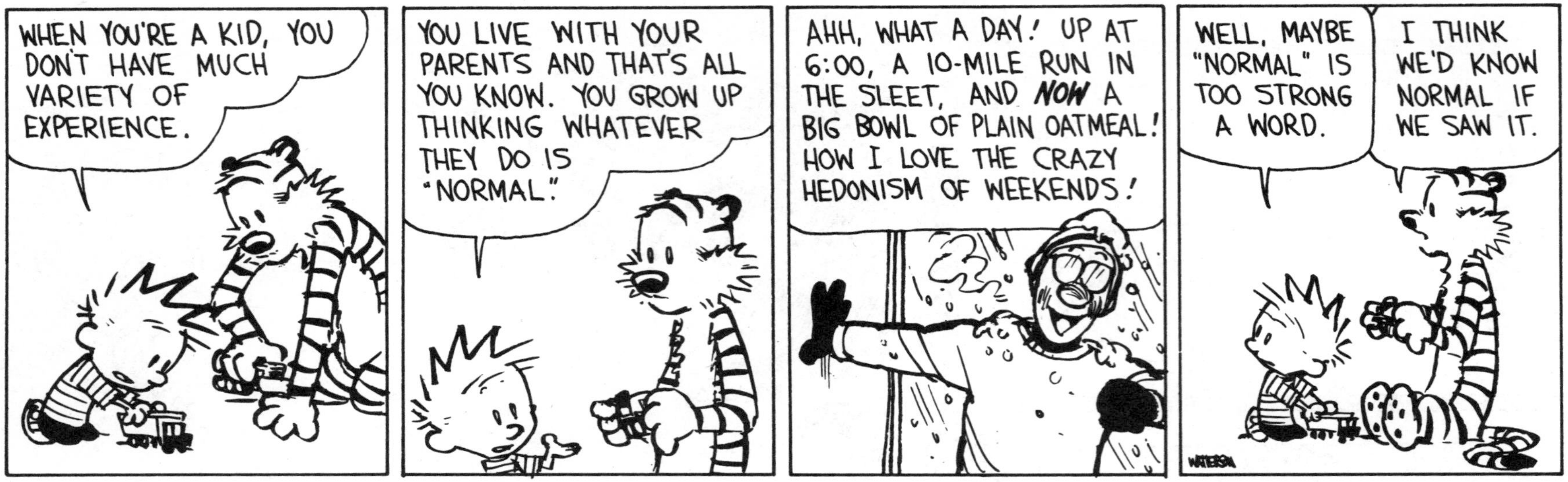
WHEN YOU'RE A KID, YOU DON'T HAVE MUCH VARIETY OF EXPERIENCE.
YOU LIVE WITH YOUR PARENTS AND THAT'S ALL YOU KNOW. YOU GROW UP THINKING WHATEVER THEY DO IS "NORMAL."
AHH, WHAT A DAY! UP AT 6:00, A 10-MILE RUN IN THE SLEET, AND NOW A BIG BOWL OF PLAIN OATMEAL! HOW I LOVE THE CRAZY HEDONISM OF WEEKENDS!
WELL, MAYBE "NORMAL" IS TOO STRONG A WORD.
I THINK WE'D KNOW NORMAL IF WE SAW IT.

This is my dad. No exaggeration.

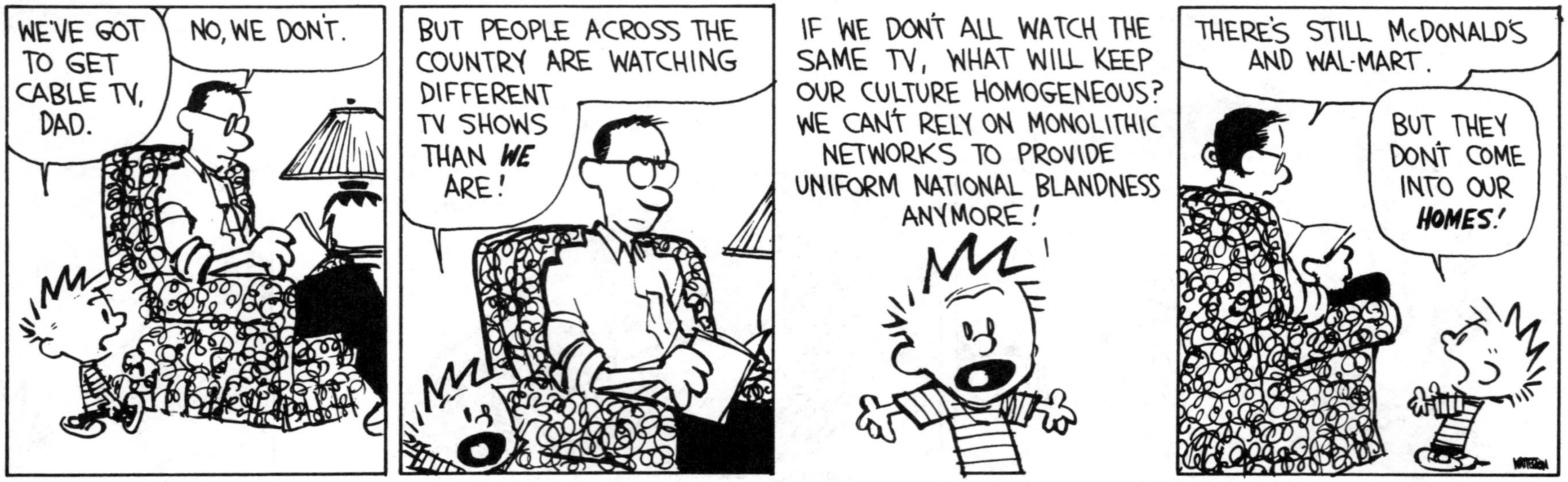
WE'VE GOT TO GET CABLE TV, DAD.
NO, WE DON'T.
BUT PEOPLE ACROSS THE COUNTRY ARE WATCHING DIFFERENT TV SHOWS THAN WE ARE!
IF WE DON'T ALL WATCH THE SAME TV, WHAT WILL KEEP OUR CULTURE HOMOGENEOUS? WE CAN'T RELY ON MONOLITHIC NETWORKS TO PROVIDE UNIFORM NATIONAL BLANDNESS ANYMORE!
THERE'S STILL McDONALD'S AND WAL-MART.
BUT THEY DON'T COME INTO OUR HOMES!

I'm sure they're working on this.

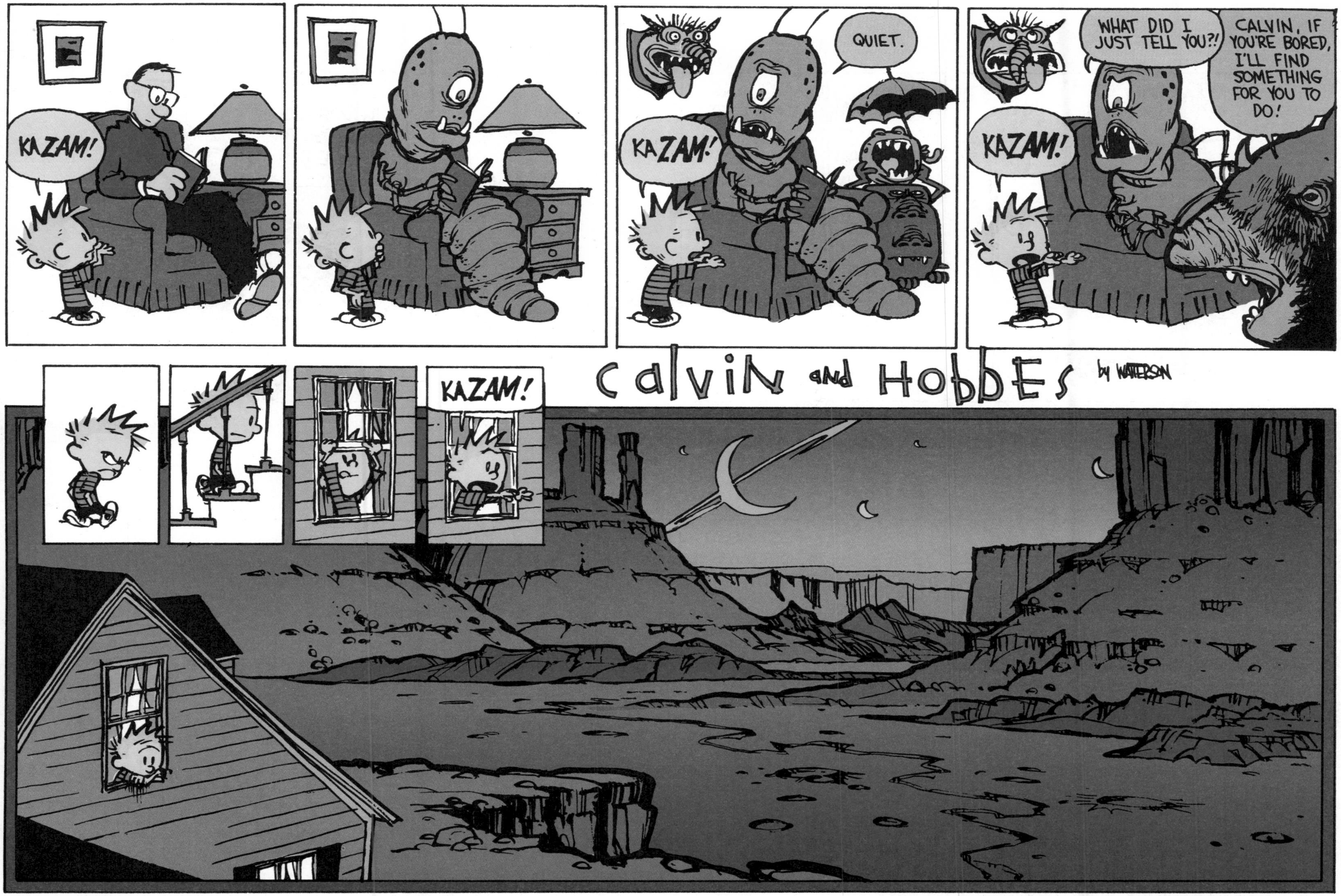
KAZAM!
QUIET.
KAZAM!
WHAT DID I JUST TELL YOU?!
CALVIN, IF YOU'RE BORED, I'LL FIND SOMETHING FOR YOU TO DO!
KAZAM!
Calvin and HOBBES
by WATTERSON
KAZAM!

Imagination is not always appreciated. In the last panel here, I faded a narrow range of colors to create an atmospheric effect, and I think this is one of my more evocative landscapes.

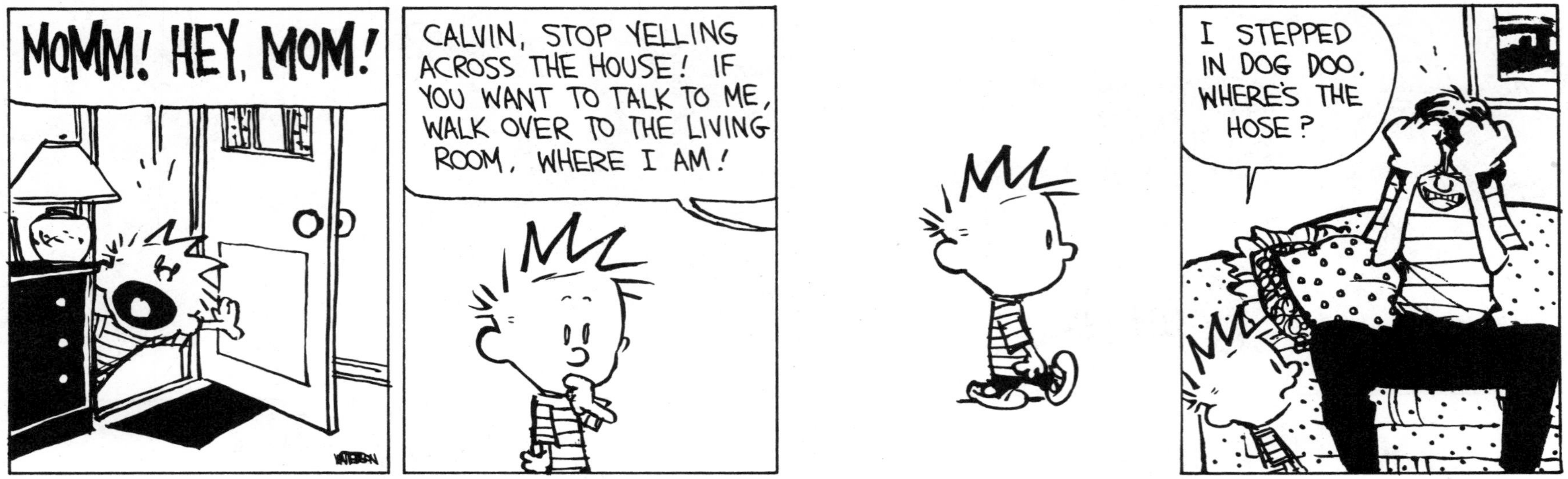
MOMM! HEY, MOM!
CALVIN, STOP YELLING ACROSS THE HOUSE! IF YOU WANT TO TALK TO ME, WALK OVER TO THE LIVING ROOM, WHERE I AM!
I STEPPED IN DOG DOO. WHERE'S THE HOSE?

Right lesson, wrong time.

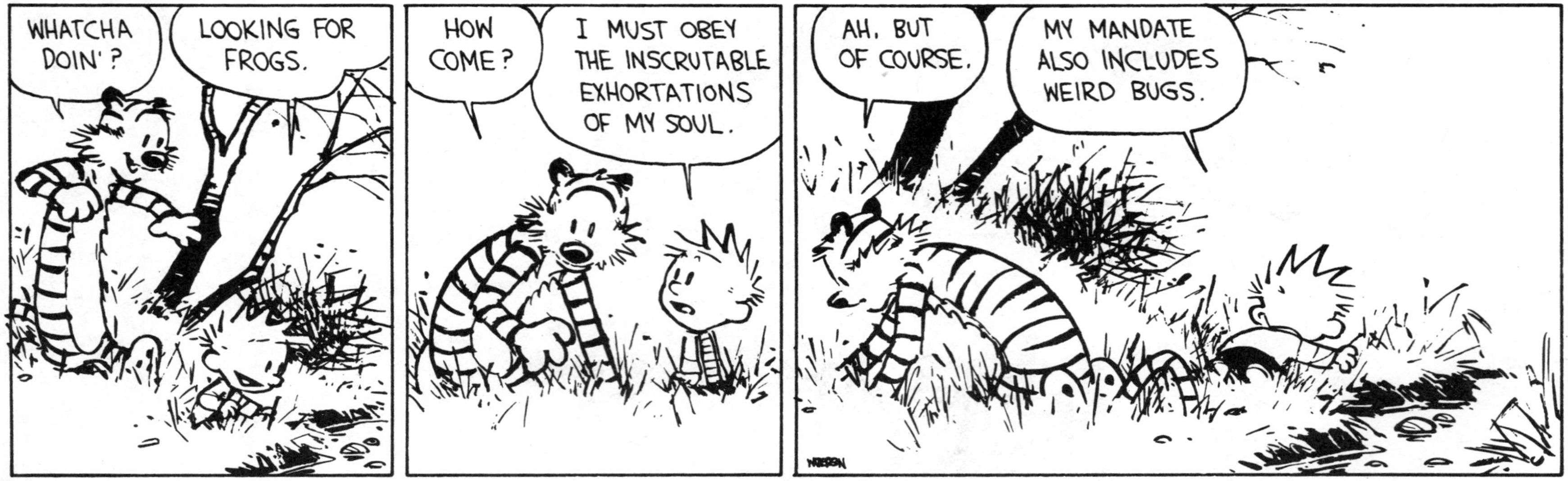
WHATCHA DOIN'?
LOOKING FOR FROGS.
HOW COME?
I MUST OBEY THE INSCRUTABLE EXHORTATIONS OF MY SOUL.
AH, BUT OF COURSE.
MY MANDATE ALSO INCLUDES WEIRD BUGS.

Calvin's vocabulary puzzles some readers, but Calvin has never been a literal six-year-old. Cumbersome words are funny to me, and I like Calvin's ability to precisely articulate stupid ideas.

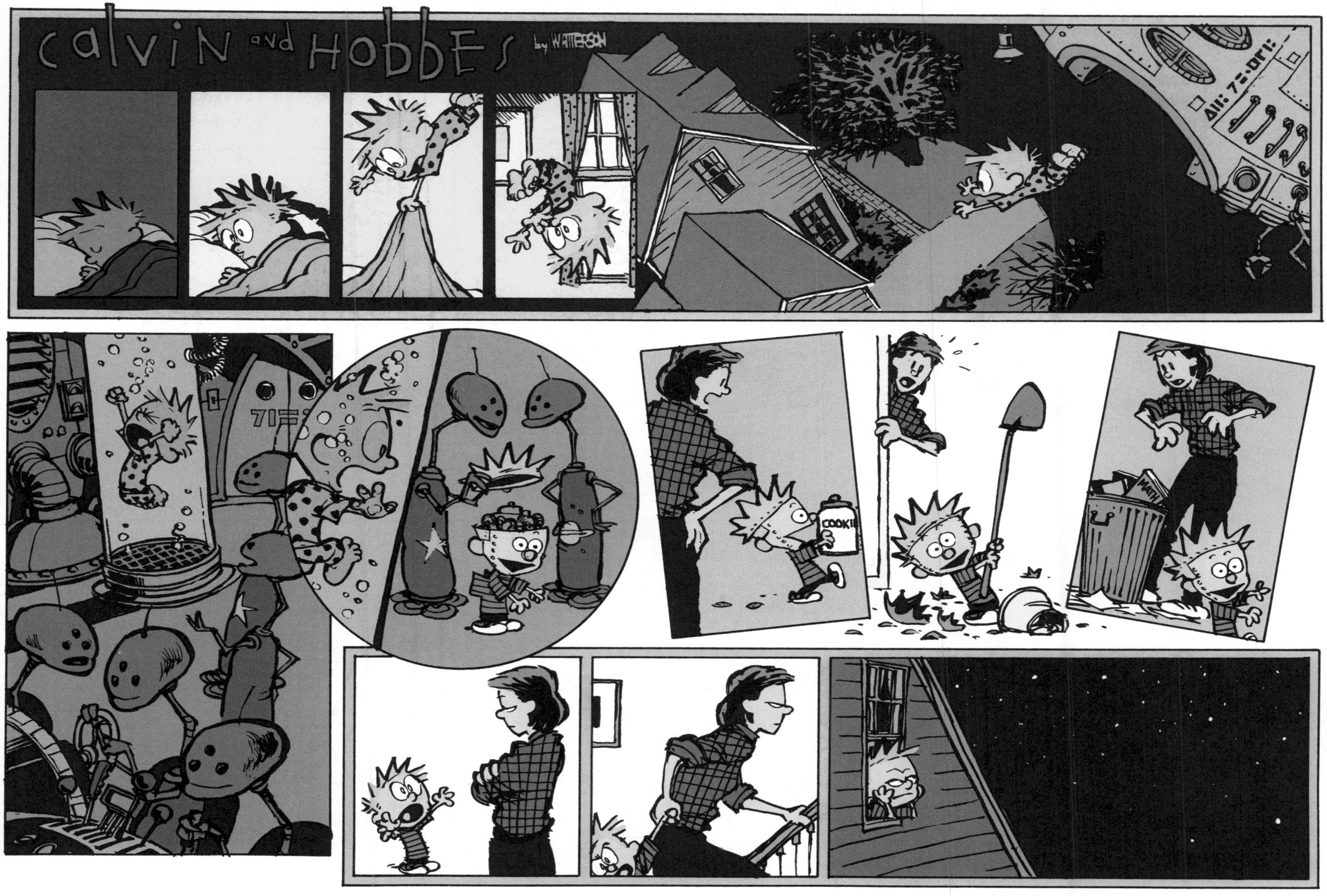
calvin and HOBBES
by WATTERSON
COOKI
MATH

With the larger Sunday strip, I find I can often tell a story with greater nuance by eliminating the dialogue altogether.

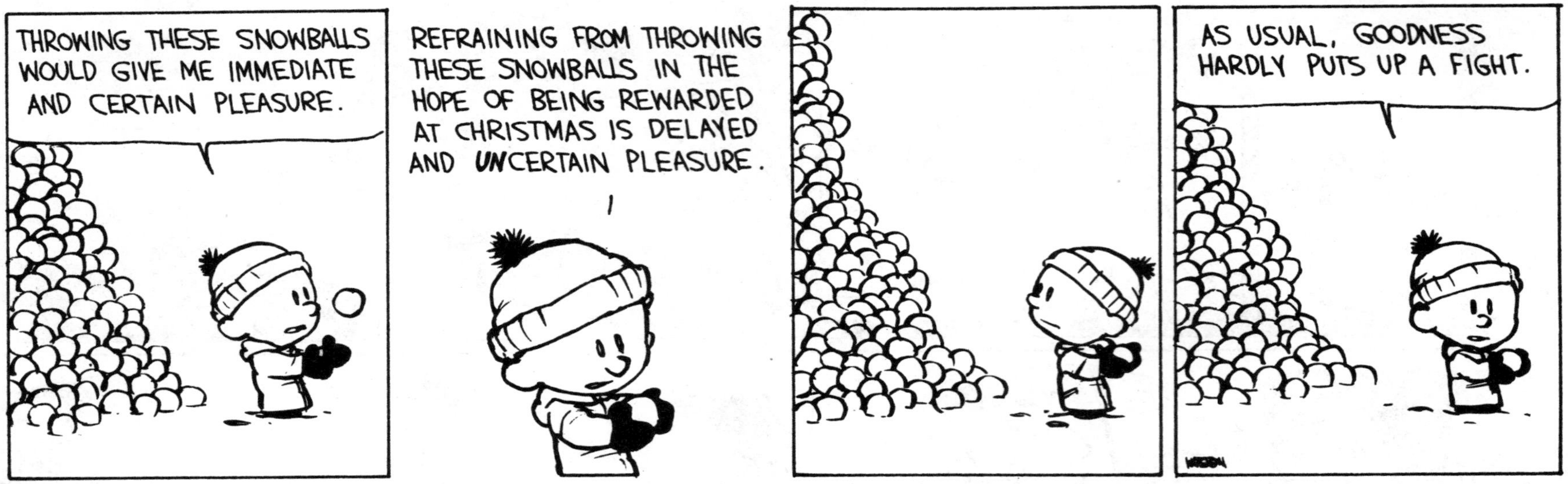
THROWING THESE SNOWBALLS WOULD GIVE ME IMMEDIATE AND CERTAIN PLEASURE.
REFRAINING FROM THROWING THESE SNOWBALLS IN THE HOPE OF BEING REWARDED AT CHRISTMAS IS DELAYED AND *UN*CERTAIN PLEASURE.
AS USUAL, GOODNESS HARDLY PUTS UP A FIGHT.

I often use the Christmas season for Calvin to wrestle with good and evil. He wants to be good, but for the wrong reasons.

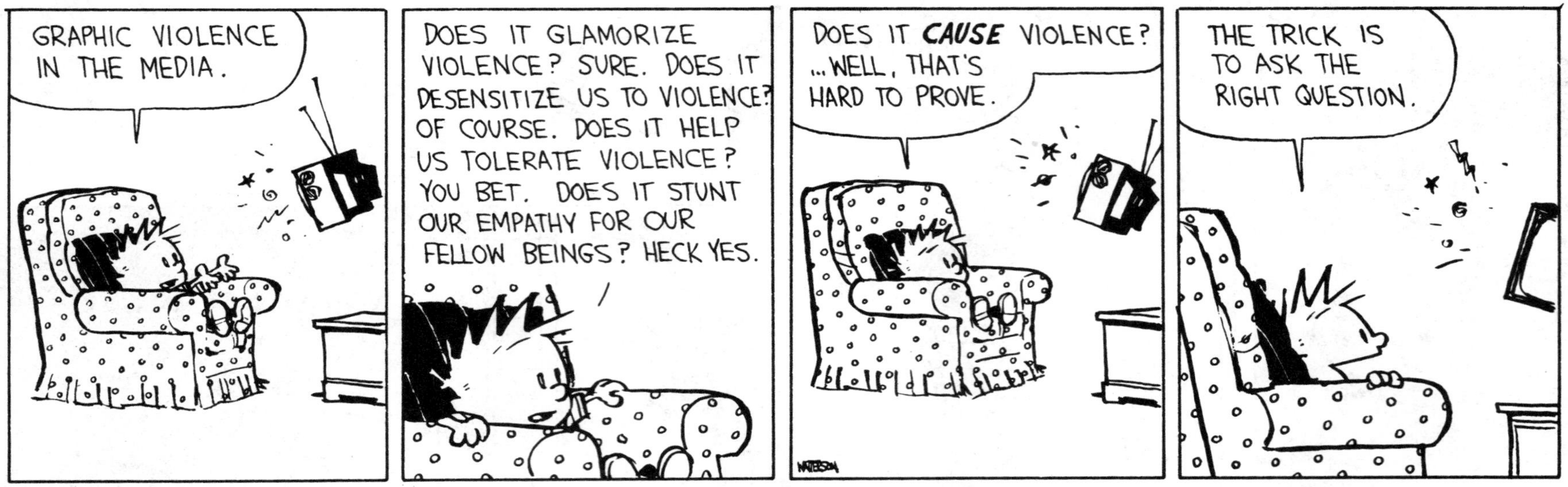
GRAPHIC VIOLENCE IN THE MEDIA.
DOES IT GLAMORIZE VIOLENCE? SURE. DOES IT DESENSITIZE US TO VIOLENCE? OF COURSE. DOES IT HELP US TOLERATE VIOLENCE? YOU BET. DOES IT STUNT OUR EMPATHY FOR OUR FELLOW BEINGS? HECK YES.
DOES IT ***CAUSE*** VIOLENCE? ...WELL, THAT'S HARD TO PROVE.
THE TRICK IS TO ASK THE RIGHT QUESTION.

What's to debate?

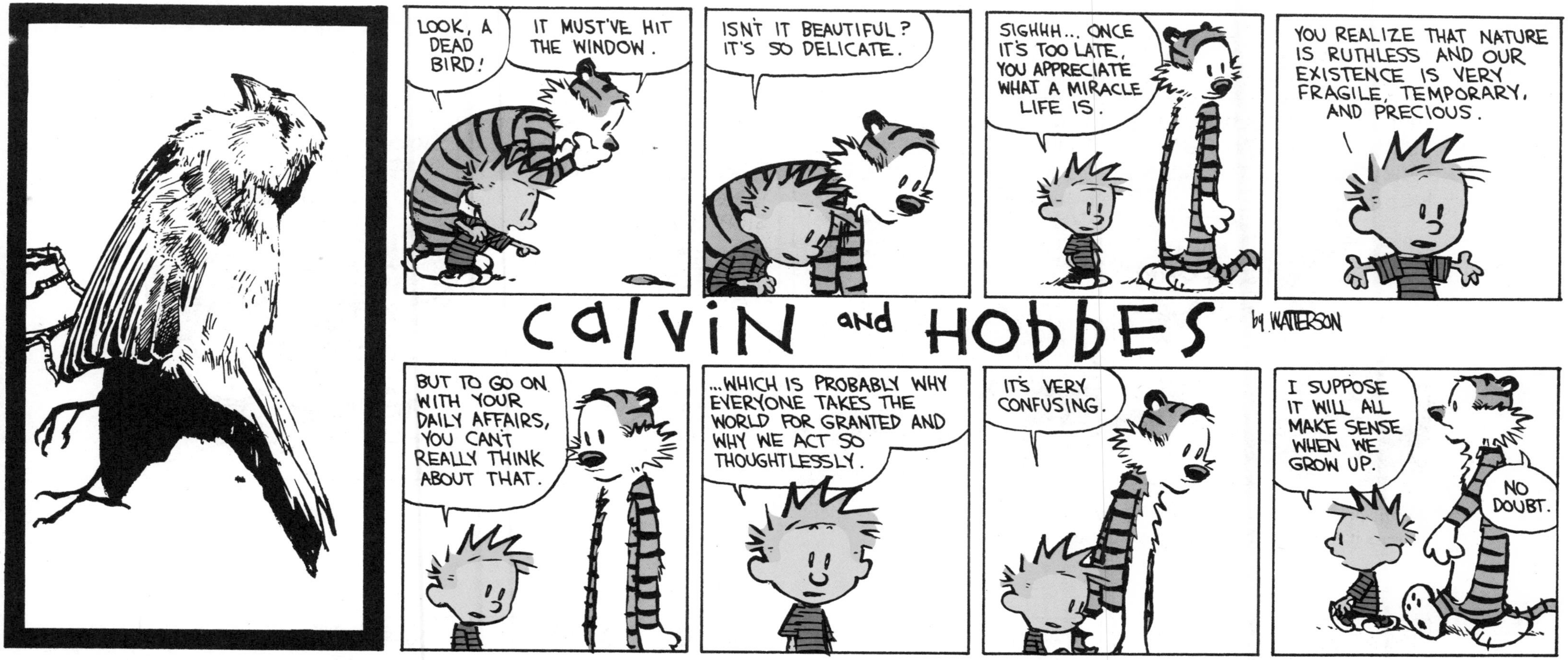
LOOK, A DEAD BIRD!
IT MUST'VE HIT THE WINDOW.
ISN'T IT BEAUTIFUL? IT'S SO DELICATE.
SIGHHH... ONCE IT'S TOO LATE, YOU APPRECIATE WHAT A MIRACLE LIFE IS.
YOU REALIZE THAT NATURE IS RUTHLESS AND OUR EXISTENCE IS VERY FRAGILE, TEMPORARY, AND PRECIOUS.
CALVIN and HOBBES
by WATTERSON
BUT TO GO ON WITH YOUR DAILY AFFAIRS, YOU CAN'T REALLY THINK ABOUT THAT.
...WHICH IS PROBABLY WHY EVERYONE TAKES THE WORLD FOR GRANTED AND WHY WE ACT SO THOUGHTLESSLY.
IT'S VERY CONFUSING.
I SUPPOSE IT WILL ALL MAKE SENSE WHEN WE GROW UP.
NO DOUBT.

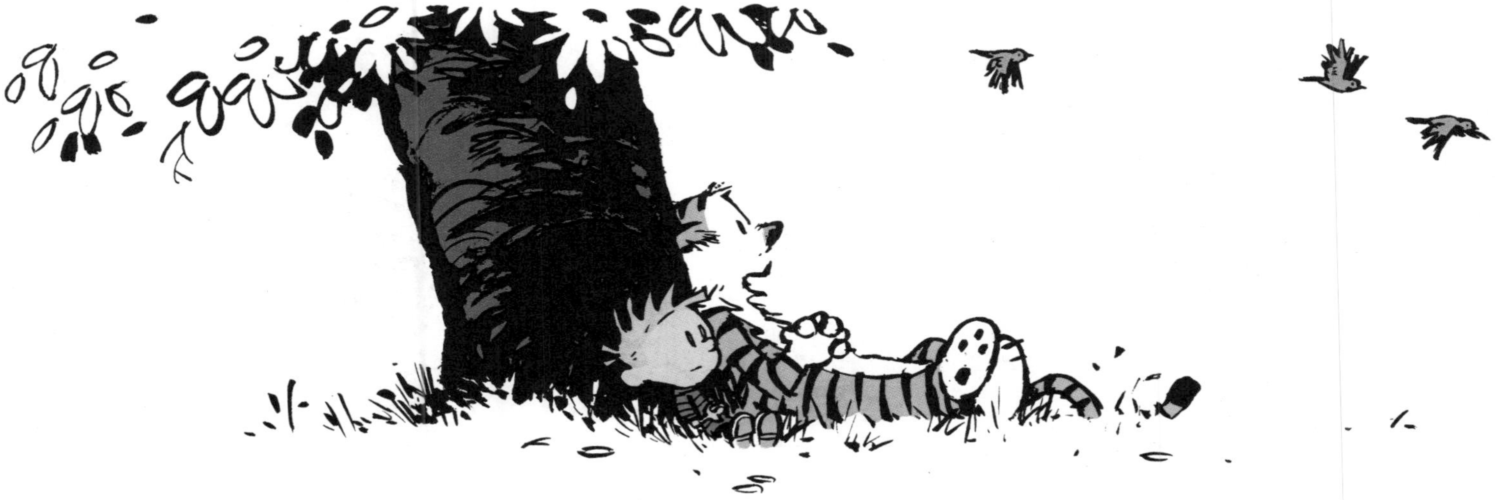

Drawing is a way for me to muse about the nature of things, and I sketched a dead bird I found with reflections similar to Calvin's. Not many Sunday strips begin with a first panel like this, and I wondered if readers would find it offensive. In fact, I received several moving letters from people who had suffered losses and found the strip meaningful. Sharing with people, I'm always impressed by how they share back.

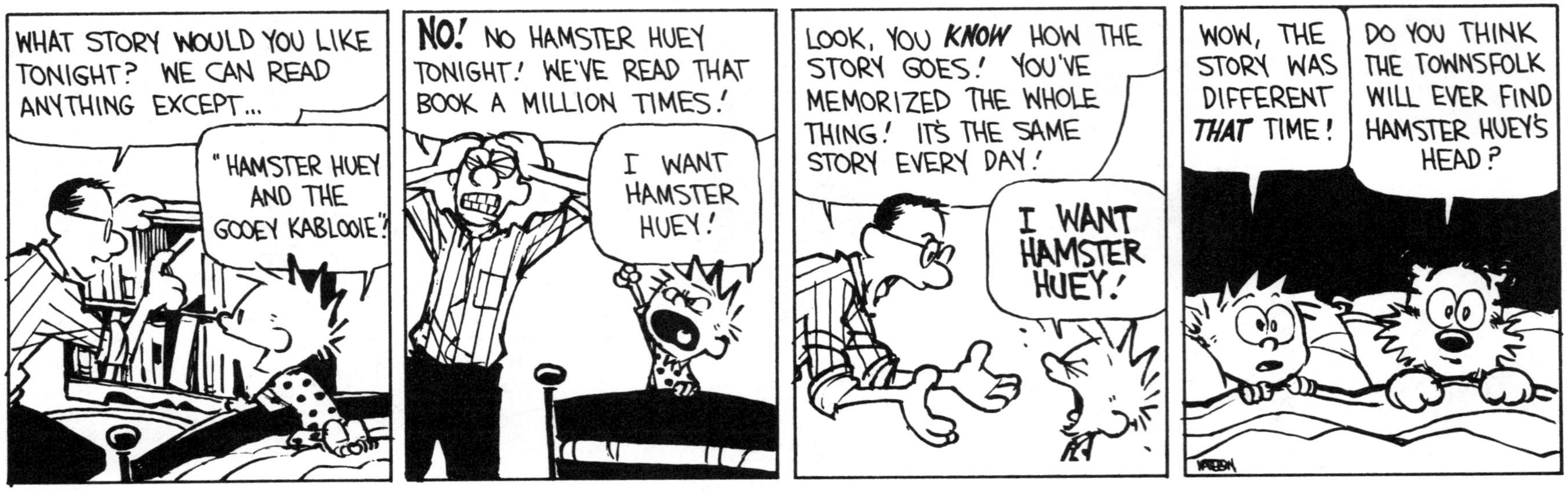
WHAT STORY WOULD YOU LIKE TONIGHT? WE CAN READ ANYTHING EXCEPT...
"HAMSTER HUEY AND THE GOOEY KABLOOIE"?
NO! NO HAMSTER HUEY TONIGHT! WE'VE READ THAT BOOK A MILLION TIMES!
I WANT HAMSTER HUEY!
LOOK, YOU KNOW HOW THE STORY GOES! YOU'VE MEMORIZED THE WHOLE THING! IT'S THE SAME STORY EVERY DAY!
I WANT HAMSTER HUEY!
WOW, THE STORY WAS DIFFERENT THAT TIME!
DO YOU THINK THE TOWNSFOLK WILL EVER FIND HAMSTER HUEY'S HEAD?

Hamster Huey and the Gooey Kablooie (like "the Noodle Incident" I've referred to in several strips) is left to the reader's imagination, where it's sure to be more outrageous.

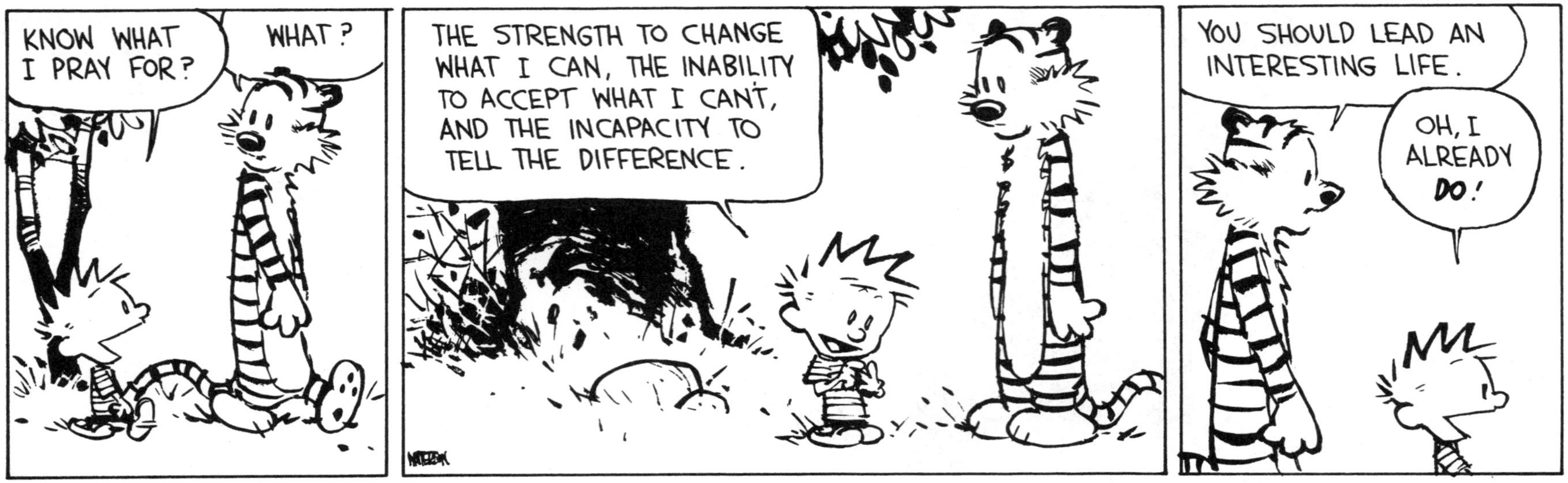
KNOW WHAT I PRAY FOR?
WHAT?
THE STRENGTH TO CHANGE WHAT I CAN, THE INABILITY TO ACCEPT WHAT I CAN'T, AND THE INCAPACITY TO TELL THE DIFFERENCE.
YOU SHOULD LEAD AN INTERESTING LIFE.
OH, I ALREADY DO!

I don't pray for this, but it's the case anyway.

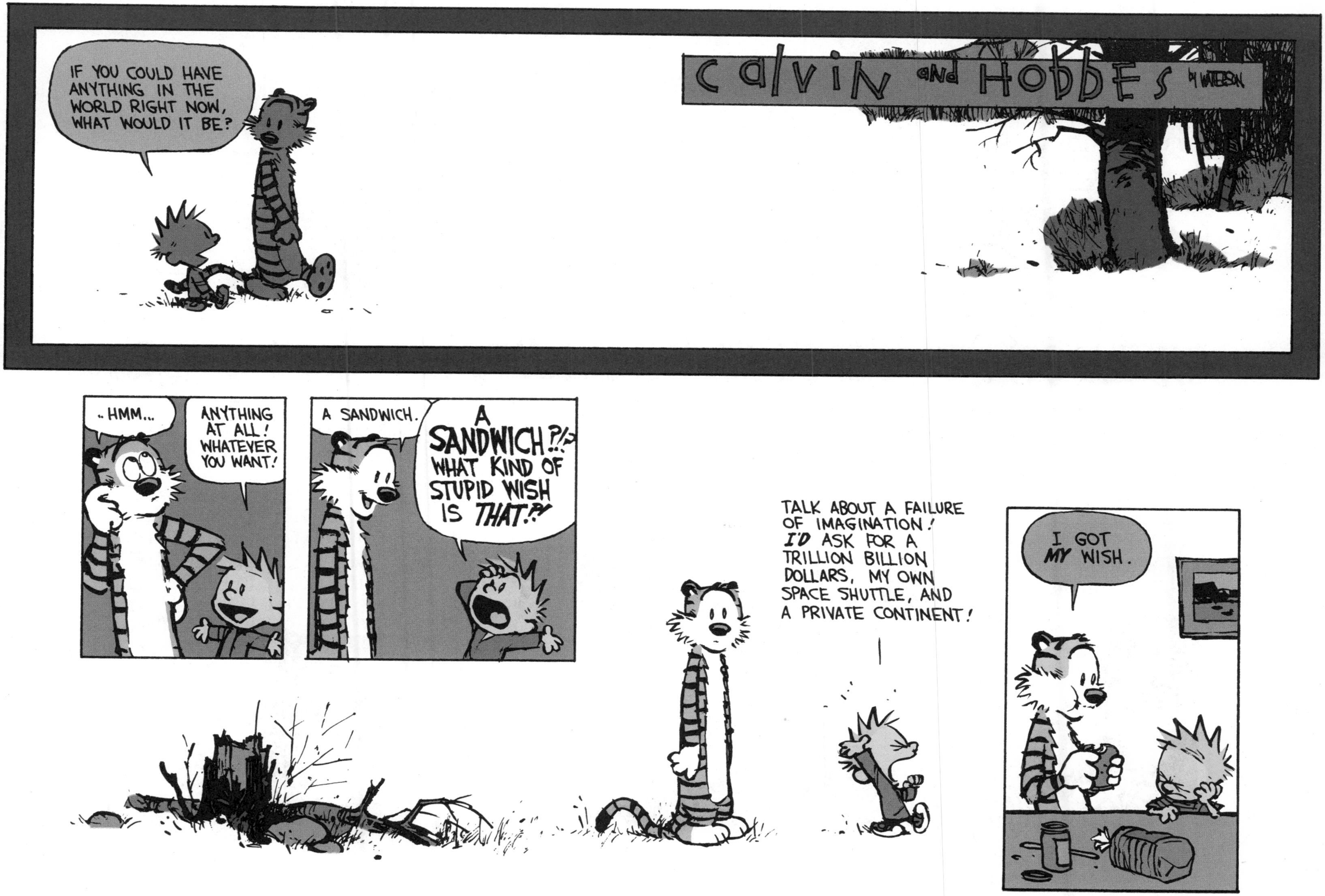
IF YOU COULD HAVE ANYTHING IN THE WORLD RIGHT NOW, WHAT WOULD IT BE?
CALVIN AND HOBBES BY WATTERSON
..HMM...
ANYTHING AT ALL! WHATEVER YOU WANT!
A SANDWICH.
A SANDWICH?!?! WHAT KIND OF STUPID WISH IS THAT?!?
TALK ABOUT A FAILURE OF IMAGINATION! I'D ASK FOR A TRILLION BILLION DOLLARS, MY OWN SPACE SHUTTLE, AND A PRIVATE CONTINENT!
I GOT MY WISH.

Some of my strips end up being little sermons, and this can be annoying and sappy if it's not handled lightly. One of the ongoing jokes in the strip is that Calvin usually learns the wrong lesson from his experiences, if he learns anything at all. Calvin's expression in the last panel suggests that he is resisting the moral here too.

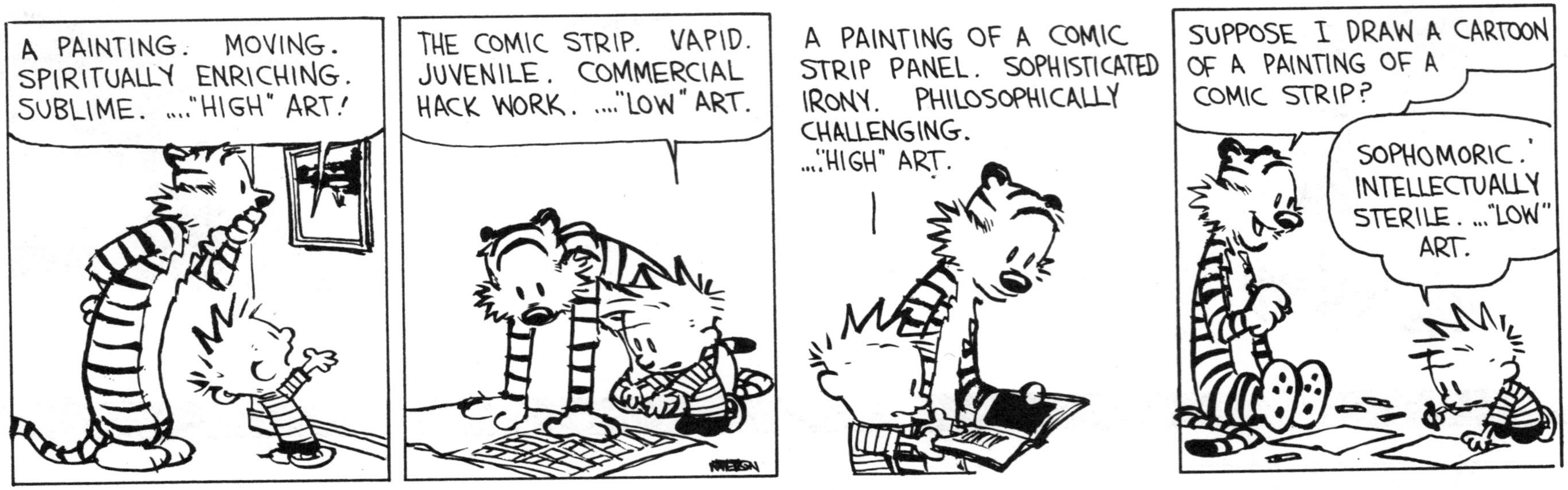
A PAINTING. MOVING. SPIRITUALLY ENRICHING. SUBLIME. ..."HIGH" ART!
THE COMIC STRIP. VAPID. JUVENILE. COMMERCIAL HACK WORK. ..."LOW" ART.
A PAINTING OF A COMIC STRIP PANEL. SOPHISTICATED IRONY. PHILOSOPHICALLY CHALLENGING. ..."HIGH" ART.
SUPPOSE I DRAW A CARTOON OF A PAINTING OF A COMIC STRIP?
SOPHOMORIC. INTELLECTUALLY STERILE. ..."LOW" ART.

I would suggest that it's not the medium, but the quality of perception and expression, that determines the significance of art. But what would a cartoonist know?

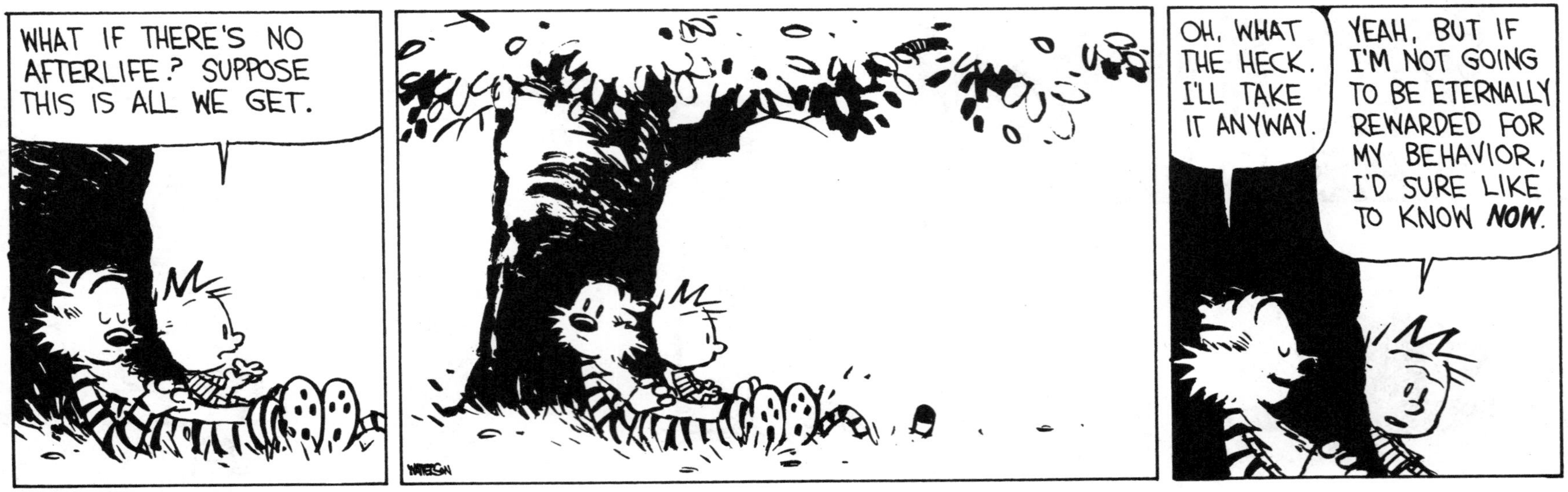
WHAT IF THERE'S NO AFTERLIFE? SUPPOSE THIS IS ALL WE GET.
OH, WHAT THE HECK. I'LL TAKE IT ANYWAY.
YEAH, BUT IF I'M NOT GOING TO BE ETERNALLY REWARDED FOR MY BEHAVIOR, I'D SURE LIKE TO KNOW ***NOW***.

I don't know how much Hobbes helps Calvin gain perspective, but Hobbes certainly helps me.

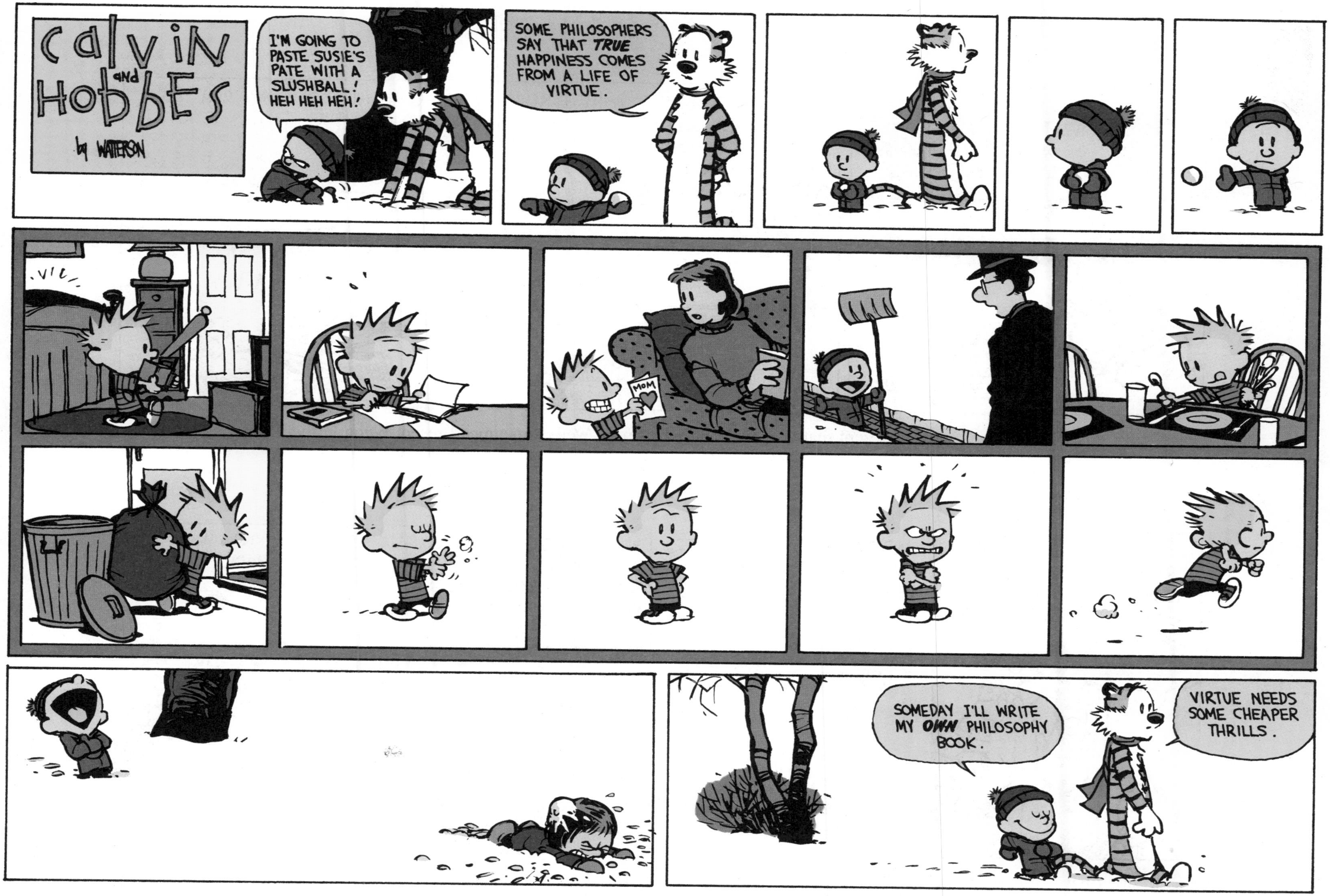
Calvin and Hobbes
by WATTERSON
I'M GOING TO PASTE SUSIE'S PATE WITH A SLUSHBALL! HEH HEH HEH!
SOME PHILOSOPHERS SAY THAT TRUE HAPPINESS COMES FROM A LIFE OF VIRTUE.
MOM
SOMEDAY I'LL WRITE MY OWN PHILOSOPHY BOOK.
VIRTUE NEEDS SOME CHEAPER THRILLS.

I don't know why we're wired this way, but we are.

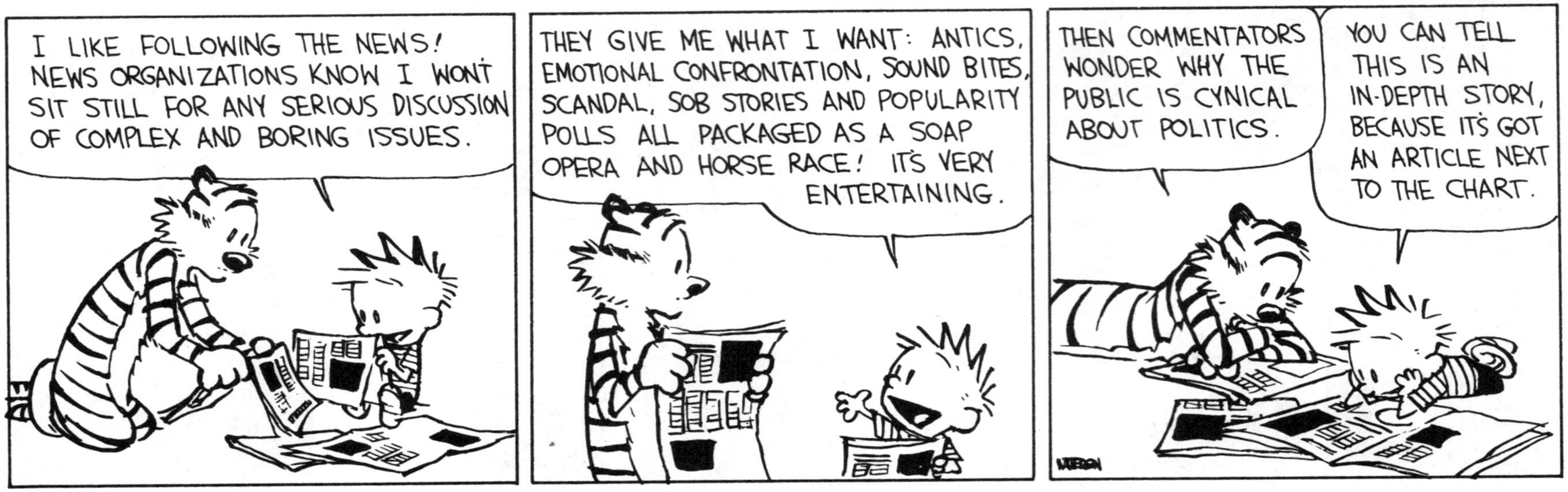
I LIKE FOLLOWING THE NEWS! NEWS ORGANIZATIONS KNOW I WON'T SIT STILL FOR ANY SERIOUS DISCUSSION OF COMPLEX AND BORING ISSUES.
THEY GIVE ME WHAT I WANT: ANTICS, EMOTIONAL CONFRONTATION, SOUND BITES, SCANDAL, SOB STORIES AND POPULARITY POLLS ALL PACKAGED AS A SOAP OPERA AND HORSE RACE! IT'S VERY ENTERTAINING.
THEN COMMENTATORS WONDER WHY THE PUBLIC IS CYNICAL ABOUT POLITICS.
YOU CAN TELL THIS IS AN IN-DEPTH STORY, BECAUSE IT'S GOT AN ARTICLE NEXT TO THE CHART.

Newspaper editors sometimes seem to resent that they have to run comics. Well, sometimes I resent being in their newspapers.

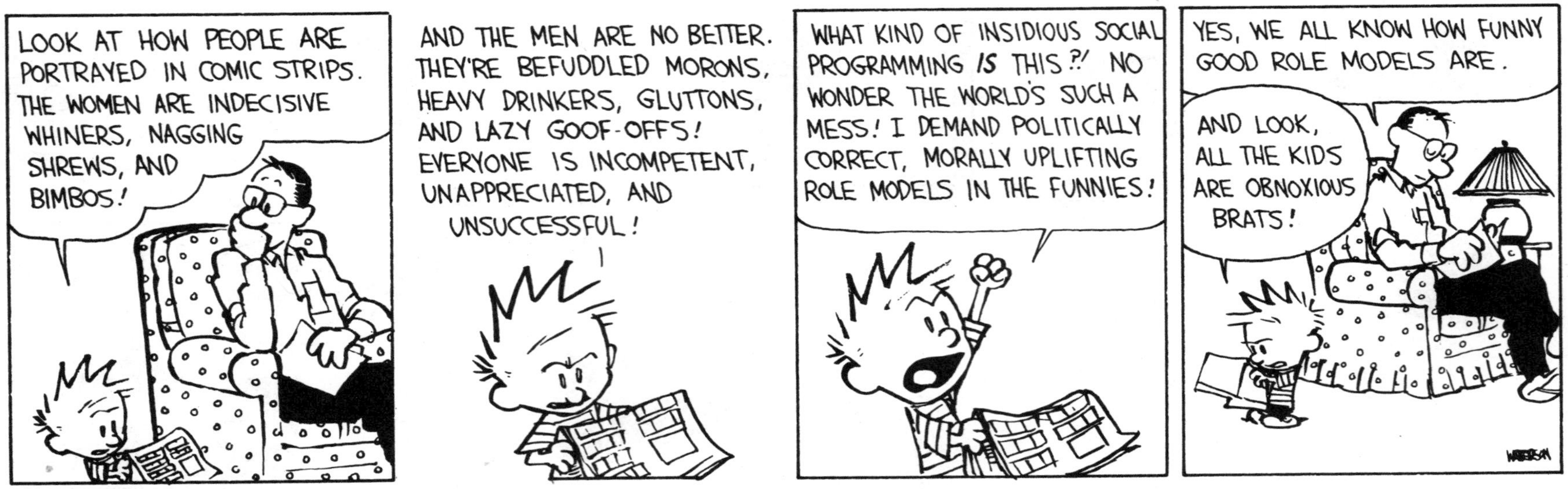
LOOK AT HOW PEOPLE ARE PORTRAYED IN COMIC STRIPS. THE WOMEN ARE INDECISIVE WHINERS, NAGGING SHREWS, AND BIMBOS!
AND THE MEN ARE NO BETTER. THEY'RE BEFUDDLED MORONS, HEAVY DRINKERS, GLUTTONS, AND LAZY GOOF-OFFS! EVERYONE IS INCOMPETENT, UNAPPRECIATED, AND UNSUCCESSFUL!
WHAT KIND OF INSIDIOUS SOCIAL PROGRAMMING *IS* THIS?! NO WONDER THE WORLD'S SUCH A MESS! I DEMAND POLITICALLY CORRECT, MORALLY UPLIFTING ROLE MODELS IN THE FUNNIES!
YES, WE ALL KNOW HOW FUNNY GOOD ROLE MODELS ARE.
AND LOOK, ALL THE KIDS ARE OBNOXIOUS BRATS!

Comic strips have historically been full of ugly stereotypes, the hallmark of writers too lazy to honestly observe the world. Offended parties often suggest the further sanitization of the comics, but one of the great strengths of cartooning is its ability to criticize through distortion. The trick is to remember that the way we describe things reveals the way we think. The cartoonist who resorts to stereotypes reveals his own bigotry.

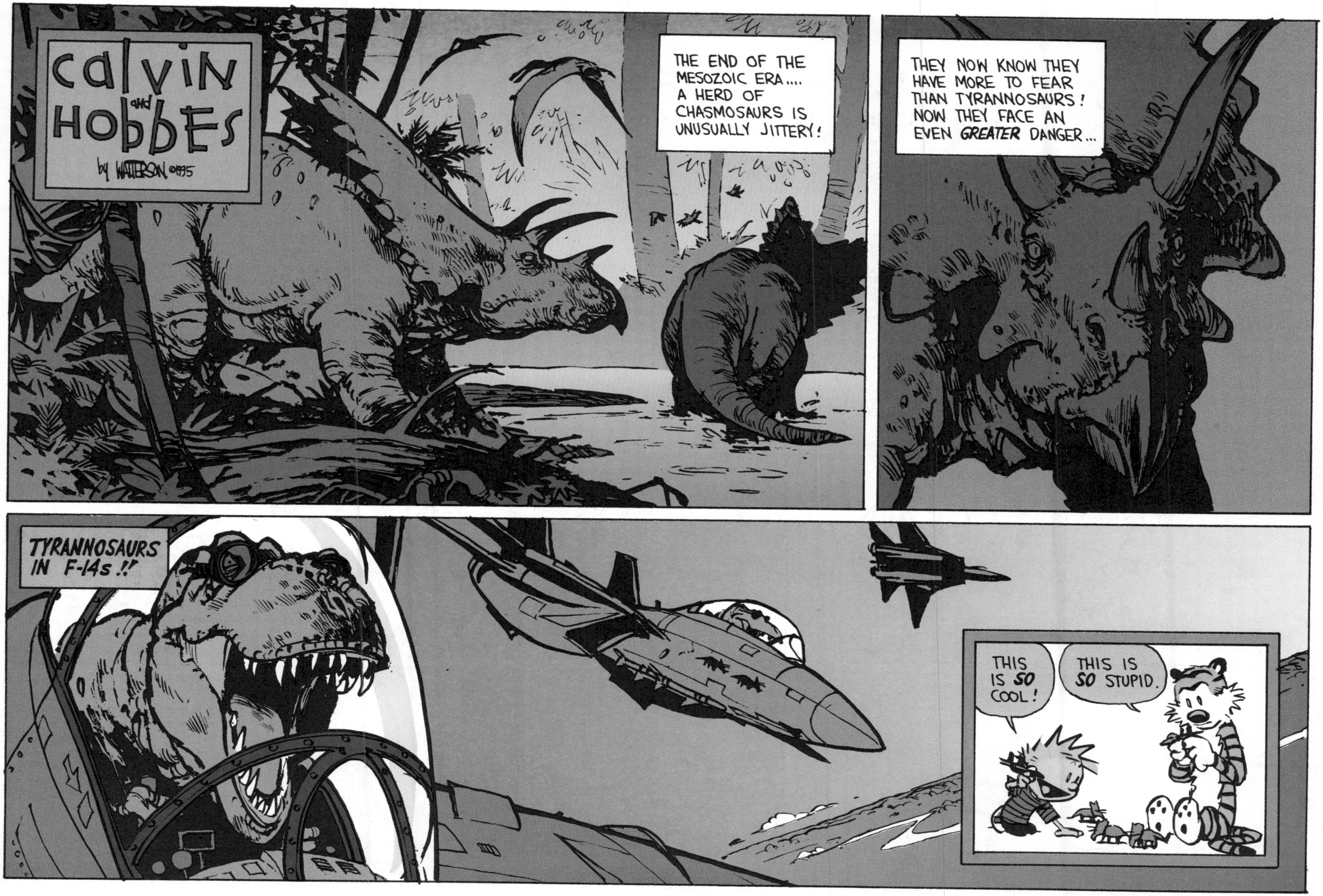
Calvin and Hobbes
by WATTERSON ©1995
THE END OF THE MESOZOIC ERA.... A HERD OF CHASMOSAURS IS UNUSUALLY JITTERY!
THEY NOW KNOW THEY HAVE MORE TO FEAR THAN TYRANNOSAURS! NOW THEY FACE AN EVEN GREATER DANGER...
TYRANNOSAURS IN F-14s!!
THIS IS SO COOL!
THIS IS SO STUPID.

The best part of being a cartoonist is the ever-present opportunity to be silly. This is a dumb strip, but I sure had fun with it.

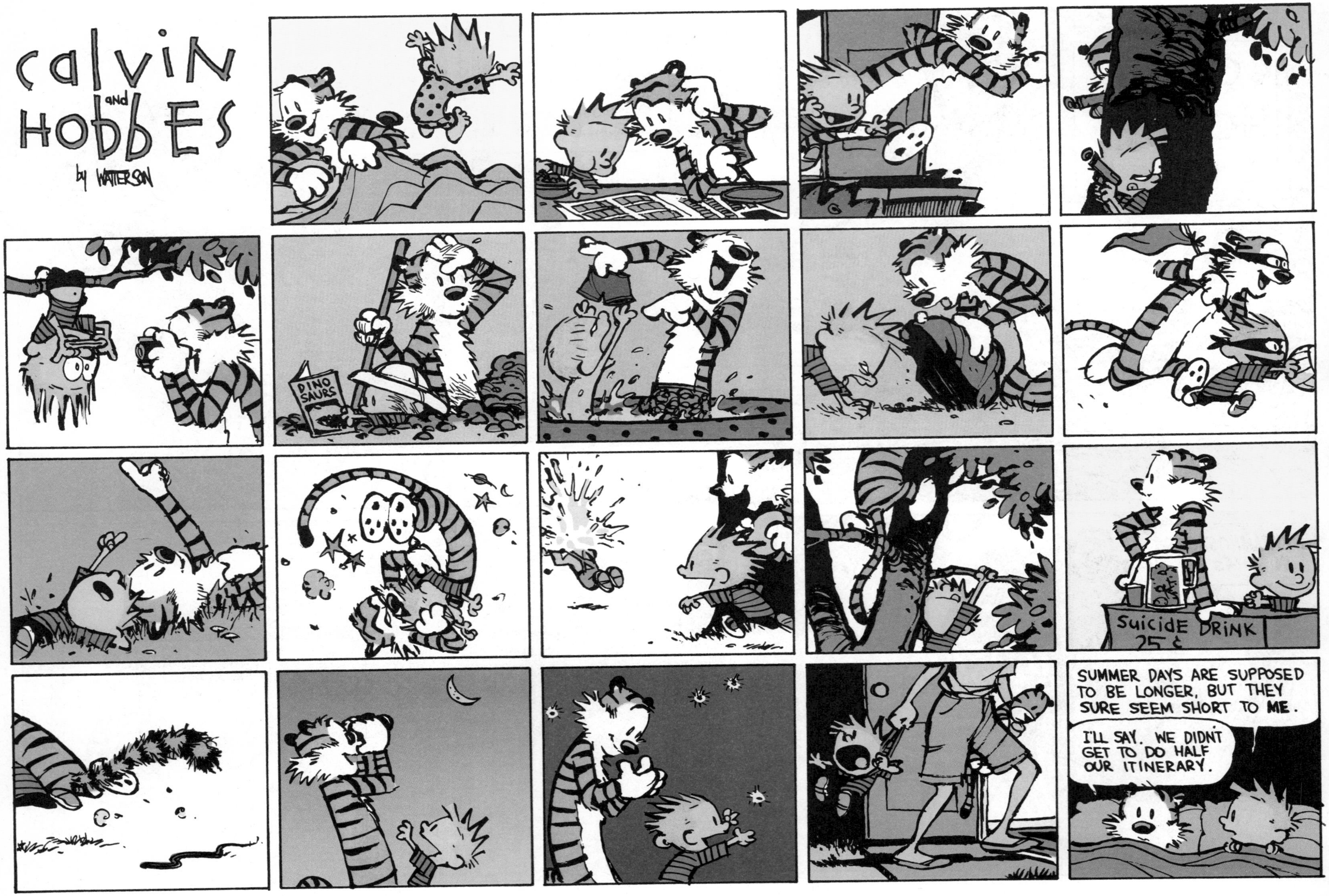
Calvin and Hobbes
by WATTERSON
DINO SAURS
SUICIDE DRINK 25¢
SUMMER DAYS ARE SUPPOSED TO BE LONGER, BUT THEY SURE SEEM SHORT TO ME.
I'LL SAY. WE DIDN'T GET TO DO HALF OUR ITINERARY.

This is how I remember summer. When the strip captures real moments—without making them saccharine and tidy—my work is very gratifying.

CARTOONING AND *CALVIN AND HOBBES*

I don't think of comics as just entertainment. It's a rare privilege to be able to talk to millions of people on a given day, so I'm eager to say something meaningful when I can. There is always pressure to write some snappy one-liner that will buy me another twenty-four hours of lead time on deadlines, but nothing depresses me like thinking I've become a joke factory to fill newspaper space. Whenever possible, I use the strip to talk about the things that are important to me.

I think the best comics (like the best novels, paintings, etc.) are personal, idiosyncratic works that reflect a unique and honest sensibility. To attract and keep an audience, art must entertain, but the significance of any art lies in its ability to express truths—to reveal and help us understand our world. Comic strips, in their own humble way, are capable of doing this.

The best comics expose human nature and help us laugh at our own stupidity and hypocrisy. They indulge in exaggeration and absurdity, helping us to see the world with fresh eyes and reminding us how important it is to play and be silly. Comics depict the ordinary, mundane events of our lives and help us remember the importance of tiny moments. They cleverly sum up our unexpressed thoughts and emotions. Sometimes they show the world from the perspective of children and animals, encouraging us to be innocent for a moment. The best comics, that is to say, are fun house mirrors that distort appearances only to help us recognize, and laugh at, our essential characteristics.

Surprise is the essence of humor, and nothing is more surprising than truth. When cartoons dig beyond glib punch lines, cheap sentimentality, and tidy stories to deeper, truthful experiences, they can really touch people and connect us all. As frustrated as I am by the way this business works, I continue to believe that comics are an art form capable of any level of beauty, intelligence, and sophistication.

I've written and drawn over three thousand *Calvin and Hobbes* strips now, and to the extent that the strip reflects my interests, values, and thoughts, my cartoons are a sort of self-portrait. The longer I've worked, the more I've used the strip to explore personal issues. When I come up with an idea that surprises me, I'm happy to offer it to anyone who shares my interests. I'm flattered when people respond to my work, but I don't feel accountable to public demand. Trying to please people encourages calculation, and the strip is valuable to me only insofar as it's honest and sincere.

It's not hard to write jokes—good characters will always have something amusing to say about their situation—but it's very difficult to keep the strip's world energized and expansive year after year. At the beginning of a strip, virtually every installment explores new territory, but it's frightening how fast stories and situations become predictable. Today's funny innovation is tomorrow's stale formula.

My early strips look crude and forced to me now, but the characters were still introducing themselves to me. The first couple of years were exploratory efforts to create an engaging world and rounded characters. I began writing longer stories when I saw how they added dimension to the characters' personalities and relationships. Lately, I've had trouble writing extended narratives that satisfy me, and I've been doing fewer of them. Instead, my enthusiasm has drifted to the visual possibilities of the larger Sunday strip. Over the years, *Calvin and Hobbes* has changed directions, but I don't control where it goes. When everything is working, I'm more surprised by the strip's destination than anybody.

The trick to writing a comic strip is to cultivate a mental playfulness—a natural curiosity and eagerness to learn. If I keep my eyes open and follow my interests, sooner or later the effort yields questions, thoughts, and ideas—unexpected paths into new territory. Like Calvin, I just head out into the yard in search of weirdness, and with the right attitude, I make discoveries.

Putting myself in the head of a fictitious six-year-old and a tiger encourages me to be more alert and inquisitive than I would otherwise be. Sometimes I resent the pressure to exploit every waking moment for strip ideas, but at its best, the strip makes me examine events and live more thoughtfully. I love the solitude of this work and the opportunity to work with ideas that interest me. This is the greatest reward of cartooning for me.

I've always loved cartoons. With *Calvin and Hobbes*, I've tried to return some of the fun, magic, and beauty I've enjoyed in other comics. It's been immensely satisfying to draw *Calvin and Hobbes*, and I will always be grateful to have had the opportunity to work in this wonderful art form.

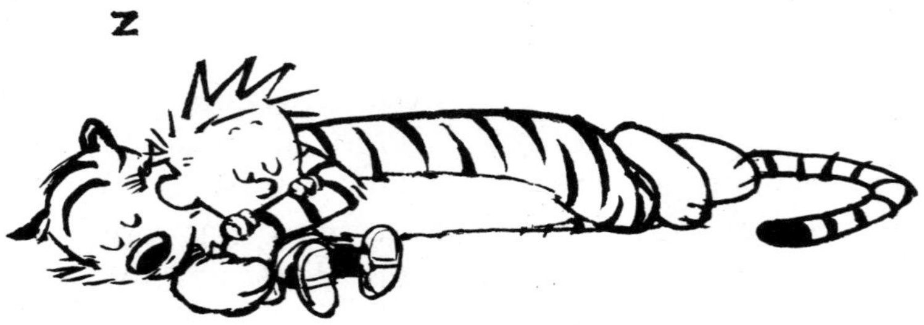
Z